A SOURCE BOOK
IN INDIAN PHILOSOPHY

A SOURCE BOOK IN
Indian Philosophy

EDITED BY

SARVEPALLI RADHAKRISHNAN
AND CHARLES A. MOORE

PRINCETON, NEW JERSEY
PRINCETON UNIVERSITY PRESS

L. C. Card: 55-6698

ISBN 0-691-01958-4

Fifth Princeton Paperback Printing, 1973

Printed in the United States of America
by Princeton University Press, Princeton, New Jersey

GREGG M. SINCLAIR

PREFACE

GENERALLY speaking, Western students of Indian philosophy are limited to secondary sources and to a few primary sources, such as translations of the *Ṛg Veda*, the more important Upaniṣads, and the *Bhagavad-gītā*. The need for primary as well as secondary sources is obvious, and it is also clear that acquaintance with only a very limited range of source material—that dealing exclusively with the religious background of Indian philosophy rather than the wide range of Indian philosophy as a whole—is highly unsatisfactory.

This *Source Book in Indian Philosophy* fulfills the two needs involved here, namely, to supply Western readers with basic source material on Indian philosophy in convenient and usable form and to present source material which represents all of the major philosophical systems and perspectives of India, not merely its earliest and most religious background. In addition to selections from the *Ṛg Veda*, the Upaniṣads, and the *Bhagavad-gītā*, this volume contains substantial selections from all the major systems of Indian philosophy, orthodox and unorthodox. These selections are adequate for a comprehensive general study of all the systems and of India's basic social philosophy.

There is a general introduction giving a brief history and outline of Indian philosophy, as well as a short explanatory introduction accompanying the selections from each major system. The introductions—prepared by Dr Radhakrishnan except where noted—are intended as guides for the study of the source material; the source material provides the basic material for study of the systems. Part of the function of this volume is to "prove" both the substantiality and the wide range of Indian philosophy and also to convince skeptical Westerners that much of Indian philosophy is *philosophy* not only in its unique Indian forms but also in accordance with the strictest standards of open-mindedness, critical analysis, and rational investigation.

A source book in Indian philosophy may appear to be of questionable merit on two counts: because, of necessity, it makes *selections* from the comprehensive material of the systems involved, and because it is extremely difficult to translate Indian philosophy, originally written in Sanskrit and Pali, into English without distorting or confusing the meanings of basic concepts. The first of these objections is well taken, but, in view of the general unavailability of complete texts for most of the systems, a source book which provides adequate selections is thought to be at least a minimum requirement on the part of anyone who is seriously concerned with Indian thought. This volume of selections is not intended as an adequate substitute for the texts themselves; it is intended to encourage the student to go to the texts, wherever possible, for fuller and more adequate study. Any volume of selections must merely scratch the surface of the vast amount of fundamental philosophizing represented in the many basic texts related to every one of the systems, orthodox and unorthodox. The selections concentrate on basic original formulations of the philosophies of the systems. All developments in the long history of Indian philosophy could not be included. In choosing the selections stress has been laid on expository material. This fails to do justice to the vast amount of polemical material in most of the systems—including, unfortunately, Śaṁkara's disproofs of the validity of all other major systems. It is further admitted that it is very difficult, at times, to translate some of the more complex terms and concepts of Indian philosophy into exact English equivalents. Nevertheless, in the selections made available here, the translations are adequate, if not perfect. Also, it would be a serious loss to philosophy if the great richness of the thought of Indian philosophers for approximately 4000 years were to be lost or abandoned, because, here and there, certain concepts cannot be expressed precisely and exactly in English. The gain to be derived from a study of translations of Indian philosophy is great; the loss suffered by virtue of the difficulty of exact linguistic or philosophical equivalents is serious at times but is never so great as to destroy the intelligibility or the significance of the material under study.

For the most part, existing translations have been used. In general, these translations are quite satisfactory, although some improvement could undoubtedly be achieved by undertaking the Herculean task of a completely new translation. In some cases, new translations are offered, and at times existing translations have been revised slightly to clarify and to correct questionable readings. This volume also includes several original translations made exclusively for this source book. These translations are of basic material which cannot be found elsewhere in English.

In addition to selections from all of the basic systems of classical

Indian philosophy, selections are given from two outstanding representatives of modern Indian thought, Sri Aurobindo and Sarvepalli Radhakrishnan. There are other important names in contemporary Indian philosophy, but these two represent the most important interpretational developments in Indian thought in the present day and offer philosophies which bridge the gap between the East and the West, philosophies which achieve synthesis by fundamentally different methods—Sri Aurobindo by intuition and mystical insight and Radhakrishnan by synthetic rationality and "enlightened intellect," his equivalent for intuition.

The difficulties of translating (as such, and especially from the Indian languages), the differing styles of the original texts, the great number of texts involved, the varieties of styles among the several translators (including the degree to which they give literal or liberal translations)—these and other unavoidable difficulties peculiar to an undertaking of this kind have posed many editorial problems. The attempt has been made throughout to meet the demands of exact scholarship as far as possible. In matters of detail:

(1) Transliteration of Sanskrit terms has been made uniform throughout the volume, except in bibliographical items, where the titles have been retained exactly as in the published volumes. The only exception is the occasional inconsistent use of ṅ or ṁ—both of which are correct—to accord with common practice.

(2) Punctuation, wherever it is misleading in the texts used, has been corrected.

(3) Capitalization has been modified so as to overcome the too profuse and sometimes confusing use of capitals, a common practice among Indian translators.

(4) Mistakes in spelling and grammar have been corrected.

(5) No attempt has been made to achieve uniformity of spelling according to the English or the American usage—the style in the translations used is retained in the selections here.

(6) Differing translations of the same Sanskrit term appearing in different selections are retained, although in these cases care has been taken to include the Sanskrit word for purposes of identification. A Sanskrit word often has different meanings in different contexts. For this reason no glossary is included.

(7) "Self" and "self" are sometimes considered preferable to "Soul" and "soul" to denote respectively the ultimate spiritual reality and the individual spiritual essence in man in much of Indian

philosophy. The word "Soul"—or "soul"—may carry Western connotations that might be misleading, although "soul" may well be used to denote the embodied individual self. The texts from which selections have been taken disagree widely on these matters. For the sake of clarity, some changes have been made, but it was not felt that the desirability of editorial consistency would justify the hundreds of changes which would be required. Also, mechanical uniformity itself may be misleading at times. The reader is strongly advised to avoid the tendency to misinterpretation in terms of traditional Western connotations.

(8) In order to avoid possible confusion, *brāhmin* (not *brāhmaṇa*) has been used to refer to the priest-teacher class or caste, and *Brahman* (not *Brahma* or Brahmā) for the Absolute in Hindu thought. (*Brahma* is also technically correct but the term is susceptible to ambiguity.)

(9) The use of parentheses and brackets is not altogether consistent. In general, brackets indicate the translator's explanatory addition to the translation, whereas parentheses indicate a concept or definition implied but not literally found in the Sanskrit text. Translators differ in this usage, however, and no attempt has been made to force all such cases into a strictly consistent style. In some cases, neither parentheses nor brackets are used to indicate material implied and necessary for a clear translation but not actually a part of the Sanskrit original.

(10) In general, the footnotes are those of the editors. Authorship is not specified except when a note is extensive or controversial.

Much of Indian philosophy is written in a style which is very different from Western style. In many cases, poetic verses or certain basic statements of aphoristic form (*sūtras*) constitute the fundamental and original texts of the systems. From time to time in the course of the development of these systems, commentaries were written to elucidate the brief and often cryptic statements of the original *sūtras*. Without these commentaries, the *sūtras* are often unintelligible. In this volume, the commentaries are printed in smaller type than the *sūtras*. This style is used, not because the commentary is unimportant, but to point up the basic *sūtras* and also to permit use of a greater amount of the indispensable commentary without enlarging the volume beyond convenient size.

This volume has been planned as part of a projected series of source books. Others in the series will concern Chinese philosophy, Buddhist philosophy, and Japanese philosophy. This series had its origin in preliminary work done with Dr Wing-tsit Chan, now Professor of

Chinese Culture and Philosophy and Chairman of the Division of the Humanities at Dartmouth College, on what was originally planned as a one-volume source book in Oriental philosophy. It was found impossible to present in one volume adequate selections from all the great systems of philosophy in the East. It was considered a much sounder policy to devote an entire volume to each of the major Oriental philosophical traditions, so as to provide adequate selections of fundamental material from all the various schools and systems involved in each of these traditions.

An expression of deep and sincere gratitude is hereby extended to the following authorities in the field who have assisted in the preparation of this volume: B. L. Atreya, Arabindu Basu, Wing-tsit Chan, S. C. Chatterjee, Haridas Chaudhuri, George P. Conger, Daniel H. H. Ingalls, T. M. P. Mahadevan, T. R. V. Murti, Johannes Rahder, P. Nagaraja Rao, S. K. Saksena (who examined the entire manuscript and made many valuable suggestions), D. T. Suzuki, and Judith Tyberg. I owe a special debt of gratitude, of course, to Dr Chan. Without his collaboration on the source book as originally planned, this volume would never have been undertaken. At the present time he is working on a source book in Chinese philosophy, which is projected as the second volume in this series.

I also wish to express my thanks to Dr Henry Allen Moe, Secretary General of the John Simon Guggenheim Memorial Foundation, and to the Foundation, for the grant which made it possible for me to go to India and to Oxford to work with Dr Radhakrishnan on this project and to undertake advanced studies in Indian philosophy at Banaras Hindu University.

Appreciation is also gladly extended to those who provided necessary financial aid which made publication of this volume possible: the Honorable Maulana Abul Kalam Azad, Minister of Education, Government of India; the John Simon Guggenheim Memorial Foundation and its Secretary General, Dr Henry Allen Moe; the Edward W. Hazen Foundation and its President, Dr Paul J. Braisted; the Watumull Foundation; and the McInerny Foundation.

Appreciation is hereby expressed to the following publishers for permission to include in this volume selections taken from their publications. These are cited in the several chapters and in addition Appendix C gives publication data of all of the English translations from which passages have been chosen: George Allen & Unwin Ltd. and Harper & Bros.; The Academy of Sciences of the USSR; The

American Oriental Society; Association Press (Calcutta); Bhandarkar Oriental Research Institute (Poona); The Central Jaina Publishing House (Arrah); E. P. Dutton & Co., Inc., *The Eastern Buddhist*; Harvard University Press; Kegan Paul, Trench, Trübner and Co., Ltd.; Alfred A. Knopf, Inc.; University of Madras; John Murray (Wisdom of the East Series); The Oriental Book Agency (Poona); Oriental Institute (Baroda); Oxford University Press; The Pali Text Society; The Panini Office (Allahabad); Routledge & Kegan Paul, Ltd.; Asiatic Society of Bengal; Shri Jain Shivetambar Education Board (Bombay); Sri Vyasa Press (Tirupati); and Mr M. S. Srinivas. Very special appreciation is expressed to Oxford University Press for permission to publish all the verses in Dr Radhakrishnan's translation of the *Dhammapada* and to George Allen & Unwin Ltd., for permission to quote all the verses in his translation of the *Bhagavad-gītā*. Both of these volumes are still in print and are highly recommended to students in this field because of Dr Radhakrishnan's superb introductions, explanations, and notes as well as the translations themselves. In some cases it was impossible to contact publishers, especially those in India, to obtain formal permission to use selections from their books. If any fault in this connection is mine, an apology is hereby extended to these publishers, including E. J. Lazarus & Co., The Bharata Press, and the Wesleyan Mission Press.

I also want to express my sincere appreciation to the personnel of Princeton University Press for assistance and encouragement—to Mr Datus C. Smith, Jr., former Director, to Mr Herbert S. Bailey, Jr., present Director, and to Miss Harriet Anderson for her understanding, patience, and help throughout the processing of this complicated and difficult volume.

I wish to express my deep gratitude to Dr Radhakrishnan for consenting to work with me on this material and for the great amount of time and effort he contributed to its completion. The honor of being united with him in an undertaking of this kind is a rare privilege which I appreciate very greatly.

I have been personally responsible for the preparation of the manuscript for submission to the publisher and therefore assume responsibility for the many changes made in punctuation, capitalization, romanization, etc., and for any errors which might be found in the text.

CHARLES A. MOORE

Honolulu, Hawaii
9 October 1954

CONTENTS

CONTENTS

CONTEMPORARY THOUGHT

GENERAL
INTRODUCTION

HISTORY OF INDIAN THOUGHT

AT the very outset, it should be emphasized that Indian philosophy has had an extremely long and complex development, much more complex than is usually realized, and probably a longer history of continuous development than any other philosophical tradition. While the historical perspective is undoubtedly of immense importance in the study of such a tradition, it is impossible to present an exact historical survey of this development. Because of the Indians' lack of concern for chronology, many of the details of the chronological sequence of the writings either are lost or no record of them was kept. In a sense, the history of Indian philosophy can be written, if only in broadest outline, but no history of philosophy can be complete without some acquaintance with the philosophers who were responsible for the doctrines and for the development of thought. However, so unhistorical, or perhaps so deeply-philosophical, was the nature of the ancient Indians that much more is known about the philosophies than about the philosophers. Relatively few of the great philosophers of ancient Indian thought are known to us and some of the most famous names to which history attributes certain philosophical doctrines or systems are now admitted to be legendary. On the one hand, we are occasionally aware of the author of some doctrines but, as in the case of Indian materialism and some other movements, original texts are not available and the details of the systems are completely unknown.

In broad outline, Indian philosophy may be said to have had four major periods of development up to the time of its serious decline about A.D. 1700. The Vedic Period is dimmed by obscurity, but it may be placed approximately between 2500 and 600 B.C. This is the period during which the Āryans, having come down into India from central Asia, settled their new homeland and gradually expanded and developed their Āryan culture and civilization. In the technical sense of the term, this can hardly be called a philosophical age. It is to be thought of as an age of groping, in which religion, philosophy, superstition, and thought were inextricably interrelated and yet in perpetual conflict. It is an age of philosophical development, however, and its culminating doctrines, those expounded in the major Upaniṣads, have determined the tone if not the precise pattern of the Indian philosophical development ever since.

The literature of this period consists of the four Vedas (*Ṛg Veda*, *Yajur Veda*, *Sāma Veda*, and *Atharva Veda*), each of which has four parts, known as Mantras, Brāhmaṇas, Āraṇyakas, and Upaniṣads. The Mantras (hymns), especially the later ones in the *Ṛg Veda*, constitute the actual beginning of Indian philosophy. By progressing from the not unusual polytheism of the early Vedas, through monotheism, to suggestions of monism, these poems and songs paved the way for the monistic tendencies of the Upaniṣads. The Brāhmaṇas are chiefly religious documents, including ritualistic precepts and sacrificial duties. The Āraṇyakas and the Upaniṣads constitute the concluding parts of the Brāhmaṇas, and in these philosophical problems are discussed. The Brāhmaṇas provide the ritual to be observed by the householder, but when the householder has reached old age, he resorts to the forest and needs a substitute for the ritual he has known as a householder. The Āraṇyakas, which come between the Brāhmaṇas and the Upaniṣads, supply this need by encouraging meditation for those who live in the forest. The Āraṇyakas form the transition link between the ritual of the Brāmaṇas and the philosophy of the Upaniṣads. While the hymns are the creation of poets, the Brāhmaṇas are the work of priests, and the Upaniṣads are the meditations of philosophers. The Upaniṣads, though in one sense a continuation of the Vedic religion, are in another sense a strong philosophical protest against the religion of the Brāhmaṇas. It is in the Upaniṣads that the tendency to spiritual monism, which in one form or another characterizes much of Indian philosophy, was first established and where intuition rather than reason was first recognized as the true guide to ultimate truth.

The second period of philosophical development is the Epic Period, dated approximately from 500 or 600 B.C. to A.D. 200. This period is characterized by the indirect presentation of philosophical doctrines through the medium of nonsystematic and nontechnical literature, especially the great epics, the *Rāmāyaṇa* and the *Mahābhārata*. In addition, however, the period includes the rise and early development of Buddhism, Jainism, Śaivism, and Vaiṣṇavism. The *Bhagavad-gītā*, which is a part of the *Mahābhārata*, ranks as one of the three most authoritative texts in Indian philosophical literature. Furthermore, the beginnings of the orthodox schools of Indian philosophy also belong to this period. Most of the systems had their beginnings about the time of the rise of Buddhism, and developed side by side for centuries. The systematic works of the major schools were written later, but the origin of the doctrines of the several schools most probably occurred during the Epic Period. This was one of the most fertile periods of philosophy in India as well as in several other parts of the world—Greece, China, Persia, and elsewhere. A great amount of philosophical or semiphilosophical material was produced during the period, and it is very probable that our knowledge of the doctrines developed at that time merely scratches the surface of the wealth, depth, and variety of philosophical speculation that took place. It was during this period that such philosophies as skepticism, naturalism, materialism, etc., arose along with the other heterodox systems of Buddhism and Jainism and what were later to be known as the orthodox systems of Hinduism. It is out of this wealth of material that the later systems—the orthodox systems of Hinduism and the unorthodox systems of the Cārvāka, Buddhism, and Jainism—were perforce brought into clearer perspective by the construction of systematic treatises.

It was also during this period that many of the Dharmaśāstras, treatises on ethical and social philosophy, were compiled. These, like the rest of the philosophical texts of the period, are classed as *smṛtis*, that is, traditional texts, as contrasted with the literature of the Vedic Period, which is known as *śruti*, revealed scriptures or authoritative texts. The Dharmaśāstras are systematic treatises concerning the conduct of life among the Āryans, describing their social organization and their ethical and religious functions and obligations.

The third period is the *Sūtra* Period, which is dated approximately from the early centuries of the Christian era. In this period the systematic treatises of the various schools were written and the systems took the basic form they were to preserve henceforth. The doctrines of each of the systems were presented in orderly, systematic, and logically developed sets of aphorisms, extremely brief, sometimes enigmatic, statements which, according to some interpretations, are merely reminders for the initiated to enable them to recall the details of philosophical systems to which they belonged and whose fuller doctrines were known only to those within the fold of the system. During this period the critical attitude in philosophy was distinctly developed along with the systematic, and the *Sūtras* themselves contain not only the positive developments of the systems but also keen and comprehensive polemics against opposing systems. Whereas during the preceding period philosophical thought and discussion had their origin, they were at that time carried on at the precritical level. In the *Sūtras*, however, we have self-conscious thought and reflection and no longer merely constructive imagination and spontaneous insights.

The six Hindu systems presented in *sūtra* form during this period are the Nyāya or logical realism; the Vaiśesika or realistic pluralism; the Sāṁkhya or evolutionary dualism; the Yoga or disciplined meditation; the Pūrva Mīmāṁsā or earlier interpretative investigations of the Vedas, relating to conduct; and the Uttara Mīmāṁsā or later investigations of the Vedas, relating to knowledge, also called Vedānta, the "end of the Vedas".

The fourth period, the Scholastic Period, is that in which commentaries were written upon the *Sūtras* in order to explain them. Without elaboration and explanation the *Sūtras* are almost unintelligible. Not only were commentaries written upon the *sūtras*, but also commentaries upon commentaries, and commentaries upon these, almost without limit. It is impossible to provide dates for this period with any great degree of certainty. It is dated generally from the *Sūtra* Period to the seventeenth century. The literature of this period is primarily explanatory, but is also strongly and sometimes grossly polemical. There is a brood of "Schoolmen," noisy controversialists, indulging in oversubtle theories and finespun arguments, who fought fiercely over details of philosophical doctrines and who were in constant philosophical conflict with representatives of other schools. Sometimes the commentaries are more confusing than enlightening. Instead of clear explanation and thought, one often finds mere words; instead of philosophy, logic-chopping. Obscurity of thought, subtlety of logic, and intolerance of opposition are marks of the worst types of commentators. The better types, however, are invaluable and are respected almost as much as the creators of the systems themselves. Śaṁkara, for example, the writer of a famous commentary on the *Sūtra* of the Vedānta system, is thought of more highly as a philosopher than is Bādarāyaṇa, the seer who wrote the original *Vedānta Sūtra* (also called the *Brahma Sūtra*). The Scholastic Period is one of explanation of the original *Sūtras*, but, like any scholastic period, it has also produced quibbling and unphilosophical debates which are relatively worthless. On the other hand, it has brought forth some of the greatest of all Indian philosophers. Among these, in addition to Śaṁkara, are Kumārila, Śrīdhara, Rāmānuja, Madhva, Vācaspati, Udayana, Bhāskara, Jayanta, Vijñānabhikṣu, and Raghunātha. These great thinkers have been much more than commentators on ancient systems, although, in their modesty, they have claimed to be no more. In fact, however, they have been, to all intents and purposes, creators of their own systems. In the guise of commentators, they have elaborated points of view which, though capable of being related to the original system of which they are supposed to be commentaries, are new expositions rather than mere explanations. For example, the three major forms of Vedānta, those developed by Śaṁkara, Rāmānuja, and Madhva, are distinct and elaborate systems, although they all stem from the same *Vedānta Sūtra* of Bādarāyaṇa. This type of development is indicative of the unique way in which Indian philosophers have maintained their traditional respect for the past and their recognition of the value of authority in philosophy, but, without seeming to break this tradition, have also carried along the free development of thought as their insight and reason directed.

While, in a sense, the Scholastic Period is still in progress, since interpretations of ancient ideas and systems are still being written, Indian philosophy lost its dynamic spirit about the sixteenth century when India became the victim of outside powers. First the Muslims and then the British assumed control of the country, not only physically but also in the realm of thought. The Muslims undermined Āryan culture and thought as far as possible, and the British, in their time, did as much as they could to belittle the thought of traditional India. For a long time, the English-educated Indians were apparently ashamed of their own philosophical tradition, and it became the mark of intelligence as well as expediency to be as European and as English in thought and in life as possible. While the coming of the British brought about a revival in education, the resulting revival of Indian thought was unintentional, to say the least. During this period indigenous reform movements like that of the Brāhmo Samāj and the Ārya Samāj took a leading part in India's philosophical and religious renaissance. More recently, especially since the nationalist movement began, and more especially since the re-establishment of India as a free and independent nation, the revival of Indian philosophy as such and the consciousness of the greatness of India's philosophical past have been the most prominent developments in the field. During the twentieth century, the Indian mind has been affected by the Western, but the Western mind has also been influenced by the Indian more than ever before, through the writings of contemporary poets, sages, and philosophers. To be sure, the revival of the Indian consciousness of the greatness of its own philosophical past has tended in recent years to develop a nationalistic tone in philosophy as well as in politics. The resulting tendency of extremists to minimize or reject the revival and development of philosophy which was effected by the contact of Indians and Westerners has not been a healthy sign. We of today are able to see further than our predecessors, since we have climbed on their shoulders. Instead, therefore, of resting content with the foundations so nobly laid in the past, we must build in harmony with ancient endeavor as well as with contemporary thought. The future development of Indian philosophy, if one may hazard a guess, will be in terms of a more synthetic approach to Indian and Western points of view.

The Spirit of Indian Philosophy

Indian philosophy, it has been noted, is extremely complex. Through the ages the Indian philosophical mind has probed deeply into many aspects of human experience and the external world. Although some methods, such as the experimental method of modern science, have been relatively less prominent than others, not only the problems of Indian philosophy but also the methods used and the conclusions reached in the pursuit of truth have certainly been as far-reaching in their extent, variety, and depth as those of other philosophical traditions. The six basic systems and the many subsystems of Hinduism, the four chief schools of Buddhism, the two schools of Jainism, and the materialism of the Cārvāka are evidence enough of the diversity of views in Indian philosophy. The variety of the Indian perspective is unquestionable. Accordingly, it is very difficult to cite any specific doctrines or methods as characteristic of Indian philosophy as a whole and applicable to all the multitudinous systems and subsystems developed through nearly four millenniums of Indian philosophical speculation.

Nevertheless, in certain respects there is what might be called a distinct spirit of Indian philosophy. This is exemplified by certain attitudes which are fairly characteristic of the Indian philosophical mind or which stand as points of view that have been emphasized characteristically by Indians in their philosophies.

(1) The chief mark of Indian philosophy in general is its concentration upon the spiritual. Both in life and in philosophy the spiritual motive is predominant in India. Except for the relatively minor materialistic school of the Cārvāka and related doctrines, philosophy in India conceives man to be spiritual in nature, is interested primarily in his spiritual destiny, and relates him in one way or another to a universe which is also spiritual in essential character. Neither man nor the universe is looked upon as physical in essence, and material welfare is never recognized as the goal of human life, except by the Cārvāka. Philosophy and religion are intimately related because philosophy itself is regarded as a spiritual adventure, and also because the motivation both in philosophy and in religion concerns the spiritual way of life in the here-and-now and the eventual spiritual salvation of man in relation to the universe. Practically all of Indian philosophy, from its beginning in the Vedas to the present day, has striven to bring about a socio-spiritual reform in the country, and philosophical literature has taken many forms, mythological, popular, or technical, as the circumstances required, in order to promote such spiritual life. The problems of religion have always given depth and power and purpose to the Indian philosophical mind and spirit.

(2) Another characteristic view of Indian philosophy is the belief in the intimate relationship of philosophy and life. This attitude of the practical application of philosophy to life is found in every school of Indian philosophy. While natural abundance and material prosperity paved the way for the rise of philosophical speculation, philosophy has never been considered a mere intellectual exercise. The close relationship between theory and practice, doctrine and life, has always been outstanding in Indian thought. Every Indian system seeks the truth, not as academic "knowledge for its own sake," but to learn the truth which shall make men free. This is not, as it has been called, the modern pragmatic attitude. It is much larger and much deeper than that. It is not the view that truth is measured in terms of the practical, but rather that the truth is the only sound guide for practice, that truth alone has efficacy as a guide for man in his search for salvation. Every major system of Indian philosophy

takes its beginning from the practical and tragic problems of life and searches for the truth in order to solve the problem of man's distress in the world in which he finds himself. There has been no teaching which remained a mere word of mouth or dogma of schools. Every doctrine has been turned into a passionate conviction, stirring the heart of man and quickening his breath, and completely transforming his personal nature. In India, philosophy is for life; it is to be lived. It is not enough to *know* the truth; the truth must be *lived*. The goal of the Indian is not to know the ultimate truth but to *realize* it, to become one with it.

Another aspect of the intimate inseparability of theory and practice, philosophy and life, in Indian philosophy is to be found in the universally prevalent demand for moral purification as an imperative preliminary for the would-be student of philosophy or searcher after truth. Śaṁkara's classic statement of this demand calls for a knowledge of the distinction between the eternal and the noneternal, that is, a questioning tendency in the inquirer; the subjugation of all desire for the fruits of action either in this life or in a hereafter, a renunciation of all petty desire, personal motive, and practical interest; tranquillity, self-control, renunciation, patience, peace of mind, and faith; and a desire for release (*mokṣa*) as the supreme goal of life.

(3) Indian philosophy is characterized by the introspective attitude and the introspective approach to reality. Philosophy is thought of as *ātmavidyā*, knowledge of the self. Philosophy can start either with the external world or with the internal world of man's inner nature, the self of man. In its pursuit of the truth, Indian philosophy has always been strongly dominated by concern with the inner life and self of man rather than the external world of physical nature. Physical science, though developed extensively in the Golden Age of Indian culture, was never considered the road to ultimate truth; truth is to be sought and found within. The subjective, then, rather than the objective, becomes the focus of interest in Indian philosophy, and, therefore, psychology and ethics are considered more important as aspects or branches of philosophy than the sciences which study physical nature. This is not to say that the Indian mind has not studied the physical world; in fact, on the contrary, India's achievements in the realm of positive science were at one time truly outstanding, especially in the mathematical sciences such as algebra, astronomy, and geometry, and in the applications of these basic sciences to numerous phases of human activity. Zoology, botany,

medicine, and related sciences have also been extremely prominent in Indian thought. Be this as it may, the Indian, from time immemorial, has felt that the inner spirit of man is the most significant clue to his reality and to that of the universe, more significant by far than the physical or the external.

(4) This introspective interest is highly conducive to idealism, of course, and consequently most Indian philosophy is idealistic in one form or another. The tendency of Indian philosophy, especially Hinduism, has been in the direction of monistic idealism. Almost all Indian philosophy believes that reality is *ultimately* one and *ultimately* spiritual. Some systems have seemed to espouse dualism or pluralism, but even these have been deeply permeated by a strong monistic character. If we concentrate our attention upon the underlying spirit of Indian philosophy rather than its variety of opinions, we shall find that this spirit is embodied in the tendency to interpret life and reality in the way of monistic idealism. This rather unusual attitude is attributable to the nonrigidity of the Indian mind and to the fact that the attitude of monistic idealism is so plastic and dynamic that it takes many forms and expresses itself even in seemingly conflicting doctrines. These are not conflicting doctrines in fact, however, but merely different expressions of an underlying conviction which provides basic unity to Indian philosophy as a whole.

Materialism undoubtedly had its day in India, and, according to sporadic records and constant and determined efforts on the part of other systems to denounce it, the doctrine apparently enjoyed widespread acceptance at one time. Nevertheless, materialism could not hold its own; its adherents have been few in number, and its positive influence has been negligible. Indian philosophy has not been oblivious to materialism; rather, it has known it, has overcome it, and has accepted idealism as the only tenable view, whatever specific form that idealism might take.

(5) Indian philosophy makes unquestioned and extensive use of reason, but intuition is accepted as the only method through which the ultimate can be known. Reason, intellectual knowledge, is not enough. Reason is not useless or fallacious, but it is insufficient. To know reality one must have an actual experience of it. One does not merely *know* the truth in Indian philosophy; one *realizes* it. The word which most aptly describes philosophy in India is *darśana*, which comes from the verbal root *dṛś*, meaning "to see." "To see" is to have a direct intuitive experience of the object, or, rather, to realize

it in the sense of becoming one with it. No complete knowledge is possible as long as there is the relationship of the subject on one hand and the object on the other. Later developments in Indian philosophy, from the time of the beginning of the systems, have all depended in large part upon reason for the systematic formulation of doctrines and systems, for rational demonstration or justification, and in polemical conflicts of system against system. Nevertheless, all the systems, except the Cārvāka, agree that there is a higher way of knowing reality, beyond the reach of reason, namely, the direct perception or experience of the ultimate reality, which cannot be known by reason in any of its forms. Reason can demonstrate the truth, but reason cannot discover or reach the truth. While reason may be the method of philosophy in its more intellectualistic sense, intuition is the only method of comprehending the ultimate. Indian philosophy is thus characterized by an ultimate dependence upon intuition, along with the recognition of the efficacy of reason and intellect when applied in their limited capacity and with their proper function.

(6) Another characteristic of Indian philosophy, one which is closely related to the preceding one, is its so-called acceptance of authority. Although the systems of Indian philosophy vary in the degree to which they are specifically related to the ancient *śruti*, not one of the systems—orthodox or unorthodox, except the Cārvāka—openly stands in violation of the accepted intuitive insights of its ancient seers, whether it be the Hindu seers of the Upaniṣads, the intuitive experience of the Buddha, or the similarly intuitive wisdom of Mahāvīra, the founder of Jainism, as we have it today. Indian philosophers have always been conscious of tradition and, as has been indicated before, the great system-builders of later periods claimed to be merely commentators, explaining the traditional wisdom of the past. While the specific doctrines of the past may be changed by interpretation, the general spirit and frequently the basic concepts are retained from age to age. Reverence for authority does not militate against progress, but it does lend a unity of spirit by providing a continuity of thought which has rendered philosophy especially significant in Indian life and solidly unified against any philosophical attitude contradicting its basic characteristics of spirituality, inwardness, intuition, and the strong belief that the truth is to be lived, not merely known.

The charge of indulging in an exaggerated respect for authority may be legitimately leveled against some of Indian philosophy, but this respect for the past is rooted in the deep conviction that those who really know reality are those who have *realized* the truth and that it is to them that we must turn ultimately, beyond all our power of reasoning, if we are to attain any comprehension of the truth which they saw and realized. As has been said, India has produced a great variety of philosophical doctrines and systems. This has been true despite universal reverence for and acceptance of the authority of the ancient seers as the true discoverers of wisdom. The variety of the systems, even in their basic conceptions, looked at in the light of the prevalent acceptance of authority, reveals the fact that this reverence has not made Indian philosophy a dogmatic religious creed, as is often alleged, but rather a single tone or trend of thought on basic issues. How completely free from traditional bias the systems are is seen, for example, by the fact that the original Sāṁkhya says nothing about the possible existence of God, although it is emphatic in its doctrine of the theoretical undemonstrability of his existence; the Vaiśeṣika and the Yoga, especially the latter, admit the existence of God, but do not consider him to be the creator of the universe; the Mīmāṁsā speaks of God but denies his importance and efficacy in the moral ordering of the world. To emphasize the point further, reference should be made also to the early Buddhist systems, which reject God, and to the Cārvākas, who deny God without qualification.

(7) Finally, there is the over-all synthetic tradition which is essential to the spirit and method of Indian philosophy. This is as old as the *Ṛg Veda*, where the seers realized that true religion comprehends all religions, so that "God is one but men call him by many names." Indian philosophy is clearly characterized by the synthetic approach to the various aspects of experience and reality. Religion and philosophy, knowledge and conduct, intuition and reason, man and nature, God and man, noumenon and phenomena, are all brought into harmony by the synthesizing tendency of the Indian mind. The Hindu is prone to believe even that all the six systems, as well as their varieties of subsystems, are in harmony with one another, in fact, that they complement one another in the total vision, which is one. As contrasted with Western philosophy, with its analytic approach to reality and experience, Indian philosophy is fundamentally synthetic. The basic texts of Indian philosophy treat not only one phase of experience and reality, but of the full content of the philosophic sphere. Metaphysics, epistemology, ethics, religion, psychology, facts, and value are not cut off one from the other but are

treated in their natural unity as aspects of one life and experience or of a single comprehensive reality.

It is this synthetic vision of Indian philosophy which has made possible the intellectual and religious tolerance which has become so pronounced in Indian thought and in the Indian mind throughout the ages. Recent squabbles between religious communities, bred of new political factionalism, are not outgrowths of the Indian mind but, instead, are antagonistic to its unique genius for adaptability and tolerance, which takes all groups and all communities into its one truth and one life.

In addition to these general characteristics of Indian philosophy from the intellectual or theoretical point of view, there is also a fundamental unity of perspective in the practical realm. This has several aspects. In the first place, there is the fact, mentioned earlier, that all philosophies in India—Hindu, Buddhist, Jaina, and Cārvāka—have a practical motivation, stemming from man's practical problems of life, his limitations and suffering, and culminating in every case except the Cārvāka in a consideration of his ultimate liberation. In every case, including the Cārvāka, the motivation is practical rather than theoretical, for the Cārvāka is interested, not in theory for its own sake, but in living a life of pleasure since it believes the world is conducive to that type of life and justifies no other. The goal of life in Hinduism, Buddhism, and Jainism is essentially the same. *Mokṣa* (liberation) is the ultimate objective for Hinduism and Jainism, and *nirvāṇa* is the goal in Buddhism. The precise meanings of liberation vary among the different schools, even among those within the framework of Buddhism and Hinduism, but the essential meaning of both *mokṣa* and *nirvāṇa* is emancipation or liberation from turmoil and suffering and freedom from rebirth. In some instances, the goal seems to be negative, consisting essentially of freedom from pain and freedom from rebirth, but in reality it is the positive achievement of a richer and fuller life and the attainment of infinite bliss. The spirit re-achieves its original purity, sometimes by becoming identical with the Absolute, sometimes by a life of communion with God, sometimes simply by the eternal existence of the pure spirit in its individuality, but in all cases free from the limitations and entanglements of life.

The several schools and systems of Indian philosophy are of one mind not only with reference to the goal of life, but also with reference to the good life on earth. The essential spirit of the philosophy of life of Hinduism, Buddhism, and Jainism is that of non-attachment. This is an attitude of mind with which the individual fulfills his part in life and lives a "normal" everyday existence in company with his fellow men, without being entangled in or emotionally disturbed by the results of his actions. He attains a mental and spiritual superiority to worldly values and is never enslaved by them. This is not negativism or escapism, for one takes part in everyday activities in accordance with his place in society. However, it is living and acting without any sense of attachment to the things of this world and without any selfishness whatsoever.

Hinduism, Buddhism, and Jainism, in all their branches, also accept the underlying doctrines of *karma* and rebirth. All of these schools believe that man must be morally and spiritually perfected before he can attain salvation. They also believe that justice is the law of the moral life exactly as cause-and-effect is the law of the natural world. What one sows one must reap. Since justice and moral and spiritual perfection are not achievable in one life, all these systems believe in rebirth, so as to provide the opportunity for moral progress and eventual perfection. Throughout Indian philosophy, from the earliest Vedas to the latest developments, the moral order of the universe has been an accepted doctrine of all Indian thinkers except the Cārvākas. *Karma* and rebirth are the instrumentalities by which the moral order of the universe is worked out in the life of man.

There is a further common element which unifies all schools of Hindu philosophy in the practical realm, although the heterodox schools, the Cārvāka, Buddhism, and Jainism, do not conform to this pattern. The way of life accepted by all schools of Hinduism, regardless of metaphysical and epistemological variations, includes the fourfold division of society, the four stages of life, and the four basic values which man seeks. In Hinduism, society is divided into four groups (*varṇa*, frequently translated as castes) determined generally according to occupational ability, namely, the priest-teacher (*brāhmin*),[1] the king or political and military leader (*kṣatriya*), the merchant (*vaiśya*), and the laborer (*śūdra*). The first three of these are called the twice-born, that is, they are religiously initiated Hindus, whereas the *śūdras* are not so accepted. The lives of the twice-born are to consist of the four stages of the student (*brahmacārin*), the householder

[1] *Brāhmin* is used throughout this volume in preference to *brāhmaṇa* to designate this group because the latter term also refers to a group of early Indian texts, and thus may lead to confusion. Technically speaking, however, "*brāhmin*" is not a correct Sanskrit term, although it is used rather widely.

(*gṛhastha*), the forest-dweller (*vānaprastha*), and the wandering monk (*sannyāsin* or *saṁnyāsin*). In this social scheme, one does not enter the life of ascetism until after he has fulfilled his obligations to his fellow man as a student and as a householder, but in the later stages of life one is to concentrate more and more upon the spiritual and upon his search for liberation. The goals of life which are accepted by all Hindus are righteousness or obedience to the moral law (*dharma*), wealth or material welfare (*artha*), pleasure (*kāma*), and emancipation (*mokṣa*). *Dharma* prevails throughout life, that is, neither pleasure nor wealth is to be obtained through violation of the rules of morality. *Mokṣa* is the ultimate goal to which all men should aspire. This social philosophy is accepted without question by all Hindus. It is presented in the literature of the Dharmaśāstras, but is not found in any elaboration or with any philosophical justification in the basic technical philosophical texts. This common ideal life of all Hindus provides a spirit of unity to the social and moral life of the country, although Buddhists and Jainas, who are greatly in the minority, do not follow the same specific pattern of life.

The Value of the Study of Indian Philosophy

The study of Indian philosophy is important historically, philosophically, and even politically. The Indian philosophical tradition is man's oldest as well as the longest continuous development of speculation about the nature of reality and man's place therein. It began with the ancient Vedas, which are probably the earliest documents of the human mind that have come down to us, and has continued age after age in progressive philosophical advance in the effort to understand life and reality. But it is not as a piece of antiquarian investigation that we of today should study Indian philosophy. Despite the tendency to respect and revere the greatness of the past, Indian thinkers of all ages have been deeply and profoundly concerned with the ultimate truth which is timeless. Nor should we study Indian philosophy as a merely provincial or geographical approach to reality. Despite charges by some Western critics who would accuse Indian philosophy of neglecting scientific method, Indian thinkers have not been anti-empirical and have not neglected nature in their study of reality; nor, in their study of man, have they been excessively restricted to those characteristics which may be peculiar to man in India. India's concentrated study of the inner nature of man is, in the end, a study of man universal.

The teachings of Indian philosophers from the days of the Vedas till today have been landmarks of human thought. Not all ideas and not all systems of Indian philosophy are deeply significant, but the heights and depths reached by Indian thinkers and seers are indications and examples of the profound powers of the human mind. Indian thought is neither merely ancient speculation nor merely provincial Indian thinking. It is man's mind and soul at their best in philosophy and religion.

Philosophically, the study of Indian philosophy is important in the search for the truth. Philosophy must include all insights and all experiences in its purview, and Indian philosophy has much to contribute. The major problems of Indian philosophy are the problems faced by thinking man ever since he first began to speculate about life and reality, but Indian philosophy also has special problems, different emphases, unique approaches and methods, and unique solutions—all of which are India's contributions to the total picture of the truth which is the substance of philosophy. The need of philosophy today is for a world perspective which will include the philosophical insights of all the world's great traditions. The goal is not a single philosophy which would annihilate differences of perspective, but there must be agreement on basic perspectives and ultimate values. Such a world philosophy should certainly incorporate the spiritual insights of the seers of ancient India and of the thinkers who have guided the many centuries of Indian philosophical speculation.

It is politically important, too, that Indian philosophy should be studied by the West. The current appeal for "one world" is too often thought of merely in the realm of politics. Political unity is impossible without philosophical understanding. Political insights, agreements, and differences are on the secondary level of man's thinking. Social and political conditions in the several areas of the world depend, in the final analysis, upon the philosophical and spiritual thought and ideals of the peoples of the world. It is to philosophy, then, that man must turn in his hope to bring the peoples of the world together in greater mutual understanding and in the intellectual and spiritual harmony without which a unified world will be impossible in any sphere, political or otherwise. The future of civilization depends upon the return of spiritual awareness to the hearts and minds of men. To this purpose the contribution of Indian philosophy, with its agelong spiritual emphasis, is inestimable and indispensable.

THE VEDIC PERIOD

CHAPTER I

THE VEDAS

WHATEVER may be the truth of the theory of the racial affinities of the Indian and the European peoples, there is no doubt that Indo-European languages derive from a common source and illustrate a relationship of the mind. The oldest Indo-European literary and philosophical monument is the *Ṛg Veda*. The name Veda, signifying wisdom, suggests that the road which the Vedic sages traveled was the road of those who seek to understand. The questions they investigate are of a philosophical character: "What god shall we adore with our oblation?"[1] "Who verily knows and who can here declare where it was born and whence comes this creation? The gods are later than this world's production. Who knows whence it first came into being?"[2]

A study of the hymns of the *Ṛg Veda* is indispensable for any adequate account of Indian thought. Whatever we may think of them, half-formed myths or crude allegories, obscure gropings or immature compositions, still they are the source of the later practices and philosophies of the Indo-Āryans, and a study of them is necessary for a proper understanding of subsequent thought.

There are four Vedas, the *Ṛg Veda*, composed of hymns, the *Yajur Veda*, which deals with sacrificial formulas, the *Sāma Veda*, which refers to melodies, and the *Atharva Veda*, which has a large number of magic formulas. For philosophical purposes, the *Yajur Veda* and the *Sāma Veda* are not of great importance. The *Atharva Veda* describes spells and incantations. There are spells for the healing of diseases, for long life, etc. It is said that in the *Atharva Veda* are to be found the beginnings of Indian medical science.

Each of the Vedas contains four sections: Saṁhitā (a collection of hymns, prayers, benedictions, sacrificial formulas, and litanies), Brāhmaṇas (prose treatises discussing the significance of sacrificial rites and ceremonies), Āraṇyakas (forest-texts), which are partly included in the Brāhmaṇas and partly reckoned as independent, and Upaniṣads.

The dates of the composition and of the collection of the hymns of the *Ṛg Veda* are unknown. It is believed, however, that a long period of time must have elapsed between the composition and the compilation of the hymns. There is evidence to indicate with some certainty that the hymns were current fifteen centuries before Christ, somewhat in the arrangement

[1] x.121. [2] x.129.

in which we have them at the present time. The *Ṛg Veda* Saṁhitā is a collection which represents the thought of several generations of thinkers, and this fact accounts both for the heterogeneity of the hymns and also for the different strata of thought which indicate marked development from "polytheistic" religion to monistic philosophy.

The *Ṛg Veda*, which comprises 1,017 hymns divided into ten books, represents the earliest phase of the evolution of religious consciousness, where we have not so much commandments of priests as the outpourings of poetic minds who are struck by the immensity of the universe and the inexhaustible mystery of life. We have worship of deities like Sūrya (sun), Agni (fire), Dyaus (sky or heaven), Maruts (storms), Vāyu or Vāta (wind), Āpas (waters), Uṣas (dawn), and Pṛthivī (earth). Even deities whose names are no longer so transparent, such as Indra, Varuṇa, Mitra, Aditi, Viṣṇu, Pūṣan, the two Aśvins, Rudra, and Parjanya, were originally related to natural phenomena. Qualities which emphasize particular important aspects of natural phenomena attained sometimes to the rank of independent deities. Savitṛ (Savitar), the inspirer or life-giver, and Vivasvān, the shining, were originally attributes, names of the sun, but later became sun-gods. Some of the deities worshiped by the different tribes, such as Pūṣan, were admitted into the Vedic pantheon. Abstract qualities like Śraddhā (faith), Manyu (anger), Gandharvas (fairies), Apsaras (heavenly damsels), and forest and field spirits were also included.

Though the *Ṛg Veda* speaks of a plurality of gods, when worship is accorded to any one of them, he becomes the chief god, the creator, preserver, and judge (or destroyer) of the universe. As several gods are exalted to this high place, the tendency is called henotheism, as distinct from monotheism where only one God is exalted as the highest.

The attributes of creation, preservation, and judgment (or destruction), it was felt early, could not be separated and ascribed to different deities. They were given to a single personality, Prajāpati, the lord of creatures, and Viśvakarman, the world-maker. The conception of *Ṛta* (the order of the world) supports this idea. If the endless variety of the world suggests numerous deities, the unity of the world implies one deity.

The beginnings of doubt are felt in the *Ṛg Veda*. It is said, "Of whom they ask, 'Where is he?' of him indeed they also say, 'He is not.'"[1] A super-personal monism develops, and the universe is explained in the Hymn of Creation[2] as an evolution out of an ultimate One. This hymn suggests the distinction between the absolute reality (*Brahman*) and the personal God (Īśvara), which dominates the subsequent development of Indian thought.

The passages quoted in this chapter are all from the *Ṛg Veda*. They are selected primarily from Books I and X, in which the philosophical material of the *Ṛg Veda* is most concentrated. In the selections an effort has been made to give representative statements of the several basic attitudes, ideas, and tendencies found in the *Ṛg Veda*. The selections are divided into six topical sections. The most important of these sections, from the point of

[1] II.12 [2] X.129.

view of philosophical content, is that termed "Monotheistic and Monistic Tendencies," where the transition from early polytheism to the more philosophical monism of later hymns is depicted.

Since the hymns often deal with more than one topic, it is not possible always to subsume the entire hymn under single topical categories. The Hymn of Creation, for example, deals with the nature of the Absolute and the relation of the Absolute to the empirical world, as well as the process of creation itself. Sometimes, because of the singleness of subject-matter and for the sake of adequate presentation of the poetic style, entire hymns are quoted.

The relative clarity of most of the hymns quoted here should not minimize the fact that almost innumerable problems and theories of interpretation are involved throughout the Vedas.

The selections have been taken from R. T. H. Griffith, *The Hymns of the Rigveda*, 2 vols. (Benares: E. J. Lazarus and Co., 3rd ed., 1920–6); A. A. Macdonell, *Hymns from the Rigveda* (London: Oxford University Press, 1922); Hermann Oldenberg, *Vedic Hymns*, Part II, Sacred Books of the East, XLVI (Oxford: Clarendon Press, 1897); Edward J. Thomas, *Vedic Hymns*, Wisdom of the East (London: John Murray, 1923). The translator's name will accompany the number of the hymn in the selections.

1. HYMNS TO GODS—POLYTHEISM

Three strata of development are found in the thought of the hymns of the *Ṛg Veda*, naturalistic polytheism, monotheism, and monism. Naturalism and anthropomorphism, as indicated in these hymns, seem to constitute the first stage or stages of Vedic thought. The hymns quoted in this section represent this first phase of the doctrine of the *Ṛg Veda*. A striking aspect of the hymns is their polytheistic character. Very many gods are named and worshiped.

Different views of the spirit of these hymns are held by competent scholars. They have been referred to as primeval child-like naïve prayers, as the allegorical representation of the attributes of the supreme Deity, as sacrificial compositions of a primitive race which attached great importance to ceremonial rites, as altogether allegorical, or as somewhat naturalistic. These varying opinions need not be looked upon as antagonistic, for they only point to the heterogeneous nature of the *Ṛg Veda* collection.

To Indra [primarily a deity of the thunderstorm][1]

x.89 (Griffith)

1. I will extol the most heroic Indra who with his might forced earth and sky asunder;
   Who hath filled all with width as man's upholder, surpassing floods and rivers in his greatness.

[1] Indra is the most prominent of the gods in the *Ṛg Veda*. He is most frequently praised for his power and heroism, as the god of battle.

2. Sūrya is he: throughout the wide expanses shall Indra turn him, swift as car-wheels, hither,
   Like a stream resting not but ever active: he hath destroyed, with light, the black-hued darkness.
3. To him I sing a holy prayer, incessant, new, matchless, common to the earth and heaven,
   Who marks, as they were backs, all living creatures: ne'er doth he fail a friend, the noble Indra.
4. I will send forth my songs in flow unceasing, like water from the ocean's depth, to Indra.
   Who to his car on both its sides securely hath fixed the earth and heaven as with an axle.
5. Rousing with draughts, the shaker, rushing onward, impetuous, very strong, armed as with arrows
   Is Soma; forest trees and all the bushes deceive not Indra with their offered likeness.
6. Soma hath flowed to him who naught can equal, the earth, the heavens, the firmament, the mountains,—
   When heightened in his ire his indignation shatters the firm and breaks the strong in pieces.
7. As an axe fells the tree so he slew Vṛtra,[1] brake down the strongholds and dug out the rivers.
   He cleft the mountain like a new-made pitcher. Indra brought forth the kine with his companions.
8. Wise art thou, punisher of guilt, O Indra. The sword lops limbs, thou smitest down the sinner,
   The men who injure, as it were a comrade, the lofty Law of Varuṇa and Mitra.[2]
9. Men who lead evil lives, who break agreements, and injure Varuṇa, Aryaman,[3] and Mitra,—
   Against these foes, O mighty Indra, sharpen, as furious death, thy bull of fiery colour.
10. Indra is sovran lord of Earth and Heaven, Indra is lord of waters and of mountains.
    Indra is lord of prosperers and sages: Indra must be invoked in rest and effort.
11. Vaster than days and nights, giver of increase, vaster than firmament and flood of ocean,

[1] Vṛtrāsura, a cloud-demon.
[2] A god of light.
[3] One of the chief Ādityas or sons of Aditi.

Vaster than bounds of earth and wind's extension, vaster than rivers and our lands is Indra.

12. Forward, as herald of refulgent morning, let thine insatiate arrow fly, O Indra,
And pierce, as 'twere a stone launched forth from heaven, with hottest blaze the men who love deception.
13. Him, verily, the moons, the mountains followed, the tall trees followed and the plants and herbage.
Yearning with love both worlds approached, the waters waited on Indra when he first had being.
14. Where was the vengeful dart when thou, O Indra, clavest the demon ever bent on outrage?
When fiends lay there upon the ground extended like cattle in the place of immolation?
15. Those who are set in enmity against us, the Ogaṇas,[1] O Indra waxen mighty,—
Let blinding darkness follow those our foemen, while these shall have bright shining nights to light them.
16. May plentiful libations of the people, and singing *ṛṣis*'[2] holy prayers rejoice thee.
Hearing with love this common invocation, come unto us, pass by all those who praise thee.
17. O Indra, thus may we be made partakers of the new favours that shall bring us profit.
Singing with love! may we the Viśvāmitras win daylight even now through thee, O Indra.
18. Call we on Maghavan, auspicious Indra, best hero in the fight where spoil is gathered,
The strong who listens, who gives aid in battles, who slays the Vṛtras, wins and gathers riches.

To Agni [the god of fire] I.1 (Oldenberg)

1. I magnify Agni, the Purohita, the divine ministrant of the sacrifice, the Hotṛ priest, the greatest bestower of treasures.
2. Agni, worthy to be magnified by the ancient *ṛṣis* and by the present ones—may he conduct the gods hither.
3. May one obtain through Agni wealth and welfare day by day, which may bring glory and high bliss of valiant offspring.

[1] Probably a hostile clan. [2] Sages.

4. Agni, whatever sacrifice and worship thou encompassest on every side, that indeed goes to the gods.
5. May Agni the thoughtful Hotṛ, he who is true and most splendidly renowned, may the god come hither with the gods.
6. Whatever good thou wilt do to thy worshipper, O Agni, that (work) verily is thine, O Aṅgiras.[1]
7. Thee, O Agni, we approach day by day, O (god) who shinest in the darkness; with our prayer, bringing adoration to thee—
8. Who art the king of all worship, the guardian of Ṛta, the shining one, increasing in thy own house.
9. Thus, O Agni, be easy of access to us, as a father is to his son. Stay with us for our happiness.

To Viṣṇu [the all-pervader] I.154 (Macdonell)

1. I will proclaim the mighty deeds of Viṣṇu,
Of him who measured out the earthly spaces;
Who, firmly propping up the higher station,
Strode out in triple regions, widely pacing.
2. Because of this his mighty deed is Viṣṇu
Lauded, like some fierce beast that is much dreaded,
That wanders as it lists, that haunts the mountains:
He in whose three wide strides abide all creatures.
3. Let my inspiring hymn go forth to Viṣṇu,
The mountain-dwelling bull, the widely pacing,
Him who has measured out with but three footsteps,
Alone, this long and far-extended station;
4. Him whose three footsteps filled with mead, unfailing,
Revel in blissful joy; who has supported
Alone the universe in three divisions:
The earth and sky and all created beings.
5. I would attain to that his dear dominion
Where men devoted to the gods do revel.
In the wide-striding Viṣṇu's highest footstep
There is a spring of mead: such is our kinship.
6. We long to go to those your dwelling-places
Where are the kine with many horns, the nimble:
For thence, indeed, the highest step of Viṣṇu,
Wide-pacing bull, shines brightly down upon us.

[1] A semi-divine patriarchal *ṛṣi* or sage.

To Agni — I.143 (Oldenberg)

1. I bring forward my most powerful, entirely new (pious) thought (i.e., hymn), the prayer of my words to Agni, the son of strength; he is the child of the Waters, the beloved one, who together with the Vasus has sat down on the Earth as a Hotṛ observing the appointed time (for sacrificing).
2. Being born in the highest heaven Agni became visible to Mātariśvan.[1] By the power of his mind, by his greatness when kindled, his flame filled Heaven and Earth with light.
3. His flames are fierce; never ageing are the flames of him who is beautiful to behold, whose face is beautiful, whose splendour is beautiful. The never sleeping, never ageing (rays) of Agni whose power is light, roll forward like streams across the nights (?).
4. Him the all-wealthy, whom the Bhṛgus have set to work on the navel of the earth, with the whole power of the world—stir up that Agni by thy prayers in his own house—(him) who alone rules over gods like Varuṇa.
5. He who is not to be kept back like the roar of the Maruts,[2] like an army that is sent forward, like the thunderbolt of heaven—Agni eats with his sharp jaws, he chews, he throws down the forests as a warrior throws down his foes.
6. Would Agni eagerly come to our hymn? Would He the Vasu together with the Vasus fulfil our desire? Will He, the driver, stir our prayers that they may be successful? (Thus thinking) I praise Him whose face is bright, with this my prayer.
7. He who has kindled him strives towards Agni as towards Mitra (or, towards a friend)—(to Agni) whose face shines with ghee, the charioteer of Ṛta. May he who when kindled becomes a racer, shining at the sacrifices, lift up our bright-coloured prayer.
8. Preserve us, O Agni, never failing with thy never-failing, kind and mighty guardians; protect our people all around with those undeceived, undismayed, never slumbering (guardians), O thou our wish!

[1] A divine being described in *Ṛg Veda* I.60.1 as bringing Agni to Bhṛgu, an ancient *ṛṣi* or sage.

[2] Storm-gods.

To BṚHASPATI [primarily the god of prayer] x.68 (Griffith)

1. Like birds who keep their watch, plashing in water, like the loud voices of the thundering rain-cloud,
   Like merry streamlets bursting from the mountain, thus to Bṛhaspati, our hymns have sounded.
2. The Son of Aṅgiras,[1] meeting the cattle, as Bhaga, brought in Aryaman among us.
   As friend of men he decks the wife and husband: as for the race, Bṛhaspati, nerve our coursers.
3. Bṛhaspati, having won them from the mountains, strewed down, like barley out of winnowing-baskets,
   The vigorous, wandering cows who aid the pious, desired of all, of blameless form, well-coloured.
4. As the Sun dews with meath the seat of Order, and casts a flaming meteor down from heaven,
   So from the rock Bṛhaspati forced the cattle, and cleft the earth's skin as it were with water.
5. Forth from mid-air with light he drave the darkness, as the gale blows a lily from the river.
   Like the wind grasping at the cloud of Vala,[2] Bṛhaspati gathered to himself the cattle.
6. Bṛhaspati, when he with fiery lightnings cleft through the weapon of reviling Vala,
   Consumed him as tongues eat what teeth have compassed: he threw the prisons of the red cows open.
7. That secret name borne by the lowing cattle within the cave Bṛhaspati discovered,
   And drave, himself, the bright kine from the mountain, like a bird's young after the eggs' disclosure.
8. He looked around on rock-imprisoned sweetness as one who eyes a fish in scanty water.
   Bṛhaspati, cleaving through with varied clamour, brought it forth like a bowl from out the timber.
9. He found the light of heaven, and fire, and morning: with lucid rays he forced apart the darkness.
   As from a joint, Bṛhaspati took the marrow of Vala as he gloried in his cattle.

[1] "Son of Aṅgiras," i.e., especially worshiped by Aṅgiras.
[2] An imprisoning deity, a demon of drought.

10. As trees for foliage robbed by winter, Vala mourned for the cows Bṛhaspati had taken.
He did a deed ne'er done, ne'er to be equalled, whereby the Sun and Moon ascend alternate.
11. Like a dark steed adorned with pearl, the fathers have decorated heaven with constellations.
They set the light in day, in night the darkness. Bṛhaspati cleft the rock and found the cattle.
12. This homage have we offered to the cloud-god who thunders out to many in succession.
May this Bṛhaspati vouchsafe us fulness of life with kine and horses, men, and heroes.

To Pṛthivī [Earth] v.84 (Macdonell)

1. Thou bearest truly, Pṛthivī,
The burden of the mountains' weight;
With might, O thou of many streams,
Thou quickenest, potent one, the soil.
2. With flowers of speech our songs of praise
Resound to thee, far-spreading one,
Who sendest forth the swelling cloud,
O bright one, like propelling speed;
3. Who, steadfast, holdest with thy might,
The forest-trees upon the ground,
When, from the lightnings of thy cloud,
The rain-floods of the sky pour down.

To Dyaus and Pṛthivī [Heaven and Earth] i.185 (Thomas)

1. Which was the former, which of them the later? How born? O sages, who discerns? They bear of themselves all that has existence. Day and Night revolve as on a wheel.
2. The two footless ones that go not uphold many a germ that goes and has feet. As a son in his own parents' lap, may Heaven and Earth protect us from fearful evil.
3. I invoke the gift of Aditi,[1] the gift free from hatred, inviolable, heavenly, invulnerable, worshipful. This, O Worlds, beget for the singer. May Heaven and Earth protect us from fearful evil.

[1] Sāyaṇa, a famous commentator on the Vedas, explains Aditi here as the space between Heaven and Earth. Henry explains the gift as sinlessness. If Sāyaṇa's meaning is taken, it would refer to the blessing of seasonable rain.

4. May we serve the two Worlds that know not suffering, that aid with help, that have Gods as sons, both of them among the Gods with alternate days and nights. May Heaven and Earth protect us from fearful evil.
5. The two maidens uniting form a pair, twin sisters in their parents' lap, caressing the navel of the world. May Heaven and Earth protect us from fearful evil.
6. The two wide great abodes I duly invoke, the two parents with the protection of the Gods, the beauteous ones, who partake of the immortal drink. May Heaven and Earth protect us from fearful evil.
7. The two wide, broad, great ones, with far limits, I implore with worship at this sacrifice, the two gracious bounteous ones who share it. May Heaven and Earth protect us from fearful evil.
8. Whatever sin we have committed against the Gods, or ever against a friend, or against a master of the house, may this prayer be a propitiation for them. May Heaven and Earth protect us from fearful evil.
9. May the blessings both of men (and of the Gods) aid me, may both attend me with protection and help. Abundance be to the more generous one rather than to the godless. Exhilarated with refreshment may we be nourished, O Gods.
10. This solemn ordinance (the sacrifice) have I Sumedhas uttered to Heaven and Earth for them first to hear. May they guard us from fault and crime. As father and mother may they protect us with their help.
11. May this, O Heaven and Earth, be true, O father and mother, that which I here implore you. Become the nearest of the Gods with your help. May we find refreshment and a well-watered camp.

To Sūrya [the sun-god] I.50 (Macdonell)

1. Aloft his beams now bring the god
Who knows all creatures that are born,
That all may look upon the Sun.
2. Away like thieves the stars depart,
By the dark nights accompanied,
At the all-seeing Sun's approach.
3. His beams, his rays, have shone afar
Athwart the many homes of men,
Flaming aloft like blazing fires.

4. Swift-moving, visible to all,
Maker of light thou art, O Sun,
Illuming all the shining space.
5. Thou risest toward the host of gods
And toward the race of men: toward all,
That they may see the heavenly light.
7. The broad air traversing, the sky,
Thou metest, Sun, the days with nights,
Seeing all creatures that are born.
8. The seven bay mares that draw thy car,
Bring thee to us, far-seeing god,
O Sūrya of the gleaming hair.
9. The Sun has yoked the seven bright mares,
The shining daughters of his car:
With that self-yoking team he speeds.
10. Athwart the darkness gazing up,
To him the higher light, we now
Have soared to Sūrya, the god
Among the gods, the highest light.

To Uṣas [Dawn] I.48 (Griffith)

1. Dawn on us with prosperity, O Uṣas, daughter of the sky,
Dawn with great glory, goddess, lady of the light, dawn thou with riches, bounteous one.
2. They, bringing steeds and kine, boon givers of all wealth, have oft sped forth to lighten us.
O Uṣas, waken up for me the sounds of joy: send us the riches of the great.
3. Uṣas hath dawned, and now shall dawn, the goddess, driver forth of cars
Which, as she cometh nigh, have fixed their thoughts on her, like glory-seekers on the flood.
4. Here Kaṇva,[1] chief of Kaṇva's race, sings forth aloud the glories of the heroes' names,—
The princes who, O Uṣas, as thou comest near, direct their thoughts to liberal gifts.
5. Like a good matron Uṣas comes carefully tending everything:
Rousing all life she stirs all creatures that have feet, and makes the birds of air fly up.

[1] A *ṛṣi* or sage.

6. She sends the busy forth, each man to his pursuit: delay she knows not as she springs.
   O rich in opulence, after thy dawning birds that have flown forth no longer rest.
7. This dawn hath yoked her steeds afar, beyond the rising of the Sun:
   Borne on a hundred chariots she, the auspicious dawn, advances on her way to men.
8. To meet her glance all living creatures bend them down: excellent one, she makes the light.
   Uṣas, the daughter of the sky, the opulent, shines foes and enmities away.
9. Shine on us with thy radiant light, O Uṣas, Daughter of the sky,
   Bringing to us great store of high felicity, and beaming on our solemn rites.
10. For in thee is each living creature's breath and life, when, Excellent! thou dawnest forth.
    Borne on thy lofty car, O lady of the light, hear, thou of wondrous wealth, our call.
11. O Uṣas, win thyself the strength which among men is wonderful.
    Bring thou thereby the pious unto holy rites, those who as priests sing praise to thee.
12. Bring from the firmament, O Uṣas, all the gods, that they may drink our *Soma* juice,[1]
    And, being what thou art, vouchsafe us kine and steeds, strength meet for praise and hero might.
13. May Uṣas, whose auspicious rays are seen resplendent round about,
    Grant us great riches, fair in form, of all good things, wealth which light labour may attain.
14. Mighty One, whom the *ṛṣis* of old time invoked for their protection and their help,
    O Uṣas, graciously answer our songs of praise with bounty and with brilliant light.
15. Uṣas, as thou with light to day hast opened the twin doors of heaven,
    So grant thou us a dwelling wide and free from foes. O goddess, give us food with kine.

[1] The drink of the gods.

16. Bring us to wealth abundant, sent in every shape, to plentiful refreshing food,
To all subduing splendour, Uṣas, mighty one, to strength, thou rich in spoil and wealth.

To Vāta (Vāyu) [the wind god] x.168 (Thomas)

1. Declare the might of Vāta's chariot. Crushing in pieces he goes. Thundering is his roar. He touches the sky as he advances, making (the clouds) ruddy, and speeds over the earth, whirling up dust.
2. Behind him rise the blasts of Vāta. They advance to him like women to a meeting. United with them, in the same car, hastens the God, the king of the whole world.
3. Hastening through the air on his ways he never rests. The friend of the Waters, the first-born, law-maintaining—where has he been born? Whence has he arisen?
4. The breath (*ātman*) of the Gods, the germ of the world, this God wanders at his will. His roarings are heard, not (seen) is his form. This Vāta let us worship with an oblation.

To Vāk [voice or speech personified][1] x.125 (Griffith)

1. I travel with the Rudras[2] and the Vasus,[3] with the Ādityas[4] and all-gods I wander.
I hold aloft both Varuṇa and Mitra, Indra and Agni, and the Pair of Aśvins.[5]
2. I cherish and sustain high-swelling Soma, and Tvaṣṭar[6] I support, Pūṣan,[7] and Bhaga.[8]
I load with wealth the zealous sacrificer who pours the juice and offers his oblation.
3. I am the queen, the gatherer-up of treasures, most thoughtful, first of those who merit worship.
Thus Gods have stablished me in many places with many homes to enter and abide in.

[1] "Vāk is speech personified, the Word, the first creation and representative of Spirit, and the means of communication between men and gods."—Griffith.
[2] Tempest-gods. [3] A class of gods.
[4] A special group of seven or eight gods.
[5] The two horsemen, twin heralds.
[6] The divine artificer of the dawn. [7] A sun-god.
[8] One of the Ādityas; the deity who bestows wealth and presides over love and marriage.

4. Through me alone all eat the food that feeds them,—each man sees, breathes, hears the word outspoken.
   They know it not, but yet they dwell beside me. Hear, one and all, the truth as I declare it.
5. I, verily, myself announce and utter the word that gods and men alike shall welcome.
   I make the man I love exceeding mighty, make him a sage, *ṛṣi*, and a *brāhmin*.
6. I bind the bow for Rudra that his arrow may strike and slay the hater of devotion.
   I rouse and order battle for the people, and I have penetrated Earth and Heaven.
7. On the world's summit I bring forth the father: my home is in the waters, in the ocean.
   Thence I extend o'er all existing creatures, and touch even yonder heaven with my forehead.
8. I breathe a strong breath like the wind and tempest, the while I hold together all existence.
   Beyond this wide earth and beyond the heavens I have become so mighty in my grandeur.

2. MONOTHEISTIC AND MONISTIC TENDENCIES[1]

The hymns in this section represent the second and third stages of the development of the thought of the *Ṛg Veda*, the transition from naturalistic polytheism to monotheism and then to the philosophical monism which constitutes the main philosophical doctrine of the Veda later to be carried over into the Upaniṣads and eventually into the most highly developed system of Indian thought, the Vedānta. All the crowding of gods and goddesses in Vedic polytheism proved a weariness to the intellect and so a tendency shows itself very early to identify one god with another or throw all the gods together. This tendency and systematization has its natural end in monotheism, which is simpler and more logical than the anarchy of a crowd of gods and goddesses thwarting each other.

The gradual idealization of the conception of God, the logic of religion which tended to make the gods flow into one another, the henotheism which has its face set in the direction of monotheism, the conception of *Ṛta* or the unity of nature, and the systematizing impulse of the human

[1] Hymns dealing with creation will be found in this section. No special section can be devoted to hymns on creation without unwise and artificial selection of parts of hymns which are not restricted to that topic exclusively.

mind—all these helped toward the displacement of polytheistic anthropomorphism by a spiritual monotheism.

Even the single great Being of the monotheistic period did not escape criticism. The mind of man is not satisfied with an anthropomorphic deity. The seeking mind did not so much care for personal comfort and happiness as for absolute truth. Whatever the emotional value of a personal God may be, the truth sets up a different standard and requires a different object of worship. Monotheism failed to satisfy the later Vedic thinkers. And thus, monotheism eventually gave way to philosophical monism, the doctrine of the impersonal, unknowable One.

To Varuṇa [chief of the gods of the natural and moral order]

viii.41 (Griffith)

1. To make this Varuṇa come forth, sing thou a song unto the band of Maruts wiser than thyself,—
   This Varuṇa who guardeth well the thoughts of men like herds of kine.
   Let all the others die away.
3. The night he hath encompassed, and stablished the morns with magic art: visible over all is he.
   His dear ones,[1] following his law, have prospered the three dawns[2] for him.
4. He, visible, o'er all the earth, stablished the quarters of the sky:
   He measured out the eastern place, that is the fold of Varuṇa: like a strong herdsman is the god.
5. He who supports the worlds of life, he who well knows the hidden names mysterious of the morning beams,
   He cherishes much wisdom, sage, as heaven brings forth each varied form.
6. In whom all wisdom centres, as the nave is set within the wheel.
   Haste ye to honour Trita,[3] as kine haste to gather in the fold, even as they muster steeds to yoke.
7. He wraps these regions as a robe; he contemplates the tribes of gods and all the works of mortal men.
   Before the home of Varuṇa all the gods follow his decree.
8. He is an ocean far-removed, yet through the heaven to him ascends the worship which these realms possess.
   With his bright foot he overthrew their magic, and went up to heaven.

[1] The nights, which give place to the dawn.
[2] Morning, noon, and evening.
[3] Varuṇa.

9. Ruler, whose bright far-seeing rays, pervading all three earths, have filled the three superior realms of heaven.
   Firm is the seat of Varuṇa: over the Seven [rivers] he rules as king.
10. Who, after his decree, o'erspread the dark ones[1] with a robe of light;
   Who measured out the ancient seat, who pillared both the worlds apart as the unborn supported heaven. Let all the others die away.

To Viśvakarman [the "all-worker," creator of the universe]
x.82 (Griffith)

1. The father of the eye, the wise in spirit, created both these worlds submerged in fatness.
   Then when the eastern ends were firmly fastened, the heavens and the earth were far extended.
2. Mighty in mind and power is Viśvakarman, maker, disposer, and most lofty presence.
   Their offerings joy in rich juice where they value One, only One, beyond the seven *ṛṣis*.
3. Father who made us, he who, as disposer, knoweth all races and all things existing,
   Even he alone, the deities' name-giver,—him other beings seek for information.
4. To him in sacrifice they offered treasures,—*ṛṣis* of old, in numerous troops, as singers,
   Who, in the distant, near, and lower region, made ready all these things that have existence.
5. That which is earlier than this earth and heaven, before the Asuras[2] and gods had being,—
   What was the germ primeval which the waters received where all the gods were seen together?
6. The waters, they received that germ primeval wherein the gods were gathered all together.
   It rested set upon the unborn's navel, that One wherein abide all things existing.
7. Ye will not find him who produced these creatures: another thing hath risen up among you.
   Enwrapt in misty cloud, with lips that stammer, hymn-chanters wander and are discontented.

[1] Nights which Varuṇa turns into days.

[2] High gods.

To Puruṣa [person or man personified] x.90 (Thomas)

1. Thousand-headed was the Puruṣa, thousand-eyed, thousand-footed. He embraced the earth on all sides, and stood beyond the breadth of ten fingers.
2. The Puruṣa is this all, that which was and which shall be. He is Lord of immortality, which he grows beyond through (sacrificial) food.
3. Such is his greatness, and still greater than that is the Puruṣa. One fourth of him is all beings. The three fourths of him is the immortal in Heaven.
4. Three fourths on high rose the Puruṣa. One fourth of him arose again here (on the earth). Thence in all directions he spread abroad, as that which eats and that which eats not.
5. From him Virāj was born, from Virāj the Puruṣa.[1] He when born reached beyond the earth behind as well as before.
6. When the Gods spread out the sacrifice with the Puruṣa as oblation, spring was its ghee, summer the fuel, autumn the oblation.
7. As the sacrifice on the strewn grass they besprinkled the Puruṣa, born in the beginning. With him the Gods sacrificed, the Sādhyas[2] and the sages.
8. From that sacrifice completely offered was the sprinkled ghee collected. He made it the beasts of the air, of the forest, and those of the village.
9. From that sacrifice completely offered were born the Verses (*Ṛg Veda*) and the *Sāman*-melodies (*Sāma Veda*). The metres were born from it. From it was born the Sacrificial formula (*Yajur Veda*).
10. From it were born horses, and they that have two rows of teeth. Cattle were born from it. From it were born goats and sheep.
11. When they divided the Puruṣa, into how many parts did they arrange him? What was his mouth? What his two arms? What are his thighs and feet called?
12. The *brāhmin* was his mouth, his two arms were made the *rājanya* (warrior), his two thighs the *vaiśya* (trader and agriculturist), from his feet the *śūdra* (servile class) was born.[3]

[1] Virāj has been interpreted as the female principle, which with the primal Puruṣa produces the concrete universe. In the *Atharva Veda* she is an independent creative principle, identified with the Spell (*brahma*), with Speech, and with Prajāpati.

[2] A class of gods or celestial beings.

[3] This is the famous passage describing the origin of the castes.

13. The moon was born from his spirit (*manas*), from his eye was born the sun, from his mouth Indra and Agni, from his breath Vāyu (wind) was born.
14. From his navel arose the middle sky, from his head the heaven originated, from his feet the earth, the quarters from his ear. Thus did they fashion the worlds.
15. Seven were his sticks that enclose (the fire), thrice seven were made the faggots. When the Gods spread out the sacrifice, they bound the Puruṣa as a victim.
16. With the sacrifice the Gods sacrificed the sacrifice. These were the first ordinances. These great powers reached to the firmament, where are the ancient Sādhyas, the Gods.

TO THE GODS — x.72 (Griffith)

1. Let us with tuneful skill proclaim these generations of the gods,
   That one may see them when these hymns are chanted in a future age.
2. These Brahmaṇaspati[1] produced with blast and smelting, like a smith.
   Existence, in an earlier age of gods, from non-existence sprang.
3. Existence, in the earliest age of gods, from non-existence sprang.
   Thereafter were the regions born. This sprang from the productive power.
4. Earth sprang from the productive power; the regions from the earth were born.
   Dakṣa was born of Aditi, and Aditi was Dakṣa's child.[2]
5. For Aditi, O Dakṣa, she who is thy daughter, was brought forth.
   After her were the blessed gods born sharers of immortal life.
6. When ye, O gods, in yonder deep close-clasping one another stood.
   Thence, as of dancers, from your feet a thickening cloud of dust arose.
7. When, O ye gods, like *yatis*,[3] ye caused all existing things to grow,
   Then ye brought Sūrya forward who was lying hidden in the sea.

[1] Lord of prayer.
[2] Aditi is infinity or the infinite; Dakṣa is force or power personified.
[3] Devotees.

8. Eight are the sons of Aditi who from her body sprang to life.
With seven she went to meet the gods: she cast Mārtāṇḍa[1] far away.
9. So with her seven sons Aditi went forth to meet the earlier age.
She brought Mārtāṇḍa thitherward to spring to life and die again.

To Viśvedevas [All gods—the pantheon as a whole]

I.164 (Griffith)

1. Of this benignant priest, with eld grey coloured, the brother midmost of the three is lightning.
The third is he whose back with oil is sprinkled. Here I behold the chief with seven made children.
2. Seven to the one-wheeled chariot yoke the courser; bearing seven names the single courser draws it.
Three-naved the wheel is, sound and undecaying, whereon are resting all these worlds of being.
3. The seven who on the seven-wheeled car are mounted have horses, seven in tale, who draw them onward.
Seven sisters utter songs of praise together, in whom the names of the seven cows are treasured.
4. Who hath beheld him as he sprang to being, seen how the boneless One supports the bony?
Where is the blood of earth, the life, the spirit? Who may approach the man who knows, to ask it?
5. Unripe in mind, in spirit undiscerning, I ask of these the gods' established places;
For up above the yearling calf the sages, to form a web, their own seven threads have woven.
6. I ask, unknowing, those who know, the sages, as one all ignorant for sake of knowledge,
What was that One who in the unborn's image hath stablished and fixed firm these worlds' six religions [regions]?
46. They call him Indra, Mitra, Varuṇa, Agni, and he is heavenly nobly-winged Garutmān.[2]
To what is one, sages give many a title: they call it Agni, Yama,[3] Mātariśvan.

[1] Sūrya, the sun. [2] The "Celestial Bird," the sun.
[3] King of the departed. See below, *Ṛg Veda* x.14.

To Viśvedevas — III.54 (Griffith)

5. What pathway leadeth to the gods? Who knoweth this of a truth, and who will now declare it?
Seen are their lowest dwelling-places only, but they are in remote and secret regions.
8. All living things they part and keep asunder: though bearing up the mighty gods they reel not.
One All is lord of what is fixed and moving, that walks, that flies, this multiform creation.

To Viśvedevas — I.89 (Griffith)

1. May power auspicious come to us from every side, never deceived, unhindered, and victorious,
That the gods ever may be with us for our gain, our guardians day by day unceasing in their care.
2. May the auspicious favour of the gods be ours, on us descend the bounty of the righteous gods.
The friendship of the gods have we devoutly sought; so may the gods extend our life that we may live.
3. We call them higher with a hymn of olden time, Bhaga, the friendly Dakṣa, Mitra, Aditi,
Aryaman, Varuṇa, Soma, the Aśvins. May Sarasvatī,[1] auspicious, grant felicity.
4. May the Wind waft to us that pleasant medicine, may Earth our Mother give it, and our Father Heaven,
And the joy-giving stones that press the *soma's* juice.
Aśvins, may ye, for whom our spirits long, hear this.
5. Him we invoke for aid who reigns supreme, the Lord of all that stands or moves, inspirer of the soul,
That Pūṣan may promote the increase of our wealth, our keeper and our guard infallible for our good.
6. Illustrious far and wide, may Indra prosper us; may Pūṣan prosper us, the Master of all wealth.
May Tārkṣya[2] with uninjured fellies prosper us; Bṛhaspati vouchsafe to us prosperity.
7. The Maruts, Sons of Pṛṣṇi, borne by spotted steeds, moving in glory, oft visiting holy rites,

[1] River-goddess; goddess of eloquence and sacred poetry.
[2] Probably a form of the sun.

Sages whose tongue is Agni, brilliant as the sun,—hither let all the gods for our protection come.

8. Gods, may we with our ears listen to what is good, and with our eyes see what is good, ye Holy Ones.
   With limbs and bodies firm may we extolling you attain the term of life appointed by the gods.
9. A hundred autumns stand before us, O ye gods, within whose space ye bring our bodies to decay;
   Within whose space our sons become fathers in turn. Break ye not in the midst our course of fleeting life.
10. Aditi is the heaven, Aditi is mid-air, Aditi is the mother and the sire and son,
    Aditi is all gods, Aditi five-classed men, Aditi all that hath been born and shall be born.

HYMN OF CREATION x.129 (Macdonell)

1. Non-being then existed not nor being:
   There was no air, nor sky that is beyond it.
   What was concealed? Wherein? In whose protection?
   And was there deep unfathomable water?
2. Death then existed not nor life immortal;
   Of neither night nor day was any token.
   By its inherent force the One breathed windless:
   No other thing than that beyond existed.
3. Darkness there was at first by darkness hidden;
   Without distinctive marks, this all was water.
   That which, becoming, by the void was covered,
   That One by force of heat came into being.
4. Desire entered the One in the beginning:
   It was the earliest seed, of thought the product.
   The sages searching in their hearts with wisdom,
   Found out the bond of being in non-being.
5. Their ray extended light across the darkness:
   But was the One above or was it under?
   Creative force was there, and fertile power:
   Below was energy, above was impulse.
6. Who knows for certain? Who shall here declare it?
   Whence was it born, and whence came this creation?
   The gods were born after this world's creation:
   Then who can know from whence it has arisen?

7. None knoweth whence creation has arisen;
And whether he has or has not produced it:
He who surveys it in the highest heaven,
He only knows, or haply he may know not.

To Prajāpati[1] [Hymn to the Unknown God] x.121 (Thomas)

1. As the Golden Germ he arose in the beginning; when born he was the one Lord of the existent. He supported the earth and this heaven. What God with our oblation shall we worship?
2. He who gives breath, who gives strength, whose command all the Gods wait upon, whose shadow is immortality, is death—what God with our oblation shall we worship?
3. Who through his greatness over that which breathes and closes the eyes is only king of the world, who is Lord of the two-footed and four-footed—what God with our oblation shall we worship?
4. Whose are the snowy mountains through his greatness, whose, as they say, are the ocean and the Rasā,[2] whose are the regions, whose the arms[3]—what God with our oblation shall we worship?
5. Through whom the mighty heaven and the earth have been fixed, through whom the sun has been established, through whom the firmament; who in the middle sky measures out the air—what God with our oblation shall we worship?
6. To whom the two realms (heaven and earth), sustained by his aid, looked up, trembling in spirit, over whom the risen sun shines—what God with our oblation shall we worship?
7. When the great waters came, bearing all as the Germ, and generating fire (Agni), then arose the one life-spirit of the Gods—what God with our oblation shall we worship?
8. Who through his greatness beheld the waters, that bore power and generated the sacrifice, who was the one God above the Gods—what God with our oblation shall we worship?
9. May he not injure us, who is the generator of the earth, he of true ordinances, who produced the heaven, who produced the shining mighty waters.

[1] Lord of creation or of creatures.
[2] A mythical river surrounding the world.
[3] Perhaps the all-embracing arms of Prajāpati. Sāyaṇa understands the four quarters, and by the regions the intermediate quarters.

10. O Prajāpati, none other than thou has encompassed all these created things.[1] May that for which we desiring have invoked thee be ours. May we become lords of wealth.

3. COSMIC LAW OR ORDER, RIGHT, TRUTH—ṚTA

One of the special forms in which the doctrine of the unity of reality appeared was in the recognition of a universal and eternal law, Ṛta. Ṛta represents the law, unity, or rightness underlying the orderliness of the universe.

There are no hymns addressed specifically to Ṛta, but brief references to the important concept are found repeatedly in hymns to Varuṇa, the dispenser of the law, Agni, Viśvedevas, etc.

To Indra — iv.23 (Griffith)

8. Eternal Law [Ṛta] hath varied food that strengthens; thought of eternal law removes transgressions.
   The praise-hymn of eternal law, arousing, glowing, hath oped the deaf ears of the living.
9. Firm-seated are eternal law's foundations; in its fair form are many splendid beauties.
   By holy law long lasting food they bring us; by holy law have cows come to our worship.
10. Fixing eternal law he [Indra], too, upholds it: swift moves the might of law and wins the booty.
   To law belong the vast deep earth and heaven: milch-kine supreme, to law their milk they render.

Creation — x.190 (Griffith)

1. From fervour[2] kindled to its height Eternal Law and Truth were born:
   Thence was the night produced, and thence the billowy flood of sea arose.
2. From that same billowy flood of sea the year was afterwards produced,
   Ordainer of the days nights [*sic*], Lord over all who close the eye.

[1] Ludwig interprets this hymn to mean essentially: "what other God than Prajāpati shall we worship?"

[2] This term could refer to the devotional ardor or asceticism of *Brahman* or "warmth."

3. Dhātar, the great creator, then formed in due order sun and moon.
He formed in order heaven and earth, the regions of the air, and light.

To Vāyu I.2 (Griffith)

8. Mitra and Varuṇa, through Law, lovers and cherishers of Law,
Have ye obtained your mighty power.

To Viśvedevas I.105 (Griffith)

12. Firm is this new-wrought hymn of praise, and meet to be told forth, O gods.
The flowing of the floods is Law, Truth is the sun's extended light. Mark this my woe, ye earth and heaven.

16. That pathway of the sun in heaven, made to be highly glorified,
Is not to be transgressed, O gods. O mortals, ye behold it not.
Mark this my woe, ye earth and heaven.

To Agni IV.5 (Griffith)

11. With reverence I declare the law, O Agni; what is, comes by thine order, Jātavedas [Agni].

To Brahmaṇaspati [lord of priests] II.23 (Griffith)

15. Bṛhaspati, that which the foe deserves not, which shines among the folk effectual, splendid,
That, Son of Law! which is with might refulgent—that treasure wonderful bestow thou on us.

To Indra IV.21 (Griffith)

1. May Indra come to us for our protection; here be the Hero praised, our feast-companion.
May he whose powers are many, waxen mighty, cherish, like Dyaus, his own supreme dominion.

2. Here magnify his great heroic exploits, most glorious one, enriching men with bounties,
Whose will is like a sovran in assembly, who rules the people, conqueror, all-surpassing.

3. Hither let Indra come from earth or heaven, hither with speech from firmament or ocean;
With Maruts, from the realm of light to aid us, or from a distance, from the seat of Order.

To Uṣas [Dawn] I.123 (Griffith)

6. ... The far-refulgent mornings make apparent the lovely treasures which the darkness covered.
7. The one departeth and the other cometh; unlike in hue day's halves march on successive.
   One hides the gloom of the surrounding parents. Dawn on her shining chariot is resplendent.
8. The same in form to-day, the same to-morrow, they still keep Varuṇa's eternal statute....
9. ... The maiden breaketh not the law of Order, day by day coming to the place appointed.
13. Obedient to the rein [*sic*] of Law Eternal give us each thought that more and more shall bless us....

To Āprīs III.4 (Oldenberg)

7. I catch hold of the two divine Hotṛs first[1]. The seven strong ones rejoice according to their wont. Teaching the right, they proclaim the right, the guardians of law, contemplating the law.

To Varuṇa II.28 (Griffith)

4. He made them flow, the Āditya, the Sustainer: the rivers run by Varuṇa's commandment.

4. ETHICAL PRINCIPLES AND SOCIAL PRACTICES

Ṛta, the law or order of the world—literally "the course of things"—provides the standard of morality. As seen in the preceding section, Ṛta represents the orderliness and eternal Law of the universe. Here, Ṛta stands for the same principle in human conduct. Orderly and consistent conduct is the essential feature of the good life. Disorder, often represented in the form of falsehood, is the greatest evil. Virtue is conformity to the cosmic law. (Ṛta also serves as the origin of the basic ethical concept of *dharma* in later Indian philosophy.) Love of fellowmen, kindness to all, and obedience to our duties to the gods and to men are enjoined. Asceticism, fasting, and abstinence are not unknown to the *Ṛg Veda*, but asceticism is not the dominant note.

[1] The Āprīs are the divine or deified beings and objects to which the propitiatory verses are addressed. The Hotṛs are Agni and perhaps Varuṇa.

To Indra-Soma vii.104 (Griffith)

8. Whoso accuses me with words of falsehood when I pursue my way with guileless spirit,
May he, the speaker of untruth, be, Indra, like water which the hollowed hand compresses.
9. Those who destroy, as is their wont, the simple, and with their evil natures harm the righteous,
May Soma give them over to the serpent, or to the lap of Nirṛti[1] consign them.
10. The fiend, O Agni, who designs to injure the essence of our food, kine, steeds, or bodies,
May he, the adversary, thief, and robber, sink to destruction, both himself and offspring.
11. May he be swept away, himself and children: may all the three earths press him down beneath them.
May his fair glory, O ye gods, be blighted, who in the day or night would fain destroy us.
12. The prudent finds it easy to distinguish the true and false: their words oppose each other.
Of these two that which is the true and honest, Soma protects, and brings the false to nothing.
13. Never doth Soma aid and guide the wicked or him who falsely claims the warrior's title.
He slays the fiend and him who speaks untruly: both lie entangled in the noose of Indra.

To Soma Pavamāna [Self-Purifying Soma][2] ix.113 (Griffith)

4. Splendid by Law! declaring Law, truth-speaking, truthful in thy works,
Enouncing faith, king Soma!...

To Āpas [Waters] vii.47 (Griffith)

3. All-purifying, joying in their nature, to paths of gods the goddesses move onward.
They never violate the laws of Indra....

[1] Death and destruction.
[2] See also *Ṛg Veda* ix.112, below.

To Maruts — vii.56 (Griffith)

12. Pure, Maruts, pure yourselves, are your oblations: to you, the pure, pure sacrifice I offer.
By Law they came to truth, the Law's observers, bright by their birth, and pure, and sanctifying.

To Varuṇa — ii.28 (Griffith)

5. Loose me from sin as from a band that binds me: may we swell, Varuṇa, thy spring of Order. . . .

To Vāyu and Others — i.23 (Griffith)

22. Whatever sin is found in me, whatever evil I have wrought,
If I have lied or falsely sworn, Waters, remove it far from me.

To Agni — iv.5 (Oldenberg)

5. They who roam about like brotherless girls, of evil conduct like women who deceive their husbands, being wicked, sinful, and untrue—they have created for themselves this deep place.

To Varuṇa — v.85 (Thomas)

7. What sin we have ever committed against an intimate, O Varuṇa, against a friend or companion at any time, a brother, a neighbour, or a stranger, that, O Varuṇa, loose from us.
8. If like gamblers at play we have cheated, whether in truth or without knowing, all that loose from us, O God. So may we be dear to thee, O Varuṇa.

To Dāna [charity or liberality] — x.117 (Macdonell)

1. The gods inflict not hunger as a means to kill:
Death frequently befalls even satiated men.
The charitable giver's wealth melts not away;
The niggard never finds a man to pity him.
2. Who, of abundant food possessed, makes hard his heart
Towards a needy and decrepit suppliant
Whom once he courted, come to pray to him for bread:
A man like this as well finds none to pity him.
3. He is the liberal man who helps the beggar
That, craving food, emaciated wanders,
And coming to his aid, when asked to succour,
Immediately makes him a friend hereafter.

4. He is no friend who gives not of his substance
To his devoted, intimate companion:
This friend should turn from him—here is no haven—
And seek a stranger elsewhere as a helper.
5. The wealthier man should give unto the needy,
Considering the course of life hereafter;
For riches are like chariot wheels revolving:
Now to one man they come, now to another.
6. The foolish man from food has no advantage;
In truth I say: it is but his undoing;
No friend he ever fosters, no companion:
He eats alone, and he alone is guilty.
7. The plough that cleaves the soil produces nurture;
He that bestirs his feet completes his journey.
The speaking *brāhmin* earns more than the silent;
A friend who gives is better than the niggard.

TO KEŚINS[1] x.136 (Griffith)

2. The *munis*,[2] girdled with the wind, wear garments soiled of yellow hue.
They, following the wind's swift course, go where the gods have gone before.
3. Transported with our *muni*hood we have pressed on into the winds:
You therefore, mortal men, behold our natural bodies and no more.
4. The *muni*, made associate in the holy work of every god,
Looking upon all varied forms flies through the region of the air.
5. The steed of Vāta, Vāyu's friend, the *muni*, by the gods impelled,
In both the oceans hath his home, in eastern and in western sea.
6. Treading the path of sylvan beasts, Gandharvas, and Apsarases,
He with long locks, who knows the wish, is a sweet most delightful friend.
7. Vāyu hath churned for him: he poundeth things most hard to bend,
When he with long loose locks hath drunk, with Rudra, water from the cup.

[1] Wearers of long, loose hair, ascetics.
[2] Ascetics. The hymn is perhaps the earliest reference to the supernormal powers attainable by ascetic practices.

To UṢAS [the Dawn][1] I.113 (Thomas)

5. The generous one, that he who lies down may go, one to his enjoyment, one to his desire, another to wealth, that those who behold little may see widely, the Dawn has awakened all living things.
6. That one may win rule, another fame, another his desire, another achieve his end, to behold their different livelihoods the Dawn has awakened all living things.

To INDRA, PARVATA, ETC.[2] III.53 (Griffith)

15. Sasarparī,[3] the gift of Jamadagnis,[4] hath lowed with mighty voice dispelling famine.
 The daughter of the Sun hath spread our glory among the gods, imperishable, deathless.
16. Sasarparī brought glory speedily to these, over the generations of the fivefold race;[5]
 Daughter of Pakṣa, she bestows new vital power, she whom the ancient Jamadagnis gave to me.

To PURUṢA x.90 (Thomas)

11. When they divided the Puruṣa, into how many parts did they arrange him? What was his mouth? What his two arms? What are his thighs and feet called?
12. The *brāhmin* was his mouth, his two arms were made the *rājanya* (warrior), his two thighs the *vaiśya* (trader and agriculturist), from his feet the *śūdra* (servile class) was born.[6]

5. THE HEREAFTER

The Vedic Indians believed in personal immortality and in the world of the gods and the world of the fathers (manes). Good men went to heaven or the world of Viṣṇu, and others to the world presided over by Yama,[7] although Yama was also thought of as the ruler of all departed spirits.

[1] This and two succeeding passages are among the earliest references to the castes.
[2] The "Genius of the Mountains and Clouds," frequently an associate of Indra.
[3] An epithet of Vāk (Voice), the daughter of the sun.
[4] This refers to an ancient story which is of no philosophical significance.
[5] The five tribes of Āryan men, the four castes and the barbarians or non-Āryans.
[6] See note to these verses in *Ṛg Veda* x.90, above.
[7] Yama is sometimes described as the ruler of the realm of all departed spirits, but at other times (I.38. 5) as presiding over a realm which departed spirits wish to avoid.

To Savitṛ [Heaven] I.35 (Griffith)

6. Three heavens there are; two Savitar's, adjacent: in Yama's world is one, the home of heroes.
As on a linch-pin, firm, rest things immortal: he who hath known it, let him here declare it.

To Yama [Ruler of the realm of departed spirits]
x.14 (Macdonell)

1. Him who has past along the mighty ridges,
And has spied out the path for many travellers,
Vivasvant's son, the gatherer of people,
Yama, the king, do thou present with offering.
2. For us has Yama first found out the pathway:
This pasture never can be taken from us.
To where have passed away our former fathers,
The later born by their own paths have travelled.
4. Upon this sacred grass sit down, O Yama,
Uniting with the Aṅgiras, our fathers.
Let spells recited by the sages bring thee;
Do thou, O king, rejoice in this oblation.
5. Come hither with the Aṅgiras, the holy:
Here with Virūpa's sons, O Yama revel,
Vivasvant I invoke, who is thy father,
When at this rite upon the straw he's seated.
6. The Aṅgiras, our fathers, the Navagvas,
The Bhṛgus and Atharvans,[1] soma-loving:
May we abide for ever in the favour
And the good graces of those holy sages.
7. Depart, depart, along those ancient pathways,
On which have passed away our former fathers:
There thou shalt see rejoicing in libations
The two kings, Varuṇa the god and Yama.
8. Unite thou with the Fathers and with Yama,
With thy good works' reward in highest heaven.
To home return, all imperfection leaving.
Unite with thine own body, full of vigour.
9. Begone, depart from here, disperse and scatter:
For him the Fathers have prepared this dwelling.

[1] Three priestly families of ancient times.

Yama bestows on him this place to rest in,
A place by waters, days and nights distinguished.
10. Run on thy path straight forward, past the two dogs,
The sons of Saramā, four-eyed and brindled.
Draw near thereafter to the bounteous Fathers,
Who revel on in company with Yama.
11. O King, to those two this dead man deliver,
The two that are thy guardian dogs, O Yama,
Four-eyed, observing men, the pathway watching.
Bestow upon the dead man health and welfare.
12. Broad-nosed and brown the messengers of Yama,
Greedy of lives they rove among the people.
May they give back to us a life propitious
Here and to-day, that we may see the sunlight.
13. For Yama press the soma juice,
To Yama offering present.
To Yama goes the sacrifice,
Announced by Agni, well-prepared.
14. To Yama offering rich in ghee
Present forthwith, and forward step.
Let him direct us to the gods,
That we may live a life prolonged.
15. To Yama as a King present
Oblation very honey-sweet.
This homage is for seers of old,
The ancient makers of the path.

To Maruts — I.38 (Griffith)

4. If, O ye Maruts, ye the sons whom Pṛṣṇi bare, were mortal, and
Immortal he who sings your praise,
5. Then never were your praiser loathed like a wild beast in pasture-land,
Nor should he go on Yama's path.

To Viṣṇu — I.154 (Thomas)

5. May I attain to that his dear place, where men devoted to the Gods are exulting; for that verily is akin to the wide-stepper, in the highest step of Viṣṇu a well of sweetness.

To Soma Pavamāna — ix.113 (Griffith)

7. O Pavamāna, place me in that deathless, undecaying world
Wherein the light of heaven is set, and everlasting lustre shines.
Flow, Indu,[1] flow for Indra's sake.

8. Make me immortal in that realm where dwells the king, Vivasvān's son,[2]
Where is the secret shrine of heaven, where are those waters young and fresh. Flow, Indu, flow for Indra's sake.

9. Make me immortal in that realm where they move even as they list,
In the third sphere of inmost heaven, where lucid worlds are full of light. Flow, Indu, flow for Indra's sake.

10. Make me immortal in that realm of eager wish and strong desire,
The region of the radiant Moon, where food and full delight are found. Flow, Indu, flow for Indra's sake.

11. Make me immortal in that realm where happiness and transports, where
Joys and felicities combine, and longing wishes are fulfilled. Flow, Indu, flow for Indra's sake.

6. SKEPTICISM AND RIDICULE OF THE GODS

The later Vedic Indian experienced not only the wonder which is so characteristic of the mood of philosophy, but also the doubt and skepticism concerning his previously accepted beliefs, the skepticism which so often prepares the way for philosophic thought. The questioning mood asserted itself very often. Skepticism was in the air. The Indian of this period—as seen in hymns quoted above, e.g., x.121, and x.129—wondered about his gods and about the possibility of knowing the ultimate source of all things, but his doubt often took the form of ridicule of accepted beliefs and of his gods. Even the very existence of his highest gods was questioned. He even offered up a prayer for faith, and a prayer to make us faithful is not possible in a time of unshaken faith.

To Indra — viii.89 (Griffith)

3. Striving for strength bring forth a laud to Indra, a truthful hymn if he in truth existeth.
One and another say, There is no Indra. Who hath beheld him? Whom then shall we honour?

[1] Indu (or Soma), the moon, is supposed to contain the celestial nectar, soma juice.
[2] Yama.

To Indra — iv.24 (Griffith)

10. Who for ten milch-kine purchaseth from me this Indra who is mine?
When he hath slain the Vṛtras let the buyer give him back to me.

To Indra — ii.12 (Macdonell)

1. He who just born as chief god full of spirit
Went far beyond the other gods in wisdom:
Before whose majesty and mighty manhood
The two worlds trembled: he, O men, is Indra.
5. Of whom, the terrible, they ask, "Where is he?"
Of him, indeed, they also say, "He is not."
The foemen's wealth, like players' stakes, he lessens.
Believe in him: for he, O men, is Indra.

To Viśvedevas — i.164 (Griffith)

4. Who hath beheld him as he sprang to being, seen how this boneless One supports the bony?
. Where is the blood of earth, the life, the spirit? Who may approach the man who knows, to ask it?
17. Beneath the upper realm, above this lower, bearing her calf at foot the cow hath risen.
Whitherward, to what place hath she departed? Where calved she? Not amid this herd of cattle.
18. Who, that the father of this calf discerneth beneath the upper realm, above the lower,
Showing himself a sage, may here declare it? Whence hath the godlike spirit had its rising?

A Song of Soma-Preparing — ix.112 (Thomas)

1. Varied truly are our thoughts. Varied are the ways of men. The joiner wants to find a breakage, the medicine-man an accident, the *brāhmin*-priest a worshipper. O Indu, flow round for Indra.
2. The smith with brittle firewood, with wings of birds (to fan the flame), with stones and glowing heat of fire, wants golden riches for himself. O Indu, flow round for Indra.
3. I'm poet, dad is medicine-man, mama[1] is grinding at the mill. With varied thoughts intent on gain we follow after wealth of cows. O Indu, flow round for Indra.

[1] The words for father and mother in the original are pet names (*tāta*, *nānā*).

4. The horse an easy car to draw, the troop of lovers jest and laugh, the frog wants too a water-pool. O Indu, flow round for Indra.

TO INDRA x.86 (Griffith)

1. Men have abstained from pouring juice; they count not Indra as a god.

TO THE FROGS VII.103 (Griffith)

1. They who lay quiet for a year, the *brāhmins* who fulfill their vows,
   The frogs have lifted up their voice, the voice Parjanya[1] hath inspired.
2. What time on these, as on a dry skin lying in the pool's bed, the floods of heaven descended,
   The music of the frogs comes forth in concert like the cows' lowing with their calves beside them.
7. As *brāhmins*, sitting round the brimful vessel, talk at the *soma* rite of Atirātra,[2]
   So, frogs, ye gather round the pool to honour this day of all the year, the first of rain-time.

TO ŚRADDHĀ x.151 (Griffith)

1. By faith is Agni kindled, through faith is oblation offered up.
   We celebrate with praises faith upon the height of happiness.
2. Bless thou the man who gives, O Faith; Faith, bless the man who fain would give.
   Bless thou the liberal worshippers: bless thou the word that I have said.
3. Even as the Deities maintained Faith in the mighty Asuras,
   So make this uttered wish of mine true for the liberal worshippers.
4. Guarded by Vāyu, gods and men who sacrifice draw near to Faith.
   Man winneth faith by yearnings of the heart, and opulence by faith.

[1] God of the rain-cloud.
[2] A ceremony accompanied by three nocturnal recitations.

CHAPTER II

THE UPANIṢADS

THE Upaniṣads are the concluding portions of the Vedas and the basis for the Vedānta philosophy, "a system in which human speculation seems to have reached its very acme," according to Max Müller. The Upaniṣads have dominated Indian philosophy, religion, and life for nearly three thousand years. Though remote in time from us, the Upaniṣads are not remote in thought. The ideal which haunted the thinkers of the Upaniṣads—the ideal of man's ultimate beatitude, the perfection of knowledge, the vision of the real in which the religious hunger of the mystic for direct vision and the philosopher's ceaseless quest for truth are both satisfied—is still our ideal.

The word "Upaniṣad" is derived from *upa*, near, *ni*, down, and *sad*, to sit. Groups of pupils sat near the teacher to learn from him the truth by which ignorance is destroyed.

There are over 200 Upaniṣads, although the traditional number is 108. Of these, the principal Upaniṣads are ten: *Īśā*, *Kena*, *Kaṭha*, *Praśna*, *Muṇḍaka*, *Māṇḍūkya*, *Taittirīya*, *Aitareya*, *Chāndogya*, and *Bṛhadāraṇyaka*. Śaṁkara, the great Vedāntic philosopher, wrote commentaries on eleven of the Upaniṣads, these ten and the *Śvetāśvatara*. He also referred to the *Kauṣītaki* and *Mahānārāyaṇa*. These, together with the *Maitrī*, constitute the fourteen principal Upaniṣads.

The dates of the Upaniṣads are difficult to determine. The ancient prose Upaniṣads, *Aitareya*, *Kauṣītaki*, *Chāndogya*, *Kena*, *Taittirīya*, and *Bṛhadāraṇyaka*, as well as the *Īśā* and *Kaṭha*, belong to the eighth and seventh centuries B.C. They are definitely pre-Buddhistic.

We do not know the names of the authors of the Upaniṣads. Some of the chief doctrines of the Upaniṣads are associated with the names of renowned sages such as Aruṇi, Yājñavalkya, Bālāki, Śvetaketu, and Śāṇḍilya. They were perhaps the early exponents of the doctrines attributed to them.

The Upaniṣads belong to *śruti* or revealed literature, and are the utterances of sages who spoke out of the fullness of their illumined experience. They are vehicles more of spiritual illumination than of systematic reflection. Their aim is practical rather than speculative. They give us knowledge as a means to spiritual freedom. Out of the wealth of suggestions and speculations contained in the Upaniṣads, various later thinkers chose elements for the construction of their own systems, not infrequently by straining the texts.

Though a logical and coherent system of metaphysics is not to be found in the Upaniṣads, there are a few fundamental doctrines which stand out as the central teachings of the early ones. The reflective tendency manifest in some of the philosophical hymns of the *Ṛg Veda* becomes more pronounced in the Upaniṣads. Hymns to gods and goddesses are replaced by a search for the reality underlying the flux of things. "What is that which, being known, everything else becomes known?"[1] There is one God of whom all the Vedic gods are manifestations. "For fear of whom fire burns, for fear of whom the sun shines, for fear of whom the winds, clouds, and death perform their offices."[2]

The real which is at the heart of the universe is reflected in the infinite depths of the self. *Brahman* (the ultimate as discovered objectively) is *Ātman* (the ultimate as discovered introspectively). *Tat tvam asi* (That art thou). Truth is within us. "When we realize the universal Self in us, when and what may anybody fear or worship?"

The Supreme in its inner being as the one self-subsistent reality cannot be defined by logical categories or linguistic symbols. It is the incomprehensible *nirguṇa* (qualityless) *Brahman*, the pure Absolute. It is envisaged as *saguṇa* (with qualities) *Brahman* or Īśvara, a personal god, when It is viewed as the constitutive reality of the many or the cause of the world, as the source, ground, and dwelling-place of selves. The Upaniṣads thus set forth the distinction between *Brahman* in itself and *Brahman* in the universe, the transcendent beyond manifestation and the transcendent in manifestation, the Self pure and essential and the Self in the individual selves.

The Upaniṣads subordinate Vedic ceremonialism and even caste duties to the supreme good of self-realization. They lay great stress on the distinction between the ignorant, narrow, selfish way which leads to transitory satisfaction and the way of wisdom which leads to eternal life. Though here and there we find passages supporting sacrificial observances, the main tendency of the Upaniṣads is against them. While the sacrifice is the abandonment of one's ego, prayer is the exploration of reality by entering the Beyond that is within, by an ascension of consciousness. The Upaniṣads speak to us of the way in which the individual self gets at the ultimate reality by an inward journey, an inner ascent. They give us the stages of the ascent in some detail.

This inner ascent requires adequate moral preparation, "The Self is not to be attained by one without fortitude, not through slackness nor without distinctive marks of discipline."[3] To see the Self one must become "calm, controlled, quiet, patiently enduring, and contented."[4]

The goal is not a heavenly state of bliss or rebirth in a better world. Negatively, it is freedom from the objective cosmic law of *karma*; positively, it is identity with the Supreme. Until we are released from the law of *karma* and reach *mokṣa* or deliverance, we will be in *saṁsāra* or the time process.

[1] *Muṇḍaka Upaniṣad* I.i.3.
[2] *Taittirīya Upaniṣad* II.vii.
[3] *Muṇḍaka Upaniṣad* III.ii.4.
[4] *Bṛhadāraṇyaka Upaniṣad* IV.iv.23.

As in the selections quoted from the *Ṛg Veda*, the purpose of passages chosen from the Upaniṣads is to emphasize the basic principles and teachings rather than the literary style. Passages from all of the most important Upaniṣads are included in order to present the rich variety of doctrines and the numerous approaches to the basic metaphysical view. To quote any of the longer Upaniṣads completely would involve much repetition and has been deemed inadvisable and unnecessary. Only two short—but important—Upaniṣads, the *Īśā* and the *Māṇḍūkya*, are included in their entirety. The sequence in which the Upaniṣads are listed conforms, not to the chronological order, but to the traditional arrangement employed in Upaniṣadic studies in India.

The selections are taken from R. E. Hume, *The Thirteen Principal Upanishads* (London: Oxford University Press, 2nd ed. rev., 1931).

Attention is called to the questionable and misleading translation of certain basic terms in the text used. To avoid confusion and possible misinterpretation the ultimate reality should be designated generally as *Brahman*, not *Brahma*, and as It, or That, not He. Also, the word "*Ātman*" or "*ātman*" (the former referring to the ultimate principle, the latter to the individual principle in man) should, for clarity, be translated as "Self" or "self," not "Soul" or "soul," respectively. These changes have been made in the selections included here. *Brahma*, though technically correct, has been changed to *Brahman* and Soul or soul to Self or self, respectively. *Puruṣa*, person, may be referred to by the personal pronoun, of course.

1. Īśā Upaniṣad

This, the smallest of all the Upaniṣads, consisting of only eighteen short verses, speaks of many important topics, including the claims of the path of knowledge and the path of action, the paradoxical nature of the *Ātman*, and the nature of the nonattached sage. Most important, however, is the doctrine that neither knowledge of the supernatural nor knowledge of the natural alone can be sufficient for true wisdom. By implication, then, this Upaniṣad tends to deny the doctrine of the unreality of the empirical world which is emphasized in some phases of later Indian philosophy.

The Upaniṣad gets its name—the full and correct form of which is *Īśāvāsyam*—from the first word of the text.

The paradoxical, transcendent, yet immanent, unity underlying the diversity of the world[1]

1. By the Lord (*Īśa*) enveloped must this all be—
Whatever moving thing there is in the moving world.
With this renounced, thou mayest enjoy.
Covet not the wealth of anyone at all.

[1] Section headings conform for the most part to those in Hume, but some have been revised and, in some instances, completely new headings have been added or substituted.

2. Even while doing deeds here,
One may desire to live a hundred years.
Thus on thee—not otherwise than this is it—
The deed adheres not on the man.
3. Devilish are those worlds called,
With blind darkness covered o'er!
Unto them, on descending, go
Whatever folk are slayers of the Self.
4. Unmoving, the One is swifter than the mind.
The sense-powers reached not It, speeding on before.
Past others running, This goes standing.
In It Mātariśvan places action.
5. It moves. It moves not.
It is far, and It is near.
It is within all this,
And It is outside of all this.
6. Now, he who on all beings
Looks as just in the Self (*Ātman*),
And on the Self as in all beings—
He does not shrink away from Him.
7. In whom all beings
Have become just the Self of the discerner—
Then what delusion, what sorrow is there,
Of him who perceives the unity!
8. He has environed. The bright, the bodiless, the scatheless,
The sinewless, the pure, unpierced by evil!
Wise, intelligent, encompassing, self-existent,
Appropriately he distributed objects through the eternal years.
9. Into blind darkness enter they
That worship ignorance;
Into darkness greater than that, as it were, they
That delight in knowledge.[1]
10. Other, indeed, they say, than knowledge!
Other, they say, than non-knowledge!
—Thus we have heard from the wise
Who to us have explained It.
11. Knowledge and non-knowledge—
He who this pair conjointly knows,

[1] The sophistry of the learned is a greater danger than the ignorance of the unlearned.

With non-knowledge passing over death,
With knowledge wins the immortal.

12. Into blind darkness enter they
Who worship non-becoming;
Into darkness greater than that, as it were, they
Who delight in becoming.

13. Other, indeed—they say—than origin!
Other—they say—than non-origin!
—Thus have we heard from the wise
Who to us have explained It.

14. Becoming and destruction—
He who this pair conjointly knows,
With destruction passing over death,
With becoming wins the immortal.

15. With a golden vessel
The Real's face is covered o'er.
That do thou, O Pūṣan, uncover
For one whose law is the Real to see.

16. O Nourisher, the sole Seer, O Controller, O Sun, offspring of Prajāpati, spread forth thy rays! Gather thy brilliance! What is thy fairest form—that of thee I see. He who is yonder, yonder Person—I myself am he!

17. [My] breath to the immortal wind! This body then ends in ashes! *Om*!
O Purpose, remember! The deed remember!
O Purpose, remember! The deed remember!

18. O Agni, by a goodly path to prosperity lead us,
Thou god who knowest all the ways!
Keep far from us crooked-going sin!
Most ample expression of adoration to thee would we render.

2. Kena Upaniṣad

As the name indicates, this Upaniṣad asks, "By whom?"—that is, who is the real power behind the functions of the universe, external in nature and internal in man. In reply the Upaniṣad gives an account of a single unitary reality, the *Ātman*, as the inspirer of the functions of both man and the universe, of sense-functions in man and the functions of the elements in the external world. While knowledge of the unqualified Absolute alone can result in emancipation, knowledge of the Absolute as God prepares the way for such knowledge.

The Upaniṣad is famous also for its saying, "It is not understood by those who [say they] understand It. It is understood by those who [say they] understand It not." This statement is intended to indicate the paradoxical nature of the inscrutability of the Absolute, the *Brahman* or *Ātman.*

[Question:] *The real agent in the individual?*

1. By whom impelled soars forth the mind projected?
By whom enjoined goes forth the earliest breathing?
By whom impelled this speech do people utter?
The eye, the ear—what god, pray, them enjoineth?

[Answer:] *The all-conditioning, yet inscrutable agent, Brahman*

2. That which is the hearing of the ear, the thought of the mind,
The voice of speech, as also the breathing of the breath,
And the sight of the eye! Past these escaping, the wise,
On departing from this world, become immortal.
3. There the eyes go not;
Speech goes not, nor the mind.
We know not, we understand not
How one would teach It.
Other, indeed, is It than the known,
And moreover above the unknown.
—Thus have we heard of the ancients
Who to us have explained It. (I.1–3)

The paradox of Its inscrutability

3. [Teacher:]
It is conceived of by him by whom It is not conceived of.
He by whom It is conceived of, knows It not.
It is not understood by those who [say they] understand It.
It is understood by those who [say they] understand It not.
4. When known by an awakening, It is conceived of; . . .
(II.3–4)

3. Kaṭha Upaniṣad

The *Kaṭha* gets its name from a school of the *Black Yajur Veda.* It is perhaps the most philosophical of the Upaniṣads. Among its important features are: the dialogue between Naciketas and Yama (the god of the world of departed spirits) on the question of the immortality of the self, in which Naciketas chooses knowledge above all worldly blessings; the theory of the superiority of the good (*śreyas*) over the pleasant (*preyas*); the view that the *Ātman* cannot be known by the senses, by reason, or by much learning, but only by intuitive insight or direct realization; and the doctrine of the body as the chariot of the self—a reminder of a similar figure used by Plato.

The story of Naciketas: knowledge preferable to the greatest earthly pleasures

1. Now verily, with zeal did Vājaśravasa give his whole possession [as a religious gift].
 He had a son, Naciketas by name.
2. Into him, boy as he was, while the sacrificial gifts were being led up, faith entered....
4. Then he said to his father: "Papa, to whom will you give me?"—a second time—a third time.
 To him then he said: "To Death I give you!"[1]

[Here follows a conversation between Death (Yama) and Naciketas. Death, just returned from a three days' absence and finding that Naciketas has not received the hospitality which is due a *brāhmin*, says, "Therefore in return choose three boons!" His first wish is that he might return to his father on earth; his second is for an understanding of the Naciketas sacrificial fire that leads to heaven. These are granted. The account of the third and most important wish follows in part:]

[Naciketas:]

20. This doubt that there is in regard to a man deceased:
 "He exists," say some; "He exists not," say others—
 This would I know, instructed by thee!
 Of the boons this is boon the third.

[Death:]

21. Even the gods had doubt as to this of yore!
 For truly, it is not easily to be understood. Subtile is this matter.
 Another boon, O Naciketas, choose!
 Press me not! Give up this one for me!

[1] Opinions and interpretations of this incident and the motivations involved vary. No attempt is made here to take a position on this debatable question.

[Naciketas:]

22. Even the gods had doubt, indeed, as to this,
And thou, O Death, sayest that it is not easily to be understood.
And another declarer of it the like of thee is not to be obtained.
No other boon the equal of it is there at all.

[Death:]

23. Choose centenarian sons and grandsons,
Many cattle, elephants, gold, and horses.
Choose a great abode of earth.
And thyself live as many autumns as thou desirest.
24. This, if thou thinkest as equal boon,
Choose—wealth and long life!
A great one on earth, O Naciketas, be thou.
The enjoyer of thy desires I make thee.
25. Whate'er desires are hard to get in the mortal world—
For all desires at pleasure make request.
These lovely maidens with chariots, with lyres—
Such [maidens], indeed, are not obtainable by men—
By these, from me bestowed, be waited on!
O Naciketas, question me not regarding dying!

[Naciketas:]

26. Ephemeral things! That which is a mortal's, O End-maker,
Even the vigor of all the powers, they wear away.
Even a whole life is slight indeed.
Thine be the vehicles! Thine be the dance and song!
27. Not with wealth is a man to be satisfied.
Shall we take wealth, if we have seen thee?
Shall we live so long as thou shalt rule?
—This, in truth, is the boon to be chosen by me.
28. When one has come into the presence of undecaying immortals,
What decaying mortal, here below, that understands,
That meditates upon the pleasures of beauty and delight,
Would delight in a life over-long?
29. This thing whereon they doubt, O Death:
What there is in the great passing-on—tell us that!
This boon, that has entered into the hidden—
No other than that does Naciketas choose. (I.1–2, 4, 20–29)

The failure of pleasure and of ignorance; the wisdom of the better knowledge

[Death:]

1. The better (*śreyas*) is one thing, and the pleasanter (*preyas*) quite another.
Both these, of different aim, bind a person.
Of these two, well it is for him who takes the better;
He fails of his aim who chooses the pleasanter.
2. Both the better and the pleasanter come to a man.
Going all around the two, the wise man discriminates.
The wise man chooses the better, indeed, rather than the pleasanter.
The stupid man, from getting-and-keeping, chooses the pleasanter.
3. Thou indeed, upon the pleasant and pleasantly appearing desires
Meditating, hast let them go, O Naciketas.
Thou art not one who has taken that garland of wealth
In which many men sink down.
4. Widely opposite and asunder are these two:
Ignorance and what is known as "knowledge."
I think Naciketas desirous of obtaining knowledge!
Many desires rend thee not.
5. Those abiding in the midst of ignorance,
Self-wise, thinking themselves learned,
Running hither and thither, go around deluded,
Like blind men led by one who is himself blind. (II.1–5)

The eternal indestructible Self

18. The wise one [i.e., the *Ātman*, the Self] is not born, nor dies.
This one has not come from anywhere, has not become anyone.
Unborn, constant, eternal, primeval, this one
Is not slain when the body is slain.
19. If the slayer think to slay,
If the slain think himself slain,
Both these understand not.
This one slays not, nor is slain.
20. More minute than the minute, greater than the great,
Is the Self that is set in the heart of a creature here.

One who is without the active will beholds Him, and becomes freed from sorrow—
When through the grace of the Creator he beholds the greatness of the Self.

22. Him who is the bodiless among bodies,
Stable among the unstable,
The great, all-pervading Self—
On recognizing Him, the wise man sorrows not.
23. This Self is not to be obtained by instruction,
Nor by intellect, nor by much learning.
He is to be obtained only by the one whom he chooses;
To such a one that Self reveals his own person.
24. Not he who has not ceased from bad conduct,
Not he who is not tranquil, not he who is not composed,
Not he who is not of peaceful mind
Can obtain Him by intelligence (*prajñā*).
25. He for whom the priesthood and the nobility
Both are as food,
And death is as a sauce—
Who really knows where He is? (II.18–20, 22–5)

The universal and the individual self

3. Know thou the self (*ātman*) as riding in a chariot,
The body as the chariot.
Know thou the intellect (*buddhi*) as the chariot-driver,
And the mind as the reins.
4. The senses, they say, are the horses;
The objects of sense, what they range over.
The self combined with senses and mind
Wise men call "the enjoyer."
7. He, however, who has not understanding,
Who is unmindful and ever impure,
Reaches not the goal,
But goes on to transmigration [rebirth].
8. He, however, who has understanding,
Who is mindful and ever pure,
Reaches the goal
From which he is born no more. . . .
10. Higher than the senses are the objects of sense.
Higher than the objects of sense is the mind;

And higher than the mind is the intellect (*buddhi*).
Higher than the intellect is the Great Self (*Ātman*).
11. Higher than the Great is the Unmanifest (*avyakta*).
Higher than the Unmanifest is the Person.
Higher than the Person there is nothing at all.
That is the goal. That is the highest course.
12. Though He is hidden in all things,
That Self shines not forth.
But He is seen by subtle seers
With superior, subtle intellect.
13. An intelligent man should suppress his speech and his mind.
The latter he should suppress in the Understanding-Self (*jñāna ātman*).
The understanding he should suppress in the Great Self.
That he should suppress in the Tranquil Self. . . .
14. Arise ye! Awake ye!
Obtain your boons and understand them!
A sharpened edge of a razor, hard to traverse,
A difficult path is this—poets declare!
15. What is soundless, touchless, formless, imperishable,
Likewise tasteless, constant, odorless,
Without beginning, without end, higher than the great, stable—
By discerning That, one is liberated from the mouth of death.
(III.3–4, 7–8, 10–15)

The immortal Self not to be sought by outward knowledge

1. The Self-existent pierced the openings [of the senses] outward;
Therefore one looks outward, not within himself.
A certain wise man, while seeking immortality,
Introspectively beheld the Self face to face.
2. The childish go after outward pleasures;
They walk into the net of widespread death.
But the wise, knowing immortality,
Seek not the stable among things which are unstable here.
3. That by which [one discerns] form, taste, smell,
Sound, and mutual touches—
It is with That indeed that one discerns.
What is there left over here!
This, verily, is That!

4. By recognizing as the great pervading Self
That whereby one perceives both
The sleeping state and the waking state,
The wise man sorrows not.
10. Whatever is here, that is there.
What is there, that again is here.
He obtains death after death
Who seems to see a difference here.
11. By the mind, indeed, is this [realization] to be attained:—
There is no difference here at all!
He goes from death to death
Who seems to see a difference here. (IV.1–4, 10–11)

One's real person (self), the same as the world-ground

8. He who is awake in those that sleep,
The Person who fashions desire after desire—
That indeed is the Pure. That is *Brahman.*
That indeed is called the Immortal.
On it all the worlds do rest;
And no one soever goes beyond it.
This, verily, is That!
9. As the one fire has entered the world
And becomes corresponding in form to every form,
So the one Inner Self (*antarātman*) of all things
Is corresponding in form to every form, and yet is outside.
10. As the one wind has entered the world
And becomes corresponding in form to every form,
So the one Inner Self of all things
Is corresponding in form to every form, and yet is outside.
11. As the sun, the eye of the whole world,
Is not sullied by the external faults of the eyes,
So the one Inner Self of all things
Is not sullied by the evil in the world, being external to it.
12. The Inner Self of all things, the One Controller,
Who makes his one form manifold—
The wise who perceive Him as standing in oneself,
They, and no others, have eternal happiness! (V.8–12)

The world-tree rooted in Brahman; [*Ways to Brahman*]

1. Its root is above, its branches below—
This eternal fig-tree!
That (root) indeed is the Pure. That is *Brahman.*
That indeed is called the Immortal.
On it all the worlds do rest,
And no one soever goes beyond it.
This, verily, is That!

2. This whole world, whatever there is,
Was created from and moves in Life.
The great fear, the upraised thunderbolt—
They who know That, become immortal.

3. From fear of Him fire doth burn.
From fear the sun gives forth heat.
From fear both Indra and Wind,
And Death as fifth, do speed along. . . .

6. The separate nature of the senses,
And that their arising and setting
Is of things that come into being apart [from himself],
The wise man recognizes, and sorrows not.

9. His form is not to be beheld.
No one soever sees Him with the eye.
He is framed by the heart, by the thought, by the mind.
They who know That become immortal.

10. When cease the five
[Sense-] knowledges, together with the mind,
And the intellect (*buddhi*) stirs not—
That, they say, is the highest course.

11. This they consider as *yoga*—
The firm holding back of the senses.
Then one becomes undistracted.
Yoga, truly, is the origin and the end.

12. Not by speech, not by mind,
Not by sight can He be apprehended.
How can He be comprehended
Otherwise than by one's saying "He is"? . . .

13. He can indeed by comprehended by the thought "He is"
And by [admitting] the real nature of both [his comprehensibility and his incomprehensibility].

When he has been comprehended by the thought "He is"
His real nature manifests itself.
14. When are liberated all
The desires that lodge in one's heart,
Then a mortal becomes immortal!
Therein he reaches *Brahman*!
15. When are cut all
The knots of the heart here on earth,
Then a mortal becomes immortal!
—Thus far is the instruction. (VI.1–3, 6, 9–15)

4. Praśna Upaniṣad

As the name indicates, this work has its origin in the *questions* (six in all) which philosophers ask of the sage Pippalāda. His answers evolve in the end quite a systematic philosophy on creation, human personality, and the metaphysical principle in man. This indicates that the Upaniṣad must have been a late work.

Questioners seek the highest Brahman from a teacher

4. To him [a questioner] then he [Pippalāda, a seer,] said: "The Lord of Creation (Prajāpati), verily, was desirous of creatures (offspring, *prajā*). He performed austerity. Having performed austerity, he produces a pair, matter (*rayi*, fem.) and life (*prāṇa*, masc.), thinking 'These two will make creatures for me in manifold ways.'"

5. The sun, verily, is life; matter, indeed, is the moon. Matter, verily, is everything here, both what is formed and what is formless. . . . (I.4, 5)

The Supreme Self, the ultimate basis of the manifold world and of the individual

7. As birds resort to a tree for a resting-place, even so, O friend, it is to the supreme Self (*Ātman*) that everything here resorts:—[1]

8. Earth and the elements of earth, water and the elements of water, heat and the elements of heat, wind and the elements of wind, space and the elements of space, sight and what can be seen, hearing and what can be heard, smell and what can be smelled, taste and what can be tasted, the skin and what can be touched, speech and what can be spoken, the hands and what can be taken,

[1] The following is a noteworthy Sāṁkhya enumeration.—Hume.

the organ of generation and what can be enjoyed, the anus and what can be excreted, the feet and what can be walked, mind (*manas*) and what can be perceived, intellect (*buddhi*) and what can be conceived, egoism (*ahaṁkāra*) and what can be connected with "me," thought (*citta*) and what can be thought, brilliance and what can be illumined, life-breath and what can be supported.

9. Truly, this seer, toucher, hearer, smeller, taster, thinker, conceiver, doer, the conscious self (*vijñānātman*), the person—his resort is in the supreme imperishable Self (*Ātman*). (IV.7–9)

5. Muṇḍaka Upaniṣad

This is the most poetical of the Upaniṣads. The philosophy expressed is mostly eclectic, and, generally speaking, the subject-matter is that which is common to all the Upaniṣads. Worthy of special mention, however, is the theory of two kinds of knowledge, a higher (*parā*) and a lower (*aparā*).

The name means "shaven," and presumably was given to this Upaniṣad because it emphasizes the life of *sannyāsa* (austerity) as contrasted with the life of sacrifice and work. The *sannyāsin* is shaved of ignorance and of concern for work or religious practices.

Two kinds of knowledge

4. [Aṅgiras said:] "There are two knowledges to be known—as indeed the knowers of *Brahman* are wont to say: a higher (*parā*) and also a lower (*aparā*).

5. Of these, the lower is the *Ṛg Veda*, the *Yajur Veda*, the *Sāma Veda*, the *Atharva Veda*. . . .

Now, the higher is that whereby that Imperishable is apprehended. . . .

6. That which is invisible, ungraspable, without family, without caste—

Without sight or hearing is It, without hand or foot,
Eternal, all-pervading, omnipresent, exceedingly subtile;
That is the Imperishable, which the wise perceive as the source of beings.

7. As a spider emits and draws in [its thread],
As herbs arise on the earth,
As the hairs of the head and body from a living person,
So from the Imperishable arises everything here. (I.i.4–7)

The supremacy of knowledge of Brahman over sacrifice

10. Thinking sacrifice and merit is the chiefest thing,
Naught better do they know—deluded!
Having had enjoyment on the top of the heaven won by good works,
They re-enter this world, or a lower.
11. They who practise austerity and faith in the forest,
The peaceful knowers who live on alms,
Depart passionless through the door of the sun,
To where is that immortal Person (*Puruṣa*), e'en the imperishable Self (*Ātman*)....
12. Having scrutinized the worlds that are built up by work, a *brāhmin*
Should arrive at indifference. The [world] that was not made is not [won] by what is done.
For the sake of this knowledge let him go, fuel in hand,
To a spiritual teacher who is learned in the scriptures and established on *Brahman*. (I.ii.10–12)

The doctrine of Brahman-Ātman

1. This is the truth:—
As, from a well-blazing fire, sparks
By the thousand issue forth of like form,
So from the Imperishable, my friend, beings manifold
Are produced, and thither also go.
2. Heavenly, formless is the Person.
He is without and within, unborn,
Breathless, mindless, pure,
Higher than the high Imperishable.
3. From Him is produced breath,
Mind, and all the senses,
Space, wind, light, water,
And earth, the supporter of all.
4. Fire is His head; His eyes, the moon and sun;
The regions of space, His ears; His voice, the revealed Vedas;
Wind, His breath; His heart, the whole world. Out of His feet, The earth. Truly, He is the Inner Self (*Ātman*) of all.
5. From him [proceeds] fire, whose fuel is the sun;
From the moon, rain; herbs, on the earth.

The male pours seed in the female.
Many creatures are produced from the Person.
7. From Him, too, gods are manifoldly produced,
The celestials, men, cattle, birds,
The in-breath and the out-breath, rice and barley, austerity,
Faith, truth, chastity, and the law.
10. The Person himself is everything here;
Work and austerity and *Brahman*, beyond death.
He who knows That, set in the secret place [of the heart]—
He here on earth, my friend, rends asunder the knot of ignorance.
(II.i.1–5, 7, 10)

The All-inclusive Brahman

1. Manifest, [yet] hidden; called "Moving-in-secret";
The great abode! Therein is placed that
Which moves and breathes and winks.
What that is, know as Being and Non-being,
As the object of desire, higher than understanding,
As what is the best of creatures!
2. That which is flaming, which is subtler than the subtle,
On which the worlds are set, and their inhabitants
That is the imperishable *Brahman*.
It is life, and It is speech and mind.
That is the real. It is immortal.
It is [a mark] to be penetrated. Penetrate It, my friend!
3. Taking as a bow the great weapon of the Upaniṣad,
One should put upon it an arrow sharpened by meditation.
Stretching it with a thought directed to the essence of That,
Penetrate that Imperishable as the mark, my friend.
4. The mystic syllable *Om* is the bow. The arrow is the Self (*Ātman*).
Brahman is said to be the mark.
By the undistracted man is It to be penetrated.
One should come to be in It, as the arrow [in the mark].
9. In the highest golden sheath
Is *Brahman*, without stain, without parts.
Brilliant is It, the light of lights—
That which knowers of the Self (*Ātman*) do know!
(II.ii.1–4, 9)

The way to Brahman

1. Two birds, fast bound companions,
Clasp close the self-same tree.
Of these two, the one eats sweet fruit;
The other looks on without eating.
2. On the self-same tree a person, sunken,
Grieves for his impotence, deluded;
When he sees the other, the Lord (*Īśa*), contented,
And his greatness, he becomes freed from sorrow.
3. When a seer sees the brilliant
Maker, Lord, Person, the *Brahman*-source,
Then, being a knower, shaking off good and evil,
Stainless, he attains supreme identity [with Him].
5. This Self (*Ātman*) is obtainable by truth, by austerity,
By proper knowledge, by the student's life of chastity constantly [practiced].
Within the body, consisting of light, pure is He
Whom the ascetics, with imperfections done away, behold.
8. Not by sight is It grasped, not even by speech,
Not by any other sense-organs, austerity, or work.
By the peace of knowledge, one's nature purified—
In that way, however, by meditating, one does behold Him who is without parts. (III.i.1–3, 5, 8)

1. ...They who, being without desire, worship the Person
And are wise, pass beyond the seed [of rebirth] here.
2. He who in fancy forms desires,
Because of his desires is born [again] here and there.
But of him whose desire is satisfied, who is a perfected self,
All desires even here on earth vanish away.
3. This Self (*Ātman*) is not to be obtained by instruction,
Nor by intellect, nor by much learning.
He is to be obtained only by the one whom He chooses;
To such a one that Self reveals His own person.
4. This Self is not to be obtained by one destitute of fortitude,
Nor through heedlessness, nor through a false notion of austerity.
But he who strives by these means, provided he knows—
Into his *Brahman*-abode this Self enters.

5. Attaining Him, the seers who are satisfied with knowledge,
Who are perfected selves, from passion free, tranquil—
Attaining Him who is the universally omnipresent, those wise,
Devout selves into the All itself do enter.
7. Gone are the fifteen parts according to their station,
Even all the sense-organs in their corresponding divinities!
One's deeds and the self that consists of understanding—
All become unified in the supreme Imperishable.
8. As the flowing rivers in the ocean
Disappear, quitting name and form,
So the knower, being liberated from name and form,
Goes unto the Heavenly Person, higher than the high.
9. He, verily, who knows that supreme *Brahman*, becomes very *Brahman*.... (III.ii.1–5, 7–9)

6. Māṇḍūkya Upaniṣad

Named for the sage-teacher Māṇḍūkya, this Upaniṣad has given to Indian thought the famous theory of the four states of consciousness, namely, waking, dreaming, profound sleep, and the fourth state (*turīya*), which alone is real. (Here these states are explained in their relationship to the mystic syllable *Om.*) Both psychologically and metaphysically this doctrine has had a great influence on subsequent Indian thought. The text is given in full.

The mystic symbolism of the syllable "Om" depicting the four states of consciousness

1. *Om!*—This syllable is this whole world.
Its further explanation is:—
The past, the present, the future—everything is just the word *Om*.
And whatever else that transcends threefold time—that, too, is just the word *Om*.
2. For truly, everything here is *Brahman*; this self is *Brahman*. This same self has four fourths.
3. The waking state, outwardly cognitive, having seven limbs, having nineteen mouths, enjoying the gross, the Common-to-all-men, is the first fourth.
4. The dreaming state, inwardly cognitive, having seven limbs, having nineteen mouths, enjoying the exquisite, the Brilliant, is the second fourth.

5. If one asleep desires no desire whatsoever, sees no dream whatsoever, that is deep sleep.

The deep-sleep state, unified, just a cognition-mass, consisting of bliss, enjoying bliss, whose mouth is thought, the cognitional, is the third fourth.

6. This is the lord of all. This is the all-knowing. This is the inner controller. This is the source of all, for this is the origin and the end of beings.

7. Not inwardly cognitive, not outwardly cognitive, not both-wise cognitive, not a cognition-mass, not cognitive, not non-cognitive, unseen, with which there can be no dealing, ungraspable, having no distinctive mark, non-thinkable, that cannot be designated, the essence of the assurance of which is the state of being one with the Self, the cessation of development, tranquil, benign, without a second (*a-dvaita*)—[such] they think is the fourth. He is the Self. He should be discerned.

8. This is the Self with regard to the word *Om*, with regard to its elements. The elements are the fourths; the fourths, the elements: the letter *a*, the letter *u*, the letter *m*.[1]

9. The waking state, the Common-to-all-men, is the letter *a*, the first element, from *āpti* (obtaining) or from *ādimatva* (being first).

He obtains, verily, indeed, all desires, he becomes first—he who knows this.

10. The sleeping state, the brilliant, is the letter *u*, the second element, from *utkarṣa* (exaltation) or from *ubhayatvā* (intermediateness).

He exalts, verily, indeed, the continuity of knowledge; and he becomes equal; no one ignorant of *Brahman* is born in the family of him who knows this.

11. The deep-sleep state, the cognitional, is the letter *m*, the third element, from *miti* ("erecting') or from *apiti* ("immerging").

He, verily, indeed, erects (*minoti*) this whole world, and he becomes its immerging—he who knows this.

12. The fourth is without an element, with which there can be no dealing, the cessation of development, benign, without a second.

Thus *Om* is the Self (*Ātman*) indeed.

He who knows this, with his self enters the Self—yea, he who knows this!

[1] In Sanskrit the vowel *o* is constitutionally a diphthong, contracted from $a+u$. *Om* therefore may be analyzed into the elements $a+u+m$.

7. Taittirīya Upaniṣad

The distinctive feature of this Upaniṣad is its description of the ethical teachings of the times as brought out in the form of a discourse between the teacher and his pupils—sometimes called a "Convocation Address." The Upaniṣad is also rightly famous for its doctrine of the "Five Sheaths" of the self—food, breath, mind, intellect, and bliss—and also for its "calculus of bliss," leading up to the ultimate bliss of *Brahman*. The Upaniṣad is so named because it is a part of the *Taittirīya Āraṇyaka*.

The fivefoldness of the world and of the individual

Earth,	Atmosphere,	Heaven,	Quarters of Heaven,	Intermediate Quarters;
fire,	wind,	sun,	moon,	stars;
water,	plants,	trees,	space,	one's body.

—Thus with regard to material existence.

Now with regard to oneself.—

Prāṇa	*Vyāna*	*Apāna*	*Udāna*	*Samāna*
breath,	breath,	breath,	breath,	breath;
sight,	hearing,	mind,	speech,	touch;
skin,	flesh,	muscle,	bone,	marrow.

Having analyzed in this manner, a seer has said: "Fivefold, verily, is this whole world. With the [knowledge of the] fivefold, indeed, one wins the fivefold." (I.7)

The excellence of Veda-knowledge—a (mystical) meditation

I am the mover[1] of the tree!
My fame is like a mountain's peak!
Exaltedly pure, like the excellent nectar in the sun,
I am a shining treasure,
Wise, immortal, indestructible![2]

Practical precepts to a student

1. Having taught the Veda, a teacher further instructs a pupil:—
Speak the truth.
Practise virtue (*dharma*).

[1] "Mover" may mean either "I am the feller of the tree of the world-delusion" (Śaṁkara) or "I am the moving (or animating) spirit of the tree of life" (Deussen).—Hume.

[2] The whole paragraph is an obscure, mystical meditation, either a preparatory invocation for the study of the Vedas, or a summary praise of its exalting and enlightening effect.—Hume.

Neglect not study of the Vedas.
Having brought an acceptable gift to the teacher, cut not off the line of progeny.
One should not be negligent of truth.
One should not be negligent of virtue.
One should not be negligent of welfare.
One should not be negligent of prosperity.
One should not be negligent of study and teaching.

2. One should not be negligent of duties to the gods and to the fathers.
Be one to whom a mother is as a god.
Be one to whom a father is as a god.
Be one to whom a teacher is as a god.
Be one to whom a guest is as a god.
Those acts which are irreproachable should be practised, and no others.
Those things which among us are good deeds should be revered by you, [3] and no others.
Whatever *brāhmins* there are who are superior to us, should be comforted [or refreshed] by you with a seat. [Revised tr.]
One should give with faith.
One should not give without faith.
One should give with plenty.
One should give with modesty.
One should give with fear.
One should give with sympathy.
Now, if you should have doubt concerning an act, or doubt concerning conduct, [4] if there should be there *brāhmins* competent to judge, apt, devoted, not harsh, lovers of virtue—as they may behave themselves in such a case, so should you behave yourself in such a case.
Now, with regard to [people] spoken against, if there should be there *brāhmins* competent to judge, apt, devoted, not harsh, lovers of virtue—as they may behave themselves with regard to such, so should you behave yourself with regard to such.
This is the teaching. This is the admonition. This is the mystic doctrine of the Veda (*veda-upaniṣad*). This is the instruction. Thus should one worship. Thus, indeed, should one worship.

(I.xi.1–4)

The all-comprehensive Brahman of the world and of the individual; knowledge thereof (is) the supreme success

Om! He who knows *Brahman*, attains the highest!
As to that this [verse] has been declared:—

He who knows *Brahman* as the real, as knowledge (*jñāna*), as the infinite,[1]
Set down in the secret place [of the heart] and in the highest heaven,
He obtains all desires,
Together with the intelligent (*vipaścit*) *Brahman*.

The progressive identification of the person

From this Self (*Ātman*), verily, space arose; from space, wind; from wind, fire; from fire, water; from water, the earth; from the earth, herbs; from herbs, food; from food, semen; from semen, the person.

This, verily, is the person that consists of the essence of food. This, indeed, is his head; this, the right side; this, the left side; this, the body (*ātman*); this, the lower part, the foundation. . . . (II.1)

From food, verily, creatures are produced,
Whatsoever [creatures] dwell on the earth.
Moreover by food, in truth, they live.
Moreover into it also they finally pass.
For truly, food is the chief of beings;
Therefore it is called a panacea.[2]
Verily, they obtain all food
Who worship *Brahman* as food.
For truly, food is the chief of beings;
Therefore it is called a panacea.
From food created things are born.
By food, when born, do they grow up.
It both is eaten and eats things.
Because of that it is called food.

Verily, other than and within that one that consists of the essence of food is the self that consists of breath. By that this is filled. This, verily, has the form of a person. . . . (II.2)

[1] Deussen proposes to emend *ānanda*, "bliss," in order to have the customary threefold definition of *Brahman* as *sat-cit-ānanda*, "being, intelligence, and bliss," and in order to introduce the great culminating thought of the chapter.—Hume.

[2] *Sarvauṣadham*, literally, "consisting of all sorts of herbs."

The gods do breathe along with breath,
As also men and beasts.
For truly, breath is the life of beings
Therefore it is called the Life-of-all....

Verily, other than and within that one that consists of breath is a self that consists of mind. By that this is filled. This, verily, has the form of a person. (II.3)

Wherefrom words turn back,
Together with the mind, not having attained—
The bliss of *Brahman* he who knows,
Fears not at any time at all.

Verily, other than and within that one that consists of mind is a self that consists of understanding. By that this is filled. This, verily, has the form of a person. (II.4)

Understanding directs the sacrifice;
And deeds also it directs.
'Tis understanding that all the gods
Do worship as *Brahman*, as chief....

Verily, other than and within that one that consists of understanding is a self that consists of bliss. By that this is filled. That one, verily, has the form of a person. According to that one's personal form is this one with the form of a person. Pleasure is its head; delight, the right side; great delight, the left side; bliss, the body (*ātman*); *Brahman* the lower part, the foundation.... (II.5)

...He desired: "Would that I were many! Let me procreate myself!" He performed austerity. Having performed austerity he created this whole world, whatever there is here. Having created it, into it, indeed, he entered. Having entered it, he became both the actual [here] and the yon, both the defined and the undefined, both the based and the non-based, both the conscious (*vijñāna*) and the unconscious, both the real and the false. As the real, he became whatever there is here. That is what they call the real.... (II.6)

The gradation of blisses up to the bliss of Brahman

This is a consideration of bliss,—

Let there be a youth, a good youth, well read, very quick, very firm, very strong. Let this whole earth be full of wealth for him. That is one human bliss.

A hundred human blisses are one bliss of the human Gandharvas [higher beings]—also of a man who is versed in the scriptures and who is not smitten with desire.

A hundred blisses of the human Gandharvas are one bliss of the divine Gandharvas—also of a man who is versed in the scriptures and who is not smitten with desire.

A hundred blisses of the divine Gandharvas are one bliss of the fathers in their long-enduring world—also of a man who is versed in the scriptures and who is not smitten with desire.

A hundred blisses of the fathers in their long-enduring world are one bliss of the gods who are born so by birth—also of a man who is versed in the scriptures and who is not smitten with desire.

A hundred blisses of the gods who are born so by birth are one bliss of the gods who are gods by work, who go to the gods by work—also of a man who is versed in the scriptures and who is not smitten with desire.

A hundred blisses of the gods who are gods by work are one bliss of the gods—also of a man who is versed in the scriptures and who is not smitten with desire.

A hundred blisses of the gods are one bliss of Indra—also of a man who is versed in the scriptures and who is not smitten with desire.

A hundred blisses of Indra are one bliss of Bṛhaspati—also of a man who is versed in the scriptures and who is not smitten with desire.

A hundred blisses of Bṛhaspati are one bliss of Prajāpati—also of a man who is versed in the scriptures and who is not smitten with desire.

A hundred blisses of Prajāpati are one bliss of Brahmā—also of a man who is versed in the scriptures and who is not smitten with desire.

Both he who is here in a person and he who is yonder in the sun—he is one.

He who knows this, on departing from this world, proceeds on to that self which consists of food, proceeds on to that self which consists of breath, proceeds on to that self which consists of mind, proceeds on to that self which consists of understanding, proceeds on to that self which consists of bliss. . . . (II.8)

Such a one, verily, the thought does not torment: "Why have I not done the good? Why have I done the evil?" He who knows this, delivers himself from these two [thoughts]. For truly, from both of these he delivers himself—he who knows this!

Such is the mystic doctrine (*upaniṣad*)! (II.9)

Bhṛgu's progressive learning through austerity of five phases of Brahman

1. Bhṛgu Vāruṇi, verily approached his father Varuṇa, and said: "Declare *Brahman*, Sir!"

To him he taught that as food, as breath, as sight, as hearing, as mind, as speech.

Then he said to him: "That, verily, whence beings here are born, that by which when born they live, that into which on deceasing they enter—that be desirous of understanding. That is *Brahman*."

He performed austerity. Having performed austerity, [2] he understood that *Brahman* is food. For truly, indeed, beings here are born from food, when born they live by food, on deceasing they enter into food.

Having understood that, he again approached his father Varuṇa, and said: "Declare *Brahman*, Sir!"

Then he said to him: "Desire to understand *Brahman* by austerity. *Brahman* is austerity (*tapas*)."

He performed austerity. Having performed austerity, [3] he understood that *Brahman* is breath. For truly, indeed, beings here are born from breath, when born they live by breath, on deceasing they enter into breath.

Having understood that, he again approached his father Varuṇa, and said: "Declare *Brahman*, Sir!"

Then he said to him: "Desire to understand *Brahman* by austerity. *Brahman* is austerity!"

He performed austerity. Having performed austerity, [4] he understood that *Brahman* is mind. For truly, indeed, beings here are born from mind, when born they live by mind, on deceasing they enter into mind.

Having understood that, he again approached his father Varuṇa, and said: "Declare *Brahman*, Sir!"

Then he said to him: "Desire to understand *Brahman* by austerity. *Brahman* is austerity."

He performed austerity. Having performed austerity, [5] he understood that *Brahman* is understanding (*vijñāna*). For truly, indeed, beings here are born from understanding, when born they live by understanding, on deceasing they enter into understanding.

Having understood that, he again approached his father Varuṇa, and said: "Declare *Brahman*, Sir!"

Then he said to him: "Desire to understand *Brahman* by austerity. *Brahman* is austerity."

He performed austerity. Having performed austerity, [6] he understood that *Brahman* is bliss. For truly, indeed, beings are born from bliss, when born they live by bliss, on deceasing they enter into bliss.

This is the knowledge of Bhṛgu Vāruṇi, established in the highest heaven. He who knows this becomes established. He becomes an eater of food, possessing food. He becomes great in offspring, in cattle, in the splendor of sacred knowledge, great in fame....

(III.1–6)

8. Aitareya Upaniṣad

As the name suggests, this Upaniṣad is only a part of the larger *Aitareya Āraṇyaka*. The idea of life after death is brought out more clearly than in other places in Upaniṣadic literature, but the Upaniṣad is most famous for its doctrine of the *Ātman* as intellect.

The Creation

1. In the beginning *Ātman* (Self), verily, one only, was here—no other winking thing whatever. He bethought himself: "Let me now create worlds."

2. He created these worlds: water, light rays, death, the waters....

3. He bethought himself: "Here now are worlds. Let me now create world-guardians." Right from the waters he drew forth and shaped a person.... (I.i.1–3)

The universal Self

1. [Question:] Who is this one?

[Answer:] We worship him as the Self.

[Question:] Which one is the Self?

[Answer:] [He] whereby one sees, or whereby one hears, or whereby one smells odors, or whereby one articulates speech, or whereby one discriminates the sweet and the unsweet; [2] that which is heart and mind—that is, consciousness, perception, discrimination, intelligence, wisdom, insight, steadfastness, thought, thoughtfulness, impulse, memory, conception, purpose, life, desire, will.

All these, indeed, are appellations of intelligence (*prajñāna*).

3. He is *Brahman*; he is Indra; he is Prajāpati; [he is] all these gods; and these five gross elements, namely, earth, wind, space,

water, light; these things and those which are mingled of the fine, as it were; origins of one sort and another; those born from an egg, and those born from a womb, and those born from sweat, and those born from a sprout; horses, cows, persons, elephants; whatever breathing thing there is here—whether moving or flying, and what is stationary.

All this is guided by intelligence, is based on intelligence. The world is guided by intelligence. The basis is intelligence. *Brahman* is intelligence. (III.v.1–3)

9. Chāndogya Upaniṣad

This is one of the oldest and best known of the Upaniṣads. Many important teachings are contained in it, but perhaps the most popular passage in the whole work is the story of Satyakāma Jābāla and his truthful mother, in which it is demonstrated that the status of the *brāhmin* is determined by character rather than by birth. The central teaching of the Upaniṣad, associated with the philosopher Āruṇi, is the basic doctrine of the identity of the *Ātman*, the psychical principle within, and the *Brahman*, the universal principle of nature. This doctrine is expressed in the very famous saying, "*Tat tvam asi* (That art thou)." In this Upaniṣad is also found a delineation of the significance of the mystic syllable *Om*, as well as some of the famous theories of creation, such as the cosmic-egg theory.

The name of the Upaniṣad is derived from "*chandoga*," the name of certain priests specializing in the *Sāma Veda*.

The sacred syllable "Om"

1. *Om!* One should meditate on this syllable [the *Udgītha*, loud chant], for one sings the loud chant [beginning] with "*Om*." [Revised tr.]

The further explanation thereof [is as follows].—

2. The essence of things here is the earth.

The essence of the earth is water.

The essence of water is plants.

The essence of plants is a person (*puruṣa*).

The essence of a person is speech.

The essence of speech is the *Ṛg* (hymn).

The essence of the *Ṛg* is the *Sāman* (chant).

The essence of the *Sāman* is the *Udgītha* (loud singing). . . .

5. The *Ṛg* is speech. The *Sāman* is breath. The *Udgītha* is this syllable "*Om*."[1] (I.i.1–2, 5)

[1] See also *Māṇḍūkya Upaniṣad*.

3. . . .As all leaves are held together by a spike, so all speech is held together by *Om*. Verily, *Om* is the world-all. Verily, *Om* is this world-all. (II.xxiii.3)

The three branches of duty

1. There are three branches of duty. Sacrifice, study of the Vedas, alms-giving—that is the first. [2] Austerity, indeed, is the second. A student of sacred knowledge (*brahmacārin*) dwelling in the house of a teacher, settling himself permanently in the house of a teacher, is the third. . . . (II.xxiii.1)

The individual self identical with the infinite Brahman

1. Verily, this whole world is *Brahman*. Tranquil, let one worship It as that from which he came forth, as that into which he will be dissolved, as that in which he breathes. . . .

2. He who consists of mind, whose body is life (*prāṇa*), whose form is light, whose conception is truth, whose self is space, containing all works, containing all desires, containing all odors, containing all tastes, encompassing this whole world, the unspeaking, the unconcerned—this Self of mine within the heart is smaller than a grain of rice, or a barley-corn, or a mustard-seed, or a grain of millet, or the kernel of a grain of millet; this Self of mine within the heart is greater than the earth, greater than the atmosphere, greater than the sky, greater than these worlds.

4. Containing all works, containing all desires, containing all odors, containing all tastes, encompassing this whole world, the unspeaking, the unconcerned—this is the Self of mine within the heart, this is *Brahman*. Into him I shall enter on departing hence. . . . (III.xiv.1–2, 4)

The cosmic egg

1. The sun is *Brahman*—this is the teaching. A further explanation thereof [is as follows]:

In the beginning this world was merely non-being. It was existent. It developed. It turned into an egg. It lay for the period of a year. It was split asunder. One of the two eggshell-parts became silver, one gold.

2. That which was of silver is this earth. That which was of gold is the sky. What was the outer membrane is the mountains. What was the inner membrane is cloud and mist. What were the veins are the rivers. What was the fluid within is the ocean.

3. Now, what was born therefrom is yonder sun. When it was born, shouts and hurrahs, all beings and all desires rose up toward it. Therefore at its rising and at its every return shouts and hurrahs, all beings and all desires rise up toward it.

4. He who, knowing it thus, reverences the sun as *Brahman*—the prospect is that pleasant shouts will come unto him and delight him—yea, delight him! (III.xix.1–4)

The story of Jābāla, a brāhmin

1. Once upon a time Satyakāma Jābāla addressed his mother Jabālā: "Madam! I desire to live the life of a student of sacred knowledge. Of what family, pray, am I?"

2. Then she said to him: "I do not know this, my dear—of what family you are. In my youth, when I went about a great deal serving as a maid, I got you. So I do not know of what family you are. However, I am Jabālā by name; you are Satyakāma by name. So you may speak of yourself as Satyakāma Jābāla."

3. Then he went to Hāridrumata Gautama, and said: "I will live the life of a student of sacred knowledge. I will become a pupil of yours, Sir."

4. To him he then said: "Of what family, pray, are you, my dear?"

Then he said: "I do not know this, Sir, of what family I am. I asked my mother. She answered me: 'In my youth, when I went about a great deal serving as a maid, I got you. So I do not know this, of what family you are. However, I am Jabālā by name; you are Satyakāma by name.' So I am Satyakāma Jābāla, Sir."

5. To him he then said: "A non-*brāhmin* would not be able to explain thus. Bring the fuel, my dear. I will receive you as a pupil. You have not deviated from the truth." (IV.iv.1–5)

Brahman as life, joy, and the void

4. . . . Then they said to him: [5] "*Brahman* is life (*prāṇa*). *Brahman* is joy. *Brahman* is the void."

Then he said: I understand that *Brahman* is life. But joy and void I do not understand."

They said: "Joy (*ka*)—verily, that is the same as the Void (*kha*). The Void—verily, that is the same as Joy. . . ." (IV.x.4–5)

Man's destiny determined by his conduct

7. . . . those who are of pleasant conduct here—the prospect is, indeed, that they will enter a pleasant womb, either the womb of a

brāhmin, or the womb of a *kṣatriya*, or the womb of a *vaiśya*. But those who are of stinking conduct here—the prospect is, indeed, that they will enter a stinking womb, either the womb of a dog, or the womb of a swine, or the womb of an outcast (*caṇḍāla*). (v.x.7)

The universal Self

1. "Aupamanyava, whom do you reverence as the *Ātman*?"

"The heaven indeed, sir, O King," said he.

"The Universal *Ātman* is, verily, that brightly shining one which you reverence as the *Ātman*. . . .

2. ". . . That, however, is only the head of the *Ātman*," said he. . . . (v.xii.1–2)

1 Then he said to Satyayajña Pauluṣi: "Prācīnayogya! Whom do you reverence as the *Ātman*?"

"The sun indeed, sir, O King," said he.

"The Universal *Ātman* is, verily, that manifold one which you reverence as the *Ātman*. . . . That, however, is only the eye of the *Ātman*," said he. . . . (v.xiii.1)

1. Then he said to Indradyumna Bhāllaveya: "Vaiyāghrapadya! Whom do you reverence as the *Ātman*?"

"The wind indeed, sir, O King," said he.

"The Universal *Ātman* is, verily, that which possesses various paths, which you reverence as the *Ātman*. . . .

2. ". . . That, however, is only the breath of the *Ātman*," said he. . . . (v.xiv.1–2)

1. Then he said to Jana: "Śārkarākṣya! Whom do you reverence as the *Ātman*?"

"Space indeed, sir, O King," said he.

"The Universal *Ātman* is, verily, that expanded one, which you reverence as the *Ātman*. . . .

2. ". . . That, however, is only the body of the *Ātman*," said he. . . . (v.xv.1–2)

1. Then he said to Buḍila Āśvatarāśvi: "Vaiyāghrapadya! Whom do you reverence as the *Ātman*?"

"Water indeed, sir, O King," said he.

"The Universal *Ātman* is, verily, that wealth, which you reverence as the *Ātman*. . . .

2. ". . . That, however, is only the bladder of the *Ātman*," said he. . . . (v.xvi.1–2)

1. Then he said to Uddālaka Āruṇi: "Gautama! Whom do you reverence as the *Ātman?*"

"The earth indeed, sir, O King," said he.

"The Universal *Ātman* is, verily, that support, which you reverence as the *Ātman*....

2. "...That, however, is only the feet of the *Ātman*," said he.... (v.xviii.1–2)

1. Then he said to them: "Verily, indeed, you here eat food, knowing this Universal *Ātman* as if something separate. He however, who reverences this Universal *Ātman* that is of the measure of the span—thus [yet], is to be measured by thinking of oneself—he eats food in all worlds, in all beings, in all selves. (v.xviii.1)

Being as the source of all

1. "In the beginning, my dear, this world was just Being (*sat*), one only, without a second. To be sure, some people say: 'In the beginning this world was just Non-being (*a-sat*), one only, without a second; from that Non-being Being was produced.'"

2. "But verily, my dear, whence could this be?" said he. "How from Non-being could Being be produced? On the contrary, my dear, in the beginning this world was just Being, one only, without a second."

3. "It bethought itself: 'Would that I were many! Let me procreate myself!'"... (vi.ii.1–3)

In sleep one reaches Being

1. Then Uddālaka Āruṇi said to Svetaketu, his son:..."When a person here sleeps, as it is called, then, my dear, he has reached Being, he has gone to his own...." (vi.viii. 1)

1. "Now, when one is sound asleep; composed, serene, and knows no dream—that is the Self (*Ātman*)," said he. "That is the immortal, the fearless. That is *Brahman*...." (viii.xi.1)

The unitary World-Self, the immanent reality of all things and of man

1. "As the bees, my dear, prepare honey by collecting the essences of different trees and reducing the essence to a unity, [2] as they are not able to discriminate 'I am the essence of this tree,' 'I am the essence of that tree'—even so, indeed, my dear, all creatures here, though they reach Being, know not 'We have reached Being.'

3. "Whatever they are in this world, whether tiger, or lion, or wolf, or boar, or worm, or fly, or gnat, or mosquito, that they become.

4. "That which is the finest essence—this whole world has that as its self. That is Reality. That is *Ātman*. That art thou [*Tat tvam asi*], Śvetaketu. . . ."

(VI.ix.1–4)

1. "These rivers, mv dear, flow, the eastern toward the east, the western toward the west. They go just from the ocean to the ocean. They become the ocean itself. As there they know not 'I am this one,' 'I am that one'—[2] even so, indeed, my dear, all creatures here, though they have come forth from Being, know not 'We have come forth from Being.' Whatever they are in this world, whether tiger, or lion, or wolf, or boar, or worm, or fly, or gnat, or mosquito, that they become.

3. "That which is the finest essence—this whole world has that as its self. That is Reality. That is *Ātman*. That art thou, Śvetaketu. . . ."

(VI.x.1–3)

1. "Bring hither a fig from there."

"Here it is, sir."

"Divide it."

"It is divided, Sir."

"What do you see there?"

"These rather fine seeds, Sir."

"Of these, please, divide one."

"It is divided, Sir."

"What do you see there?"

"Nothing at all, Sir."

2. Then he said to him: "Verily, my dear, that finest essence which you do not perceive—verily, my dear, from that finest essence this great Nyagrodha (sacred fig) tree thus arises.

3. Believe me, my dear," said he, "that which is the finest essence—this whole world has that as its self. That is Reality. That is *Ātman*. That art thou, Śvetaketu. . . ."

(VI.xii.1–3)

1. "Place this salt in the water. In the morning come unto me."

Then he did so.

Then he said to him: "That salt you placed in the water last evening—please bring it hither."

Then he grasped for it, but did not find it, as it was completely dissolved.

2. "Please take a sip of it from this end," said he. "How is it?"

"Salt."

"Take a sip from the middle," said he. "How is it?"

"Salt."

"Take a sip from that end," said he. "How is it?"

"Salt."

"Set it aside. Then come unto me."

He did so, saying, "It is always the same."

Then he said to him: "Verily, indeed, my dear, you do not perceive Being here. Verily, indeed, it is here.

3. That which is the finest essence—this whole world has that as its self. That is Reality. That is *Ātman*. That art thou, Śvetaketu."

(vi.xiii.1–3)

Progressive worship of Brahman up to the universal Self

5. "He who reverences name as *Brahman*—as far as name goes, so far he has unlimited freedom, he who reverences name as *Brahman*."

(vii.i.5)

2. "Speech, assuredly, is more than name.... Verily, if there were no speech, neither right nor wrong would be known, neither true nor false, neither good nor bad, neither pleasant nor unpleasant. Speech, indeed, makes all this known. Reverence speech." (vii.ii.1)

1. "Mind (*manas*), assuredly, is more than speech.... Truly the self (*ātman*) is mind. Truly, the world is mind. Truly, *Brahman* is mind." (vii.iii.1)

1. "Conception (*saṁkalpa*), assuredly, is more than mind."

(vii.iv.1)

1. "Thought (*citta*), assuredly, is more than conception. Verily, when one thinks, then he forms a conception, then he has in mind, then he utters speech, and he utters it in name....

2. "Truly, indeed, thought is the union-point, thought is the self (*ātman*), thought is the support of these things. Reverence thought."

(vii.v.1–2)

1. "Meditation (*dhyāna*), assuredly, is more than thought."

(vii.vi.1)

1. "Understanding (*vijñāna*), assuredly, is more than meditation. Verily, by understanding one understands the *Ṛg Veda*, the *Yajur Veda*, the *Sāma Veda*, the *Atharva Veda*." (vii.vii.1)

1. "Strength, assuredly, is more than understanding. Indeed, one man of strength causes a hundred men of understanding to tremble." (VII.viii.1)

1. "Food, assuredly, is more than strength. Therefore, if one should not eat for ten days, even though he might live, yet verily he becomes a non-seer, a non-hearer, a non-thinker, a non-perceiver, a non-doer, a non-understander." (VII.ix.1)

1. "Water, verily, is more than food. Therefore, when there is not a good rain, living creatures sicken with the thought, 'Food will become scarce.'" (VII.x.1)

1. "Heat, verily, is more than water. That, verily, seizes hold of the wind, and heats the ether (*ākāśa*). Then people say: 'It is hot! It is burning hot! Surely it will rain!'" (VII.xi.1)

1. "Space (*ākāśa*), assuredly, is more than heat. In space, verily, are both sun and moon, lightning, stars and fire. Through space one calls out; through space one hears; through space one answers. In space one enjoys himself; in space one does not enjoy himself. In space one is born; unto space one is born. Reverence space." (VII.xii.1)

1. "Memory, verily, is more than space. Therefore, even if many not possessing memory should be assembled; indeed they would not hear any one at all, they would not think, they would not understand...." (VII.xiii.1)

1. "Hope, assuredly, is more than memory. When kindled by hope, verily, memory learns the sacred sayings; [kindled by hope] one performs sacred works, longs for sons and cattle, for this world and the yonder. Reverence hope." (VII.xiv.1)

1. "Life (*prāṇa*, breath), verily, is more than hope. Just as, verily, the spokes are fastened in the hub, so on this vital breath everything is fastened. Life goes on with vital breath (*prāṇa*). Vital breath gives life."

4. "For, indeed, vital breath is all these things. Verily, he who sees this, thinks this, understands this, becomes a superior speaker." (VII.xv.1, 4)

1. "But he, verily, speaks superiorly who speaks superiorly with truth.... But one must ... desire to understand the truth." (VII.xvi.1)

1. "Where one sees nothing else, hears nothing else, understands nothing else—that is a plenum. But where one sees something else—that is the small. Verily, the plenum is the same as the immortal; but the small is the same as the mortal." (VII.xxiv.1)

1. That [plenum], indeed, is below. It is above. It is to the west. It is to the east. It is to the south. It is to the north. It, indeed, is this whole world.

"I [the ego], indeed, am below. I am above. I am to the west. I am to the east. I am to the south. I am to the north. I, indeed, am this whole world.

2. "... The Self (*Ātman*), indeed, is below. The Self is above. The Self is to the west. The Self is to the east. The Self is to the south. The Self is to the north. The Self, indeed, is this whole world.

"Verily, he who sees this, who thinks this, who understands this, who has pleasure in the Self, who has delight in the Self, who has intercourse with the Self, who has bliss in the Self—he is autonomous; he has unlimited freedom in all worlds. But they who know otherwise than this are heteronomous; they have perishable worlds; in all worlds they have no freedom." (VII.xxv.1–2)

1. Verily, for him who sees this, who thinks this, who understands this, vital breath arises from the Self (*Ātman*); hope, from the Self; memory, from the Self; space, from the Self; heat, from the Self; water, from the Self, appearance and disappearance, from the Self; food, from the Self; strength, from the Self; understanding, from the Self; meditation, from the Self; thought, from the Self; conception, from the Self; mind, from the Self; speech, from the Self; name, from the Self; sacred sayings, from the Self; sacred works, from the Self; indeed this whole world, from the Self. (VII.xxvi.1)

The progressive instruction of Indra by Prajāpati concerning the real Self

1. "The Self, which is free from evil, ageless, deathless, sorrowless, hungerless, thirstless, whose desire is the Real, whose conception is the Real—He should be searched out, Him one should desire to understand. He obtains all worlds and all desires who has found out and who understands that Self."—Thus spake Prajāpati.

2. Then both the gods and the devils heard it. Then they said: "Come! Let us search out that Self, the Self by searching out whom one obtains all worlds and all desires!"

Then Indra from among the gods went forth unto him, and Virocana from among the devils. Then, without communicating with each other, the two came into the presence of Prajāpati, fuel in hand [in token of discipleship].

3. Then for thirty-two years the two lived the chaste life of a student of sacred knowledge (*brahmacarya*).

Then Prajāpati said to the two: "Desiring what have you been living?"

Then the two said: "The Self, which is free from evil, ageless, deathless, sorrowless, hungerless, thirstless, whose desire is the Real, whose conception is the Real—He should be searched out, Him one should desire to understand. He obtains all worlds and all desires who has found out and who understands that Self.—Such do people declare to be your words, sir. We have been living desiring Him."

4. Then Prajāpati said to the two: "That Person who is seen in the eye—He is the Self of whom I spoke. That is the immortal, the fearless. That is *Brahman*."

"But this one, sir, who is observed in water and in a mirror—which one is he?"

"The same one, indeed, is observed in all these," said he.

(viii.vii.1–4)

1. "Look at yourself in a pan of water. Anything that you do not understand of the Self, tell me."

Then the two looked in a pan of water.

Then Prajāpati said to the two: "What do you see?"

Then the two said: "We see everything here, sir, a Self corresponding exactly, even to the hair and fingernails!"

2. Then Prajāpati said to the two: "Make yourselves well-ornamented, well-dressed, adorned, and look in a pan of water."

Then the two made themselves well-ornamented, well-dressed, adorned, and looked in a pan of water.

Then Prajāpati said to the two: "What do you see?"

3. Then the two said: "Just as we ourselves are here, sir, well-ornamented, well-dressed, adorned—so there, sir, well-ornamented, well-dressed, adorned."

"That is the Self," said he. "That is the immortal, the fearless. That is *Brahman*."

Then with tranquil heart the two went forth.

4. Then Prajāpati glanced after them, and said: "They go without having comprehended, without having found the Self. Whosoever

shall have such a doctrine (*upaniṣad*), be they gods or be they devils, they shall perish."

Then with tranquil heart Virocana came to the devils. To them he then declared this doctrine: "Oneself (*ātman*) is to be made happy here on earth. Oneself is to be waited upon. He who makes his own self (*ātman*) happy here on earth, who waits upon himself—he obtains both worlds, both this world and the yonder."

5. Therefore even now here on earth they say of one who is not a giver, who is not a believer, who is not a sacrificer, "Oh! devilish!" for such is the doctrine of the devils. They adorn the body (*śarīra*) of one deceased with what they have begged, with dress, with ornament, as they call it, for they think that thereby they will win yonder world. (viii.viii.1–5)

1. But then Indra, even before reaching the gods, saw this danger: "Just as, indeed, that one [i.e., the bodily self] is well-ornamented when this body (*śarīra*) is well-ornamented, well-dressed when this is well-dressed, adorned when this is adorned, even so that one is blind when this is blind, lame when this is lame, maimed when this is maimed. It perishes immediately upon the perishing of this body. I see nothing enjoyable in this."

2. Fuel in hand, back again he came. Then Prajāpati said to him: "Desiring what, O Maghavan (Munificent One), have you come back again, since you along with Virocana went forth with tranquil heart?"

Then he said: "Just as, indeed, that one [i.e., the bodily self] is well-ornamented when this body is well-ornamented, well-dressed when this is well-dressed, adorned when this is adorned, even so it is blind when this is blind, lame when this is lame, maimed when this is maimed. It perishes immediately upon the perishing of this body. I see nothing enjoyable in this."

3. "He is even so, O Maghavan," said he. "However, I will explain this further to you. Live with me thirty-two years more."

Then he lived with him thirty-two years more.

To him [i.e., to Indra] he [i.e., Prajāpati] then said:— (viii.ix.1–3)

1. "He who moves about happy in a dream—he is the Self," said he. "That is the immortal, the fearless. That is *Brahman*."

Then with tranquil heart he [i.e., Indra] went forth.

Then, even before reaching the gods, he saw this danger: "Now, even if this body is blind, that one [i.e., the Self, *Ātman*] is not blind. If this is lame, he is not lame. Indeed, he does not suffer defect through defect of this. [2] He is not slain with one's murder. He is not lame with one's lameness. Nevertheless, as it were, they kill him; as it were, they unclothe him; as it were, he comes to experience what is unpleasant; as it were, he even weeps. I see nothing enjoyable in this."

3. Fuel in hand, back again he came. Then Prajāpati said to him: "Desiring what, O Maghavan, have you come back again, since you went forth with tranquil heart?"

Then he said: "Now, sir, even if this body is blind, that one [i.e., the Self] is not blind. If this is lame, he is not lame. Indeed, he does not suffer defect through defect of this. [4] He is not slain with one's murder. He is not lame with one's lameness. Nevertheless, as it were, they kill him; as it were, they unclothe him; as it were, he comes to experience what is unpleasant; as it were, he even weeps. I see nothing enjoyable in this."

"He is even so, O Maghavan," said he. "However, I will explain this further to you. Live with me thirty-two years more."

Then he lived with him thirty-two years more.

To him [i.e., to Indra] he [i.e., Prajāpati] then said:—

(viii.x.1–4)

1. "Now, when one is sound asleep, composed, serene, and knows no dream—that is the Self," said he. "That is the immortal, the fearless. That is *Brahman*."

Then with tranquil heart he went forth.

Then, even before reaching the gods, he saw this danger: "Assuredly, indeed, this one does not exactly know himself (*ātmānam*) with the thought 'I am he,' nor indeed the things here. He becomes one who has gone to destruction. I see nothing enjoyable in this."

2. Fuel in hand, back again he came. Then Prajāpati said to him: "Desiring what, O Maghavan, have you come back again, since you went forth with tranquil heart?"

Then he [i.e., Indra] said: "Assuredly, this [self] does not exactly know himself with the thought 'I am he,' nor indeed the things here. He becomes one who has gone to destruction. I see nothing enjoyable in this."

3. "He is even so, O Maghavan," said he. "However, I will explain this further to you, and there is nothing else besides this. Live with me five years more."

Then he lived with him five years more.—That makes one hundred and one years. Thus it is that people say, "Verily, for one hundred and one years Maghavan lived the chaste life of a student of sacred knowledge (*brahmacarya*) with Prajāpati."—

To him [i.e., to Indra] he [i.e., Prajāpati] then said:—

(VIII.xi.1–3)

1. "O Maghavan, verily, this body (*śarīra*) is mortal. It has been appropriated by Death (Mṛtyu). [But] it is the standing-ground of that deathless, bodiless Self. Verily, he who is incorporate has been appropriated by pleasure and pain. Verily, there is no freedom from pleasure and pain for one while he is incorporate. Verily, while one is bodiless, pleasure and pain do not touch him.

2. "The wind is bodiless. Clouds, lightning, thunder—these are bodiless. Now as these, when they arise from yonder space and reach the highest light, appear each with its own form, [3] even so that serene one (*samprasāda*), when he rises up from this body and reaches the highest light, appears with his own form. Such a one is the supreme person (*uttama puruṣa*). There such a one goes around laughing, sporting, having enjoyment with women or chariots or friends, not remembering the appendage of this body. As a draft-animal is yoked in a wagon, even so this spirit (*prāṇa*) is yoked in this body.

4. "Now, when the eye is directed thus toward space, that is the seeing person (*cākṣuṣa puruṣa*); the eye is [the instrument] for seeing. Now, he who knows 'Let me smell this'—that is the Self; the nose is [the instrument] for smelling. Now, he who knows 'Let me utter this'—that is the Self; the voice is [the instrument] for utterance. Now, he who knows 'Let me hear this'—that is the Self; the ear is [the instrument] for hearing.

5. "Now, he who knows 'Let me think this'—that is the Self; the mind (*manas*) is his divine eye (*daiva cakṣu*). He verily, with that divine eye the mind, sees, desires here, and experiences enjoyment.

6. "Verily, those gods who are in the Brahmā-world reverence that Self. Therefore all worlds and all desires have been appropriated by them. He obtains all worlds and all desires who has found out and who understands that Self."

Thus spake Prajāpati—yea, thus spake Prajāpati! (VIII.xii.1–6)

Final words to the departing pupil

This did Brahmā tell to Prajāpati; Prajāpati, to Manu; Manu, to human beings (*prajā*).

He who according to rule has learned the Veda from the family of a teacher, in time left over from doing work for the teacher; he who, after having come back again, in a home of his own continues Veda-study in a clean place and produces [sons and pupils]; he who has concentrated all his senses upon the Self; he who is harmless (*ahiṁsant*) toward all things elsewhere than at holy places (*tīrtha*)—he, indeed, who lives thus throughout his length of life, reaches the Brahmā-world and does not return hither again—yea, he does not return hither again! (VIII.XV)

10. Bṛhadāraṇyaka Upaniṣad

This Upaniṣad is the longest—the name means "great forest-book"—the most famous, and one of the oldest of all the Upaniṣads. In it is found, among many other valuable passages, the famous discourse between the great philosopher Yājñavalkya—perhaps the greatest of the Upaniṣadic sages—and his wife Maitreyī. It is in this discourse that we find one of the best expressions of the philosophical idealism of the Upaniṣads. Nowhere else is the notion of the transcendental *Ātman* as universal and undifferentiated consciousness better portrayed.

It is this Upaniṣad which has made famous the doctrine of "*Neti, Neti*" ("not this, not this"), the mystical doctrine of the indescribability of the Absolute.

Important passages in this Upaniṣad are devoted to the effort to define *Brahman*, and to a consideration of the various theories of the nature of the ultimate.

The creation of the manifold world from the unitary Self

1. In the beginning this world was Self (*Ātman*) alone in the form of a Person. Looking around, he saw nothing else than himself. He said first: "I am." Thence arose the name "I." Therefore even today, when one is addressed, he says first just "It is I" and then speaks whatever name he has. Since before all this world he burned up (√ *uṣ*) all evils, therefore he is a person (*pur-uṣ-a*). He who knows this, verily, burns up him who desires to be ahead of him.

2. He was afraid. Therefore one who is alone is afraid. This one then thought to himself: "Since there is nothing else than myself, of what am I afraid?" Thereupon, verily, his fear departed, for of what

should he have been afraid? Assuredly it is from a second that fear arises.

3. Verily, he had no delight. Therefore one alone has no delight. He desired a second. He was, indeed, as large as a woman and a man closely embraced. He caused that self to fall into two pieces. Therefrom arose a husband and a wife. Therefore this [is true]: "Oneself is like a half-fragment,"... Therefore this space is filled by a wife. He copulated with her. Therefrom human beings were produced.

4. [She changed herself into the forms of various animals; he did likewise.] ... Thus, indeed, he created all....

5. He knew: "I, indeed, am this creation, for I emitted it all from myself." Thence arose creation. Verily, he who has this knowledge comes to be in that creation of his.

7. Verily, at that time the world was undifferentiated. It became differentiated just by name and form, as the saying is: "He has such a name, such a form."...

He entered in here, even to the fingernail-tips, as a razor would be hidden in a razor-case, or fire in a fire-holder. Him they see not, for [as seen] he is incomplete. When breathing, he becomes breath by name; when speaking, voice; when seeing, the eye; when hearing, the ear; when thinking, the mind: these are merely the names of his acts. Whoever worships one or another of these—he knows not; for he is incomplete with one or another of these. One should worship with the thought that he is just one's self, for therein all these become one. That same thing, namely, this self, is the trace of this All, for by it one knows this All.... He finds fame and praise who knows this....

10. Verily, in the beginning this world was *Brahman*.

It knew only itself: "I am *Brahman*!" Therefore it became the All. Whoever of the gods became awakened to this, he indeed became it; likewise in the case of seers, likewise in the case of men....

...Whoever thus knows "I am *Brahman*!" becomes this All; even the gods have not power to prevent his becoming thus, for he becomes their self...

11. Verily, in the beginning this world was *Brahman*, one only. Being one, he was not developed. He created still further a superior form, the *kṣātra*hood, even those who are *kṣātras* (rulers) among the gods: Indra, Varuṇa, Soma, Rudra, Parjanya, Yama, Mṛtyu, Īśāna....

12. He was not yet developed. He created the *viś* (the commonalty), those kinds of gods that are mentioned in numbers: the Vasus, the Rudras, the Ādityas, the Viśvedevas, the Maruts.

13. He was not yet developed. He created the *śūdra* caste, Pūṣan. Verily, this [earth] is Pūṣan, for she nourishes (√*puṣ*) everything that is.

14. He was not yet developed. He created still further a better form, Law (*dharma*). This is the power of the *kṣatriya* class, viz., Law. Therefore there is nothing higher than Law. So a weak man controls a strong man by Law, just as if by a king. Verily, that which is Law is truth....

17. In the beginning this world was just the Self, one only. He wished: "Would that I had a wife; then I would procreate. Would that I had wealth; then I would offer sacrifice." So far as he does not obtain any one of these, he thinks that he is, assuredly, incomplete. Now his completeness is as follows: his mind truly is his self (*ātman*); his voice is his wife; his breath is his offspring; his eye is his worldly wealth, for with his eye he finds; his ear is his heavenly [wealth], for with his ear he hears it; his body (*ātman*), indeed, is his work, for with his body he performs work....

(I.iv.1–5, 7, 10–14, 17)

Progressive definition of Brahman as the world-source

2–13. Gārgya [a seer] said: "The Person who is yonder in the sun ... moon ... lightning ... here in space ... wind ... fire ... water ... mirror ... the sound here which follows after one as he goes ... the Person who is here in the quarters of heaven ... who consists of shadow ... who is in the body (*ātman*)—him, indeed, I worship as *Brahman*!..."

20. Ajātaśatru said: "As a spider might come out with his thread, as small sparks come forth from the fire, even so from this Self come forth all vital energies, all worlds, all gods, all beings. The mystic meaning (*upaniṣad*) thereof is the Real of the real. Vital energies, verily, are the real. He is their Real." (II.i.2–13, 20)

The two forms of Brahman

1. There are, assuredly, two forms of *Brahman*: the formed and the formless, the mortal and the immortal, the stationary and the moving, the actual and the yon.

2. This is the formed—whatever is different from the wind and the atmosphere. This is mortal; this is stationary; this is actual. The

essence of this formed, mortal, stationary, actual [*Brahman*] is yonder [sun] which gives forth heat, for this is the essence of the actual.

3. Now the formless is the wind and the atmosphere. This is immortal, this is moving, this is the yon.... Thus with reference to the divinities. (II.iii.1–3)

The conversation of Yājñavalkya and Maitreyī concerning the pantheistic Self

1. "Maitreyi!" said Yājñavalkya, "lo, verily, I am about to go forth from this state. Behold! let me make a final settlement for you and that Kātyāyanī."

2. Then said Maitreyī: "If now, sir, this whole earth filled with wealth were mine, would I be immortal thereby?"

"No," said Yājñavalkya. "As the life of the rich, even so would your life be. Of immortality, however, there is no hope through wealth."

3. Then said Maitreyī: "What should I do with that through which I may not be immortal? What you know, sir—that, indeed, tell me!"

4. Then said Yājñavalkya: "Ah! Lo, dear (*priyā*) as you are to us, dear is what you say! Come, sit down. I will explain to you. But while I am expounding, do you seek to ponder thereon."

5. Then said he: "Lo, verily, not for love of the husband is a husband dear, but for love of the Self (*Ātman*) a husband is dear.

"Lo, verily, not for love of the wife is a wife dear, but for love of the Self a wife is dear.

"Lo, verily, not for love of the sons are sons dear, but for love of the Self sons are dear.

"Lo, verily, not for love of the wealth is wealth dear, but for love of the Self wealth is dear.

"Lo, verily, not for love of *brāhmin*hood is *brāhmin*hood dear, but for love of the Self *brāhmin*hood is dear.

"Lo, verily, not for love of *kṣātra*hood is *kṣātra*hood dear, but for love of the Self *kṣātra*hood is dear.

"Lo, verily, not for love of the worlds are the worlds dear, but for love of the Self the worlds are dear.

"Lo, verily, not for love of the gods are the gods dear, but for love of the Self the gods are dear.

"Lo, verily, not for love of the beings (*bhūta*) are beings dear, but for love of the Self beings are dear.

"Lo, verily, not for love of all is all dear, but for love of the Self all is dear.

"Lo, verily, it is the Self (*Ātman*) that should be seen, that should be hearkened to, that should be thought on, that should be pondered on, O Maitreyi. Lo, verily, with the seeing of, with the hearkening to, with the thinking of and with the understanding of the Self, this world-all is known.

6. "*Brāhmin*hood has deserted him who knows *brāhmin*hood in aught else than the Self.

"*Kṣātra*hood has deserted him who knows *kṣātra*hood in aught else than the Self.

"The worlds have deserted him who knows the worlds in aught else than the Self.

"The gods have deserted him who knows the gods in aught else than the Self.

"Beings have deserted him who knows beings in aught else than the Self.

"Everything has deserted him who knows everything in aught else than the Self.

"This *brāhmin*hood, this *kṣātra*hood, these worlds, these gods, these beings, everything here is what this Self is.

7. "It is—as, when a drum is being beaten, one would not be able to grasp the external sounds, but by grasping the drum or the beater of the drum the sound is grasped.

8. "It is—as, when a conch-shell is being blown, one would not be able to grasp the external sounds, but by grasping the conch-shell or the blower of the conch-shell the sound is grasped.

9. "It is—as, when a lute is being played, one would not be able to grasp the external sounds, but by grasping the lute or the player of the lute the sound is grasped.

10. "It is—as, from a fire laid with damp fuel, clouds of smoke separately issue forth, so, lo, verily, from this great Being (*bhūta*) has been breathed forth that which is *Ṛg Veda*, *Yajur Veda*, *Sāma Veda*, [Hymns] of the Atharvans and Aṅgirases, Legend (*itihāsa*), Ancient Lore (*purāṇa*), Sciences (*vidyā*), Mystic Doctrines (*upaniṣad*), Verses (*śloka*), Aphorisms (*sūtra*), Explanations (*anuvyākhyāna*), and Commentaries (*vyākhyāna*). From it, indeed, are all these breathed forth.

11. "It is—as of all waters the uniting-point is the sea, so of all touches the uniting-point is the skin, so of all tastes the uniting-point is the tongue, so of all smells the uniting-point is the nostrils, so of

all forms the uniting-point is the eye, so of all sounds the uniting-point is the ear, so of all intentions (*saṁkalpa*) the uniting-point is the mind (*manas*), so of all knowledges the uniting-point is the heart, so of all acts (*karma*) the uniting-point is the hands, so of all pleasures (*ānanda*) the uniting-point is the generative organ, so of all evacuations the uniting-point is the anus, so of all journeys the uniting-point is the feet, so of all the Vedas the uniting-point is speech.

12. "It is—as a lump of salt cast in water would dissolve right into the water; there would not be [any] of it to seize forth, as it were (*iva*), but wherever one may take, it is salty indeed—so, lo, verily, this great Being (*bhūta*), infinite, limitless, is just a mass of knowledge (*vijñāna-ghana*).

"Arising out of these elements (*bhūta*), into them also one vanishes away. After death there is no consciousness (*na pretya saṁjñā 'sti*). Thus, lo, say I." Thus spake Yājñavalkya.

13. Then spake Maitreyī: "Herein, indeed, you have bewildered me, sir—in saying (*iti*): 'After death there is no consciousness'!"

Then spake Yājñavalkya: "Lo, verily, I speak not bewilderment (*moha*). Sufficient, lo, verily, is this for understanding.

14. "For where there is a duality (*dvaita*), as it were (*iva*), there one sees another; there one smells another; there one hears another; there one speaks to another; there one thinks of another; there one understands another. Where, verily, everything has become just one's own self, then whereby and whom would one smell? then whereby and whom would one see? then whereby and whom would one hear? then whereby and to whom would one speak? then whereby and on whom would one think? then whereby and whom would one understand? Whereby would one understand him by whom one understands this All? Lo, whereby would one understand the understander?" (II.iv.1–14)

The fettered self and its fate at death

12. "Yājñavalkya," said he [Jāratkārava Ārtabhāga], "when a man dies, what does not leave him?"

"The name. Endless, verily, is the name. Endless are the All-gods. An endless world he wins thereby."

13. "Yājñavalkya," said he, "when the voice of a dead man goes into fire, his breath into wind, his eye into the sun, his mind into the moon, his hearing into the quarters of heaven, his body into the earth, his self (*ātman*) into space, the hairs of his head into plants, the hairs

of his body into trees, and his blood and semen are placed in water, what then becomes of this person?"

"Ārtabhāga, my dear, take my hand. We two only will know of this. This is not for us two [to speak of] in public."

The two went away and deliberated. What they said was *karma* (action). What they praised was *karma*. Verily, one becomes good by good action, bad by bad action.

Thereupon Jāratkārava Ārtabhāga held his peace.

(III.ii.12, 13)

1. Then Uṣasta Cākrāyaṇa questioned him. "Yājñavalkya," said he, "explain to me him who is the *Brahman* present and not beyond our ken, him who is the Self in all things. . . ."

"He is your self (*ātman*), which is in all things. . . ." (III.iv.1)

The practical way of knowing Brahman—by asceticism

[Yājñavalkya said:] "He who passes beyond hunger and thirst, beyond sorrow and delusion, beyond old age and death—*brāhmins* who know such a Self overcome desire for sons, desire for wealth, desire for worlds, and live the life of mendicants. For desire for sons is desire for wealth, and desire for wealth is desire for worlds, for both these are merely desires. Therefore let a *brāhmin* become disgusted with learning and desire to live as a child. When he has become disgusted both with the state of childhood and with learning, then he becomes an ascetic. When he has become disgusted both with the non-ascetic state and with the ascetic state, then he becomes a *brāhmin*."

"By what means would he become a *brāhmin*?"

"By that means by which he does become such a one. Aught else than this Self (*Ātman*) is wretched." (III.v)

The regressus to Brahman, the ultimate world-ground

Then Gārgī Vācaknavī questioned him. "Yājñavalkya," said she, "since all this world is woven, warp and woof, on water, on what, pray, is the water woven, warp and woof?"

"On wind, O Gārgi."

"On what then, pray, is the wind woven, warp and woof?"

"On the atmosphere-worlds, O Gārgi."

"On what then, pray, are the atmosphere-worlds woven, warp and woof?"

"On the worlds of the Gandharvas, O Gārgi."

"On what then, pray, are the worlds of the Gandharvas woven, warp and woof?"

"On the worlds of the sun, O Gārgi."

"On what then, pray, are the worlds of the sun woven, warp and woof?"

"On the worlds of the moon, O Gārgi."

"On what then, pray, are the worlds of the moon woven, warp and woof?"

"On the worlds of the stars, O Gārgi."

"On what then, pray, are the worlds of the stars woven, warp and woof?"

"On the worlds of the gods, O Gārgi."

"On what then, pray, are the worlds of the gods woven, warp and woof?"

"On the worlds of Indra, O Gārgi."

"On what then, pray, are the worlds of Indra woven, warp and woof?"

"On the worlds of Prajāpati, O Gārgi."

"On what then, pray, are the worlds of Prajāpati woven, warp and woof?"

"On the worlds of *Brahman*, O Gārgi."

"On what then, pray, are the worlds of *Brahman* woven, warp and woof?"

Yājñavalkya said: "Gārgi, do not question too much, lest your head fall off. In truth, you are questioning too much about a divinity about which further questions cannot be asked. Gārgi, do not over-question." (III.vi)

The immortal universal Self, the Inner Controller

15. [Yājñavalkya said:] "He who, dwelling in all things, yet is other than all things, whom all things do not know, whose body all things are, who controls all things from within—He is your Self, the Inner Controller, the Immortal....

23. "He is the unseen Seer, the unheard Hearer, the unthought Thinker, the ununderstood Understander. Other than He there is no seer. Other than He there is no hearer. Other than He there is no thinker. Other than He there is no understander. He is your Self, the Inner Controller, the Immortal." (III.vii.15, 23)

The ultimate warp of the world—the unqualified Imperishable

6. She [Gārgī Vācaknavī] said: "That, O Yājñavalkya, which is above the sky, that which is beneath the earth, that which is between these two, sky and earth, that which people call the past and the present and the future—across what is that woven, warp and woof?"

7. He said: ". . . across space alone is that woven, warp and woof." "Across what then, pray, is space woven, warp and woof?"

8. He said: "That, O Gārgi, *brāhmins* call the Imperishable. It is not coarse, not fine, not short, not long, not glowing [like fire], not adhesive [like water], without shadow and without darkness, without air and without space, without stickiness, (intangible), odorless, tasteless, without eye, without ear, without voice, without wind, without energy, without breath, without mouth, (without personal or family name, unaging, undying, without fear, immortal, stainless, not uncovered, not covered), without measure, without inside and without outside. . . .

11. "Verily, O Gārgi, that Imperishable is the unseen Seer, the unheard Hearer, the unthought Thinker, the ununderstood Understander. Other than It there is naught that sees . . . hears . . . thinks . . . understands. Across this Imperishable, O Gārgi, is space woven, warp and woof." (III.viii.6–8, 11)

Regressus of the numerous gods to the unitary Brahman

1. Then Vidagdha Śākalya questioned him. "How many gods are there, Yājñavalkya?"

He answered in accord with the following *Nivid* (invocationary formula): "As many as are mentioned in the *Nivid* of the "Hymn to All the Gods," namely, three hundred and three, and three thousand and three [=3306]."

"Yes," said he, "but just how many gods are there, Yājñavalkya?"

"Thirty-three."

"Yes," said he, "but just how many gods are there, Yājñavalkya?"

"Six."

"Yes," said he, "but just how many gods are there, Yājñavalkya?"

"Three."

"Yes," said he, "but just how many gods are there, Yājñavalkya?"

"Two."

"Yes," said he, "but just how many gods are there, Yājñavalkya?"

"One and a half."

"Yes," said he, "but just how many gods are there, Yājñavalkya?"

"One...."

9. ... "Which is the one god?"

"Breath," said he. "They call him *Brahman*, the Yon."

(III.ix.1, 9)

The self as the light of man, and its various states

2. "Yājñavalkya, what light does a person here have?"...

6. "...The self (*ātman*), indeed, is his light," said he, "for with the self, indeed, as his light one sits, moves around, does his work, and returns."

7. "Which is the self?"...

"The person here who among the senses is made of knowledge, who is the light in the heart. He, remaining the same, goes along both worlds, appearing to think, appearing to move about, for upon becoming asleep he transcends this world and the forms of death.

8. "Verily, this person, by being born and obtaining a body, is joined with evils. When he departs, on dying, he leaves evils behind.

9. "Verily, there are just two conditions of this person: the condition of being in this world and the condition of being in the other world. There is an intermediate third condition, namely, that of being in sleep. By standing in this intermediate condition one sees both those conditions, namely, being in this world and being in the other world. Now whatever the approach is to the condition of being in the other world, by making that approach one sees the evils [of this world] and the joys [of yonder world].

"When one goes to sleep, he takes along the material of this all-containing world, himself tears it apart, himself builds it up, and dreams by his own brightness, by his own light. Then this person becomes self-illuminated.

10. "There are no chariots there, no spans, no roads. But he projects from himself chariots, spans, roads. There are no blisses there, no pleasures, no delights. But he projects from himself blisses, pleasures, delights. There are no tanks there, no lotus-pools, no streams. But he projects from himself tanks, lotus-pools, streams. For he is a creator.

30. "Verily, while he does not there know, he is verily knowing, though he does not know (what is [usually] to be known); for there is no cessation of the knowing of a knower, because of his imperishability [as a knower]. It is not, however, a second thing, other than himself and separate, which he may know.

31. "Verily, where there seems to be another, there the one might see ... smell ... taste ... speak to ... hear ... think of ... touch ... know the other.

32. "An ocean, a seer alone without duality, becomes he whose world is *Brahman*, O King!"—thus Yājñavalkya instructed him. "This is a man's highest path. This is his highest achievement. This is his highest world. This is his highest bliss. On a part of just this bliss other creatures have their living." (IV.iii.2, 6–10, 30–2)

The self of the unreleased, and of the released, after death

5. Verily, this self is *Brahman*, made of knowledge, of mind, of breath, of seeing, of hearing, of earth, of water, of wind, of space, of energy and of non-energy, of desire and of non-desire, of anger and of non-anger, of virtuousness and of non-virtuousness. It is made of everything. This is what is meant by the saying "made of this, made of that."

According as one acts, according as one conducts himself, so does he become. The doer of good becomes good. The doer of evil becomes evil. One becomes virtuous by virtuous action, bad by bad action.

But people say: "A person is made [not of acts, but] of desires only." [In reply to this I say:] As is his desire, such is his resolve; as is his resolve, such the action he performs; what action he performs, that he procures for himself.

6. On this point there is this verse:

> Where one's mind is attached—the inner self
> Goes thereto with action, being attached to it alone.
>   Obtaining the end of his action,
>   Whatever he does in this world,
>   He comes again from that world
>   To this world of action.

—So the man who desires.

Now the man who does not desire.—He who is without desire, who is freed from desire, whose desire is satisfied, whose desire is the Self—his breaths do not depart. Being very *Brahman*, he goes to *Brahman*.

12. If a person knew the Self (*Ātman*).
With the thought "I am he!"
With what desire, for love of what
Would he cling unto the body?

13. He who has found and has awakened to the Self
That has entered this conglomerate abode—
He is the maker of everything, for he is the creator of all;
The world is his: indeed, he is the world itself.

19. By the mind alone is It [the ancient, primeval *Brahman*] to be perceived.
There is on earth no diversity.
He gets death after death,
Who perceives here seeming diversity.

20. As a unity only is It to be looked upon—
This indemonstrable, enduring Being,
Spotless, beyond space,
The unborn Self, great, enduring.

21. By knowing Him only, a wise
brāhmin should get for himself intelligence;
He should not meditate upon many words,
For that is a weariness of speech.

22. Verily, he is the great, unborn Self, who is this [person] consisting of knowledge among the senses. In the space within the heart lies the ruler of all, the lord of all, the king of all. He does not become greater by good action nor inferior by bad action. He is the lord of all, the overlord of beings, the protector of beings. He is the separating dam for keeping these worlds apart.

Such a one the *brāhmins* desire to know by repetition of the Vedas, by sacrifices, by offerings, by penance, by fasting. On knowing him, in truth, one becomes an ascetic. Desiring him only as their home, mendicants wander forth.... (IV.iv.5–6, 12–13, 19–22)

The universal Self

15. For where there is a duality, as it were, there one sees another; there one smells another; there one tastes another; there one speaks to another; there one hears another; there one thinks of another; there one touches another; there one understands another. But where everything has become just one's own self, then whereby and whom would one see? ... smell? ... taste? ... speak [to]? ... hear? ... think [of]? ... touch? ... understand? whereby would one understand him by means of whom one understands this All?

That Self (*Ātman*) is not this, it is not that [this] (*neti, neti*). It is unseizable, for it cannot be seized; indestructible, for it cannot be destroyed; unattached, for it does not attach itself; is unbound, does not tremble, is not injured. . . . (IV.V.15)

The three cardinal virtues

. . . This same thing does the divine voice here, thunder, repeat: *Da! Da! Da!* that is, restrain yourselves, give, be compassionate. One should practise this same triad: self-restraint, giving, compassion. (V.ii.3)

11. Śvetāśvatara Upaniṣad

This is one of the later Upaniṣads. In it some of the ideas of the Sāṁkhya and Yoga philosophies—both of which are dualistic systems—and of Advaita (non-dualism) find clear expression. The Upaniṣad does not expound any single doctrine or philosophy in particular, but it gives an eloquent exposition of the best thought of the times. The emphasis, however, is in the direction of theism rather than on the Absolutism stressed in most of the Upaniṣads.

The Upaniṣad gets its name from the name or title of the sage who is said to have taught it to his disciples.

Conjectures concerning the First Cause

1. . . . What is the cause: *Brahman?* Whence are we born?
Whereby do we live? And on what are we established?
Overruled by whom, in pains and pleasures,
Do we live our various conditions, O ye theologians?
2. Time, or inherent nature, or necessity, or chance,
Or the elements, or a [female] womb, or a [male] person are to be considered [as the cause];
Not a combination of these, because of the existence of the self (*ātman*).
The self certainly is impotent over the cause of pleasure and pain.
3. Those who followed after meditation and abstraction (*yoga*)
Saw the self-power of God (*deva*) hidden in his own qualities.
He is the One who rules over all these causes,
From "time" to "the self."
6. In this which vitalizes all things, which appears in all things, the Great—
In this Brahmā-wheel the self flutters about,
Thinking that itself and the Actuator are different.
When favored by Him, it attains immortality. (I.1–3, 6)

The saving knowledge of the one inclusive Brahman

7. This has been sung as the supreme *Brahman.*
In it there is a triad. It is the firm support, the Imperishable.
By knowing what is therein, *Brahman*-knowers
Become merged in *Brahman*, intent thereon, liberated from the womb [i.e., from rebirth].

10. What is perishable, is primary matter. What is immortal and imperishable, is Hara (the "Bearer," the self).
Over both the perishable and the self the One God rules.
By meditation upon Him, by union with Him, and by entering into His being
More and more, there is finally cessation from every illusion.

11. By knowing God there is a falling off of all fetters;
With distresses destroyed, there is cessation of birth and death.
By meditating upon Him there is a third stage at the dissolution of the body,
Even universal lordship; being absolute, his desire is satisfied.

12. That Eternal should be known as present in the self.
Truly there is nothing higher than that to be known.
When one recognizes the enjoyer, the object of enjoyment, and the universal Actuator,
All has been said. This is the threefold *Brahman.*

16. The Self (*Ātman*), which pervades all things
As butter is contained in cream,
Which is rooted in self-knowledge and austerity—
This is *Brahman*, the highest mystic doctrine (*upaniṣad*)!
This is *Brahman*, the highest mystic doctrine! (I.7, 10–12, 16)

Knowing the one Supreme Person overcomes death

7. Higher than this[1] is *Brahman.* The Supreme, the Great,
Hidden in all things, body by body,
The One embracer of the universe—
By knowing Him as Lord (*Īśa*) men become immortal.

8. I know this mighty Person
Of the color of the sun, beyond darkness.
Only by knowing Him does one pass over death.
There is no other path for going there.

[1] Either "higher than this [terrible Vedic god, Rudra]," or "higher than this [world]." —Hume.

9. Than whom there is naught else higher,
Than whom there is naught smaller, naught greater,
The One stands like a tree established in heaven.
By Him, the Person, this whole world is filled.
10. That which is beyond this world
Is without form and without ill.
They who know That, become immortal;
But others go only to sorrow. (III.7–10)

The one God of the manifold world

1. The One who, himself without color, by the manifold application of his power
Distributes many colors in his hidden purpose,
And into whom, its end and its beginning, the whole world dissolves—He is God (*deva*)!
May he endow us with clear intellect!
9. Sacred poetry (*chandas*)—the sacrifices, the ceremonies, the ordinances,
The past, the future, and what the Vedas declare—
This whole world the illusion-maker (*māyin*) projects out of this [*Brahman*].
And in it by illusion (*māyā*) the other is confined.
10. Now, one should know that Nature (*Prakṛiti*) is illusion (*māyā*),
And that the Mighty Lord (*maheśvara*) is the illusion-maker (*māyin*).
This whole world is pervaded
With beings that are parts of Him.
19. Not above, not across,
Nor in the middle has one grasped Him.
There is no likeness of Him
Whose name is Great Glory.
20. His form is not to be beheld.
No one soever sees Him with the eye.
They who thus know Him with heart and mind
As abiding in the heart become immortal. (IV.1, 9–10, 19–20)

Liberation through knowledge of the one God

13. Him who is without beginning and without end, in the midst of confusion,
The Creator of all, of manifold form,

The One embracer of the universe—
By knowing God one is released from all fetters. (v.13)

The one God, Creator and Lord, in and over the world

1. Some sages discourse of inherent nature;
   Others likewise, of time. Deluded men!
   It is the greatness of God in the world
   By which this Brahmā-wheel is caused to revolve.
2. He by whom this whole world is constantly enveloped
   Is intelligent, the author of time, possessor of qualities, omniscient.
   Ruled o'er by Him, [his] work revolves—
   This which is regarded as earth, water, fire, air, and space!
9. Of Him there is no ruler in the world,
   Nor lord; nor is there any mark of Him.... (vi.1–2, 9)

12. Kauṣītaki Upaniṣad

Sage Kauṣītaki is the philosopher of this Upaniṣad, which excels in the delineation of *prāṇa* (the breathing spirit) as the prime mover of the universe. *Prāṇa* is ultimately identified with the higher subjective reality as well.

The subject of all knowledge, the permanent object of knowledge

...These ten existential elements [speech, smell, form, sound, taste, deed, pleasure and pain, bliss—delight—and—procreation, going, mind], verily, are with reference to intelligence. The ten intelligential elements [speaker, smeller, seer, hearer, discerner of taste, doer, discerner of pleasure and pain, discerner of bliss—delight—and—procreation, goer, thinker] are with reference to existence. For truly, if there were no elements of being, there would be no elements of intelligence. Verily, if there were no elements of intelligence, there would be no elements of being. For truly, from either alone no appearance whatsoever would be effected.

And this is not a diversity. But as of a chariot the felly is fixed on the spokes and the spokes are fixed on the hub, even so these elements of being are fixed on the elements of intelligence, and the elements of intelligence are fixed on the breathing spirit (*prāṇa*).

This same breathing spirit, in truth, is the intelligential self (*prajñātman*); [it is] bliss, ageless, immortal.

He does not become greater with good action, nor indeed lesser with bad action.

This one, truly, indeed, causes him whom he wishes to lead up from these worlds, to perform good action. This one, also, indeed causes him whom he wishes to lead downward, to perform bad action.

He is the world-protector. He is the world-sovereign. He is the lord of all.

"He is my self"—this one should know. "He is my self"—this one should know. (III.8)

13. Maitri Upaniṣad

Here, the inspiring sage is Maitri, from whom the work gets its name. This Upaniṣad is important for its very clear account of the two forms of the *Ātman*, the noumenal and the phenomenal, or the *Ātman* and the *bhūtātman* (literally, the changing self,—or the "elemental self"). The latter reaps the fruits of good and bad actions while the former abides "in its own greatness."

Rejection of evanescent worldly desires; craving for liberation

3. "...in this ill-smelling, unsubstantial body, which is a conglomerate of bone, skin, muscle, marrow, flesh, semen, blood, mucus, tears, rheum, feces, urine, wind, bile, and phlegm, what is the good of enjoyment of desires? In this body, which is afflicted with desire, anger, covetousness, delusion, fear, despondency, envy, separation from the desirable, union with the undesirable, hunger, thirst, senility, death, disease, sorrow, and the like, what is the good of enjoyment of desires?

4. And we see that this whole world is decaying, as these gnats, mosquitoes, and the like, the grass, and the trees that arise and perish.

But, indeed, what of these?... Among other things, there is the drying up of great oceans, the falling away of mountain peaks, the deviation of the fixed pole-star, the cutting of the wind-cords [of the stars], the submergence of the earth, the retreat of the celestials from their station.

In this sort of cycle of existence (*saṁsāra*) what is the good of enjoyment of desires, when after a man has fed on them there is seen repeatedly his return here to earth?

Be pleased to deliver me. In this cycle of existence I am like a frog in a waterless well. Sir [Śākāyanya, one who knows the true nature of the *Ātman*], you are our way of escape—yea, you are our way of escape!" (I.3–4)

The primeval Person progressively differentiated himself

6. [Śākāyanya said: . . .] "Verily, in the beginning Prajāpati stood alone. He had no enjoyment, being alone. He then, by meditating upon himself, created numerous offspring.

He saw them inanimate and lifeless, like a stone, standing like a post. He had no enjoyment. He then thought to himself: "Let me enter within, in order to animate them." . . .

7. Verily, this Self (*Ātman*)—poets declare—wanders here on earth from body to body, unovercome, as it seems, by the bright or the dark fruits of action. He who on account of his unmanifestness, subtility, imperceptibility, incomprehensibility, and selflessness is [apparently] unabiding and a doer in the unreal—he, truly, is not a doer, and he is abiding. Verily, he is pure, steadfast and unswerving, stainless, unagitated, desireless, fixed like a spectator, and self-abiding. As an enjoyer of righteousness, he covers himself with a veil made of qualities; [but] he remains fixed—yea, he remains fixed! (II.6–7)

The great Self, and the individual suffering, transmigrating self

1. . . . "Sir, if thus you describe the greatness of this Self, there is still another, different one. Who is he, called self, who, being overcome by the bright or the dark fruits of action, enters a good or an evil womb, so that his course is downward or upward and he wanders around, overcome by the pairs of opposites?"

2. [Then he said:] "There is indeed another, different self, called 'the elemental self'. . . .

"The five subtile substances are spoken of by the word 'element.' Likewise, the five gross elements are spoken of by the word 'element.' Now, the combination of these is said to be 'the body.' Now, he, assuredly, indeed, who is said to be in 'the body' is said to be 'the elemental self.' Now, its immortal self is like 'the drop of water on the lotus leaf.'[1]

"This [elemental self], verily, is overcome by Nature's qualities.

". . . In thinking 'This is I' and 'That is mine,' he binds himself with his self, as does a bird with a snare. . . ." (III.1–2)

[1] That is, unaffected by externals.

The rule for the elemental self's complete union with the universal Self

1. ..."Sir,... What is the rule for this elemental self, whereby, on quitting this body, it may come to complete union with the Self?" Then he said...

3. "The antidote, assuredly, indeed, for this elemental self is this: study of the knowledge of the Veda, and pursuit of one's regular duty. Pursuit of one's regular duty, in one's own stage of the religious life—that, verily, is the rule! Other rules are like a bunch of grass. With this, one tends upwards; otherwise, downwards. That is one's regular duty, which is set forth in the Vedas. Not by transgressing one's regular duty does one come into a stage of the religious life. Some one says: 'He is not in any of the stages of the religious life! Verily, he is one who practises austerity!' That is not proper. [However], if one does not practise austerity, there is no success in the knowledge of the Self nor perfection of works....

4. Therefore, by knowledge (*vidyā*), by austerity (*tapas*), and by meditation (*cintā*) *Brahman* is apprehended...

So when this chariot-rider is liberated from those things wherewith he was filled full and overcome, then he attains complete union with the *Ātman*." (IV.1, 3–4)

The indescribable Self

7. For thus has it been said: "Now, where knowledge is of a dual nature, there, indeed, one hears, sees, smells, tastes, and also touches; the self knows everything. Where knowledge is not of a dual nature, being devoid of action, cause, or effect, unspeakable, incomparable, indescribable—what is that? It is impossible to say!" (VI.7)

The infinite Brahman, and the Yoga method of attaining pure unity with it

17. Verily, in the beginning this world was *Brahman*, the limitless One—limitless to the east, limitless to the south, limitless to the west, limitless to the north, and above and below, limitless in every direction. Truly, for him east and the other directions exist not, nor across, nor below, nor above.

Incomprehensible is that supreme Self, unlimited, unborn, not to be reasoned about, unthinkable—He whose self is space! In the dissolution of the world He alone remains awake. From that space

He, assuredly, awakes this world, which is a mass of thought. It is thought by Him, and in Him it disappears.

His is that shining form which gives heat in yonder sun and which is the brilliant light in a smokeless fire, as also the fire in the stomach which cooks food. For thus has it been said: "He who is in the fire, and he who is here in the heart, and he who is yonder in the sun—he is one."

To the unity of the One goes he who knows this.

18. The precept for effecting this [unity] is this: restraint of the breath, withdrawal of the senses, meditation, concentration, contemplation, absorption. Such is said to be the sixfold *yoga*. . . .

30. . . . Verily, freedom from desire is like the choicest extract from the choicest treasure. For, a person who is made up of all desires, who has the marks of determination, conception, and self-conceit, is bound. Hence, in being the opposite of that, he is liberated. . . .

34. . . . *Saṁsāra* [cycle of existence] is just one's own thought;
With effort he should cleanse it, then.
What is one's thought, that he becomes;
This is the eternal mystery.

For by tranquillity of thought,
Deeds, good and evil, one destroys.
With self serene, stayed on the Self,
Delight eternal one enjoys!

As firmly as the thought of man
Is fixed within the realm of sense—
If thus on *Brahman* it were fixed,
Who would not be released from bond? . . .

By making mind all motionless,
From sloth and from distraction freed,
When unto mindlessness one comes,
Then that is the supreme estate! . . .

The mind, in truth, is for mankind
The means of bondage and release;
For bondage, if to objects bound;
From objects free—that's called release! . . .

(vi.17–18, 30, 34)

THE EPIC PERIOD

THE EPIC PERIOD

THE Epic Period derives its name from the two epics, the *Rāmāyaṇa* and the *Mahābhārata*. The *Rāmāyaṇa* deals with the conflict of the Āryans with the then natives of India and of the penetration of the Āryan culture. The *Mahābhārata* records the conflict between two claimants to the throne, and besides reflecting the culture of the age the story is said to symbolize the struggle between the forces of good and evil. Though the events related in the epics belong to an earlier period, the composition of the epics belongs to the Epic Period, which had its origin about the sixth century before Christ. This period, like every period in which civilizations converge and conflict, was one of great intellectual activity, enlargement of life, and many-sided developments. While there were orthodox developments of Brahmanism, as in the *Bhagavad-gītā* (a part of the *Mahābhārata*), of Manu, and of Kauṭilya, there were also strong radical and heretical systems, such as the Cārvāka, the Jaina, and the Buddhist.

Brahmanism in this period was readjusting itself to the needs of the different communities which were being taken into the Āryan fold. Apart from the great work of synthesis attempted in the *Bhagavad-gītā*, we have also the Pāśupata, the Bhāgavata, and the Tantra systems of thought and practice. The *Mahābhārata*, which in a spirit of accommodation admitted the beliefs and teachings of the various tribes, was interested in making itself a work attractive to all the people of India. It thus became a miscellany of history and mythology, politics and law, philosophy and theology. In all this variety there was a direction of unity, and the main principles of the Āryan culture were the formative motives. The authoritativeness of the Vedas was accepted. New gods were identified with Vedic deities. Śiva, Śakti, and Viṣṇu became prominent. Emphasis on the personal God with devotion (*bhakti*) to him developed. Philosophical tendencies which later became systematized in the systems of philosophy (*darśanas*) were suggested.

In the *Mahābhārata* we find the elaboration of the orthodox social code, with the four aims of life (*puruṣārthas*), namely, righteousness (*dharma*), wealth (*artha*), worldly enjoyment (*kāma*), and spiritual freedom (*mokṣa*); the four stages of life, the student (*brahmacarya*), the householder (*gārhasthya*), the forest-dweller (*vānaprastha*), and the wandering ascetic (*sannyāsa*); and the four castes, the priest-teacher (*brāhmin*), the warrior (*kṣatriya*), the trader (*vaiśya*), and the worker (*śūdra*).

In the *Code of Manu* detailed instructions regarding the then social rules and practices are given. The metaphysical and cosmological speculations found in Manu are not of much importance since they are mentioned only to give the intellectual background of the social code. While in Manu's system there is scope for some progress, the main emphasis is on the conservation of the social order. It glorified custom and convention at a time when they were being undermined. There are, however, flashes of great insight in the book.

Some passages from Kauṭilya's *Artha-śāstra* (*Treatise on the Science of Economics and Politics*) are given to show that ancient Indian thinkers were not uninterested in practical and theoretical problems of economics and politics. The detailed discussions about the nature of sovereignty, representative institutions, peace and war, the validity of punishment, the principles of taxation, the police and moral functions of the state, etc., indicate that the political thinkers of ancient India combined idealism with a high degree of realism.

Because of its very great influence upon subsequent Indian thought and life, the *Bhagavad-gītā* is reproduced in full.

Short and miscellaneous passages are quoted from other sections of the *Mahābhārata* to indicate the nonabsolutist realism of the ethical thought and practice of the times.

The selections for these chapters have been taken from:

The Bhagavadgītā, with an Introductory Essay, Sanskrit Text, English Translation and Notes by S. Radhakrishnan (New York: Harper & Bros., 1948).

The Mahābhārata, translated by Pratap Chandra Ray (Calcutta: Bharata Press, 1890).

The Laws of Manu, translated by G. Bühler: Sacred Books of the East, xxv (Oxford: Clarendon Press, 1886).

Kauṭilya's Arthaśāstra, translated by Dr. R. Shamasastry (Mysore: Wesleyan Mission Press, 2nd ed., 1923).

CHAPTER III

THE *BHAGAVAD-GĪTĀ*

THE *Bhagavad-gītā* is a religious classic rather than a philosophical treatise. It is set forth not as a metaphysical system thought out by an individual thinker or school of thinkers but as a tradition which has emerged from the religious life of mankind. As the colophon indicates, the *Bhagavad-gītā* is both metaphysics and ethics, *brahmavidyā* and Yoga-śāstra, the science of reality and the art of union with reality.

The *Gītā* derives its main inspiration from the Upaniṣads and integrates into a comprehensive synthesis the different elements of the Vedic cult of sacrifice, the Upaniṣadic teaching of the Absolute *Brahman*, the Bhāgavata theism, the Sāṁkhya dualism, and the Yoga meditation. It is a part of the *Mahābhārata*, and its authorship is attributed to Vyāsa.

Metaphysics. The *Bhagavad-gītā* takes up the Upaniṣadic conception of *Brahman* as absolute reality, and points out that the impersonality of the Absolute is not its whole significance. It develops the theistic side of the Upaniṣadic teaching by giving us a God who exceeds the infinite and the mere finite. In the *Gītā* the Supreme is at once the transcendental, the cosmic, and the individual reality. In its transcendental aspect the Supreme is the pure Self unaffected by any action or experience, detached, and unconcerned. In its dynamic aspect, it not only supports but also governs the whole cosmic action. The same Supreme which is one in all and above all is present in the individual.

The emphasis of the *Gītā* is on the Supreme as the personal God who creates the perceptible world by His nature (*prakṛti*). He is responsible for the creation, preservation, and destruction of the universe.

The *Gītā* is interested in the process of redeeming the world, and so this aspect of Viṣṇu is emphasized. Kṛṣṇa represents the Viṣṇu aspect of the Supreme. The *Gītā* makes out that Kṛṣṇa is an incarnation (*avataraṇa*) or descent of the Divine into the human frame. If the Infinite God is manifested in finite existence throughout time, its special manifestation at one given moment and through the assumption of one single human nature by the Divine person is but the free fulfillment of that same movement by which the Divine plenitude freely fulfills itself and inclines toward the finite. The theory of *avatāra* is an eloquent expression of the law of the spiritual world. If God is looked upon as the savior of man, He must manifest Himself whenever the forces of evil threaten to destroy human values.

The world for the *Gītā* is the scene of an active struggle between good and evil in which God is deeply interested. He pours out all his wealth of love in helping man to resist all that makes for error, ugliness, and evil.

Ethics. The *Gītā* is a comprehensive Yoga-śāstra (treatise on *yoga*), large, flexible, many-sided, which includes various phases of the self's development and ascent into the Divine. The different *yogas* are special applications of the inner discipline which leads to the liberation of the self and to a new understanding of the unity and meaning of mankind. This goal of union with God may be attained by *jñāna-yoga* (the way of knowledge), *bhakti-yoga* (the way of devotion), or *karma-yoga* (the way of action). Knowledge, devotion, and work are complementary both when we seek the goal and after we attain it. We may climb the mountain from different paths but the view from the summit is identical for all.

Chapter 1. The Hesitation and Despondency of Arjuna

The question

Dhṛtarāṣṭra said:

1. In the field of righteousness, the field of the Kurus,[1] when my people and the sons of Pāṇḍu had gathered together, eager for battle, what did they do, O Saṁjaya?[2]

Saṁjaya said:

2. Then, Duryodhana the prince, having seen the army of the Pāṇḍavas drawn up in battle order, approached his teacher and spoke this word:

3. Behold, O Teacher, this mighty army of the sons of Pāṇḍu organized by thy wise pupil, the son of Drupada.

4. Here are heroes, great bowmen equal in battle to Bhīma[3]

[1] Kurukṣetra is the land of the Kurus, a leading clan of the period. It is a vast field near Hastināpura in the neighborhood of modern Delhi. When Dhṛtarāṣṭra, the blind king of the Kurus, decided to give his throne to Yudhiṣṭhira, who is also known as Dharmarāja, the embodiment of virtue, in preference to his own eldest son, Duryodhana, the latter, by tricks and treachery, secured the throne for himself and attempted to destroy Yudhiṣṭhira and his four brothers. Kṛṣṇa, the head of the Yādava clan, sought to bring about a reconciliation between the cousins. When all attempts failed, a fratricidal war between the Kauravas and the Pāṇḍavas became inevitable. Kṛṣṇa proposed that he and his vassals would join the two sides and left the choice to the parties. The vassals were selected by Duryodhana, and Kṛṣṇa himself joined the Pāṇḍavas as the charioteer of Arjuna.

[2] Saṁjaya is the charioteer of the blind king, Dhṛtarāṣṭra, who reports to him the events of the war. (Many of the other names used in the text are without philosophical significance and no attempt will be made to explain them.)

[3] Bhīma is Yudhiṣṭhira's Commander-in-Chief, though nominally Dhṛṣṭadyumna holds that office.

and Arjuna[1]—Yuyudhāna, Virāṭa, and Drupada, a mighty warrior;

5. Dhṛṣṭaketu, Cekitāna and the valiant King of Kāśi, also Purujit, Kuntibhoja and Śaibya, the foremost of men;

6. Yudhāmanyu, the strong and Uttamauja, the brave; and also the son of Subhadrā and sons of Draupadī, all of them great warriors.

7. Know also, O best of the twiceborn,[2] the leaders of my army, those who are most distinguished among us. I will name them now for thine information:

8. Thyself and Bhīṣma and Karṇa and Kṛpa, ever victorious in battle; Asvatthāman, Vikarṇa, and also the son of Somadatta;

9. And many other heroes who have risked their lives for my sake. They are armed with many kinds of weapons and are all well skilled in war.

10. Unlimited is this army of ours which is guarded by Bhīṣma, while that army of theirs, which is guarded by Bhīma, is limited.

11. Therefore do ye all support Bhīṣma, standing firm in all the fronts, in your respective ranks.

12. In order to cheer him up, the aged Kuru, his valiant grandsire, roared aloud like a lion and blew his conch.

13. Then conches and kettledrums, tabors and drums and horns suddenly blared forth and the noise was tumultuous.

14. When stationed in their great chariot yoked to white horses, Kṛṣṇa and Arjuna blew their celestial conches.

15. Kṛṣṇa blew his Pāñcajanya and Arjuna his Devadatta and Bhīma of terrific deeds blew his mighty conch, Pauṇḍra.

16. Prince Yudhiṣṭhira, the son of Kuntī, blew his Anantavijaya and Nakula and Sahadeva blew their Sughoṣa and Maṇipuṣpaka.

17. And the king of Kāśi, the Chief of archers, Śikhaṇḍin, the great warrior, Dhṛṣṭadyumna and Virāṭa and the invincible Sātyaki;

18. Drupada and the sons of Draupadī, O Lord of earth, and the strong-armed son of Subhadrā, on all sides blew their respective conches.

19. The tumultuous uproar resounding through earth and sky rent the hearts of Dhṛtarāṣṭra's sons.

[1] Arjuna is the friend of Kṛṣṇa and the great hero of the Pāṇḍavas. Other names used for Arjuna are Bhārata (descended of Bhārata), Dhanaṁjaya (winner of wealth), Guḍākeśa (having the hair in a ball), Pārtha (son of Pṛthā), Paraṁtapa (oppressor of the enemy).

[2] One who is twice-born is one who is invested with the sacred thread, the symbol of initiation into the life of spirit, which is the aim of education.

20. Then Arjuna, whose banner bore the crest of Hanumān, looked at the sons of Dhṛtarāṣṭra drawn up in battle order; and as the flight of missiles [almost] started, he took up his bow.

21. And, O Lord of earth, he spoke this word to Hṛṣīkeśa (Kṛṣṇa): Draw up my chariot, O Acyuta (Kṛṣṇa),[1] between the two armies.

22. So that I may observe these men standing, eager for battle, with whom I have to contend in this strife of war.

23. I wish to look at those who are assembled here, ready to fight and eager to achieve in battle what is dear to the evil-minded son of Dhṛtarāṣṭra.

24. Thus addressed by Guḍākeśa (Arjuna), Hṛṣīkeśa (Kṛṣṇa) drew up that best of chariots, O Bhārata (Dhṛtarāṣṭra), between the two armies.

25. In front of Bhīṣma, Droṇa, and all the chiefs he said: "Behold, O Pārtha (Arjuna), these Kurus assembled here."

26. There saw Arjuna standing fathers and grandfathers, teachers, uncles, brothers, sons and grandsons, as also companions;

27. And also fathers-in-law and friends in both the armies. When the son of Kuntī (Arjuna) saw all these kinsmen thus standing arrayed,

28. He was overcome with great compassion and uttered this in sadness:

The Distress of Arjuna

When I see my own people arrayed and eager for fight, O Kṛṣṇa,

29. My limbs quail, my mouth goes dry, my body shakes and my hair stands on end.

30. The bow Gāṇḍīva slips from my hand, and my skin too is burning all over. I am not able to stand steady. My mind is reeling.

31. And I see evil omens, O Keśava (Kṛṣṇa), nor do I foresee any good by slaying my own people in the fight.

32. I do not long for victory, O Kṛṣṇa, nor kingdom nor pleasures. Of what use is kingdom to us, O Kṛṣṇa, or enjoyment or even life?

33. Those for whose sake we desire kingdom, enjoyments and pleasures—they stand here in battle, renouncing their lives and riches:

[1] Acyuta (immovable) is another name for Kṛṣṇa. Other names used for Kṛṣṇa are Madhusūdana (slayer of the demon Madhu), Arisūdana (slayer of enemies), Govinda (herdsman or giver of enlightenment), Vāsudeva (son of Vasudeva), Yādava (descendent of Yadu), Keśava (having fine hair), Mādhava (the husband of Lakṣmī), Hṛṣīkeśa (lord of the senses, *hṛṣīka*, *īśā*), Janārdana (the liberator of men).

34. Teachers, fathers, sons, and also grandfathers; uncles and fathers-in-law, grandsons and brothers-in-law, and other kinsmen.

35. These I would not consent to kill, though killed myself, O Madhusūdana (Kṛṣṇa), even for the kingdom of the three worlds; how much less for the sake of the earth?

36. What pleasure can be ours, O Kṛṣṇa, after we have slain the sons of Dhṛtarāṣṭra? Only sin will accrue to us if we kill these criminals.

37. So it is not right that we slay our kinsmen, the sons of Dhṛtarāṣṭra. Indeed, how can we be happy, O Mādhava (Kṛṣṇa), if we kill our own people?

38. Even if these whose minds are overpowered by greed see no wrong in the destruction of the family and no crime in treachery to friends;

39. Why should we not have the wisdom to turn away from this sin, O Janārdana (Kṛṣṇa), we who see the wrong in the destruction of the family?

40. In the ruin of a family, its ancient laws are destroyed: and when the laws perish, the whole family yields to lawlessness.

41. And when lawlessness prevails, O Vārṣṇeya (Kṛṣṇa), the women of the family become corrupted, and when women are corrupted, confusion of castes arises.

42. And to hell does this confusion bring the family itself as well as those who have destroyed it. For the spirits of their ancestors fall, deprived of their offerings of rice and water.

43. By the misdeeds of those who destroy a family and create confusion of *varṇas* [castes], the immemorial laws of the race and the family are destroyed.

44. And we have heard it said, O Janārdana (Kṛṣṇa), that the men of the families whose laws are destroyed needs must live in hell.

45. Alas, what a great sin have we resolved to commit in striving to slay our own people through our greed for the pleasures of the kingdom!

46. Far better would it be for me if the sons of Dhṛtarāṣṭra, with weapons in hand, should slay me in the battle, while I remain unresisting and unarmed.

47. Having spoken thus on the field of battle, Arjuna sank down on the seat of his chariot, casting away his bow and arrow, his spirit overwhelmed by sorrow.

In the Upaniṣad of the *Bhagavad-gītā*, the science of the Absolute, the scripture of *yoga*, and the dialogue between Śrīkṛṣṇa and Arjuna, this is the first chapter, entitled "The Depression of Arjuna."[1]

Chapter 2: Sāṁkhya Theory[2] and Yoga Practice

Kṛṣṇa's rebuke and exhortation to be brave

Saṁjaya said:

1. To him who was thus overcome by pity, whose eyes were filled with tears and troubled and who was much depressed in mind, Madhusūdana (Kṛṣṇa) spoke this word.

The Blessed Lord said:

2. Whence has come to thee this stain (this dejection) of spirit in this hour of crisis? It is unknown to men of noble mind [not cherished by the Āryans]; it does not lead to heaven; on earth it causes disgrace, O Arjuna.

3. Yield not to this unmanliness, O Pārtha (Arjuna), for it does not become thee. Cast off this petty faintheartedness and arise, O Oppressor of the foes (Arjuna).

Arjuna said:

4. How shall I strike Bhīṣma and Droṇa, who are worthy of worship, O Madhusūdana (Kṛṣṇa), with arrows in battle, O Slayer of foes (Kṛṣṇa)?

5. It is better to live in this world by begging than to slay these honoured teachers. Though they are mindful of their gains, they are my teachers, and by slaying them, I would enjoy in this world delights which are smeared with blood.

6. Nor do we know which for us is better, whether we conquer them or they conquer us. The sons of Dhṛtarāṣṭra, whom if we slew we should not care to live, are standing before us in battle array.

7. My very being is stricken with the weakness of sentimental pity. With my mind bewildered about my duty, I ask Thee. Tell me, for certain, which is better. I am Thy pupil; teach me, who am seeking refuge in Thee.

[1] This is the usual colophon, which is not a part of the text. There are slight variations in the titles of the chapters in the different versions, but they are not worth recording.

[2] The teacher explains in brief in verses 11–38 the wisdom of the Sāṁkhya philosophy. The Sāṁkhya does not refer to Kapila's system but to the teaching of the Upaniṣads.

Sāṁkhya and Yoga are not in the *Gītā* discordant systems. They have the same aim but differ in their methods.

8. I do not see what will drive away this sorrow which dries up my senses even if I should attain rich and unrivalled kingdom on earth or even the sovereignty of the gods.

Saṁjaya said:

9. Having thus addressed Hṛṣīkeśa (Kṛṣṇa), the mighty Guḍākeśa (Arjuna) said to Govinda (Kṛṣṇa), "I will not fight," and became silent.

10. To him thus depressed in the midst of the two armies, O Bhārata (Dhṛtarāṣṭra), Hṛṣīkeśa (Kṛṣṇa), smiling as it were, spoke this word.

The distinction between self and body: we should not grieve for what is imperishable

The Blessed Lord said:

11. Thou grievest for those whom thou shouldst not grieve for, and yet thou speakest words about wisdom. Wise men do not grieve for the dead or for the living.

12. Never was there a time when I was not, nor thou, nor these lords of men, nor will there ever be a time hereafter when we shall cease to be.[1]

13. As the soul passes in this body through childhood, youth and age, even so is its taking on of another body. The sage is not perplexed by this.

14. Contacts with their objects, O son of Kuntī (Arjuna), give rise to cold and heat, pleasure and pain. They come and go and do not last forever; these learn to endure, O Bhārata (Arjuna).

15. The man who is not troubled by these, O Chief of men (Arjuna), who remains the same in pain and pleasure, who is wise, makes himself fit for eternal life.

16. Of the non-existent there is no coming to be; of the existent there is no ceasing to be. The conclusion about these two has been perceived by the seers of truth.

17. Know thou that that by which all this is pervaded is indestructible. Of this immutable being, no one can bring about the destruction.

18. It is said that these bodies of the eternal embodied soul, which is indestructible and incomprehensible, come to an end. Therefore fight, O Bhārata (Arjuna).

[1] While the Sāṁkhya system postulates a plurality of souls, the *Gītā* reconciles this with unity.

19. He who thinks that this slays and he who thinks that this is slain; both of them fail to perceive the truth; this one neither slays nor is slain.

20. He is never born, nor does he die at any time, nor having once come to be does he again cease to be. He is unborn, eternal, permanent, and primeval. He is not slain when the body is slain.

21. He who knows that it is indestructible and eternal, uncreate and unchanging—how can such a person slay any one, O Pārtha (Arjuna), or cause any one to slay?

22. Just as a person casts off worn-out garments and puts on others that are new, even so does the embodied soul cast off worn-out bodies and take on others that are new.

23. Weapons do not cleave this self; fire does not burn him; waters do not make him wet; nor does the wind make him dry.

24. He is uncleavable. He cannot be burnt. He can be neither wetted nor dried. He is eternal, all-pervading, unchanging, and immovable. He is the same forever.

25. He is said to be unmanifest, unthinkable, and unchanging. Therefore, knowing him as such, thou shouldst not grieve.

We should not grieve over what is perishable

26. Even if thou thinkest that the self is perpetually born and perpetually dies, even then, O Mighty-armed (Arjuna), thou shouldst not grieve,

27. For to the one that is born death is certain, and certain is birth for the one that has died. Therefore, for what is unavoidable thou shouldst not grieve.

28. Beings are unmanifest in their beginnings, manifest in the middles, and unmanifest again in their ends, O Bhārata (Arjuna). What is there in this for lamentation?

29. One looks upon Him as a marvel; another likewise speaks of Him as a marvel; another hears of Him as a marvel; and even after hearing, no one whatsoever has known Him.

30. The dweller in the body of every one, O Bhārata (Arjuna), is eternal and can never be slain. Therefore, thou shouldst not grieve for any creature.

Appeal to a sense of duty

31. Further, having regard for thine own duty, thou shouldst not falter; there exists no greater good for a *kṣatriya* [warrior] than a war enjoined by duty.

32. Happy are the *kṣatriyas*, O Pārtha (Arjuna), for whom such a war comes of its own accord as an open door to heaven.

33. But if thou doest not this lawful battle, then thou wilt fail thy duty and glory and will incur sin.

34. Besides, men will ever recount thy ill-fame, and for one who has been honoured ill-fame is worse than death.

35. The great warriors will think that thou hast abstained from battle through fear, and they by whom thou wast highly esteemed will make light of thee.

36. Many unseemly words will be uttered by thine enemies, slandering thy strength. Could anything be sadder than that?

37. Either slain thou shalt go to heaven; or victorious thou shalt enjoy the earth; therefore arise, O Son of Kuntī (Arjuna), resolve on battle.

38. Treating alike pleasure and pain, gain and loss, victory and defeat, then get ready for battle. Thus thou shalt not incur sin.

The insight of Yoga

39. This is the wisdom of the Sāṁkhya given to thee, O Pārtha (Arjuna). Listen now to the Yoga. If your intelligence accepts it, thou shalt cast away the bondage of works.

40. In this path, no effort is ever lost and no obstacle prevails; even a little of this righteousness (*dharma*) saves from great fear.

41. In this, O joy of the Kurus (Arjuna), the resolute understanding is single; but the thoughts of the irresolute are many-branched and endless.

No wisdom for the worldly-minded

42–43. The undiscerning, who rejoice in the letter of the Veda, who contend that there is nothing else, whose nature is desire, and who are intent on heaven, proclaim these flowery words that result in rebirth as the fruit of actions and lay down various specialized rites for the attainment of enjoyment and power.

44. The intelligence which is to be trained, of those who are devoted to enjoyment and power and whose minds are carried away by these words [of the Veda], is not well-established in the Self [or concentration].

45. The action of the threefold modes[1] is the subject matter of the Veda; but do thou become free, O Arjuna, from this threefold

[1] The three modes (*guṇas*) are goodness (*sattva*), passion (*rajas*), and dullness or inertia (*tamas*). These are the primary constituents of nature and are the bases of all substances.

nature; be free from the dualities [the pairs of opposites]; be firmly fixed in purity, not caring for acquisition and preservation; and be possessed of the Self.

46. As is the use of a pond in a place flooded with water everywhere, so is that of all the Vedas for the *brāhmin* who understands.[1]

Work without concern for the results

47. To action alone hast thou a right and never at all to its fruit; let not the fruits of action be thy motive; neither let there be in thee any attachment to inaction.

48. Fixed in *yoga*, do thy work, O winner of wealth (Arjuna), abandoning attachment, with an even mind in success and failure, for evenness of mind is called *yoga*.

49. Far inferior indeed is mere action to the discipline of intelligence, O winner of wealth (Arjuna); seek refuge in intelligence. Pitiful are those who seek for the fruits of their action.

50. One who has yoked his intelligence [with the Divine] (or is established in his intelligence) casts away even here both good and evil. Therefore strive for *yoga*; *yoga* is skill in action.

51. The wise who have united their intelligence [with the Divine], renouncing the fruits which their action yields and freed from the bonds of birth, reach the sorrowless state.

52. When thine intelligence shall cross the whirl of delusion, then shalt thou become indifferent to what has been heard and what is yet to be heard.[2]

53. When thine intelligence, which is bewildered by the Vedic texts, shall stand unshaken and stable in spirit (*samādhi*), then shalt thou attain to insight (*yoga*).

The characteristics of the perfect sage

Arjuna said:

54. What is the description of the man who has this firmly founded wisdom, whose being is steadfast in spirit, O Keśava (Kṛṣṇa)? How does the man of settled intelligence speak; how does he sit; how does he walk?

The Blessed Lord said:

55. When a man puts away all the desires of his mind, O Pārtha

[1] That is, for those of illumined consciousness or spiritual insight ritual observances are of little value.

[2] Scriptures are unnecessary for the man who has attained insight.

(Arjuna), and when his spirit is content in itself, then is he called stable in intelligence.

56. He whose mind is untroubled in the midst of sorrows and is free from eager desire amid pleasures, he from whom passion, fear, and rage have passed away—he is called a sage of settled intelligence.

57. He who is without affection on any side, who does not rejoice or loathe as he obtains good or evil—his intelligence is firmly set [in wisdom].

58. He who draws away the senses from the objects of sense on every side as a tortoise draws in his limbs into the shell—his intelligence is firmly set [in wisdom].

59. The objects of sense turn away from the embodied soul who abstains from feeding on them, but the taste for them remains. Even the taste turns away when the Supreme is seen.

60. Even though a man may ever strive [for perfection] and be ever so discerning, O Son of Kuntī (Arjuna), his impetuous senses will carry off his mind by force.

61. Having brought all the senses under control, he should remain firm in *yoga*, intent on Me; for he, whose senses are under control, his intelligence is firmly set.

62. When a man dwells in his mind on the objects of sense, attachment to them is produced. From attachment springs desire, and from desire comes anger.

63. From anger arises bewilderment, from bewilderment loss of memory, and from loss of memory the destruction of intelligence; and from the destruction of intelligence he perishes.

64. But a man of disciplined mind, who moves among the objects of sense, with the senses under control and free from attachment and aversion—he attains purity of spirit.

65. And in that purity of spirit, there is produced for him an end of all sorrow; the intelligence of such a man of pure spirit is soon established [in the peace of the self].

66. For the uncontrolled, there is no intelligence; nor for the uncontrolled is there the power of concentration; and for him without concentration, there is no peace; and for the unpeaceful, how can there be happiness?

67. When the mind runs after the roving senses, it carries away the understanding, even as a wind carries away a ship on the waters.

68. Therefore, O Mighty-armed (Arjuna), he whose senses are all withdrawn from their objects—his intelligence is firmly set.

69. What is night for all beings is the time of waking for the disciplined soul; and what is the time of waking for all beings is night for the sage who sees (or the sage of vision).[1]

70. He unto whom all desires enter as waters into the sea, which, though ever being filled, is ever motionless, attains to peace, and not he who hugs his desires.

71. He who abandons all desires and acts free from longing, without any sense of mineness or egotism—he attains to peace.

72. This is the divine state, O Pārtha (Arjuna); having attained thereto, one is not again bewildered; fixed in that state at the end [at the hour of death] one can attain to the bliss of God.

This is the second chapter, entitled "The *Yoga* of Knowledge."

Chapter 3: Karma-Yoga or the Method of Work

Why then work at all?

Arjuna said:

1. If thou deemest that the path of understanding is more excellent than the path of action, O Janārdana (Kṛṣṇa), why then dost thou urge me to do this savage deed, O Keśava (Kṛṣṇa)?

2. With an apparently confused utterance thou seemest to bewilder my intelligence. Tell me, then, decisively the one thing by which I can attain to the highest good.

Life is work; unconcern for results is needful

The Blessed Lord said:

3. O blameless One, in this world a twofold way of life has been taught of yore by Me, the path of knowledge for men of contemplation and that of works for men of action.

4. Not by abstention from work does a man attain freedom from action; nor by mere renunciation does he attain to his perfection.

5. For no one can remain even for a moment without doing work; every one is made to act helplessly by the impulses born of nature.

6. He who restrains his organs of action but continues in his mind to brood over the objects of sense, whose nature is deluded, is said to be a hypocrite [a man of false conduct].

[1] When all beings are attracted by the glitter of sense-objects, the sage is intent on understanding reality. He is wakeful to the nature of reality to which the unwise is asleep or indifferent.

7. But he who controls the senses by the mind, O Arjuna, and without attachment engages the organs of action in the path of work, he is superior.

The importance of sacrifice

8. Do thou thine allotted work, for action is better than inaction; even the maintenance of thy physical life cannot be effected without action.

9. Save work done as and for a sacrifice[1] this world is in bondage to work. Therefore, O son of Kuntī (Arjuna), do thy work as a sacrifice, becoming free from all attachment.

10. In ancient days the Lord of creatures created men along with sacrifice, and said, "By this shall ye bring forth and this shall be unto you that which will yield the milk of your desires."

11. By this foster ye the gods and let the gods foster you; thus fostering each other you shall attain to the supreme good.

12. Fostered by sacrifice, the gods will give the enjoyments you desire. He who enjoys these gifts without giving to them in return is verily a thief.

13. The good people who eat what is left from the sacrifice are released from all sins, but those wicked people who prepare food for their own sake—verily they eat their sin.

14. From food creatures come into being; from rain is the birth of food; from sacrifice rain comes into being, and sacrifice is born of work.

15. Know the origin of *karma* [of the nature of sacrifices] to be in *Brahman* [the Veda], and the *Brahman* springs from the Imperishable. Therefore the *Brahman*, which comprehends all, ever centres round the sacrifice.

16. He who does not, in this world, turn the wheel thus set in motion, is evil in his nature, sensual in his delight, and he, O Pārtha (Arjuna), lives in vain.

Be satisfied in the Self

17. But the man whose delight is in the Self alone, who is content with the Self, who is satisfied with the Self—for him there exists no work that needs to be done.

18. Similarly, in this world he has no interest whatever to gain by the actions that he has done and none to be gained by the actions

[1] All work is to be done in a spirit of sacrifice, for the sake of the Divine.

that he has not done. He does not depend on all these beings for any interest of his.

19. Therefore, without attachment, perform always the work that has to be done, for man attains to the highest by doing work without attachment.

Set an example to others

20. It was even by works that Janaka[1] and others attained to perfection. Thou shouldst do works also with a view to the maintenance of the world.[2]

21. Whatsoever a great man does, the same is done by others as well. Whatever standard he sets, the world follows.

22. There is not for me, O Pārtha (Arjuna), any work in the three worlds which has to be done or anything to be obtained which has not been obtained; yet I am engaged in work.

23. For, if ever I did not engage in work unwearied, O Pārtha (Arjuna), men would in every way follow my path.

24. If I should cease to work, these worlds would fall in ruin, and I should be the creator of disordered life and destroy these people.

25. As the unlearned act from attachment to their work, so should the learned also act, O Bhārata (Arjuna), but without any attachment, with the desire to maintain the world-order.

26. Let him not unsettle the minds of the ignorant who are attached to action. The enlightened man doing all works in a spirit of *yoga* should set others to act (as well).

The Self is no doer

27. While all kinds of work are done by the modes of nature (*guṇas*), he whose soul is bewildered by the self-sense thinks, "I am the doer."

28. But he who knows the true character of the distinction of the soul from the modes of nature and their works, O Mighty-armed (Arjuna), understanding that it is the modes which are acting on the modes themselves, does not get attached.

29. Those who are misled by the modes of nature get attached to

[1] Janaka was the king of Mithilā and the father of Sītā, the wife of Rāma. Janaka ruled, giving up his personal sense of being the worker.

[2] "The maintenance of the world" (*lokasaṁgraha*) stands for the unity of the world, the interconnectedness of society. If the world is not to sink into a condition of physical misery and moral degradation, if the common life is to be decent and dignified, religious ethics must control social action.

the works produced by them. But let no one who knows the whole unsettle the minds of the ignorant who know only a part.

30. Resigning all thy works to Me, with thy consciousness fixed in the Self, being free from desire and egoism, fight, delivered from thy fever.

31. Those men, too, who, full of faith and free from cavil, constantly follow this teaching of Mine are released from the bondage of works.

32. But those who slight My teaching and do not follow it, know them to be blind to all wisdom, lost and senseless.

Nature and duty

33. Even the man of knowledge acts in accordance with his own nature. Beings follow their nature. What can repression accomplish?

34. For every sense-attachment and [every] aversion are fixed in regard to the objects of that sense. Let no one come under their sway, for they are his two enemies.

35. Better is one's own law though imperfectly carried out than the law of another carried out perfectly. Better is death in the fulfilment of one's own law, for to follow another's law is perilous.

The enemy is desire and anger

Arjuna said:

36. But by what is a man impelled to commit sin, as if by force, even against his will, O Vārṣṇeya (Kṛṣṇa)?

The Blessed Lord said:

37. This is craving, this is wrath, born of the mode of passion, all devouring and most sinful. Know this to be the enemy here.

38. As fire is covered by smoke, as a mirror by dust, as an embryo is enveloped by the womb, so is this covered by that [passion].

39. Enveloped is wisdom, O Son of Kuntī (Arjuna), by this insatiable fire of desire, which is the constant foe of the wise.

40. The senses, the mind, and the intelligence are said to be its seat. Veiling wisdom by these, it deludes the embodied soul.

41. Therefore, O Best of Bhāratas (Arjuna), control thy senses from the beginning and slay this sinful destroyer of wisdom and discrimination.

42. The senses, they say, are great; greater than the senses is the mind; greater than the mind is the intelligence; but greater than the intelligence is he [the self].

43. Thus knowing him who is beyond the intelligence, steadying the [lower] self by the Self, smite, O Mighty-armed (Arjuna), the enemy in the form of desire, so hard to get at.

This is the third chapter, entitled "The *Yoga* of Works."

Chapter 4: The Way of Knowledge

The tradition of jñāna (knowledge)-yoga

The Blessed Lord said:

1. I proclaimed this imperishable *yoga* to Vivasvān; Vivasvān told it to Manu; and Manu spoke it to Iṣvāku.

2. Thus handed down from one to another, the royal sages knew it till that *yoga* was lost to the world through long lapse of time, O Oppressor of the foe (Arjuna).

3. This same ancient *yoga* has been today declared to thee by Me; for thou art My devotee and My friend; and this is the supreme secret.

Arjuna said:

4. Later was Thy birth and earlier was the birth of Vivasvat. How, then, am I to understand that thou didst declare it to him in the beginning?

The theory of avatārs

The Blessed Lord said:

5. Many are My lives that are past, and thine also, O Arjuna; all of them I know but thou knowest not, O Scourge of the foe (Arjuna).

6. Though I am unborn, and My self is imperishable, though I am the lord of all creatures, yet, establishing Myself in My own nature, I come into [empiric] being through My power (*māyā*).

7. Whenever there is a decline of righteousness and rise of unrighteousness, O Bhārata (Arjuna), then I send forth [create incarnate] Myself.

8. For the protection of the good, for the destruction of the wicked, and for the establishment of righteousness, I come into being from age to age.

9. He who knows thus in its true nature My divine birth and works is not born again, when he leaves his body but comes to Me, O Arjuna.

10. Delivered from passion, fear, and anger, absorbed in Me,

taking refuge in Me, many purified by the austerity of wisdom have attained to My state of being.

11. As men approach me so do I accept them: men on all sides follow my path, O Pārtha (Arjuna).

12. Those who desire the fruition of their works on earth offer sacrifices to the gods [the various forms of the one Godhead], for the fruition of works in this world of men is very quick.

The desireless nature of God's work

13. The fourfold order[1] was created by Me according to the divisions of quality and work. Though I am its creator, know Me to be incapable of action or change.

Action without attachment does not lead to bondage

14. Works do not defile Me; nor do I have yearning for their fruit. He who knows Me thus is not bound by works.

15. So knowing was work done also by the men of old who sought liberation. Therefore do thou also work as the ancients did in former times.

Action and inaction

16. What is action? What is inaction?—as to this even the wise are bewildered. I will declare to thee what action is, knowing which thou shalt be delivered from evil.

17. One has to understand what action is, and likewise one has to understand what is wrong action, and one has to understand about inaction. Hard to understand is the way of work.

18. He who in action sees inaction and action in inaction—he is wise among men, he is a *yogin*, and he has accomplished all his work.

19. He whose undertakings are all free from the will of desire, whose works are burned up in the fire of wisdom—him the wise call a man of learning.

20. Having abandoned attachment to the fruit of works, ever content, without any kind of dependence, he does nothing though he is ever engaged in work.

21. Having no desires, with his heart and self under control, giving up all possessions, performing action by the body alone, he commits no wrong.

[1] The fourfold order is the caste system. The emphasis is on *guṇa* (aptitude) and *karma* (function), and not *jāti* (birth). The *varṇa*, or the order to which we belong, is independent of sex, birth, and breeding.

22. He who is satisfied with whatever comes by chance, who has passed beyond the dualities (of pleasure and pain), who is free from jealousy, who remains the same in success and failure—even when he acts, he is not bound.

Sacrifice and its symbolic value

23. The work of a man whose attachments are sundered, who is liberated, whose mind is firmly founded in wisdom, who does work as a sacrifice, is dissolved[1] entirely.

24. For him the act of offering is God; the oblation is God. By God is it offered into the fire of God. God is that which is to be attained by him who realizes God in his works.

25. Some *yogins* offer sacrifices to the gods, while others offer sacrifice by the sacrifice itself into the fire of the Supreme.

26. Some offer hearing and the other senses into the fires of restraint; others offer sound and the other objects of sense into the fires of sense.

27. Some again offer all the works of their senses and the works of the vital force into the fire of the *yoga* of self-control, kindled by knowledge.

28. Some likewise offer as sacrifice their material possessions, or their austerities, or their spiritual exercises, while others of subdued minds and severe vows offer their learning and knowledge.

29. Others again who are devoted to breath control, having restrained the paths of *prāṇa* (the outgoing breath) and *apāna* (the incoming breath), pour as sacrifice *prāṇa* into *apāna* and *apāna* into *prāṇa*.

30. While others, restricting their food, pour as sacrifice their life breaths into life breaths.[2] All these are knowers of sacrifice [know what sacrifice is] and by sacrifice have their sins destroyed.

31. Those who eat the sacred food that remains after a sacrifice attain to the eternal Absolute; this world is not for him who offers no sacrifice; how, then, any other world, O Best of the Kurus (Arjuna)?

32. Thus many forms of sacrifice are spread out in the face of *Brahman* [i.e., set forth as the means of reaching the Absolute]. Know thou that all these are born of work, and so knowing thou shalt be freed.

[1] That is, his action does not bind him to cosmic existence.
[2] That is, some practice control of breath.

Wisdom and work

33. Knowledge as a sacrifice is greater than any material sacrifice, O scourge of the foe (Arjuna), for all works without any exception culminate in wisdom.

34. Learn that by humble reverence, by inquiry, and by service. The men of wisdom who have seen the truth will instruct thee in knowledge.

In praise of wisdom

35. When thou hast known it, thou shalt not fall again into this confusion, O Pāṇḍava (Arjuna), for by this thou shalt see all existences without exception in the Self, then in Me.

36. Even if thou shouldst be the most sinful of all sinners, thou shalt cross over all evil by the boat of wisdom alone.

37. As the fire which is kindled turns its fuel to ashes, O Arjuna, even so does the fire of wisdom turn to ashes all work.

38. There is nothing on earth equal in purity to wisdom. He who becomes perfected by *yoga* finds this of himself, in his self [*ātman*] in course of time.

Faith is necessary for wisdom

39. He who has faith, who is absorbed in it [i.e., wisdom], and who has subdued his senses, gains wisdom, and having gained wisdom he attains quickly the supreme peace.

40. But the man who is ignorant, who has no faith, who is of a doubting nature, perishes. For the doubting soul [*ātman*] there is neither this world nor the world beyond, nor any happiness.

41. Works do not bind him who has renounced all works by *yoga*, who has destroyed all doubt by wisdom, and who ever possesses his soul, O winner of wealth (Arjuna).

42. Therefore, having cut asunder with the sword of wisdom this doubt in thy heart that is born of ignorance, resort to *yoga* and stand up, O Bhārata (Arjuna).

This is the fourth chapter, entitled "The *Yoga* of [Divine] Knowledge."

Chapter 5: True Renunciation

Sāṁkhya and Yoga lead to the same goal

Arjuna said:

1. Thou praisest, O Kṛṣṇa, the renunciation of works and again their unselfish performance. Tell me for certain which one is the better of these two.

The Blessed Lord said:

2. The renunciation of works and their unselfish performance both lead to the soul's salvation. But of the two, the unselfish performance of works is better than their renunciation.[1]

3. He who neither loathes nor desires should be known as one who has ever the spirit of renunciation; for, free from dualities, he is released easily, O Mighty-armed (Arjuna), from bondage.

4. The ignorant speak of renunciation [Sāṁkhya] and practice of works [Yoga] as different, not the wise. He who applies himself well to one gets the fruit of both.

5. The status which is obtained by men of renunciation is reached by men of action also. He who sees that the ways of renunciation and of action are one—he sees truly.

6. But renunciation, O Mighty-armed (Arjuna), is difficult to attain without *yoga*; the sage who is trained in *yoga* [the way of works] attains soon to the Absolute.

7. He who is trained in the way of works, and is pure in soul, who is master of his self and who has conquered the senses, whose soul becomes the self of all beings—he is not tainted by works, though he works.

8. The man who is united with the Divine and knows the truth thinks, "I do nothing at all," for in seeing, hearing, touching, smelling, tasting, walking, sleeping, breathing,

9. In speaking, emitting, grasping, opening and closing the eyes he holds that only the senses[2] are occupied with the objects of the senses.

10. He who works, having given up attachment, resigning his actions to God, is not touched by sin, even as a lotus leaf is untouched by water.

[1] The Sāṁkhya method involves the renunciation of works and the Yoga insists on their performance in the right spirit. The two ways are not inconsistent. In Sāṁkhya, *jñāna* (insight) is emphasized. In Yoga, volitional effort is stressed. In one, we know the Self by thinking away the alien elements; in the other, we will them away.

[2] "Only the senses": that is, not the self.

11. The *yogins* [men of action] perform works merely with the body, mind, understanding or merely with the senses, abandoning attachment, for the purification of their selves.

12. The self in union with the Divine attains to peace well-founded, by abandoning attachment to the fruits of works, but he whose self is not in union with the Divine is impelled by desire, and is attached to the fruit of action, and is therefore bound.

The enlightened self

13. The embodied self who has controlled his nature, having renounced all actions by the mind [inwardly], dwells at ease in the city of nine gates,[1] neither working nor causing work to be done.

14. The Sovereign Self does not create for the people agency, nor does He act. Nor does He connect works with their fruits. It is nature that works out these.

15. The All-pervading Spirit does not take on the sin or the merit of any. Wisdom is enveloped by ignorance; thereby creatures are bewildered.

16. But for those in whom ignorance is destroyed by wisdom—for them wisdom lights up the Supreme Self like the sun.

17. Thinking of That, directing one's whole conscious being to That, making That their whole aim, with That as the sole object of their devotion, they reach a state from which there is no return, their sins washed away by wisdom.

18. Sages see with an equal eye, a learned and humble *brāhmin*, a cow, an elephant, or even a dog, or an outcaste.

19. Even here on earth the created world is overcome by those whose mind is established in equality. God is flawless and the same in all. Therefore are these persons established in God.

20. One should not rejoice on obtaining what is pleasant or sorrow on obtaining what is unpleasant. He who is thus firm of understanding and unbewildered—such a knower of God is established in God.

21. When the self is no longer attached to external contacts [objects], one finds the happiness that is in the Self. Such a one who is in union with God enjoys undying bliss.

22. Whatever pleasures are born of contacts with objects are only

[1] The nine gates are the two eyes, the two ears, the two nostrils, the mouth, and the two organs of excretion and generation.

sources of pain: they have a beginning and an end, O Son of Kuntī (Arjuna); no wise man delights in them.

23. He who is able to resist the rush of desire and anger—even here before he gives up his body, he is a *yogin*, he is the happy man.

Peace from within

24. He who finds his happiness within, his joy within, and likewise his light only within, that *yogin* becomes divine and attains to the beatitude of God.

25. The holy men whose sins are destroyed, whose doubts [dualities] are cut asunder, whose minds are disciplined, and who rejoice in doing good to all creatures attain to the beatitude of God.

26. To those austere souls who are delivered from desire and anger and who have subdued their minds and have knowledge of the Self—near to them lies the beatitude of God.

27–28. Shutting out all external objects, fixing the vision between the eyebrows, making even the inward and the outward breaths moving within the nostrils, the sage who has controlled the senses, mind, and understanding, who is intent on liberation, who has cast away desire, fear and anger—he is ever freed.

29. And having known Me as the Enjoyer of sacrifices and austerities, the Great Lord of all the worlds, the Friend of all beings, he [the sage] attains peace.

This is the fifth chapter, entitled "The *Yoga* of Renunciation of Action."

Chapter 6: The True Yoga

Renunciation and action are one

The Blessed Lord said:

1. He who does the work which he ought to do without seeking its fruit is the *sannyāsin* [renouncer], he is the *yogin*, not he who does not light the sacred fire, and performs no rites.

2. What they call renunciation, that know to be disciplined activity, O Pāṇḍava (Arjuna), for no one becomes a *yogin* who has not renounced his selfish purpose.

The pathway and the goal

3. Work is said to be the means of the sage who wishes to attain to *yoga*; when he has attained to *yoga*, serenity is said to be the means.

4. When one does not get attached to the objects of sense or to works, and has renounced all purposes, then he is said to have attained to *yoga*.

5. Let a man lift himself by himself; let him not degrade himself; for the Self alone is the friend of the self and the Self alone is the enemy of the self.

6. For him who has conquered his [lower] self by the [higher] Self his Self is a friend, but for him who has not possessed his [higher] Self, his very Self will act in enmity, like an enemy.

7. When one has conquered one's [lower] self and has attained to the calm of self-mastery, his Supreme Self abides ever concentrate:[1] he is at peace in cold and heat, in pleasure and pain, in honour and dishonour.

8. The ascetic (*yogi*) whose soul is satisfied with wisdom and knowledge, who is unchanging and master of his senses, to whom a clod, a stone, and a piece of gold are the same, is said to be controlled [in *yoga*].

9. He who is equal-minded among friends, companions, and foes, among those who are neutral and impartial, among those who are hateful and related, among saints and sinners—he excels.

Eternal vigilance over body and mind is essential

10. Let the *yogin* try constantly to concentrate his mind [on the Supreme Self] remaining in solitude and alone, self-controlled, free from desires, and longing for possessions.

11. He should set in a clean place his firm seat, neither too high nor too low, covered with sacred grass, a deerskin, and a cloth, one over the other.

12. There taking his place on the seat, making his mind one-pointed, and controlling his thought and sense, let him practise *yoga* for the purification of the self.[2]

13. Holding the body, head, and neck erect and still, looking fixedly at the tip of his nose, without looking around [without allowing his eyes to wander].

14. Serene and fearless, firm in the vow of celibacy, subdued in mind, let him sit, harmonized, his mind turned to Me and intent on Me alone.

15. The *yogin* of subdued mind, ever keeping himself thus harmonized, attains to peace, the supreme *nirvāṇa*, which abides in Me.

[1] That is, established in itself, self-established.

[2] "*Yoga*" here means *dhyāna-yoga*, meditation.

16. Verily, *yoga* is not for him who eats too much or abstains too much from eating. It is not for him, O Arjuna, who sleeps too much or keeps awake too much.

17. For the man who is temperate in food and recreation, who is restrained in his actions, whose sleep and waking are regulated, there ensues discipline (*yoga*) which destroys all sorrow.

The perfect yogi [*yogī, or yogin*]

18. When the disciplined mind is established in the Self alone, liberated from all desires, then is he said to be harmonized [in *yoga*].

19. As a lamp in a windless place flickereth not, to such is likened the *yogi* of subdued thought who practises union with the Self [or discipline of himself].

20. That in which thought is at rest, restrained by the practice of concentration, that in which he beholds the Self through the self and rejoices in the Self,

21. That in which he finds this supreme delight, perceived by the intelligence and beyond the reach of the senses, wherein established, he no longer falls away from the truth,

22. That, on gaining which he thinks that there is no greater gain beyond it, wherein established he is not shaken even by the heaviest sorrow—

23. Let that be known by the name of *yoga*, this disconnection from union with pain. This *yoga* should be practised with determination, with heart undismayed.

24. Abandoning without exception all desires born of [selfish] will, restraining with the mind all the senses on every side,

25. Let him gain, little by little, tranquillity by means of reason controlled by steadiness, and, having fixed the mind on the Self, let him not think of anything else.

26. Whatsoever makes the wavering and unsteady mind wander away let him restrain and bring it back to the control of the Self alone,

27. For supreme happiness comes to the *yogin* whose mind is peaceful, whose passions are at rest, who is stainless and has become one with God.

28. Thus making the self ever harmonized, the *yogin*, who has put away sin, experiences easily the infinite bliss of contact with the Eternal.

29. He whose self is harmonized by *yoga* sees the Self abiding in all beings and all beings in the Self; everywhere he sees the same.

30. He who sees Me everywhere and sees all in Me—I am not lost to him nor is he lost to Me.

31. The *yogin* who, established in oneness, worships Me abiding in all beings lives in Me, howsoever he may be active,

32. He, O Arjuna, who sees with equality everything, in the image of his own self, whether in pleasure or in pain—he is considered a perfect *yogi*.

Control of mind is difficult but possible

Arjuna said:

33. This *yoga* declared by you to be of the nature of equality [evenness of mind], O Madhusūdana (Kṛṣṇa), I see no stable foundation for, on account of restlessness,

34. For the mind is verily fickle, O Kṛṣṇa; it is impetuous, strong, and obstinate. I think that it is as difficult to control as the wind.

The Blessed Lord said:

35. Without doubt, O Mighty-armed (Arjuna), the mind is difficult to curb and restless, but it can be controlled, O Son of Kuntī (Arjuna), by constant practice and non-attachment.

36. *Yoga* is hard to attain, I agree, by one who is not self-controlled; but by the self-controlled it is attainable by striving through proper means.

Arjuna said:

37. He who cannot control himself though he has faith, with the mind wandering away from *yoga*, failing to attain perfection in *yoga*—what way does he go, O Kṛṣṇa?

38. Does he not perish like a rent cloud, O Mighty-armed (Kṛṣṇa), fallen from both and without any hold and bewildered in the path that leads to the Eternal?

39. Thou shouldst dispel completely this, my doubt, O Kṛṣṇa, for there is none else than Thyself who can destroy this doubt.

The Blessed Lord said:

40. O, Pārtha (Arjuna), neither in this life nor hereafter is there destruction for him, for never does any one who does good, dear friend, tread the path of woe.

41. Having attained to the world of the righteous and dwelt there for very many years, the man who has fallen away from *yoga* is again born in the house of such as are pure and prosperous.

42. Or he may be born in the family of *yogins* who are endowed with wisdom. For such a birth as this is more difficult to obtain in the world.

43. There he regains the mental impressions of union [with the Divine] which he had developed in his previous life, and with this [as the starting point] he strives again for perfection, O Joy of the Kurus (Arjuna).

44. By his former practice, he is carried on irresistibly. Even the seeker after the knowledge of *yoga* goes beyond the Vedic rule.[1]

45. But the *yogi* who strives with assiduity, cleansed of all sins, perfecting himself through many lives, then attains to the highest goal.

The perfect yogi

46. The *yogin* is greater than the ascetic; he is considered to be greater than the man of knowledge, greater than the man of ritual works; therefore, do thou become a *yogin*, O Arjuna.

47. And of all *yogins*, he who full of faith worships Me, with his inner self abiding in me,—him I hold to be the most attuned to me [in *yoga*].

This is the sixth chapter, entitled "The *Yoga* of Meditation."

Chapter 7: God and the World

God is nature and spirit

The Blessed Lord said:

1. Hear then, O Pārtha (Arjuna), how, practising *yoga*, with the mind clinging to Me, with Me as thy refuge, thou shalt know Me in full, without any doubt.

2. I will declare to thee in full this wisdom together with knowledge[2] by knowing which there shall remain nothing more here left to be known.

3. Among thousands of men scarcely one strives for perfection, and of those who strive and succeed scarcely one knows Me in truth.

[1] "Vedic rule" refers to the Veda and the injunctions set forth in it. By practicing the Vedic rule, we are helped to get beyond it.

[2] *Jñāna* is interpreted as wisdom, the direct spiritual illumination, and *vijñāna* as the detailed rational knowledge of the principles of existence.

The two natures of the Lord

4. Earth, water, fire, air, ether, mind, and understanding, and self-sense—this is the eightfold division of My nature.

5. This is My lower nature. Know My other and higher nature which is the soul, by which this world is upheld, O Mighty-armed (Arjuna).

6. Know that all beings have their birth in this. I am the origin of all this world and its dissolution as well.

7. There is nothing whatever that is higher than I, O Winner of wealth (Arjuna). All that is here is strung on me as rows of gems on a string.

8. I am the taste in the waters, O Son of Kuntī (Arjuna). I am the light in the moon and the sun. I am the syllable *Aum* in all the Vedas. I am the sound in ether and manhood in men.

9. I am the pure fragrance in earth and brightness in fire. I am the life in all existences and the austerity in ascetics.

10. Know Me, O Pārtha (Arjuna), to be the eternal seed of all existences. I am the intelligence of the intelligent. I am the splendour of the splendid.

11. I am the strength of the strong, devoid of desire and passion. In beings am I the desire which is not contrary to law,[1] O Lord of the Bhāratas (Arjuna).

12. And whatever states of being there may be, be they harmonious, passionate, slothful—know thou that they are all from Me alone. I am not in them; they are in Me.

The modes of Nature confuse men

13. Deluded by these threefold modes of nature (*guṇas*) this whole world does not recognize Me who am above them and imperishable.

14. This divine *māyā* [power] of Mine, consisting of the modes, is hard to overcome. But those who take refuge in Me alone cross beyond it.

The state of evildoers

15. The evildoers who are foolish, low in the human scale, whose minds are carried away by illusion and who partake of the nature of demons do not seek refuge in Me.

[1] "Law" (*dharma*) refers to the moral law. Desire as such is not evil. Selfish desire requires to be rooted out. The desire for union with the Divine is not wrong.

Different kinds of devotion

16. The virtuous ones who worship Me are of four kinds, the man in distress, the seeker for knowledge, the seeker for wealth, and the man of wisdom, O Lord of the Bhāratas (Arjuna).

17. Of these, the wise one, who is ever in constant union with the Divine, whose devotion is single-minded, is the best, for I am supremely dear to him and he is dear to Me.

18. Noble indeed are all these, but the sage, I hold, is verily Myself, for, being perfectly harmonized, he resorts to Me alone as the highest goal.

19. At the end of many lives, the man of wisdom resorts to Me, knowing that Vāsudeva [the Supreme] is all that is. Such a great soul is very difficult to find.

Toleration

20. But those whose minds are distorted by desires resort to other gods, observing various rites, constrained by their own natures.

21. Whatever form[1] any devotee with faith wishes to worship, I make that faith of his steady.

22. Endowed with that faith, he seeks the worship of such a one and from him he obtains his desires, the benefits being decreed by Me alone.

23. But temporary is the fruit gained by these men of small minds. The worshippers of the gods go to the gods but My devotees come to Me.

The power of ignorance

24. Men of no understanding think of Me, the unmanifest, as having manifestation, not knowing My higher nature, changeless and supreme.

25. Veiled by My creative power (*yogamāyā*), I am not revealed to all. This bewildered world knows Me not, the unborn, the unchanging.

26. I know the beings that are past, that are present, O Arjuna, and that are to come, but Me no one knows.

27. All beings are born deluded, O Bhārata (Arjuna), overcome by the dualities which arise from wish and hate, O Conqueror of the foe (Arjuna).

[1] That is, whatever form of the Divine.

The object of knowledge

28. But those men of virtuous deeds in whom sin has come to an end [who have died to sin], freed from the delusion of dualities, worship Me steadfast in their vows.

29. Those who take refuge in Me and strive for deliverance from old age and death—they know the *Brahman* [or the Absolute] entire; they know the Self and all about action.

30. Those who know Me as the One that governs the material and the divine aspects, and all sacrifices—they, with their minds harmonized, have knowledge of Me even at the time of their departure from here.

This is the seventh chapter, entitled "The *Yoga* of Wisdom and Knowledge."

Chapter 8: The Course of Cosmic Evolution

Arjuna questions

Arjuna said:

1. What is *Brahman* [or the Absolute]? What is the Self, and what is action, O the Best of persons? What is said to be the basis of the elements? What is called the basis of the gods?

2. What is the basis of sacrifice in this body, and how, O Madhusūdana (Kṛṣṇa)? How, again, art Thou to be known at the time of departure by the self-controlled?

Kṛṣṇa answers

The Blessed Lord said:

3. *Brahman* [or the Absolute] is the indestructible, the Supreme [higher than all else], essential nature is called the Self. *Karma* is the name given to the creative force that brings beings into existence.

4. The basis of all created things is the mutable nature; the basis of the divine elements is the cosmic spirit. And the basis of all sacrifices, here in the body, is Myself, O Best of embodied beings (Arjuna).

The soul goes to that on which it is set at the moment of dissolution

5. And whoever, at the time of death, gives up his body and departs, thinking of Me alone, he comes to My status of being; of that there is no doubt.

6. Thinking of whatever state (of being) he at the end gives up his body, to that being does he attain, O Son of Kuntī (Arjuna), being ever absorbed in the thought thereof.

7. Therefore, at all times remember Me and fight. When thy mind and understanding are set on Me, to Me alone shalt thou come without doubt.

8. He who meditates on the Supreme Person with his thought attuned by constant practice and not wandering after anything else—he, O Pārtha (Arjuna), reaches the Person, Supreme and Divine.

9. He who meditates on the Seer, the ancient, the ruler, subtler than the subtle, the supporter of all, whose form is beyond conception, who is sun-coloured beyond the darkness.

10. He who does so, at the time of his departure, with a steady mind, devotion, and strength of *yoga*, and setting well his life force in the centre of the eyebrows—he attains to this Supreme Divine Person.

11. I shall briefly describe to thee that state which the knowers of the Veda call the Imperishable, which ascetics freed from passion enter and desiring which they lead a life of self-control.

12. All the gates of the body[1] restrained, the mind confined within the heart, one's lifeforce fixed in the head, established in concentration by *yoga*,

13. He who utters the single syllable *Aum*[2] which is *Brahman*, remembering Me as he departs, giving up his body—he goes to the highest goal.

14. He who constantly meditates on Me, thinking of none else—by him who is a *yogin* ever disciplined [or united with the Supreme], I am easily reached.

15. Having come to Me, these great souls do not get back to rebirth, the place of sorrow, impermanent, for they have reached the highest perfection.

16. From the realm of Brahmā downwards, all worlds are subject to return to rebirth, but on reaching Me, O Son of Kuntī (Arjuna), there is no return to birth again.

17. Those who know that the day of Brahmā is of the duration of a thousand ages and that the night of Brahmā is a thousand ages long—they are the knowers of day and night.

18. At the coming of day, all manifested things come forth from

[1] See above, v.13.

[2] *Aum* stands for the inexpressible Absolute.

the unmanifested, and at the coming of night they merge in that same, called the unmanifested.

19. This very same multitude of existences arising again and again merges helplessly at the coming of night, O Pārtha (Arjuna), and streams forth into being at the coming of day.

20. But beyond this unmanifested, there is yet another Unmanifested Eternal Being who does not perish even when all existences perish.

21. This Unmanifested is called the Imperishable. Him they speak of as the Supreme Status. Those who attain to Him return not. That is My supreme abode.

22. This is the Supreme Person, O Pārtha (Arjuna), in whom all existences abide and by whom all this is pervaded, who can, however, be gained by unswerving devotion.

The two ways

23. Now I shall declare to thee, O Best of Bhāratas (Arjuna), the time in which *yogins*, departing, never return, and also that wherein, departing, they return.

24. Fire, light, day, the bright half of the month, the six months of the northern path of the sun, then going forth the men who know the Absolute go to the Absolute.

25. Smoke, night, so also the dark half of the month, the six months of the southern path of the sun, then going forth the *yogi* obtains the lunar light and returns.[1]

26. Light and darkness, these paths are thought to be the world's everlasting paths. By the one he goes not to return, by the other he returns again.

27. The *yogin* who knows these paths, O Pārtha (Arjuna), is never deluded. Therefore, at all times, O Arjuna, be thou firm in *yoga*.

28. The *yogin*, having known all this, goes beyond the fruits of meritorious deeds assigned to the study of the Vedas, sacrifices, austerities, and gifts, and attains to the supreme and primal status.

This is the eighth chapter, entitled "The *Yoga* of the Imperishable Absolute."

[1] Our dead ancestors (*pitṛs*) are said to live in the world of the moon and remain there till the time of their return to earth.

Chapter 9: The Lord is more than His Creation

The sovereign mystery

The Blessed Lord said:

1. To Thee, who dost not cavil, I shall declare this profound secret of wisdom combined with knowledge, by knowing which thou shalt be released from evil.

2. This is sovereign knowledge, sovereign secret, supreme sanctity, known by direct experience, in accord with the law, very easy to practise and imperishable.

3. Men who have no faith in this way, not attaining to Me, O Oppressor of the foe (Arjuna), return to the path of mortal living (*saṁsāra*).

The incarnate Lord as the supreme reality

4. By Me all this universe is pervaded through My unmanifested form. All beings abide in Me but I do not abide in them.[1]

5. And (yet) the beings do not dwell in Me; behold My divine mystery. My spirit which is the source of all beings sustains the beings but does not abide in them.[2]

6. As the mighty air moving everywhere ever, abides in the etheric space, know thou that in the same manner all existences abide in Me.

7. All beings, O Son of Kuntī (Arjuna), pass into nature which is My own at the end of the cycle; and at the beginning of the next cycle I send them forth.

8. Taking hold of nature which is My own, I send forth again and again all this multitude of beings which are helpless, being under the control of Nature (*prakṛti*).

9. Nor do these works bind Me, O winner of wealth (Arjuna), for I am seated as if indifferent, unattached in those actions.

10. Under My guidance, Nature (*prakṛti*) gives birth to all things, moving and unmoving, and by this means, O Son of Kuntī (Arjuna), the world revolves.

[1] This whole universe owes its being to the Transcendent Godhead and yet the forms of this universe do not contain or express Him adequately. His absolute reality is far above the appearance of things in space and time.

[2] The Supreme is the source of all phenomena but is not touched by them. That is the *yoga* of divine power. Though He creates existences, God transcends them to such a degree that we cannot even say that He dwells in them. Even the idea of immanence of God is, strictly speaking, untenable. All existences are due to His double nature but as His higher proper nature is *Ātman* which is unconnected with the work of *prakṛti*, it is also true that beings do not dwell in Him or He in them. They are one and yet separate.

Devotion to the Supreme brings its great reward: lesser devotions bring lesser rewards

11. The deluded despise Me clad in human body, not knowing My higher nature as Lord of all existences.

12. Partaking of the deceptive nature of fiends and demons, their aspirations are vain, their actions vain, and their knowledge vain, and they are devoid of judgment.

13. The great-souled, O Pārtha (Arjuna), who abide in the divine nature, knowing [Me as] the imperishable source of all beings, worship Me with an undistracted mind.

14. Always glorifying Me, strenuous and steadfast in vows, bowing down to Me with devotion, they worship Me, ever disciplined.

15. Others, again, sacrifice with the sacrifice of wisdom and worship Me as the one, as the distinct and as the manifold, facing in all directions.

16. I am the ritual action, I am the sacrifice, I am the ancestral oblation, I am the medicinal herb, I am the sacred hymn, I am also the melted butter, I am the fire, and I am the offering.

17. I am the father of this world, the mother, the supporter, and the grandsire. I am the object of knowledge, the purifier. I am the syllable *Aum*, and I am the *ṛk*, the *sāma* and the *yajus*[1] as well.

18. I am the goal, the upholder, the lord, the witness, the abode, the refuge, and the friend. I am the origin and the dissolution, the ground, the resting place, and the imperishable seed.

19. I give heat; I withhold and send forth the rain. I am immortality and also death; I am being as well as non-being, O Arjuna.

20. The knowers of the three Vedas who drink the *soma* juice and are cleansed of sin, worshipping Me with sacrifices, pray for the way to heaven. They reach the holy world of Indra [the lord of heaven] and enjoy in heaven the pleasures of the gods.

21. Having enjoyed the spacious world of heaven, they enter [return to] the world of mortals, when their merit is exhausted; thus conforming to the doctrine enjoined in the three Vedas and desirous of enjoyments, they obtain the changeable [what is subject to birth and death].

22. But those who worship Me, meditating on Me alone—to them who ever persevere, I bring attainment of what they have not and security in what they have.

[1] That is, the *Ṛg Veda*, the *Sāma Veda*, and the *Yajur Veda*.

23. Even those who are devotees of other gods, worship them with faith—they also sacrifice to Me alone, O Son of Kuntī (Arjuna), though not according to the true law,

24. For I am the enjoyer and lord of all sacrifices. But these men do not know Me in My true nature, and so they fall.

25. Worshippers of the gods go to the gods, worshippers of the manes[1] go to the manes, sacrificers to the spirits go to the spirits, and those who sacrifice to Me come to Me.

Devotion and its effects

26. Whosoever offers to Me with devotion a leaf, a flower, a fruit, or water—that offering of love, of the pure of heart, I accept.

27. Whatever thou doest, whatever thou eatest, whatever thou offerest, whatever thou givest away, whatever austerities thou dost practise—do that, O Son of Kuntī (Arjuna), as an offering to Me.

28. Thus shalt thou be freed from the good and evil results which are the bonds of action. With thy mind firmly set on the way of renunciation, thou shalt become free and attain to Me.

29. I am alike to all beings. None is hateful or dear to Me. But those who worship Me with devotion—they are in Me and I also in them.

30. Even if a man of the most vile conduct worships me with undistracted devotion, he must be reckoned as righteous for he has rightly resolved.

31. Swiftly does he become a soul of righteousness and obtain lasting peace. O Son of Kuntī (Arjuna), know thou for certain that My devotee perishes never.

32. For those who take refuge in Me, O Pārtha (Arjuna), though they are lowly born, women, *vaiśyas* (merchants or traders), as well as *śūdras* (workers)—they also attain to the highest goal—

33. How much more, then, holy *brāhmins* (priest-teachers) and devoted royal saints, having entered this impermanent sorrowful world, do thou worship Me.

34. On Me fix thy mind; to Me be devoted; worship Me; revere Me; thus having disciplined thyself, with Me as thy goal, to Me shalt thou come.

This is the ninth chapter, entitled "The *Yoga* of Sovereign Knowledge and Sovereign Mystery."

[1] Ancestors.

Chapter 10: God is the Source of all: to know Him is to know all

The Immanence and Transcendence of God

The Blessed Lord said:

1. Again, O Mighty-armed (Arjuna), hearken to My supreme word. From a desire to do thee good, I will declare it to thee, now that thou art taking delight [in My words].

2. Neither the hosts of gods nor the great sages know any origin of Me for I am the source of the gods and the great sages in every way.

3. He who knows Me, the unborn, without beginning, also the mighty lord of the worlds, he, among mortals is undeluded and freed from all sins.

4. Understanding, knowledge, freedom from bewilderment, patience, truth, self-control and calmness; pleasure and pain, existence and non-existence, fear and fearlessness.

5. Non-violence, equal-mindedness, contentment, austerity, charity, fame and ill-fame, the different states of beings proceed from Me alone.

6. The seven great sages of old, and the four Manus also are of My nature and born of My mind and from them are all these creatures in the world.[1]

7. He who knows in truth this glory and power of Mine is united [with Me] by unfaltering *yoga*; of this there is no doubt.

Knowledge and devotion

8. I am the origin of all; from Me all [the whole creation] proceeds. Knowing this, the wise worship Me, endowed with meditation.

9. Their thoughts [are fixed] in Me, their lives [are wholly] given up to Me, enlightening each other and ever conversing of Me, they are contented and rejoicing in Me.

10. To these who are in constant union with Me and worship Me with love, I grant the power of understanding by which they come unto Me.

11. Out of compassion for those same ones, remaining within My own true state, I destroy the darkness born of ignorance by the shining lamp of wisdom.

[1] These are the powers in charge of the many processes of the world. Manu according to tradition is the first man at the beginning of each new race of beings.

The Lord is the seed and perfection of all that is

Arjuna said:

12. Thou art the Supreme *Brahman*, the Supreme Abode and the Supreme Purifier, the Eternal, Divine Person, the First of the gods, the Unborn, the All-pervading.

13. All the sages say this of Thee, as well as the divine seer Nārada, so also Asita, Devala, Vyāsa and Thou thyself declarest it to me.

14. I hold as true, all this that thou sayest to me, O Keśava (Kṛṣṇa); neither the gods nor the demons, O Lord, know Thy manifestation.

15. Verily Thou Thyself knowest Thyself by Thyself, O Supreme Person; the Source of beings, the Lord of creatures; the God of gods, the Lord of the world!

16. Thou shouldst tell me of Thy divine manifestations, without exception, whereby, pervading these worlds, Thou dost abide [in them and beyond].

17. How may I know Thee, O *Yogin*, by constant meditation? In what various aspects art Thou, O Blessed Lord, to be thought of by me?

18. Relate to me again in detail, O Janārdana (Kṛṣṇa), of Thy power and manifestation; for I am not satiated with hearing Thy nectar-like speech.

The Blessed Lord said:

19. Yes, I will declare to thee of My divine forms but only of those which are prominent, O best of the Kurus (Arjuna), for there is no end to my extent (the details).

20. I, O Guḍākeśa (Arjuna), am the self seated in the hearts of all creatures. I am the beginning, the middle and the very end of beings.

21. Of the Ādityas I am Viṣṇu; of the lights (I am) the radiant sun; I am Marīci of the Maruts; of the stars I am the moon.

22. Of the Vedas I am the *Sāma Veda*; of the gods I am Indra; of the senses I am mind and of beings I am consciousness.

23. Of the Rudras I am Śaṁkara (Śiva); of the Yakṣas and the Rākṣasas (I am) Kubera; of the Vasus I am Agni (Fire) and of mountain-peaks I am Meru.

24. Of the household priests, O Pārtha (Arjuna), know Me to be the chief—Bṛhaspati; of the (war) generals I am Skanda; of the lakes I am the ocean.

25. Of the great sages I am Bhṛgu; of utterances, I am the single syllable *Aum*; of offerings I am the offering of silent meditation and of unmovable things (I am) the Himālaya.

26. Of all trees (I am) the Aśvattha and of divine seers (I am) Nārada; among the Gandharvas (I am) Citraratha and of the perfected ones (I am) Kapila the sage.

27. Of horses, know me to be Ucchaihśravas, born of nectar; of lordly elephants (I am) Airāvata and of men (I am) the monarch.

28. Of weapons I am the thunderbolt; of the cows I am the cow of plenty; of the progenitors I am the God of love; of the serpents I am Vāsuki.

29. Of the *nāgas* I am Ananta; of the dwellers in water I am Varuṇa; of the (departed) ancestors I am Aryama; of those who maintain law and order, I am Yama.

30. Of the Titans I am Prahlāda; of calculators I am Time; of beasts I am the King of beasts (lion) and of birds (I am) the son of Vinatā (Garuḍa).

31. Of purifiers I am the wind; of warriors I am Rāma; of fishes I am the alligator and of rivers I am the Ganges.

32. Of creations I am the beginning, the end and also the middle, O Arjuna; of the sciences (I am) the science of the self; of those who debate I am the dialectic.

33. Of letters I am (the letter) A and of compounds (I am) the dual; I also am imperishable time and I the creator whose face is turned on all sides.

34. I am death, the all-devouring and (am) the origin of things that are yet to be; and of feminine beings, (I am) fame, prosperity, speech, memory, intelligence, firmness and patience.

35. Likewise, of hymns (I am) Bṛhatsāman, of metres (I am) *gāyatrī*; of months (I am) Mārgaśīrṣa and of seasons (I am) the flower-bearer (spring).

36. Of the deceitful I am the gambling; of the splendid I am the splendour; I am victory; I am effort and I am the goodness of the good.

37. Of the Vṛṣṇis I am Vāsudeva; of the Pāṇḍavas (I am) the Winner of wealth (Arjuna); of the sages I am Vyāsa also and of the poets (I am) the poet Uśanā.

38. Of those who chastise I am the rod (of chastisement); of those that seek victory I am the wise policy; of things secret I am the silence and of the knowers of wisdom I am the wisdom.

39. And further, whatsoever is the seed of all existences that am I, O Arjuna; nor is there anything, moving or unmoving that can exist without Me.

40. There is no end to My divine manifestations, O Conqueror of the foe (Arjuna). What has been declared by Me is only illustrative of My infinite glory.

41. Whatsoever being there is, endowed with glory and grace and vigour, know that to have sprung from a fragment of My splendour.

42. But what need is there, O Arjuna, for such detailed knowledge by you? I support this entire universe pervading it with a single fraction of Myself.

This is the tenth chapter, entitled "The *Yoga* of Manifestation."

Chapter 11: The Lord's Transfiguration

Arjuna wishes to see the universal form of God

Arjuna said:

1. The supreme mystery, the discourse concerning the Self which thou hast given out of grace for me—by this my bewilderment is gone from me.

2. The birth and passing away of things have been heard by me in detail from Thee, O Lotus-eyed (Kṛṣṇa), as also Thy imperishable majesty.

3. As Thou hast declared Thyself to be, O Supreme Lord, even so it is. (But) I desire to see Thy divine form, O Supreme Person.

4. If Thou, O Lord, thinkest that by me, It can be seen, then reveal to me, Thy Imperishable Self, O Lord of *yoga* (Kṛṣṇa).

The Revelation of the Lord

The Blessed Lord said:

5. Behold, O Pārtha (Arjuna), My forms, a hundredfold, a thousandfold, various in kind, divine, of various colours and shapes.

6. Behold, the Ādityas, the Vasus, the Rudras, the two Aśvins and also the Maruts. Behold, O Bhārata (Arjuna), many wonders never seen before.

7. Here today, behold the whole universe, moving and unmoving and whatever else thou desirest to see, O Gudākeśa (Arjuna), all unified in My body.

8. But thou canst not behold Me with this [human] eye of yours; I will bestow on thee the supernatural eye. Behold My divine power.

Saṁjaya describes the form

Saṁjaya said:

9. Having thus spoken, O King, Hari, the great lord of *yoga*, then revealed to Pārtha (Arjuna), His Supreme and Divine Form.[1]

10. Of many mouths and eyes, of many visions of marvel, of many divine ornaments, of many divine uplifted weapons.

11. Wearing divine garlands and raiments, with divine perfumes and ointments, made up of all wonders, resplendent, boundless, with face turned everywhere.

12. If the light of a thousand suns were to blaze forth all at once in the sky, that might resemble the splendour of that exalted Being.

13. There the Pāṇḍava (Arjuna) beheld the whole universe, with its manifold divisions gathered together in one, in the body of the God of gods.

Arjuna addresses the Lord

14. Then he, the Winner of wealth (Arjuna), struck with amazement, his hair standing on end, bowed down his head to the Lord, with hands folded [in salutation], said:

15. In Thy body, O God, I see all the gods and the varied hosts of beings as well, Brahmā, the Lord seated on the lotus throne and all the sages and heavenly *nāgas*.

16. I behold Thee, infinite in form on all sides, with numberless arms, bellies, faces and eyes, but I see not Thy end or Thy middle or Thy beginning, O Lord of the universe, O Form Universal.

17. I behold Thee with Thy crown, mace and discus, glowing everywhere as a mass of light, hard to discern, [dazzling] on all sides with the radiance of the flaming fire and sun, incomparable.

18. Thou art the Imperishable, the Supreme to be realized. Thou art the ultimate resting-place of the universe; Thou art the undying guardian of the eternal law. Thou art the Primal Person, I think.[2]

19. I behold Thee as one without beginning, middle or end, of infinite power, of numberless arms, with the moon and the sun as Thine eyes, with Thy face as a flaming fire, whose radiance burns up this universe.

[1] This is Kṛṣṇa's transfiguration where Arjuna sees all the creatures in heaven and earth in the Divine Form.

[2] Arjuna states that the Supreme is both *Brahman* and Īśvara, Absolute and God.

20. This space between heaven and earth is pervaded by Thee alone, also all the quarters [directions of the sky]. O Exalted One, when this wondrous, terrible form of Thine is seen, the three worlds tremble.

21. Yonder hosts of gods enter Thee and some, in fear, extol Thee, with folded hands, and bands of great seers and perfected ones cry "hail" and adore Thee with hymns of abounding praise.

22. The Rudras, the Ādityas, the Vasus, the Sādhyas; the Viśvas, the two Aśvins, the Maruts and the manes and the hosts of Gandharvas, Yakṣas, Asuras and Siddhas, all gaze at Thee and are quite amazed.

23. Seeing Thy great form, of many mouths and eyes, O Mighty-armed, of many arms, thighs and feet, of many bellies, terrible with many tusks, the worlds tremble and so do I.

24. When I see Thee touching the sky, blazing with many hues, with the mouth opened wide, and large glowing eyes, my inmost soul trembles in fear and I find neither steadiness nor peace, O Viṣṇu!

25. When I see Thy mouths terrible with their tusks, like Time's devouring flames, I lose sense of the directions and find no peace. Be gracious, O Lord of gods, Refuge of the worlds!

26. All yonder sons of Dhṛtarāṣṭra together with the hosts of kings and also Bhīṣma, Droṇa and Karṇa along with the chief warriors on our side too,—

27. Are rushing into Thy fearful mouths set with terrible tusks. Some caught between the teeth are seen with their heads crushed to powder.

28. As the many rushing torrents of rivers race towards the ocean, so do these heroes of the world of men rush into Thy flaming mouths.

29. As moths rush swiftly into a blazing fire to perish there, so do these men rush into Thy mouths with great speed to their own destruction.

30. Devouring all the worlds on every side with Thy flaming mouths, thou lickest them up. Thy fiery rays fill this whole universe and scorch it with their fierce radiance, O Viṣṇu!

31. Tell me who Thou art with form so terrible. Salutation to Thee, O Thou Great Godhead, have mercy. I wish to know Thee [who art] the Primal One, for I know not Thy working.

God as the judge

The Blessed Lord said:

32. Time am I, world-destroying, grown mature, engaged here in subduing the world. Even without thee [thy action], all the warriors standing arrayed in the opposing armies shall cease to be.

33. Therefore arise thou and gain glory. Conquering thy foes, enjoy a prosperous kingdom. By Me alone are they slain already. Be thou merely the occasion, O Savyasācin (Arjuna).

34. Slay Droṇa, Bhīṣma, Jayadratha, Karṇa and other great warriors as well, who are already doomed by Me. Be not afraid. Fight, thou shalt conquer the enemies in battle.

Saṁjaya said:

35. Having heard this utterance of Keśava (Kṛṣṇa), Kirīṭin (Arjuna), with folded hands and trembling, saluted again and prostrating himself with great fear, spoke in a faltering voice to Kṛṣṇa.

Arjuna's hymn of praise

Arjuna said:

36. O Hṛṣīkeśa (Kṛṣṇa), rightly does the world rejoice and delight in Thy magnificence. The Rākṣasas are fleeing in terror in all directions and all the hosts of perfected ones are bowing down before Thee (in adoration).

37. And why should they not do Thee homage, O Exalted One, who art greater than Brahmā, the original creator? O Infinite Being, Lord of the gods, Refuge of the universe, Thou art the Imperishable, the being and the non-being and what is beyond that.

38. Thou art the First of gods, the Primal Person, the Supreme Resting Place of the world. Thou art the knower and that which is to be known and the supreme goal. And by Thee is this universe pervaded, O Thou of infinite form!

39. Thou art Vāyu [the wind], Yama [the destroyer], Agni [the fire], Varuṇa [the sea-god] and Śaśānka [the moon], and Prajāpati, the grandsire [of all]. Hail, hail to Thee, a thousand times. Hail, hail to Thee again and yet again.

40. Hail to Thee in front, [hail] to Thee behind and hail to Thee on every side, O All; boundless in power and immeasurable in might, Thou dost penetrate all and therefore Thou art All.

41. For whatsoever I have spoken in rashness to Thee, thinking that Thou art my companion and unaware of this [fact of] Thy

greatness, "O Kṛṣṇa, O Yādava, O Comrade"; out of my negligence or may be through fondness,

42. And for whatsoever disrespect was shown to Thee in jest, while at play or on the bed or seated or at meals, either alone or in the presence of others, I pray, O Unshaken One, forgiveness from Thee, the Immeasurable.

43. Thou art the father of the world of the moving and the unmoving. Thou art the object of its worship and its venerable teacher. None is equal to Thee; how then could there be one greater than Thee in the three worlds, O Thou of incomparable greatness?

44. Therefore bowing down and prostrating my body before Thee, Adorable Lord, I seek Thy grace. Thou, O God, shouldst bear with me as a father to his son, as a friend to his friend, as a lover to his beloved.

45. I have seen what was never seen before and I rejoice but my heart is shaken with fear. Show me that other [previous] form of Thine, O God, and be gracious, O Lord of the gods and Refuge of the Universe!

46. I wish to see Thee even as before with Thy crown, mace, and disc in Thy hand. Assume Thy four-armed shape, O Thou of a thousand arms and of universal form.[1]

The Lord's grace and assurance

The Blessed Lord said:

47. By My grace, through My divine power, O Arjuna, was shown to thee this supreme form, luminous, universal, infinite and primal which none but thee has seen before.

48. Neither by the Vedas, [nor by] sacrifices nor by study nor by gifts nor by ceremonial rites nor by severe austerities can I with this form be seen in the world of men by any one else but thee, O hero of the Kurus (Arjuna).

49. May you not be afraid, may you not be bewildered seeing this terrific form of Mine. Free from fear and glad at heart, behold again this other [former] form of Mine.

Saṁjaya said:

50. Having thus spoken to Arjuna, Vāsudeva (Kṛṣṇa) revealed to him again His own form. The Exalted One, having assumed again the form of grace, comforted the terrified Arjuna.

[1] Arjuna is asking Kṛṣṇa to assume the shape of Viṣṇu of whom He is said to be an incarnation.

Arjuna said:

51. Beholding again this Thy gracious human form, O Janārdana (Kṛṣṇa), I have now become collected in mind and am restored to my normal nature.

The Blessed Lord said:

52. This form of Mine which is indeed very hard to see, thou hast seen. Even the gods are ever eager to see this form.

53. In the form in which thou hast seen Me now, I cannot be seen either by the Vedas or by austerities or by gifts or by sacrifices.

54. But by unswerving devotion to Me, O Arjuna, I can be thus known, truly seen and entered into, O Oppressor of the foe (Arjuna).

55. He who does work for Me, he who looks upon Me as his goal, he who worships Me, free from attachment, who is free from enmity to all creatures, he goes to Me, O Pāṇḍava (Arjuna).

This is the eleventh chapter, entitled "The Vision of the Cosmic Form."

Chapter 12: Worship of the Personal Lord is better than Meditation of the Absolute

Devotion and contemplation

Arjuna said:

1. Those devotees who, thus ever harmonized, worship Thee and those, again, who worship the Imperishable and the Unmanifested—which of these have the greater knowledge of *yoga*?

The Blessed Lord said:

2. Those who fixing their minds on Me worship Me, ever harmonized and possessed of supreme faith—them do I consider most perfect in *yoga*.

3. But those who worship the Imperishable, the Undefinable, the Unmanifested, the Omnipresent, the Unthinkable, the Unchanging and the Immobile, the Constant,

4. By restraining all the senses, being even-minded in all conditions, rejoicing in the welfare of all creatures—they come to Me indeed [just like the others].

5. The difficulty of those whose thoughts are set on the Unmanifested is greater, for the goal of the Unmanifested is hard to reach by the embodied beings.

Different approaches

6. But those who, laying all their actions on Me, intent on Me, worship, meditating on Me, with unswerving devotion,

7. These whose thoughts are set on Me, I straightway deliver from the ocean of death-bound existence, O Pārtha (Arjuna).

8. On Me alone fix thy mind, let thy understanding dwell in Me; In Me alone shalt thou live thereafter. Of this there is no doubt.

9. If, however, thou art not able to fix thy thought steadily on Me, then seek to reach Me by the practice of concentration, O winner of wealth (Arjuna).

10. If thou art unable even to seek by practice, then be as one whose supreme aim is My service; even performing actions for My sake, thou shalt attain perfection.

11. If thou art not able to do even this, then, taking refuge in My disciplined activity, renounce the fruit of all action, with the self subdued.

12. Better indeed is knowledge than the practice of concentration; better than knowledge is meditation; better than meditation is the renunciation of the fruit of action; on renunciation follows immediately peace.

The true devotee

13. He who has no ill will to any being, who is friendly and compassionate, free from egoism and self-sense, even-minded in pain and pleasure, and patient,

14. The *yogi* who is ever content, self-controlled, unshakable in determination, with mind and understanding given up to Me—he, My devotee, is dear to Me.

15. He from whom the world does not shrink and who does not shrink from the world and who is free from joy and anger, fear and agitation—he too is dear to Me.

16. He who has no expectation, is pure, skilful in action, unconcerned, and untroubled, who has given up all initiative in action—he, My devotee, is dear to Me.

17. He who neither rejoices nor hates, neither grieves nor desires, and who has renounced good and evil—he who is thus devoted is dear to Me.

18. He who [behaves] alike to foe and friend, also to good and evil repute, and who is alike in cold and heat, pleasure and pain, and who is free from attachment,

19. He who holds equal blame and praise, who is silent [restrained in speech], content with anything that comes, who has no fixed abode and is firm in mind—that man who is devoted is dear to Me.

20. But those who with faith, holding Me as their supreme aim, follow this immortal wisdom—those devotees are exceedingly dear to Me.

This is the twelfth chapter, entitled "The *Yoga* of Devotion."

Chapter 13: The Body called the Field, the Soul called the Knower of the Field, and Discrimination between them

The field and the knower of the field

Arjuna said:

Prakṛti and *puruṣa*, the field and the knower of the field,[1] knowledge and the object of knowledge—these I should like to know, O Keśava (Kṛṣṇa).[2]

The Blessed Lord said:

1. This body, O Son of Kuntī (Arjuna), is called the field, and him who knows this those who know thereof call the knower of the field.

2. Know Me as the Knower of the field in all fields, O Bhārata (Arjuna). The knowledge of the field and its knower do I regard as true knowledge.

3. Hear briefly from Me what the field is, of what nature, what its modifications are, whence it is, what he [the knower of the field] is, and what his powers are.

4. This has been sung by sages in many ways and distinctly, in various hymns and also in well-reasoned and conclusive expressions of the aphorisms of the Absolute [*Brahma Sūtra*].[3]

5. The great [five gross] elements, self-sense, understanding, as also the unmanifested, the ten senses and mind, and the five objects of the senses,[4]

[1] *Prakṛti* (Nature) is unconscious activity, and *puruṣa* (the self) is inactive consciousness. The body is called the field in which events happen; all growth, decline, and death take place in it. The conscious principle, inactive and detached, which lies behind all active states as witness, is the knower of the field. See also below, Chapter XII, on the Sāṁkhya system.

[2] This verse is not found in some editions. If it is included, the total number of verses in the *Bhagavad-gītā* will be 701 and not 700, which is the number traditionally accepted. So we do not include it in the numbering of the verses.

[3] The *Gītā* suggests that it is expounding the truths already contained in the Vedas, the Upaniṣads, and the *Brahma Sūtra* or the aphorisms of *Brahman* later systematized by Bādarāyaṇa.

[4] See below, Chapter XII.

6. Desire and hatred, pleasure and pain, the aggregate [the organism], intelligence, and steadfastness described—this in brief is the field along with its modifications.

Knowledge

7. Humility [absence of pride], integrity [absence of deceit], non-violence, patience, uprightness, service of the teacher, purity of body and mind, steadfastness, and self-control,

8. Indifference to the objects of sense, self-effacement, and the perception of the evil of birth, death, old age, sickness, and pain,

9. Non-attachment, absence of clinging to son, wife, home, and the like, and a constant equal-mindedness to all desirable and undesirable happenings,

10. Unswerving devotion to Me with wholehearted discipline, resort to solitary places, dislike for a crowd of people,

11. Constancy in the knowledge of the Spirit, insight into the end of the knowledge of Truth—this is declared to be true knowledge, and all that is different from it is non-knowledge.

12. I will describe that which is to be known and by knowing which life eternal is gained. It is the Supreme *Brahman* who is beginningless and who is said to be neither existent nor non-existent.

The knower of the field

13. With his hands and feet everywhere, with eyes, heads, and faces on all sides, with ears on all sides, He dwells in the world, enveloping all.

14. He appears to have the qualities of all the senses and yet is without any of the senses, unattached and yet supporting all, free from the *guṇas* [dispositions of *prakṛti*] and yet enjoying them.

15. He is without and within all beings. He is unmoving as also moving. He is too subtle to be known. He is far away and yet is He near.

16. He is undivided [indivisible] and yet He seems to be divided among beings. He is to be known as supporting creatures, destroying them and creating them afresh.

17. He is the Light of lights, said to be beyond darkness. Knowledge, the object of knowledge, and the goal of knowledge—He is seated in the hearts of all.

The fruit of knowledge

18. Thus the field, also knowledge and the object of knowledge have been briefly described. My devotee who understands thus becomes worthy of My state.

Nature and spirit

19. Know thou that *prakṛti* [Nature] and *puruṣa* [soul] are both beginningless; and know also that the forms and modes are born of *prakṛti*.[1]

20. Nature is said to be the cause of effect, instrument, and agent-(ness) and the soul is said to be the cause, in regard to the experience of pleasure and pain.

21. The soul in nature enjoys the modes born of nature. Attachment to the modes is the cause of its births in good and evil wombs.

22. The Supreme Spirit in the body is said to be the Witness, the Permitter, the Supporter, the Experiencer, the Great Lord and the Supreme Self.

23. He who thus knows soul (*puruṣa*) and Nature (*prakṛti*) together with the modes (*guṇas*)—though he act in every way, he is not born again.

Different roads to salvation

24. By meditation some perceive the Self in the self by the self; others by the path of knowledge and still others by the path of works.

25. Yet others, ignorant of this [these paths of *yoga*], hearing from others, worship; and they too cross beyond death by their devotion to what they have heard.

26. Whatever being is born, moving or unmoving, know thou, O Best of the Bhāratas (Arjuna), that it is sprung through the union of the field and the knower of the field.

27. He who sees the Supreme Lord abiding equally in all beings, never perishing when they perish—he, verily, sees,

28. For, as he sees the Lord present, equally everywhere, he does not injure his true Self by the self and then he attains to the supreme goal.

29. He who sees that all actions are done only by Nature (*prakṛti*) and likewise that the self is not the doer—he verily sees.

[1] The *puruṣa* described in this section is not the multiple *puruṣa* of the Sāṁkhya (see below, Chapter XII). The *Gītā* does not look upon *prakṛti* and *puruṣa* as two independent elements as the Sāṁkhya does, but looks upon them as the inferior and the superior forms of one and the same Supreme.

30. When he sees that the manifold state of beings is centred in the One and from which alone they spread out, then he attains *Brahman.*

31. Because this Supreme Self, imperishable, is without beginning, without qualities, so, O Son of Kuntī (Arjuna), though It dwells in the body, It neither acts nor is tainted.

32. As the all-pervading ether is not tainted, by reason of its subtlety, even so the Self that is present in every body does not suffer any taint.

33. As the one sun illumines this whole world, so does the Lord of the field illumine this entire field, O Bhārata (Arjuna).

34. Those who perceive thus by their eye of wisdom the distinction between the field and the knower of the field, and the deliverance of beings from Nature (*prakṛti*)—they attain to the Supreme.

This is the thirteenth chapter, entitled "The *Yoga* of the Distinction between the Field and the Knower of the Field."

Chapter 14: The Mystical Father of All Beings

The highest knowledge

The Blessed Lord said:

1. I shall again declare that supreme wisdom, of all wisdom the best, by knowing which all sages have passed from this world to the highest perfection.

2. Having resorted to this wisdom and become of like nature to Me, they are not born at the time of creation; nor are they disturbed at the time of dissolution.

3. Great *brahma* (*prakṛti*) is My womb: in that I cast the seed and from it is the birth of all beings, O Bhārata (Arjuna).

4. Whatever forms are produced in any wombs whatsoever, O Son of Kuntī (Arjuna), great *brahma* is their womb and I am the Father who casts the seed.

Goodness, passion and dullness

5. The three modes (*guṇas*) goodness (*sattva*), passion (*rajas*), and dullness (*tamas*) born of nature (*prakṛti*) bind down in the body, O Mighty-armed (Arjuna), the imperishable dweller in the body.

6. Of these, goodness (*sattva*) being pure, causes illumination and health. It binds, O blameless one, by attachment to happiness and by attachment to knowledge.

7. Passion (*rajas*), know thou, is of the nature of attraction, springing from craving and attachment. It binds fast, O Son of Kuntī (Arjuna), the embodied one by attachment to action.

8. But dullness (*tamas*), know thou, is born of ignorance and deludes all embodied beings. It binds, O Bhārata (Arjuna), by [developing the qualities of] negligence, indolence and sleep.

9. Goodness attaches one to happiness, passion to action, O Bhārata (Arjuna), but dullness, veiling wisdom, attaches to negligence.

10. Goodness prevails, overpowering passion and dullness, O Bhārata (Arjuna). Passion prevails, [overpowering] goodness and dullness and even so dullness prevails [overpowering] goodness and passion.

11. When the light of knowledge streams forth in all the gates of the body, then it may be known that goodness has increased.

12. Greed, activity, the undertaking of actions, unrest and craving—these spring up, O Best of the Bhāratas (Arjuna), when *rajas* (passion) increases.

13. Unillumination, inactivity, negligence, and mere delusion—these arise, O Joy of the Kurus (Arjuna), when dullness increases.

14. When the embodied soul meets with dissolution, when goodness prevails, then it attains to the pure worlds of those who know the Highest,

15. Meeting with dissolution when passion prevails, it is born among those attached to action; and if it is dissolved when dullness prevails, it is born in the wombs of the deluded.

16. The fruit of good action is said to be of the nature of "goodness" and pure; while the fruit of passion is pain, the fruit of dullness is ignorance.

17. From goodness arises knowledge and from passion greed, negligence and error arise from dullness, as also ignorance.

18. Those who are established in goodness rise upwards; the passionate remain in the middle [regions]; the dull steeped in the lower tendencies sink downwards.

19. When the seer perceives no agent other than the modes, and knows also that which is beyond the modes, he attains to My being.

20. When the embodied soul rises above these three modes that spring from the body, it is freed from birth, death, old age, and pain and attains life eternal.

The character of him who is beyond the three modes

Arjuna said:

21. By what mark is he, O Lord, who has risen above the three modes characterized? What is his way of life? How does he get beyond the three modes?

The Blessed Lord said:

22. He, O Pāṇḍava (Arjuna), who does not abhor illumination, activity, and delusion when they arise nor longs for them when they cease;

23. He who is seated like one unconcerned, unperturbed by the modes, who stands apart, without wavering, knowing that it is only the modes that act;

24. He who regards pain and pleasure alike, who dwells in his own self, who looks upon a clod, a stone, a piece of gold as of equal worth, who remains the same amidst the pleasant and the unpleasant things, who is firm of mind, who regards both blame and praise as one;

25. He who is the same in honour and dishonour and the same to friends and foes, and who has given up all initiative of action, he is said to have risen above the modes;

26. He who serves Me with unfailing devotion of love, rises above the three modes, he too is fit for becoming *Brahman*.

27. For I am the abode of *Brahman*, the Immortal and the Imperishable, of eternal law and of absolute bliss.

This is the fourteenth chapter entitled "The *Yoga* of the Differentiation of the Three Modes."

Chapter 15: The Tree of Life

The cosmic tree

The Blessed Lord said:

1. They speak of the imperishable *aśvattham* (peepal tree) as having its root above and branches below. Its leaves are the Vedas and he who knows this is the knower of the Vedas.[1]

2. Its branches extend below and above, nourished by the modes, with sense objects for its twigs; and below, in the world of men, stretch forth the roots resulting in actions.

[1] The world is a living organism united with the Supreme. According to ancient belief, the Vedic sacrificial cult is said to sustain the world and so the hymns are said to be the leaves which keep the tree with its trunk and branches alive.

3. Its real form is not thus perceived here, nor its end nor beginning nor its foundation. Having cut off this firm-rooted *aśvattham* (peepal tree) with the strong sword of non-attachment.

4. Then, that path must be sought from which those who have reached it never return, saying, "I seek refuge only in that Primal Person from whom has come forth this ancient current of the world" [this cosmic process].

5. Those who are freed from pride and delusion, who have conquered the evil of attachment, who, all desires stilled, are ever devoted to the Supreme Spirit, who are liberated from the dualities of pleasure and pain and are undeluded, go to that eternal state.

Manifested life is only a part

6. The sun does not illumine that, nor the moon nor the fire. That is My supreme abode from which those who reach it never return.

The Lord as the life of the universe

7. A fragment [or fraction] of My own self, having become a living soul, eternal, in the world of life, draws to itself the senses of which the mind is the sixth, that rest in nature.

8. When the lord takes up a body and when he leaves it, he takes these [the senses and mind] and goes even as the wind carries perfumes from their places.

9. He enjoys the objects of the senses, using the ear, the eye, the touch sense, the taste sense, and the nose as also the mind.

10. When He departs or stays or experiences, in contact with the modes, the deluded do not see [the indwelling soul] but they who have the eye of wisdom [or whose eye is wisdom] see.

11. The sages also striving perceive Him as established in the self, but the unintelligent, whose souls are undisciplined, though striving, do not find Him.

12. That splendour of the sun that illumines this whole world, that which is in the moon, that which is in the fire, that splendour, know as Mine.

13. And entering the earth, I support all beings by My vital energy; and becoming the sapful *soma* [moon], I nourish all herbs [or plants].

14. Becoming the fire of life in the bodies of living creatures and mingling with the upward and downward breaths, I digest the four kinds of food.

15. And I am lodged in the hearts of all; from Me are memory and knowledge as well as their loss. I am indeed He who is to be known by all the Vedas. I indeed [am] the author of the Vedānta and I too the knower of the Vedas.

The Supreme Person

16. There are two persons in this world, the perishable and the imperishable; the perishable is all these existences and the unchanging is the imperishable.

17. But other than these, the Highest Spirit called the Supreme Self who, as the Undying Lord, enters the three worlds and sustains them.

18. As I surpass the perishable and am higher even than the imperishable, I am celebrated as the Supreme Person in the world and in the Veda.

19. He who, undeluded, thus knows Me, the Highest Person, is the knower of all and worships Me with all his being [with his whole spirit], O Bhārata (Arjuna).

20. Thus has this most secret doctrine been taught by Me, O blameless one. By knowing this, a man will become wise and will have fulfilled all his duties, O Bhārata (Arjuna).

This is the fifteenth chapter entitled "The *Yoga* of the Supreme Person."

CHAPTER 16: THE NATURE OF THE GODLIKE AND THE DEMONIAC MIND

Those of divine nature

The Blessed Lord said:

1. Fearlessness, purity of mind, steadfastness in knowledge and concentration, charity, self-control and sacrifice, study of the scriptures, austerity, and uprightness,

2. Non-violence, truth, freedom from anger, renunciation, tranquillity, aversion to fault finding, compassion to living beings, freedom from covetousness, gentleness, modesty, and steadiness [absence of fickleness],

3. Vigour, forgiveness, fortitude, purity, freedom from malice and excessive pride—these, O Pāṇḍava (Arjuna), are the endowments of him who is born with the divine nature.

The demoniac

4. Ostentation, arrogance, excessive pride, anger, as also harshness and ignorance, these, O Pārtha (Arjuna), are the endowments of him who is born with the demoniac nature.

Their respective results

5. The divine endowments are said to make for deliverance and the demoniac for bondage. Grieve not, O Pāṇḍava (Arjuna), thou art born with the divine endowments [for a divine destiny].

The nature of the demoniac

6. There are two types of beings created in the world—the divine and the demoniac. The divine have been described at length. Hear from me, O Pārtha (Arjuna), about the demoniac.

7. The demoniac do not know about the way of action or the way of renunciation. Neither purity, nor good conduct, nor truth is found in them.

8. They say that the world is unreal, without a basis, without a Lord, not brought about in regular causal sequence, caused by desire, in short.

9 Holding fast to this view, these lost souls of feeble understanding, of cruel deeds, rise up as the enemies of the world for its destruction.

10. Giving themselves up to insatiable desire, full of hypocrisy, excessive pride and arrogance, holding wrong views through delusion, they act with impure resolves.

11. Obsessed with innumerable cares which would end only with [their] death, looking upon the gratification of desires as their highest aim, assured that this is all.

12. Bound by hundreds of ties of desire, given over to lust and anger, they strive to amass hoards of wealth, by unjust means, for the gratification of their desires.

13. "This today has been gained by me: this desire I shall attain, this is mine and this wealth also shall be mine [in the future].

14. "This foe is slain by me and others also I shall slay. I am the lord, I am the enjoyer, I am successful, mighty and happy.

15. "I am rich and well-born. Who is there like unto me? I shall sacrifice, I shall give, I shall rejoice," thus they [say], deluded by ignorance.

16. Bewildered by many thoughts, entangled in the meshes of delusion and addicted to the gratification of desires, they fall into a foul hell.

17. Self-conceited, obstinate, filled with the pride and arrogance of wealth, they perform sacrifices which are so only in name with ostentation and without regard to rules.

18. Given over to self-conceit, force, and pride and also to lust and anger, these malicious people despise Me dwelling in the bodies of themselves and others.

19. These cruel haters, worst of men, I hurl constantly these evil-doers only into the wombs of demons in this cycle of births and deaths.

20. Fallen into the wombs of demons, these deluded beings from birth to birth, do not attain to Me, O Son of Kuntī (Arjuna), but go down to the lowest state.

The triple gate of hell

21. The gateway of this hell leading to the ruin of the soul is threefold, lust, anger, and greed. Therefore these three one should abandon.

22. The man who is released from these, the three gates to darkness, O son of Kuntī (Arjuna), does what is good for his soul and then reaches the highest state.

23. But he who discards the scriptural law and acts as his desires prompt him, he does not attain either perfection of happiness or the highest goal.

24. Therefore let the scripture be thy authority for determining what should be done and what should not be done. Knowing what is declared by the rules of the scripture, thou shouldst do thy work in this world.

This is the sixteenth chapter entitled "The *Yoga* of the Distinction between the Divine and the Demoniac Endowments."

Chapter 17: The Three Modes Applied to Religious Phenomena

Three kinds of faith

Arjuna said:

1. Those who, neglecting the ordinances of scriptures, offer sacrifices filled with faith—what is their position, O Kṛṣṇa? Is it one of goodness or of passion or of dullness?

The Blessed Lord said:

2. The faith of the embodied is of three kinds, born of their nature, good, passionate, and dull. Hear now about it.

3. The faith of every individual, O Bhārata (Arjuna), is in accordance with his nature. Man is of the nature of his faith: what his faith is, that, verily, he is.

4. Good men worship the gods, the passionate worship the demigods, and the demons and the others [who are] the dull, worship the spirits and ghosts.

5. Those men, vain and conceited and impelled by the force of lust and passion, who perform violent austerities, which are not ordained by the scriptures,

6. Being foolish oppress the group of elements in their body and Me also dwelling in the body. Know these to be demoniac in their resolves.

Three kinds of food

7. Even the food which is dear to all is of three kinds. So are the sacrifices, austerities, and gifts. Hear thou the distinction of these.

8. The foods which promote life, vitality, strength, health, joy, and cheerfulness, which are sweet, soft, nourishing, and agreeable are dear to the "good."

9. The foods that are bitter, sour, saltish, very hot, pungent, harsh, and burning, producing pain, grief, and disease are liked by the "passionate."

10. That which is spoiled, tasteless, putrid, stale, refuse, and unclean is the food dear to the "dull."

Three kinds of sacrifice

11. That sacrifice which is offered, according to the scriptural law, by those who expect no reward and believe firmly that it is their duty to offer the sacrifice, is "good."

12. But that which is offered in expectation of reward or for the sake of display, know, O best of the Bhāratas (Arjuna), that sacrifice to be "passionate."

13. The sacrifice which is not in conformity with the law, in which no food is distributed, no hymns are chanted, and no fees are paid, which is empty of faith, they declare to be "dull."

Three kinds of penance

14. The worship of the gods, of the twice-born, of teachers and of the wise, purity, uprightness, continence, and non-violence, this is said to be the penance of the body.

15. The utterance [of words] which gives no offence, which is truthful, pleasant, and beneficial and the regular recitation of the Veda—this is said to be the penance of speech.

16. Serenity of mind, gentleness, silence, self-control, the purity of mind—this is called the penance of mind.

17. This threefold penance practised with utmost faith by men of balanced mind without the expectation of reward, they call "good."

18. That penance which is performed in order to gain respect, honour, and reverence and for the sake of show is said to be "passionate"; it is unstable and not lasting.

19. That penance which is performed with a foolish obstinacy by means of self-torture or for causing injury to others is said to be "dull."

Three kinds of gifts

20. That gift which is made to one from whom no return is expected, with the feeling that it is one's duty to give and which is given in proper place and time and to a worthy person, that gift is held to be "good."

21. But that gift which is made with the hope of a return or with the expectation of future gain or when it hurts to give is held to be "passionate."

22. And that gift which is made at a wrong place or time or to an unworthy person, without proper ceremony or with contempt, that is declared to be "dull."

The mystical utterance: Aum Tat Sat

23. "*Aum Tat Sat*"—this is considered to be the threefold symbol of *Brahman*.[1] By this were ordained of old the *brāhmins*, the Vedas and the sacrifices.

24. Therefore with the utterance of "*aum*" the acts of sacrifice, gift, and penance enjoined in the scriptures are always undertaken by the expounders of *Brahman*.

25. And with the utterance of the word "*tat*" the acts of sacrifice

[1] "*Aum*" expresses the absolute supremacy, "*tat*" the universality, and "*sat*" the reality of *Brahman*.

and penance and the various acts of giving are performed by the seekers of salvation, without aiming at the reward.

26. The word "*sat*" is employed in the sense of reality and goodness; and so also, O Pārtha (Arjuna), the word "*sat*" is used for praiseworthy action.

27. Steadfastness in sacrifice, penance, gift is also called "*sat*" and so also any action for such purposes is called "*sat*."

28. Whatever offering or gift is made, whatever penance is performed, whatever rite is observed, without faith, it is called "*asat*," O Pārtha (Arjuna); it is of no account hereafter or here.

This is the seventeenth chapter entitled, "The *Yoga* of the Threefold Division of Faith."

Chapter 18: Conclusion

Renunciation is to be practised not towards work but to the fruits of work

Arjuna said:

1. I desire, O Mighty-armed (Kṛṣṇa), to know the true nature of renunciation and of relinquishment, O Hṛṣīkeśa (Kṛṣṇa), severally O Keśiniṣūdana (Kṛṣṇa).

The Blessed Lord said:

2. The wise understand by "renunciation" the giving up of works prompted by desire: the abandonment of the fruits of all works, the learned declare, is relinquishment.

3. "Action should be given up as an evil," say some learned men; others declare that "acts of sacrifice, gift, and penance are not to be given up."

4. Hear now from Me, O Best of the Bhāratas (Arjuna), the truth about relinquishment: relinquishment, O Best of men (Arjuna), has been explained as threefold.

5. Acts of sacrifice, gift, and penance are not to be relinquished but should be performed. For sacrifice, gift, and penance are purifiers of the wise.

6. But even these works ought to be performed, giving up attachment and desire for fruits. This, O Pārtha (Arjuna), is my decided and final view.

7. Verily the renunciation of any duty that ought to be done is not right. The abandonment of it through ignorance is declared to be of the nature of "dullness."

8. He who gives up a duty because it is painful or from fear of physical suffering performs only the relinquishment of the "passionate" kind and does not gain the reward of relinquishment.

9. But he who performs a prescribed duty as a thing that ought to be done, renouncing all attachment and also the fruit—his relinquishment is regarded as one of "goodness."

10. The wise man, who renounces, whose doubts are dispelled, whose nature is of goodness, has no aversion to disagreeable action and no attachment to agreeable action.

11. It is indeed impossible for any embodied being to abstain from work altogether. But he who gives up the fruit of action—he is said to be the relinquisher.

12. Pleasant, unpleasant, and mixed—threefold is the fruit of action accruing after death to those who have not relinquished: there is none whatever for those who have renounced.

13. O Mighty-armed (Arjuna), learn of Me, these five factors for the accomplishment of all actions, as stated in the Sāṁkhya doctrine:

14. The seat of action[1] and likewise the agent, the instruments of various sorts, the many kinds of efforts, and providence being the fifth.

15. Whatever action a man undertakes by his body, speech, or mind, whether it is right or wrong, these five are its factors.

16. Such being the case, the man of perverse mind who, on account of his untrained understanding, looks upon himself as the sole agent —he does not see truly.

17. He who is free from self-sense, whose understanding is not sullied, though he slay these people—he slays not nor is he bound [by his actions].

Knowledge and action

18. Knowledge, the object of knowledge, and the knowing subject, are the threefold incitement to action: the instrument, the action, and the agent are the threefold composite of action.

19. Knowledge, action, and the agent are said, in the science of modes, to be of three kinds only, according to difference in the modes.[2] Hear thou duly of these also.

[1] The "seat" refers to the physical body.

[2] The Sāṁkhya system is referred to and it is authoritative in some matters though not in regard to the highest truth.

Three kinds of knowledge

20. The knowledge by which the one Imperishable Being is seen in all existences, undivided in the divided—know that that knowledge is of "goodness."

21. The knowledge which sees multiplicity of beings in the different creatures, by reason of their separateness—know that that knowledge is of the nature of "passion."

22. But that which clings to one single effect as if it were the whole, without concern for the cause, without grasping the real, and narrow is declared to be of the nature of "dullness."

Three kinds of work

23. An action which is obligatory, which is performed without attachment, without love or hate by one undesirous of fruit—that is said to be of the nature of "goodness."

24. But that action which is done in great strain by one who seeks to gratify his desires or is impelled by self-sense is said to be of the nature of "passion."

25. The action which is undertaken through ignorance, without regard to consequences or to loss and injury and without regard to one's human capacity—that is said to be of the nature of "dullness."

Three kinds of doer

26. The doer who is free from attachment, who has no speech of egotism, full of resolution and zeal, and who is unmoved by success or failure—he is said to be of the nature of "goodness."

27. The doer who is swayed by passion, who eagerly seeks the fruit of his works, who is greedy, of violent nature, impure, who is moved by joy and sorrow—he is said to be of "passionate" nature.

28. The doer who is unbalanced, vulgar, obstinate, deceitful, malicious, indolent, despondent, and procrastinating—he is said to be of the nature of "dullness."

Three kinds of understanding

29. Hear now the threefold distinction of understanding as also of steadiness, O Winner of wealth (Arjuna), according to the modes, to be set forth fully and separately.

30. The understanding which knows action and non-action, what ought to be done and what ought not to be done, what is to be feared

and what is not to be feared, what binds and what frees the soul—that understanding, O Pārtha (Arjuna), is of the nature of "goodness."

31. That by which one knows in a mistaken way the right and the wrong, what ought to be done and what ought not to be done—that understanding, O Pārtha (Arjuna), is of the nature of "passion."

32. That which, enveloped in darkness, conceives as right what is wrong and sees all things in a perverted way [contrary to the truth]—that understanding, O Pārtha (Arjuna), is of the nature of "dullness."

Three kinds of steadiness

33. The unwavering steadiness by which, through concentration, one controls the activities of the mind, the life breaths, and the senses—that, O Pārtha (Arjuna), is of the nature of "goodness."

34. The steadiness by which one holds fast to duty, pleasure, and wealth, desiring the fruit of each on its occasion—that, O Pārtha (Arjuna), is of the nature of "passion."

35. That steadiness by which a fool does not give up sleep, fear, grief, depression, and arrogance—that, O Pārtha (Arjuna), is of the nature of "dullness."

Three kinds of happiness

36. And now hear from Me, O Best of the Bhāratas (Arjuna), the three kinds of happiness: That in which a man comes to rejoice by long practice and in which he reaches the end of his sorrow,

37. That happiness which is like poison at first and like nectar at the end, which springs from a clear understanding of the Self, is said to be of the nature of "goodness."

38. That happiness which arises from the contact of the senses and their objects and which is like nectar at first but like poison at the end—such happiness is recorded to be "passionate."

39. That happiness which deludes the soul both at the beginning and at the end, and which arises from sleep, sloth, and negligence—that is declared to be of the nature of "dullness."

Various duties determined by one's nature (svabhāva) and station (svadharma)

40. There is no creature either on earth or, again, among the gods in heaven which is free from the three modes born of nature.

41. Of *brāhmins*, of *kṣatriyas*, and *vaiśyas*, as also of *śūdras*, O Conqueror of the foe (Arjuna), the activities are distinguished, in accordance with the qualities born of their nature.

42. Serenity, self-control, austerity, purity, forbearance and uprightness, wisdom, knowledge, and faith in religion—these are the duties of the *brāhmin*, born of his nature.

43. Heroism, vigour, steadiness, resourcefulness, not fleeing even in a battle, generosity, and leadership—these are the duties of a *kṣatriya*, born of his nature.

44. Agriculture, tending cattle, and trade are the duties of a *vaiśya*, born of his nature; work of the character of service is the duty of a *śūdra*, born of his nature.

45. Devoted each to his own duty man attains perfection. How one devoted to one's own duty attains perfection, that do thou hear.

46. He from whom all beings arise and by whom all this is pervaded—by worshipping Him through the performance of his own duty does man attain perfection.

47. Better is one's own law though imperfectly carried out than the law of another carried out perfectly. One does not incur sin when one does the duty ordained by one's own nature.

48. One should not give up the work suited to one's nature, O Son of Kuntī (Arjuna), though it may be defective, for all enterprises are clouded by defects as fire by smoke.

Karma-yoga and absolute perfection

49. He whose understanding is unattached everywhere, who has subdued his self and from whom desire has fled—he comes through renunciation to the supreme state transcending all work.

Perfection and Brahman

50. Hear from me in brief, O Son of Kuntī (Arjuna), how, having attained perfection, he attains to the *Brahman*, that supreme consummation of wisdom.

51. Endowed with a pure understanding, firmly restraining oneself, turning away from sound and other objects of sense and casting aside attraction, and aversion,

52. Dwelling in solitude, eating but little, controlling speech, body, and mind, and ever engaged in meditation and concentration and taking refuge in dispassion,

53. And casting aside self-sense, force, arrogance, desire, anger, possession, egoless, and tranquil in mind, he becomes worthy of becoming one with *Brahman*.

The highest devotion

54. Having become one with *Brahman*, and being tranquil in spirit, he neither grieves nor desires. Regarding all beings as alike he attains supreme devotion to Me.

55. Through devotion he comes to know Me, what My measure is and who I am in truth; then, having known Me in truth, he forthwith enters into Me.

Application of the teaching to Arjuna's case

56. Doing continually all actions whatsoever, taking refuge in Me, he reaches by My grace the eternal, undying abode.

57. Surrendering in thought all actions to Me, regarding Me as the Supreme, and resorting to steadfastness in understanding, do thou fix thy thought constantly on Me.

58. Fixing thy thought on Me, thou shalt, by My grace, cross over all difficulties; but if, from self-conceit, thou wilt not listen [to Me], thou shalt perish.

59. If indulging in self-conceit, thou thinkest, "I will not fight," vain is this, thy resolve. Nature will compel thee.

60. That which, through delusion, thou wishest not to do, O Son of Kuntī (Arjuna), that thou shalt do even against thy will, fettered by thy own acts, born of thy nature.

61. The Lord abides in the hearts of all beings, O Arjuna, causing them to turn round by His power as if they were mounted on a machine.

62. Flee unto Him for shelter with all thy being, O Bhārata (Arjuna). By His grace shalt thou obtain supreme peace and eternal abode.

63. Thus has wisdom more secret than all secrets been declared to thee by Me. Reflect on it fully and do as thou choosest.

Final appeal

64. Listen again to My supreme word, the most secret of all. Well beloved art thou of Me, therefore I shall tell thee what is good for thee.

65. Fix thy mind on Me; be devoted to Me; sacrifice to Me; prostrate thyself before Me; so shalt thou come to Me. I promise thee truly, for thou art dear to Me.

66. Abandoning all duties, come to Me alone for shelter. Be not grieved, for I shall release thee from all evils.

The reward of following the doctrine

67. Never is this to be spoken by thee to one who is not austere in life or who has no devotion in him or who is not obedient or who speaks ill of Me.

68. He who teaches this supreme secret to My devotees, showing the highest devotion to Me, shall doubtless come to Me.

69. There is none among men who does dearer service to Me than he; nor shall there be another dearer to Me in the world.

70. And he who studies this sacred dialogue of ours, by him I would be worshipped through the sacrifice of knowledge, so I hold.

71. And the man who listens to it with faith and without scoffing, even he, being liberated, shall attain to the happy worlds of the righteous.

72. O Pārtha (Arjuna), has this been heard by thee with thy thought fixed to one point? O Winner of wealth (Arjuna), has thy distraction of thought caused by ignorance been dispelled?

Conclusion

Arjuna said:

73. Destroyed is my delusion, and recognition has been gained by me through Thy grace, O Acyuta (Kṛṣṇa). I stand firm with my doubts dispelled. I shall act according to Thy word.

Saṁjaya said:

74. Thus have I heard this wonderful dialogue between Vāsudeva (Kṛṣṇa) and the high-souled Pārtha (Arjuna) causing my hair to stand on end.

75. By the grace of Vyāsa, I heard this supreme secret, this *yoga* taught by Kṛṣṇa himself, the Lord of *yoga*, in person.

76. O King, as I recall again and again this dialogue, wondrous and holy, of Keśava (Kṛṣṇa) and Arjuna, I thrill with joy again and again.

77. And as often as I recall that most wondrous form of Hari (Kṛṣṇa), great is my astonishment, O King, and I thrill with joy again and again.

78. Wherever there is Kṛṣṇa, the lord of *yoga*, and Pārtha (Arjuna), the archer, I think, there will surely be fortune, victory, welfare, and morality.

This is the eighteenth chapter, entitled "The *Yoga* of Release by Renunciation."

Here the *Bhagavad-gītā-Upaniṣad* ends.[1]

[1] The *Bhagavad-gītā* and the *Brahma Sūtra* have the same status as the Upaniṣads; for this reason the *Gītā* may be called *Bhagavad-gītā-Upaniṣad*.

CHAPTER IV

THE MAHĀBHĀRATA

1. General rules of conduct

. . . Abstention from injury, truthfulness of speech, justice, compassion, self-restraint.

Procreation (of offspring) [with] one's own wife, amiability, modesty, patience,—the practice of these is the best of all religions as said by . . . Manu himself. . . . (Śāntiparva 21.11–12)

Refusal to appropriate what is not given, gift, study (of scriptures), penance, abstention from injury, truth, freedom from wrath, and worship of the gods in sacrifices,—these are the characteristics of virtue. (Śāntiparva 37.10)

Abstention from injury, by act, thought, and word, in respect of all creatures, compassion, and gift [charity], constitute behavior that is worthy of praise.

That act or exertion by which others are not benefited, or that act in consequence of which one has to feel shame, should never be done. (Śāntiparva 124.65–6)

. . . it is difficult to say what righteousness is. It is not easy to indicate it. No one, in discoursing upon righteousness, can indicate it accurately.

Righteousness was declared (by Brahmā) for the advancement and growth of all creatures. Therefore, that which leads to advancement and growth is righteousness.

Righteousness was declared for restraining creatures from injuring one another. Therefore, that is righteousness which prevents injury to creatures. (Śāntiparva 109.9–11)

. . . I know morality, which is eternal, with all its mysteries. It is nothing else than that ancient morality which is known to all, and which consists of universal friendliness, and is fraught with beneficence to all creatures.

That mode of living which is founded upon a total harmlessness towards all creatures or (in case of actual necessity) upon a minimum of such harm, is the highest morality. (Śāntiparva 262.5–6)

There is no expiation for them that cast off the duties and practices of their order and class, country, and family, and those that abandon their very creed. (Śāntiparva 37.20)

2. Expediency and moderation

That again which is virtue may, according to time and place, be sin. Thus appropriation (of what belongs to others), untruth, and injury and killing, may, under special circumstances, become virtue.

Acts that are (apparently) evil, when undertaken from considerations connected with the gods, the scriptures, life itself, and the means by which life is sustained, produce consequences that are good. (Śāntiparva 37.11, 14)

Know, O child, these two truths with certainty, viz., that might is not always meritorious and forgiveness also is not always meritorious! He that forgiveth always suffereth many evils. Therefore it is that... the learned applaud not a constant habit of forgiveness.

Listen now...to the demerits of those that are never-forgiving! The man of wrath who, surrounded by darkness, always inflicteth, by help of his own energy, various kinds of punishments on persons whether they deserve them or not, is necessarily separated from his friends in consequence of that energy of his. Such a man is hated by both relatives and strangers. Such a man, because he insulteth others, suffereth loss of wealth and reapeth disregard and sorrow and hatred and confusion and enemies....He...is an object of alarm to the world. People always do him an injury when they find a hole. Therefore, should men never exhibit might in excess nor forgiveness on all occasions. (Vanaparva 6.8 ff.)

[It is said]: "To tell the truth is consistent with righteousness. There is nothing higher than truth." I shall now, O Bhārata, say unto thee that which is not generally known to men.

There where falsehood would assume the aspect of truth, truth should not be said. There, again, where truth would assume the aspect of falsehood, even falsehood should be said....

(Śāntiparva 109.4–5)

It is always proper to speak the truth. It is better again to speak what is beneficial than to speak what is true. I hold that this is truth which is fraught with the greatest benefit to all creatures.

(Śāntiparva 329.13)

...In seasons of distress, a person by even speaking an untruth acquires the merit of speaking the truth, even as a person who accomplishes an unrighteous act acquires by that very means the merit of having done a righteous act. Conduct is the refuge of righteousness. Thou shouldst know what righteousness is, aided by conduct.

(Śāntiparva 259.6)

Know that the *kṣatriya* [warrior or king] is the protector and the destroyer of the people. Therefore, a *kṣatriya* in distress should take (by force) what he can, with a view to (ultimately) protect the people.

No person in this world...can support life without injuring other creatures. The very ascetic leading a solitary life in the depths of the forest is no exception. (Śāntiparva 130.27–8)

The irresistible course of time affects all mortals. All earthly things, ripened by time, suffer destruction.

Some, O King, slay some men. The slayers, again, are slain by others. This is the language of the world. In reality, however, no one slays, and no one is slain.

Some one thinks men slay (their fellow men). Another thinks men do not slay. The truth is that the birth and destruction of all creatures have been ordained to happen in consequence of their very nature.

(Śāntiparva 25.14–16)

3. Destiny and effort

All acts, good and bad, done in past lives come to the doer. Knowing that everything one enjoys or endures at present is the result of the acts of past lives, the self urges the understanding on different directions (so that it may act in such a way as to avoid all unpleasant fruits). (Śāntiparva 299.42)

...And think also how thou hast been forced by the Supreme Ordainer to do such an act (as the slaughter of so many human beings)!

As a weapon made by a smith or carpenter is under the control of the person that is handling it, and moves as he moves it, similarly this universe, controlled by actions done in time, moves as those actions move it. (Śāntiparva 34.21–2)

...thou shouldst always exert with promptitude,...for without promptitude of exertion mere destiny never accomplishes the objects cherished by kings.

These two, viz., exertion and destiny, are equal (in their operation). Of them, I regard exertion to be superior, for destiny is ascertained from the results of what is begun with exertion.

(Śāntiparva 58.14–15)

Learning, penances, vast wealth, indeed, everything, can be earned by exertion. Exertion, as it occurs in embodied creatures, is governed by intelligence.

The king...should never depend upon destiny....

(Śāntiparva 120.45, 54)

4. Conventional conduct

...Conduct [conventional practice] is the root of prosperity. Conduct is the enhancer of fame.

It is conduct that prolongs life. It is conduct that destroys all calamities and evils. Conduct has been said to be superior to all the branches of knowledge.

It is conduct that begets righteousness, and it is righteousness that prolongs life. Conduct is the most efficacious rite of propitiating the deities (for bringing about auspiciousness of every kind).

(Anuśāsanaparva 104.155–7)

5. Non-attachment and asceticism

A complete disregard for all (worldly) things, perfect contentment, abandonment of hope of every kind, and patience,—these constitute the highest good of one that has subjugated one's senses and acquired a knowledge of self.

No need of attaching thyself to things of this world. Attachment to worldly objects is productive of evil.

Relatives, sons, spouses, the body itself, and all one's possessions stored with care, are unsubstantial and prove of no service in the next world. Only acts, good and bad, that one does, follow one to the other world. (Śāntiparva 329.19, 29, 32)

That man is said to be truly learned and truly possessed of wisdom who abandons every act, who never indulges in hope, who is completely dissociated from all worldly surroundings, and who has renounced everything that appertains to the world.

That person, who, without being attached thereto, enjoys all objects of sense with the aid of the senses that are completely under his control, who is possessed of a tranquil self, who is never moved by joy or sorrow, who is engaged in *yoga*-meditation, who lives in companionship with the deities presiding over his senses and dissociated also from them, and who, though endowed with a body, never regards himself as identifiable with it, becomes emancipated and very soon attains to that which is his highest good.

(Śāntiparva 330.14–16)

Whatever objects, amongst things that are desired, are cast off, become sources of happiness. The man that pursues objects of desire meets with destruction in the course of the pursuit.

Neither the happiness that is derived from a gratification of the senses nor that great felicity which one may enjoy in heaven, approaches to even a sixteenth part of the felicity which arises from the destruction of all desire. (Śāntiparva 47–8)

. . . Freedom from attachment, emancipation from desire, contentment, tranquility, truth, self-restraint, forgiveness, and universal compassion, are the qualities that have now come to me.

. . . Pure happiness has now come to me.

(Śāntiparva 177.43, 48)

The understanding of the man unconversant with *yoga* can never be directed towards emancipation. One unconversant with *yoga* can never have happiness. Patience and the resolution to cast off sorrow, these two indicate the advent of happiness.

(Śāntiparva 287.16)

6. True knowledge versus renunciation

. . one becomes cleansed of all sins by means of knowledge alone, living the while in [the] Supreme Brahmā [deity].

The wearing of brown cloths, shaving of the head, bearing of the triple stick, and the *kamaṇḍalu* [the begging bowl]—these are the outward signs of one's mode of life. These have no value in aiding one to the attainment of emancipation.

When, notwithstanding the adoption of these emblems of a particular mode of life, knowledge alone becomes the cause of one's emancipation from sorrow, it would appear that the adoption of mere emblems is perfectly useless.

Or, if, beholding the mitigation of sorrow in it, thou hast betaken thyself to these emblems of *sannyāsa* [asceticism], why then should not the mitigation of sorrow be beheld in the umbrella and the sceptre to which I have betaken myself?

Emancipation does not exist in poverty; nor is bondage to be found in affluence. One attains to emancipation through knowledge alone, whether one is indigent or affluent.

For these reasons, know that I am living in a condition of freedom, though ostensibly engaged in the enjoyment of religion [*dharma*], wealth, and pleasure, in the form of kingdom and spouses, which constitute a field of bondage (for the generality of men).

The bonds constituted by kingdom and affluence, and the bondage of attachments, I have cut off with the sword of renunciation whetted on the stone of the scriptures bearing upon emancipation.

(Śāntiparva 321.46–52)

7. Against worldly goods

The desire for wealth can never be fraught with happiness. If acquired, great is the anxiety that the acquirer feels. If lost after acquisition, that is felt as death. Lastly, respecting acquisition itself, it is very uncertain.

Wealth cannot be got by even the surrender of one's person. What can be more painful than this? When acquired, one is never gratified with its measure, but one continues to seek it.

Like the sweet water of the Ganges, wealth only increases one's hankering. (Śāntiparva 177.26–8)

8. Happiness and sorrow

In this respect it is said that they [who] are possessed of wisdom, beholding that the world of life is overwhelmed with sorrow both bodily and mental, and with happiness that is sure to end in misery, never suffer themselves to be stupefied.

He that is wise will strive to rescue himself from sorrow. The happiness of living creatures is unstable both here and hereafter.

Happiness is said to be of two kinds, viz., bodily and mental. Both in this and the other world, the visible and the invisible fruits (of action) are specified (in the Vedas) for the sake of happiness. There is nothing more important than happiness among the fruits or consequences of the triple aggregate.[1] Happiness is desirable. It is an attribute of the self. Both virtue and profit are sought for its sake. Virtue is its root. This, indeed, is its origin. All acts have for their end the attainment of happiness. (Śāntiparva 190.6–7, 9)

There is only sorrow in this world but no happiness. . . .

Sorrow comes after happiness, and happiness after sorrow. One does not always suffer sorrow or always enjoy happiness.

Happiness always ends in sorrow, and sometimes proceeds from sorrow itself. He, therefore, that desires eternal happiness must abandon both.

Be it happiness or sorrow, be it agreeable or disagreeable, whatever comes should be borne with an unaffected heart.

They that are highly stupid and they that are masters of their self enjoy happiness here. They, however, that occupy an intermediate place suffer misery.

. . . There is no end of grief, and grief arises from happiness itself.

Happiness and misery, prosperity and adversity, gain and loss, death and life, in their turn, wait upon all creatures. For this reason the wise man of tranquil self would neither be elated with joy nor be depressed with sorrow. (Śāntiparva 25.22–4, 26–7, 30–31)

When one reflects properly (one's heart being purified by such reflection), one comes to know that the things of this world are as valueless as straw. Without doubt, one is then freed from attachment in respect of those things.

When the world, . . . which is full of defects, is so constituted, every man of intelligence should strive for the attainment of the emancipation of his self.

. . . Behold, all creatures,—the superior, the middling, and the inferior,—in consequence of their respective acts, are entangled in grief!

I do not regard even my own self to be mine. On the other hand, I regard the whole world to be mine. I again think that all this (which I see) is as much mine as it belongs to others! Grief cannot approach me in consequence of this thought.

[1] Virtue, wealth, and pleasure.

Having acquired such an understanding, I do not yield either to joy or grief.

As two pieces of wood floating on the ocean come together at one time and are again separated, even such is the union of (living) creatures in this world.

Sons, grandsons, kinsmen, relatives, are all of this kind. One should never feel affection for them, for separation with them is certain.

Grief arises from the disease constituted by desire. Happiness again results from the disease of desire being cured. From joy springs sorrow, and sorrow arises repeatedly.

Sorrow comes after joy, and joy after sorrow. The joys and sorrows of human beings are revolving on a wheel.

After happiness sorrow has come to thee. Thou shalt again have happiness. No one suffers sorrow forever, and no one enjoys happiness forever. (Śāntiparva 174.4–5, 13–17, 19–21)

CHAPTER V

THE LAWS OF MANU

THERE are four great aims of human life, *dharma* or righteousness, *artha* or wealth, *kāma* or enjoyment, and *mokṣa* or spiritual freedom. The literature of *dharma* deals with law and custom governing the development of the human individual and the proper relations of the different groups of society. The *Code of Manu*, a metrical work of 2,685 verses, deals with religion, law, custom, and politics. The author is familiar with Vedic literature and refers to previous teachers and traditions of *dharma*. The book discusses certain philosophical topics and offers solutions based on the Sāṁkhya and the Vedānta, but its aim is not the exposition of a philosophical system. It is essentially a *dharma-śāstra*. It gives respectability to custom and convention at a time when they were being undermined. The *Code* believes in the fourfold order of society as a means of social cooperation for the common good, though the system has not functioned in the interests of social coherence. The functional basis, as distinct from that based on birth, has been stressed. Each one has to perform the function for which his nature best suits him. Manu believes in the four stages of development and the four supreme ends of life.

A high place is given to women. "Where women are honoured there the gods are pleased; but where they are not honoured no sacred rite yields rewards" (III.56). Again: "In that family where the husband is pleased with his wife and the wife with her husband, happiness will assuredly be lasting" (III.60). "If a suitable husband is not found, a girl may stay in her father's house as a spinster till the end of her life" (IX.89).

The moral code, for Manu, is not a static one. It is to be learned in each generation from what wise men who are good and free from hatred and attachment declare (II.1).

There are, according to Manu, four ways of determining right and wrong. Veda, *smṛti*, *ācāra* (good conduct), and conscience. While the three former make for social order, social progress is achieved by the last. We should do what appeals to our conscience (*ātmanaḥ priyam*) (II.12).

1. One's actions and mental attitude determine one's destiny

(The means of gaining the chief good)

81. . . . with whatever disposition of mind (a man) performs any act, he reaps its result in a (future) body endowed with the same quality. (xii.81)

3. Action, which springs from the mind, from speech, and from the body, produces either good or evil results; by action are caused the (various) conditions of men, the highest, the middling, and the lowest.

4. Know that the mind is the instigator here below, even to that (action) which is connected with the body, (and) which is of three kinds, has three locations, and falls under ten heads.

5. Coveting the property of others, thinking in one's heart of what is undesirable, and adherence to false (doctrines), are the three kinds of (sinful) mental action.

6. Abusing (others, speaking) untruth, detracting from the merits of all men, and talking idly, shall be the four kinds of (evil) verbal action.

7. Taking what has not been given, injuring (creatures) without the sanction of the law, and holding criminal intercourse with another man's wife, are declared to be the three kinds of (wicked) bodily action.

8. (A man) obtains (the result of) a good or evil mental (act) in his mind, (that of) a verbal (act) in his speech, (that of) a bodily (act) in his body.

9. In consequence of (many) sinful acts committed with his body, a man becomes (in the next birth) something inanimate, in consequence (of sins) committed by speech, a bird, or a beast, and in consequence of mental (sins he is re-born in) a low caste.

11. That man who keeps this threefold control (over himself) with respect to all created beings and wholly subdues desire and wrath, thereby assuredly gains complete success. (xii.3–9, 11)

104. Austerity and sacred learning are the best means by which a *brāhmin* secures supreme bliss; by austerities he destroys guilt, by sacred learning he obtains the cessation of (births and) deaths. (xii.104)

95. All those traditions (*smṛti*) and all those despicable systems of philosophy, which are not based on the Veda, produce no reward after death; for they are declared to be founded on darkness.

(xii.95)

238. Giving no pain to any creature, let him slowly accumulate spiritual merit, for the sake (of acquiring) a companion to the next world,...

239. For in the next world neither father, nor mother, nor wife, nor sons, nor relations stay to be his companions; spiritual merit alone remains (with him).

240. Single is each being born; single it dies; single it enjoys (the reward of its) virtue; single (it suffers the punishment of its) sin.

(iv.238–40)

155. Let him, untired, follow the conduct of virtuous men, connected with his occupations, which has been fully declared in the revealed texts and in the sacred tradition (*smṛti*) and is the root of the sacred law.

156. Through virtuous conduct he obtains long life, through virtuous conduct desirable offspring, through virtuous conduct imperishable wealth; virtuous conduct destroys (the effect of) inauspicious marks.

157. For a man of bad conduct is blamed among people, constantly suffers misfortunes, is afflicted with diseases, and [is] short-lived.

158. A man who follows the conduct of the virtuous, has faith and is free from envy, lives a hundred years, though he be entirely destitute of auspicious marks.

172. Unrighteousness, practised in this world, does not at once produce its fruit, like a cow; but, advancing slowly, it cuts off the roots of him who committed it.

173. If (the punishment falls) not on (the offender) himself, (it falls) on his sons, if not on the sons, (at least) on his grandsons; but an iniquity (once) committed, never fails to produce to him who wrought it.

174. He prospers for a while through unrighteousness, then he gains great good fortune, next he conquers his enemies, but (at last) he perishes (branch and) root.

175. Let him always delight in truthfulness, (obedience to) the sacred law, conduct worthy of an Āryan, and purity;...

(iv.155–8, 172–5)

40. Those endowed with Goodness reach the state of gods, those endowed with Activity the state of men, and those endowed with Darkness ever sink to the condition of beasts; that is the threefold course of transmigrations.

50. The sages declare *Brahman*, the creators of the universe, the law, the Great One, and the Undiscernible One (to constitute) the highest order of beings produced by Goodness. (XII.40, 50)

2. General pattern of the social order

87. The student, the householder, the hermit, and the ascetic, these (constitute) four separate orders, which all spring from (the order of) householders.

88. But all (or) even (any of) these orders, assumed successively in accordance with the Institutes (of the sacred law), lead the *brāhmin* who acts by the preceding (rules) to the highest state.

89. And in accordance with the precepts of the Veda and of the traditional texts, the housekeeper [householder] is declared to be superior to all of them [the other three orders]; for he supports the other three.

90. As all rivers, both great and small, find a restingplace in the ocean, even so men of all orders find protection with householders.

91. By twice-born men belonging to (any of) these four orders, the tenfold law must be ever carefully obeyed.

92. Contentment, forgiveness, self-control, abstention from unrighteously appropriating anything, (obedience to the rules of) purification, coercion of the organs [control of the senses], wisdom, knowledge (of the supreme Self), truthfulness, and abstention from anger (form) the tenfold law. (VI.87–92)

63. Abstention from injuring (creatures), veracity, abstention from unlawfully appropriating (the goods of others), purity, and control of the organs, Manu has declared to be the summary of the law for the four castes. (X.63)

1. Let the three twice-born castes, discharging their (prescribed) duties, study (the Veda); but among them the *brāhmin* (alone) shall teach it, not the other two; that is an established rule.

2. The *brāhmin* must know the means of subsistence (prescribed) by law for all, instruct the others, and himself live according to (the law).

3. On account of his pre-eminence, on account of the superiority of his origin, on account of his observance of (particular) restrictive rules, and on account of his particular sanctification, the *brāhmin* is the lord of (all) castes.

4. The *brāhmin*, the *kṣatriya*, and the *vaiśya* castes are the twice-born ones, but the fourth, the *śūdra*, has one birth only; there is no fifth (caste). (x.1–4)

31. But for the sake of the prosperity of the worlds, he [the Lord] caused the *brāhmin*, the *kṣatriya*, the *vaiśya*, and the *śūdra* to proceed from his mouth, his arms, his thighs, and his feet.[1] (i.31)

87. But in order to protect this universe He, the most resplendent one, assigned separate (duties and) occupations to those who sprang from his mouth, arms, thighs, and feet. (i.87)

45. All those tribes in this world, which are excluded from the (community of) those born from the mouth, the arms, the thighs, and the feet (of *Brahman*), are called Dasyus, whether they speak the language of the Mlekkhas [*Mlecchas*] (barbarians) or that of the Āryans. (x.45)

41. (A King) who knows the sacred law, must inquire into the laws of castes, of districts, of guilds, and of families, and (thus) settle the peculiar law of each.

42. For men who follow their particular occupations and abide by their particular duty, become dear to people, though they may live at a distance.

46. What may have been practised by the virtuous, by such twice-born men as are devoted to the law, that he shall establish as law, if it be not opposed to the (customs of) countries, families, and castes. (viii.41–2, 46)

5. In all castes those (children) only which are begotten in the direct order on wedded wives, equal (in caste and married as) virgins, are to be considered as belonging to the same caste (as their fathers).[2] (x.5)

24. By adultery (committed by persons) of (different) castes, by marriages with women who ought not to be married, and by the

[1] See *Ṛg Veda* x.90.

[2] The text, x.6 ff., contains elaborate and detailed treatment of many combinations of castes, assigning names and occupations to all such mixed castes, and describing the status of present and later generations of descendants.

neglect of the duties and occupations (prescribed) to each, are produced (sons who owe their origin) to a confusion of the castes.
(x.24)

352. Men who commit adultery with the wives of others, the king shall cause to be marked by punishments which cause terror, and afterwards banish.

353. For by (adultery) is caused a mixture of the castes among men; thence (follows) sin, which cuts up even the roots and causes the destruction of everything. (VIII.352–3)

3. THE FOUR ORDERS (OR *āśramas*) AND THEIR DUTIES

87. The student, the householder, the hermit, and the ascetic, these (constitute) four separate orders,... (VI.87 [Repeated])

(*a*) *The Student*

165. An Āryan must study the whole Veda together with the Rahasyas [Upaniṣads], performing at the same time various kinds of austerities and the vows prescribed by the rules (of the Veda).
(II.165)

36. In the eighth year after conception, one should perform the initiation (*upanāyana*) of a *brāhmin*, in the eleventh [year] after conception (that) of a *kṣatriya*, but in the twelfth that of a *vaiśya*.
(II.36)

68. Thus has been described the rule for the initiation of the twice-born, which indicates a (new) birth, and sanctified; learn (now) to what duties they must afterwards apply themselves.

69. Having performed the (rite of) initiation, the teacher must first instruct the (pupil) in (the rules of) personal purification, of conduct, of the fire-worship [fire sacrifice], and of the twilight [morning and evening] devotions. (II.68–9)

108. Let an Āryan who has been initiated, (daily) offer fuel in the sacred fire, beg food, sleep on the ground and do what is beneficial to his teacher, until (he performs the ceremony of) *Samāvartana* [the rite of returning home] (on returning home). (II.108)

173. The (student) who has been initiated must be instructed in the performance of the vows [acts of discipline, *vrata*], and gradually learn the Veda, observing the prescribed rules. (II.173)

175. . . . a student who resides with his teacher must observe the following restrictive rules, duly controlling all his organs, in order to increase his spiritual merit.

176. Every day, having bathed, and being purified, he must offer libations of water to the gods, sages and manes, worship (the images of) the gods, and place fuel on (the sacred fire).

177. Let him abstain from honey, meat, perfumes, garlands, substances (used for) flavouring (food), women, all substances turned acid, and from doing injury to living creatures.

178. From anointing (his body), applying collyrium to his eyes, from the use of shoes and of an umbrella (or parasol), from (sensual) desire, anger, covetousness, dancing, singing, and playing (musical instruments),

179. From gambling, idle disputes, backbiting, and lying, from looking at and touching women, and from hurting others.

180. Let him always sleep alone, . . .

182. Let him fetch a pot full of water, flowers, cowdung, earth, and *Kuśa* grass, as much as may be required (by his teacher), and daily go to beg food. (II.175–80, 182)

188. He who performs the vow (of studentship) shall constantly subsist on alms, (but) not eat the food of one (person only);[1] the subsistence of a student on begged food is declared to be equal (in merit) to fasting. (II.188)

199. Let him not pronounce the mere name of his teacher (without adding an honorific title) behind his back even, and let him not mimic his gait, speech, and deportment.

201. By censuring (his teacher), though justly, he will become (in his next birth) an ass, by falsely defaming him, a dog; he who lives on his teacher's substance, will become a worm, and he who is envious (of his merit), a (larger) insect. (II.199, 201)

225. The teacher, the father, the mother, and an elder brother must not be treated with disrespect, especially by a *brāhmin*, though one be grievously offended (by them).

226. The teacher is the image of *Brahman*, the father the image of Prajāpati (the lord of created beings), the mother the image of the earth, and an (elder) full brother the image of oneself.

(II.225–6)

[1] That is, he will not beg always from the same house.

233. By honouring his mother he gains this (nether) world, by honouring his father the middle sphere, but by obedience to his teacher the world of *Brahman.*

234. All duties have been fulfilled by him who honours those three; but to him who honours them not, all rites remain fruitless.

237. By (honouring) these three all that ought to be done by man, is accomplished; that is clearly the highest duty, every other (act) is a subordinate duty. (II.233–4, 237)

145. The teacher is ten times more venerable than a sub-teacher, the father a hundred times more than the teacher, but the mother a thousand times more than the father.

146. Of him who gives natural birth and him who gives (the knowledge of) the Veda, the giver of the Veda is the more venerable father; for the birth for the sake of the Veda (ensures) eternal (rewards) both in this (life) and after death.

148. But that birth which a teacher acquainted with the whole Veda, in accordance with the law, procures for him through the Sāvitrī, is real, exempt from age and death. (II.145–6, 148)

1. The vow (of studying) the three Vedas under a teacher must be kept for thirty-six years, or for half that time, or for a quarter, or until the (student) has perfectly learnt them. (III.1)

(*b*) *Householder*

77. As all living creatures subsist by receiving support from air, even so (the members of) all orders subsist by receiving support from the householder.

78. Because men of the three (other) orders are daily supported by the householder with (gifts of) sacred knowledge and food, therefore (the order of) householders is the most excellent order. (III.77–8)

89. And in accordance with the precepts of the Veda and of the traditional texts, the housekeeper [householder] is declared to be superior to all of them [the other three orders]; for he supports the other three.

90. As all rivers, both great and small, find a resting-place in the ocean, even so men of all orders find protection with householders. (VI.89–90 [Repeated])

2. (A student) who has studied in due order the three Vedas, or two, or even one only, without breaking the (rules of) studentship, shall enter the order of householders.

4. Having bathed, with the permission of his teacher, and performed according to the rule the rite on returning home, a twice-born man shall marry a wife of equal caste who is endowed with auspicious (bodily) marks. (III.2, 4)

12. For the first marriage of twice-born men (wives) of equal caste are recommended; but for those who through desire proceed (to marry again) the following females, (chosen) according to the (direct) order (of the castes), are most approved.

13. It is declared that a *śūdra* woman alone (can be) the wife of a *śūdra*, she and one of his own caste (the wives) of a *vaiśya*, those two and one of his own caste (the wives) of a *kṣatriya*, those three and one of his own caste (the wives) of a *brāhmin*. (III.12–13)

75. Let (every man) in this (second order, at least) daily apply himself to the private recitation of the Veda, and also to the performance of the offering to the gods; for he who is diligent in the performance of sacrifices, supports both the movable and the immovable creation. (III.75)

1. Having dwelt with a teacher during the fourth part[1] of (a man's) life, a *brāhmin* shall live during the second quarter (of his existence) in his house, after he has wedded a wife.

2. A *brāhmin* must seek a means of subsistence which either causes no, or at least little pain (to others), and live (by that) except in times of distress.

3. For the purpose of gaining bare subsistence, let him accumulate property by (following those) irreproachable occupations (which are prescribed for) his (caste), without (unduly) fatiguing his body.

11. Let him never, for the sake of subsistence, follow the ways of the world; let him live the pure, straightforward, honest life of a *brāhmin*.

12. He who desires happiness must strive after a perfectly contented disposition and control himself; for happiness has contentment for its root, the root of unhappiness is the contrary (disposition).

15. Whether he be rich or even in distress, let him not seek wealth through pursuits to which men cleave, nor by forbidden occupations, nor (let him accept presents) from any (giver whosoever he may be).

[1] The first quarter.

16. Let him not, out of desire (for enjoyments), attach himself to any sensual pleasures, and let him carefully obviate an excessive attachment to them, by (reflecting on their worthlessness in) his heart.

17. Let him avoid all (means of acquiring) wealth which impede the study of the Veda; (let him maintain himself) anyhow, but study, because that (devotion to the Veda-study secures) the realisation of his aims.

18. Let him walk here (on earth), bringing his dress, speech, and thoughts to a conformity with his age, his occupation, his wealth, his sacred learning, and his race.

19. Let him daily pore over those Institutes of science which soon give increase of wisdom, those which teach the acquisition of wealth, those which are beneficial (for other worldly concerns), and likewise over the *Nigamas* which explain the Veda. (IV.1–3, 11–12, 15–19)

21. Let him never, if he is able (to perform them), neglect the sacrifices to the sages, to the gods, to the *bhūtas* [elementary forces], to men, and to the manes. (IV.21)

169. (Living) according to the (preceding) rules, he must never neglect the five (great) sacrifices, and, having taken a wife, he must dwell in (his own) house during the second period of his life. (V.169)

(*c*) *The forest-dweller*

1. A twice-born *snātaka*,[1] who has thus lived according to the law in the order of householders, may, taking a firm resolution and keeping his organs in subjection, dwell in the forest, duly (observing the rules given below).

2. When a householder sees his (skin) wrinkled, and (his hair) white, and the sons of his sons, then he may resort to the forest.

3. Abandoning all food raised by cultivation, and all his belongings, he may depart into the forest, either committing his wife to his sons, or accompanied by her.

4. Taking with him the sacred fire and the implements required for domestic (sacrifices), he may go forth from the village into the forest and reside there, duly controlling his senses.

5. Let him offer those five great sacrifices according to the rule, with various kinds of pure food fit for ascetics, or with herbs, roots, and fruit.

[1] One who has completed his studentship.

8. Let him be always industrious in privately reciting the Veda; let him be patient in hardships, friendly (towards all), of collected mind, ever liberal, and never a receiver of gifts, and compassionate towards all living creatures.

26. Making no effort (to procure) things that give pleasure, chaste, sleeping on the bare ground, not caring for any shelter, dwelling at the roots of trees.

27. From *brāhmins* (who live as) ascetics, let him receive alms, (barely sufficient) to support life, or from other householders of the twice-born (castes) who reside in the forest.

28. Or (the hermit) who dwells in the forest may bring (food) from a village, receiving it either in a hollow dish (of leaves), in (his naked) hand, or in a broken earthen dish, and may eat eight mouthfuls.

29. These and other observances must a *brāhmin* who dwells in the forest diligently practise, and in order to attain complete (union with) the (supreme) Self, (he must study) the various sacred texts contained in the Upaniṣads,

30. (As well as those rites and texts) which have been practised and studied by the sages (*ṛṣis*), and by *brāhmin* householders, in order to increase their knowledge (of *Brahman*), and their austerity, and in order to sanctify their bodies;

31. Or let him walk, fully determined and going straight on, in a north-easterly direction, subsisting on water and air, until his body sinks to rest.

32. A *brāhmin*, having got rid of his body by one of those modes practised by the great sages, is exalted in the world of *Brahman*, free from sorrow and fear. (vi.1–5, 8, 26–32)

(*d*) *The wandering ascetic*

33. . . . having thus passed the third part of (a man's natural term of) life in the forest, he may live as an ascetic during the fourth part of his existence, after abandoning all attachment to worldly objects.

34. He who after passing from order to order, after offering sacrifices and subduing his senses, becomes, tired with (giving) alms and offerings of food, an ascetic, gains bliss after death.

36. Having studied the Vedas in accordance with the rule, having begat sons according to the sacred law, and having offered sacrifices according to his ability, he may direct his mind to (the attainment of) final liberation.

37. A twice-born man who seeks final liberation, without having studied the Vedas, without having begotten sons, and without having offered sacrifices, sinks downwards.

38. Having performed the *Iṣṭi*,[1] sacred to the Lord of creatures (Prajāpati), where (he gives) all his property as a sacrificial fee, having reposited the sacred fires in himself, a *brāhmin* may depart from his house (as an ascetic).

41. Departing from his house fully provided with the means of purification, let him wander about absolutely silent, and caring nothing for enjoyments that may be offered (to him).

42. Let him always wander alone, without any companion, in order to attain (final liberation), fully understanding that the solitary (man, who) neither forsakes nor is forsaken, gains his end.

43. He shall neither possess a fire, nor a dwelling, he may go to a village for his food, (he shall be) indifferent to everything, firm of purpose, meditating (and) concentrating his mind on *Brahman*.

45. Let him not desire to die, let him not desire to live; let him wait for (his appointed) time, as a servant (waits) for the payment of his wages.

49. Delighting in what refers to the Self, sitting (in the postures prescribed by the Yoga), independent (of external help), entirely abstaining from sensual enjoyments, with himself for his only companion, he shall live in this world, desiring the bliss (of final liberation).

65. By deep meditation let him recognise the subtile nature of the supreme Self, and its presence in all organisms, . . .

73. Let him recognise by the practise of meditation the progress of the individual soul through beings of various kinds, (a progress) hard to understand for unregenerate men.

74. He who possesses the true insight (into the nature of the world), is not fettered by his deeds; but he who is destitute of that insight, is drawn into the circle of births and deaths.

75. By not injuring any creatures, by detaching the senses (from objects of enjoyment), by the rites prescribed in the Veda, and by rigorously practising austerities, (men) gain that state (even) in this (world).

80. When by the disposition (of his heart) he becomes indifferent to all objects, he obtains eternal happiness both in this world and after death.

[1] A sacrifice.

81. He who has in this manner gradually given up all attachments and is freed from all the pairs (of opposites), reposes in *Brahman* alone.

83. Let him constantly recite (those texts of) the Veda which refer to the sacrifice, (those) referring to the deities, and (those) which treat of the Self and are contained in the concluding portions of the Veda (Vedānta).

85. A twice-born man who becomes an ascetic, after the successive performance of the above-mentioned acts, shakes off sin here below and reaches the highest *Brahman*.

(vi.33–4, 36–8, 41–3, 45, 49, 65, 73–5, 80–81, 83, 85)

4. Duties of members of the four castes[1]

(*a*) *Brāhmin* (Priest or Teacher)

97. It is better (to discharge) one's own (appointed) duty incompletely than to perform completely that of another; for he who lives according to the law of another (caste) is instantly excluded from his own. (x.97)

74. *Brāhmins* who are intent on the means (of gaining union with) *Brahman* and firm in (discharging) their duties, shall live by duly performing the following six acts (which are enumerated) in their (proper) order.

75. Teaching, studying, sacrificing[2] for himself, sacrificing for others, making gifts and receiving them are the six acts (prescribed) for a *brāhmin*.

76. But among the six acts (ordained) for him three are his means of subsistence, (viz.,) sacrificing[2] for others, teaching, and accepting gifts from pure men. (x. 74–6)

77. (Passing) from the *brāhmin* to the *kṣatriya*, three acts (incumbent on the former) are forbidden, (viz.,) teaching, sacrificing[2] for others, and, thirdly, the acceptance of gifts.

78. The same are likewise forbidden to a *vaiśya*, that is a settled rule; for Manu, the lord of creatures (Prajāpati), has not prescribed them for (men of) those two (castes).

79. To carry arms for striking and for throwing (is prescribed) for *kṣatriyas* as a means of subsistence; to trade, (to rear) cattle, and

[1] See also previous references to status and duties of a *brāhmin*.

[2] That is, performing sacrifices.

agriculture for *vaiśyas*; but their duties are liberality, the study of the Veda, and the performance of sacrifices.

80. Among the several occupations the most commendable are, teaching the Veda for a *brāhmin*, protecting (the people) for a *kṣatriya*, and trade for a *vaiśya*.

81. But a *brāhmin*, unable to subsist by his peculiar occupations just mentioned, may live according to the law applicable to *kṣatriyas*; for the latter is next to him in rank.

82. If it be asked, "How shall it be, if he cannot maintain himself by either (of these occupations?" the answer is), he may adopt a *vaiśya's* mode of life, employing himself in agriculture and rearing cattle.

83. But a *brāhmin*, or a *kṣatriya*, living by a *vaiśya's* mode of subsistence, shall carefully avoid (the pursuit of) agriculture, (which causes) injury to many beings and depends on others.

85. But he who, through a want of means of subsistence, gives up the strictness with respect to his duties, may sell, in order to increase his wealth, the commodities sold by *vaiśyas*, making (however) the (following) exceptions.

92. By (selling) flesh, salt, and lac a *brāhmin* at once becomes an outcaste; by selling milk he becomes (equal to) a *śūdra* in three days.

93. But by willingly selling in this world other (forbidden) commodities, a *brāhmin* assumes after seven nights the character of a *vaiśya*.

95. A *kṣatriya* who has fallen into distress, may subsist by all these (means); but he must never arrogantly adopt the mode of life (prescribed for his) betters.

98. A *vaiśya* who is unable to subsist by his own duties, may even maintain himself by a *śūdra's* mode of life, avoiding (however) acts forbidden (to him), and he should give it up, when he is able (to do so).

99. But a *śūdra*, being unable to find service with the twice-born and threatened with the loss of his sons and wife (through hunger), may maintain himself by handicrafts.

101. A *brāhmin* who is distressed through a want of means of subsistence and pines (with hunger), (but) unwilling to adopt a *vaiśya's* mode of life and resolved to follow his own (prescribed) path, may act in the following manner.

102. A *brāhmin* who has fallen into distress may accept (gifts) from

anybody; for according to the law it is not possible (to assert) that anything pure can be sullied.

103. By teaching, by sacrificing for, and by accepting gifts from despicable (men) *brāhmins* (in distress) commit not sin; for they (are as pure) as fire and water.

104. He who, when in danger of losing his life, accepts food from any person whatsoever, is no more tainted by sin than the sky by mud. (x.77–83, 85, 92–3, 95, 98–9, 101–4)

(*b*) *Kṣatriya* (King or Prince or Warrior)

1. I will declare the duties of kings, (and) show how a king should conduct himself, . . . and how (he can obtain) highest success.

2. A *kṣatriya* who has received according to the rule the sacrament prescribed by the Veda, must duly protect this whole (world).

3. For, when these creatures, being without a king, through fear dispersed in all directions, the Lord created a king for the protection of this whole (creation),

8. Even an infant king must not be despised, (from an idea) that he is a (mere) mortal; for he is a great deity in human form.

13. Let no (man), therefore, transgress that law which the king decrees with respect to his favourites, nor (his orders) which inflict pain on those in disfavour.

14. For the (king's) sake the Lord formerly created his own son, Punishment, the protector of all creatures, (an incarnation of) the law, formed of *Brahman's* glory.

18. Punishment alone governs all created beings, punishment alone protects them, punishment watches over them while they sleep; the wise declare punishment (to be identical with) the law.

19. If (punishment) is properly inflicted after (due) consideration, it makes all people happy; but inflicted without consideration, it destroys everything.

20. If the king did not, without tiring, inflict punishment on those worthy to be punished, the stronger would roast the weaker, like fish on a spit;

22. The whole world is kept in order by punishment, for a guiltless man is hard to find; through fear of punishment the whole world yields the enjoyments (which it owes).

24. All castes would be corrupted (by intermixture), all barriers would be broken through, and all men would rage (against each other) in consequence of mistakes with respect to punishment.

26. They declare that king to be a just inflicter of punishment, who is truthful, who acts after due consideration, who is wise, and who knows (the respective value of) virtue, pleasure, and wealth.

35. The king has been created (to be) the protector of the castes and orders, who, all according to their rank, discharge their several duties.

87. A king who, while he protects his people, is defied by (foes), be they equal in strength, or stronger, or weaker, must not shrink from battle, remembering the duty of *kṣatriyas*.

88. Not to turn back in battle, to protect the people, to honour the *brāhmins*, is the best means for a king to secure happiness.

89. Those kings who, seeking to slay each other in battle, fight with the utmost exertion and do not turn back, go to heaven.

99. Let him strive to gain what he has not yet gained; what he has gained let him carefully preserve; let him augment what he preserves, and what he has augmented let him bestow on worthy men.

100. Let him know that these are the four means for securing the aims of human (existence); let him, without ever tiring, properly employ them.

144. The highest duty of a *kṣatriya* is to protect his subjects, for the king who enjoys the rewards, just mentioned, is bound to (discharge that) duty.

198. He should (however) try to conquer his foes by conciliation, by (well-applied) gifts, and by creating dissension, used either separately or conjointly, never by fighting, (if it can be avoided).

199. For when two (princes) fight, victory and defeat in the battle are, as experience teaches, uncertain; let him therefore avoid an engagement.

205. All undertakings (in) this (world) depend both on the ordering of fate and on human exertion; but among these two (the ways of) fate are unfathomable; in the case of man's work action is possible. (VII.1–3, 8, 13–14, 18–20, 22, 24, 26, 35, 87–89, 99–100, 144, 198–9, 205)

410. (The king) should order a *vaiśya* to trade, to lend money, to cultivate the land, or to tend cattle, and a *śūdra* to serve the twice-born castes.

418. (The king) should carefully compel *vaiśyas* and *śūdras* to perform the work (prescribed) for them; for if these two (castes) swerved

from their duties, they would throw this (whole) world into confusion.

420. A king who thus brings to a conclusion all the legal business enumerated above, and removes all sin, reaches the highest state (of bliss). (VIII.410, 418, 420)

(*c*) *Vaiśya* (Tradesman)

326. After a *vaiśya* has received the sacraments and has taken a wife, he shall be always attentive to the business whereby he may subsist and to (that of) tending cattle.

327. For when the Lord of creatures (Prajāpati) created cattle, he made them over to the *vaiśya*; to the *brāhmins* and to the king he entrusted all created beings.

328. A *vaiśya* must never (conceive this) wish, "I will not keep cattle"; and if a *vaiśya* is willing (to keep them), they must never be kept by (men of) other (castes).

329. (A *vaiśya*) must know the respective value of gems, of pearls, of coral, of metals, of (cloth) made of thread, of perfumes, and of condiments.

330. He must be acquainted with the (manner of) sowing of seeds, and of the good and bad qualities of fields, and he must perfectly know all measures and weights.

331. Moreover, the excellence and defects of commodities, the advantages and disadvantages of (different) countries, the (probable) profit and loss on merchandise, and the means of properly rearing cattle.

332. He must be acquainted with the (proper) wages of servants, with the various languages of men, with the manner of keeping goods, and (the rules of) purchase and sale.

333. Let him exert himself to the utmost in order to increase his property in a righteous manner, and let him zealously give food to all created beings. (IX.326–33)

(*d*) *Śūdras* (Workers)

334. ...to serve *brāhmins* (who are) learned in the Vedas, householders, and famous (for virtue) is the highest duty of a *śūdra*, which leads to beatitude.

335. (A *śūdra* who is) pure, the servant of his betters, gentle in his speech, and free from pride, and always seeks a refuge with *brāhmins*, attains (in his next life) a higher caste. (IX.334–5)

413. But a *śūdra*, whether bought or unbought, he may compel to do servile work; for he was created by the Self-existent (*Svayambhū*) to be the slave of a *brāhmin*.

414. A *śūdra*, though emancipated by his master, is not released from servitude; since that is innate in him, who can set him free from it? (VIII.413–14)

121. If a *śūdra*, (unable to subsist by serving *brāhmins*), seeks a livelihood, he may serve *kṣatriyas*, or he may also seek to maintain himself by attending on a wealthy *vaiśya*.

122. But let a (*śūdra*) serve *brāhmins*, either for the sake of heaven, or with a view to both (this life and the next); for he who is called the servant of a *brāhmin* thereby gains all his ends.

123. The service of *brāhmins* alone is declared (to be) an excellent occupation for a *śūdra*; for whatever else besides this he may perform will bear him no fruit.

126. A *śūdra* cannot commit an offence, causing loss of caste, and he is not worthy to receive the sacraments; he has no right to (fulfill) the sacred law (of the Āryans, yet) there is no prohibition against (his fulfilling certain portions of) the law.

127. (*Śūdras*) who are desirous to gain merit, and know (their) duty, commit no sin, but gain praise, if they imitate the practice of virtuous men without reciting sacred texts.

128. The more a (*śūdra*), keeping himself free from envy, imitates the behaviour of the virtuous, the more he gains, without being censured, (exaltation in) this world and the next.

(x.121–3, 126–8)

5. Status and Duties of Women

55. Women must be honoured and adorned by their fathers, brothers, husbands, and brothers-in-law, who desire (their own) welfare.

56. Where women are honoured, there the gods are pleased; but where they are not honoured, no sacred rite yields rewards.

57. Where the female relations live in grief, the family soon wholly perishes; but that family where they are not unhappy ever prospers.

58. The houses on which female relations, not being duly honoured, pronounce a curse, perish completely, as if destroyed by magic.

59. Hence men who seek (their own) welfare, should always

honour women on holidays and festivals with (gifts of) ornaments, clothes, and (dainty) food.

60. In that family, where the husband is pleased with his wife and the wife with her husband, happiness will assuredly be lasting.

(III.55–60)

2. Day and night women must be kept in dependence by the males (of) their (families), and, if they attach themselves to sensual enjoyments, they must be kept under one's control.

3. Her father protects (her) in childhood, her husband protects (her) in youth, and her sons protect (her) in old age; a woman is never fit for independence.

4. Reprehensible is the father who gives not (his daughter in marriage) at the proper time; reprehensible is the husband who approaches not (his wife in due season), and reprehensible is the son who does not protect his mother after her husband has died.

6. Considering that the highest duty of all castes, even weak husbands (must) strive to guard their wives.

7. He who carefully guards his wife, preserves (the purity of) his offspring, virtuous conduct, his family, himself, and his (means of acquiring) merit.

18. For women no (sacramental) rite (is performed) with sacred texts, thus the law is settled; women (who are) destitute of strength and destitute of (the knowledge of) Vedic texts, (are as impure as) falsehood (itself), that is a fixed rule.

45. He only is a perfect man who consists (of three persons united), his wife, himself, and his offspring; thus (says the Veda), and (learned) *brāhmins* propound this (maxim) likewise, "The husband is declared to be one with the wife." (IX.2–4, 6–7, 18, 45)

67. The nuptial ceremony is stated to be the Vedic sacrament for women (and to be equal to the initiation), serving the husband (equivalent to) the residence in (the house of the) teacher, and the household duties (the same) as the (daily) worship of the sacred fire.

(II.67)

147. By a girl, by a young woman, or even by an aged one, nothing must be done independently, even in her own house.

148. In childhood a female must be subject to her father, in youth to her husband, when her lord is dead to her sons; a woman must never be independent.

149. She must not seek to separate herself from her father, husband, or sons; by leaving them she would make both (her own and her husband's) families contemptible.

150. She must always be cheerful, clever in (the management of her) household affairs, careful in cleaning her utensils, and economical in expenditure.

151. Him to whom her father may give her, or her brother with her father's permission, she shall obey as long as he lives, and when he is dead, she must not insult (his memory).

152. For the sake of procuring good fortune to (brides), the recitation of benedictory texts, and the sacrifice to the Lord of creatures (Prajāpati) are used at weddings; (but) the betrothal (by the father or guardian) is the cause of (the husband's) dominion (over his wife).

153. The husband who wedded her with sacred texts, always gives happiness to his wife, both in season and out of season, in this world and in the next.

154. Though destitute of virtue, or seeking pleasure (elsewhere), or devoid of good qualities, (yet) a husband must be constantly worshipped as a god by a faithful wife.

155. No sacrifice, no vow, no fast must be performed by women apart (from their husbands); if a wife obeys her husband, she will for that (reason alone) be exalted in heaven.

156. A faithful wife, who desires to dwell (after death) with her husband, must never do anything that might displease him who took her hand, whether he be alive or dead.

157. At her pleasure let her emaciate her body by (living on) pure flowers, roots, and fruit; but she must never even mention the name of another man after her husband has died.

160. A virtuous wife who after the death of her husband constantly remains chaste, reaches heaven, though she have no son, just like those chaste men.

164. By violating her duty towards her husband, a wife is disgraced in this world, (after death) she enters the womb of a jackal, and is tormented by diseases (the punishment of) her sin.

165. She who, controlling her thoughts, words, and deeds, never slights her lord, resides (after death) with her husband (in heaven), and is called a virtuous (wife).

167. A twice-born man, versed in the sacred law, shall burn a wife of equal caste who conducts herself thus and dies before him,

with (the sacred fires used for) the *Agnihotra*,[1] and with the sacrificial implements.

168. Having thus, at the funeral, given the sacred fires to his wife who dies before him, he may marry again, and again kindle (the fires). (v.147–57, 160, 164–5, 167–8)

6. The gaining of supreme bliss

102. In whatever order (a man) who knows the true meaning of the Veda-science may dwell, he becomes even while abiding in this world, fit for the union with *Brahman*. (xii.102)

83. Studying the Veda, (practising) austerities, (the acquisition of true) knowledge, the subjugation of the organs, abstention from doing injury, and serving the *Guru* [preceptor] are the best means for attaining supreme bliss.

84. (If you ask) whether among all these virtuous actions, (performed) here below, (there be) one which has been declared more efficacious (than the rest) for securing supreme happiness to man,

85. (The answer is that) the knowledge of the Self is stated to be the most excellent among all of them; for that is the first of all sciences, because immortality is gained through that. (xii.83–5)

91. He who sacrifices to the Self (alone), equally recognising the Self in all created beings, and all created beings in the Self, becomes (independent like) an autocrat and self-luminous.

125. He who thus recognises the Self through the Self in all created beings, becomes equal (-minded) towards all, and enters the highest state, *Brahman*.

126. A twice-born man who recites these Institutes, revealed by Manu, will be always virtuous in conduct, and will reach whatever condition he desires. (xii.91, 125–6)

[1] A fire sacrifice.

CHAPTER VI

KAUṬILYA'S *ARTHA-ŚĀSTRA*

ONE of the four aims of human effort is *artha* or material advantage which includes political and economic power. The *Artha-śāstra* is a treatise on politics and diplomacy. Its author, Kauṭilya, the minister of the first Mauryan emperor, gives us an account of the law and administration of the Magadha empire. The work is dated 321–296 B.C.

Kauṭilya refers to the views of five different schools on subjects of polity. While both Dharma- and Artha-śāstras deal with man in society, the former deals with social life from the standpoint of religion and moral order, and the latter from that of policy and utility.

For Kauṭilya, *artha* or wealth is the chief end of life, and the other aims of life, spiritual and artistic, depend upon an economic foundation.

Kauṭilya's *Artha-śāstra* deals, among others, with such subjects as accounts, coinage, commerce, forests, army and navy, weights and measures, agriculture, and law. It also discusses the rules of administration, selection of ministers, principles of taxation, economic development of the country, and the maintenance of discipline in the army.

Though Kauṭilya devotes a section of his work to republican states, he prefers monarchical government. He suggests that the State is established by the weak as a protection against the strong. The king should be vigilant about the wellbeing of his subjects. "The happiness of the subjects is the happiness of the king; their welfare, his; his own pleasure is not his good, but the pleasure of his subjects is his good." Kauṭilya lays down elaborate rules for the selection of successors to kings and the training to be given to them.

BOOK 1: CONCERNING DISCIPLINE

CHAPTER 1: THE LIFE OF A KING

Salutation to Śukra and Bṛhaspati

This *Artha-śāstra* is made as a compendium of almost all the Artha-śāstras, which, in view of acquisition and maintenance of the earth, have been composed by ancient teachers.

Of this work, the following are the contents by sections and books:

Book 1. Concerning Discipline[1]

The end of sciences; association with the aged; restraint of the organs of sense; the creation of ministers; the creation of councillors and priests; ascertaining by temptations purity or impurity in the character of ministers; the institution of spies; protection of parties for or against one's own cause in one's own state; winning over the factions for or against an enemy's cause in an enemy's state; the business of council meeting; the mission of envoys; protection of princes; the conduct of a prince kept under restraint; treatment of a prince kept under restraint; the duties of a king; duty towards the harem; personal safety.

Book 2. The Duties of Government Superintendents

Formation of villages; division of land; construction of forts; buildings within the fort; the duty of the chamberlain; the business of collection of revenue by the collector-general; the business of keeping up accounts in the office of accountants; detection of what is embezzled by government servants out of state revenue; examination of the conduct of government servants; the procedure of forming royal writs; the superintendent of the treasury; examination of gems that are to be entered into the treasury; conducting mining operations and manufacture; the superintendent of gold; the duties of the state goldsmith in the high road; the superintendent of store-house; the superintendent of commerce; the superintendent of forest produce; the superintendent of the armoury; the superintendent of weights and measures; measurement of space and time; the superintendent of tolls; the superintendent of weaving; the superintendent of agriculture; the superintendent of liquor; the superintendent of slaughterhouse; the superintendent of prostitutes; the superintendent of ships; the superintendent of cows; the superintendent of horses; the superintendent of elephants; the superintendent of chariots; the superintendent of infantry; the duty of the commander-in-chief; the superintendent of passports; the superintendent of pasture lands; the duty of revenue collectors; spies in the guise of householders, merchants, and ascetics; the duty of a city superintendent.

[1] Though chapter titles have been retained, the portions selected often deal with a restricted phase of the subject.

Book 3. Concerning Law

Determination of forms of agreements; determination of legal disputes; concerning marriage; division of inheritance; buildings; non-performance of agreements; recovery of debts; concerning deposits; rules regarding slaves and labourers; co-operative undertakings; rescission of purchase and sale; resumption of gifts, and sale without ownership; ownership; robbery; defamation; assault; gambling and betting and miscellaneous.

Book 4. Removal of Thorns

Protection of artisans; protection of merchants; remedies against national calamities; suppression of the wicked living by foul means; detection of youths of criminal tendency by ascetic spies; seizure of criminals on suspicion or in the very act; examination of sudden death; trial and torture to elicit confession; protection of all kinds of government departments; fines in lieu of mutilation of limbs; death with or without torture; sexual intercourse with immature girls; atonement for violating justice.

Book 5. Conduct of Courtiers

Concerning the awards of punishments; replenishment of the treasury; concerning subsistence to government servants; the conduct of a courtier; time-serving; consolidation of the kingdom and absolute sovereignty.

Book 6. The Source of Sovereign States

The elements of sovereignty; concerning peace and exertion.

Book 7. The End of Sixfold Policy

The sixfold policy; determination of deterioration, stagnation, and progress; the nature of alliance; the character of equal, inferior and superior kings; forms of agreement made by an inferior king; neutrality after proclaiming war or after concluding a treaty of peace; marching after proclaiming war or after making peace; the march of combined powers; considerations about marching against an assailable enemy and a strong enemy; causes leading to the dwindling, greed and disloyalty of the army; considerations about the combination of powers; the march of combined powers; agreement of peace with or without definite terms; and peace with renegades;

peace and war by adopting the double policy; the attitude of an assailable enemy; friends that deserve help; agreement for the acquisition of a friend or gold; agreement of peace for the acquisition of land; agreement for undertaking a work; considerations about an enemy in the rear; recruitment of lost power; measures conducive to peace with a strong and provoked enemy; the attitude of a conquered enemy; the attitude of a conquered king; making peace and breaking it; the conduct of a Madhyama king; of a neutral king and of a circle of states.

Book 8. Concerning Vices and Calamities

The aggregate of the calamities of the elements of sovereignty; considerations about the troubles of the king and his kingdom; the aggregate of the troubles of men; the group of molestations; the group of obstructions; and the group of financial troubles; the group of troubles of the army; and the group of troubles of a friend.

Book 9. The Work of an Invader

The knowledge of power, place, time, strength and weakness; the time of invasion; the time for recruiting the army; the form of equipment; the work of arraying a rival force; considerations of annoyance in the rear; remedies against internal and external troubles; consideration about loss of men; wealth and profit. Internal and external dangers; persons associated with traitors and enemies; doubts about wealth and harm; and success to be obtained by the employment of alternative strategic means.

Book 10. Relating to War

Encampment; march of the camp; protection of the army in times of distress and attack; forms of treacherous fights; encouragement to one's own army; the fight between one's own and enemy's armies; battlefields; the work of infantry, cavalry, chariots and elephants; distinctive array of troops in respect of wings, flanks and front; distinction between strong and weak troops; battles with infantry, cavalry, chariots and elephants; the array of the army like a staff, a snake, a circle or in detached order; the array of the army against that of an enemy.

Book 11. The Conduct of Corporations

Causes of dissension; secret punishment.

Book 12. Concerning a Powerful Enemy

The duties of a messenger; battle of intrigue; slaying the commander-in-chief, and inciting a circle of states; spies with weapons, fire, and poison; destruction of supply of stores, and of granaries; capture of the enemy by means of secret contrivances or by means of the army; and complete victory.

Book 13. Strategic Means to Capture a Fortress

Sowing the seeds of dissension; enticement of kings by secret contrivances; the work of spies in a siege; the operation of a siege; restoration of peace in a conquered country.

Book 14. Secret Means

Means to injure an enemy; wonderful and delusive contrivances; remedies against the injuries of one's own army.

Book 15. The Plan of a Treatise

Paragraphical divisions of this treatise.

Such are the contents of this science. There are on the whole 15 books, 150 chapters, 180 sections and 6,000 *ślokas.*[1]

This *Śāstra,*[2] bereft of undue enlargement and easy to grasp and understand, has been composed by Kauṭilya in words the meaning of which has been definitely settled.

Chapter 2: The End [Purposes] of Sciences

Ānvīkṣikī (science of logic), the three Vedas,[3] *Vārtā* (agriculture, cattle-breeding and trade), and *Daṇḍanīti* (science of government)[4] are what are called the four sciences.

The school of Manu hold that there are only three sciences: the three Vedas, *Vārtā* and the science of government, inasmuch as the science of *Ānvīkṣikī* is nothing but a special branch of the Vedas.

The school of Bṛhaspati say that there are only two sciences: *Vārtā* and the science of government, inasmuch as the three Vedas are merely an abridgment for a man experienced in affairs temporal.

The school of Uśanas declare that there is only one science, and

[1] Thirty-two syllables make one *śloka*.

[2] This is in *śloka*-metre.

[3] The text uses the phrase "Triple Vedas." Throughout this section corrections of punctuation and transliteration and typographical errors in the text have been made. Numerous unnecessary Sanskrit terms have been omitted.

[4] Literally, the science of punishment.

that the science of government; for, they say, it is in that science that all other sciences have their origin and end.

But Kauṭilya holds that four, and only four, are the sciences; wherefore it is from these sciences that all that concerns righteousness and wealth is learnt, therefore they are so called.

Ānvīkṣikī comprises the Philosophy of Sāṁkhya, Yoga, and Lokāyata (atheism).

Righteous and unrighteous acts are learnt from the three Vedas; wealth and non-wealth from *Vārtā*; the expedient and the inexpedient, as well as potency and impotency from the science of government.

When seen in the light of these sciences, the science of *Ānvīkṣikī* is most beneficial to the world, keeps the mind steady and firm in weal and woe alike, and bestows excellence of foresight, speech and action.

Light to all kinds of knowledge, easy means to accomplish all kinds of acts and receptacle of all kinds of virtues, is the science of *Ānvīkṣikī* ever held to be.

Chapter 3. The End of Sciences

...Harmlessness, truthfulness, purity, freedom from spite, abstinence from cruelty, and forgiveness are duties common to all.

The observance of one's own duty leads one to *svarga* [heaven] and infinite bliss. When it is violated, the world will come to an end owing to confusion of castes and duties.

Hence the king shall never allow people to swerve from their duties; for whoever upholds his own duty, ever adhering to the customs of the Āryas, and following the rules of caste and divisions of religious life, will surely be happy both here and hereafter. For the world, when maintained in accordance with injunctions of the three Vedas, will surely progress, but never perish.

Chapter 4: The End of Sciences

Vārtā and *Daṇḍanīti*[1]

...That sceptre on which the well-being and progress of the sciences of logic, the three Vedas [*Ṛg Veda*, *Sāma Veda*, *Yajur Veda*], and commerce depend is known as punishment. That which treats of *Daṇḍa* is the law of punishment or science of government.

...whoever imposes severe punishment becomes repulsive to the people; while he who awards mild punishment becomes contemptible.

[1] For definition of these terms, see first sentence of chapter 2.

But whoever imposes punishment as deserved becomes respectable. For punishment, when awarded with due consideration, makes the people devoted to righteousness and to works productive of wealth and enjoyment; while punishment, when ill-awarded under the influence of greed and anger or owing to ignorance, excites fury even among hermits and ascetics dwelling in forests, not to speak of householders.

But when the law of punishment is kept in abeyance, it gives rise to such disorder as is implied in the proverb of fishes (A great fish swallows a small one); for in the absence of a magistrate, the strong will swallow the weak; but under his protection the weak resist the strong.

This people, consisting of four castes and four orders of religious life, when governed by the king with his sceptre, will keep to their respective paths, ever devotedly adhering to their respective duties and occupations.

Chapter 5: Association with the Aged

Hence the (first) three sciences (out of the four) are dependent for their well-being on the science of government. *Daṇḍa*, punishment, which alone can procure safety and security of life, is, in its turn, dependent on discipline.

Discipline is of two kinds: artificial and natural; for instruction can render only a docile being conformable to the rules of discipline, and not an undocile being. The study of sciences can tame only those who are possessed of such mental faculties as obedience, hearing, grasping, retentive memory, discrimination, inference, and deliberation, but not others devoid of such faculties....

The king who is well educated and disciplined in sciences, devoted to good government of his subjects, and bent on doing good to all people will enjoy the earth unopposed.

Chapter 7: Restraint of the Organs of Sense

The Life of a Saintly King

...wealth, and wealth alone, is important, inasmuch as charity and desire depend upon wealth for their realisation....

Sovereignty is possible only with assistance. A single wheel can never move. Hence he shall employ ministers and hear their opinion.

Chapter 10: Ascertaining by Temptations Purity or Impurity in the Character of Ministers

...Teachers have decided that, in accordance with ascertained purity, the king shall employ in corresponding works those ministers whose character has been tested under the three pursuits of life, religion, wealth and love, and under fear....

Chapter 11: The Institution of Spies

Assisted by the council of his ministers tried under espionage, the king shall proceed to create spies: spies under the guise of a fraudulent disciple, a recluse, a householder, a merchant, an ascetic practising austerities, a classmate or a colleague, a fire-brand, a poisoner, and a mendicant woman.

A skilful person capable of guessing the mind of others is a fraudulent disciple....

One who is initiated in asceticism and is possessed of foresight and pure character is a recluse....

A cultivator, fallen from his profession, but possessed of foresight and pure character, is termed a householder spy....

A trader, fallen from his profession, but possessed of foresight and pure character, is a merchant spy....

A man with shaved head or braided hair and desirous to earn livelihood is a spy under the guise of an ascetic practising austerities....

Honoured by the king with awards of money and titles, these five institutes of espionage shall ascertain the purity of character of the king's servants.

Chapter 13: Protection of Parties for or Against One's Own Cause in One's Own State

Having set up spies over his prime ministers, the king shall proceed to espy both citizens and country people.

Classmate spies formed as opposing factions shall carry on disputations in places of pilgrimage, in assemblies, houses, corporations, and amid congregations of people. One spy may say:

"This king is said to be endowed with all desirable qualities; he seems to be a stranger to such tendencies as would lead him to oppress citizens and country people by levying heavy fines and taxes."

Against those who seem to commend this opinion, another spy may interrupt the speaker and say:

"People suffering from anarchy, as illustrated by the proverbial tendency of a large fish swallowing a small one, first elected Manu, the Vaivasvata, to be their king; and allotted one-sixth of the grains grown and one-tenth of merchandise as sovereign dues. Fed by this payment, kings took upon themselves the responsibility of maintaining the safety and security of their subjects, and of being answerable for the sins of their subjects when the principle of levying just punishments and taxes has been violated. Hence hermits, too, provide the king with one-sixth of the grains gleaned by them, thinking that 'it is a tax payable to him who protects us.' It is the king in whom the duties of both the rewarder and the punisher are blended, and he is a visible dispenser of punishments and rewards; whoever disregards kings will be visited with divine punishments, too. Hence kings shall never be despised."

Thus treacherous opponents of sovereignty shall be silenced.

. . . Those who are inebriated with feelings of enmity may be put down by punishment in secret or by making them incur the displeasure of the whole country. Or, having taken the sons and wives of such treacherous persons under state protection, they may be made to live in mines, lest they may afford shelter to enemies.

. . . Thus in his own state a wise king shall guard factions among his people, friendly or hostile, powerful or powerless, against the intrigue of foreign kings.

Chapter 19: The Duties of a King

If a king is energetic, his subjects will be equally energetic. If he is reckless, they will not only be reckless likewise, but also eat into his works. Besides, a reckless king will easily fall into the hands of his enemies. Hence the king shall ever be wakeful.

. . . When in the court, he shall never cause his petitioners to wait at the door, for when a king makes himself inaccessible to his people and entrusts his work to his immediate officers, he may be sure to engender confusion in business, and to cause thereby public disaffection, and himself a prey to his enemies.

. . . Of a king, the religious vow is his readiness to action; satisfactory discharge of duties is his performance of sacrifice; equal attention to all is the offer of fees and ablution towards consecration.

In the happiness of his subjects lies his happiness; in their welfare his welfare; whatever pleases himself he shall not consider as good, but whatever pleases his subjects he shall consider as good.

Hence the king shall ever be active and discharge his duties; the root of wealth is activity, and of evil its reverse.

In the absence of activity acquisitions present and to come will perish; by activity he can achieve both his desired ends and abundance of wealth.

Chapter 20: Duty Towards the Harem

On a site naturally best fitted for the purpose, the king shall construct his harem, consisting of many compartments, one within the other, enclosed by a parapet and a ditch, and provided with a door.

He shall construct his own residential palace after the model of his treasury-house; or he may have his residential abode in the centre of the delusive chamber, provided with secret passages made into the walls; or in an underground chamber provided with the figures of goddesses and of altars carved on the wooden door-frame, and connected with many underground passages for exit; or in an upper storey provided with a staircase hidden in a wall, with a passage for exit made in a hollow pillar, the whole building being so constructed with mechanical contrivance as to be caused to fall down when necessary.

Or considering the danger from his own classmates, such contrivances as the above, mainly intended as safeguards against danger, may be made on occasions of danger or otherwise as he deems fit. . . .

BOOK 3: CONCERNING LAW

Chapter 1: Determination of Forms of Agreement; Determination of Legal Disputes

. . . In virtue of his power to uphold the observance of the respective duties of the four castes and of the four divisions of religious life, and in virtue of his power to guard against the violation of the *dharmas*, the king is the fountain of justice.

Sacred law, evidence, history, and edicts of kings are the four legs of Law. Of these four in order, the later is superior to the one previously named.

Dharma is eternal truth holding its sway over the world; *vyavahāra*, evidence, is in witnesses; *cāritra*, history, is to be found in the tradition of the people; and the order of kings is what is called *śāsana*.

As the duty of a king consists in protecting his subjects with justice, its observance leads him to heaven. He who does not protect his people or upsets the social order wields his royal sceptre in vain.

It is power and power alone which, only when exercised by the king with impartiality and in proportion to guilt, either over his son or his enemy, maintains both this world and the next.

The king who administers justice in accordance with sacred law, evidence, history, and edicts of kings, which is the fourth, will be able to conquer the whole world bounded by the four quarters.

Whenever there is disagreement between history and sacred law or between evidence and sacred law, then the matter shall be settled in accordance with sacred law.

But whenever sacred law is in conflict with rational law, then reason shall be held authoritative; for there the original text on which the sacred law has been based is not available....

Chapter 2: Concerning Marriage. The Duty of Marriage, The Property of a Woman, and Compensations for Re-Marriage

Marriage is the basis of all disputes (*vyavahāra*).[1]

The giving in marriage of a maiden well-adorned is called *brāhma*-marriage. The joint-performance of sacred duties by a man and a woman is known as *prājāpatya* marriage.

The giving in marriage of a maiden for a couple of cows is called *ārṣa*. The giving in marriage of a maiden to an officiating priest in a sacrifice is called *daiva*. The voluntary union of a maiden with her lover is called *gandharva*. Giving a maiden after receiving plenty of wealth is termed *asura*. The abduction of a maiden is called *rākṣasa*. The abduction of a maiden while she is asleep and in intoxication is called *paiśāca* marriage.[2]

...Any kind of marriage is approvable, provided it pleases all those that are concerned in it.

[1] Literally, *vyavahāra* means transactions rather than disputes.

[2] These were the eight forms of marriage recognized in ancient India.

Chapter 15: Rescission of Purchase and Sale (Marriage Contracts)

[As regards marriages among the three higher castes, rejection of a bride before the rite of *pāṇigrahaṇa*, clasping of hands, is valid; but among the *śūdras*, before nuptials. Even in the case of a couple that has gone through the rite of *pāṇigrahaṇa*],[1] rejection of a bride whose guilt of having lain with another man has been afterwards detected is valid. But never so in the case of brides and bridegrooms of pure character and high family. Any person who has given a girl in marriage without announcing her guilt of having lain with another shall not only be punished with a fine of 96 *paṇas*,[2] but also be made to return the *śulka*[3] and *strīdhana*.[4] Any person receiving a girl in marriage without announcing the blemishes of the bridegroom shall not only pay double the above fine, but also forfeit the *śulka* and *strīdhana* he paid for the bride.

BOOK 5: THE CONDUCT OF COURTIERS

Chapter 1: Concerning the Awards of Punishments

Measures necessary to remove the thorns of public peace, both in fortified cities and country parts, have been dealt with. We shall now proceed to treat of measures to suppress treason against the king and his kingdom.

With regard to those chiefs who, though living by service under the king, are inimically disposed towards him or have taken the side of his enemy, a spy with secret mission or one in the guise of an ascetic and devoted to the king's cause shall set to work, as described before; or a spy trained in the art of sowing the seeds of dissension may set to work, as will be described in connection with the "Invasion of an Enemy's Villages."

The king in the interests of righteousness may inflict punishment in secret on those courtiers or confederacy of chiefs who are dangerous to the safety of the kingdom and who cannot be put down in open daylight. . . .

[1] The portion within the brackets is supplied from the Munich Manuscript.
[2] A unit of money.
[3] Dowery.
[4] Literally, the wife's money.

Chapter 2: Replenishment of the Treasury

The king who finds himself in a great financial trouble and needs money, may collect revenue by demand. In such parts of his country as depend solely upon rain for water and are rich in grain, he may demand of his subjects one-third or one-fourth of their grain, according to their capacity. He shall never demand of such of his subjects as live in tracts of middle or low quality; nor of people who are of great help in the construction of fortifications, gardens, buildings, roads for traffic, colonisation of waste lands, exploitation of mines, and formation of forest preserves for timber and elephants; nor of people who live on the border of his kingdom or who have not enough subsistence. He shall, on the other hand, supply with grain and cattle those who colonise waste lands....

BOOK 6: THE SOURCE OF SOVEREIGN STATES

Chapter 1: The Elements of Sovereignty

The king, the minister, the country, the fort, the treasury, the army and the friend are the elements of sovereignty.

Of these, the best qualities of the king are:

Born of a high family, godly, possessed of valour, seeing through the medium of aged persons, virtuous, truthful, not of a contradictory nature, grateful, having large aims, highly enthusiastic, not addicted to procrastination, powerful to control his neighbouring kings, of resolute mind, having an assembly of ministers of no mean quality, and possessed of a taste for discipline—these are the qualities of an inviting nature.

Inquiry, hearing, perception, retention in memory, reflection, deliberation, inference and steadfast adherence to conclusions are the qualities of the intellect.

Valour, determination of purpose, quickness, and probity are the aspects of enthusiasm.

Possessed of a sharp intellect, strong memory, and keen mind, energetic, powerful, trained in all kinds of arts, free from vice, capable of paying in the same coin by way of awarding punishments or rewards, possessed of dignity, capable of taking remedial measures against dangers, possessed of foresight, ready to avail himself of opportunities when afforded in respect of place, time, and manly efforts, clever enough to discern the causes necessitating the cessation of treaty or war with an enemy, or to lie in wait keeping treaties, obligations and pledges, or to avail himself of his enemy's weak points, making jokes with no loss of dignity or secrecy, never browbeating and casting haughty and stern looks, free from passion, anger, greed, obstinacy, fickleness, haste and back-biting habits, talking to others with a smiling face, and observing customs as taught by aged persons—such is the nature of self-possession.

The qualifications of a minister have been described in the beginning, middle, and at the close of the work.

Possessed of capital cities both in the centre and the extremities of the kingdom, productive of subsistence not only to its own people, but also to outsiders on occasions of calamities, repulsive to enemies, powerful enough to put down neighbouring kings, free from miry, rocky, uneven, and desert tracts, as well as from conspirators, tigers, wild beasts, and large tracts of wilderness, beautiful to look at, containing fertile lands, mines, timber and elephant forests, and pasture grounds, artistic, containing hidden passages, full of cattle, not depending upon rain for water, possessed of land and waterways, rich in various kinds of commercial articles, capable of bearing the burden of a vast army and heavy taxation, inhabited by agriculturists of good and active character, full of intelligent masters and servants, and with a population noted for its loyalty and good character—these are the qualities of a good country.

The excellent qualities of forts have already been described.

Justly obtained either by inheritance or by self-acquisition, rich in gold and silver, filled with an abundance of big gems of various colours and of gold coins, and capable to withstand calamities of long duration is the best treasury.

Coming down directly from father and grandfather of the king, ever strong, obedient, happy in keeping their sons and wives well contented, not averse to making a long sojourn, ever and everywhere invincible, endowed with the power of endurance, trained in fighting various kinds of battles, skilful in handling various forms of weapons, ready to share in the weal or woe of the king, and consequently not falling foul with him, and purely composed of soldiers of *kṣatriya* caste, is the best army.

Coming down directly from father and grandfather, long-standing, open to conviction, never falling foul, and capable of making preparations for war quickly and on a large scale, is the best friend.

Not born of a royal family, greedy, possessed of a mean assembly of ministers, with disloyal subjects, ever doing unrighteous acts, of loose character, addicted to mean pleasures, devoid of enthusiasm, trusting to fate, indiscreet in action, powerless, helpless, impotent and ever injurious, is the worst enemy. Such an enemy is easily uprooted.

Excepting the enemy, these seven elements, possessed of their excellent characteristics are said to be the limb-like elements of sovereignty.

A wise king can make even the poor and miserable elements of his sovereignty happy and prosperous; but a wicked king will surely destroy the most prosperous and loyal elements of his kingdom.

Hence a king of unrighteous character and of vicious habits will, though he is an emperor, fall a prey either to the fury of his own subjects or to that of his enemies.

But a wise king, trained in politics, will, though he possesses a small territory, conquer the whole earth with the help of the best-fitted elements of his sovereignty, and will never be defeated.

Chapter 2: Concerning Peace and Exertion

Acquisition and security of property are dependent upon peace and industry.

Effort to achieve the results of works undertaken is industry.

Absence of disturbance to the enjoyment of the results achieved from works is peace.

The application of the six-fold royal policy is the source of peace and industry.

Deterioration, stagnation, and progress are the three aspects of position.

Those causes of human make which affect position are policy and impolicy; fortune and misfortune are providential causes. Causes, both human and providential, govern the world and its affairs.

What is unforeseen is providential; here, the attainment of that desired and which seemed almost lost is termed fortune.

What is anticipated is human; and the attainment of a desired end as anticipated is due to policy.

What produces unfavourable results is impolicy. This can be foreseen; but misfortune due to providence cannot be known.

The king who, being possessed of good character and best-fitted elements of sovereignty, is the fountain of policy, is termed the conqueror.

The king who is situated anywhere immediately on the circumference of the conqueror's territory is termed the enemy.

The king who is likewise situated close to the enemy, but separated from the conqueror only by the enemy, is termed the friend of the conqueror.

A neighbouring foe of considerable power is styled an enemy; and when he is involved in calamities or has taken himself to evil ways, he becomes assailable; and when he has little or no help, he becomes destructible; otherwise (i.e., when he is provided with some help), he deserves to be harassed or reduced. Such are the aspects of an enemy....

Strength is of three kinds: power of deliberation is intellectual strength; the possession of a prosperous treasury and a strong army is the strength of sovereignty; and martial power is physical strength.

The end is also of three kinds: that which is attainable by deliberation is the end of deliberation; that which is attainable by the strength of sovereignty is the end of sovereignty; and that which is to be secured by perseverance is the end of martial power.

The possession of power and happiness in a greater degree makes a king superior to another; in a less degree, inferior; and in an equal degree, equal. Hence a king shall always endeavour to augment his own power and elevate his happiness....

BOOK 7: THE END [PURPOSE] OF THE SIX-FOLD POLICY

Chapter 1: The Six-fold Policy and Determination of Deterioration, Stagnation and Progress

The Circle of States is the source of the six-fold policy.

My teacher says that peace, war, observance of neutrality, marching, alliance, and making peace with one and waging war with another are the six forms of state policy.

But Vātavyādhi holds that there are only two forms of policy, peace and war, inasmuch as the six forms result from these two primary forms of policy.

While Kauṭilya holds that, as their respective conditions differ, the forms of policy are six.

Of these, agreement with pledges is peace; offensive operation is war; indifference is neutrality; making preparations is marching; seeking the protection of another is alliance; and making peace with one and waging war with another, is termed a double policy. These are the six forms.

Whoever is inferior to another shall make peace with him; whoever is superior in power shall wage war; whoever thinks, "No enemy can hurt me, nor am I strong enough to destroy my enemy," shall observe neutrality; whoever is possessed of necessary means shall march against his enemy; whoever is devoid of necessary strength to defend himself shall seek the protection of another; whoever thinks that help is necessary to work out an end shall make peace with one and wage war with another. Such is the aspect of the six forms of policy.

Of these, a wise king shall observe that form of policy which, in his opinion, enables him to build forts, to construct buildings and commercial roads, to open new plantations and villages, to exploit mines and timber and elephant forests, and at the same time to harass similar works of his enemy.

Whoever thinks himself to be growing in power more rapidly both in quality and quantity than his enemy, and the reverse of his enemy, may neglect his enemy's progress for the time.

If any two kings, hostile to each other, find the time of achieving the results of their respective works to be equal, they shall make peace with each other.

No king shall keep that form of policy, which causes him the loss of profit from his own works, but which entails no such loss on the enemy; for it is deterioration.

Whoever thinks that in the course of time his loss will be less than his acquisition as contrasted with that of his enemy, may neglect his temporary deterioration.

If any two kings, hostile to each other, and deteriorating, expect to acquire equal amount of wealth in equal time, they shall make peace with each other.

That position in which neither progress nor retrogression is seen is stagnation.

Whoever thinks his stagnancy to be of a shorter duration and his prosperity in the long run to be greater than his enemy's may neglect his temporary stagnation.

My teacher says that if any two kings, who are hostile to each other, and are in a stationary condition, expect to acquire equal amount of wealth and power in equal time, they shall make peace with each other.

"Of course," says Kauṭilya, "there is no other alternative."

Or if a king thinks:

"...keeping the agreement of peace, I can undertake productive works of considerable importance and destroy at the same time those of my enemy; or apart from enjoying the results of my own works, I shall also enjoy those of my enemy in virtue of the agreement of peace; or I can destroy the works of my enemy by employing spies and other secret means; or by holding out such inducements as a happy dwelling, rewards, remission of taxes, little work and large profits and wages, I can empty my enemy's country of its population, with which he has been able to carry his own works; or being allied with a king of considerable power, my enemy will have his own works destroyed; or I can prolong my enemy's hostility with another king whose threats have driven my enemy to seek my protection; or being allied with me, my enemy can harass the country of another king who hates me; or oppressed by another king, the subjects of my enemy will immigrate into my country, and I can, therefore, achieve the results of my own works very easily; or being in a precarious condition due to the destruction of his works, my enemy will not be so powerful as to attack me; or by exploiting my own resources in alliance with any two friendly kings, I can augment my resources; or if a Circle of States is formed by my enemy as one of its members, I can divide them and combine with the others; or by threats or favour, I can catch hold of my enemy, and when he desires to be a member of my own Circle of States, I can make him incur the displeasure of the other members and fall a victim to their own fury"—if a king thinks thus, then he may increase his resources by keeping peace.

Or if a king thinks:

"...neither is my enemy strong enough to destroy my works, nor am I his; or if he comes to fight with me like a dog with a boar, I can increase his afflictions without incurring any loss in my own works," then he may observe neutrality and augment his own resources.

Or if a king thinks:

"...by marching my troops it is possible to destroy the works of my enemy; and as for myself, I have made proper arrangements to safeguard my own works," then he may increase his resources by marching.

Or if a king thinks:

"...I am strong enough neither to harass my enemy's works nor to defend my own against my enemy's attack," then he shall seek protection from a king of superior power, and endeavour to pass from the stage of deterioration to that of stagnancy and from the latter to that of progress.

Or if a king thinks:

"...by making peace with one, I can work out my own resources, and by waging war with another, I can destroy the works of my enemy," then he may adopt that double policy and improve his resources.

Thus, a king in the circle of sovereign states shall, by adopting the six-fold policy, endeavour to pass from the state of deterioration to that of stagnation, and from the latter to that of progress.

Chapter 2: The Nature of Alliance

When the advantages derivable from peace and war are of equal character, one should prefer peace; for disadvantages, such as the loss of power and wealth, sojourning, and sin, are ever attending upon war.

The same holds good in the case of neutrality and war.

Of the two forms of policy, double policy and alliance, double policy, i.e., making peace with one and waging war with another is preferable; for whoever adopts the double policy enriches himself, being ever attentive to his own works, whereas an allied king has to help his ally at his own expense.

One shall make an alliance with a king who is stronger than one's neighbouring enemy; in the absence of such a king, one should ingratiate oneself with one's neighbouring enemy, either by supplying money or army or by ceding a part of one's territory and by keeping oneself aloof; for there can be no greater evil to kings than alliance with a king of considerable power, unless one is actually attacked by one's enemy.

A powerless king should behave as a conquered king towards his immediate enemy; but when he finds that the time of his own ascendancy is at hand, due to a fatal disease, internal troubles, increase of enemies, or a friend's calamities that are vexing his enemy, then under the pretence of performing some expiatory rites to avert the danger of his enemy, he may get out of the enemy's court; or if he is in his own territory, he should not go to see his suffering enemy; or if he is near to his enemy, he may murder the enemy when opportunity affords itself.

A king who is situated between two powerful kings shall seek protection from the stronger of the two; or from one of them on whom he can rely; or he may make peace with both of them on equal terms. Then he may begin to set one of them against the other by telling each that the other is a tyrant causing utter ruin to himself, and thus cause dissension between them. When they are divided, he may put down each separately by secret or covert means. Or, throwing himself under the protection of any two immediate kings of considerable power, he may defend himself against an immediate enemy. Or, having made an alliance with a chief in a stronghold, he may adopt the double policy, i.e., make peace with one of the two kings and wage war with another. Or, he may adapt himself to circumstances, depending upon the causes of peace and war in order. Or, he may make friendship with traitors, enemies, and wild chiefs who are conspiring against both the kings. Or, pretending to be a close friend of one of them, he may strike the other at the latter's weak point by employing enemies and wild tribes. Or, having made friendship with both, he may form a Circle of States. Or, he may make an alliance with the *madhyama* or the neutral king; and with this help he may put down one of them or both. Or when hurt by both, he may seek protection from a king of righteous character among the *madhyama* king, the neutral king, and their friends or equals, or from any other king whose subjects are so disposed as to increase his happiness and peace, with whose help he may be able to recover his lost position, with whom his ancestors were in close intimacy or blood relationship, and in whose kingdom he can find a number of powerful friends.

Of two powerful kings who are on amicable terms with each other, a king shall make alliance with one of them who likes him and whom he likes; this is the best way of making alliance.

Chapter 3: The Character of Equal, Inferior and Superior Kings; and Forms of Agreement Made by an Inferior King

A king desirous of expanding his own power shall make use of the six-fold policy.

Agreements of peace shall be made with equal and superior kings; and an inferior king shall be attacked.

Whoever goes to wage war with a superior king will be reduced to the same condition as that of a foot-soldier opposing an elephant.

Just as the collision of an unbaked mud-vessel with a similar vessel is destructive to both, so war with an equal king brings ruin to both.

Like a stone striking an earthen pot, a superior king attains decisive victory over an inferior king.

If a superior king discards the proposal of an inferior king for peace, the latter should take the attitude of a conquered king, or play the part of an inferior king towards a superior.

When a king of equal power does not like peace, then the same amount of vexation as his opponent has received at his hands should be given to him in return; for it is power that brings about peace between any two kings: no piece of iron that is not made red-hot will combine with another piece of iron.

When an inferior king is all submissive, peace should be made with him; for when provoked by causing him troubles and anger, an inferior king, like a wild fire, will attack his enemy and will also be favoured by his Circle of States.

When a king in peace with another finds that greedy, impoverished, and oppressed as are the subjects of his ally, they do not yet immigrate into his own territory lest they might be called back by their master, then he should, though of inferior power, proclaim war against his ally.

When a king at war with another finds that greedy, impoverished, and oppressed as are the subjects of his enemy, still they do not come to his side in consequence of the troubles of war, then he should, though of superior power, make peace with his enemy or remove the troubles of war as far as possible.

When one of the two kings at war with each other and equally involved in trouble finds his own troubles to be greater than his enemy's, and thinks that by getting rid of his enemy's trouble his enemy can successfully wage war with him, then he should, though possessing greater resources, sue for peace.

When, either in peace or war, a king finds neither loss to his enemy nor gain to himself, he should, though superior, observe neutrality.

When a king finds the troubles of his enemy irremediable, he should, though of inferior power, march against the enemy.

When a king finds himself threatened by imminent danger or troubles, he should, though superior, seek the protection of another.

When a king is sure to achieve his desired ends by making peace with one and waging war with another, he should, though superior, adopt the double policy.

Thus it is that the six forms of policy are applied together. . . .

Chapter 5: Consideration about Marching against an Assailable Enemy; Causes Leading to the Dwindling, Greed, and Disloyalty of the Army; and Considerations about the Combination of Powers

. . . By insulting the good and commending the wicked; by causing unnatural and unrighteous slaughter of life; by neglecting the observance of proper and righteous customs; by doing unrighteous acts and neglecting righteous ones; by doing what ought not to be done and not doing what ought to be done; by not paying what ought to be paid and exacting what ought not to be taken; by not punishing the guilty and severely punishing the less guilty; by arresting those who are not to be caught hold of and leaving those who are to be arrested; by undertaking risky works and destroying profitable ones; by not protecting the people against thieves and by robbing them of their wealth; by giving up manly enterprise and condemning good work; by hurting the leaders of the people and despising the worthy; by provoking the aged, by crooked conduct, and by untruthfulness; by not applying remedies against evils and neglecting works in hand; and by carelessness and negligence of himself in maintaining the security of person and property of subjects, the king causes impoverishment, greed, and disaffection to appear among his subjects; when a people are impoverished, they become greedy; when they are greedy, they become disaffected; when disaffected, they voluntarily go to the side of the enemy or destroy their own master.

Hence, no king should give room to such causes as would bring about impoverishment, greed or disaffection among his people. If, however, they appear, he should at once take remedial measures against them.

Which of the three is the worst—an impoverished people? greedy people? or disaffected people?

An impoverished people are ever apprehensive of oppression and destruction by over-taxation, etc., and are therefore desirous of getting rid of their impoverishment, or of waging war or of migrating elsewhere.

A greedy people are ever discontented and they yield themselves to the intrigues of an enemy.

A disaffected people rise against their master along with his enemy.

When the dwindling of the people is due to want of gold and grain, it is a calamity fraught with danger to the whole of the kingdom and can be remedied with difficulty. The dearth of efficient men can be made up by means of gold and grain. Greed is partial and is found among a few chief officers, and it can be got rid of or satisfied by allowing them to plunder an enemy's wealth. Disaffection or disloyalty can be got rid of by putting down the leaders; for in the absence of a leader or leaders, the people are easily governed and they will not take part in the intrigues of enemies. When a people are too nervous to endure the calamities, they first become dispersed, when their leaders are put down; and when they are kept under restraint, they endure calamities.

Having well considered the causes which bring about peace or war, one should combine with kings of considerable power and righteous character and march against one's enemy. . . .

Though actuated with feelings of true friendship, the conqueror has reason to fear his ally, though of equal power, when the latter attains success in his mission; having succeeded in his mission, an ally of equal power is likely to change his attitude even towards the conqueror of superior power.

An ally of superior power should not be relied upon, for prosperity changes the mind. Even with little or no share in the spoils, an ally of superior power may go back, appearing contented; but some time afterwards, he may not fail to sit on the lap of the conqueror and carry off twice the amount of share due to him.

Having been satisfied with mere victory, the leading conqueror should discharge his allies, having satisfied them with their shares he may allow himself to be conquered by them instead of attempting to conquer them in the matter of spoils; it is thus that a king can win the good graces of his Circle of States.

Chapter 17: Making Peace and Breaking It

The words *śama* (quiet), *sandhi* (agreement of peace), and *samādhi* (reconcilement) are synonymous. . . .

My teacher says that peace, dependent upon honesty or oath, is mutable, while peace with a security or a hostage is immutable.

No, says Kauṭilya, peace, dependent upon honesty or oath, is immutable both in this and the next world. It is for this world only that a security or a hostage is required for strengthening the agreement.

Honest kings of old made their agreement of peace with this declaration: "We have joined in peace." In case of any apprehension of breach of honesty, they made their agreement by swearing by fire, water, plough, the brick of a fort wall, the shoulder of an elephant, the hips of a horse, the front of a chariot, a weapon, seeds, scents, juice, wrought gold, or bullion gold, and by declaring that these things will destroy and desert him who violates the oath.

In order to avoid the contingency of violation of oath, peace made with the security of such persons as ascetics engaged in penance, or nobles, is peace with a security. In such a peace, whoever takes as security a person capable of controlling the enemy gains more advantages, while he who acts to the contrary is deceived. . . .

Whoever is rising in power may break the agreement of peace. . . .

Chapter 18: The Conduct of a Madhyama King, a Neutral King, and of a Circle of States

. . . When, after having put down the enemy, and after having grown in power, a friend becomes unsubmissive, the conqueror should cause the friend to incur the displeasure of a neighbour and of the king who is next to the neighbour.

Or the conqueror may employ a scion of the friend's family or an imprisoned prince to seize his lands; or the conqueror may so act that his friend, desirous of further help, may continue to be obedient.

The conqueror should never help his friend when the latter is more and more deteriorating; a politician should so keep his friend that the latter neither deteriorates nor grows in power.

When, with the desire of getting wealth, a wandering friend, i.e., a nomadic king makes an agreement with the conqueror, the latter should so remove the cause of the friend's flight that he never flies again.

When a friend is as accessible to the conqueror as to the latter's enemy, the conqueror should first separate that obstinate friend from the enemy, and then destroy him, and afterwards the enemy also.

When a friend remains neutral, the conqueror should cause him to incur the displeasure of his immediate enemies; and when he is worried in his wars with them, the conqueror should oblige him with help.

When, owing to his own weakness, a friend seeks protection both from the conqueror and the latter's enemy, the conqueror should help him with the army, so that he never turns his attention elsewhere.

Or having removed him from his own lands, the conqueror may keep him in another tract of land, having made some previous arrangements to punish or favour the friend.

Or the conqueror may harm him when he has grown powerful, or destroy him when he does not help the conqueror in danger and when he lies on the conqueror's lap in good faith.

When an enemy furiously rises against his own enemy, i.e., the conqueror's friend under troubles, the former should be put down by the latter himself with troubles concealed.

When a friend keeps quiet after rising against an enemy under troubles, that friend will be subdued by the enemy himself after getting rid of his troubles.

Whoever is acquainted with the science of polity should clearly observe the conditions of progress, deterioration, stagnation, reduction, and destruction, as well as the use of all kinds of strategic means.

Whoever thus knows the inter-dependence of the six kinds of policy plays at his pleasure with kings, bound round, as it were, in chains skilfully devised by himself.

BOOK 8: CONCERNING VICES AND CALAMITIES

CHAPTER 1: THE AGGREGATE OF THE CALAMITIES OF THE ELEMENTS OF SOVEREIGNTY

When calamities happen together, the form of consideration should be whether it is easier to take an offensive or defensive attitude. National calamities, coming from Providence or from man, happen from one's misfortune or bad policy. The word, vices or calamities, means the reverse or absence of virtue, the preponderance of vices, and occasional troubles. That which deprives a person of his happiness is termed vices or calamities.

My teacher says that of the calamities, viz., the king in distress, the minister in distress, the people in distress, distress due to bad fortifications, financial distress, the army in distress, and an ally in distress—that which is first mentioned is more serious than the one coming later in the order of enumeration.

No, says Bhāradvāja, of the distress of the king and of his minister, ministerial distress is more serious; deliberations in council, the attainment of results as anticipated while deliberating in council, the accomplishment of works, the business of revenue collection and its expenditure, recruiting the army, the driving out of the enemy and of wild tribes, the protection of the kingdom, taking remedial measures against calamities, the protection of the heir apparent, and the installation of princes constitute the duties of ministers. In the absence of ministers, the above works are ill-done; and, like a bird deprived of its feathers, the king loses his active capacity. In such calamities, the intrigues of the enemy find a ready scope. In ministerial distress, the king's life itself comes into danger, for a minister is the mainstay of the security of the king's life.

No, says Kauṭilya, it is verily the king who attends to the business of appointing ministers, priests, and other servants including the superintendents of several departments, the application of remedies against the troubles of his people, and of his kingdom, and the adoption of progressive measures; when his ministers fall into troubles, he employs others; he is ever ready to bestow rewards on the worthy and inflict punishments on the wicked; when the king is well off, by his welfare and prosperity, he pleases the people; of what kind the king's character is, of the same kind will be the character of his people; for their progress or downfall, the people depend upon the king; the king is, as it were, the aggregate of the people.

Viśālākṣa says that of the troubles of the minister and of the people, the troubles of the people are more serious: finance, army, raw products, free labour, carriage of things, and collection of necessaries are all secured from the people. There will be no such things in the absence of people, next to the king and his minister.

No, says Kauṭilya, all activities proceed from the minister: activities such as the successful accomplishment of the works of the people, security of person and property from internal and external enemies, remedial measures against calamities, colonization and improvement of wild tracts of land, recruiting the army, collection of revenue, and bestowal of favour.

The school of Parāśara say that of the distress of the people and distress due to bad fortifications, the latter is a more serious evil; for it is in fortified towns that the treasury and the army are secured; they (fortified towns) are a secure place for the people; they are a stronger power than the citizens or country people; and they are a powerful defensive instrument in times of danger for the king. As to the people, they are common both to the king and his enemy.

No, says Kauṭilya, for forts, finance, and the army depend upon the people; likewise buildings, trade, agriculture, cattle-rearing, bravery, stability, power, and abundance of things. In countries inhabited by people, there are mountains and islands as natural forts; in the absence of an expansive country, forts are resorted to. When a country consists purely of cultivators, troubles due to the absence of fortifications are apparent; while in a country which consists purely of warlike people, troubles that may appear are due to the absence of an expansive and cultivated territory.

Piśuna says that of the troubles due to the absence of forts and to want of finance, troubles due to want of finance are more serious; the repair of fortifications and their maintenance depend upon finance; by means of wealth, intrigue to capture an enemy's fort may be carried on; by means of wealth, the people, friends, and enemies can be kept under control; by means of it, outsiders can be encouraged and the establishment of the army and its operations conducted. It is possible to remove the treasury in times of danger, but not the fort.

No, says Kauṭilya, for it is in the fort that the treasury and the army are safely kept, and it is from the fort that secret war intrigue, control over one's partisans, the upkeep of the army, the reception of allies and the driving out of enemies and of wild tribes are successfully practised. In the absence of forts, the treasury is to the enemy, for it seems that for those who own forts there is no destruction.

Kauṇapadanta says that of distress due to want of finance or to an inefficient army, that which is due to the want of an efficient army is more serious; for control over one's own friends and enemies, the winning over the army of an enemy, and the business of administration are all dependent upon the army. In the absence of the army, it is certain that the treasury will be lost, whereas lack of finance can be made up by procuring raw products and lands or by seizing an enemy's territory.

The army[1] may go to the enemy, or murder the king himself, and bring about all kinds of troubles. But finance is the chief means of observing virtuous acts and of enjoying desires. Owing to a change in place, time, and policy, either finance or the army may be a superior power; for the army is sometimes the means of securing the wealth acquired; but wealth is always the means of securing both the treasury and the army. Since all activities are dependent upon finance, financial troubles are more serious.

Vātavyādhi says that of the distress of the army and of an ally, the distress of an ally is more serious—an ally, though he is not fed and is far off, is still serviceable; he drives off not only the rear-enemy and the friends of the rear-enemy, but also the frontal enemy and wild tribes; he also helps his friend with money, army, and lands on occasions of troubles.

No, says Kauṭilya, the ally of him who has a powerful army keeps the alliance; and even the enemy assumes a friendly attitude; when there is a work that can be equally accomplished either by the army or by an ally, then preference to the army or to the ally should depend on the advantages of securing the appropriate place and time for war and the expected profit. In times of sudden expedition and on occasions of troubles from an enemy, a wild tribe, or local rebels, no friend can be trusted. When calamities happen together, or when an enemy has grown strong, a friend keeps up his friendship as long as money is forthcoming. Thus the determination of the comparative seriousness of the calamities of the various elements of sovereignty. . . .

Chapter 2: Considerations about the Troubles of the King and of His Kingdom

The king and his kingdom are the primary elements of the state.

The troubles of the king may be either internal or external. Internal troubles are more serious than external troubles, which are like the danger arising from a lurking snake. Troubles due to a minister are more serious than other kinds of internal troubles. Hence, the king should keep under his own control the powers of finance and the army.

. . . a people will naturally obey a high-born king though he is

[1] A line or two introducing the opinion of Kauṭilya against Kauṇpadanta seem to have been lost here.

weak, for the tendency of a prosperous people is to follow a high-born king. Also they render the intrigues of a strong but base-born person unavailing, as the saying is, that possession of virtues makes for friendship....

Chapter 3: The Aggregate of the Trouble of Men

Ignorance and absence of discipline are the causes of a man's troubles. An untrained man does not perceive the injuries arising from vices. We are going to treat of them (vices):

...Anger is always a necessary quality for the prevention of sin....

No, says Kauṭilya, anger brings about enmity with, and troubles from, an enemy, and is always associated with pain. Addiction to pleasure (*kāma*) occasions contempt and loss of wealth, and throws the addicted person into the company of thieves, gamblers, hunters, singers, players on musical instruments, and other undesirable persons. Of these, enmity is more serious than contempt, for a despised person is caught hold of by his own people and by his enemies, whereas a hated person is destroyed. Troubles from an enemy are more serious than loss of wealth, for loss of wealth causes financial troubles, whereas troubles from an enemy are injurious to life. Suffering on account of vices is more serious than keeping company with undesirable persons, for the company of undesirable persons can be got rid of in a moment, whereas suffering from vices causes injury for a long time. Hence, anger is a more serious evil....

The reception of what is condemned is due to desire; and anger consists in oppressing the good; since both these are productive of many evils, both of them are held to be the worst evils.

Hence, he who is possessed of discretion should associate with the aged, and, after controlling his passions, abandon both anger and desire, which are productive of other evils and destructive of the very basis of life.

BOOK 9: THE WORK OF AN INVADER

Chapter 1: The Knowledge of Power, Place, Time, Strength, and Weakness; the Time of Invasion

The conqueror should know the comparative strength and weakness of himself and of his enemy; and having ascertained the power, place, time, the time of marching and of recruiting the army, the consequences, the loss of men and money, and profits and danger, he should march with his full force; otherwise, he should keep quiet.

My teacher says that of enthusiasm and power, enthusiasm is better:...

No, says Kauṭilya, he who is possessed of power over-reaches, by the sheer force of his power, another who is merely enthusiastic. Having acquired, captured, or bought another enthusiastic king as well as brave soldiers, he can make his enthusiastic army of horses, elephants, chariots, and others to move anywhere without obstruction. Powerful kings, whether women, young men, lame, or blind, conquered the earth by winning over or purchasing the aid of enthusiastic persons.

My teacher says that of power (money and army) and skill in intrigue, power is better; for a king, though possessed of skill for intrigue becomes a man of barren mind if he has no power; for the work of intrigue is well defined. He who has no power loses his kingdom as sprouts of seeds in drought vomit their sap.

No, says Kauṭilya, skill for intrigue is better; he who has the eye of knowledge, and is acquainted with the science of polity, can, with little effort, make use of his skill for intrigue, and can succeed by means of conciliation and other strategic means and by spies and chemical appliances in over-reaching even those kings who are possessed of enthusiasm and power. Thus of the three acquirements, viz., enthusiasm, power, and skill for intrigue, he who possesses more of the quality mentioned later than the one mentioned first in the order of enumeration will be successful in over-reaching others....

Chapter 7: Doubts about Wealth and Harm; and Success to be Obtained by the Employment of Alternate Strategic Means

...As virtue is the basis of wealth and as enjoyment is the end of wealth, success in achieving that kind of wealth which promotes virtue, wealth and enjoyment is termed success in all. Thus, varieties of success.

Such providential visitations as fire, floods, disease, pestilence, fever, famine, and demoniac troubles are dangerous.

Success in averting these is to be sought by worshipping gods and *brāhmins*.

Whether demoniacal troubles are absent, or are too many, or

normal, the rites prescribed in the *Atharva Veda*, as well as the rites undertaken by accomplished ascetics, are to be performed for success.

BOOK 14: SECRET MEANS

Chapter 1: Means to Injure an Enemy

In order to protect the institution of the four castes, such measures as are treated of in secret science shall be applied against the wicked. Through the instrumentality of such men or women of [the] *Mleccha*[1] class as can put on disguises appropriate to different countries, arts, or professions, or as can put on the appearance of a hump-backed, dwarfish, or short-sized person, or of a dumb, deaf, idiot, or blind person, *kālakūṭa*[2] and other manifold poisons should be administered in the diet and other physical enjoyments of the wicked. Spies lying in wait or living as inmates in the same house may make use of weapons on occasions of royal sports or musical and other entertainments. Spies, under the disguise of night-walkers or of firekeepers may set fire to the houses of the wicked. . . .

BOOK 15: THE PLAN OF A TREATISE

Chapter 1

The subsistence of mankind is termed *artha*, wealth; the earth which contains mankind is termed *artha*, wealth; that science which treats of the means of acquiring and maintaining the earth is the *Arthaśāstra*, *Science of Polity*. . . .

Thus this *Śāstra*, conforming to these paragraphic divisions, is composed as a guide to acquire and secure this and the other world.

In the light of this *Śāstra* one can not only set on foot righteous, economical, and aesthetical acts and maintain them, but also put down unrighteous, uneconomical, and displeasing acts.

This *Śāstra* has been made by him who from intolerance of misrule quickly rescued the scriptures and the science of weapons and the earth which had passed to the Nanda king.

[1] Literally, barbarian; i.e., one of the lowest.

[2] A poison.

THE HETERODOX SYSTEMS

CHAPTER VII

CĀRVĀKA

THIS system assumed various forms of philosophical skepticism, logical fatalism, and religious indifferentism. Its origins can be traced as far back as the *Ṛg Veda.* It is mentioned in the Epics as well as in the Dialogues of the Buddha. Even the *Bhagavad-gītā*[1] refers to it.

The main work on the system, the *Bṛhaspati Sūtra* (600 B.C.), is not available, and we have to reconstruct the doctrines of materialism from statements of the position and criticism of it found in polemical and other works.

The doctrine is called Lokāyata, as it holds that only this world (*loka*) exists and there is no beyond. There is no future life. Perception is the only source of knowledge; what is not perceived does not exist. The materialists deny the validity of inference, as inference depends on universal connections, and perceived data, which are particulars, do not warrant belief in universal connections. As perception is the only form of valid knowledge, matter, which alone is cognized by the senses, is the only reality. The ultimate principles are the four elements: earth, water, fire, and air.

Consciousness is a material and transitory modification of these elements and will disappear when these elements, from which it is produced, are dissolved. That intelligence which is found to be embodied in modified forms of the nonintelligent elements is produced in the same way in which the red color is produced from the combination of betel, areca nut, and lime.

The soul is only the body qualified by intelligence. It has no existence apart from the body. Four different varieties of materialism are mentioned, according as the soul is identified with the body, the senses, the breath, or the organ of thought. The postulates of religion, God, freedom, and immortality, are illusions. Nature is indifferent to good and evil, and history does not bear witness to Divine Providence. Pleasure and pain are the central facts of life. Virtue and vice are not absolute values but mere social conventions.

The materialistic theory is a bold attempt to rid the age of the

[1] XVI.8. See references also in Śāntiparva, 1414, 1430–42, and Śalyaparva, 3619 (of the *Mahābhārata*); *Viṣṇu Purāṇa* III.xviii.14–26; The *Laws of Manu* II.II; III.150, 161; IV.30, 61, 163; V.89; VIII.22, 309; IX.65, 66; XII.33, 95, 96.

oppression of the past and prepare the ground for the great constructive efforts of speculation. It is one of the three major heterodox theories—the others being Buddhism and Jainism—in that it did not draw its theories from the Veda and Upaniṣads and did not attempt to justify its teachings by reference to those basic orthodox texts.

The selections included here are somewhat miscellaneous. There has been an attempt to be fairly exhaustive in the presentation of material stating the positive principles of the materialistic doctrine. Both of the old and standard summaries of the system, the pertinent chapters of the *Sarvadarśanasaṁgraha* (14th century A.D.) and of the *Sarvasiddhāntasaṁgraha* of Śaṁkara, are given in full. The selection from the well-known ancient drama, *Prabodha-candrodaya* (*The Rise of the Moon of Intellect*) is included in order to call attention to the prominence of the materialistic movement. The *Tattvopaplavasiṁha* (seventh century A.D.) is the only extant treatise which may be considered an authentic text of the school. It is an "upsetting of all principles," that is, a polemical treatise against all of the other schools of Indian philosophy. It is not considered worth while to enter into the very lengthy polemical side of the treatise, however, and so only one chapter, that against the orthodox theory of inference, translated especially for this volume, has been included.

The selections have been taken from (A) Mādhava Ācārya, *Sarvadarśanasaṁgraha*, translated by E. B. Cowell and A. E. Gough (London: Kegan Paul, Trench, Trübner & Co., Ltd., 1904), pp. 2–11; (B) Śaṁkara, *Sarvasiddhāntasaṁgraha*, translated by Prem Sundar Bose (Calcutta, 1929), pp. 4–6; (C) Jayarāśi Bhaṭṭa, *Tattvopaplavasiṁha*, Ch. VII, translated by S. N. Shastri and S. K. Saksena, revised by S. C. Chatterjee, from *Tattvopaplavasiṁha*, edited by Pandit Sukhlalji Sanghavi and Rasiklal C. Parikh, Gaekwad's Oriental Series, LXXXVII (Baroda: Oriental Institute, 1940); (D) Kṛṣṇa Miśra, *Prabodha-candrodaya*, translated by J. Taylor (Bombay, 1811), pp. 19–22.

A. *SARVADARŚANASAṀGRAHA*

The efforts of Cārvāka are indeed hard to be eradicated, for the majority of living beings hold by the current refrain—

> While life is yours, live joyously;
> None can escape Death's searching eye:
> When once this frame of ours they burn,
> How shall it e'er again return?

The mass of men, in accordance with the Śāstras of policy and enjoyment, considering wealth and desire the only ends of man and denying the existence of any object belonging to a future world, are found to follow only the doctrine of Cārvāka. Hence another name for that school is Lokāyata,—a name well accordant with the thing signified.

In this school the four elements, earth, &c., are the original principles; from these alone, when transformed into the body, intelligence is produced, just as the inebriating power is developed from the mixing of certain ingredients; and when these are destroyed, intelligence at once perishes also. They quote the *śruti* [Vedic text] for this [*Bṛhadāraṇyaka Upaniṣad* II.iv.12]: "Springing forth from these elements, itself solid knowledge, it is destroyed when they are destroyed, —after death no intelligence remains." Therefore the soul is only the body distinguished by the attribute of intelligence, since there is no evidence for any self distinct from the body, as such cannot be proved, since this school holds that perception is the only source of knowledge and does not allow inference, &c.

The only end of man is enjoyment produced by sensual pleasures. Nor may you say that such cannot be called the end of man as they are always mixed with some kind of pain, because it is our wisdom to enjoy the pure pleasure as far as we can, and to avoid the pain which inevitably accompanies it; just as the man who desires fish takes the fish with their scales and bones, and having taken as many as he wants, desists; or just as the man who desires rice, takes the rice, straw and all, and having taken as much as he wants, desists. It is not therefore for us, through a fear of pain, to reject the pleasure which our nature instinctively recognises as congenial. Men do not refrain from sowing rice, because forsooth there are wild animals to devour it; nor do they refuse to set the cooking-pots on the fire, because forsooth there are beggars to pester us for a share of the contents. If any one were so timid as to forsake a visible pleasure, he would indeed be foolish like a beast, as has been said by the poet—

The pleasure which arises to men from contact with sensible objects,
Is to be relinquished as accompanied by pain,—such is the reasoning of fools;
The berries of paddy, rich with the finest white grains,
What man, seeking his true interest, would fling away because covered with husk and dust?

If you object that, if there be no such thing as happiness in a future world, then how should men of experienced wisdom engage in the *Agnihotra*[1] and other sacrifices, which can only be performed with great expenditure of money and bodily fatigue, your objection cannot be accepted as any proof to the contrary, since the *Agnihotra*, &c.,

[1] Sacrificial offering to fire.

are only useful as means of livelihood, for the Veda is tainted by the three faults of untruth, self-contradiction, and tautology; then again the impostors who call themselves Vaidic [or Vedic] pandits are mutually destructive, as the authority of the *jñāna-kāṇḍa* (section on knowledge) is overthrown by those who maintain that of the *karma-kāṇḍa* (section on action), while those who maintain the authority of the *jñāna-kāṇḍa* reject that of the *karma-kāṇḍa*; and lastly, the three Vedas themselves are only the incoherent rhapsodies of knaves, and to this effect runs the popular saying—

The *Agnihotra*, the three Vedas, the ascetic's three staves, and smearing oneself with ashes,—
Bṛhaspati says these are but means of livelihood for those who have no manliness nor sense.

Hence it follows that there is no other hell than mundane pain produced by purely mundane causes, as thorns, &c.; the only Supreme is the earthly monarch whose existence is proved by all the world's eyesight; and the only liberation is the dissolution of the body. By holding the doctrine that the soul is identical with the body, such phrases as "I am thin," "I am black," &c., are at once intelligible, as the attributes of thinness, &c., and self-consciousness will reside in the same subject (the body); and the use of the phrase "my body" is metaphorical like "the head of Rāhu" [Rāhu being really *all head*].

All this has been thus summed up—

In this school there are four elements, earth, water, fire, and air;
And from these four elements alone is intelligence produced,—
Just like the intoxicating power from *kiṇva*,[1] &c., mixed together;
Since in "I am fat," "I am lean," these attributes abide in the same subject,
And since fatness, &c., reside only in the body, it alone is the soul and no other,
And such phrases as "my body" are only significant metaphorically.

"Be it so," says the opponent; "your wish would be gained if inference, &c., had no force of proof; but then they have this force; else, if they had not, then how, on perceiving smoke, should the thoughts of the intelligent immediately proceed to fire; or why, on

[1] An intoxicating herb.

hearing another say, 'There are fruits on the bank of the river,' do those who desire fruit proceed at once to the shore?"

All this, however, is only the inflation of the world of fancy.

Those who maintain the authority of inference accept the sign or middle term as the causer of knowledge, which middle term must be found in the minor and be itself invariably connected with the major. Now this invariable connection must be a relation destitute of any condition accepted or disputed; and this connection does not possess its power of causing inference by virtue of its existence, as the eye, &c., are the cause of perception, but by virtue of its being known. What then is the means of this connection's being known?

We will first show that it is not perception. Now perception is held to be of two kinds, external and internal [i.e., as produced by the external senses, or by the inner sense, mind]. The former is not the required means; for although it is possible that the actual contact of the senses and the object will produce the knowledge of the particular object thus brought in contact, yet as there can never be such contact in the case of the past or the future, the universal proposition which was to embrace the invariable connection of the middle and major terms in every case becomes impossible to be known. Nor may you maintain that this knowledge of the universal proposition has the general class as its object, because, if so, there might arise a doubt as to the existence of the invariable connection in this particular case [as, for instance, in this particular smoke as implying fire].

Nor is internal perception the means, since you cannot establish that the mind has any power to act independently towards an external object, since all allow that it is dependent on the external senses, as has been said by one of the logicians, "The eye, &c., have their objects as described; but mind externally is dependent on the others."

Nor can inference be the means of the knowledge of the universal proposition, since in the case of this inference we should also require another inference to establish it, and so on, and hence would arise the fallacy of an *ad infinitum* retrogression.

Nor can testimony be the means thereof, since we may either allege in reply, in accordance with the Vaiśeṣika doctrine of Kaṇāda, that this is included in the topic of inference; or else we may hold that this fresh proof of testimony is unable to leap over the old barrier that stopped the progress of inference, since it depends itself on the recognition of a sign in the form of the language used in the child's presence by the old man; and, moreover, there is no more reason for our believing on another's word that smoke and fire are invariably connected than for our receiving the *ipse dixit* of Manu, &c. [which, of course, we Cārvākas reject].

And again, if testimony were to be accepted as the only means of the knowledge of the universal proposition, then in the case of a man to whom the fact of the invariable connection between the middle and major terms had not been pointed out by another person, there could be no inference of one thing [as fire] on seeing another thing [as smoke]; hence, on your own showing, the whole topic of inference for oneself would have to end in mere idle words.

Then again, comparison, &c., must be utterly rejected as the means of the knowledge of the universal proposition, since it is impossible that they can produce the knowledge of the unconditioned connection [i.e., the universal proposition], because their end is to produce the knowledge of quite another connection, viz., the relation of a name to something so named.

Again, this same absence of a condition, which has been given as the definition of an invariable connection [i.e., a universal proposition], can itself never be known; since it is impossible to establish that all conditions must be objects of perception; and therefore, although the absence of perceptible things may be itself perceptible, the absence of non-perceptible things must be itself non-perceptible; and thus, since we must here too have recourse to inference, &c., we cannot leap over the obstacle which has already been planted to bar them. Again, we must accept as the definition of the condition, "it is that which is reciprocal or equipollent in extension with the major term though not constantly accompanying the middle." These three distinguishing clauses, "not constantly accompanying the middle term," "constantly accompanying the major term," and "being constantly accompanied by it" [i.e., reciprocal], are needed in the full definition to stop respectively three such fallacious conditions, in the argument to prove the non-eternity of sound, as "being produced," "the nature of a jar," and "the not causing audition"; wherefore the definition holds,—and again it is established by the *śloka* of the great doctor beginning "*samāsama*."[1]

[1] This refers to an obscure *śloka* of Udayanācārya, "where a reciprocal and a non-reciprocal universal connection (i.e., universal propositions which severally do and do not distribute their predicates) relate to the same argument (as e.g., to prove the existence of smoke), there that non-reciprocating term of the second will be a fallacious middle, which is not invariably accompanied by the other reciprocal of the first."

But since the knowledge of the condition must here precede the knowledge of the condition's absence, it is only when there is the knowledge of the condition, that the knowledge of the universality of the proposition is possible, i.e., a knowledge in the form of such a connection between the middle term and major term as is distinguished by the absence of any such condition; and, on the other hand, the knowledge of the condition depends upon the knowledge of the invariable connection. Thus we fasten on our opponents as with adamantine glue the thunderbolt-like fallacy of reasoning in a circle. Hence by the impossibility of knowing the universality of a proposition it becomes impossible to establish inference, &c.

The step which the mind takes from the knowledge of smoke, &c., to the knowledge of fire, &c., can be accounted for by its being based on a former perception or by its being an error; and that in some cases this step is justified by the result is accidental just like the coincidence of effects observed in the employment of gems, charms, drugs, &c.

From this it follows that fate, &c., do not exist, since these can only be proved by inference. But an opponent will say, if you thus do not allow *adṛṣṭa*,[1] the various phenomena of the world become destitute of any cause. But we cannot accept this objection as valid, since these phenomena can all be produced spontaneously from the inherent nature of things. Thus it has been said—

The fire is hot, the water cold, refreshing cool the breeze of morn;
By whom came this variety? from their own nature was it born.

And all this has been also said by Bṛhaspati—

There is no heaven, no final liberation, nor any soul in another world,
Nor do the actions of the four castes, orders, &c., produce any real effect.
The *Agnihotra*, the three Vedas, the ascetic's three staves, and smearing oneself with ashes,
Were made by Nature as the livelihood of those destitute of knowledge and manliness.
If a beast slain in the *Jyotiṣṭoma* rite[2] will itself go to heaven,
Why then does not the sacrificer forthwith offer his own father?
If the *Śrāddha*[3] produces gratification to beings who are dead,

[1] The unseen force. [2] A Vedic sacrifice. [3] Oblations to the dead.

Then here, too, in the case of travellers when they start, it is needless to give provisions for the journey.
If beings in heaven are gratified by our offering the *Śrāddha* here,
Then why not give the food down below to those who are standing on the housetop?
While life remains let a man live happily, let him feed on ghee[1] even though he runs in debt;
When once the body becomes ashes, how can it ever return again?
If he who departs from the body goes to another world,
How is it that he comes not back again, restless for love of his kindred?
Hence it is only as a means of livelihood that *brāhmins* have established here
All these ceremonies for the dead—there is no other fruit anywhere.
The three authors of the Vedas were buffoons, knaves, and demons.
All the well-known formulas of the pandits, *jarpharī*, *turpharī*, &c.[2]
And all the obscene rites for the queen commanded in the *Aśvamedha*,[3]
These were invented by buffoons, and so all the various kinds of presents to the priests,
While the eating of flesh was similarly commanded by night-prowling demons.

Hence in kindness to the mass of living beings must we fly for refuge to the doctrine of Cārvāka. Such is the pleasant consummation.

B. *SARVASIDDHĀNTASAṀGRAHA*

1. According to the Lokāyatika doctrine the four elements alone are the ultimate principles—earth, water, fire and air; there is none other.

2. Only the perceived exists; the unperceivable does not exist, by reason of its never having been perceived; even the believers in the invisible never say that the invisible has been perceived.

3. If the rarely perceived be taken for the unperceived, how can

[1] Clarified butter. [2] See *Ṛg Veda* x.106.
[3] A Vedic sacrificial ritual: the "horse sacrifice."

they call it the unperceived? How can the ever-unperceived, like things such as the horns of a hare, be an existent?

4. Others should not here postulate [the existence of] merit and demerit from happiness and misery. A person is happy or miserable through [the laws of] nature; there is no other cause.

5. Who paints the peacocks, or who makes the cuckoos sing? There exists here no cause excepting nature.

6. The soul is but the body characterised by the attributes signified in the expressions, "I am stout," "I am youthful," "I am grown up," "I am old," etc. It is not something other than that [body].

7. The consciousness that is found in the modifications of non-intelligent elements [i.e., in organisms formed out of matter] is produced in the manner of the red colour out of the combination of betel, areca-nut and lime.

8. There is no world other than this; there is no heaven and no hell; the realm of Śiva and like regions are invented by stupid impostors of other schools of thought.

9. The enjoyment of heaven lies in eating delicious food, keeping company of young women, using fine clothes, perfumes, garlands, sandal paste, etc.

10. The pain of hell lies in the troubles that arise from enemies, weapons, diseases; while liberation (*mokṣa*) is death which is the cessation of life-breath.

11. The wise therefore ought not to take pains on account of that [i.e., liberation]; it is only the fool who wears himself out by penances, fasts, etc.

12. Chastity and other such ordinances are laid down by clever weaklings. Gifts of gold and land, the pleasure of invitations to dinner, are devised by indigent people with stomachs lean with hunger.

13. The construction of temples, houses for water-supply, tanks, wells, resting places, and the like, is praised only by travellers, not by others.

14. The *Agnihotra* ritual, the three Vedas, the triple staff,[1] the ash-smearing, are the ways of gaining a livelihood for those who are lacking in intellect and energy,—so thinks Bṛhaspati.

15. The wise should enjoy the pleasures of this world through the proper visible means of agriculture, keeping cattle, trade, political administration, etc.

[1] A triple staff carried by a priest.

C. *TATTVOPAPLAVASIṀHA*

Jayarāśi, who gives the title of *Tattvopaplavasiṁha* to this work, undertakes to refute and attack the tenets of other schools of thought. Herein he essays to refute inference, which is acknowledged as one of the established means of evidence by the school of logic (Nyāya) propounded by Gautama and his followers. He first quotes the definition of inference as put forth by the logicians and advances arguments with hair-breadth distinctions to dismantle the definition and exclude all possibility of inference. His main attack is against the formation of the major premise on which is built the entire edifice of syllogistic inference. According to him, the formation of the premise is dependent upon direct perception of a universal principle and this is not possible.

1. Then he proceeds to dislodge the theory of inference based upon the knowledge of the effect (e.g., smoke), because the "effectness" (*kāryatva*) of the so-called effect is not established. According to him, nothing is an effect which is not destructible and without the latter being established the former cannot be substantiated.

2. Incidentally and arising out of the above, there follows a discussion on the relation of opposition as such, in which he puts forth a number of alternatives each landing the opponent into difficulties.

3. Next, he refutes the very basis of all inference, namely, the determination of the relation between cause and effect, and thereby removes the possibility of inference of the cause through the perception of the effect and vice versa.

4. Finally, he disproves the inference of the impermanence of sound, etc., due to their being created, and closes his argument by ruling out the inference even of the sequential relation between sunrise and sunset and vice versa. (C. A. M.)

REFUTATION OF INFERENCE

Inference, then, is now being examined—Well, what is inference? "Inference is preceded by it [perception]" (*Nyāya Sūtra* I.i.5). Why is this so? It is explained thus: In a kitchen, one apprehends the relation between fire and smoke through the function of the eyes, etc. By this a connection between them is formed in the mind; thereafter, the sign [smoke] is perceived in something for a second time. Then one remembers the universal relation [between the smoke and fire]. After this, there is a consideration of the thing [the hill] as related to smoke which is pervaded by [universally related to] fire, and this leads to the inference [of fire in the thing] from the sign [the smoke].

In the absence of one, there is an absence of the other, for the one precedes the other. In this world, no effect is seen to have taken place without its cause; perception is declared to be the cause, and in its absence how can there be any possibility of inference? If there were [such a] possibility, it would be a case of an event being produced without a cause. In the absence of perception, it is said, "It is impossible to apprehend an invariable relation [between events]."

There is another reason why the knowledge of an invariable relation cannot be established. Is it the cognition of a relation between two universals, or between two particulars, or between a universal and a particular? If it be the cognition of a relation between two universals, then that is incorrect for the universal itself is not demonstrated (*anupapatti*). That it is not demonstrated has already been shown. Nor is it possible to conceive of such a relation subsisting between a universal and a particular object because of the indemonstrability [or impossibility, *asaṁbhavāt*] of universals.

Nor is it [possible to think of] such a relation between two particulars for there are innumerable cases of particular fires and particular smokes, and also because [as proved by us][1] no common element exists among the many particulars. Even if that were possible, the numberlessness [of individual objects] would still persist. Or, if that [the numberlessness], too, were to disappear, then there would be no existence of particulars and, in their absence, tell me, by reference to what would the relation be apprehended?

Moreover, perception is not competent to establish any relation among particulars on account of the remoteness of time, place, and the essence [of things]. Nor is it possible to have any knowledge of a relation without the perception of the related terms, because that is the basis of the relation and of the knowledge of it. Nor is it the case that all the related terms are perceived at the time when the relation is being perceived, for they do not appear to be perceived at all [at the time]. It is not logical to regard something as perceived unless it appears to be perceived, as that would be an undue assumption; otherwise, when, as the result of a palatal perception, the taste of an object is being experienced, the perception of its color (*rūpa*) would also occur.

Well, then, if [it be argued that] the existence of such a relation could be apprehended in the case of a few particular objects that are present at the time of apprehending the relation of invariability, though not with regard to all of them, then only those particular objects [that are present at the time of perception] can be taken as

[1] See *Tattvopaplavasiṁha*, p. 47.

signs (or marks, *gamaka*) [for inference], and not the others. A relation subsisting between one pair of terms cannot serve as the ground of inference for another [pair], for that would be an undue extension. Indeed, a visual contact being established between the eye of Devadatta and a jar, no knowledge of water, etc., can be had, for it is an essential characteristic of a contact that it gives rise to the knowledge of an object with reference only to a particular time and place.

...Individual objects differ; hence, upon the contact of one, another cannot be perceived, due to the difference in their form. Should the difference in form not be recognized, all varieties of smoke on a mountain would fall into the category of smoke, which having taken place, the perception of smoke could not give rise to the inference of fire, because the relation [of invariability] subsisting between them is as unknown [to the perceiver] as it is to a resident of a Coconut Island. Without the knowledge of such a relation, the inferred fire is only like the god of the goblins.

If from the cognition of that which is related to fire [smoke] you argue to a cognition of the relation [between the two], then there is the fallacy of undue assumption [*atiprasaṅga*). Therefore, the smokes are like the cognitions of the signs... [and this] cannot, on the right view, be explained in any way. Thus, in fact, why is it not acceptable that the knowledge of the one [smoke] does not depend upon the [knowledge of the] other [fire]?... [Well, if it be argued that even without the cognition of the relation of interdependence, smoke by itself is competent to give rise to the knowledge of fire on a mountain], then, it is to be asked whether the smokeness in smoke has just arisen, or had arisen long before, or has arisen due to some other cause, or without any cause.... [In the absence of any conclusive factor to prove any one of the first three alternatives, the only alternative left is to believe] in the accidental rise of the phenomenon, for complex, indeed, is the nature of this universe. In the case of its being accidental, it is not valid to object that it will have no relation to a fixed time and place, for even in the case of the accidental rise of a phenomenon, its non-reference to time and place has not been observed. Thus, also, a phenomenon which has arisen without a cause can have its existence with reference to a particular time and place. Under such circumstances, even after the perception of smoke, there could be no inferential knowledge of fire, for it is simply not admissible.

1. *In order to refute inference based on the effect, the fact of there being an effect is now disproved.*

Also on account of what follows, there could be no knowledge of the inferred object, for smoke cannot be proved to be an effect. It cannot be [regarded as] an effect, because the cessation of its existence is not apprehended.[1] If it be said that it [the destruction of smoke] is directly perceived, then, is the direct perception in a positive or in a negative form? If it is in the positive form, is the object of that perception smoke, or something else, or nothing? If the perception is of smoke, then the perception, having smoke as its object, can establish only the existence of smoke and not its negation. If the perception is of something else, then, being of that nature, it cannot establish the negation of smoke; for cognition establishes the existence of that thing only which is its object. If the perception is of nothing, then, like a dumb, blind, and deaf person, it neither affirms nor denies anything.

If the said perception is of a negative nature, then, has it for its object the smoke, or something else, or nothing? If it has smoke as its object, then, being rooted in the being of its object, it establishes the object's existence and obviously cannot deny its existence; if it has something else as its object, then, being related to something else, and having that as its content, it cannot deny the existence of smoke. If it has nothing for its object, it is, again, like a dunce, incompetent to affirm or deny anything.

If it be said that destruction is only the end of existence and it becomes the object of perception, then, too, the argument is not very skillful, for destruction is a different object altogether. Any perception relating thereto can establish only the fact of destruction, and cannot, therefore, deny the *existence* of something. To be sure, the destruction [of something] being perceived, it cannot prove the *end of existence* of anything, because perceptions are limited to their own objects and establish [only] their existence. Hence, what denial can it make of anything?

If [it were to be remarked that] in the knowledge of the destruction [of smoke] there is no awareness of the nature of smoke, and this is, in essence, the denial of smoke, then, even the three worlds[2] could be denied, for in the perception of the destruction [of smoke] there is no awareness of the three worlds. That does not mean that the three worlds are destroyed.

[1] In Indian thought, whatever is produced in time must end in time.

[2] Earth, sky, and heaven.

2. *Incidentally, the concept of the relation of opposition itself is criticized.*

Again, if the denial of smoke means being opposed to smoke, what, then, is the meaning of opposition? Is it being not-that, or non-simultaneity of existence, or its not being perceived although its opposite exists, or its being an effect of that, or its being the cause of that, or its being an agent of an action different from that [which issues from its opposite], or its being produced by altogether different causes, or its not depending on that on which the opposed depends?

(i) If opposition were in the form of being not-that, then it would mean the denial of the three worlds, and not of the smoke only, because there is here opposition in the form of not being the three worlds.

(ii) If non-simultaneity [of existence] is the meaning of opposition, then there would occur mutual opposition between past, present, and future....

(iii) If opposition consists in a thing's not being perceived while its opposite exists, then, it is observed that an object is not perceived also due to the obstruction of distance, etc. They [such obstructions] do not prove its non-existence, just as, in the absence of a lamp, the jar, smoke, etc., are not perceived, but this does not mean that they do not exist.

[If it be said that] ordinarily things which are not perceived for reasons of distance and the like become perceived subsequently, while here, in the case of the destruction of objects like the smoke or the jar, it is not so, then [let it be seen] by whom they are not perceived. Are they not perceived by a particular individual or by all perceivers? If the existence [of the unperceived object] be denied because it is not perceived by a particular individual, then this is obviously wrong, for it is quite possible for someone else to perceive what another does not perceive because of distance, hiddenness, or the like. This being so, and destruction having taken place, it is quite possible that one may not perceive what others do.

If, however, [an object] is not perceived by any perceiver, then what is [the basis of] this inference? That "all perceivers are destitute of this knowledge" is a proposition for which there is no inference, because of the extreme difficulty of knowing other minds and [because of] their difference from our minds.

Again, an object having been destroyed, [it is to be considered] whether its imperceptibility is with regard to some fixed time and place or forever? If it be with regard to some fixed time and place, the absence of its existence is not cognized because there is cognition only of what exists. If it be for all time and all places, then, that, too, is incorrect, because there is no determining evidence, without which nothing can be acceptable.

Furthermore, how can an object after destruction, having become deprived of all its distinguishing marks [name, form, color, etc.], retain the character of being an object? And, when does it lose all its characteristics—during the time of its cognizability, or at the time when it ceases to be cognized? If it be the former, it is curious that it should be cognizable and yet be without its characteristics.

If it be said that [it loses its characteristics] at the time when it ceases to be cognized, then that also is absurd, for an object may not be cognized because of distance or cover, etc., and yet it may be existent and not be deprived of its characteristics. Moreover, even if there is a complete incognizability after destruction, this cannot establish the absence of its existence, just as imperceptibility due to various other reasons including the above-mentioned ones, namely, distance or cover, etc., [does not establish it].

(iv) If opposition consists in being the effect of something, then, because of its being the effect of the stick, etc., also, [the destruction of the jar] would be opposed to them also [and not only to the jar]. [If it is said that the stick is not directly responsible for the destruction of the jar, but is so only through its action], then this, too, is not tenable, for the action [of destruction] is not perceived independently of the stick.[1]

(v) If the essence of opposition lies in being the cause of that to which it is opposed, then that, too, is wrong, because the destruction [of the jar or smoke] does not create the jar or smoke. Even they[2] do not admit that. Moreover, if opposition lies in being a cause, then non-existence will become opposed to the knowledge of non-existence [since the former produces the latter].

(vi) If opposition consists in being the cause of different actions with different effects, then everything in this world will be opposed to everything else.

(vii) If opposition consists in being produced by different causes, then that, too, is incorrect, for the jar and its destruction are both capable of being produced by one and the same Devadatta. If

[1] Literally: Nor is there any special function, for we do not perceive any special activity in relation to it (destruction).

[2] The Naiyāyikas, who oppose the view expressed here.

opposition between existent and non-existent objects is said to lie in their being produced by their invariable causes, then all things will be opposed to one another, because of their being respectively produced by invariable causes. Moreover, it [this view] would result in opposition between eternal and non-eternal objects, for the eternal are uncaused and, if caused, objects are not eternal.

(viii) If dependence and independence be the marks of opposition, then there would be opposition between the self and knowledge [of the self], and the destruction of the jar would become opposed to everything else because the relation of dependence and independence is common to both. Besides, the genitive case [destruction *of* the jar] cannot stand without relation, as [for example] "Devadatta's eye or Devadatta's horse" definitely indicates the relation between Devadatta and the object stated. If the absence of the jar could be affirmed without any relation, then this universe could also be said to have been destroyed, for want of relatedness [between the universe and its non-existence] is present here as well.

3. *Showing the impossibility of understanding the relation of cause and effect.*

From this it follows also that there is no possibility of understanding the relation of cause and effect. If the effect is perceived after the cause, then it is to be considered whether the effect is perceived after the perception of the unqualified cause or the qualified cause. If it follows [the perception of the effect of] the unqualified cause, the statement is incorrect, for the unqualified cause is imperceptible and hence is incapable of being experienced. If it follows the perception of the qualified cause, then, too, [the statement] is erroneous, inasmuch as a qualified cause cannot even be the cause,[1] let alone produce an effect.

Besides, when yarn [is held to be] the cause of cloth—is it so because the yarn precedes and survives the cloth, or because it is perceived first? If the cause is what precedes and survives [the effect], then we cannot have any specific cause of the sound which is produced by ether, for simultaneously there would be several things that would produce so many other things which would precede and survive the sound.

If [it be said that] only those antecedents which are established by positive and negative instances as the causes of particular effects

[1] Because it cannot be associated with the feature of the effect until the effect is produced, and, once it is associated with the effect, it cannot evidently be the cause.

are to be so acknowledged, because it is only for such causes that an invariable effect can be found, then what is meant by "positive" and "negative"? Is it the cause or something else that is positively and negatively related? If it is the cause, then nothing determines a cause to be necessarily the cause. If it be something different, one does not know what it is, and, without this knowledge, it is not possible to know whether it preceded the other, or both arose together, or they were never produced at all.

On the other hand, if [it be said that] the sequence [of cause and effect] is to be determined in the order of their cognition, then [what has been said above] is applicable to the process of cognition as well, for it is only the reality as it exists that is cognized and not any other thing. It is seen that, though produced simultaneously, the two horns of the cow[1] are perceived successively, and also with regard to cowness and existence, both of which are uncaused. So, also, it is seen that the perception of thread follows the perception of cloth; similarly, there is the simultaneous perception of two things, and there is no difference between the two, and no cause-and-effect relation between them. That there is no difference has been explained previously. Similarly, knowledge is not different from the object of knowledge, as both are forms of existence and they have no other form—in fact, they are one and the same.

For this reason also, the cognition of cause and effect is not cognized; the generated cognition does not cognize itself, there being no second cognition other than that cognition. If it be said that even without a secondary act of cognition it is self-cognized, why can we not say that it is not self-cognized, the absence of a secondary act of cognition being common to both?

For the reason given above, knowledge cannot also be a cognition of the object itself. [If you ask] how it is that there is no knowledge of the object, well, the answer is: Is knowledge [of an object] to be had because of the mere existence of an object, or because of its being produced by the object? If an object is known because of its mere existence, then the whole world should be known, because mere existence is present there, too. If you say that knowledge is produced by the object, then, since it [knowledge] is produced as much by the eyes, the light, God, etc., knowledge of these would also arise. [If you say that] an object [in producing knowledge] shows no special activity because no such activity is found, and it is only in the absence

[1] *Goviṣāṇayoḥ* may mean either the cow and its horns or the two horns of the cow.

of such a special activity that an object can produce a particular effect [knowledge], [that is] true, [but here it is not so] as it is not evidenced by experience, for an effect is an outcome of the entire collocation of causes and conditions. Thus, [according to your view] like the knowledge of an object, this would lead to knowledge of the entire group of causes. [If you say that] it will not take in the other causal conditions, then it will also not be the perception even of the object, and, in the absence of that, there would be no cognition of the relation of cause and effect; and, that not being known, there would be no inference of the cause from the perception of the effect.

Again, after seeing the effect, does the person inferring remember or cognize the cause? To remember it is impossible unless he has first cognized it.

If he cognizes the cause, then, does he cognize the qualified cause or an unqualified cause? If it be the former, that is wrong, as its relation [to the effect] is not proved, and without such a relation its cognition is not possible.

Well, if what he cognizes is an unqualified cause, then [it is to be determined] whether such a cause exists or is non-existent. To say that it exists does not stand to reason, for a cause is said to be a cause by virtue of some activity as, for example, one is said to be a staff-holder because he has a staff, or an object is called a substance on account of substantiality in it. According to your own view, a cause is not capable of subsisting for any length of time without producing a number of effects. If you say that it does not produce [effects] even though possessed of the power of producing them, then it would wholly cease to be a cause and nothing would ever be produced. If, however, he cognizes what is non-existent, it is curious, indeed, that a man cognizes what is non-existent!

Again, after having observed the effect [smoke, etc.], is what is known the cause, or the causal priority, or the effect as preceded by the cause? If the cause is cognized, then it comes to this: "There is a cause, for there is an effect"—and this inference is as good as "The crow has a soul, for it is black."

If it is the priority of the cause of an effect that is inferred, then, does that priority consist in its [the effect's] relation to the existence of the cause, or mere existence, or some other type [of existence]? If the inference is with regard to its relation to the existence of the cause, then that is not correct, for that would be the object of perception, and there is no propriety in speaking of inference where there is perception, [for, otherwise,] even the ground of the inference [the effect] would become the object of inference. As is said, of common objects there is the proving of what is already known. By common objects are meant those that may be objects of both perception and inference.

If the existence [of the causal priority] alone is the object of inference, then that also is the object of perception, and inference is not required. Here also it is to be observed that commonness in means of evidence[1] proves only what is already known, or establishes what is already existent. That neither of them[2] is true has been discussed above.

If causal priority stands for some other characters and that is inferred, then, being within the range of the definition of perception, that also is the object of perception and does not require any other means of being known. Nor is there any cause of non-perception, like obstruction, remoteness, etc., [of the object]. Otherwise, even the jar, etc., would not be perceived. As is said, "In the case of unique particularity, there is no perception." Particularity is the object of inference alone, and we do not know anything related to it. In the absence of such knowledge there can be no inference from a sign to the thing signified. Moreover, according to you [Naiyāyikas] there is no reality beyond the six categories,[3] and if any other is now accepted by you it will go against your own position. If [it be argued that] causal priority is another character and it is inferred from the sign [e.g., smoke], then such causes as space, God, etc., are not known.

If [it be said that] what is cognized is the effect as preceded by the cause, then the statement shows only stupidity of mind. Why? Because, the effect in its own essential nature [as smoke] being perceived, what is the necessity of inference? Here the same fallacy of "proving the already known" occurs. If it be said that knowledge of the universal can be had by both perception and inference, then, if the universal is disputable [or unreal], the means of establishing the universal will also be unnecessary. Moreover, if the effect [itself] is to be known even through inference, there would be no means of knowing the cause of anything, and, the cause not being known, its reference to time, place, etc., would be impossible.

[1] That is, known by both perception and inference.
[2] "Neither of them," i.e., what is already known or what is already existent.
[3] I.e., substance, quality, action, universality, inherence, and negation.

Also, by seeing the cause, it is not possible to infer the effect, for, according to you, it is the entire group of causal conditions that is the cause of the effect. If that [totality of causes] is not perceived, then there will be no other means which will yield knowledge of it. Further, when the sign is perceived, there is the recollection of the universal relation and, after that, there is consideration of the sign as pervaded by the inferrable object. But the collection of causal conditions does not persist so long.

[To meet this difficulty, if you would like to add that] from the perception of a part of the collection of causal conditions the effect can be inferred, then that, too, is not right, for a part of the collection of causal conditions is not the producer [of the effect], and something is said to be a producer when it produces [the effect]. But that which has this capacity of producing [the effect] does not persist when the inferrable is cognized. And that which is not a part of the collection of causal conditions cannot bring about knowledge of the effect, for that would be an undue assumption.

4. *Demonstrating the impossibility of inference of the impermanence [of an object] from its being an effect.*

The inference of the impermanence of an object due to its being an effect cannot be established. The impermanence of an object means (1) its relation to the existence of its cause, or (2) its own existence, or (3) some other character, or (4) the destruction of sound [as an example], or (5) the nature of the sound itself. As for the first three alternatives, the flaws involved therein have already been explained.

If it is the destruction of the sound that is inferred, then that is incorrect, because there is no cognition of the relation of destruction to it [the sound]. So long as the sound exists, there is no destruction of it, and in the absence of that [the destruction] there is no cognition of a relation, a relation being impossible with only one term. Moreover, non-existence cannot be the object of any cognition. Even if it were so, it would not be a sign of sound. Even if it were the sign of sound, non-existence is not the object of cognition, that being but absence. By this one must understand that between sunrise and sunset the relation of the inferrable and the inferent is repudiated.

D. *PRABODHA-CANDRODAYA*

PASSION: (*Smiling.*) Uncivilized ignorant fools, who imagine that spirit is something different from body, and reaps the reward of actions in a future state; we might as well expect to find excellent fruit drop from trees growing in the air. But assuming the existence of what is the mere creature of their own imagination, they deceive the people. They falsely affirm the existence of that which does not exist; and by their frequent disputations endeavour to bring reproach upon the *nāstikas*[1] who maintain the words of truth. Who has seen the soul existing in a state separate from the body? Does not life result from the ultimate configuration of matter? Consider this attentively. They not only deceive themselves, but likewise deceive the world. On what grounds do they establish distinctions among beings formed with bodies possessing the same parts and organs, as a mouth, etc.? Why do they affirm that this woman belongs to one person, and this thing to another; these are distinctions which I do not know. Those who enquire whether slaying animals, indulgence at pleasure in the tender passions, or taking what belongs to another, be lawful or unlawful, do not act conformably to the principal end of life. (*Meditating proudly.*) The *Śāstra*[2] whose doctrines are obvious to all, and which is founded on the evidence of the senses; which admits only the elements of earth, water, fire, air; which maintains that sustenance and love are the objects of human existence; which asserts that matter possesses intelligence; which denies the existence of separate spirits, and affirms that death is blessedness, was written by Vācaspati,[3] a believer in this system; he delivered it to a materialist, who taught it to his disciples, and these disciples instructed their followers. Thus it has become widely diffused in the world.

(A MATERIALIST and one of his pupils enter.)

MATERIALIST: My son, you know that Legislation [the law of punishment by fear of which alone are men influenced in their conduct] is the only Science, and that it comprises everything else. The three Vedas are a cheat. Behold if Heaven be obtained through the officiating priest, sacrificial rites, and the destruction of the substances employed, why is not abundance of excellent fruit obtained

[1] Unbelievers in the Vedas.
[2] That is, the *Cārvāka-śāstra*.
[3] The same as Bṛhaspati.

from the ashes of a tree which has been burnt up by the fire of the forest. If the victims slain in sacrifices ascend to heaven, why are not parents offered up in sacrifice by their children? If funeral oblations nourish the deceased, why is not the flame of an extinguished taper renovated by pouring on oil?

PUPIL: Venerable tutor, if to gratify the appetites be the principal end of life, why do these men renounce sensual pleasures, and submit to pain arising from the severest mortifications?

MATERIALIST: These fools are deceived by the lying Śāstras, and are fed with the allurements of hope. But can begging, fasting, penance, exposure to the burning heat of the sun, which emaciate the body, be compared with the ravishing embraces of women with large eyes, whose prominent breasts are compressed with one's arms?

PUPIL: Do these pilgrims indeed torture themselves in order to remove the happiness which is mingled with this miserable existence?

MATERIALIST: (*Smiling.*) You ignorant boy, such are the fooleries of these unenlightened men. They conceive that you ought to throw away the pleasures of life, because they are mixed with pain; but what prudent man will throw away unpeeled rice which incloses excellent grain because it is covered with the husk?

PASSION: These opinions which are supposed to be verified by futurity, merely gratify the ear. (*Looking with joy.*) Materialist, you are my beloved friend.

MATERIALIST: (*Looks at the great King Passion and advances towards him.*) May thou be victorious. Materialist salutes thee.

PASSION: My friend, you are welcome, sit down here.

MATERIALIST: (*Sitting down.*) Vice [Kali, the name of the present or sinful age] prostrates himself at your feet.

PASSION: The felicity of Vice, I hope, is unimpaired.

MATERIALIST: By your bounty all are happy. Having accomplished what he was ordered to perform, he now desires to touch your feet; for blessed is he who after destroying the enemies of his Lord beholds his gracious face with exceeding joy, and prostrates himself at his lotus foot.

PASSION: What exploits have been performed by Vice?

MATERIALIST: He has caused the most virtuous men to forsake the road commanded in the Vedas, and to follow their own inclinations. This achievement, however, belongs neither to Vice nor myself; for it was your Majesty who inspired us with courage. The people who are doomed to inferior duties, and who were created last[1] have renounced the three Vedas; who then are Quiet, Mortification and others?[2] Besides, those who read the Vedas do it merely for the sake of subsistence. The teacher Bṛhaspati has declared that the performance of sacrifice, reading the Vedas, penances, and rubbing the body with ashes, are the means by which ignorant, weak men contrive to support themselves. . . .

[1] The military, husbandry, and the servile classes.
[2] These are characters in the play.

CHAPTER VIII

JAINISM

THE Jainas are the followers of Vardhamāna (Mahāvīra) (599 B.C.–527 B.C.), who systematized the doctrine of the three *tīrthaṅkaras* (founders of the path), Ṛṣabha, Ajitanātha, and Ariṣṭanemi (all of ancient date, mentioned in the *Yajur Veda*).

The Jaina system does not accept the authority of the Veda. It commends the truth of its system on the ground of its accordance with reality. Its scheme of the universe is said to be grounded in logic and experience.

Its central features are its realistic classification of being, its theory of knowledge with its celebrated doctrines of *syādvāda* and *saptabhaṅgī*, and its ascetic ethics.

The Jainas admit five kinds of knowledge, (1) *mati* or ordinary cognition, which includes memory, recognition, and induction; (2) *śruti* or knowledge derived through signs, symbols, or words, which includes association, attention, understanding, and *naya* or aspects of the meanings of things; (3) *avadhi* or direct knowledge of things at a distance in time or space (clairvoyance); (4) *manaḥparyāya* or direct knowledge of the thoughts of others; and (5) *kevala* or perfect knowledge, which is all-comprehensive. The first three are liable to error, not the last two.

Consciousness is the essence of the self (or soul); its manifestations are perception and intelligence. The former is simple apprehension, while the latter is conceptual knowledge. The Jainas adopt the mediate theory of perception, and hold that things are extramental realities. The relation between knowledge and its object is an external one with regard to physical objects, though it is different in the case of self-consciousness. As light reveals itself and other objects, so *jñāna* (wisdom) reveals itself and others. In knowing any object the self knows itself simultaneously.

In its perfect condition the soul is pure *jñāna* and *darśana*, i.e., knowledge and intuition. In its imperfect condition there are disturbing media, passions and emotions, which cause the inflow of matter and prevent the soul from exercising its natural function in full measure. Souls are substances characterized by intelligence, and differences among souls are due to the degrees of their connection with matter.

A prominent feature of Jaina logic is its doctrine of *naya* (aspects or standpoints). Knowledge is either of the thing as it is in itself (*pramāṇa*) or of the thing in its relation (*naya*). *Nayas* give us knowledge of a thing from particular standpoints and these relative views are abstractions from which reality is regarded. The *nayas* are said to be seven in number. In the *saptabhaṅgī* (seven forms), we use judgments in seven different ways to discriminate the several qualities of an object. Jainism holds that all knowledge is only probable or partial. It gives us a "somehow," a "perhaps," or a "maybe" (*syād*). This is the doctrine of *syādvāda*. (This doctrine is described in detail in the introduction and the selections of section B of this chapter.)

The whole universe is traced to the everlasting, uncreated, independent categories of *jīva* and *ajīva*, the conscious and the nonconscious. Animate beings are composed of soul and body. The souls are distinct from matter and are eternal. Nonconsciousness (*ajīva*) is divided into two main classes, those without form (*arūpa*) such as *dharma* (principle of motion), *adharma* (principle of rest), space, and time, and those with form (*rūpa*) such as *pudgala* or matter. The Jainas believe in the atomic structure of the universe.

The cause of the soul's embodiment is the presence in it of what is called karmic matter. The self is never separated from matter until its final release. The way to deliverance is through the three "jewels" of right faith, right knowledge, and right conduct. Belief in real existence or the *tattvas* is right faith. Knowledge of real nature without doubt or error is right knowledge. The practice of the five virtues, (1) *ahiṁsā* (non-violence), (2) truth-speaking, (3) non-stealing, (4) chastity, and (5) non-attachment to worldly things, constitutes right conduct. The Jainas were the first to make *ahiṁsā*, non-violence, into a rule of life.

The state of "release" for the Jainas is one of distinctiveness of the selves endowed with the qualities that are generally attributed to the divine principle in other systems, such as perfect tranquillity, perfect knowledge, and perfect power.

Selections in section A of this chapter are based upon *Śrī* Umāsvāti Ācārya, *Tattvārthādhigama Sūtra* (after third century A.D.), translated by J. L. Jaini, Sacred Books of the Jainas, II (Arrah, India: The Central Jaina Publishing House, 1920). For the sake of clarity some of the translations have been revised; and to facilitate the reading parentheses have been omitted at many places.

The selection in section B was translated by S. K. Saksena and C. A. Moore—and revised by Helen M. Johnson—from *Malliṣeṇa's* (thirteenth century) *Syādvādamañjarī with Anyayoga-vyavaccheda-dvātriṃśikā of Hemacandra* (1088–1172), edited by A. B. Dhruva, Sanskrit and Prakrit Series, LXXXIII (Bombay: S. K. Belvalkar, Bhandarkar Oriental Research Institute, 1933). The selection in section C is from Siddhasena Divākara, *Sanmati Tarka*; Pandita Sukhlalji Sanghavi and Pandita Bechardasji Doshi, trans., *Siddhasena Divākara's Sanmati Tarka* (Bombay: Shri Jain Shivetamber Education Board, 1939), Chap. I.

A. *TATTVĀRTHĀDHIGAMA SŪTRA*

Chapter I

1. Right belief,[1] right knowledge, right conduct—these together constitute the path to liberation.

2. Belief in things ascertained as they are is right belief.

3. This is attained by intuition or understanding.

4. The categories (*tattvas*) are souls [or selves] (*jīva*), non-souls, inflow (*āsrava*) of karmic matter[2] into the self, bondage (*bandha*) of self by karmic matter, stoppage (*saṁvara*) of inflow of karmic matter into the self, shedding (*nirjarā*) of karmic matter by the self, and liberation (*mokṣa*) of the self from matter.[3]

5. By name, representation, privation, present condition (*bhāva*), their aspects are known.

6. Understanding (*adhigama*) is derived from external sources, e.g., precept and scriptures. It is attained by means of right knowledge (*pramāṇa*) and partial knowledge (*naya*).[4]

7. Understanding is attained by [considering a thing with reference to its] description, inherence, cause, place, duration, and classification.

8. Also by existence, number, place, extent, time, interval of time, quality, and quantity.

9. Knowledge [is of five kinds]: ordinary cognition (*mati*), scriptural knowledge (*śruti*), extraordinary knowledge (*avadhi*), mental knowledge (*manaḥparyāya*), and perfect knowledge (*kevala*).

10. They constitute the two[5] means of right knowledge (*pramāṇas*).

11. The first two kinds of knowledge are mediate.

12. The remaining three are immediate.

13. Ordinary cognition, remembrance, recognition, induction (*cintā*), and deduction (*abhinibodha*) are not different in meaning.

14. It [ordinary cognition] is acquired by the help of the senses and the mind.

20. Scriptural knowledge is always preceded by ordinary cognition. . . .

[1] Right belief is not identical with faith. Its authority is neither external nor autocratic. It is reasoned knowledge. One cannot doubt its testimony. So long as there is doubt, there is no right belief. But doubt must not be suppressed. It must be destroyed.

[2] This and other items in the list will be explained in the course of the passages to follow.

[3] Many sacred books of the Jainas treat of nine categories (*padārthas*—basic things or principles). They add merit and demerit to the seven realities listed here. The present text assumes that these are included in the third and fourth principles given here since they are determined or caused by merit or demerit.

[4] See section C of this chapter for an exposition of the doctrine of *naya*; also below, I, 33.

[5] The two means are immediate (*pratyakṣa*) and mediate (*parokṣa*).

23. Mental knowledge [is of two kinds]: of simple mental things and of complex mental things.

25. Between extraordinary and mental knowledge [the differences relate to their] purity, place, inherence, and subject-matter.

26. The subject-matter of ordinary cognition and scriptural knowledge is [the six] substances but not all their modifications.

27. The subject-matter of extraordinary knowledge is matter.[1]

28. The subtlest form of that [matter] is the subject-matter of mental knowledge.

29. The subject-matter of perfect knowledge is all the substances and all their modifications.

31. Ordinary, scriptural, and extraordinary knowledge may be wrong knowledge.

33. The points of view (*naya*) are: figurative, general, distributive, actual, descriptive, specific, and active.

[Note: *Dravyārthika* (substantial), relating to the substance. Its sub-kinds are:

Figurative (*naigama*): Not literal. Taking something for granted. Speaking of a past or future event as a present one. Speaking of a thing in hand, as a completed fact.

General or Common (*saṁgraha*): A class as a whole. A class of things, denoted by the same word.

Distributive (*vyavahāra*): To divide or separate a general term into its classes, orders, kinds and species.

Note: *Paryāyārthika* (modal), relating to the modification of substances. This is:

Actual (*ṛjusūtra*): the actual condition (1) at a particular instant and (2) for a long time.

Descriptive (*śabda*): This includes grammatical correctness and propriety of expression.

Specific (*samabhirūḍha*): Giving a word one fixed meaning out of several which it has had.

Active (*evaṁbhūta*): Restricting a name to the very activity which is connoted by the name.

Note: *Naya* may be distinguished from *nikṣepa*. *Nikṣepa* is an aspect of the thing itself. *Naya* is a point of view from which we make some statement about the thing.... If we consider the statement merely as such, its point of view is *naya*; if we consider the fact which justifies the point of view it is *nikṣepa*.

[1] This also includes embodied souls, but not the modifications of matter and souls.

Of the seven *nayas*, the first four figurative, general, distributive, and actual, are object stand-point, i.e., stand-points relating to the object considered. The remaining three, descriptive, specific, and active, are word stand-point, i.e., related to the word by which the object is expressed.

Each of the seven stand-points has a greater extent or denotation than the one which follows it. Figurative has thus the greatest, and active the least extent. Figurative deals with real and unreal. General deals with real only. Distributive with only a part of the real. Descriptive with only the expression of the real. Specific with only one particular expression. Active with only that particular expression which applies to the thing in its present activity.

The principal stand-points are seven. But in practice the stand-points can obviously be many more, according to the point of view from which the thing is considered or spoken of.][1]

Chapter II

7. The self's (*jīva*) essence is life, the capacity of being liberated, and the incapacity of becoming liberated.[2]

8. The distinctive characteristic of self is attention.

10. Selves are [of two kinds]: worldly and liberated.

11. Worldly selves are [of two kinds]: with mind and without mind.

12. Worldly selves are again [of two kinds]: mobile and immobile.

13. Immobile selves are earth-bodied, water-bodied, fire-bodied, air-bodied, and vegetable-bodied.

14. Mobile selves are with two senses, etc.[3]

15. There are five senses.

21. The function of the mind is the cognition of scriptural knowledge.

22. Up to the vegetable-bodied ones, selves have one sense [i.e., touch].

23. Worms, ants, bumblebees, and men each have one more than the one preceding.

24. Those with minds are knowers (*saṁjñinaḥ*).

[1] This bracketed passage is essentially the translator's explanation of the *nayas*. For a more detailed treatment, see section C, this chapter.

[2] Mundane souls are of two kinds, one having the capacity of being liberated, the other, the incapacity of being liberated.

[3] That is, they are with two, three, four, or five senses.

36. Bodies are [of five kinds]: physical, fluid, assimilative, splendorous, and karmic.

37. Each successive one is more subtle than the one preceding it.

40. The splendorous[1] and karmic bodies are not subject to obstruction.

41. And their connection [with the self] is without beginning.

42. These are possessed by all worldly selves.

Chapter V

1. Non-living bodies (*ajīvakāyas*) are: the medium of motion (*dharma*), the medium of rest (*adharma*), space (*ākāśa*), and matter (*pudgala*).

2. These are called substances (*dravyas*).

3. Selves are also substances.

4. The above five extensive substances are permanent in their nature, and with time (*kāla*), are fixed as the sole constituents of the Universe, and are devoid of touch, taste, smell and colour.

5. But matter is qualitative [i.e., has touch, taste, smell and colour.] [Note.—In *sūtras* 3 and 5, the plural is used to indicate that selves are infinite and distinct, so also are the particles of matter.]

6. Up to space [i.e., *dharma*, *adharma*, and *ākāśa* are] one substance each. They are indivisible wholes.

7. These three are not capable of moving from place to place. Time substance also is incapable of motion.

8. There are innumerable *pradeśas* [units of space occupied by an atom of matter] of *dharma*, *adharma* and each self. The number of *pradeśas* in *dharma*, *adharma*, a self, and Lokākāsa, i.e., the Universe [i.e., all except pure space] is the same, i.e., it is innumerable in all.

9. The points of space are infinite.

10. Material particles are numerable and innumerable.[2]

13. Motion and rest pervade the whole universe.

15. The place of selves is in one or more of the innumerable parts [of the universe].

16. Depending upon greatness or smallness of space, the self [occupies space] as does the light from a lamp.[3]

[1] This term refers to supernatural bodies which usually inhabit other worlds more lustrous than this world.

[2] That is, according to their different compositions.

[3] That is, in a small room the light occupies a smaller space than if the lamp is in a larger room.

17. To support motion and rest is the function of the principle of motion (*dharma*) and the principle of rest (*adharma*) respectively.

18. The function of space is to give place [to all the other substances].

19. The function of matter is to form the basis of bodies, speech, mind, and breath.

20. The function of matter is also to make possible worldly enjoyment, pain, life, and death.

21. The function of selves is to support each other.

22. And the function of time is [to explain] existence in the present, change, movement, and long or short duration.

23. Material substances are possessed of touch, taste, smell, and color.

25. Matter [has two forms]: atom and molecule.

29. The distinctive characteristic of substance is being.

30. Being is a simultaneous possession of coming into existence, going out of existence, and permanence.

31. Permanence means the indestructibility of the essence of the substance.

32. The determination of substances is achieved by giving prominence [to their essence] and a secondary place [to their changeable condition.][1]

38. Substance is possessed of attributes and modifications.

39. Time is also a substance.

41. Attributes depend upon substance and cannot be the substratum of another attribute.

42. Modification is change of attribute.

Chapter VI

1. *Yoga* is the activity of body, speech, and mind.

2. *Yoga* is the inflow of karmic matter into the soul.

3. Inflow [is of two kinds]: good, of virtue or meritorious *karmas*; bad, of vice or demeritorious *karmas*.

4. [Souls] affected with the passions have mundane [inflow].[2] [Those] without the passions have only transient [inflow].[3]

6. The differences in inflow arise from differences in: intensity [of

[1] In the second section of this chapter this *sūtra* is translated thus: "By the given is the non-given established."

[2] This refers to the inflow of karmic matter which leads to cycles of birth and rebirth.

[3] Transient inflow will lead to fewer rebirths.

desire], mildness, intentional character of the act, unintentional character of the act, dependence, and power to do the act.

12. Compassion for all living beings, compassion for those who have taken vows, charity, self-control with attachment, etc., contemplation, forgiveness, and contentment—these are the causes of the inflow of pleasure-bearing karmic matter.

13. The inflow of right-belief-deluding karmic matter is caused by defaming the omniscient ones (*kevalis*), the scriptures, the brotherhood (*saṅgha*), the religion (*dharma*), and the celestial beings (*devas*).

14. The inflow of right-conduct-deluding karmic matter is caused by the intense thought-activity produced by the rise of the passions.

22. The inflow of bad-body-making karmic matter is caused by the deceitful working of the mind, body, or speech, and by wrangling.

23. The inflow of good-body-making karmic matter is caused by the opposite of the above.

24. The inflow of the body-making[1] karmic matter of a *tīrthaṅkara* [a founder of the path] is caused by meditation on: purity of right-belief, reverence for means of liberation, faultless observance of vows and subdual of passions, ceaseless pursuit of right knowledge, perpetual apprehension of mundane miseries, renunciation according to capacity, the practice of austerities according to one's capacity, protecting the saints, serving the meritorious, devotion to omniscient ones (*arhats*), devotion to heads of the order of saints, devotion to teaching-saints, devotion to scriptures, non-neglect of duties, propagation of the path of liberation, and affection for one's brothers on the path of liberation.

25. The inflow of low-family-determining karmic matter is caused by speaking ill of others, praising oneself, concealing the good qualities of others, and proclaiming in oneself the good qualities which one does not possess.

26. The inflow of the other is caused by the opposite of the above.

Chapter VII

1. The vow is to be free from injury (*hiṁsā*), falsehood, theft, unchastity, and worldly attachment.

2. Vows [are of two kinds]: lesser vow and greater vow.[2]

[1] That is, high-family-determining karmic matter.

[2] "Lesser and greater" refer, respectively, to limited and total abstention from the five faults of the preceding *sūtra*.

3. For the fixing of these five vows in the mind, there are five meditations for each.

4. The five meditations [for the vow against injury] are carefulness of speech, carefulness of mind, care in walking, care in lifting and laying down things, and thoroughly seeing to one's food and drink.[1]

5. And the five meditations [for the vow against falsehood] are giving up anger, greed, cowardice and frivolity, and speaking in accordance with scriptural injunctions.

6. The five meditations [for the vow against theft] are residence in a solitary place, residence in a deserted place, residence in a place where one is not likely to be interfered with by others, purity of alms, and not disputing with disciples of the same faith as to "mine" and "thine."

7. The five meditations [for the vow against unchastity] are renunciation of hearing stories inciting attachment for women, renunciation of seeing their beautiful bodies, renunciation of remembrance of past enjoyment of women, renunciation of aphrodisiacs, and renunciation of beautifying one's own body.

8. The five meditations [for the vow against worldly attachment] are giving up of love and hatred for the pleasing and displeasing objects of the senses.

11. And one must meditate upon compassion for all living beings, delight at the sight of beings more advanced than ourselves [on the path of liberation], pity for the afflicted, and indifference toward those who mistreat you.

12. For the apprehension of the miseries of the world and renunciation of sense-pleasures, we should meditate upon the nature of the world and of our physical bodies.

19. Those who take vows are householders [laymen] and houseless [ascetics].

20. One whose vows are lesser is a householder.

21. The householder must also limit his activity to a fixed place, limit the above also to a shorter period of time, not commit purposeless sin, contemplate the soul, fast, limit one's enjoyment of consumable and non-consumable things, and eat only after the guests [saints] have been fed with a part of the food.

22. The householder is also the observer in the last moments of his life of peaceful death.

[1] This last means that one should take care not to destroy living beings in one's food and drink.

23. Scepticism, desire of sense-pleasures, disgust at anything [sick or deformed], thinking admiringly of wrong-believers, and praising wrong-believers are defects in a man of right belief.

Chapter VIII

1. The causes of bondage are wrong belief, non-renunciation, carelessness, passions, and union (*yoga*) of the soul with the mind, body, and speech.[1]

2. The soul, owing to its being with passion, assimilates matter which is fit to form *karmas*. This is bondage.

4. The main divisions of the nature of *karma* are knowledge-obscuring, perception (*darśana*)-obscuring, feeling-*karma*, deluding, age-determining, body-making, family-determining, and obstructive.

21. There is the maturing and fruition of *karmas*.

23. After fruition the *karmas* fall off.

25. Meritorious *karmas* are the pleasure-bearing, good-age-producing, good-body-producing, and high-family-determining.

26. The *karmas* other than these are demeritorious *karmas*.

Chapter IX

1. There is stoppage of inflow of karmic matter into the soul.

2. It is produced by preservation, carefulness, observances, meditation, conquest of sufferings, and good conduct.

3. By austerities is caused the shedding of karmic matter and [the stoppage of inflow].

4. Preservation is proper control over mind, speech, and body.

5. Carefulness is to take proper care in walking, speaking, eating, lifting and laying, and in excreting.

6. The observances are forgiveness, humility, straight-forwardness, contentment, truth, restraint, austerities, renunciation, not taking the non-self for one's own self [non-attachment], and chastity, all of the highest degree.

7. The meditations are transitoriness, unprotectedness, the cycle of life and death (*saṁsāra*), loneliness, separateness, inflow, shedding, the nature of the universe, difficulty of attainment of the right path, and the nature of the right path.

18. Right conduct consists of equanimity, recovery of equanimity, absolute non-injury, freedom from subtle passion, and passionless conduct.

[1] Forty-two subclasses are listed in the commentary.

19. External austerities are fasting, eating less than one's fill, taking a vow to accept food from a householder [only if a certain condition is fulfilled, without letting anyone know about the vow], daily renunciation of delicacies, sleeping in a lonely place, and mortification of the body.

20. The others, that is, internal austerities, are expiation, reverence, service, study, giving up attachment to the body, and concentration.

27. Concentration is confining one's thoughts to one particular object.

28. Concentration [is of four kinds]: painful concentration, wicked concentration, righteous concentration, and pure concentration.

29. The last two are the causes of liberation.

35. Wicked concentration is delight in hurtfulness, falsehood, theft, and preservation of objects of sense-enjoyment.

36. Righteous concentration is contemplation on the subject-matter of scriptural teaching, the removal of wrong belief, the knowledge and conduct of people, the fruition of *karmas*, and the nature and constitution of the Universe.

39. [The four kinds of] pure concentration are absorption in the different attributes of the soul, absorption in one aspect of the soul, concentrated upon the subtlest movements in the soul, and total absorption of the soul in itself.

Chapter X

1. Perfect knowledge is gained by destroying the deluding *karmas* and then by simultaneous destruction of knowledge- and perception-obscuring *karmas* and of obstructive *karmas*.

2. Liberation is the freedom from all karmic matter, owing to the non-existence of the cause of bondage and to the shedding of the *karmas*.

4. After the soul is released, there remain perfect right-belief. perfect right-knowledge, perfect perception, and the state of having accomplished all.

B. *SYĀDVĀDAMAÑJARĪ*

The *Syādvādamañjarī* by Malliṣeṇa is a 13th-century commentary on the famous Jaina work *An Examination in Thirty-two Stanzas of the Doctrines of Other Systems* by the great Jaina scholar Hemacandra (1088–1172). The *Syādvādamañjarī* has come to be regarded as one of the most celebrated works on Jaina metaphysics and logic. By virtue of its systematic presentation of thought and its lucidity of style, though technically only a commentary, the book has been ranked almost as an original piece of work. It is also the best available source for a basic explanation of the fundamental logical doctrines of Jainism.

The thirty-two stanzas of Hemacandra, though clothed in devotional language, criticize with skill the philosophical systems of the Hindus, the Buddhists, and the Cārvākas. As the name of the original work suggests, most of the stanzas are occupied with criticism of non-Jaina systems.

Only about the last ten stanzas deal with important Jaina theories. The commentary on four of these stanzas (XXIII, XXIV, XXV, and XXVIII) has been translated here. These stanzas deal with the doctrine of "points of view" (*naya*) as represented in the theory of *syādvāda* (conditional predication) and *saptabhaṅgī* (seven modes). This logical and epistemological theory leads to the celebrated Jaina metaphysical doctrine of the "many-sidedness of reality" (*anekāntavāda*).

The doctrine of *syādvāda*, briefly stated, amounts to the assertion that reality, whatever it is, expresses itself in multiple forms, with the result that no absolute predication is possible. This view in general is called *anekāntavāda*, the doctrine that reality has many (literally, "not-one") aspects, leading to the possibility of only relative predication. Herein Jaina logic is opposed to the views of the other systems, which in opposition to it are called *ekāntavāda*, the doctrine that reality has but one true nature, thus grounding the possibility of absolute predication. This doctrine of the many-sidedness of reality is a result of the doctrine of *nayas*, points of view. A *naya*, in one of its major meanings, is a standpoint from which statements are made about things.

Syādvāda means, literally, the doctrine of relativism as usually expressed by adding the prefix "somehow" or "in a certain sense"—sometimes translated "maybe," or "perhaps"—before a statement.

Why are there only seven possible standpoints, no more and no less? Because, first, we may desire to make a statement of affirmation about a thing with regard to its substance, time, place, or qualities; or, second, we may desire to make a statement of negation; or, third, we may combine both these forms of affirmation and negation and say that in one sense it is and in another sense it is not; or, fourth, we may say of a thing that it is indescribable, when we are in difficulty about the possibility of a precise word for a thing. These give us four formal points of view. The first three combined with the fourth possibility, that of indescribability, give us the seven possible forms of a statement technically represented as:

1. Somehow a thing is.
2. Somehow it is not.
3. Somehow it both is and is not.
4. Somehow it is indescribable.
5. Somehow it is and is indescribable.
6. Somehow it is not and is indescribable.
7. Somehow it is, is not, and is indescribable.

Thus understood, no absolute affirmation or negation is possible about anything, for the nature of things is too complex to be exhausted in any single definite predication. Thus, all predications are predications only from a certain point of view.

The non-Jaina critics of *syādvāda* have often found fault with this doctrine on the ground that it makes contradictory statements about a thing possible. This criticism is regarded by the adherent of this doctrine as actually missing the very point, for, according to this doctrine, contradictions are avoided only when statements are made from different points of view. Jaina logic admits that contradictory statements cannot be made about the same thing in the same sense at the same time and place, but stresses the fact that contradiction can be avoided only by their own doctrine of *syādvāda*, in which every statement is made only from a particular point of view. The charge of contradiction lies, if at all, at the door of the absolutist, who affirms or denies a statement about a thing from no point of view, as it were, which, according to the Jaina logician, is invalid. (C. A. M.)

XXIII. When it is integrated, an entity is without modifications; and this same entity is without substance when it is differentiated. Thou didst bring to light the doctrine of seven modes which is expressed by means of [two] kinds of statement[1]—a doctrine which is comprehensible to the most intelligent people.

An entity described as a whole is "integrated"; it is "without modifications" when it is described with no intended reference to the modifications. That is called "entity" in which reside qualities and modifications. There are six substances: medium of motion, medium of rest, space, matter, time, and soul. This is the meaning: When it is desired to speak of a single entity only—self, pot, etc., conscious or unconscious—having the form of substance only, without intending any reference to its modifications even though they are present, then it is called "without modifications"—i.e., it has the form of pure substance only—because it is designated as a unit with the characteristics of the entire body of modifications included. This is the meaning.

As [one says] "this soul," "this pot," etc., because of the non-distinctness of the substance and the modifications, so the standpoints attached to the substance-category, i.e., the simple, collective, etc., acknowledge substance only because of the non-separateness of it and the modifications.

"Differentiated," i.e., described with distinctions by virtue of its capacity for different forms. On the other hand, this same entity is non-substance only, i.e., having the form of pure modifications only without any intended reference to the underlying substance. This is the meaning.

For when the soul is considered with reference to the several modifications, giving precedence to the modifications, knowledge, perception, etc.,

[1] That is, synthetic and analytical statements.

then the modifications only stand out, but not some substance called "self." Similarly, a "pot," when differentiated in regard to parts, round lip, broad bottom, belly, upper and lower parts, etc., is modifications only, but not an entity beyond them called "pot." This is why those who follow the standpoint of the modification-category quote:

> "The parts alone stand out, located thus and so,
> But no partless owner of them is understood at all."

And thus, even though an entity consists of both substance and modifications, it has a substance-form through emphasis on the substance-standpoint as primary and the subordination of modification-standpoint; and it has a modification-form through emphasis on the modification-standpoint as primary and the subordination of the substance-standpoint, and it has the form of both through emphasis on both standpoints. Hence, the chief teacher Umāsvāti says: "By the establishment of what is emphasized as primary and what is subordinated." Such an entity consisting of both substance and modifications, thou alone—and no one else—didst bring to light. By these words there is understanding of certainty through emphasis.

Surely, "substance" stands for some particular name and idea, and "modifications" stands for other names and ideas; so how can there be a single entity with the nature of both? He removes such a doubt by means of a qualifier, "by kinds of statement." The modes (i.e., kinds of assertion) to the number of seven in regard to that entity [of the first line of the original] are explained by the two kinds of statement called "statement in regard to the whole" and "statement in regard to the parts."

Now, what are these "seven modes" and what are these "kinds of statement"? It is said: When in regard to a single entity, soul, etc., in virtue of an inquiry relating to modifications, existence, etc., one by one, without contradiction—i.e., with avoidance of conflict with direct perception, etc.—made with consideration of affirmation and negation singly and jointly, a statement adorned with the word "somehow" is made in seven ways to be described hereafter, this is called the "seven-mode doctrine," as follows:

(1) Somehow [or, from one point of view] everything *does* exist [or certainly exists]. This is the first mode, by way of affirmation.

(2) Somehow [or, from one point of view] everything does not exist. This is the second mode, by way of negation.

(3) It is certain that from one point of view everything exists and that from another point of view it does not exist. This is the third mode, by way of affirmation and negation successively.

(4) Somehow everything is certainly indescribable. This is the fourth mode, by way of simultaneous affirmation and negation.

(5) Somehow everything *does* exist and somehow it is certainly indescribable. This is the fifth mode, by way of affirmation and also by way of simultaneous affirmation and negation.

(6) Somehow everything does not exist and somehow it is indescribable. This is the sixth mode, by way of negation and by way of simultaneous affirmation and negation.

(7) Somehow everything *does* exist, somehow it *does not* exist, and somehow it is certainly indescribable. This is the seventh mode, by way of affirmation and negation successively and by way of simultaneous affirmation and negation.

Here, somehow (from one point of view) everything, pot, etc., certainly exists in the form of its own substance, place, time, and nature; but certainly does not exist in the form of another substance, place, time, and nature. For instance: A pot exists in an earthen form in respect to substance and does not exist in an aqueous form, etc.; it exists in Pātaliputra in respect to place, but does not exist in Kānyakubja, etc.,; it exists in the cool season in respect to time, but not in spring, etc.; it exists with a black color in respect to nature, but does not exist with a red, etc., color. Otherwise, the loss of its own form would result from changing into another form. And the "certainly" has been used here in the mode to exclude a meaning not intended; otherwise, from the non-mention of its own particular meaning there would result an *unintended* equivalence of the statement. It has been said:

In a statement "certainly" must be used just to exclude an unintended meaning.

Because otherwise in some cases an unstated equivalent of it [the statement] would result.

Nevertheless, if only so much as "the pot certainly exists" were used, there would be no ascertainment of the pot's own particular form, because of its existence in all forms through the existence of the pillar, etc., also. For the ascertainment of this [the particular form] the word "somehow" is used. Somehow (from one point of view) the (pot) certainly exists with reference to its own substance, etc., but not with reference to other substances, etc. This is the meaning. That [i.e., word "somehow"], even when it is not used, is to be understood certainly by intelligent people, like the word "certainly" which denotes exclusion [of what is not intended]. It has been said:

This [i.e., word "somehow"], even when it is not used, is to be understood by intelligent people in all cases from the meaning,

Like the word "certainly," whose purpose is to exclude what is unsuitable, etc.

This is the first mode.

Somehow (i.e., from one point of view) the pot, etc., certainly do not exist. For on the false assumption of the non-existence of an entity in respect to its own substance, etc., as well as other substances, etc., there would be no particularity of an entity because of the lack of its own particular form.

Therefore, the existence of an entity [in its own form] is inherently bound up with its non-existence [in another form], and its non-existence with that [existence]. And their primariness and secondariness depend upon the meaning. In the same way one must understand the following modes in accordance with the teacher's statement: "By the establishment of what is emphasized as primary and what is subordinated."

This is the second mode.

The third is quite clear.

When one wishes to designate a single entity with the two modifications, existence and non-existence, emphasized as primary simultaneously, the entity, such as soul, etc., is indescribable because of the lack of an adequate word. Thus, the two qualities, existence and non-existence, cannot be stated simultaneously in regard to one thing by the term "existent," because that is incapable of expressing its non-existence; nor, similarly, by the term "non-existent," because that is incapable of expressing its existence....

So that, from the lack of an inclusive term an entity is overcome by simultaneous existence and non-existence emphasized as primary and is therefore "indescribable." But it is not indescribable in every way, because [if it were] it would be inexpressible even by the word "indescribable." This is the fourth.

The remaining three are easily understood.

Nor should it be said that "'seven-modes' are certainly incongruous because of the infinite modes arising from the admitted infinite modifications which can be affirmed or denied in a single entity." [This should not be said] because there is a possibility of *seven* modes *only* with respect to the affirmation and negation of each modification in a single entity, though [the seven-modes—or, the groups of seven-modes—may be] infinite [because of the infinite modifications].

It has been said above that the many-sided nature of an entity...is comprehensible to supremely intelligent people. Because the many-sided nature [of an entity] may be easily deduced by the exposition of the seven-mode system, that also has been discussed.

The absolutists, the supremely unintelligent, seeing that in it [i.e., the seven-mode system] the entity is endowed with contradictory modifications, point out the contradiction. He [Hemacandra] describes their fall from the path of authoritative knowledge.

XXIV. Non-existence, when it is referred to different aspects, is not contradictory [to existence] in things; and existence and indescribability [are not contradictory]. Because they have not recognized this at all, afraid of contradiction, the dull-witted fall slain by the absolutist view.

In "things" (objects), conscious and unconscious, "non-existence" (non-isness) is "not contradictory" (not affected by contradiction)—i.e., does not embrace contradiction to existence. This is the meaning. Not only is non-existence not contradictory [to existence], but existence and indescribability...also are not contradictory. This is the meaning.

And so, existence is not contradictory to non-existence; indescribability in the form of affirmation and negation is not contradictory, one to the other [i.e., affirmation and negation]; or, rather, indescribability does not carry contradiction to describability. And freedom from contradiction of the whole seven-mode doctrine is understood from this triad of modes called non-existence, existence, and indescribability, because these three alone are the chief modes and the remaining modes are included in these through combinations.

"Surely these modifications are mutually contradictory. How then can they be associated in one and the same entity?" He gives the reason by means of a qualifier: "referred to different aspects" ("aspects," that is, "properties," "different parts"; "different," that is, "a variety of them"; "referred to," that is, "with emphasis on": this is the adjective of non-existence). Non-existence in existing objects is not contradictory, when it is referred to different aspects, and, dividing the compound [i.e., existence-indescribability], this must be applied to existence and indescribability. When they are referred to different aspects, existence and indescribability also are not contradictory.

This is the meaning: Where two things are mutually exclusive, such as cold and heat, there is contradiction which is defined as the impossibility of their existing together. But such is not the case here, because existence and non-existence occur by reason of the non-universal nature of both. For in a pot, etc., existence does not exclude non-existence, because [if it did] existence even in other forms would result. And so there would be no status as objects of other objects except that [the pot], because of the accomplishment by it alone of [all] actions to be effected by [all] the objects in the three worlds. And non-existence does not exclude existence, because [if it did] non-existence [of an entity] even in its own form would follow. And so, universal emptiness would follow because of absence of matter. There would be a contradiction in case existence and non-existence were referred to the same aspect. But that is not so here, because in whatever part existence is, non-existence also is not in *that* part. However, existence belongs to one aspect, and non-existence belongs to another aspect. For existence [of an entity] is in regard to its own form and non-existence in regard to another form.

For in one and the same multicolored cloth as a whole blueness is seen in one part and other colors in other parts—for blueness is an aspect of the color of indigo, etc., and the other colors are aspects of various coloring substances. So, in the jewel *mecaka* [which is many-colored], a variety of colors is to be understood as aspects of various color-substances. Nor does it follow from these examples that existence and non-existence belong to different parts, because of the one-ness of the multiple-colored cloth, etc., as a whole, . . .

If even so Your Honor [the opponent] is not satisfied, what is to be said of the familiar sight of mutually contradictory modifications, such as the status of father, son, maternal uncle, sister's son, paternal uncle, brother, etc., of one and the same man because of various different relationships?

And the same thing should be said of indescribability, etc. [The dull-witted] have not recognized at all that an entity is devoid of contradiction because of different aspects of the kind described.

Describing the Blessed One's teaching[1] by means of a four fold designation of basic divisions of the many-sided doctrine, though it includes all substances and all modifications, he [Hemacandra] says:

XXV. Somehow one and the same thing is perishable and eternal; somehow it is of similar and dissimilar form; somehow it is describable and indescribable; somehow it is existent and non-existent.

(1) "Somehow," the adverb signifying many-sidedness, must be used with all the eight terms. "One and the same thing," i.e., one and the same entity to which they belong. "Somehow," i.e., from one standpoint, "perishable," i.e., of a nature to perish, non-eternal. Somehow "eternal," i.e., having the modification of non-perishing. This is the meaning. This is the first proposition called "eternal and non-eternal."

(2) Likewise, somehow "similar," i.e., having a generic form as the source of similarity; "dissimilar," i.e., of different forms, consisting of different evolutions, having a particular form as the source of difference. This is the meaning. Here we have the second division in the form of generality and particularity.

(3) Likewise, somehow "describable," i.e., expressible; somehow "indescribable," i.e., inexpressible. This is the meaning.... Here we have the third division in the form of describable and indescribable.

(4) Likewise, somehow, "existent," i.e., actually, in the form of being; somehow, "non-existent," i.e., the reverse of that. Here is the fourth division known as "existent and non-existent."

Now by the description of [the doctrines of] false standpoints, standpoints, and medium of cognition (*pramāṇa*), because of the statement that "knowledge is attained by medium of cognition and standpoints," extolling... the refutation of the path of false standpoints, which is contradictory to the "somehow" doctrine, he says:

XXVIII. With the words, "it *does* exist [or, it certainly exists], it exists, somehow it exists," an object would be defined in three ways· by false standpoints, by standpoints, and by medium of cognition.

Thou, seeing the real truth, didst avoid the path of false standpoints by following the path of standpoints and medium of cognition.

An object is defined in three ways. By what three ways? He says: by false standpoints, by standpoints, and by medium of cognition. Because an object, distinguished by one aspect, is "led," i.e., defined by these [i.e., they are called] "standpoints."...A thing, distinguished by many-

[1] This is not a literal translation, but an interpretation of a figure of speech referring to a sentence in the text which has been omitted.

sidedness, is "measured," i.e., defined by it—for that reason it is called "medium of cognition," belonging to the "somehow" doctrine, characterized by direct and indirect perception. . . . By what description should an object be defined? He says: "by it *does* exist, it exists, and somehow it exists." . . . [Of these] "it *does* exist" is a false standpoint; "it exists" is a standpoint; and "somehow it exists" is the medium of cognition. Thus, a false standpoint says merely "it *does* exist," for example, "the pot *does* exist." This point of view admits absolute existence alone in an entity and by the rejection of other modifications determines the attribute [and no other] which is acceptable to itself. And its status as a false standpoint is due to its false form; and the falsity of its form is due to the rejection of other modifications, though they exist, in it [the entity].

Likewise, from the description "it exists," there is a standpoint, for by the words "the pot exists" it emphasizes in the pot the modification "existence," acceptable to itself, and resorts to an elephant's-eye-closure in regard to the other modifications. And this is not a false standpoint, because it does not reject the other modifications, and it is not the medium of cognition because it is not adorned with the word "somehow."

Now, the medium of cognition, by the words "somehow it exists," says "somehow the entity exists." And its status as a medium of cognition is due to the fact that it is not contradicted by anything seen or wished to be seen and due to the presence of contradiction in the alternative. For every entity is existent in its own form and non-existent in another form. This has been said again and again. "Existent" is merely for illustration; in the same way, non-existence, permanence and impermanence, describability and indescribability, generality and particularity, etc., must be understood.

Now follows some description of the nature of false standpoints, standpoints and medium of cognition. Of these, first, the nature of the standpoint-method, because without a knowledge of it, the nature of the false-standpoint-method would be hard to understand. And here the mention of the false-standpoint-method first by the *Ācārya* [Hemacandra] was made to show the order of importance. Of these, the standpoint-method is the consideration of one aspect of an object [the whole of which is] understood by the medium of cognition. It is called a "lead" because it leads, i.e., makes reach, i.e., raises an entity particularized by one modification acceptable to itself to the point of understanding, [though] it is endowed with infinite modifications. . . . And standpoints are infinite because of an entity's infinite modifications and because of the standpoint-view of the speaker's meanings which are satisfied by one modification, and so the elders say:

"As many as are the ways of speaking about a thing, so many are the statements of the standpoint-method."

Nevertheless, seven standpoints have been taught by ancient scholars by making seven meanings all-inclusive.

C. SANMATI TARKA

1.3. The noumenal [substantial, relating to substance] (*dravyārthika*) and the phenomenal [modal, relating to modifications or conditions] (*paryāyārthika*), i.e., the analytical methods of inquiry, are the two fundamental methods (the two *nayas*, standpoints) that cover the general and the particular viewpoints of things as stated by *Tīrthaṅkaras*. All other analytical methods of inquiry fall under these two heads only.

1.4. The fundamental nature of *dravyāstika* in its extreme form is what is called [the general or common] (*saṁgraha*) *naya*, and limited generalizations as regards particular things come under the head of [the distributive] (*vyavahāra*) *naya*.

1.5. [The actual] (*ṛjusūtra*) *naya* is the very foundation of the *paryāyāstika naya*. [Descriptive] (*śabda*) and other minor *nayas* are, of course, subtle varieties of *ṛjusūtra*, its branches and twigs.

1.6. Name (*nāma*), picture (*sthāpanā*) and potentiality (*drayva*) are the varieties of [the aspect of a thing itself] (*nikṣepa*) which are applicable to *dravyāstika* while *bhāva* (present condition) includes under it *paryāyāstika*.

1.12. There cannot be a thing which is devoid of its modifications of birth and decay. On the other hand, modifications cannot exist without an abiding or eternal something—a permanent substance, for birth, decay and stability (continuance)—these three constitute the characteristic of a substance or entity.

1.13. These three characteristics of birth, decay and stability must dwell together in harmony to make a real definition of a thing in its integral form. Each *naya*, therefore, if taken independently, isolated from the other, can never yield an adequate idea of an entity. Both these, therefore, divorced from each other, are wrong in their standpoints.

1.14. There is no third *naya*. Moreover, it cannot be said that truth cannot be adequately expressed by these two *nayas*, for if we combine both these standpoints in their particular aspects we can certainly arrive at the truth by the method of *anekānta* (the versatility [plurality] of aspects).

1.15. As these two *nayas* when taken in their exclusiveness are false *nayas*, all other *nayas* also are wrong when taken in their isolated standpoints, for the subsequent *nayas* occupy themselves in viewing the different aspects of the thing which is the subject of these two principal *nayas*.

1.17. This worldly life cannot be accounted for from the *dravyāstika* standpoint. It is equally unaccountable from the *paryāyāstika* point of view. For the former holds that there is only one element and stable thing; while the latter holds that birth and decay are the true characteristics of a thing.

1.18. From the point of view of those who hold that an entity is unchangeable, happiness and misery cannot stand; in the opinion of those who hold that things eternally change the idea of happiness and misery can never hold good.

1.21. All the *nayas*, therefore, in their exclusively individual standpoints are absolutely faulty. If, however, they consider themselves as supplementary to each other, they are right in their viewpoints.

1.23. . . .every *naya* in its own sphere is right, but if all of them arrogate to themselves the whole truth and disregard the views of rival *nayas* then they do not attain the status of a right view.

1.25. . . .if all the *nayas* arrange themselves in a proper way and supplement to each other, then alone they are worthy of being termed as "the whole truth" or the right view in its entirety. But in this case they merge their individuality in the collective whole.

1.27. All the *nayas* are right in their own respective spheres—but if they encroach upon the province of other *nayas* and they try to refute their views they are wrong.

1.28. A man who holds the view of the cumulative character of truth (*anekāntajña*) never says that a particular view is right or that a particular view is wrong.

1.36. If we desire to describe a thing simultaneously from the standpoint of its own particularising elements and the particularising elements of another thing, it baffles description and is said to be indescribable.

1.37. If we desire to say that a thing partly exists from one point of view (or in a certain sense) and does not exist from another point of view—that thing is said to exist and not to exist.

1.38. If we desire to say that one part of a thing exists and another exists and does not exist at the same time the thing is said to be existing and indescribable.

1.39. If we desire to say that one part of a certain thing does not exist and another part does and does not exist at the same time, the thing is said to be not existing and indescribable.

1.40. If one part of a thing does and does not exist and another does and does not exist at the same time—the thing is said to be existing, not existing and indescribable.

1.47. As it is impossible to separate milk from water when they both are intermingled with each other, similarly it is neither possible nor logical to separate two things (such as the soul and the matter in the present case) when they are inextricably blended together or when one permeates the other. No one can point out in such cases that this is one thing and this—another. It is not possible to distribute the *paryāyas* (conditions or modifications) of a composite thing into its component parts.

1.48. All the modifications in a body such as form and others should be described as inextricably mixed together. Similarly in the case of the soul all the attributes of it in the state of its temporal existence should be described as interpenetrating.

1.53. The right Jaina view consists of the combination of these two *nayas* with all their attendant statements.

1.54. A wise speaker sometimes places before his audience even one of the two *nayas* having regard to their various mental levels, for that speaker is justified in stating one particular standpoint of one *naya* only, with a view to lead them in the long run to all-comprehensive truth.

CHAPTER IX

BUDDHISM

BUDDHISM had a history of a thousand years in India and, as the centuries rolled by, its doctrines varied. The teaching of the Buddha, the Hīnayāna (early) and the Mahāyāna (later) forms, and the several specific schools constitute the history of Buddhism.

The Buddha takes up some of the thoughts of the Upaniṣads and gives to them a new orientation. The Buddha is not so much formulating a new scheme of metaphysics and morals as rediscovering an old norm and adapting it to the new conditions of thought and life.

His Four Noble Truths are that there is suffering, that it has a cause, that it can be suppressed, and that there is a way to accomplish this. All things pass away, dreams and hopes, fears and desires. None can resist the universal supremacy of death.

The Buddha postulates that life is a stream of becoming. There is nothing permanent in the empirical self. One thing is dependent on another. This is the law of dependent origination (*pratītyasamutpāda*). Even the self is a composite of *samjñā* (perception), *vedanā* (feeling), *saṁskāras* (volitional dispositions), *vijñāna* (intelligence), and *rūpa* (form). All these forms change according to the law of *karma.*

The cause of suffering is traced to ignorance and selfish craving (*avidyā* and *taṅhā*). When we get rid of ignorance and its practical consequence of selfishness, we attain *nirvāṇa,* which is described negatively as freedom from ignorance, selfishness, and suffering, and positively as the attainment of wisdom (*prajñā*) and compassion (*karuṇā*).

The path to the attainment of *nirvāṇa,* to the elimination of ignorance and selfishness, is the famous eightfold path of morality.

The Buddha does not affirm a positive reality underlying the world of change, a self underlying the empirical series of mental happenings, and the positive character of *nirvāṇa.* While he is not prepared to dogmatize on these issues, it would be improper to look upon him as a skeptic, or an agnostic, or an atheist. As he is deeply interested in the ethical remaking of man, as he feels that metaphysical disputations would take us away from the task of individual change, he keeps silent on the nature of the absolute reality, the self, and *nirvāṇa.* But his silence is not a cloak for ignorance or skepticism. Whereof we cannot speak we must keep silent. This is the great tradition of the mysticism of the Upaniṣads.

As Buddhism spread, different answers were given to these central metaphysical issues. The Hīnayāna developed the doctrine of the transitoriness of substances or individuals. The goal of existence is defined as *nirvāṇa*, whose content is not further specified. It upholds the ideal of the saint (*arhat*), who frees himself from bondage to *karma* by his own ideals. The Buddha is not so much a savior as an example. The worship of the Buddha is merely an act of commemoration. The popular gods were introduced into Buddhism in its more religious form to serve as objects for meditation.

The Mahāyāna gives us a positive philosophy which believes in the reality of an Absolute (*bhūtatathatā*), the essence of existence. Religiously, this is the *dharmakāya* (embodied law). The world of experience is phenomenal, an expression of the absolute reality. The Buddha himself is a personification of the law. Here we have the transformation of the *dharmakāya* into the *saṁbhogakāya* (enjoyment-body). It is the *ādibuddha* (original *Buddha*) answering to *Saguṇa Brahman*, or Īśvara, in Hinduism.

While the *arhat* is the ideal of the *Hīnayāna*, the *bodhisattva* (a would-be Buddha) is the ideal of the Mahāyāna. A *bodhisattva*, out of the abundance of his love, engages himself in the task of teaching every sentient being. *Nirvāṇa*, for Mahāyāna, is not annihilation, but attainment.

In the course of the development of Buddhist thought many philosophical schools arose. Chief among these are four, the Vaibhāṣika (direct realism) and the Sautrāntika (indirect realism) schools which belong to the Hīnayāna, and the Yogācāra (idealism) and the Mādhyamika (relativism—sometimes called nihilism) which belong to the Mahāyāna.

In view of plans for a Source Book in Buddhist Philosophy, only basic philosophical principles and schools are represented here.

Since selections in this chapter are taken from so many texts, documentary references will be given with each selection, and not in the introduction, as in other chapters. *The Dhammapada* is quoted in its entirety.

A. *HĪNAYĀNA*

1. The Three Characteristics[1]

Whether Buddhas arise, O priests, or whether Buddhas do not arise, it remains a fact and the fixed and necessary constitution of being that all its constituents are transitory. This fact a Buddha discovers and masters, and when he has discovered and mastered it, he announces, teaches, publishes, proclaims, discloses, minutely explains, and makes it clear, that all the constituents of being are transitory.

Whether Buddhas arise, O priests, or whether Buddhas do not arise, it remains a fact and the fixed and necessary constitution of

[1] *Aṅguttara-nikāya* iii.134; in H. C. Warren, *Buddhism in Translations*, Harvard Oriental Series, 3, sixth issue (Cambridge, Mass.: Harvard University Press, 1915), Foreword.

being, that all its constituents are misery. This fact a Buddha discovers and masters, and when he has discovered and mastered it, he announces, teaches, publishes, proclaims, discloses, minutely explains, and makes it clear, that all the constituents of being are misery.

Whether Buddhas arise, O priests, or whether Buddhas do not arise, it remains a fact and the fixed and necessary constitution of being, that all its elements are lacking in an ego [substantial, permanent self-nature]. This fact a Buddha discovers and masters, and when he has discovered and mastered it, he announces, teaches, publishes, proclaims, discloses, minutely explains, and makes it clear, that all the elements of being are lacking in an ego.

2. The First Sermon[1]

These two extremes, O monks, are not to be practised by one who has gone forth from the world. What are the two? That conjoined with the passions, low, vulgar, common, ignoble, and useless, and that conjoined with self-torture, painful, ignoble, and useless. Avoiding these two extremes the Tathāgata[2] has gained the knowledge of the Middle Way, which gives sight and knowledge, and tends to calm, to insight, enlightenment, *nirvāṇa*.

What, O monks, is the Middle Way, which gives sight...? It is the noble Eightfold Path, namely, right views, right intention, right speech, right action, right livelihood, right effort, right mindfulness, right concentration. This, O monks, is the Middle Way....

(1) Now this, O monks, is the noble truth of pain: birth is painful, old age is painful, sickness is painful, death is painful, sorrow, lamentation, dejection, and despair are painful. Contact with unpleasant things is painful, not getting what one wishes is painful. In short the five *khandhas* of grasping are painful.[3]

(2) Now this, O monks, is the noble truth of the cause of pain: that craving which leads to rebirth, combined with pleasure and lust, finding pleasure here and there, namely, the craving for passion, the craving for existence, the craving for non-existence.

(3) Now this, O monks, is the noble truth of the cessation of pain:

[1] *Saṁyutta-nikāya* v.420; in Edward J. Thomas, *The Life of Buddha as Legend and History* (New York: Alfred A. Knopf, 1927), pp. 87–8.

[2] "Tathāgata" is a name for the Buddha. Literally it means one who has "thus come."

[3] The five *khandhas* (groups or aggregates) are form, feeling (or sensation), perception (volitional disposition), predispositions (or impressions), and consciousness. These will be described in detail later in this chapter.

the cessation without a remainder of that craving, abandonment, forsaking, release, non-attachment.

(4) Now this, O monks, is the noble truth of the way that leads to the cessation of pain: this is the noble Eightfold Path, namely, right views, right intention, right speech, right action, right livelihood, right effort, right mindfulness, right concentration....

As long as in these noble truths my threefold knowledge and insight duly with its twelve divisions[1] was not well purified, even so long, O monks, in the world with its gods, Māra,[2] Brahmā,[3] with ascetics, *brāhmins*, gods, and men, I had not attained the highest complete enlightenment. Thus I knew.

But when in these noble truths my threefold knowledge and insight duly with its twelve divisions was well purified, then, O monks, in the world...I had attained the highest complete enlightenment. Thus I knew. Knowledge arose in me; insight arose that the release of my mind is unshakable; this is my last existence; now there is no rebirth.

3. The Synopsis of Truth[4]

Thus have I heard. Once when the Lord was staying at Benares in the Isipatana deerpark, he addressed the almsmen as follows: It was here in this very deerpark at Benares that the Truth-finder, *Arahat* [*arhat*] all-enlightened, set a-rolling the supreme Wheel of the Doctrine—which shall not be turned back from its onward course by recluse or *brāhmin*, god or Māra or Brahmā or by anyone in the universe,—the announcement of the Four Noble Truths, the teaching, declaration, and establishment of those Four Truths, with their unfolding, exposition, and manifestation.

What are these four?—The announcement, teaching...and manifestation of the Noble Truth of suffering[5]—of the origin of suffering—of the cessation of suffering—of the path that leads to the cessation of suffering.

Follow, almsmen, Sāriputta and Moggallāna and be guided by them; they are wise helpers unto their fellows in the higher life....

[1] See section 4, this chapter.

[2] The goddess of temptation.

[3] God in the role of creator.

[4] *Majjhima-nikāya*, iii.248–52: in *Further Dialogues of the Buddha*, ii, translated by Lord Chalmers, Sacred Books of the Buddhists, vi (London: Oxford University Press, 1927), pp. 296–9.

[5] "Suffering" has been substituted for the translator's "ill" in this selection. Other frequent translations are "misery" and "pain."

Sāriputta is able to announce, teach...and manifest the Four Noble Truths in all their details.

Having thus spoken, the Blessed One arose and went into his own cell.

The Lord had not been gone long when the reverent Sāriputta proceeded to the exposition of the Truth-finder's Four Noble Truths, as follows:

What, reverend sirs, is the Noble Truth of suffering?—Birth is a suffering; decay is a suffering; death is a suffering; grief and lamentation, pain, misery and tribulation are sufferings; it is a suffering not to get what is desired;—in brief all the factors of the fivefold grip on existence are suffering.

Birth is, for living creatures of each several class, the being born or produced, the issue, the arising or the re-arising, the appearance of the impressions,[1] the growth of faculties.

Decay, for living creatures of each several class, is the decay and decaying, loss of teeth, grey hair, wrinkles, a dwindling term of life, sere faculties.

Death, for living creatures of each several class, is the passage and passing hence, the dissolution, disappearance, dying, death, decease, the dissolution of the impressions, the discarding of the dead body.

Grief is the grief, grieving, and grievousness, the inward grief and inward anguish of anyone who suffers under some misfortune or is in the grip of some type of suffering.

Lamentation is the lament and lamentation, the wailing and the lamenting of anyone who suffers under some misfortune or is in the grip of some type of suffering.

Pain is any bodily suffering or bodily evil, and suffering bred of bodily contact, any evil feeling.

Misery is mental suffering and evil, any evil feeling of the mind.

Tribulation is the tribulation of heart and mind, the state to which tribulation brings them, in anyone who suffers under some misfortune or is in the grip of some type of suffering.

There remains not to get what is desired. In creatures subject to birth—or decay—or death—or grief and lamentation, pain, misery, and tribulation—the desire arises not to be subject thereto but to escape them. But escape is not to be won merely by desiring it; and failure to win it is another suffering.

[1] "Impressions," "dispositions" or "predispositions" would appear to be a better translation of *saṁskāras* than the translator's "plastic forces."

What are in brief all the factors of the fivefold grip on existence which are sufferings?—They are: the factors of form, feeling, perception, impressions, and consciousness.

The foregoing, sirs, constitutes the Noble Truth of suffering.

What now is the Noble Truth of the origin of suffering? It is any craving that makes for re-birth and is tied up with passion's delights and culls satisfaction now here now there—such as the craving for sensual pleasure, the craving for continuing existence, and the craving for annihilation.

Next, what is the Noble Truth of the cessation of suffering?—It is the utter and passionless cessation of this same craving,—the abandonment and rejection of craving, deliverance from craving, and aversion from craving.

Lastly, what is the Noble Truth of the Path that leads to the cessation of suffering?—It is just the Noble Eightfold Path, consisting of right outlook, right resolves, right speech, right acts, right livelihood, right endeavour, right mindfulness and right rapture of concentration.

Right outlook is to know suffering, the origin of suffering, the cessation of suffering, and the path that leads to the cessation of suffering.

Right resolves are the resolve to renounce the world and to do no hurt or harm.

Right speech is to abstain from lies and slander, from reviling, and from tattle.

Right acts are to abstain from taking life, from stealing, and from lechery.

Right livelihood is that by which the disciple of the Noble One supports himself, to the exclusion of wrong modes of livelihood.

Right endeavour is when an almsman brings his will to bear, puts forth endeavour and energy, struggles and strives with all his heart, to stop bad and wrong qualities which have not yet arisen from ever arising, to renounce those which have already arisen, to foster good qualities which have not yet arisen, and, finally, to establish, clarify, multiply, enlarge, develop, and perfect those good qualities which are there already.

Right mindfulness is when realizing what the body is—what feelings are—what the heart is—and what the mental states are—an almsman dwells ardent, alert, and mindful, in freedom from the wants and discontents attendant on any of these things.

Right rapture of concentration is when, divested of lusts and divested of wrong dispositions, an almsman develops, and dwells in, the first ecstasy with all its zest and satisfaction, a state bred of aloofness and not divorced from observation and reflection. By laying to rest observation and reflection, he develops and dwells in inward serenity, in [the] focussing of heart, in the zest and satisfaction of the second ecstasy, which is divorced from observation and reflection and is bred of concentration—passing thence to the third and fourth ecstasies.

This, sirs, constitutes the Noble Truth of the Path that leads to the cessation of suffering. . . .

4. Dependent Origination

(a) *Saṁyutta-nikāya*[1]

That things have being, O Kaccāna, constitutes one extreme of doctrine; that things have no being is the other extreme. These extremes, O Kaccāna, have been avoided by the Tathāgata, and it is a middle doctrine he teaches:—

On ignorance depends *karma*;
On *karma* depends consciousness;
On consciousness depend name and form;
On name and form depend the six organs of sense;
On the six organs of sense depends contact;
On contact depends sensation;
On sensation depends desire;
On desire depends attachment;
On attachment depends existence;
On existence depends birth;
On birth depend old age and death, sorrow, lamentation, misery, grief, and despair. Thus does this entire aggregation of misery arise.

But on the complete fading out and cessation of ignorance ceases *karma*;
On the cessation of *karma* ceases consciousness;
On the cessation of consciousness cease name and form;
On the cessation of name and form cease the six organs of sense;
On the cessation of the six organs of sense ceases contact;
On the cessation of contact ceases sensation;
On the cessation of sensation ceases desire;

[1] xxii.90, H. C. Warren, *Buddhism in Translations*, p. 166.

On the cessation of desire ceases attachment;

On the cessation of attachment ceases existence;

On the cessation of existence ceases birth;

On the cessation of birth cease old age and death, sorrow, lamentation, misery, grief, and despair. Thus does this entire aggregation of misery cease.

(b) *Visuddhi-magga*[1]

Inasmuch as it is dependently on each other and in unison and simultaneously that the factors which constitute dependence originate the elements of being, therefore did the Sage call these factors dependent origination.

For the ignorance etc., which have been enumerated as constituting dependence, when they originate any of the elements of being, namely, *karma* and the rest, can only do so when dependent on each other and in case none of their number is lacking. Therefore it is dependently on each other and in unison and simultaneously that the factors which constitute dependence originate the elements of being, not by a part of their number nor by one succeeding the other. Accordingly the Sage, skilful in the art of discovering the signification of things, calls this dependence by the name of dependent origination.

And in so doing, by the first of these two words is shown the falsity of such heresies as that of the persistence of existences, and, by the second word, a rejection of such heresies as that existences cease to be, while by both together is shown the truth.

By the first:—The word "dependent," as exhibiting a full complement of dependence and inasmuch as the elements of being are subject to that full complement of dependence, shows an avoidance of such heresies as that of the persistence of existences, the heresies, namely, of the persistence of existences, of uncaused existences, of existences due to an overruling power, of self-determining existences. For what have persistent existences, uncaused existences, etc., to do with a full complement of dependence?

By the second:—The word "origination," as exhibiting an origination of the elements of being and inasmuch as the elements of being originate by means of a full complement of dependence, shows a rejection of such heresies as that of the annihilation of existences, the heresies, namely, of the annihilation of existences, of nihilism, of the inefficacy of *karma*. For if the elements of being are

[1] xvii, H. C. Warren, *Buddhism in Translations*, pp. 168–70.

continually originating by means of an antecedent dependence, whence can we have annihilation of existence, nihilism, and an inefficacy of *karma*?

By both together:—By the complete phrase "dependent origination," inasmuch as such and such elements of being come into existence by means of an unbroken series of their full complement of dependence, the truth, or middle course, is shown. This rejects the heresy that he who experiences the fruit of the deed is the same as the one who performed the deed, and also rejects the converse one that he who experiences the fruit of a deed is different from the one who performed the deed, and leaning not to either of these popular hypotheses, holds fast by nominalism.

5. The Theory of No-Soul [or Self]

(a) *Saṁyutta-nikāya*[1]

The body, monks, is soulless. If the body, monks, were the soul, this body would not be subject to sickness, and it would be possible in the case of the body to say, "Let my body be thus, let my body not be thus." Now, because the body is soulless, monks, therefore the body is subject to sickness, and it is not possible in the case of the body to say, "Let my body be thus, let my body not be thus."

Feeling is soulless...perception is soulless...the aggregates are soulless....

Consciousness is soulless. For if consciousness were the soul, this consciousness would not be subject to sickness, and it would be possible in the case of consciousness to say, "Let my consciousness be thus, let my consciousness not be thus."

Now, because consciousness is soulless, therefore consciousness is subject to sickness, and it is not possible in the case of consciousness to say, "Let my consciousness be thus, let my consciousness not be thus."

What think you, monks, is the body permanent or impermanent?

Impermanent, Lord.

But is the impermanent painful or pleasant?

Painful, Lord.

But is it fitting to consider what is impermanent, painful, and subject to change as, "this is mine, this am I, this is my soul"?

No indeed, Lord.

[1] iii.66, in E. J. Thomas, *The Life of Buddha*, pp. 88–9.

[And so of feeling, perception, the aggregates, and consciousness.] Therefore in truth, monks, whatever body, past, future, or present, internal or external, gross or subtle, low or eminent, near or far, is to be looked on by him who duly and rightly understands, as, "all this body is not mine, not this am I, not mine is the soul." [And so of feeling, etc.]

Thus perceiving, monks, the learned noble disciple feels loathing for the body, for feeling, for perception, for the aggregates, for consciousness. Feeling disgust he becomes free from passion, through freedom from passion he is emancipated, and in the emancipated one arises the knowledge of his emancipation. He understands that destroyed is rebirth, the religious life has been led, done is what was to be done, there is nought [for him] beyond this world.

(b) *Milindapañha*[1]

Then drew near Milinda the king to where the venerable Nāgasena was; and having drawn near, he greeted the venerable Nāgasena; and having passed the compliments of friendship and civility, he sat down respectfully at one side. And the venerable Nāgasena returned the greeting; by which, verily, he won the heart of king Milinda.

And Milinda the king spoke to the venerable Nāgasena as follows:—

"How is your reverence called? *Bhante* [Lord], what is your name?"

"Your majesty, I am called Nāgasena; my fellow-priests, your majesty, address me as Nāgasena; but whether parents give one the name Nāgasena, or Sūrasena, or Vīrasena, or Sīhasena, it is, nevertheless, your majesty, but a way of counting, a term, an appellation, a convenient designation, a mere name, this Nāgasena; for there is no ego here to be found."

And Milinda the king spoke to the venerable Nāgasena as follows: "*Bhante* Nāgasena, if there is no ego to be found, who is it, then, furnishes you priests with the priestly requisites,—robes, food, bedding, and medicine, the reliance of the sick? Who is it makes use of the same? Who is it keeps the precepts? Who is it applies himself to meditation? Who is it realizes the Paths, the Fruits, and *nirvāṇa*? Who is it destroys life? Who is it takes what is not given him? Who is it commits immorality? Who is it tells lies? Who is it drinks

[1] 251 (or II.i.1), in H. C. Warren, *Buddhism in Translations*, pp. 129–33.

intoxicating liquor? Who is it commits the five crimes that constitute "proximate *karma*'?[1] In that case, there is no merit; there is no demerit; there is no one who does or causes to be done meritorious or demeritorious deeds; neither good nor evil deeds can have any fruit or result. *Bhante* Nāgasena, neither is he a murderer who kills a priest, nor can you priests, *bhante* Nāgasena, have any teacher, preceptor, or ordination. When you say, 'My fellow-priests, your majesty, address me as Nāgasena,' what, then, is this Nāgasena? Pray, *bhante*, is the hair of the head Nāgasena"?

"Nay, verily, your majesty."

"Is the hair of the body Nāgasena"?

"Nay, verily, your majesty."

"Are nails ... teeth ... skin ... flesh ... sinews ... bones ... marrow of the bones ... kidneys ... heart ... liver ... pleura ... spleen ... lungs ... intestines ... mesentery ... stomach ... faeces ... bile ... phlegm ... pus ... blood ... sweat ... fat ... tears ... lymph ... saliva ... snot ... synovial fluid ... urine ... brain of the head Nāgasena"?

"Nay, verily, your majesty."

"Is now, *bhante*, form Nāgasena"?

"Nay, verily, your majesty."

"Is sensation Nāgasena"?

"Nay, verily, your majesty."

"Is perception Nāgasena"?

"Nay, verily, your majesty."

"Are the predispositions Nāgasena"?

"Nay, verily, your majesty."

"Is consciousness Nāgasena?"

"Nay, verily, your majesty."

"Are, then, *bhante*, form, sensation, perception, the predispositions, and consciousness unitedly Nāgasena?"

"Nay, verily, your majesty."

"Is it, then, *bhante*, something besides form, sensation, perception, the predispositions, and consciousness which is Nāgasena?"

"Nay, verily, your majesty."

"*Bhante*, although I question you very closely, I fail to discover any Nāgasena. Verily, now, *bhante*, Nāgasena is a mere empty sound. What Nāgasena is there here? *Bhante*, you speak a falsehood, a lie: there is no Nāgasena."

[1] That is, *karma* that bears fruit in this life.

Then the venerable Nāgasena spoke to Milinda the king as follows:—

"Your majesty, you are a delicate prince, an exceedingly delicate prince; and if, your majesty, you walk in the middle of the day on hot sandy ground, and you tread on rough grit, gravel, and sand, your feet become sore, your body tired, the mind is oppressed, and the body-consciousness suffers. Pray, did you come afoot, or riding?"

"*Bhante*, I do not go afoot: I came in a chariot."

"Your majesty, if you came in a chariot, declare to me the chariot. Pray, your majesty, is the pole the chariot?"

"Nay, verily, *bhante*."

"Is the axle the chariot?"

"Nay, verily, *bhante*."

"Are the wheels the chariot?"

"Nay, verily, *bhante*."

"Is the chariot-body the chariot?"

"Nay, verily, *bhante*."

"Is the banner-staff the chariot?"

"Nay, verily, *bhante*."

"Is the yoke the chariot?"

"Nay, verily, *bhante*."

"Are the reins the chariot?"

"Nay, verily, *bhante*."

"Is the goading-stick the chariot?"

"Nay, verily, *bhante*."

"Pray, your majesty, are pole, axle, wheels, chariot-body, banner-staff, yoke, reins, and goad unitedly the chariot?"

"Nay, verily, *bhante*."

"Is it, then, your majesty, something else besides pole, axle, wheels, chariot-body, banner-staff, yoke, reins, and goad which is the chariot?"

"Nay, verily, *bhante*."

"Your majesty, although I question you very closely, I fail to discover any chariot. Verily now, your majesty, the word chariot is a mere empty sound. What chariot is there here? Your majesty, you speak a falsehood, a lie: there is no chariot. Your majesty, you are the chief king in all the continent of India; of whom are you afraid that you speak a lie? Listen to me, my lords, ye five hundred Yonakas, and ye eighty thousand priests! Milinda the king here says thus: 'I came in a chariot'; and being requested, 'Your majesty, if you came in a chariot, declare to me the chariot,' he fails to produce any chariot. Is it possible, pray, for me to assent to what he says?"

When he had thus spoken, the five hundred Yonakas applauded the venerable Nāgasena and spoke to Milinda the king as follows:—

"Now, your majesty, answer, if you can."

Then Milinda the king spoke to the venerable Nāgasena as follows:—

"*Bhante* Nāgasena, I speak no lie: the word 'chariot' is but a way of counting, term, appellation, convenient designation, and name for pole, axle, wheels, chariot-body, and banner-staff."

"Thoroughly well, your majesty, do you understand a chariot. In exactly the same way, your majesty, in respect of me, Nāgasena is but a way of counting, term, appellation, convenient designation, mere name for the hair of my head, hair of my body... brain of the head, form, sensation, perception, the predispositions, and consciousness. But in the absolute sense there is no ego here to be found. And the priestess Vajirā, your majesty, said as follows in the presence of the Blessed One:—

"'Even as the word of "chariot" means
That members join to frame a whole;
So when the groups appear to view,
We use the phrase, "a living being."'"

"It is wonderful, *bhante* Nāgasena! It is marvellous, *bhante* Nāgasena! Brilliant and prompt is the wit of your replies. If the Buddha were alive, he would applaud. Well done, well done, Nāgasena! Brilliant and prompt is the wit of your replies."

(c) *Visuddhi-magga*[1]

Just as the word "chariot" is but a mode of expression for axle, wheels, chariot-body, pole, and other constituent members, placed in a certain relation to each other, but when we come to examine the members one by one, we discover that in the absolute sense there is no chariot; and just as the word "house" is but a mode of expression for wood and other constituents of a house, surrounding space in a certain relation, but in the absolute sense there is no house; and just as the word "fist" is but a mode of expression for the fingers, the thumb, etc., in a certain relation; and the word "lute" for the body of the lute, strings, etc.; "army" for elephants, horses, etc.;

[1] xviii, H. C. Warren, *Buddhism in Translations*, pp. 132–5.

"city" for fortifications, houses, gates, etc.; "tree" for trunk, branches, foliage, etc., in a certain relation, but when we come to examine the parts one by one, we discover that in the absolute sense there is no tree; in exactly the same way the words "living entity" and "ego" are but a mode of expression for the presence of the five attachment groups,[1] but when we come to examine the elements of being one by one, we discover that in the absolute sense there is no living entity there to form a basis for such figments as "I am," or "I"; in other words, that in the absolute sense there is only name and form. The insight of him who perceives this is called knowledge of the truth.

He, however, who abandons this knowledge of the truth and believes in a living entity must assume either that this living entity will perish or that it will not perish. If he assume that it will not perish, he falls into the heresy of the persistence of existences; or if he assume that it will perish, he falls into that of the annihilation of existences. And why do I say so? Because, just as sour cream has milk as its antecedent, so nothing here exists but what has its own antecedents. To say, "The living entity persists," is to fall short of the truth; to say, "It is annihilated," is to outrun the truth. Therefore has the Blessed One said:—

"There are two heresies, O priests, which possess both gods and men, by which some fall short of the truth, and some outrun the truth; but the intelligent know the truth.

"And how, O priests, do some fall short of the truth?

"O priests, gods and men delight in existence, take pleasure in existence, rejoice in existence, so that when the doctrine for the cessation of existence is preached to them their minds do not leap toward it, are not favorably disposed toward it, do not rest in it, do not adopt it.

"Thus, O priests, do some fall short of the truth.

"And how, O priests, do some outrun the truth?

"Some are distressed at, ashamed of, and loathe existence, and welcome the thought of non-existence, saying, 'See here! When they say that on the dissolution of the body this ego is annihilated, perishes, and does not exist after death, that is good, that is excellent, that is as it should be.'

"Thus, O priests, do some outrun the truth.

[1] The "attachment groups" are the *khandhas*. See introduction to this chapter and the First Sermon, above.

"And how, O priests, do the intelligent know the truth?

"We may have, O priests, a priest who knows things as they really are, and knowing things as they really are, he is on the road to aversion for things, to absence of passion for them, and to cessation from them.

"Thus, O priests, do the intelligent know the truth."

(d) *Saṁyutta-nikāya*[1]

Thus have I heard.

On a certain occasion the venerable Sāriputta was dwelling at Sāvatthi in Jetavana monastery in Anāthapiṇḍika's Park.

Now at that time the following wicked heresy had sprung up in the mind of a priest named Yamaka: "Thus do I understand the doctrine taught by the Blessed One, that on the dissolution of the body the priest who has lost all depravity is annihilated, perishes, and does not exist after death."

And a number of priests heard the report:...

Then drew near these priests to where the venerable Yamaka was; and having drawn near, they greeted the venerable Yamaka; and having passed the compliments of friendship and civility, they sat down respectfully at one side. And seated respectfully at one side, these priests spoke to the venerable Yamaka as follows: "Is the report true, brother Yamaka, that the following wicked heresy has sprung up in your mind: [The above statement is repeated.] ...

"Say not so, brother Yamaka. Do not traduce the Blessed One; for it is not well to traduce the Blessed One. The Blessed One would never say that on the dissolution of the body the saint who has lost all depravity is annihilated, perishes, and does not exist after death."

Nevertheless, in spite of all these priests could say, the venerable Yamaka persisted obstinately to adhere to his pestiferous delusion:...

And when these priests found themselves unable to detach the venerable Yamaka from this wicked heresy, then these priests arose from their seats and drew near to where the venerable Sāriputta was. And having drawn near they spoke to the venerable Sāriputta as follows: ...Brother Sāriputta, the following wicked heresy has sprung up in the mind of a priest named Yamaka....

[1] xxii.85, H. C. Warren, *Buddhism in Translations*, pp. 138–45.

Then the venerable Sāriputta spoke to the venerable Yamaka as follows:...

"What think you, brother Yamaka? Is form permanent, or transitory?"

"It is transitory, brother."

"And that which is transitory—is it evil, or is it good?"

"It is evil, brother."

"And that which is transitory, evil, and liable to change—is it possible to say of it: 'This is mine; this am I; this is my ego'?"

"Nay, verily, brother."

"Is sensation...perception...the predispositions...consciousness, permanent or transitory?"

"It is transitory, brother."

"And that which is transitory—is it evil, or is it good?"

"It is evil, brother."

"And that which is transitory, evil, and liable to change—is it possible to say of it: 'This is mine; this am I; this is my ego'?"

"Nay, verily, brother."

"Accordingly, brother Yamaka, as respects all form whatsoever, past, future, or present, be it subjective or existing outside, gross or subtile, mean or exalted, far or near, the correct view in the light of the highest knowledge is as follows: 'This is not mine; this am I not; this is not my ego.'

"Perceiving this, brother Yamaka, the learned and noble disciple conceives an aversion for form,...for sensation,...for perception,... for the predispositions, ..for consciousness. And in conceiving this aversion he becomes divested of passion, and by the absence of passion he becomes free, and when he is free he becomes aware that he is free; and he knows that rebirth is exhausted, that he has lived the holy life, that he has done what it behooved him to do, and that he is no more for this world.

"What think you, brother Yamaka? Do you consider form as the saint?"

"Nay, verily, brother."

"Do you consider sensation...perception...the predispositions ...consciousness as the saint?"

"Nay, verily, brother."

"What think you, brother Yamaka? Do you consider the saint as comprised in form?"

"Nay, verily, brother."

"Do you consider the saint as distinct from form?"

"Nay, verily, brother."

"Do you consider the saint as comprised in sensation? . . . as distinct from sensation? . . . as comprised in perception? . . . as distinct from perception? . . . as comprised in the predispositions? . . . as distinct from the predispositions? . . . as comprised in consciousness? . . . as distinct from consciousness?"

"Nay, verily, brother."

"What think you, brother Yamaka? Are form, sensation, perception, the predispositions, and consciousness unitedly the saint?"

"Nay, verily, brother."

"What think you, brother Yamaka? Do you consider the saint as a something having no form, sensation, perception, predispositions, or consciousness?"

"Nay, verily, brother."

"Considering now, brother Yamaka, that you fail to make out and establish the existence of the saint in the present life, is it reasonable for you to say: 'Thus do I understand the doctrine taught by the Blessed One, that on the dissolution of the body the priest who has lost all depravity is annihilated, perishes, and does not exist after death'?"

"Brother Sāriputta, it was because of my ignorance that I held this wicked heresy; but now that I have listened to the doctrinal instruction of the venerable Sāriputta, I have abandoned that wicked heresy and acquired the true doctrine."

"But if others were to ask you, brother Yamaka, as follows: 'Brother Yamaka, the priest who is a saint and has lost all depravity, what becomes of him on the dissolution of the body, after death?' what would you reply, brother Yamaka, if you were asked that question?"

"I would reply, brother, as follows, if I were asked that question: 'Brethren, the form was transitory, and that which was transitory was evil, and that which was evil has ceased and disappeared. The sensation . . . perception . . . predispositions . . . consciousness was transitory, and that which was transitory was evil, and that which was evil has ceased and disappeared.' Thus would I reply, brother, if I were asked that question."

(e) *Visuddhi-magga*[1]

Therefore has it been said as follows:—

"Misery only doth exist, none miserable,
No doer is there; naught save the deed is found.
Nirvāṇa is, but not the man who seeks it.
The Path exists, but not the traveler on it."

6. Questions Which Tend Not to Edification[2]

Thus have I heard.

...Vaccha, the wandering ascetic, spoke to the Blessed One as follows:—

"How is it, Gotama? Does Gotama hold that the world is eternal, and that this view alone is true, and every other false?"

"Nay, Vaccha. I do not hold that the world is eternal, and that this view alone is true, and every other false."

"But how is it, Gotama? Does Gotama hold that the world is not eternal, and that this view alone is true, and every other false?"

"Nay, Vaccha. I do not hold that the world is not eternal, and that this view alone is true, and every other false."

"How is it, Gotama? Does Gotama hold that the world is finite,..."

"How is it, Gotama? Does Gotama hold that the soul and the body are identical,..."

"How is it, Gotama? Does Gotama hold that the saint exists after death,..."

"How is it, Gotama? Does Gotama hold that the saint both exists and does not exist after death, and that this view alone is true, and every other false?"

"Nay, Vaccha. I do not hold that the saint both exists and does not exist after death, and that this view alone is true, and every other false."

"But how is it, Gotama? Does Gotama hold that the saint neither exists nor does not exist after death, and that this view alone is true, and every other false?"

"Nay, Vaccha. I do not hold that the saint neither exists nor does not exist after death, and that this view alone is true, and every other false...

[1] xvi, H. C. Warren, *Buddhism in Translations*, p. 146.

[2] *Majjhima-nikāya* i.483–8, in H. C. Warren, *Buddhism in Translations*, pp. 123–8.

"Vaccha, the theory that the world is eternal is a jungle, a wilderness, a puppet-show, a writhing, and a fetter, and is coupled with misery, ruin, despair, and agony, and does not tend to aversion, absence of passion, cessation, quiescence, knowledge, supreme wisdom, and *nirvāṇa*. . . .

"Vaccha, the theory that the saint neither exists nor does not exist after death is a jungle, a wilderness, a puppet-show, a writhing, and a fetter, and is coupled with misery, ruin, despair, and agony, and does not tend to aversion, absence of passion, cessation, quiescence, knowledge, supreme wisdom, and *nirvāṇa*.

"This is the objection I perceive to these theories, so that I have not adopted any one of them."

"But has Gotama any theory of his own?"

"The Tathāgata, O Vaccha, is free from all theories; but this, Vaccha, does the Tathāgata know,—the nature of form, and how form arises, and how form perishes; the nature of sensation, and how sensation arises, and how sensation perishes; the nature of perception, and how perception arises, and how perception perishes; the nature of the predispositions, and how the predispositions arise, and how the predispositions perish; the nature of consciousness, and how consciousness arises, and how consciousness perishes. Therefore say I that the Tathāgata has attained deliverance and is free from attachment, inasmuch as all imaginings, or agitations, or false notions concerning an ego or anything pertaining to an ego have perished, have faded away, have ceased, have been given up and relinquished."

"But, Gotama, where is the priest reborn who has attained to this deliverance for his mind?"

"Vaccha, to say that he is reborn would not fit the case."

"Then, Gotama, he is not reborn."

"Vaccha, to say that he is not reborn would not fit the case."

"Then, Gotama, he is both reborn and is not reborn."

"Vaccha, to say that he is both reborn and not reborn would not fit the case."

"Then, Gotama, he is neither reborn nor not reborn."

"Vaccha, to say that he is neither reborn nor not reborn would not fit the case. . . ."

"Gotama, I am at a loss what to think in this matter, and I have become greatly confused, and the faith in Gotama inspired by a former conversation has now disappeared."

"Enough, O Vaccha! Be not at a loss what to think in this matter, and be not greatly confused. Profound, O Vaccha, is this doctrine, recondite, and difficult of comprehension, good, excellent, and not to be reached by mere reasoning, subtile, and intelligible only to the wise; and it is a hard doctrine for you to learn, who belong to another sect, to another faith, to another persuasion, to another discipline, and sit at the feet of another teacher. Therefore, Vaccha, I will now question you, and do you make answer as may seem to you good. What think you, Vaccha? Suppose a fire were to burn in front of you, would you be aware that the fire was burning in front of you?"

"Gotama, if a fire were to burn in front of me, I should be aware that a fire was burning in front of me."

"But suppose, Vaccha, some one were to ask you, 'On what does this fire that is burning in front of you depend?' what would you answer, Vaccha?"

"Gotama, if some one were to ask me, 'On what does this fire that is burning in front of you depend?' I would answer, Gotama, 'It is on fuel of grass and wood that this fire that is burning in front of me depends.'"

"But, Vaccha, if the fire in front of you were to become extinct, would you be aware that the fire in front of you had become extinct?"

"Gotama, if the fire in front of me were to become extinct, I should be aware that the fire in front of me had become extinct."

"But, Vaccha, if some one were to ask you, 'In which direction has that fire gone,—east, or west, or north, or south?' what would you say, O Vaccha?"

"The question would not fit the case, Gotama. For the fire which depended on fuel of grass and wood, when that fuel has all gone, and it can get no other, being thus without nutriment, is said to be extinct."

"In exactly the same way, Vaccha, all form by which one could predicate the existence of the saint, all that form has been abandoned, uprooted, pulled out of the ground like a palmyra-tree, and become non-existent and not liable to spring up again in the future. The saint, O Vaccha, who has been released from what is styled form, is deep, immeasurable, unfathomable, like the mighty ocean. To say that he is reborn would not fit the case. To say that he is not reborn would not fit the case. To say that he is both reborn and not reborn would not fit the case. To say that he is neither reborn nor not reborn would not fit the case.

"All sensation....

"All perception....

"All the predispositions. . . .

"All consciousness by which one could predicate the existence of the saint, all that consciousness has been abandoned, uprooted, pulled out of the ground like a palmyra-tree, and become non-existent and not liable to spring up again in the future. The saint, O Vaccha, who has been released from what is styled consciousness, is deep, immeasurable, unfathomable, like the mighty ocean. To say that he is reborn would not fit the case. To say that he is not reborn would not fit the case. To say that he is both reborn and not reborn would not fit the case. To say that he is neither reborn nor not reborn would not fit the case."

7 Ethics—The Way of Life

(a) *The Dhammapada* (*The Path of Virtue*)[1]

Chapter I: The Twin-Verses

1. (The mental) natures are the result of what we have thought, are chieftained by our thoughts, are made up of our thoughts. If a man speaks or acts with an evil thought, sorrow follows him (as a consequence) even as the wheel follows the foot of the drawer (i.e., the ox which draws the cart). (1)

2. (The mental) natures are the result of what we have thought, are chieftained by our thoughts, are made up of our thoughts. If a man speaks or acts with a pure thought, happiness follows him (in consequence) like a shadow that never leaves him. (2)

3. "He abused me, he struck me, he overcame me, he robbed me"—in those who harbour such thoughts hatred will never cease. (3)

4. "He abused me, he struck me, he overcame me, he robbed me"—in those who do not harbour such thoughts hatred will cease. (4)

5. Not at any time are enmities appeased here through enmity but they are appeased through non-enmity. This is the eternal law. (5)

6. Some (who are not learned) do not know that we must all come to an end here; but those who know this, their dissensions cease at once by their knowledge. (6)

7. As the wind throws down a tree of little strength, so indeed does Māra (the tempter) overthrow him who lives looking for pleasures, uncontrolled in his senses, immoderate in eating, indolent, and of low vitality. (7)

[1] S. Radhakrishnan, *The Dhammapada* with introductory essays, Pāli text, English translation and notes (London, New York, Toronto: Oxford University Press, 2nd imp., 1954).

8. As the wind does not throw down a rocky mountain, so Māra indeed does not overthrow him who lives unmindful of pleasures, well controlled in his senses, moderate in eating, full of faith (in the Buddha, the law, and the *saṅgha* or community), and of high vitality. (8)

9. He who will wear the yellow robe without having cleansed himself from impurity, who is devoid of truth and self-control, is not deserving of the yellow robe. (9)

10. But he who puts away depravity, is well grounded in all virtues, and is possessed of self-restraint and truth is indeed worthy of the yellow robe. (10)

11. They who imagine truth in untruth and see untruth in truth, never arrive at truth but follow vain imaginings (desires). (11)

12. But they who know truth as truth and untruth as untruth arrive at truth and follow right desires. (12)

13. As rain breaks through an ill-thatched house, so passion makes its way into an unreflecting mind. (13)

14. As rain does not break through a well-thatched house, so passion does not make its way into a reflecting mind. (14)

15. The evil-doer grieves in this world, he grieves in the next; he grieves in both. He grieves, he is afflicted, seeing the evil of his own actions. (15)

16. The righteous man rejoices in this world, he rejoices in the next; he rejoices in both. He rejoices and becomes delighted, seeing the purity of his own actions. (16)

17. The evil-doer suffers in this world, he suffers in the next; he suffers in both. He suffers (thinking) "evil has been done by me." He suffers even more when he has gone to the evil place. (17)

18. The righteous man rejoices in this world, he rejoices in the next; he rejoices in both. He rejoices (thinking) "good has been done by me." He rejoices still more when he has gone to the good place. (18)

19. Even if he recites a large number of scriptural texts but, being slothful, does not act accordingly, he is like a cowherd counting the cows of others, he has no share in religious life. (19)

20. Even if he recites only a small number, if he is one who acts rightly in accordance with the law, he, having forsaken passion, hatred, and folly, being possessed of true knowledge and serenity of mind, being free from worldly desires both in this world and the next, has a share in the religious life. (20)

Chapter II: Vigilance

1. Vigilance is the abode of eternal life, thoughtlessness is the abode of death. Those who are vigilant (who are given to reflection) do not die. The thoughtless are as if dead already. (21)

2. The wise who have clearly understood this reflectiveness delight in reflectiveness and rejoice in the knowledge of the Āryas. (22)

3. These wise ones, meditative, persevering, always putting forth strenuous effort attain to *nirvāṇa*, the highest freedom and happiness. (23)

4. If a person is reflective, if he rouses himself, if he is ever-mindful, if his deeds are pure, if he acts with consideration, if he is self-restrained and lives according to law, his glory will increase. (24)

5. The wise man, by rousing himself, by vigilance, by restraint, by control, may make for himself an island which the flood cannot overwhelm. (25)

6. Fools, men of inferior intelligence, fall into sloth; the wise man guards his vigilance as his best treasure. (26)

7. Give not yourselves over to sloth or to the intimacy with lust and sensual pleasures. He who meditates with earnestness attains great joy. (27)

8. When the wise man drives away sloth by strenuous effort, climbing the high tower of wisdom, he gazes sorrowless on the sorrowing crowd below. The wise person gazes on the fools even as one on the mountain peak gazes upon the dwellers on the plain (below). (28)

9. Earnest among the slothful, awake among the sleepy, the wise man advances even as a racehorse does, leaving behind the hack. (29)

10. By vigilance did Indra rise to the lordship of the gods. People praise vigilance; thoughtlessness is always deprecated. (30)

11. A mendicant who delights in vigilance, who looks with fear on thoughtlessness (who sees danger in it), moves about like a fire consuming every bond, small or large. (31)

12. A mendicant who delights in vigilance, who looks with fear on thoughtlessness, cannot fall away (from his perfect state) (but) is close to *nirvāṇa*. (32)

Chapter III: Thought

1. Just as a fletcher makes straight his arrow, the wise man makes straight his trembling, unsteady thought which is difficult to guard and difficult to hold back (restrain). (33)

2. Even as a fish taken from his watery home and thrown on the dry ground (moves about restlessly), this thought quivers all over in order to escape the dominion of Māra (the tempter or Death). (34)

3. The control of thought, which is difficult to restrain, fickle, which wanders at will, is good; a tamed mind is the bearer of happiness. (35)

4. Let the wise man guard his thought, which is difficult to perceive, which is extremely subtle, which wanders at will. Thought which is well guarded is the bearer of happiness. (36)

5. They who will restrain their thought, which travels far, alone, incorporeal, seated in the cave (of the heart), will be freed from the fetters of death. (37)

6. If a man's thought is unsteady, if it does not know the true law, if the serenity of mind is troubled, (in him) wisdom is not perfected. (38)

7. There is no fear for him whose thought is untroubled (by faults), whose thought is unagitated, who has ceased to think of good and evil, who is awake (watchful, vigilant). (39)

8. Knowing that this body is (fragile) like a jar, making this thought firm like a fortress, let him attack Māra (the tempter) with the weapon of wisdom, protect what he has conquered and remain attached to it. (40)

9. Before long, alas, will this body lie on the earth, despised, bereft of consciousness, useless like a burnt faggot. (41)

10. Whatever an enemy may do to an enemy, whatever a hater may do to a hater, a wrongly directed mind will do no greater harm. (42)

11. Not a mother, not a father, nor any other relative will do so much; a well-directed mind will do us greater service. (43)

Chapter IV: Flowers

1. Who shall conquer this world and this world of Yama (the lord of the departed) with its gods? Who shall find out the well-taught path of virtue even as a skilled person finds out the (right) flower? (44)

2. The disciple will conquer this world and this world of Yama with its gods. The disciple will find out the well-taught path of virtue even as a skilled person finds out the (right) flower. (45)

3. Knowing that this body is like froth, knowing that it is of the nature of a mirage, breaking the flowery shafts of Māra, he will go where the king of death will not see him. (46)

4. Death carries off a man who is gathering (life's) flowers, whose mind is distracted, even as a flood carries off a sleeping village. (47)

5. Death overpowers a man even while he is gathering (life's) flowers and whose mind is distracted even before he is satiated in his pleasures. (48)

6. Even as a bee gathers honey from a flower and departs without injuring the flower or its colour or scent, so let a sage dwell in his village. (49)

7. Not the unworthy actions of others, not their (sinful) deeds of commission or omission, but one's own deeds of commission and omission should one regard. (50)

8. Like a beautiful flower, full of colour but without scent, are the well-spoken but fruitless words of him who does not act (as he professes to). (51)

9. But like a beautiful flower full of colour and full of scent are the well-spoken and fruitful words of him who acts (as he professes to). (52)

10. As many kinds of garlands can be made from a heap of flowers, so many good works should be achieved by a mortal when once he is born. (53)

11. The scent of flowers does not travel against the wind, nor that of sandalwood, nor of *tagara* and *mallikā* flowers, but the fragrance of good people travels even against the wind. A good man pervades every quarter. (54)

12. Sandalwood or *tagara*, a lotus flower or a *vassikī*, among these kinds of perfumes the perfume of virtue is unsurpassed. (55)

13. Little is the scent that comes from *tagara* or sandalwood, the perfume of those who possess virtue rises up to the gods as the highest. (56)

14. Of those who possess these virtues, who live without thoughtlessness, who are freed by perfect knowledge, Māra the tempter never finds their way. (57)

15. Just as on a heap of rubbish thrown upon the highway grows the lotus sweetly fragrant and delighting the heart. (58)

16. Even so among those blinded mortals who are like rubbish the disciple of the truly enlightened Buddha shines with exceeding glory by his wisdom. (59)

Chapter V: The Fool

1. Long is the night to him who is awake, long is the *yojana* (a space of nine or twelve miles) to him who is weary; long is the chain of existence to the foolish who do not know the true law. (60)

2. If on a journey (a traveller) does not meet his better or equal let him firmly pursue his journey by himself; there is no companionship with a fool. (61)

3. The fool is tormented thinking "these sons belong to me," "this wealth belongs to me." He himself does not belong to himself. How, then, can sons be his? How can wealth be his? (62)

4. The fool who knows his foolishness is wise at least to that extent; but a fool who thinks himself wise is called a fool indeed. (63)

5. If a fool be associated with a wise man even all his life, he does not perceive the truth even as a spoon (does not perceive) the taste of soup. (64)

6. But if a thoughtful man be associated with a wise man even for a minute, he will soon perceive the truth even as the tongue (perceives) the taste of soup. (65)

7. Fools of little understanding, being enemies to themselves, wander about doing evil deeds which bear bitter fruits. (66)

8. That deed is not well done, which, having been done, brings remorse, whose reward one receives weeping and with a tearful countenance. (67)

9. But that deed is well done, which, having been done, does not bring remorse, whose reward one receives delighted and happy. (68)

10. So long as an evil deed does not bear fruit, the fool thinks that it is like honey; but when it bears fruit, then the fool suffers grief. (69)

11. Let a fool month after month eat his food with the tip (of a blade) of *kuśa* grass; nevertheless he is not worth the sixteenth part of those who have well understood the law. (70)

12. An evil deed, like newly drawn milk, does not turn (at once); smouldering, like fire covered by ashes, it follows the fool. (71)

13. The knowledge that a fool acquires, far from being to his advantage, destroys his bright share of merit and cleaves his head. (72)

14. Let the fool wish for false reputation, for precedence among the mendicants, for lordship in convents, and worship among other groups. (73)

15. "Let both the householders and the monks think that this is done by me. Let them follow my pleasure in what should be done and what should not be done." Such is the wish of the fool and so his desire and pride increase. (74)

16. One is the road that leads to gain; another is the road that leads to *nirvāṇa*. Let the mendicant, the disciple of the Buddha, having learnt this, not seek the respect of men but strive after wisdom. (75)

Chapter VI: The Wise Man

1. If a person sees a wise man who reproaches him (for his faults), who shows what is to be avoided, he should follow such a wise man as he would a revealer of hidden treasures. It fares well and not ill with one who follows such a man. (76)

2. Let him admonish, let him instruct, let him restrain from the impure. He becomes beloved of the good and hated by the evil. (77)

3. One should not associate with friends who are evil-doers nor with persons who are despicable; associate with friends who are virtuous, associate with the best of men. (78)

4. He who drinks in the law lives happily with a serene mind. The wise man ever rejoices in the law made known by the elect (or the Āryas). (79)

5. Engineers (who build canals and aqueducts) lead the water (wherever they like), fletchers make the arrow straight, carpenters carve the wood; wise people fashion (discipline) themselves. (80)

6. As a solid rock is not shaken by the wind, so wise men are not moved amidst blame and praise. (81)

7. Even as a deep lake is clear and calm, so also wise men become tranquil after they have listened to the laws. (82)

8. Good people walk on whatever happens to them. Good people do not prattle, yearning for pleasures. The wise do not show variation (elation or depression), whether touched by happiness or else by sorrow. (83)

9. He who, for his own sake or for the sake of another, does not wish for a son or wealth or a kingdom, if he does not wish for his

own prosperity by unfair means he certainly is virtuous, wise, and religious. (84)

10. Few amongst men are those who reach the farther shore: the other people here run along (this) shore. (85)

11. But those who, when the law has been well preached to them, follow the law, will pass to the other shore, [beyond] the dominion of death which is difficult to overcome. (86)

12. Let the wise man leave the way of darkness and follow the way of light. After going from his home to a homeless state, that retirement so hard to love. (87)

13. Let him there look for enjoyment. Putting away all pleasures, calling nothing his own, let the wise man cleanse himself from all the impurities of the heart. (88)

14. Those whose minds are well grounded in the (seven) elements of enlightenment, who without clinging to anything rejoice in freedom from attachment, whose appetites have been conquered, who are full of light, attain *nirvāṇa* in this world. (89)

Chapter VII: The *Arhat* (The Saint)

1. There is no suffering for him who has completed his journey, who is freed from sorrow, who has freed himself on all sides, who has shaken off all fetters. (90)

2. The thoughtful exert themselves; they do not delight in an abode; like swans who have left their lake they leave their house and home. (91)

3. Those who have no accumulation (of property), who eat according to knowledge, who have perceived (the nature of) release and unconditioned freedom, their path is difficult to understand like that (the flight) of birds through the sky. (92)

4. He whose passions are destroyed, who is indifferent to food, who has perceived (the nature of) release and unconditioned freedom, his path is difficult to understand like that of birds through the sky. (93)

5. Even the gods envy him whose senses are subdued like horses well tamed by the charioteer, who is free from pride and free from taints. (94)

6. Such a man who is tolerant like the earth, like a threshold; who does his duty, who is like a lake free from mud: to a man like that there is no cycle of births and deaths. (95)

7. His thought is calm, calm is his word as well as his deed when he has obtained freedom through true knowledge and has become tranquil. (96)

8. The man who is free from credulity, who knows the uncreated, who has severed all ties, who has put an end to all occasions (for the performance of good or bad actions), who has renounced all desires, he, indeed, is exalted among men. (97)

9. That place is delightful where saints dwell, whether in the village or in the forest, in deep water or on dry land. (98)

10. Forests are delightful (to saints); where (ordinary) people find no delight there the passionless will find delight, for they do not seek for the pleasures of sense. (99)

Chapter VIII: The Thousands

1. Better than a thousand utterances composed of meaningless words is one sensible word on hearing which one becomes peaceful. (100)

2. Better than a thousand verses composed of meaningless words is one word of a verse on hearing which one becomes peaceful. (101)

3. Better than reciting a hundred verses composed of meaningless words is one text on hearing which one becomes peaceful. (102)

4. If a man were to conquer in battle a thousand times a thousand men, and another conquer one, himself, he indeed is the greatest of conquerors. (103)

5. Conquest of self is indeed better than the conquest of other persons; of one who has disciplined himself, who always practises self-control. (104)

6. Not even a god nor a *gandharva* [fairy] nor Māra along with Brahmā could turn into defeat the victory of such a one (who has conquered himself). (105)

7. If a man month after month for a hundred years should sacrifice with a thousand (sacrifices), and if he but for one moment pay homage to a man whose self is grounded in knowledge, better is that homage than what is sacrificed for a hundred years. (106)

8. If a man for a hundred years tend the (sacrificial) fire in the forest, and if he but for one moment pay homage to a man whose self is grounded in knowledge, better is that homage than what is sacrificed for a hundred years. (107)

9. Whatever a man sacrifice in this world as an offering or oblation

for a year in order to gain merit—the whole of it is not worth a quarter (of the better offering). Homage paid to the righteous is better. (108)

10. To him who constantly practises reverence and respects the aged, four things will increase, life (length of days), beauty, happiness, strength. (109)

11. But he who lives a hundred years, wicked and unrestrained, a life of one day is better if a man is virtuous and reflecting. (110)

12. And he who lives a hundred years, ignorant and unrestrained, a life of one day is better for one who is wise and reflecting. (111)

13. And he who lives a hundred years, idle and weak, a life of one day is better if a man strenuously makes an effort. (112)

14. And he who lives a hundred years, not perceiving beginning and end (birth and death), a life of one day is better if a man perceives beginning and end. (113)

15. And he who lives a hundred years not perceiving the deathless state, a life of one day is better if a man perceives the deathless state. (114)

16. And he who lives a hundred years not perceiving the highest law, a life of one day is better if a man perceives the highest law. (115)

Chapter IX: Evil Conduct

1. A man should hasten towards the good; he should restrain his thoughts from evil. If a man is slack in doing what is good, his mind (comes to) rejoice in evil. (116)

2. If a man commits sin, let him not do it again and again. Let him not set his heart on it. Sorrowful is the accumulation of evil conduct. (117)

3. If a man does what is good, let him do it again and again. Let him set his heart on it. Happiness is the outcome of good conduct. (118)

4. Even an evil-doer sees happiness so long as his evil deed does not ripen; but when the evil deed has ripened, then does the evil-doer see evil. (119)

5. Even a good man sees evil as long as his good deed does not ripen; but when his good deed ripens, then the good man sees the good (in store for him). (120)

6. Think not lightly of evil (saying) that "it will not come near me." Even a water-pot is filled by the falling of drops of water. A fool becomes full of evil even if he gathers it little by little. (121)

7. Think not lightly of good (saying) that "it will not come near me." Even a water-pot is filled by the falling of drops of water. A wise man becomes full of goodness even if he gathers it little by little. (122)

8. As a merchant ill-attended and having much wealth shuns a dangerous road, as a man who loves his life avoids poison, so should (a wise man) avoid evil actions. (123)

9. If there be no wound on a person's hand he might touch poison with his hand. Poison does not harm one who has no wound. No evil (befalls) him who does no evil. (124)

10. Whoever does wrong to an innocent person or to one who is pure and sinless, evil recoils on that fool even as fine dust thrown against the wind (recoils on the person throwing it). (125)

11. Some enter the womb; evil-doers go to hell; the good go to heaven; those free from worldly desires attain *nirvāṇa.* (126)

12. Neither in the sky nor in the midst of the sea nor by entering into the clefts of mountains is there known a place on earth where, stationing himself, a man can escape from (the consequences of) his evil deed. (127)

13. Neither in the sky nor in the midst of the sea nor by entering into the clefts of mountains is there known a place on earth where, stationing himself, death cannot overcome (him). (128)

Chapter X: Punishment

1. All men tremble at punishment, all men fear death. Likening others to oneself, one should neither slay nor cause to slay. (129)

2. All men tremble at punishment: all men love life. Likening others to oneself, one should neither slay nor cause to slay. (130)

3. He who seeking his own happiness inflicts pain (strikes with a stick) on beings who (like himself) are desirous of happiness does not obtain happiness after death. (131)

4. He who seeking his own happiness does not inflict pain (strike with a stick) on beings who (like himself) are desirous of happiness obtains happiness after death. (132)

5. Do not speak anything harsh. Those who are spoken to will answer you (in the same way). Since angry talk is painful, retaliation will touch you. (133)

6. If you make yourself as still as a broken gong you have attained *nirvāṇa*, for agitation is not known to you. (134)

7. Just as a cowherd with his staff drives the cows into the pasture-ground, so old age and death drive the life of sentient beings (into a new existence). (135)

8. But a fool committing evil deeds does not know (what is in store for him). The stupid man burns indeed through his own deeds, like one burnt by fire. (136)

9. He who inflicts punishment on those who do not deserve punishment and offends against those who are without offence soon comes to one of these ten states. (137)

10. He may have cruel suffering, infirmity, injury of the body, heavy afflictions (dread diseases), or loss of mind, (138)

11. or a misfortune proceeding from the king or a fearful accusation, loss of relations, or destruction of treasures, (139)

12. or lightning fire burns his houses and when his body is dissolved the fool goes to hell. (140)

13. Not nakedness, not matted hair, not dirt (literally mud), not fasting, not lying on the ground, not rubbing with ashes (literally dust), not sitting motionless purify a mortal who is not free from doubt. (141)

14. He who though adorned (dressed in fine clothes) fosters the serene mind, is calm, controlled, is established (in the Buddhist way of life), is chaste, and has ceased to injure all other beings, he indeed is a *brāhmin*, an ascetic (*samāna*), a friar (a *bhikkhu*). (142)

15. Is there in the world any man so restrained by modesty that he avoids censure as a well-trained horse avoids the whip? (143)

16. Like a well-trained horse when touched by a whip, be strenuous and swift and you will, by faith, by virtue, by energy, by meditation, by discernment of the law, put aside this great sorrow (of earthly existence), endowed with knowledge and (good) behaviour and mindfulness. (144)

17. Engineers (who build canals and aqueducts) lead the water (where they like); fletchers make the arrow straight; carpenters carve the wood; good people fashion (discipline) themselves. (145)

Chapter XI: Old Age

1. Why is there laughter, why is there joy while this world is always burning? Why do you not seek a light, you who are shrouded in darkness (ignorance)? (146)

2. Behold this painted image, a body full of wounds, put together,

diseased, and full of many thoughts in which there is neither permanence nor stability. (147)

3. This body is worn out, a nest of diseases and very frail. This heap of corruption breaks to pieces, life indeed ends in death. (148)

4. What delight is there for him who sees these white bones like gourds cast away in the autumn? (149)

5. Of the bones a citadel is made, plastered over with flesh and blood, and in it dwell old age and death, pride and deceit. (150)

6. The splendid chariots of kings wear away; the body also comes to old age but the virtue of the good never ages, thus the good teach to each other. (151)

7. A man who has learnt but little grows old like an ox; his flesh increases but his knowledge does not grow. (152)

8. I have run through a course of many births looking for the maker of this dwelling and finding him not; painful is birth again and again. (153)

9. Now are you seen, O builder of the house, you will not build the house again. All your rafters are broken, your ridgepole is destroyed, your mind, set on the attainment of *nirvāṇa*, has attained the extinction of desires. (154)

10. Men who have not practised celibacy (proper discipline), who have not acquired wealth in youth, pine away like old cranes in a lake without fish. (155)

11. Men who have not practised celibacy, who have not acquired wealth in youth, lie like worn out bows, sighing after the past. (156)

Chapter XII: The Self

1. If a man holds himself dear, let him diligently watch himself. The wise man should be watchful during one of the three watches. (157)

2. Let each man first establish himself in what is proper, then let him teach others. (If he do this) the wise man will not suffer. (158)

3. If a man so shapes his life as he directs others, then, subduing himself well, he might indeed subdue (others), since the self is indeed difficult to subdue. (159)

4. The self is the lord of self; who else could be the lord? With self well subdued a man finds a lord who is difficult to obtain. (160)

5. The evil done by oneself, born of oneself, produced by oneself, crushes the fool even as a diamond breaks a precious stone. (161)

6. As a creeper overpowers the entwined *sāl* tree, he whose impiety is great reduces himself to the state which his enemy wishes for him. (162)

7. Evil deeds, deeds which are harmful to oneself, are easy to do. What is beneficial and good, that is very difficult to do. (163)

8. The foolish man who scorns the teaching of the saintly, the noble, and the virtuous and follows false doctrine, bears fruit to his own destruction even like the *khaṭṭaka* reed. (164)

9. By oneself, indeed, is evil done; by oneself is one injured. By oneself is evil left undone; by oneself is one purified. Purity and impurity belong to oneself. No one purifies another. (165)

10. Let no one neglect his own task for the sake of another's, however great; let him, after he has discerned his own task, devote himself to his task. (166)

Chapter XIII: The World

1. Do not follow evil law. Do not live in thoughtlessness. Do not follow false doctrine. Do not be a friend of the world. (167)

2. Get up (rouse yourself), do not be thoughtless. Follow the law of virtue. He who practises virtue lives happily in this world as well as in the world beyond. (168)

3. Follow the law of virtue, do not follow the law of sin. He who practises virtue lives happily in this world as well as in the world beyond. (169)

4. Look upon the world as a bubble: look upon it as a mirage. Him who looks thus upon the world the king of death does not see. (170)

5. Come, look at this world resembling a painted royal chariot. The foolish are sunk in it; for the wise there is no attachment for it. (171)

6. He who formerly was thoughtless and afterwards became reflective (sober) lights up this world like the moon when freed from a cloud. (172)

7. He whose evil conduct is covered by good conduct lights up this world like the moon when freed from a cloud. (173)

8. This world is blinded, few only can see here. Like birds escaped from the net a few go to heaven. (174)

9. The swans go on the path of the sun, they go through the sky by means of their miraculous power. The wise are led out of this world, having conquered Māra (the tempter) and his hosts. (175)

10. He who violates the one law (the Buddha's doctrine), who speaks falsely, scoffs at another world, there is no evil he will not do. (176)

11. Verily, the niggardly do not go to the world of the gods. Fools, indeed, do not praise giving. But the wise man, rejoicing in charity, becomes on that (account) happy in the other world. (177)

12. Better than absolute sovereignty on earth, better than going to heaven, better than lordship over all the worlds is the reward of reaching the stream (the attainment of the first step in sanctification). (178)

Chapter XIV: The Buddha (The Awakened)

1. He whose conquest is not conquered again, into whose conquest no one in this world enters, by what track can you lead him, the awakened, of infinite perception, the trackless? (179)

2. He whom no desire net-like or poisonous can lead astray, by what track can you lead him, the awakened, of infinite perception, the trackless? (180)

3. Even the gods emulate those wise men who are given to meditation, who delight in the peace of emancipation (from desire), the enlightened, the thoughtful. (181)

4. Difficult is it to obtain birth as a human being; difficult is the life of mortals; difficult is the hearing of the true law, difficult is the rise of *buddha*hood (or enlightenment). (182)

5. The eschewing of all evil, the perfecting of good deeds, the purifying of one's mind, this is the teaching of the Buddhas (the awakened). (183)

6. Patience which is long suffering is the highest austerity. The awakened declare *nirvāṇa* to be the highest (of things). He verily is not an anchorite who oppresses (others); he is not an ascetic who causes grief to another. (184)

7. Not reviling, not injuring, (practising) restraint according to the law, moderation in eating, dwelling in solitude, diligence in higher thought, this is the teaching of the awakened. (185)

8. There is no satisfaction of one's passions even by a shower of gold pieces. He who knows that "passions are of small enjoyment and productive of pain" is a wise man. (186)

9. Even in celestial pleasures he finds no delight. The disciple who is fully awakened delights only in the destruction of all desires. (187)

10. Men driven by fear go to many a refuge, to mountains, and to forests, to sacred trees, and shrines. (188)

11. That, verily, is not a safe refuge, that is not the best refuge. After having got to that refuge a man is not delivered from all pains. (189)

12. But he who takes refuge in the Buddha, the Law, and the Order, he perceives, in his clear wisdom, the four noble truths. (190)

13. Suffering, the origin of suffering, the cessation of suffering, and the noble eightfold path which leads to the cessation of suffering. (191)

14. That, verily, is a safe refuge, that is the best refuge; after having got to that refuge a man is delivered from all pains. (192)

15. An exalted person (a Buddha) is difficult to be found. He is not born everywhere. Wherever such a wise one is born that household prospers. (193)

16. Blessed is the birth of the awakened; blessed is the teaching of the true law; blessed is concord in the Order; blessed is the austerity of those who live in concord. (194)

17. He who pays homage to those who are worthy of homage, whether the awakened or their disciples, those who have overcome the host (of evils) and crossed beyond the stream of sorrow. (195)

18. He who pays homage to such as have found deliverance and are free from fear, this his merit cannot be measured by anyone. (196)

Chapter XV: Happiness

1. Let us live happily then, hating none in the midst of men who hate. Let us dwell free from hate among men who hate. (197)

2. Let us live happily then, free from disease in the midst of those who are afflicted with disease. Let us dwell free from disease among men who are afflicted with disease. (198)

3. Let us live happily then, free from care in the midst of those who are careworn; let us dwell free from care among men who are careworn. (199)

4. Let us live happily then, we who possess nothing. Let us dwell feeding on happiness like the shining gods. (200)

5. Victory breeds hatred; the conquered dwells in sorrow. He who has given up (thoughts of both) victory and defeat, he is calm and lives happily. (201)

6. There is no fire like passion, no ill like hatred, there is no sorrow

like this physical existence (individuality), there is no happiness higher than tranquillity. (202)

7. Greediness is the worst of diseases; propensities are the greatest of sorrows. To him who has known this truly, *nirvāṇa* is the highest bliss. (203)

8. Health is the greatest of gifts, contentment is the greatest wealth; trust is the best of relationships. *Nirvāṇa* is the highest happiness. (204)

9. Having tasted the sweetness of solitude and the sweetness of tranquillity he becomes free from fear and free from sin while he drinks the sweetness of the joy of the law. (205)

10. The sight of the noble is good; to live with them (in their company) is always happiness. He will be always happy who does not see fools. (206)

11. He who consorts with a fool suffers a long time. Association with fools as with an enemy is always (productive of) pain. Association with the wise, as meeting with one's kinsfolk, is (productive of) happiness. (207)

12. Therefore, even as the moon follows the path of the constellations one should follow the wise, the intelligent, the learned, the much enduring, the dutiful, the noble: such a good and wise man (one should follow). (208)

Chapter XVI: Pleasure

1. He who gives himself to the distractions (of the world) and does not give himself to meditation, giving up his own welfare and grasping at pleasure, will envy him who exerts himself in meditation. (209)

2. Let no man cling to what is pleasant or unpleasant. Not to see what is pleasant is pain as also (it is pain) to see what is unpleasant. (210)

3. Therefore, do not take a liking to anything; loss of the loved object is evil. There are no bonds for him who has neither likes nor dislikes. (211)

4. From the liked arises grief; from the liked arises fear. To one who is free from liking there is no grief. How (then can there be) fear? (212)

5. From affection arises grief; from affection arises fear. To one who is free from affection there is no grief. How (then can there be) fear? (213)

6. From enjoyment arises grief, from enjoyment arises fear. To one who is free from enjoyment there is no grief. How (then can there be) fear? (214)

7. From desire arises grief, from desire arises fear. To one who is free from desire there is no grief. How (then can there be) fear? (215)

8. From craving arises grief, from craving arises fear. To one who is free from craving there is no grief. How (then can there be) fear? (216)

9. Him who is endowed with virtue and insight, who is established in the law, who is truthful, who minds his own affairs, him the world holds dear. (217)

10. He in whom a desire for the Ineffable has arisen, who is replete with mind, whose thought is freed from desires, he is called one who ascends the stream. (218)

11. When a man who has been long away returns safe from afar, kinsmen, friends, and well-wishers receive him gladly. (219)

12. Even so his good deeds receive the good man who has gone from this world to the next, as kinsmen receive a friend on his return. (220)

Chapter XVII: Anger

1. Let a man put away anger, let him renounce pride. Let him get beyond all worldly attachments; no sufferings befall him who is not attached to name and form (phenomenal existence), who calls nothing his own. (221)

2. He who curbs his rising anger like a chariot gone astray (over the plain), him I call a real charioteer; others but hold the reins (and do not deserve to be called charioteers). (222)

3. Let a man overcome anger by non-anger (gentleness), let him overcome evil by good, let him overcome the miser by liberality, let him overcome the liar by truth. (223)

4. One should speak the truth, not yield to anger, even if asked for a little. By these three means one will certainly come into the presence of the gods. (224)

5. The sages who injure none, who always control their body, go to the unchangeable place, where, having gone, they do not grieve. (225)

6. Those who are ever vigilant (wakeful), who study by day and by night, who strive after *nirvāṇa*, their taints come to an end. (226)

7. This is an old saying, O Atula, this is not (a saying) only of to-day. "They blame him who remains silent, they blame him who talks much, they blame also him who speaks in moderation." There is not anyone in the world who is not blamed. (227)

8. There never was, nor will be, nor is there now to be found anyone who is (wholly) blamed, anyone who is (wholly) praised. (228)

9. But he whom the discriminating praise observing day after day, as without blemish, wise, endowed with meditative wisdom and virtue, (229)

10. who is worthy to blame him who is like a gold coin from the Jambu river? Even the gods praise him; he is praised even by Brahmā. (230)

11. Let one be watchful of bodily irritation. Let him practise restraint of the body. Having abandoned the sins of the body let him practise virtue with his body. (231)

12. Let one be watchful of speech-irritation. Let him practise restraint of speech. Having abandoned the sins of speech let him practise virtue with his speech. (232)

13. Let one be watchful of mind-irritation. Let him practise restraint of mind. Having abandoned the sins of mind let him practise virtue with his mind. (233)

14. The wise who control their body, who likewise control their speech, the wise who control their mind are indeed well controlled. (234)

Chapter XVIII: Impurity

1. You are now like a withered leaf; even the messengers of death have come near you. You stand at the threshold of departure (at the gate of death) and you have made no provision (for your journey). (235)

2. Make for yourself an island (refuge), strive quickly, be wise. When your impurities are purged and you are free from sin you will reach heaven, the land of the elect. (236)

3. Your life has come near to an end, you are arrived in the presence of Yama (the king of death). There is no resting-place for you on the way and you have made no provision (for your journey). (237)

4. Make for yourself an island, strive quickly, be wise. When your impurities are purged and you are free from sin, you will not again enter into birth and old age. (238)

5. As a smith removes the impurities of silver, even so let a wise man remove the impurities of himself one by one, little by little, and from time to time. (239)

6. Impurity arising from iron eats into it though born from itself, likewise the evil deeds of the transgressor lead him to the evil state. (240)

7. Non-recitation is the impurity of the seeker, non-exertion is the impurity of house; indolence is the impurity of (personal) appearance, and thoughtlessness is the impurity of the watchful. (241)

8. Bad conduct is the impurity of a woman; niggardliness is the impurity of the giver; evil deeds are impurities in this world and in the next. (242)

9. But there is an impurity greater than all impurities. Ignorance is the greatest impurity. O mendicants, having cast away that impurity, be free from all impurities. (243)

10. Life is easy to live for one who is shameless, who is of (the boldness of) a crow hero, for the mischief-maker, for the slanderer, for the impudent, and for the impure. (244)

11. But life is hard to live for one who has a sense of modesty, who always seeks for what is pure, who is disinterested, not impudent, who lives in purity, the man of insight. (245)

12. He who destroys life, who speaks untruth, who in this world takes what is not given to him, who goes to another man's wife, (246)

13. and he who gives himself to drinking intoxicating liquors, he, even in this world, digs up his own root. (247)

14. Know this, O man, that evil things befall the unrestrained. Let not greed and wrong-doing bring you to grief for a long time. (248)

15. Men give (alms) according to their faith or according to their friendliness. Therefore, he who frets about the drink and food given to others does not, either by day or by night, enjoy peace of mind. (249)

16. He in whom this spirit (of envy) is destroyed, removed by the very root, he, indeed, by day and by night, enjoys peace of mind. (250)

17. There is no fire like passion, no capturer like hatred; there is no net (snare) like delusion, no torrent like craving. (251)

18. The fault of others is easily seen; our own is difficult to see. A man winnows others' faults like chaff, but his own faults he hides even as a cheat hides an unlucky throw. (252)

19. To him who is observant of the faults of others, who is ever censorious, his own passions increase and he is far from the destruction of passions. (253)

20. There is no path in the sky, there is no recluse (adopting the Buddhist path) outside (of us), mankind delights in worldliness; the Buddhas are free from worldliness. (254)

21. There is no path in the sky, there is no recluse outside (of us). Nothing in the phenomenal world is eternal, there is no instability to the awakened. (255)

Chapter XIX: The Righteous

1. He who carries out his purpose by violence is not therein righteous (established in the law). He is wise who decides both advantage and disadvantage. (256)

2. He who guides others by a procedure that is non-violent and equitable, he is said to be a guardian of the law, wise and righteous. (257)

3. A man is not learned simply because he talks much. He who is tranquil, free from hatred, free from fear, he is said to be learned. (258)

4. A man is not a supporter of the law simply because he talks much, but he who, little learned, discerns it by his body, he who does not neglect the law, he, indeed, is the supporter of the law. (259)

5. A man is not an elder simply because his head (hair) is grey. His age is ripe, but he is called grown old in vain. (260)

6. He in whom dwell truth, virtue, non-violence, restraint, control, he who is free from impurity and is wise, he is called an elder. (261)

7. Not by mere talk, not by the beauty of the complexion, does a man who is envious, greedy, and wicked become of good disposition. (262)

8. He in whom these (envy, greed, and wickedness) are destroyed, removed by the very root, he who is free from guilt and is wise, is said to be handsome. (263)

9. Not by tonsure does one who is undisciplined and who speaks untruth become a religious man. How can one who is full of desire and greed be a religious man? (264)

10. But he who always quiets the evil tendencies, small or large, he is called a religious man because he has quieted all evil. (265)

11. He is not a mendicant simply because he begs others (for

alms). He who adopts the whole law is a mendicant, not he who adopts only a part. (266)

12. But he who is above good and evil and is chaste, who comports himself in the world with knowledge, he, indeed, is called a mendicant. (267)

13. By (observing) silence a man does not become a sage if he be foolish and ignorant; but that wise man, who, holding (as it were) the scale, takes what is good, (268)

14. and avoids the evil, he is the sage, is a sage for that (very) reason. He who in this world weighs both sides is called a sage on that (very) account. (269)

15. A man is not noble (or elect) because he injures living creatures. He is called noble because he does not injure living beings. (270)

16. Not only by disciplined conduct and vows, not only by much learning, nor moreover by the attainment of meditative calm nor by sleeping solitary, (271)

17. do I reach the happiness of release which no worldling can attain. O mendicant, do not be confident (rest not content) so long as you have not reached the extinction of impurities. (272)

Chapter XX: The Path

1. Of paths the eightfold is the best; of truths the (best are) four sayings (truths); of virtues freedom from attachment is the best; of men (literally two-footed beings) he who is possessed of sight. (273)

2. This is the path; there is none other that leads to the purifying of insight. You follow this (path). This will be to confuse (escape from) Māra (Death, sin). (274)

3. Going on this path, you will end your suffering. This path was preached by me when I became aware of the removal of the thorns (in the flesh). (275)

4. You yourself must strive. The Blessed Ones are (only) preachers. Those who enter the path and practise meditation are released from the bondage of Māra (Death, sin). (276)

5. "All created things are impermanent (transitory)." When one by wisdom realizes (this), he heeds not (is superior to) (this world of) sorrow; this is the path to purity. (277)

6. "All created things are sorrowful." When one by wisdom realizes (this) he heeds not (is superior to) (this world of) sorrow; this is the path to purity. (278)

7. "All the elements of being are non-self." When one by wisdom realizes (this), he heeds not (is superior to) (this world of) sorrow; this is the path to purity. (279)

8. He who does not get up when it is time to get up, who, though young and strong, is full of sloth, who is weak in resolution and thought, that lazy and idle man will not find the way to wisdom. (280)

9. Guarding his speech, restraining well his mind, let a man not commit anything wrong with his body. He who keeps these three roads of action clear will achieve the way taught by the wise. (281)

10. From meditation springs wisdom; from lack of meditation there is loss of wisdom. Knowing this twofold path of progress and decline, a man should place himself in such a way that his wisdom increases. (282)

11. Cut down the (whole) forest, not the tree (only); danger comes out of the forest. Having cut down both the forest and desire, O mendicants, do you attain freedom. (283)

12. As long indeed as the desire, however small, of a man for women is not destroyed, so long is his mind attached (to existence) as a sucking calf is to its mother. (284)

13. Cut out the love of self as you would an autumn lily with the hand. Cherish the path to peace, to *nirvāṇa* pointed out by the Buddha. (285)

14. "Here I shall dwell in the rain, here in winter and summer" thus the fool thinks; he does not think of the obstacle (of life). (286)

15. As a great flood carries off a sleeping village, death takes off and goes with that man who is giddy (with the possession of) children and cattle, whose mind is distracted (with the desire for worldly goods). (287)

16. Sons are no protection, nor father, nor relations; for one who is seized by death, there is no safety in kinsmen. (288)

17. Realizing the significance of this, the wise and righteous man should even quickly clear the path leading to release. (289)

Chapter XXI: Miscellaneous Verses

1. If, by surrendering a pleasure of little worth one sees a larger pleasure, the wise man will give up the pleasure of little worth, and look to the larger pleasure. (290)

2. He who desires happiness for himself by inflicting suffering on others, he, entangled in the bonds of hatred, is not freed from hatred. (291)

3. If, giving up what should be done, what should not be done is done, in those unrestrained and careless, the taints increase. (292)

4. But those whose mindfulness is always alert to (the nature of) the body, who do not aim at what should not be done, who steadfastly do what should be done, the impurities of these mindful and wise people come to an end. (293)

5. A (true) *brāhmin* goes scatheless though he have killed father and mother and two kings of the warrior caste and a kingdom with all its subjects. (294)

6. A (true) *brāhmin* goes scatheless though he have killed father and mother and two holy kings and an eminent man as the fifth. (295)

7. The disciples of Gautama are always well awake; their thought is always, day and night, set on the Buddha. (296)

8. The disciples of Gautama are always well awake; their thought is always, day and night, set on the Law. (297)

9. The disciples of Gautama are always well awake; their thought is always, day and night, set on the Order. (298)

10. The disciples of Gautama are always well awake; their thought is always, day and night, set on the (nature of the) body. (299)

11. The disciples of Gautama are always well awake; their mind, day and night, delights in abstinence from harm (compassion, love). (300)

12. The disciples of Gautama are always well awake; their mind, day and night, delights in meditation. (301)

13. It is hard to leave the world as a recluse and hard to enjoy. Hard also is it to live at home as a householder. Living with the unsympathetic is painful. The life of a wanderer is beset with pain. Therefore let no man be a wanderer, let no one fall into suffering. (302)

14. Whatever region a man of faith, endowed with virtue, with fame, and prosperity is allotted, even there he is revered. (303)

15. Good people shine from afar like the Himālaya mountains but the wicked are not seen, like arrows shot in the night. (304)

16. Let one sit alone, sleep alone, act alone without being indolent, subdue his self by means of his self alone: he would find delight in the extinction of desires. (305)

CHAPTER XXII: THE DOWNWARD COURSE (HELL)

1. He who speaks what is not (real) goes to hell; he also who having done a thing says, "I do not do it." After death both become equal, being men with evil deeds in the next existence. (306)

2. Many men who are clad in yellow robes are ill-behaved and unrestrained. Such evil-doers by their evil deeds go to hell. (307)

3. Better is it for an irreligious unrestrained (person) to swallow a ball of red-hot iron than enjoy the charity of the land. (308)

4. An unthinking man who courts another's wife gains four things, access of demerit, broken rest, thirdly blame, and fourthly hell. (309)

5. There is access of demerit as well as the way to the evil state; there is the short-lived pleasure of the frightened in the arms of the frightened, and a heavy penalty from the ruler. Therefore do not run after another man's wife. (310)

6. As a blade of grass when wrongly handled cuts the hand, so also asceticism when wrongly tried leads to hell. (311)

7. An act carelessly performed, a vow improperly observed, unwilling obedience to the code of chastity brings no great reward. (312)

8. If anything is to be done let one do it vigorously. A recluse who is careless only bespatters himself the more with dust. (313)

9. An evil deed left undone is better, for an evil deed causes suffering later. A good deed done is better for doing: it does not cause suffering. (314)

10. As a frontier town is well-guarded within and without, so guard the self. Do not let a moment glide by, for they who allow the moments to pass by suffer when they are consigned to hell. (315)

11. They who are ashamed of what they ought not to be ashamed of and are not ashamed of what they ought to be ashamed of, such men, following false doctrines, enter the evil path. (316)

12. They who fear when they ought not to fear and do not fear when they ought to fear, such men, following false doctrines, enter the evil path. (317)

13. Those who discern evil where there is no evil and see nothing evil in what is evil, such men, following false doctrines, enter the evil path. (318)

14. Those who discern evil as evil and what is not evil as not evil, such men, following the true doctrines, enter the good path. (319)

Chapter XXIII: The Elephant

1. I shall endure hard words even as the elephant in battle endures the arrow shot from the bow; the majority of people are, indeed, ill natured. (320)

2. They lead a tamed elephant into battle; the king mounts a tamed elephant. The tamed is the best among men, he who endures patiently hard words. (321)

3. Good are mules when tamed, so also the Sindhu horses of good breed and the great elephants of war. Better than these is he who has tamed himself. (322)

4. For with these animals does no man reach the untrodden country (*nirvāṇa*) where a tamed man goes on a tamed nature (with his self well-tamed). (323)

5. The elephant called Dhanapālaka is hard to control when the temples are running with a pungent sap (in the time of rut). He does not eat a morsel (of food) when bound. The elephant thinks longingly of the elephant-grove. (324)

6. If one becomes a sluggard or a glutton rolling himself about in gross sleep, like a hog fed on wash, that foolish one, again and again, comes to birth. (325)

7. This mind of mine would wander formerly as it liked, as it desired, as it pleased. I shall now control it thoroughly even as the rider holding the hook controls the elephant in a state of rut. (326)

8. Be not thoughtless, guard your thoughts. Extricate yourself out of the evil way as an elephant sunk in the mud. (327)

9. If you find a companion, intelligent, one who associates with you, who leads a good life, lives soberly, overcoming all dangers, walk with him delighted and thoughtful. (328)

10. If you do not find a companion, intelligent, one who associates with you, who leads a good life, lives soberly, walk alone like a king who has renounced the kingdom he has conquered or like an elephant (roaming at will) in the forest. (329)

11. It is better to live alone; there is no companionship with a fool. Let a man walk alone with few wishes like an elephant (roaming at will) in the elephant-forest. Let him commit no sin. (330)

12. Companions are pleasant when an occasion (or need) arises; contentment is pleasant when mutual. At the hour of death merit is pleasant. The giving up of all sorrow is pleasant. (331)

13. To havē a mother is happiness in the world; to have a father

is happiness in the world; to have a recluse is happiness in the world; to have a sage is happiness in the world. (332)

14. Happy is virtue lasting to old age; happy is faith firmly rooted; happy is the attainment of wisdom; happy is the avoidance of sins. (333)

Chapter XXIV: Thirst (or Craving)

1. The craving of a thoughtless man grows like a creeper. Like a monkey wishing for fruit in a forest he bounds hither and thither (from one life to another). (334)

2. Whomsoever this fierce craving, full of poison, overcomes in the world, his sorrows increase like the abounding *biraṇa* grass. (335)

3. He who overcomes in this world this fierce craving, difficult to subdue, sorrows fall off from him like water drops from a lotus leaf. (336)

4. I declare to you this good (counsel). "Do ye, as many as are gathered here, dig up the root of craving as one digs up the *biraṇa* grass to find the *usira* root, that Māra (Death) may not destroy you again and again even as the river destroys the reeds (on the bank)." (337)

5. As a tree, even though it has been cut down, grows again if its root is firm and uninjured (i.e., safe), even so if the adherences of craving are not destroyed, this suffering returns to us again and again. (338)

6. Him whose thirty-six streams flowing towards pleasures of sense are strong, whose thoughts are set on passion, the waves carry away that misguided man. (339)

7. The streams flow everywhere; the creeper (of passion) keeps on springing up. If you see that creeper sprung up, cut its root by means of wisdom. (340)

8. To creatures happen pleasures and wide-ranging endearments. Hugging those pleasures they hanker after them. Those men indeed undergo birth and old age. (341)

9. Men driven on by craving run about like a hunted hare. Fast bound in its fetters, they undergo suffering for a long time, again and again. (342)

10. Men driven on by craving run about like a hunted hare. Let, therefore, the mendicant, wishing for himself freedom from passion, shake off craving. (343)

11. He who having got rid of the forest (of desire) gives himself over to the life of the forest (desire), he who, free from the forest (of desire), runs back to the forest (of desire),—look at him, though free, he runs into bondage. (344)

12. Wise people do not say that that fetter is strong which is made of iron, wood, or fibre, but the attachment to earrings made of precious stones, to sons, and wives is passionately impassioned. (345)

13. Wise people call strong this fetter which drags down, yields, and is difficult to unfasten. After having cut this, people renounce the world, free from longings and forsaking the pleasures of sense. (346)

14. Those who are slaves to passions follow the stream (of craving) as a spider the web which he has made himself. Wise people, when they have cut this (craving), leave the world, free from cares, leaving all sorrow behind. (347)

15. Give up what is before, give up what is behind, give up what is in the middle, passing to the farther shore of existence. When your mind is wholly freed you will not again return to birth and old age. (348)

16. Craving increases more to a creature who is disturbed by thoughts, full of strong passions, yearning for what is pleasant; he indeed makes his fetters strong. (349)

17. He who delights in quieting his thoughts, always reflecting, dwells on what is not pleasant, he will certainly remove, nay, he will cut the bonds of death. (350)

18. He who has reached the good, who is fearless, who is without craving and without sin, he has broken the thorns of existence, this body is his last. (351)

19. He who is without craving, without appropriation, who is skilful in understanding words and their meanings, who knows the order of letters (which are before and which are after), he is called the great sage, the great person. This is his last body. (352)

20. "I have conquered all, I know all, in all conditions of life I am free from taint. I have renounced all and with the destruction of craving I am freed. Having learnt myself, to whom shall I point as teacher?" (353)

21. The gift of the law surpasses all gifts; the flavour of the law surpasses all flavours, the delight in the law surpasses all delights. The destruction of craving conquers all sorrows. (354)

22. Riches destroy the foolish, not those who seek the beyond (the other shore). By a craving for riches the foolish person destroys himself as he destroys others. (355)

23. Weeds are the bane of fields and passion the bane of this mankind; therefore offerings made to those free from passion bring great reward. (356)

24. Weeds are the bane of fields and hatred is the bane of this mankind; therefore offerings made to those free from hatred bring great reward. (357)

25. Weeds are the bane of fields and folly is the bane of this mankind; therefore offerings made to those free from folly bring great reward. (358)

26. Weeds are the bane of fields; desire is the bane of this mankind; therefore offerings made to those freed from desire bring great reward. (359)

Chapter XXV: The Mendicant

1. Restraint in the eye is good; good is restraint in the ear; in the nose restraint is good; good is restraint in the tongue. (360)

2. In the body restraint is good, good is restraint in speech; in thought restraint is good, good is restraint in all things. A mendicant who is restrained in all things is freed from all sorrow. (361)

3. He who controls his hand, he who controls his feet, he who controls his speech, he who is well-controlled, he who delights inwardly, who is collected, who is alone and content, him they call a mendicant. (362)

4. The mendicant who controls his tongue, who speaks wisely, not uplifted (puffed up), who illuminates the meaning and the law, his utterance is sweet. (363)

5. He whose pleasance is the law, who delights in the law, meditates on the law, follows the law, that mendicant does not fall from the true law. (364)

6. He should not overvalue what he himself receives; he should not envy others. A mendicant who envies others does not obtain tranquillity. (365)

7. Even the gods praise that mendicant who though he receives little does not overvalue what he receives, whose life is pure and strenuous. (366)

8. He, indeed, is called a mendicant who does not count as his own any name and form, who does not grieve from having nothing. (367)

9. The mendicant who lives in friendliness and calm (has faith) in the doctrine of the Buddha, he will attain the tranquil, blessed place where (bodily) existence is at rest. (368)

10. Empty the boat, O mendicant; when emptied it will go lightly. Having cut off passion and hatred then you will go to freedom. (369)

11. Cut off the five, get rid of the five, master (rise above) the five. A mendicant who has freed himself from the five fetters[1] is called "one who has crossed the flood" (of rebirth). (370)

12. Meditate, O mendicant, be not negligent. Let not your thought delight in sensual pleasures, that you may not for your negligence have to swallow the iron ball, that you may not cry out when burning, "This is suffering!" (371)

13. There is no meditation for one who is without wisdom, no wisdom for one without meditation; he in whom there are meditation and wisdom, he indeed is close to *nirvāṇa*. (372)

14. A mendicant who with a tranquil heart has entered an empty house, he has a more than human (divine) delight, through his right discernment of the law. (373)

15. Whenever he comprehends the origin and destruction of the elements of the body he obtains joy and happiness, which is life eternal to those who know. (374)

16. This is the beginning here to a wise mendicant, control of the senses, contentment, restraint under the law (according to the precepts of the *pāṭimokkha*),[2] cultivation of friends who are noble, of pure life, and zealous (not slothful). (375)

17. Let him live a life of friendship. Let him be an adept in the discharge of his duties, then his happiness being much he will make an end of suffering. (376)

18. As the *vassikā* plant sheds its withered flowers, O mendicants, so you should get rid of passion and hatred. (377)

19. That mendicant is said to be calmed who has a calmed body, a calmed speech, and a calmed mind, who is well-established, who has rejected the baits of the world. (378)

20. Rouse your self by your self, examine your self by your self. Thus guarded by your self and attentive you, mendicant, will live happy. (379)

21. For self is the lord of self; self is the refuge of self; therefore curb yourself even as a merchant curbs a fine horse. (380).

[1] Greed, hatred, folly, pride, and false doctrines.

[2] Name of a collection of precepts for the governance of the Order.

22. The mendicant full of delight, calm (with faith) in the doctrine of the Buddha, will certainly reach the peaceful state, the cessation of natural existence and happiness. (381)

23. The mendicant who, though young, applies himself to the doctrine of the Buddha, he illuminates this world like the moon when freed from a cloud. (382)

Chapter XXVI: The *Brāhmin*

1. O *brāhmin*, cut off the stream, be energetic, drive away desires. Knowing the destruction of all that is made (or the elements of existence) you know the uncreated, O *brāhmin*. (383)

2. When the *brāhmin* has reached the other shore in both laws, to him who knows all bonds vanish. (384)

3. Him I call a *brāhmin* for whom there is neither this shore nor that shore, nor both, who is free from fear and free from shackles. (385)

4. Him I call a *brāhmin* who is meditative, free from passion, settled, whose work is done, free from taints, and who has attained the highest end (of sainthood). (386)

5. The sun shines by day, the moon lights up the night, the warrior shines in his armour, the *brāhmin* shines in his meditation, but the awakened shines all day and night by his radiance (of spirit). (387)

6. Because he has put aside evil he is called a *brāhmin*; because he lives in serenity he is called a *samāna*;[1] because he puts away his impurities he is called *pabbajita*.[2] (388)

7. One should not attack a *brāhmin*; let not the *brāhmin* free (his anger) on him (the evil-doer); woe to him who slays a *brāhmin* and more woe to him who sets free (his anger) on him (the evil-doer). (389)

8. It is no slight benefit to a *brāhmin* when he holds his mind back from the pleasures of life. Wherever the wish to injure desists, even there is cessation of suffering. (390)

9. Him I call a *brāhmin* who does not hurt by body, speech, or mind, who is controlled in these three things. (391)

10. Him who has understood the law as taught by the well-awakened (fully enlightened) one, him should a man worship reverentially, even as the *brāhmin* worships the sacrificial fire. (392)

[1] From "*sam*," to be equable.

[2] From "*pabbaj*," to cast out.

11. Not by matted hair, not by lineage, not by caste does one become a *brāhmin*. He is a *brāhmin* in whom there are truth and righteousness. He is blessed. (393)

12. What is the use of matted hair, O fool, what of the raiment of goat-skins? Thine inward nature is full of wickedness; the outside thou makest clean. (394)

13. Him I call a *brāhmin* who wears cast-off garments, lean, spread over with veins, solitary, and who practises meditation in the forest. (395)

14. I do not call him a *brāhmin* because of his origin or of his mother. If he be with goods he is called *bhovādi*.[1] Him I call a *brāhmin* who is free from goods and free from attachment. (396)

15. Him I call a *brāhmin* who has cut all the fetters, who never trembles (in fear), who has passed beyond attachments, who is separated (from what is impure). (397)

16. Him I call a *brāhmin* who has cut the strap and the thong and the chain with its appurtenances, who has burst the bar and is awakened. (398)

17. Him I call a *brāhmin* who, though he has committed no offence, bears patiently reproach, ill-treatment, imprisonment; who has endurance for his force and strength for his army. (399)

18. Him I call a *brāhmin* who is free from anger, who is careful of religious duties, observes the moral rules, pure, controlled, and wears his last body. (400)

19. Him I call a *brāhmin* who, like water on the leaf of a lotus or a mustard seed on the point of an awl, does not cling to pleasures. (401)

20. Him I call a *brāhmin* who, even here, knows the end of his suffering, who has laid aside his burden, who is detached. (402)

21. Him I call a *brāhmin* whose wisdom is deep, who possesses knowledge, who discerns the right way and the wrong, and who has attained the highest end. (403)

22. Him I call a *brāhmin* who keeps away from both householders (laymen) and the houseless (mendicants), who does not frequent houses and has but few wants. (404)

23. Him I call a *brāhmin* who lays aside the rod with regard to creatures, moving or unmoving, and neither kills nor causes (their) death. (405)

24. Him I call a *brāhmin* who is without hostility among those who

[1] One who says "*bho*," the familiar form of address to inferiors or equals.

are hostile, who is peaceful among those with uplifted staves, who is unattached among those who are attached. (406)

25. Him I call a *brāhmin* whose passion and hatred, pride and hypocrisy have fallen like a mustard seed from the point of an awl. (407)

26. Him I call a *brāhmin* who utters true speech, free from harshness, clearly understood, by which no one is offended. (408)

27. Him I call a *brāhmin* who does not take, here in the world, what is not given him, be it long or short, small or large, good or bad. (409)

28. Him I call a *brāhmin* who has no desires for this world or for the next, who is free from desires and who is separated (from impurities). (410)

29. Him I call a *brāhmin* who has no desires, who is free from doubt by knowledge (of the truth), who has reached the depth of the eternal. (411)

30. Him I call a *brāhmin* who here has passed beyond the attachments of good and evil, who is free from grief, free from passion, free from impurity. (412)

31. Him I call a *brāhmin* who like the moon is stainless, pure, serene, undisturbed, in whom joyance is extinguished. (413)

32. Him I call a *brāhmin* who has gone beyond this miry road of rebirth and delusion, difficult (to cross), who has crossed over, who has reached the other shore, who is meditative, unagitated, not doubting, not grasping, and calm. (414)

33. Him I call a *brāhmin* who, in this world, giving up all sensual pleasures, wanders about without a home, in whom all desire for existence is extinguished. (415)

34. Him I call a *brāhmin* who, in this world, giving up all craving, wanders about without a home, in whom all craving for existence is extinguished. (416)

35. Him I call a *brāhmin* who, casting off attachment to human things, rises above attachment to heavenly things, is separated from all attachments. (417)

36. Him I call a *brāhmin* who gives up what is pleasurable and what is unpleasurable, who is cooled and is free from any seeds (of renewed existence), the hero who has conquered all the worlds. (418)

37. Him I call a *brāhmin* who knows everywhere the perishing of living things and their uprising, who is free from attachment, living aright, and who is awakened. (419)

38. Him I call a *brāhmin* whose path the gods do not know, nor spirits nor men, whose taints are extinct and who has attained sainthood. (420)

39. Him I call a *brāhmin* for whom there is nothing before, behind, or between, who has nothing and is without attachment. (421)

40. Him I call a *brāhmin* who is fearless (like a bull), noble, heroic, the all-wise, who has overcome (death), the sinless who has accomplished his study, the awakened. (422)

41. Him I call a *brāhmin* who knows his former abodes (lives), who perceives heaven and hell, has reached the end of births, is a sage whose knowledge is perfect and has accomplished all that has to be accomplished. (423)

(b) *Iti Vuttaka* (*As It Was Said*)[1]

Void of zeal, unscrupulous,
Sluggish, lacking energy—
Who is full of sloth and torpor,
Shameless and irreverent—
Such a monk cannot become
Fit to reach supreme insight.

But heedful, in his musing shrewd,
Ardent, scrupulous and zealous,
Cutting the bond of birth-and-eld,
In this very life (on earth)
One may reach insight supreme. (II.i.7)

For self-restraint and for abandoning,
Heedless of what men say, this Brahmā-life
Did that Exalted One proclaim as going
Unto the plunge into *nibbāna's* stream.

This is the way whereon great souls, great seers,
Have fared; and they who, as the Buddha taught,
Attain to that will make an end of ill,[2]
E'en they who what the Teacher taught perform. (II.i.8)

For seeing into things and understanding,
Heedless of what men say, this Brahmā-life

[1] In *The Minor Anthologies of the Pali Canon*, Part II, translated by F. L. Woodward (London: Oxford University Press, 1935), pp. 135–75, *passim*.

[2] Or, suffering.

Did that Exalted One proclaim as going
Unto the plunge into *nibbāna's* stream.... (II.i.9)

This is the way whereon great souls, great seers
Have fared; and they who, as the Buddha taught,
Attain to that will make an end of Ill,[1]
E'en they who what the Teacher taught perform. (II.i.9)

One who hath wisdom should be strongly thrilled
At thrilling times. A monk discreet and ardent
Should thoroughly examine things by wisdom.
So dwelling ardent, living a life of peace,
And not elated, but to calmness given,
He should attain the ending of the cankers. (II.i.10)

Thro' falling from the insight lo! the world
With *deva* world on name and shape is bent
In the belief that this thing is the truth.
But best of all things in the world is insight
By which one to *nibbāna* goes, and knows
Rightly the utter end of birth-and-death.

Those thoughtful ones who fully are awake,
Who insight have and their last body wear,
Both *devas* and mankind long to behold. (II.ii.4)

The born, become, produced, compounded, made,
And thus not lasting, but of birth-and-death
An aggregate, a nest of sickness, brittle,
A thing by food supported, come to be,—
'Twere no fit thing to take delight in such.

Th'escape therefrom, the real, beyond the sphere
Of reason, lasting, unborn, unproduced,
The sorrowless, the stainless path that ends
The things of woe, the peace from worries—bliss. (II.ii.6)

These two *nibbāna*-states are shown by him
Who seeth, who is such and unattached.
One state is that in this same life possessed
With base remaining, tho' becoming's stream
Be cut off. While the state without a base
Belongeth to the future, wherein all
Becomings utterly do come to cease.

[1] Or, suffering.

They who, by knowing this state uncompounded,
Have heart's release, by cutting off the stream,
They who have reached the core of *dhamma*, glad
To end—such have abandoned all becomings. (II.ii.7)

They who with heart at peace discriminate,
Thoughtful and musing, rightly *dhamma* see,
Their passions they do closely scrutinize.
For being fain for seriousness and seeing
Peril in wantonness, they are not the sort
To fail, but to *nibbāna* they are close. (II.ii.8)

Enjoying *dhamma*, loving *dhamma*, pondering
On *dhamma*, calling it to mind, a monk
From very *dhamma* doth not fall away.
Whether he walk or stand or sit or lie,
In self-restraining mind he goes to peace. (III.iv.7)

Three profitable ways[1] of thought should one pursue,
And three unprofitable ways[2] should put away,
He surely doth control a train of thought sustained,
As a rain-shower lays accumulated dust,
He surely with a mind that lays its thought to rest,
In this same life on earth hath reached the place of peace.
(III.iv.8)

(c) *Udāna* (*Verses of Uplift*)[3]

Behold this manifold world, by ignorance afflicted,
Come into being and thus with what has become delighted,
Yet from becoming not released. Yea, all becomings
Wherever and in whatsoever state they be—
All are impermanent and ill and doomed to change.

In one who sees as it really is by perfect wisdom
The craving to become is left; he joys not in its slaying.
But craving's utter ending, utter stopping, is *nibbāna*.
Thus become cool, that monk, no more reborn, no more becomes.
Beaten is Māra. He's won the fight, escaped all more-becomings.
(III.10)

Monks, there exists that condition wherein is neither earth nor water nor fire nor air: wherein is neither the sphere of infinite space

[1] That is, thinking about renunciation, goodwill, and harmlessness.
[2] That is, thinking about lust, ill-will, and harming others.
[3] In *The Minor Anthologies of the Pali Canon*, Part II, translated by F. L. Woodward, pp. 40, 97, *passim*.

nor of infinite consciousness nor of nothingness nor of neither-consciousness-nor-unconsciousness; where there is neither this world nor a world beyond nor both together nor moon-and-sun. Thence, monks, I declare is no coming to birth; thither is no going from life; therein is no duration; thence is no falling; there is no arising. It is not something fixed, it moves not on, it is not based on anything. That indeed is the end of ill. (VIII.1.)

B. *MAHĀYĀNA*

1. The Treatise in Twenty Stanzas on Representation-Only[1]

In the *Mahāyāna* it is established that the three worlds are representation-only.[2] According to the scriptures it is said that the three worlds are only mind. Mind, thought, consciousness, discernment are different names. What is here spoken of as mind includes mental activities also in its meaning. "Only" excludes external objects; it does not do away with mental associates. When inner representations arise, seemingly external objects appear, as persons having bad eyes see hairs and flies....

To this doctrine there are supposed objections....

I. If representations are without real objects,
Then their spatial and temporal determination,
The indetermination of the perceiving stream of consciousness
And their action must be unfounded.

II. Place and time are determined as in a dream;
The selves are not determined, just as the ghosts [in their abode]
Together behold the same river of pus etc., [and]
As in dreams there is function in the loss of [semen].

That is, as in a dream although there are no real objects, yet it is in a certain place that such things as a village, a garden, a man, or a woman are seen, not in all places, and in this place it is at a certain time that this village, garden, etc., are seen, not at all times....

That is, just as the hungry ghosts through ripening the same kind of deeds assemble together as many selves and all see the pus river, in this

[1] The *Viṁśatikā* of Vasubandhu (4th century A.D.), translated by Clarence H. Hamilton: *Wei Shih Er Shih Lun*, or *The Treatise in Twenty Stanzas on Representation-only*, American Oriental Series, XIII (New Haven: American Oriental Society, 1938).

[2] A better translation of *vijñaptimātratā* would be "ideation only," since "representation" suggests rather than denies external reality.

it is not determined that only one sees.... From this [we see that] though there are no real objects apart from consciousness, yet the principle of the indetermination of the stream which perceives is explained.

Again as in dream, although the objects are unreal, they yet have function such as the loss of semen, etc....

III. All[1] [are exemplified] as [those] in hell
Together behold the infernal guards, etc.,
And their ability to inflict torments;
Therefore the four principles are still established.

IV. As the animals in heaven
Those in hell are not, indeed;
For the asserted animals and ghosts
Suffer not that bitterness.

V. If you grant that from the force of deeds
Special elements are born
Which produce such transformations,
Why not admit [the process to be] consciousness?

VI. The impression of the deed is in one place;
You assert its fruit to be in another;
That the consciousness which is impressed has the fruit
You deny. What is the reason?

[Objector] ...if it is only consciousness which appears as if colored, etc., and there is no separate colored, etc., object, then the Buddha ought not to have said that there are "bases" of cognition, visual, and so on.

[Answer] This teaching is not a reason, for it has a different meaning....

VII. Conforming to the creatures to be converted
The World-honored One with secret intention
Said there are bases of cognition, visual, etc.,
Just as there are beings of apparitional birth.

...he did not say that creatures of apparitional birth really exist, because he said, "There is neither creature nor self but only elements and causes."...The bases are not really existent apart.

[Question] In accordance with what inner meaning does he speak of ten bases, visual, etc.?...

VIII. [Perceptive] consciousness is born from its own seed
And develops into an apparent object aspect.

[1] All four principles just mentioned.

To establish the distinction of inner and outer bases of cognition,
Buddha says there are ten of these.

[Question] What advantage is there in this teaching of an inner meaning?

IX. By reason of this teaching one enters into
[The doctrine of] the egolessness of the individual:
The asserted non-substantiality of elements
One enters again by reason of the remainder of the teaching,

[Objection] If by knowing that all elements of every kind are non-existent we enter into the insubstantiality of elements, then representation-only is also, in the end, non-existent. How can representation-only be sustained?

[Answer] It is not the man who knows that all elements of every kind are non-existent who obtains the name of having "entered the insubstantiality of elements"; but he who penetrates the insubstantiality of the elements of the "self-natures" and the "special characters" conceived by the imagination of the ignorant, is thus named him who has "entered the insubstantiality of elements." . . .

[Question] Again, how do we know that Buddha intended such an inner meaning when he said there are bases of sense cognition? Are there not separate, really existing outer elements, having color-and-form, etc., which become severally the objects of visual, etc. consciousness?

X. That realm is neither one [thing],
Nor is it many atoms;
Again, it is not an agglomeration, etc.,
Because the atom is not proved.

. . . the external object cannot logically be one, because we cannot grasp the substance of the whole apart from the parts. Also it logically is not many, because we cannot apprehend the atoms separately. . . .

XI. One atom joined with six others
Must consist of six parts.
If it is in the same place with six
The aggregate must be as one atom.

If one atom on each of its six sides joins with another atom it must consist of six parts, because the place of one does not permit of being the place of the others. If there are six atoms in one atom's place then all the aggregates must be as one atom in quantity, because though revolving in mutual confrontation they do not exceed that quantity; and so aggregates also must be invisible.

XII. Since [it is stated that] atoms do not join,
Of what, then, is the joining of the aggregates?
If joining is not proved [of the latter]
It is not because they have no spatial divisions.

If you...say that aggregates also do not join one another, then you should not say that atoms are without combination because of having no spatial divisions. Aggregates have spatial divisions, and yet you do not grant their combination. Therefore the non-combining of atoms is not due to their lack of spatial division. For this reason the single real atom is not proved. Whether atomic combination is or is not admitted, the mistake is still as we have said. Whether spatial division of atoms is or is not admitted, both views are greatly in error....

XIII. If the atom has spatial divisions,
It logically should not make a unity.
If it has none, there should be neither shadow nor occultation;
Aggregates being no different would likewise be without these two.

...The fault of multiplicity is as explained before. Unity also is irrational.

XIV. Assuming unity, there must be no walking progressively,
At one time, no grasping and not grasping,
And no plural, disconnected condition;
Moreover, no scarcely perceptible, tiny things.

...if one step is taken it reaches everywhere...a unitary thing cannot at one time be both obtained and not obtained. A single place, also, ought not to contain disconnected things such as elephants, horses, etc. If the place contains one, it also contains the rest. How can we say that one is distinguished from another? Granting two [things present], how comes it that in one place there can be both occupancy and non-occupancy, that there can be a seeing of emptiness between?...

[Question] The existence or non-existence of anything is determined by means of proof. Among all means of proof immediate perception is the most excellent. If there are no external objects how is there this awareness of objects such as are now immediately evident to me?...

XV. Immediate awareness is the same as in dreams, etc.
At the time when immediate awareness has arisen,
Seeing and its object are already non-existent;
How can it be admitted that perception exists?

[According to] those who hold the doctrine of momentariness, at the time when this awareness arises the immediate objects, visible [tangible, audible] etc. are already destroyed. How can you admit that at this time there is immediate perception?...

If you wish thus to prove the existence of external objects from "first experiencing, later remembering," this theory also fails....

XVI [first part] As has been said, the apparent object is a representation.
It is from this that memory arises.

[Question] If, in waking time as well as in a dream, representations may arise although there are no true objects, then, just as the world naturally knows that dream objects are non-existent, why is it not naturally known of the objects in waking time?...

XVI [second part] Before we have awakened we cannot know
That what is seen in the dream does not exist.

After this, the purified knowledge of the world which is obtained takes precedence; according to the truth it is clearly understood that those objects are unreal. The principle is the same.

[Objection] If for all sentient beings representations arise as apparent objects because of transformation and differentiation in their own streams of consciousness, and are not born from external things acting as objects, then how explain the fact that those sentient beings through contact with good or evil friends, or through hearing true or false doctrines, are determined to two kinds of representation since there are neither friends nor teaching?...

XVII [first part] By the power of reciprocal influence
The two representations become determined.

That is to say, because a distinct representation in one stream of consciousness occasions the arising of a distinct representation in another stream of consciousness, each becomes determined, but not by external objects....

XVII [second part] The mind by sleep is weakened:
Dream and waking retributions are not the same.

[Question] If only representations exist...how are sheep, etc., killed by anybody?

XVIII. Because of transformation in another's representation
The act of killing and injuring occurs;
Just as the mental power of a demon, etc.,
Causes another to lose his memory.

XIX. The emptiness of Daṇḍaka forest, etc.,
How [came it] from a *ṛṣi's* anger?

"Mental punishment is a great crime."
How again can this be proved?

[Question] If only representations exist, does knowledge of another's mind know another's mind or not?...

If it cannot know, why speak of knowledge of another's mind? If it can know, representation-only is of necessity not proved.

[Answer] Although it knows the mind of another it does not know it exactly....

XX. How does knowledge of another's mind
Know its object inexactly?
Just as the knowledge in knowing one's own mind
Does not know [it] as the Buddha's object.

[Question] Why is this knowledge of one's own mind not an exact knowing of its object?

[Answer] Because of ignorance. Both knowledges of the object, because each is covered over and darkened by ignorance, do not know it as the ineffable object reached by the pure knowledge of a Buddha. These two, in their objects, do not know exactly because of the false appearing of seemingly external objects; and because the distinction between what is apprehended and the apprehender is not yet discontinued.

[Conclusion]

The doctrines and implications of representation-only are of kinds infinitely diverse for decision and selection; difficult is it to fathom their profundities. Without being a Buddha, who is able to comprehend their total extent?

XXI. I, according to my ability,
Have briefly demonstrated the principles of representation-only;
Among these all [other] kinds,
Difficult to think, are reached by Buddhas [alone].

2. The Thirty Verses on the Mind-Only Doctrine[1]

I. Because our ideation gives rise to the false ideas of the ego and *dharmas* (elements of existence),
There are various revulsions of appearances.

[1] The *Triṁśikā* of Vasubandhu, translated from the Chinese version of Hsüan Tsang (A.D. 596–664) by Wing-tsit Chan especially for this book.

This ideation, depending on the mind, goes through certain transformations.
These transformations are of three kinds.

II. They are the consciousness of "ripening in a different life,"
The consciousness of intellection, and the consciousness of the discrimination of the objective world.
First of all, the *ālaya* (ideation-store) consciousness,
Which brings into fruition all seeds [or effects of good and evil deeds].

III. [In its state of pure consciousness], it is not conscious of its clingings and impressions.
In both its objective and subjective functions, it is always associated with touch,
Volition, feeling, thought, and cognition.
But it is always indifferent to its associations.

IV. It is not affected by the darkness of ignorance or by the memory [of the distinction of good and evil].
The same is true in the case of touch, etc.
It is always flowing like a torrent,
And is abandoned in the state of the *arhat*.

V. The second transformation
Is called the mind-consciousness,
Which, while it depends on the ideation-store consciousness, in turn conditions it.
Its nature and characteristic consists of intellection.

VI. It is always accompanied by the four evil desires,
Namely, ignorance of the self, view of the self [as being real and permanent],
Self-pride, and self-love,
And by touch, etc. [volition, feeling, thought, and cognition].

VII. It is free from the memory [of the distinction of good and evil] but not from the darkness of ignorance.
It follows its objects in their emergence and dependence.
It is abandoned by the *arhat* when he arrives at the state of complete extinction of sensation and thought,
And transcends this mundane world.

VIII. Next comes the third transformation,
Which consists of the last six categories of discrimination [the

consciousness of touch, sight, hearing, smell, taste, and the sense-center consciousness].

Its nature and characteristic consists of the discrimination of objects.

It is neither good nor evil.

IX. Mental functions consist of general mental functions,
Particular mental functions, good functions, evil functions,
Minor evil functions, and indeterminate mental functions.
They all impress the mind in three ways [of joy, of suffering, and of indifference].

X. General mental functions are touch, etc. [volition, feeling, thought, cognition].
Particular mental functions are desire,
Resolve, remembrance, concentration, and wisdom,
Each depending on different conditions.

XI. Good mental functions are belief, sense of shame, bashfulness,
The three roots of the absence of covetousness, etc. [the absence of hatred and the absence of attachment],
Energy, repose of mind, vigilance,
Equanimity, and non-injury.

XII. Evil mental functions are covetousness, hatred,
Attachment, arrogance, doubt, and false view.
Minor evil mental functions are anger,
Enmity, concealment, affliction, envy, parsimony,

XIII. Deception, fraudulence, injury, pride,
Absence of the sense of shame, absence of bashfulness,
High-mindedness, low-mindedness,
Unbelief, indolence,

XIV. Idleness, forgetfulness,
Distraction, and non-discernment.
Indeterminate mental functions are repentance, drowsiness,
Reflection, and investigation, the former two composing a different class from the latter.

XV. Based on the mind-consciousness
The five consciousnesses [of the senses] manifest themselves in concomitance with the objective world.
Sometimes the senses manifest themselves together, and sometimes not,
Just as waves are dependent on the water.

XVI. The sense-center consciousness always arises and manifests itself,
Except when born in the realm of the absence of thought,
In the state of unconsciousness, in the two forms of concentration,
In sleep, and in that state where the spirit is depressed or absent.

XVII. Thus the various consciousnesses are but transformations.
That which discriminates and that which is discriminated
Are, because of this, both unreal.
For this reason, everything is mind only.

XVIII. As the result of various ideations which serve as seeds,
Different transformations take place.
The revulsion-energy of these ideations
Gives rise to all sorts of discrimination.

XIX. Due to the habit-energy of various *karmas*
The habit-energy of both the six organs and their objects is influenced.
As the previous "ripening in a different life" is completed,
Succeeding "ripenings in a different life" are produced.

XX. Because of false discriminations,
Various things are falsely discriminated.
What is grasped by such false discrimination
Has no self-nature whatsoever.

XXI. The self-nature which results from dependence on others
Is produced by the condition of discrimination.
The difference between the Absolute (perfect wisdom) and the dependent
Is that the former is eternally free from what is grasped by false discrimination.

XXII. Thus the Absolute and the dependent
Are neither the same nor different;
As in the case of impermanence and permanence,
The one can be seen only in the other.

XXIII. From the three aspects of entity,
The three aspects of non-entity are established.
Therefore the Enlightened One abstrusely preached
That all *dharmas* have no entity.

xxiv. The first is the non-entity of phenomenon.
The second is the non-entity of self-existence.
The last is the non-entity of the ultimate existence
Of the falsely discriminative ego and *dharmas* now to be eliminated.

xxv. The supreme truth of all *dharmas*
Is nothing other than the True Norm [suchness].
It is forever true to its nature,
Which is the true nature of mind-only.

xxvi. Inasmuch as consciousness in its unawakened state
Is not in the abode of the reality of mind-only,
The six sense-organs, their objects, and the seeds of evil desires
Cannot be controlled and extirpated.

xxvii. To hold something before oneself,
And to say that it is the reality of mind-only,
Is not the state of mind-only,
Because it is the result of grasping.

xxviii. But when [the objective world which is] the basis of conditioning as well as the wisdom [which does the conditioning]
Are both eliminated,
The state of mind-only is realized,
Since the six sense-organs and their objects are no longer present.

xxix. Without any grasping and beyond thought
Is the supra-mundane wisdom [of *bodhisattva*hood].
Because of the abandonment of the habit-energy of various *karmas* and the six sense-organs as well as their objects,
The revulsion from relative knowledge to perfect wisdom is attained.

xxx. This is the realm of passionlessness or purity,
Which is beyond description, is good, and is eternal,
Where one is in the state of emancipation, peace, and joy.
This is the law of the Great Buddha.

3. The *Mahāyāna Viṁśaka*, or Twenty Verses on the Great Vehicle[1]

Adoration to Mañjuśrī-kumāra-bhūtā.

Adoration to the Three Treasures.

I. The Buddha who is undefiled and enlightened, elucidates well, being full of mercy, that which is not a word nor is to be expressed in words: therefore I adore the Buddha's power which is beyond thought.

II. From the absolute point of view there is no birth, here again is there no annihilation; the Buddha is like sky, so are beings; they are of one nature.

III. There is no birth on the other side, nor on this side; *nirvāṇa* too in its self-nature exists not. Thus, when surveyed by a knowledge which knows all things, empty are the created.

IV. The self-nature of all things is regarded as like shadows; they are in substance pure, serene, non-dualistic, and same as suchness.

V. [To think of] self or of no-self is not the truth; they are discriminated by the confused; pleasure and pain are relative; so are passions and emancipation from them.

VI. Transmigration in the six paths of existence, the excellence and enjoyability of the heavenly world, or the great painfulness of the purgatories—all these come from apprehending the external world as reality.

VII. One suffers very much when there is nothing pleasurable; even when there are things to enjoy, they pass away because they are impermanent; but it is so settled that goods indeed come from good deeds.

VIII. Things are produced by false discrimination where there is no origination, so, when the purgatories, etc., are manifested, the erroneous are burned like a forest fire.

IX. Like unto things magic-created, so are the deeds of sentient beings who take the external world for reality. The six paths of existence are in substance magic-creations, and they exist conditionally.

X. As the painter painting a terrible monster is himself frightened thereby, so is the fool frightened with transmigration.

[1] Selected from the *Mahāyāna Viṁśaka* of Nāgārjuna (2nd century A.D.), translated by Susumu Yamaguchi: *Nāgārjuna's Mahāyāna Viṁśaka, The Eastern Buddhist* (IV, No. 2, Kyoto, 1927), pp. 169–71.

XI. As a stupid child making a muddy pool is himself drowned in it, so are sentient beings drowned in the mire of false discrimination and unable to get out of it.

XII. As they regard non-existence as existence they suffer the feeling of pain. In the external world as well as in thought they are bound by the poison of false discrimination.

XIII. Seeing that beings are weak, one with a heart of love and wisdom is to discipline oneself for perfect enlightenment in order to benefit them.

XIV. Again, if one with such a heart accumulates [spiritual] provisions, one attains, from the relative point of view, supreme enlightenment and is delivered from the bondage of false discrimination. Such an enlightened one is a friend of the world.

XV. When a man perceives the true meaning of reality as it becomes, he understands that the paths of existence are empty, and cuts asunder [the chain of] the first, middle, and last.

XVI. Thus regarded, *saṁsāra*[1] and *nirvāṇa* have no real substance. Passions have not any substance. Such notions as the first, middle, and last are done away with when their self-nature is understood.

XVII. As perception takes place in a dream which when awakened disappears, so it is with sleeping in the darkness of ignorance: when awakened, transmigrations no more obtain.

XVIII. When things created by magic are seen as such, they have no existence; such is the nature of all things.

XIX. They are all nothing but mind, they are established as phantoms; therefore a blissful or an evil existence is matured according to deeds good or evil.

XX. When the mind-wheel ceases to exist all things indeed cease to exist; thus there is no ego in the nature of all things and therefore their nature is pure indeed.

XXI. When the ignorant wrapped in the darkness of ignorance conceive eternity or bliss in objects as they appear or as they are in themselves, they drift in the ocean of transmigration.

XXII. Where the great ocean of birth and death is filled with waters of false discrimination, who could ever reach the other shore unless carried by the raft of the Mahāyāna?

XXIII. When it is rightly understood that the world arises conditioned by ignorance, where could false discrimination obtain?

[1] Cycle of birth and death.

4. The *Mādhyamika-Śāstra*, or Treatise on the Middle Doctrine[1]

1. *Examination of Causality*[2]

Thus it is that Buddha wished to put in a strong light [the principle of relativity, i.e.,] the fact that entities are produced only in the sense of being coordinated. He therefore maintains that they neither are produced at random, nor from a unique cause, nor from a variety of causes; he denies that they are identical with their causes, that they are different from them, or that they are both [partly identical and partly non-identical]. By this negative method he discloses the true relative character of all the relative entities [of everyday life]. This is relative existence or dependent origination, because nothing really new is produced. From the transcendentalist's point of view it is a condition where nothing disappears, [nor something new appears], etc., and in which there is no motion. It is a condition characterised by the eight above-mentioned characteristics, "nothing disappears," etc. The whole of this treatise is intended by its author to prove that the condition of interdependence [or the principle of relativity] does not allow for something in the universe to disappear, or for something new to appear.

The principle of relativity [being the central law of all existence] can be characterised by an infinite number of finite characteristics, but only eight have been selected, because they are predominant in the sense of having given opportunity for discussion.

It is also called [*nirvāṇa*] the quiescence [or equalisation] of all plurality, because when it is critically realised there is for the philosopher absolutely no differentiation of existence to which our words [and concepts] could be applied. That very essence of relativity is called [*nirvāṇa*] the quiescence of plurality, for which there are no words.

Thoughts and feelings do not arise in this [undifferentiated whole], there is no subject and no object of knowledge, there is [consequently] no turmoil like birth, old age, and death, there is eternal bliss. . . .

DEDICATION

The Perfect Buddha,
The foremost of all Teachers I salute.
He has proclaimed
The principle of [universal] relativity,
'Tis like blissful [*nirvāṇa*],
Quiescence of plurality.

[1] The *Mādhyamika-śāstra* of Nāgārjuna, Chapters I and XXV with commentary by Candrakīrti; translated by Th. Stcherbatsky: *The Conception of Buddhist Nirvāṇa* (Leningrad: Academy of Sciences of the USSR, 1927), pp. 69–78, *passim*.

[2] *Ibid.*, chapter I.

There nothing disappears,
Nor anything appears;
Nothing has an end,
Nor is there anything eternal;
Nothing is identical [with itself],
Nor is there anything differentiated;
Nothing moves,
Neither hither nor thither.

I. There absolutely are no things,
Nowhere and none, that arise [anew],
Neither out of themselves, nor out of non-self,
Nor out of both, nor at random.

II. Four can be the conditions
[Of everything produced],
Its cause, its object, its foregoing moment,
Its most decisive factor.

III. In these conditions we can find
No self-existence of the entities.
Where self-existence is deficient,
Relational existence also lacks.

IV. No energies in causes,
Nor energies outside them.
No causes without energies,
Nor causes that possess them.

V. Let those facts be causes
With whom coordinated other facts arise.
Non-causes will they be,
So far the other facts have not arisen.

VI. Neither non-*ens* nor *ens*
Can have a cause.
If non-*ens*, whose the cause?
If *ens*, whatfor the cause?

VII. Neither an *ens* nor a non-*ens*,
Nor any *ens*-non-*ens*,
No element is really turned out.
How can we then assume
The possibility of a producing cause?

VIII. A mental *ens* is reckoned as an element,
Separately from its objective [counterpart].
Now, if it [begins] by having no objective counterpart,
How can it get one afterwards?

IX. If [separate] elements do not exist,
Nor is it possible for them to disappear.
The moment which immediately precedes
Is thus impossible. And if 'tis gone,
How can it be a cause?

X. If entities are relative,
They have no real existence.
The [formula] "this being, that appears"
Then loses every meaning.

XI. Neither in any of the single causes
Nor in all of them together
Does the [supposed] result reside.
How can you out of them extract
What in them never did exist?

XII. Supposing from these causes does appear
What never did exist in them,
Out of non-causes, then,
Why does it not appear?

XIII. The result is cause-possessor,
But causes are not even self-possessors.
How can result be cause-possessor,
If of non-self-possessors it be a result?

XIV. There is, therefore, no cause-possessor,
Nor is there an effect without a cause.
If altogether no effect arises,
[How can we then distinguish]
Between the causes and non-causes?

2. *Examination of Nirvāṇa*[1]

I. If every thing is relative,
No [real] origination, no [real] annihilation,
How is *nirvāṇa*, then, conceived?
Through what deliverance, through what annihilation?

[1] *Ibid.*, chapter XXV.

II. Should every thing be real in substance,
No [new] creation, no [new] destruction,
How would *nirvāṇa*, then, be reached?
Through what deliverance, through what annihilation?

III. What neither is released, nor is it ever reached,
What neither is annihilation, nor is it eternality,
What never disappears, nor has it been created,
This is *nirvāṇa*. It escapes precision.

IV. *Nirvāṇa*, first of all, is not a kind of *ens*,
It would then have decay and death.
There altogether is no *ens*
Which is not subject to decay and death.

V. If *nirvāṇa* is *ens*,
It is produced by causes,
Nowhere and none the entity exists
Which would not be produced by causes.

VI. If *nirvāṇa* is *ens*,
How can it lack substratum?
There whatsoever is no *ens*
Without any substratum.

VII. If *nirvāṇa* is not an *ens*,
Will it be, then, a non-*ens*?
Wherever there is found no *ens*,
There neither is a [corresponding] non-*ens*.

VIII. Now, if *nirvāṇa* is a non-*ens*,
How can it, then, be independent?
For sure, an independent non-*ens*
Is nowhere to be found.

IX. Coordinated here or caused are [separate things],
We call this world phenomenal;
But just the same is called *nirvāṇa*,
When from causality abstracted.

X. The Buddha has declared
That *ens* and non-*ens* should be both rejected.
Neither as *ens* nor as a non-*ens*
Nirvāṇa therefore is conceived.

XI. If *nirvāṇa* were both *ens* and non-*ens*,
Final deliverance would be also both

Reality and unreality together.
This never could be possible!

XII. If *nirvāṇa* were both *ens* and non-*ens*,
Nirvāṇa could not be uncaused.
Indeed the *ens* and the non-*ens*
Are both dependent on causation.

XIII. How can *nirvāṇa* represent
An *ens* and a non-*ens* together?
Nirvāṇa is, indeed, uncaused;
Both *ens* and non-*ens* are productions.

XIV. How can *nirvāṇa* represent
[The place] of *ens* and of non-*ens* together,
As light and darkness [in one spot]
They cannot simultaneously be present.

XV. If it were clear, indeed,
What an *ens* means, and what a non-*ens*,
We could then understand the doctrine
About *nirvāṇa* being neither *ens* nor non-*ens*.

XVI. If *nirvāṇa* is neither *ens* nor non-*ens*,
No one can really understand
This doctrine which proclaims at once
Negation of them both together.

XVII. What is the Buddha after his *nirvāṇa*?
Does he exist or does he not exist,
Or both, or neither?
We never will conceive it!

XVIII. What is the Buddha, then, at lifetime?
Does he exist, or does he not exist,
Or both, or neither?
We never will conceive it!

XIX. There is no difference at all.
Between *nirvāṇa* and *saṁsāra*.
There is no difference at all
Between *saṁsāra* and *nirvāṇa*.

XX. What makes the limit of *nirvāṇa*
Is also then the limit of *saṁsāra*.
Between the two we cannot find
The slightest shade of difference.

xxi. [Insoluble are antinomic] views
Regarding what exists beyond *nirvāṇa*,
Regarding what the end of this world is,
Regarding its beginning.

xxii. Since everything is relative [we do not know],
What is finite and what is infinite?
What means finite and infinite at once?
What means negation of both issues?

xxiii. What is identity, and what is difference?
What is eternity, what non-eternity?
What means eternity and non-eternity together?
What means negation of both issues?

xxiv. The bliss consists in the cessation of all thought,
In the quiescence of plurality.
No [separate] reality was preached at all,
Nowhere and none by Buddha!

In this case how can the reproach made above affect us! Our view is that *nirvāṇa* represents quiescence, i.e., the non-applicability of all the variety of names and [non-existence of] particular objects. This very quiescence, so far as it is the natural [genuine] quiescence [of the world], is called bliss. The quiescence of plurality is also a bliss because of the cessation of speech or because of the cessation of thought. It is also a bliss because, by putting an end to all defiling agencies, all individual existences are stopped. It is also a bliss because, by quenching all defiling forces, all instinct [and habits of thought] have been extirpated without residue. It is also a bliss because, since all the objects of knowledge have died away, knowledge itself has also died.

Addenda

[In Northern Buddhism, the Three "Seals" are:]

All that exists is impermanent.
All elements are selfless.
Nirvāṇa is serenity, peace.[1]

[1] *Saṁyutta-nikāya*, Vol. x, *sūtra* 261 (Taishō-Tripiṭaka, Vol. ii, p. 66). See also *Mahāprajñāpāramitā-sūtra*, Vol. xxxii, *sūtra* 49. (Taishō, Vol. xxv, No. 1509, p. 368.)

[Reason *vs.* Faith]

Yes, Kālāmas, you may well doubt, you may well waver. In a doubtful matter wavering does arise.

Now look you, Kālāmas. Be ye not misled by report or tradition or hearsay. Be not misled by proficiency in the collections, nor by mere logic or inference, nor after considering reasons, nor after reflection on and approval of some theory, nor because it fits becoming, nor out of respect for a recluse (who holds it). But, Kālāmas, when you know for yourselves: These things are unprofitable, these things are blameworthy, these things are censured by the intelligent; these things, when performed and undertaken, conduce to loss and sorrow,—then indeed do ye reject them, Kālāmas. [E.g.] greed . . . malice . . . illusion.

Come now, Kālāmas, . . . if at any time ye know of yourselves: These things are profitable, they are blameless, they are praised by the intelligent; these things, when performed and undertaken, conduce to profit and happiness,—then, Kālāmas, do ye, having undertaken them, abide therein. [E.g.] freedom from greed . . . freedom from malice . . . freedom from illusion.[1]

"As the wise test gold by burning, cutting and rubbing it (on a piece of touchstone), so are you to accept my words after examining them and not merely out of regard for me."[2]

[After explaining his basic doctrines to a group of listeners, the Buddha says:]

Now, Almsmen, would you, knowing and seeing all this, harken back to the past, wondering [what is true]? . . . would you be perplexed in the present? . . . would you say, "We revere our teacher, and it is because of this that we affirm this? . . . would you say, "Oh, we were told this by a recluse or recluses; we do not affirm it ourselves?" . . . would you look out for another teacher?—[to all of which the disciples reply,] "No, sir."

"Do you not affirm only what you have of yourselves known, seen, and discussed?"

"Yes, sir."

"Quite right, Almsmen. You have by me been introduced to this Doctrine. . . . All I have said was to bring out that this Doctrine was immediate in its gifts here and now, open to all, a guide Onwards to be mastered for himself by every intelligent man."[3]

[1] *Aṅguttara-nikāya*, i. 189, or III. 7. 65.

[2] *Jñānasāra-samuccaya* 31.

[3] *Majjhima-nikāya* i. 265.

THE ORTHODOX SYSTEMS

THE ORTHODOX SYSTEMS[1]

1. *The Rise of the Systems*

THE age of Buddha [563–483 B.C.] represents the great springtide of philosophic spirit in India. The progress of philosophy is generally due to a powerful attack on a historical tradition when men feel themselves compelled to go back on their steps and raise once more the fundamental questions which their fathers had disposed of by the older schemes. The revolt of Buddhism and Jainism, even such as it was, forms an era in the history of Indian thought, since it finally exploded the method of dogmatism and helped to bring about a critical point of view. For the great Buddhist thinkers, logic was the main arsenal where were forged the weapons of universal destructive criticism. Buddhism served as a cathartic in clearing the mind of the cramping effects of ancient obstructions.... The need for laying the foundations deeper resulted in the great movement of philosophy which produced the six systems of thought, where cold criticism and analysis take the place of poetry and religion. The conservative schools were compelled to codify their views and set forth logical defences of them. The critical side of philosophy became as important as the speculative. The philosophical views of the presystematic period set forth some general reflections regarding the nature of the universe as a whole, but did not realise that a critical theory of knowledge is the necessary basis of any fruitful speculation. Critics forced their opponents to employ the natural methods relevant to life and experience, and not some supernatural revelation, in the defence of their speculative schemes.... The force of thought which springs straight from life and experience as we have it in the Upaniṣads, or the epic greatness of soul which sees and chants the God-vision as in the *Bhagavad-gītā* give place to more strict philosophising...the spirit of the times required that every system of thought based on reason should be recognised as a *darśana*. All logical attempts to gather the floating conceptions of the world into some great general ideas were regarded as *darśanas*. They all help us to see some aspect of the truth. This conception led to the view that the

[1] S. Radhakrishnan, *Indian Philosophy,* II, George Allen & Unwin, Ltd., 1931, pp. 17–28.

apparently isolated and independent systems were really members of a larger historical plan. Their nature could not be completely understood so long as they were viewed as self-dependent, without regard to their place in the historic interconnection.

2. *Relation to the Vedas*

The adoption of the critical method served to moderate the impetuosity of the speculative imagination and helped to show that the pretended philosophies were not so firmly held as their professors supposed. But the iconoclastic fervour of the materialists, the sceptics and some followers of Buddhism destroyed all grounds of certitude. The Hindu mind did not contemplate this negative result with equanimity. . . . It cannot be that the hopes and aspirations of sincere souls like the *ṛṣis* of the Upaniṣads are irrevocably doomed. It cannot be that centuries of struggle and thought have not brought the mind one step nearer to the solution. . . . The seers of the Upaniṣads are the great teachers in the school of sacred wisdom. They speak to us of the knowledge of God and spiritual life. If the unassisted reason of man cannot attain any hold on reality by means of mere speculation, help may be sought from the great writings of the seers who claim to have attained spiritual certainty. Thus strenuous attempts were made to justify by reason what faith implicitly accepts. This is not an irrational attitude, since philosophy is only an endeavour to interpret the widening experience of humanity. The one danger that we have to avoid is lest faith should furnish the conclusions for philosophy.

Of the systems of thought or *darśanas*, six became more famous than others, viz., Gautama's Nyāya, Kaṇāda's Vaiśeṣika, Kapila's Sāṁkhya, Patañjali's Yoga, Jaimini's Pūrva Mīmāṁsā and Bādarāyaṇa's Uttara Mīmāṁsā or the Vedānta. They are the Brahmanical systems, since they all accept the authority of the Vedas. The systems of thought which admit the validity of the Vedas are called *āstika*, and those which repudiate it *nāstika*. The *āstika*, or *nāstika* character of a system does not depend on its positive or negative conclusions regarding the nature of the supreme spirit, but on the acceptance or non-acceptance of the authority of the Vedas. . . .

The philosophical character of the systems is not much compromised by the acceptance of the Veda. The distinction between *śruti* and *smṛti* is well known, and where the two conflict, the former is to prevail. The *śruti* itself is divided into the *karma-kāṇḍa* (the Saṁhitās and the Brāhmaṇas) and the *jñāna-kāṇḍa* (the Upaniṣads).

The latter is of higher value, though much of it is set aside as mere *arthavāda* or non-essential statements. All these distinctions enable one to treat the Vedic testimony in a very liberal spirit. The interpretations of the Vedic texts depend on the philosophical predilections of the authors. While employing logical methods and arriving at truths agreeable to reason, they were yet anxious to preserve their continuity with the ancient texts. They did not wish it to be thought that they were enunciating something completely new. While this may involve a certain want of frankness with themselves, it helped the spread of what they regarded as the truth. Critics and commentators of different schools claim for their views the sanction of the Veda and exercise their ingenuity in forcing that sanction when it is not spontaneously yielded. In the light of the controversies of subsequent times, they read into the language of the Vedas opinions on questions of which they knew little or nothing. The general conceptions of the Vedas were neither definite nor detailed, and so allowed themselves to be handled and fashioned in different ways by different schools of thought. Besides, the very vastness of the Vedas, from which the authors could select out of free conviction any portion for their authority, allowed room for original thought.

3. *The Sūtras*

When the Vedic literature became unwieldy and the Vedic thinkers were obliged to systematise their views, the *Sūtra* literature arose. The principal tenets of the *darśanas* are stated in the form of *sūtras* or short aphorisms. They are intended to be as short as possible, free from doubt, able to bring out the essential meaning and put an end to many doubts; and they must not contain anything superfluous or erroneous. They try to avoid all unnecessary repetition and employ great economy of words. The ancient writers had no temptation to be diffuse, since they had to rely more on memory than on printed books. This extreme conciseness makes it difficult to understand the *Sūtras* without a commentary.

The different systems developed in different centres of philosophical activity. The views had been growing up through many generations even before they were summed up in the *Sūtras*. They are not the work of one thinker or of one age but of a succession of thinkers spread over a number of generations. As the *Sūtras* presuppose a period of gestation and of formation, it is difficult for us to trace their origin.... The systems must have evolved at a much earlier period than that in which the *Sūtras* were formulated. The whole tone and manner of the philosophical *Sūtras* suggests that they belong approximately to the same period. The authors of the *Sūtras* are not the founders or originators of the systems but only their compilers or formulators. This fact accounts for the cross references in the philosophical *Sūtras*, and it must be noted that the various systems had been growing side by side with one another during the period which preceded the formation of the *Sūtras*. To the early centuries after Buddha and before the Christian era belongs the crystallisation of the different systems out of the complex solution. Oral tradition and not books were the repositories of the philosophical views. It may be that, through lapse of oral tradition, several important works perished, and many of those that have reached us are not even pure. Some of the earlier important *Sūtras*,...as well as large quantities of philosophical literature, are lost to us, and with them also much useful information about the chronological relations of the different systems. Max Müller assigns the gradual formation of the *Sūtras* to the period from Buddha to Aśoka [third century B.C.], though he admits that, in the cases of the Vedānta, the Sāṁkhya and the Yoga, a long previous development has to be allowed. This view is confirmed by the evidence of Kauṭilya's *Artha-śāstra* [300 B.C.]. Up till then, the orthodox Ānvīkṣikī or logical systems were divided mainly into two schools, the Pūrva Mīmāṁsā and the Sāṁkhya. Though the references in Buddhist texts are very vague, it may be said that the Buddhist *Sūtras* assume a knowledge of the six systems. The vivid intellectual life of the early centuries after Buddha flowed in many streams parallel to one another, though the impulse to codify them was due to the reaction against the systems of revolt. These systems of thought undergo modifications at the hands of later interpreters, though the resultant system is still fathered on the original systematiser....The greatest thinkers of India profess to be simply scholiasts; but in their attempts to expound the texts, they improve on them. Each system has grown in relation to others which it keeps always in view. The development of the six systems has been in progress till the present day, the successive interpreters defending the tradition against the attacks of its opponents.

In the case of every *darśana*, we have first of all a period of philosophic fermentation, which at a particular stage is reduced to *sūtras* or aphorisms. This is succeeded by the writing of commentaries on the aphorisms, which are followed by glosses, expositions and explanatory compendia, in which the original doctrines undergo modifications, corrections and amplifications. The commentaries use the form of the dialogue, which has come down from the time of the Upaniṣads as the only adequate form for the exposition of a complex theme. The commentator by means of the dialogue is enabled to show the relation of the view he is expounding to the diverse trains of thought suggested by the rival interlocutors. The ideas are re-stated and their superiority to other conceptions established.

4. *Common Ideas*

The six systems agree on certain essentials. The acceptance of the Veda implies that all the systems have drawn from a common reservoir of thought. The Hindu teachers were obliged to use the heritage they received from the past, in order to make their views readily understood. While the use of the terms *avidyā* [ignorance], *māyā* [illusion or appearance], *puruṣa* [person, self], *jīva* [self, soul] shows that the dialect of speculation is common to the different systems, it is to be noted that the systems are distinguished by the different significations assigned to those terms in the different schools. It frequently happens in the history of thought that the same terms and phrases are used by different schools in senses which are essentially distinct. Each system sets forth its special doctrine by using, with necessary modifications, the current language of the highest religious speculation. In the systems, philosophy becomes self-conscious. The spiritual experiences recorded in the Vedas are subjected to a logical criticism. The question of the validity and means of knowledge forms an important chapter of each system. Each philosophical scheme has its own theory of knowledge, which is an integral part or a necessary consequence of its metaphysics. Intuition, inference and the Veda are accepted by the systems. Reason is subordinated to intuition. Life cannot be comprehended in its fulness by logical reason. Self-consciousness is not the ultimate category of the universe. There is something transcending the consciousness of self, to which many names are given—Intuition, Revelation, Cosmic Consciousness, and God-vision. We cannot describe it adequately, so we call it the super-consciousness. When we now and then have glimpses of this higher form, we feel that it involves a purer illumination and a wider compass. As the difference between mere consciousness and self-consciousness constitutes the wide gulf separating the animal from man, so the difference between self-consciousness and super-consciousness constitutes all the difference between man as he is and man as he ought to be. The philosophy of India takes its stand on the spirit which is above mere logic, and holds that culture based on mere logic or science may be efficient, but cannot be inspiring.

All the systems protest against the scepticism of the Buddhists, and erect a standard of objective reality and truth as opposed to an eternal, unstable flux. The stream of the world has been flowing on from eternity, and this flow is not merely mental, but is objective; and it is traced to the eternal *prakṛti* [Nature] or *māyā* or atoms. "That in which the world resides, when divested of name and form, some call *prakṛti*, others *māyā*, others atoms." It is assumed that whatever has a beginning has an end. Everything that is made up of parts can be neither eternal nor self-subsistent. The true individual is indivisible. The real is not the universe extended in space and time; for its nature is becoming and not being. There is something deeper than this—atoms and selves, or *puruṣa* and *prakṛti*, or *Brahman*.

All the systems accept the view of the great world rhythm. Vast periods of creation, maintenance and dissolution follow each other in endless succession. This theory is not inconsistent with belief in progress; for it is not a question of the movement of the world reaching its goal times without number, and being again forced back to its starting-point. Creations and dissolutions do not mean the fresh rise and the total destruction of the cosmos. The new universe forms the next stage of the history of the cosmos, where the unexhausted potencies of good and evil are provided with the opportunities of fulfilment. It means that the race of man enters upon and retravels its ascending path of realisation. This interminable succession of world ages has no beginning.

Except perhaps the Pūrva Mīmāṁsā, all the systems aim at the practical end of salvation. The systems mean by release (*mokṣa*) the recovery by the self of its natural integrity, from which sin and error drive it. All the systems have for their ideal complete mental poise and freedom from the discords and uncertainties, sorrows and sufferings of life, "a repose that ever is the same," which no doubts disturb and no rebirths break into. The conception of *jīvan-mukti*, or liberation in life, is admitted in many schools.

It is a fundamental belief of the Hindus that the universe is law-abiding to the core, and yet that man is free to shape his own destiny in it. The systems believe in rebirth and preexistence. Our life is a step on a road, the direction and goal of which are lost in the infinite. On this road, death is never an end or an obstacle but at most the beginning of new steps. The development of the self is a continuous process, though it is broken into stages by the recurring baptism of death.

Philosophy carries us to the gates of the promised land, but cannot let us in; for that, insight or realisation is necessary. We are like children stranded in the darkness of *saṁsāra* [world and life of change or appearance], with no idea of our true nature, and inclined to imagine fears and to cling to hopes in the gloom that surrounds us. Hence arises the need for light, which will free us from the dominion of passions and show us the real, which we unwittingly are, and the unreal in which we ignorantly live. Such a kind of insight is admitted as the sole means to salvation, though there are differences regarding the object of insight. The cause of bondage is ignorance, and so release can be had through insight into the truth. The ideal of the systems is practically to transcend the merely ethical level. The holy man is compared to the fair lotus unsullied by the mire in which it grows. In his case the good is no more a goal to be striven after, but is an accomplished fact. While virtue and vice may lead to a good or bad life within the circle of *saṁsāra*, we can escape from *saṁsāra* through the transcending of the moralistic individualism. All systems recognise as obligatory unselfish love and disinterested activity, and insist on *cittaśuddhi* (cleansing of the heart) as essential to all moral culture. In different degrees they adhere to the rules of caste (*varṇa*) and stages of life (*āśramas*).

A history of Indian philosophy. . . is beset with innumerable difficulties. The dates of the principal writers and their works are not free from doubt; and in some cases the historicity of well-known authors is contested. While many of the relevant works are not available, even the few that are published have not all been critically studied. A historical treatment of Indian philosophy has not been taken up by the great Indian thinkers themselves. . . .

In obedience to custom, which it would be vain to try to unsettle, we shall start [in dealing with the six systems of Hinduism] with the Nyāya and the Vaiśeṣika theories, which give us an analysis of the world of experience, and pass on to the Sāṁkhya and the Yoga, which try to explain experience by bold speculative ventures; and we shall conclude with a discussion of the Mīmāṁsās, which attempt to show that the revelations of *śruti* are in harmony with the conclusions of philosophy. Such a treatment has at least the support of sound logic though not of sound chronology.

CHAPTER X

NYĀYA

Of the six systems of thought which arose in this period, the Nyāya and the Vaiśeṣika systems represent the analytic type of philosophy. The history of the Nyāya literature extends over twenty centuries and the long history of the thought and the vast amount of significant literature[1] in this one system is typical of all the systems. The distinctive character of the Nyāya philosophy is its critical examination of the objects of knowledge by means of the canons of logical proof. Systems of Hindu thought generally accept the fundamental principles of the Nyāya logic. The physical and metaphysical views of the Nyāya—atomistic realism—are essentially the same as those of the Vaiśeṣika.

"*Nyāya*" literally means that by which the mind is led to a conclusion. We are led to conclusions by arguments or reasoning. These arguments are either valid or invalid. "*Nyāya*" in popular usage means "right" or "just," and so Nyāya becomes the science of right or just reasoning. It is, in a wider sense, the science of demonstration or correct knowledge (*pramāṇa-śāstra*). In knowledge we can distinguish four factors: subject (*pramātṛ*), object (*prameya*), the resulting state of cognition (*pramiti*), and the means of knowledge (*pramāṇa*). The nature of knowledge as valid or invalid depends on the last, *pramāṇa*. By means of the *pramāṇas* we are led to a right apprehension of objects and are enabled to test the validity of knowledge.

Intuition (*pratyakṣa*) is the most important. Though it meant sense-perception originally, it soon came to include all immediate apprehension, whether through the aid of the senses or not. Gautama's definition of sense-perception mentions the different factors involved, the senses (*indriyas*), their objects (*arthas*), the contact of the two (*sannikarṣa*), and the cognition (*jñāna*) produced by the contact. There are five sense-organs, eye, ear, nose, tongue, and skin, which are of the same nature as the five elements, light, ether, earth, water, and air, whose special qualities of color, sound, smell, taste, and tangibility are manifested by them. Mind (*manas*) is a prerequisite of perception. It mediates between the self and the senses.

There are two kinds of perception, determinate and indeterminate. In the former we acquire knowledge of the genus to which the perceived object belongs, the specific qualities which distinguish it from other

[1] See S. Radhakrishnan, *Indian Philosophy*, II, George Allen & Unwin Ltd., 1931, pp. 36–41.

members of the class, and the union between the two. These specific elements are absent in indeterminate perception, which is of the type of simple apprehension. The latter is the starting point of all knowledge, though it is not itself knowledge. There are several views of this distinction between determinate and indeterminate perception. Later logicians, e.g., Dharmakīrti, distinguished four kinds of perception: sense-perception, mental perception, self-consciousness, and Yogic intuition.

Inference (*anumāna*) means, literally, knowledge which follows other knowledge. It is also defined as knowledge which is preceded by perception. It includes both deductive and inductive inference. There can be no inference without a universal connection (*vyāpti*). We infer that the mountain is on fire from the fact that there is smoke on the mountain, because smoke is universally connected with fire. The Nyāya syllogism has five elements: (1) the proposition to be established (the hill is on fire); (2) the reason (because it smokes); (3) the example (whatever has smoke has fire, for example, a kitchen); (4) the application (so does this hill); and (5) the statement of the conclusion (the hill is on fire). There are requirements to which each of these five members of an argument must conform. For example—in an interesting contrast to Western traditional formal logic—the third member, the example, indicates that the universal proposition which is the logical ground of the inference is based on particular and factual instances. Attempts have been made to reduce the number of members of the syllogism to three. All are agreed that the essentials of the inference are the universal relation and the reason (the minor premise). General propositions are traced to an enumeration of instances, positive and negative, intuition of the universal, and indirect proof by which it is shown that no other hypothesis can account for the facts.

Upamāna is comparison or analogy by which we gain knowledge of a thing from its similarity to another. The similarity should be essential, not superficial.

Śabda, verbal knowledge or testimony, refers to authority. Under this, Naiyāyikas discuss words, their meanings, and whether they refer to individual, or form, or genus.

The Nyāya thinkers believe that non-existence (*abhāva*) can be inferred, and so it need not be given an independent place—along with the other forms of knowledge.

We find in the Nyāya discussions of memory, doubt, fallacies of reasoning, etc. The test of truth is successful action.

The main selections from the Nyāya system—and from all six systems—which follow consist of *sūtras*, short aphoristic statements, and explanatory commentaries on these *sūtras*. In general, the *sūtras* are taken from *The Nyāya Sūtras of Gotama* (3rd century B.C.), translated by S. C. Vidyābhuṣaṇa, tr., Sacred Books of the Hindus, VIII (Allahabad: The Panini Office, 1930), and the commentaries—the portion in smaller type—are from *Gautama's Nyāyasūtras* with Vātsyāyaṇa's *Bhāṣya*, translated by Ganganatha Jha (Poona: Oriental Book Agency, 1939). Jha's translation of the *sūtras* is used occasionally and is so noted. Sometimes a new, alternate translation is suggested.

In the case of a few difficult passages, the commentary is taken from the volume of the Sacred Book of the Hindus—in which case it is noted thus: [S.B.H.]—although these commentaries are not literal translations of the original *bhāṣya* (commentary).

While the Nyāya is a comprehensive system and includes extensive exposition of metaphysical and psychological principles, the system, as noted above, is especially important for its logical doctrines, and so these are included at length in the selections, while Books III and IV are omitted entirely. The substance of the material of these two books will be included in the sister-system, Vaiśeṣika, in the next chapter.

A short selection is added from Udayana Ācārya's (10th century A.D.) *Kusumāñjali*: *The Kusumāñjali or Hindu Proof of the Existence of a Supreme Being*, with the commentary of Hari Dasa Bhattacarya, translated by E. B. Cowell (Calcutta: Baptist Mission Press, 1864).

A. THE *NYĀYA SŪTRA*

Book I—Chapter I

Statement of subject matter, purpose, and relation of the treatise[1]

1.[2] Supreme felicity is attained by the knowledge about the true nature of the sixteen categories, viz., means of right knowledge, object of right knowledge, doubt, purpose, familiar instance, established tenet, members [of a syllogism], confutation, ascertainment, discussion, wrangling, cavil, fallacy, quibble, futility, and occasion for rebuke.[3]

2. Pain, birth, activity, faults [defects] and misapprehension [wrong notion]—on the successive annihilation of these in the reverse order, there follows release.

From...wrong notion proceeds attachment to the agreeable and aversion for the disagreeable: and under the influence of this attachment and aversion, there appear the defects,—such as envy, jealousy, deceit, avarice and the like.

Urged by these defects, when the man acts, he commits...misdeeds....

What are meant by "activity" in this connection (in the *sūtra*) are the results of activity,...

The "activity" described above (in the form of merit and demerit) becomes the cause of mean and respectable birth (respectively);...

[1] Such sectional headings are not a part of the original text.

[2] These numbers indicate the *sūtras*.

[3] These categories are treated in order in succeeding sections of the text.

When there is birth, there is pain;...

When "true knowledge" is attained, "wrong notions" disappear; on the disappearance of "wrong notions" the "defects" disappear; the disappearance of "defects" is followed by the disappearance of "activity" (merit and demerit); when there is no activity there is no "birth"; on the cessation of birth there is cessation of pain; cessation of pain is followed by final release, which is the "highest good."

Definition of the instruments of right cognition

3. Perception, inference, comparison and word (verbal testimony)—these are the means of right knowledge.

Among the four kinds of cognition, perception is the most important;... when [a man] has once perceived the thing directly, his desires are at rest, and he does not seek for any other kind of knowledge;...

4. Perception is that knowledge which arises from the contact of a sense with its object, and which is determinate [well-defined], unnameable [not expressible in words], and non-erratic [unerring].

...the name is not (necessarily present and) operative at the time that the apprehension of the thing takes place; it becomes operative (and useful) only at the time of its being spoken of, or communicated to other persons....

...if the definition of sense-perception consisted of only two terms—"that which is produced by the sense-object contact" and "that which is not representable by words,"—then the apprehension of water [in the case of a mirage]...would have to be regarded as "sense-perception." ...That cognition is erroneous in which the thing is apprehended as what it is not; while, when a thing is perceived as what it is, the perception is not erroneous.

When the man observes from a distance, and sees (something rising from the earth), the cognition that he has is in the (doubtful) form—"this is smoke, or this is dust"; inasmuch as this doubtful cognition is also produced by the contact of the sense-organ with the object, it would have to be regarded as sense-perception, if this were defined simply as "that which is produced by the contact of the sense-organ with the object." With a view to guard against this, the author has added the further qualification that the cognition should be well-defined.

5. Inference is knowledge which is preceded by perception, and is of three kinds, viz., *a priori*, *a posteriori* and "commonly seen."

6. Comparison [analogy] is the knowledge of a thing through its similarity to another thing previously well known.

7. Word (verbal testimony) is the instructive assertion of a reliable person.

Definition of the objects of right cognition

9. Soul (self), body, senses, objects of sense, intellect, mind, activity, fault, transmigration [rebirth], fruit, pain, and release—are the objects of right knowledge.

10. Desire, aversion, volition, pleasure, pain, and intelligence are the marks of the soul.[1]

11. Body is the site of gesture [actions], senses, and sentiments [objects].

"How is the body the vehicle of objects [or sentiments]?"

That is to be regarded as the vehicle of objects in which receptacle there appear the feelings of pleasure and pain caused by the contact of the sense-organs with those objects;—and such a receptacle is the body.

12. Nose, tongue, eye, skin, and ear are the senses produced from elements.

13. Earth, water, light, air, and ether—these are the [material] elements.

14. Smell, taste, colour, touch, and sound are objects of the senses and qualities of the earth, etc.

15. Intellect [*buddhi*], apprehension [*upalabdhi*], and knowledge [*jñāna*]—these are not different from one another.

It is not possible for cognition to belong to the unconscious instrument *buddhi*; as if it were, then *buddhi* could be a conscious entity; while there is a single conscious entity, apart from the aggregate of the body, and the sense-organs. Though the sentence composing the *sūtra* is for the purpose of providing the definition of one of the *objects of cognition*, yet it is taken as implying the other fact (the refutation of the Sāṁkhya theory) by the force of the argument (implied in the mention of the synonyms). [According to the Sāṁkhya philosophy, intellect (*buddhi*), which is the first thing evolved out of primordial matter (*prakṛti*), is altogether different from knowledge (*jñāna*), which consists in the reflection of external objects on the self (*puruṣa*), the abode of transparent consciousness.]

16. The mark of the mind is that there do not arise (in the self) more acts of knowledge than one at a time.

. . . even though at one and the same time several perceptible objects . . . are in close proximity to the respective perceptive sense-organs, . . . yet there is no simultaneous cognition of them; and from this we infer that there is some other cause [namely, the mind], by whose proximity cogni-

[1] These are all marks or indications of (or arguments for) the existence of a permanent and common agent in man, because without such a permanent agent none of these functions would be possible since they all require remembrance, continuity, and identity of the self (or soul) throughout experience.

tion appears.... If the proximity of sense-organs to their objects, by themselves, independently of the contact of the mind, were the sole cause of cognitions, then it would be quite possible for several cognitions to appear simultaneously.

17. Activity is that which makes the voice, mind, and body begin their action.

[or]

Activity consists in the efforts or operation of voice, mind, and body.

18. Faults have the characteristic of causing activity. [The faults are] attachment, aversion, and ignorance.

19. Transmigration means re-births.

Having died, when [the self] is born again in an animate body, this being born again constitutes the rebirth of that [self] which is born.... The recurrence of this process of birth and death should be regarded as without beginning, and ending only with final release.

20. Fruit is the thing produced by activity and faults.

Fruition consists in the experiencing of pleasure and pain, as every action leads to pleasure and pain.

21. Pain has the characteristic of causing uneasiness.

...Every thing (i.e., body, etc., and also pleasure and pain), being intermingled with i.e., invariably accompanied by, never existing apart from—pain, is inseparable from pain; and as such is regarded as pain itself. Finding everything to be intermingled with pain, when one wishes to get rid of pain, he finds that birth (or life) itself is nothing but pain; and thus becomes disgusted (with life); and being disgusted, he loses all attachment; and being free from attachment, he becomes released.

22. Release is the absolute deliverance from pain.

When there is a relinquishing of the birth that has been taken and the non-resumption of another—this condition, which is without end (or limit) is known as "final release."... This condition of immortality, free from fear, imperishable (unchanging), consisting in the attainment of bliss, is called "*Brahman.*"

Definition of the pre-requisites of a process of ratiocination or reasoning (*nyāya*)

23. Doubt, which is a conflicting judgment about the precise character of an object, arises from the recognition of properties common to many objects, or of properties not common to any of the objects, from conflicting testimony, and from irregularity of perception and non-perception.

24. Purpose [or motive] is that with an eye to which one proceeds to act.

25. A familiar instance [or example] is the thing about which an ordinary man and an expert entertain the same opinion.

[The familiar instance aids in overthrowing contradicting opinions and in confirming one's opinions, and serves as "one of the essential factors of the inferential process."]

Definition of the tenet which is the basis of reasoning (nyāya)

26. An established tenet is a dogma resting on the authority of a certain school, hypothesis, or implication.

Definition of reasoning (nyāya)

32. The members (of a syllogism) are proposition, reason, example, application, and conclusion.

33. The proposition is the declaration of what is to be established.

[Example:] Sound is non-eternal.

34. The reason is the means for establishing what is to be established through the homogeneous or affirmative character of the example.

[Example: Sound is non-eternal] because sound has the character of being a product; as a matter of fact, everything that is a product is non-eternal.

35. Likewise through heterogeneous or negative character.

For example,—Sound is non-eternal, because it has the character of being produced, [and] that which has not the character of being produced is always eternal, e.g., such substances as the self and the like.

36. A homogeneous [or affirmative] example is a familiar instance which is known to possess the property to be established, and which implies that this property is invariably contained in the reason given.

...the form of the inference being: Sound is non-eternal, because it has the character of being produced, just like such things as the dish....

37. A heterogeneous [or negative] example is a familiar instance which is known to be devoid of the property to be established, and which implies that the absence of this property is invariably rejected in the reason given.

E.g., Sound is non-eternal, because it has the character of being produced—everything *not* having the character of being produced is eternal, for instance, the self....

38. The 're-affirmation' is that which, on the strength of the instance, re-asserts the subject as being 'so' [i.e., as possessing the character which has been found, in the instance, to be concomitant with what is to be established]—or as being 'not so' [i.e., as not possessing the character which has been found in the instance to be concomitant with the negation of what is to be established. [Jha]

(*a*) When the instance cited is the homogeneous one, which is similar to the subject,—e.g., when the dish is cited as the example. . .—we have the re-affirmation [application] stated in the form, sound is so—i.e., sound is a product.

(*b*) When the instance cited is the heterogeneous one, which is dissimilar to the subject,—e.g., when the self is cited as an example. . . —the re-affirmation [application] is stated in the form, sound is not so. . . .

39. Conclusion is the re-stating of the proposition, after the reason has been mentioned.

Definition of processes subsidiary to reasoning (*nyāya*)

40. Confutation, which is carried on for ascertaining the real character of a thing of which the character is not known, is reasoning which reveals the character by showing the absurdity of all contrary characters.

41. Ascertainment [demonstrated truth] is the removal of doubt, and the determination of a question, by hearing two opposite sides.

Book I—Chapter II

Definition of controversy

1. Discussion consists in the putting forward (by two persons) of a conception and a counter-conception, in which there is supporting and condemning by means of proofs and reasonings,—neither of which is quite opposed to the main doctrine (or thesis), and both of which are carried on in full accordance with the method of reasoning through the five factors. [Jha]

2. Wrangling [disputation], which aims at gaining victory, is the defence or attack of a proposition in the manner aforesaid, by quibbles, futilities, and other processes which deserve rebuke.

3. Cavil is a kind of wrangling, which consists in mere attacks on the opposite side.

Definition of fallacious marks of inference

4. Fallacies of a reason are the erratic [inconclusive], the contradictory, the equal to the question [neutral], the unproved, and the mistimed.

5. The erratic [inconclusive] is the reason which leads to more conclusions than one.

As for example, in the reasoning "Sound is eternal because it is intangible—the jar which is tangible has been found to be non-eternal,—and sound is not tangible,—therefore, being intangible, sound must be eternal,"—we find that the character of intangibility has been put forward as proving the character of eternality; while as a matter of fact the two characters do not bear to each other the relation of proof and proved....

6. The contradictory is the reason which opposes what is to be established.

7. Equal to the question [the "neutral reason"] is the reason which provokes the very question, for the solution of which it was employed.

That reasoning, in which what is put forward as the reason is the character that is admitted (by both parties) to be common (to that which is to be established and its reverse), is "equal to doubt" (in not leading to a certain conclusion); and such a reason, therefore, has been called "indecisive";...

8. The unproved is the reason which stands in need of proof, in the same way as the proposition does.

[As an example:] ..."Shadow is a substance,"—the proposition; to prove which is put forward the reason "because it has motion"; and this reason does not differ from the proposition, inasmuch as it is still to be proved;...

9. The mistimed is the reason which is adduced when the time is passed in which it might hold good.

Definition of fraud or quibble

10. Quibble [casuistry] is the opposition offered to a proposition by the assumption of an alternative meaning.

11. It is of three kinds, viz., quibble in respect of a term, quibble in respect of a genus, and quibble in respect of a metaphor.

12. Quibble in respect of a term [verbal casuistry] consists in wilfully taking the term in a sense other than that intended by a speaker who has happened to use it ambiguously.

13. Generalising casuistry [quibble in respect to genus] consists in

the urging of an absurd signification, which is rendered possible by the use of a too generic term. [Jha]

That word is called "too generic" which, while applying to the thing desired to be spoken of, also over-reaches it; e.g., the *brāhmin*hood—which is denoted by the term "*brāhmin*"—is, sometimes found to be concomitant with "learning and character" and sometimes it is found to over-reach it, i.e., not concomitant with it. . . .[1]

14. Quibble in respect of a metaphor consists in denying the proper meaning of a word by taking it literally, while it was used metaphorically, and *vice versa*.

Defects of reasoning due to the incapacity of the reasoner

18. Futility consists in offering objections founded on mere similarity or dissimilarity.

19. An occasion for rebuke [a clincher] arises when one misunderstands, or does not understand at all.

The man who misapprehends things becomes defeated; and "clincher" consists in this defeat.

Book II—Chapter I

Re-examination of doubt

1. Some say that doubt cannot arise from the recognition of common and uncommon properties, whether conjointly or separately.

2. It is further said that doubt cannot arise, either from conflicting testimony, or from the irregularity of perception and non-perception.

3. In the case of conflicting testimony there is, according to them, a strong conviction (on each side).

4. Doubt, they say, does not arise from the irregularity of perception and non-perception, because in the irregularity itself there is regularity.

5. Likewise, there is, they say, the chance of an endless doubt, owing to the continuity of its cause.

6. In reply, it is stated that the recognition of properties common to many objects, etc., are certainly causes of doubt, if there is no reference to the precise characters of the objects: there is no chance of no-doubt or of endless-doubt.

7. Examination should be made in this way of each case where there is room for doubt.

[1] This is the case when the term is used to refer to the group "*brāhmin*" in a general sense regardless of the actual possession or non-possession of "learning and character."

Detailed examination of perception

21. An objector may say that the definition of perception as given before is untenable, because incomplete.

22. Perception, it is said, cannot arise unless there is conjunction of self with mind.

24. The self, we point out, has not been excluded from our definition, inasmuch as knowledge is a mark of the self.

25. The mind, too, has not been omitted from our definition, inasmuch as we have spoken of the non-simultaneity of acts of knowledge.

26. Inasmuch as it is only the contact of the sense-organ and the object that forms the (distinctive) cause (or feature) of perception, it has been mentioned (in the *sūtra*) by means of words directly expressing it. [Jha]

Consideration of the view that perception is the same as inference

31. Perception, it may be urged, is inference, because it illumines only a part as a mark of the whole.

When the observer cognises the tree, what he actually perceives is only its part nearest to himself; and certainly that one part is not the "tree.' So that (when the man cognises the "tree" as a whole) what happens is that there is an inference of it (from the perception of its one part), just like the inference of fire from the apprehension of smoke.

32. But this is not so, for perception is admitted of at least that portion which it actually illumines.

Examination of the nature of the composite whole

33. There is, some say, doubt about the whole, because the whole has yet to be established.

34. If there were no whole, there would, it is replied, be non-perception of all.

...as for substance in its atomic condition, this could never be an object of perception, as atoms are beyond the reach of the sense-organs...and yet as a matter of fact, all these, substance and the rest, are found to be objects of perception, and actually apprehended as such....

35. There is a whole, because we can hold, pull, etc.

If there were no whole, we could not have held or pulled an entire thing by holding or pulling a part of it. We say, "one jar," "one man," etc. This use of "one" would vanish, if there were no whole.

36. [In answer to what has been just urged by the *siddhāntin*,[1] the *pūrvapakṣin*[2] might urge that]—"the said conception (of 'one' in regard to the many) would be similar to the notion that we have in regard to such (collective) things as the 'army' and the 'forest'";—but even so the conception would not be possible; as atoms are beyond the reach of the senses.[3] [Jha—37]

Examination of inference

37. Inference, some say, is not a means of right knowledge, as it errs in certain cases, e.g., when a river is banked, when something is damaged, and when similarity misleads, etc.

If we see a river swollen, we infer that there has been rain; if we see the ants carrying off their eggs, we infer that there will be rain; and if we hear a peacock scream, we infer that clouds are gathering. These inferences, says an objector, are not necessarily correct, for a river may be swollen because embanked, the ants may carry off their eggs because their nests have been damaged, and the so-called screaming of a peacock may be nothing but the voice of a man.

38. It is not so, because our inference is based on something else than the part, fear and likeness.

. . . the "falsity" that has been urged does not apply to inference; it is clear that what is not an inference has been mistaken for inference. . . .

Introductory examination of the nature of time, especially the present[4]

39. There is, some say, no present time because when a thing falls, we can know only the time through which it has fallen and the time through which it will yet fall.

40. If there is no present time, there will, it is replied, be no past and future times, because they are related to it.

41. The past and future cannot be established by a mere mutual reference.

42. If there were no present time, sense perception would be impossible, [and therefore no] knowledge would be possible.

[1] One who holds the true doctrine, in this case the follower of the Nyāya school.

[2] One who opposes the accepted doctrine.

[3] The commentary presents many arguments to prove the reality of the composite as distinct from its parts.

[4] It has been asserted (in the *bhāṣya* [commentary], under *sūtra* I.i.5) that inference is applicable to all three points of time because it apprehends the three points of time. Against this also an objection has been raised (by Buddhists); the objection and the reply are given in the following *sūtras*.

Perception is brought about by the contact of the sense-organ with the object; and that which is not present...cannot be in contact with a sense-organ;...

43. We can know both the past and the future, for we can conceive of a thing as [having been] made and as about to be made.

Examination of analogy [comparison]

44. Comparison, some say, is not a means of right knowledge, as it cannot be established either through complete or considerable or partial similarity.

45. This objection does not hold good, for comparison is established through similarity in a high degree.

Examination of testimony (lit., word) in general

49. Verbal testimony, say some, is inference, because the object revealed by it is not perceived but inferred.

52. In reply, we say that there is reliance on the matter signified by a word [testimony], because the word has been used by a reliable person.

Examination of the Veda [word or testimony] in particular, i.e., scripture

57. The Veda, some say, is unreliable, as it involves [in detail] the faults of untruth, contradiction, and tautology.

58. The so-called untruth in the Veda comes from some defect in the act, operator or materials of sacrifice.

59. Contradiction would occur if there were alteration of the time agreed upon.

60. There is no tautology, because reiteration is of advantage.

68. The Veda is reliable like the spell [incantations] and medical science [scripture], because of the reliability of their authors.

Book II—Chapter II

Examination of the fourfold division of the means of right knowledge [pramāṇas]

1. Some say that the means of right knowledge are more than four, because rumour [tradition or hearsay], presumption, probability [deduction], and non-existence [antithesis] are also valid.

2. This, we reply, is no contradiction, since rumour is included in verbal testimony, and presumption, probability, and non-existence are included in inference.

3. Presumption, some say, is not valid, because it leads to uncertainty.

4. We reply: if there is any uncertainty, it is due to your supposing that to be a presumption which is not really so.

Examination of the doctrine of the non-eternality of sound or words [*śabda*][1]

13. Sound is not eternal, because it has a beginning [a cause] and is cognised by our sense and is spoken of as artificial.

14. Some will not accept this argument, because the non-existence of a jar and the genus of it are eternal, and eternal things are also spoken of as if they were artificial.

[E.g., We speak of the part of a self, the part of space, etc., a thing having parts being non-eternal, whereas self and space are admitted to be eternal.]

15. There is, we reply, no opposition because there is distinction between what is really eternal and what is partially eternal, [or: between the real (direct) and the figurative (indirect) denotation of the word "eternal"].

16. It is only the things cognised by our sense as belonging to a certain genus that must, we say, be inferred to be non-eternal.

. . . what we mean is that the fact of sound being apprehended through sense-contact leads to the inference that in every phenomenon of sound there is a series of sounds; and this fact. . . proves that each of these sounds is non-eternal.

18. Sound is non-eternal, because neither do we perceive it before pronunciation, nor do we notice any veil [obstruction] which covers it.[2]

Examination of the nature and potency of words

59. There is doubt as to what a word (noun) really means, as it invariably presents to us an individual, form and genus.[3]

60. Some say that the word (noun) denotes individual, because it is only in respect of individuals that we can use "that," "collection,"

[1] "Word is the assertion of a reliable person," meaning that it is only sound of a particular kind that can be the means of right cognition; which implies that there are several kinds of "sound" [*śabda*]. Now in regard to all this "*śabda*, sound," in general, we proceed to consider whether it is eternal or non-eternal.

[2] That is, so as to explain its non-apprehension.

[3] That is, as inseparable from one another.

"giving," "taking," "number," "waxing," "waning," "colour," "compound" and "propagation."[1]

61. A word (noun) does not denote an individual, because there is no fixation of [restriction to] the latter.

...what is denoted by the word "cow" is not the mere individual by itself, without any qualifications, and as apart from the universal (to which it belongs),—but the individual as qualified by (and along with) the universal....

62. Though a word does not literally bear a certain meaning [referring to an individual], it is used figuratively to convey the same, as in the case of *brāhmin*, scaffold [platform], mat, king, flour, sandalwood, Ganges, cart, food, and man, in consideration of association, place, design, function, measure, containing, vicinity, conjunction, sustenance, and supremacy.

What is meant by "one thing being spoken of as another which is not the same as that" is that a thing is spoken of by means of a word which is not directly expressive of it. For example, in the expression "feed the stick," the word "stick" is applied to the *brāhmin* accompanied by (carrying) the stick, by reason of "association."

63. Some say that the word (noun) denotes form by which an entity is recognised.

64. "Inasmuch as the 'washing' etc. (laid down as to be done to the 'cow') cannot be done to the 'cow' of clay, even though it is endowed with individuality and configuration,—it must be the universal (that is denoted by the word)." [Jha]

65. In reply, we say that it is not genus [universal] alone that is meant by a word (noun), because the manifestation of genus depends on the form and individuality.

66. The meaning of a word (noun) is, according to us, the genus, form and individual.

67. An individual is that which has a definite form and is the abode of particular qualities.

68. The form is that which [indicates or] is called the token of the genus.

69. The "universal" is the cause (or basis) of comprehensive cognition. [Jha]

[1] In all such instances, such as "collection (or group) of cows," "he gives the cows," "the number of cows," etc., the individual entities are referred to.—Ed.

Book V—Chapter I

The futile rejoinders [fallacious opposition]

1. Futilities[1] are as follows:—(1) Balancing the homogeneity, (2) balancing the heterogeneity, (3) balancing an addition, (4) balancing a subtraction, (5) balancing the questionable, (6) balancing the unquestionable, (7) balancing the alternative, (8) balancing the reciprocity, (9) balancing the co-presence, (10) balancing the mutual absence, (11) balancing the infinite regression, (12) balancing the counter-example, (13) balancing the non-produced, (14) balancing the doubt, (15) balancing the controversy, (16) balancing the non-reason, (17) balancing the presumption, (18) balancing the non-difference, (19) balancing the non-demonstration, (20) balancing the perception, (21) balancing the non-perception, (22) balancing the non-eternality, (23) balancing the eternality and (24) balancing the effect.

2. If against an argument based on a homogeneous or heterogeneous example[2] one offers an opposition based on the same kind of example, the opposition will be called "balancing the homogeneity" or "balancing the heterogeneity."

3. The proposition would [should] be established in the same manner as the fact of a certain animal being the "cow" is established by the presence in it of the class-character of the "cow."—[Jha]

If the opposition...is to be valid it must be based on the example, homogeneous or heterogeneous, exhibiting a universal connection between the reason and the predicate such as we discern between a cow and cowhood or a universal disconnection between the reason and the absence of the predicate such as we discern between a cow and absence of cowhood. [S.B.H.]

4. Based upon the difference in the properties of the subject and of the example, there occur (futilities called) "balancing an addition," "balancing a subtraction," "balancing the questionable," "balancing the unquestionable," and "balancing the alternative"; and based upon the fact that [subject and example] both require proof, there occurs "balancing the reciprocity." [Revised translation —Ed.]

[1] Futilities are defined in *sūtra* I.ii.18 as the "offering of objections founded on mere similarity or dissimilarity."

[2] See *sūtras* I.i.36–7.

If against an argument based on a certain character of the example one offers an opposition based on an additional character thereof, the opposition will be called "balancing an addition."

If against an argument based on a certain character of the example one offers an opposition based on another character wanting in it, the opposition will be called "balancing a subtraction."

If one opposes an argument by maintaining that the character of the example is as questionable as that of the subject, the opposition will be called "balancing the questionable."

If one opposes an argument by alleging that the character of the subject is as unquestionable as that of the example, the opposition will be called "balancing the unquestionable."

If one opposes an argument by attributing alternative character to the subject and the example, the opposition will be called "balancing the alternative."

If one opposes an argument by alleging reciprocity—that is, that both subject and example equally require proof—of the subject and the example, the opposition will be called "balancing the reciprocity." [S.B.H.]

5. This is [or: such arguments are], we say, no opposition because there is a difference between the subject and the example although the conclusion is drawn from a certain equality [similarity] of their characters.

7. If, against an argument based on the co-presence of the reason and the predicate or on the mutual absence of them, one offers an opposition based on the same kind of co-presence or mutual absence, the opposition will, on account of the reason being non-distinguished from or being-non-conducive to the predicate, be called "balancing the co-presence" or "balancing the mutual absence."

Is it by becoming united with the *probandum* (proposition) that the *probans* (reason) would establish it? Or by not becoming united with it? It cannot establish it by becoming united with it; because by becoming united with it, it would become non-different from it, and as such could not establish it. When of two things both are existent, and become united, —which could be the "*probans*" (reason), the "establisher," and which the "*probandum*" (proposition), the "established"? If, on the other hand, the *probans* (reason) does not become united with the *probandum* (proposition)—then (on that very account) it could not establish it;...

8. This is, we say, no opposition because we find the production of pots by means of clay as well as the oppression of persons by spells.

Neither of the above rejoinders is valid, because there are instances (1) where the cause (the potter) is present with the clay to produce the jar, and (2) where the cause (the exorcist) is absent from the effect (the person whom he kills by means of a spell administered from a distance).[1]

[1] This is a free rendering of a difficult passage.

9. If one opposes an argument on the ground of the example having been established by a series of reasons or on the ground of the existence of a mere counter-example, the opposition will be called "balancing the infinite regression" or "balancing the counter-example."

10. The example does not, we say, require a series of reasons for its establishment just as a lamp does not require a series of lamps to be brought in for its illumination.

11. The example, we say, cannot be set aside as unreasonable only because a counter-example is advanced as the reason.

[or]

If the counter-example is an effective reason, the example also cannot but be an effective reason. [Jha]

12. If one opposes an argument on the ground that the property connoted by the reason is absent from the thing denoted by the subject while the subject is not yet produced, the opposition will be called "balancing the non-produced."

13. [Answer:] Since it is only when it has been produced that the thing is what it is, and since what is urged as the ground (for the proposition) does then subsist in it,—the presence of the ground cannot be denied. [Jha]

14. If one opposes an argument on the ground of a doubt arising from the homogeneity of the eternal and the non-eternal because the example and its genus (or type) are equally objects of perception, the opposition will be called "balancing the doubt."

The opponent alleges that sound is homogeneous with a pot as well as pot-ness inasmuch as both are objects of perception; but since the pot is non-eternal and pot-ness (the genus of pots or pot-type) is eternal there arises a doubt as to whether the sound is non-eternal or eternal. [S.B.H., with slight revision.]

15. This is, we say, no opposition because we do not admit that eternality can be established by the homogeneity with the genus: a doubt that arises from a knowledge of the homogeneity vanishes from that of the heterogeneity, and that which arises in both ways never ends.

Sound cannot be said to be eternal on the mere ground of its homogeneity with pot-ness (the genus of pots or pot-type) but must be pronounced to be non-eternal on the ground of its heterogeneity from the same in respect of being a product. [S.B.H.]

16. By reason of similarity to both, there arises vacillation—(opposition) based upon this reasoning is ["balancing the controversy"].[1] [Jha]

By reason of the similarity (of sound) to both, eternal and non-eternal things, there is likelihood of the two contrary views [i.e., the original proposition as well as its contrary];—this is what is meant by the term "vacillation."...

17. This is, we say, no opposition because it provokes a controversy which has an opposing side.

...The opposition called "balancing the controversy" cannot set aside the main argument because it leads to a controversy which supports one side quite as strongly as it is opposed by the other side. [S.B.H.]

18. "Balancing the non-reason" is an opposition which is based on the reason being shown to be impossible at all the three times.

The reason or sign is impossible at all the three times because it cannot [as a significant reason for the predicate] precede, succeed, or be simultaneous with the predicate or significate. [S.B.H.]

19. There is, we say, no impossibility at the three times because the predicate or significate is established by the reason or sign.

...we find that the accomplishing of what is to be accomplished, as also the knowing of what is to be known, is brought about by a cause;... [similarly] the cause [i.e., the reason] is the means of accomplishing what is to be accomplished, and of the knowing of what is to be made known.

20. There is, we further say, no opposition of that which is to be opposed, because the opposition itself is impossible at all the three times.

...[Similarly] the denial cannot exist, either before, or after, or together with, what is denied—and since there can be no "denial" at all (of the reason urged by the first party), it follows that the reason (being undeniable) is firmly established.

21. If one advances an opposition on the basis of a presumption, the opposition will be called "balancing the presumption."

[For example,] the opponent alleges that if sound is non-eternal on account of its homogeneity with non-eternal things (e.g., in respect of its being a product), it may be concluded by presumption that sound is eternal on account of its homogeneity with eternal things (e.g., in respect of its being incorporeal). [S.B.H.]

[1] Such brackets here and in succeeding passages indicate that the names of the types of fallacies, etc., used in S.B.H. have been substituted for those used by Jha.

22. If things unsaid could come by presumption, there would, we say, arise a possibility of the opposition itself being hurt on account of the presumption being erratic and conducive to an unsaid conclusion.

...If one says that "sound is non-eternal because of its homogeneity with non-eternal things," the presumption that naturally follows is that "sound is eternal because of its homogeneity with eternal things" and *vice versa.* There is no rule that presumption should be made in one case and not in the case opposed to it; and in the event of two mutually opposed presumptions no definite conclusion would follow. [S.B.H.]

23. "If the presence of a single (common) property were to make the two things non-different,—then all things would have to be regarded as non-different, because the property of 'existence' is present in all";—this contention constitutes ["balancing the non-different"]. [Jha]

The single (common property, in the case in question, is that of coming after effort; and because this single property is present in sound and in the jar, if these two things be regarded as non-different,—i.e., both be regarded as "non-eternal";—then all things should have to be regarded as non-different....

24. The above denial does not hold; because in the case of some (common property) the presence of certain (other properties) of the similar thing is possible, while in the case of others such presence is not possible. [Jha]

25. ["Balancing the demonstration"] is based upon the presence of grounds for both (views). [Jha]

26. This denial has no force; because the presence of ground in support (of the original proposition) is admitted. [Jha]

27. If an opposition is offered on the ground that we perceive the character of the subject even without the intervention of the reason, the opposition will be called "balancing the perception."

28. Inasmuch as the property in question may be due to some other cause,—the denial has no force at all. [Jha]

29. If against an argument proving the non-existence of a thing by the non-perception thereof, one offers an opposition aiming at proving the contrary by the non-perception of the non-perception, the opposition will be called "balancing the non-perception."

30. The reasoning through non-perception is not, we say, sound, because non-perception is merely the negation of perception.

32. If by reason of "similarity" two things be regarded as having

analogous properties, then all things should have to be regarded as "non-eternal,"—this contention constitutes ["balancing the non-eternality"]. [Jha]

"When the first party says that—'Sound should be regarded as non-eternal, by reason of its similarity to the jar, which is non-eternal,'—he becomes faced with the undesirable contingency of having to regard all things as non-eternal, by reason of their similarity (consisting of existence) to the jar, which is non-eternal."[1]

33. If rejection can be based upon "similarity," there should be rejection also of the denial (set up by the opponent), as there is a similarity between the denial and that which it is sought to deny. [Jha]

. . . the said "denial" has this similarity to the original view that both are equipped with the factors of reasoning, proposition and the rest. . . .

34. What serves as the reason is that property which is definitely known to subsist in the example, as being an infallible indicator of the proposition; and since such a reason can be of both kinds, there can be no non-difference (among all things). [Jha]

35. If one opposes an argument by attributing eternality to all non-eternal things on the ground of these being eternally non-eternal, the opposition will be called "balancing the eternal."

36. Inasmuch as the everlasting character of the "non-eternality" in the subject of denial (sound) [is admitted by the opponent], the "non-eternality" of the non-eternal thing (sound) becomes established; so that there can be no basis for the denial. [Jha]

37. If one opposes an argument by showing the diversity of the effect of efforts, the opposition will be called "balancing the effect."

. . . "Coming into existence after effort" we find in the case of the jar, etc., and we also find the "manifestation" of things concealed under some obstruction, by the removal of the obstruction [and this also is the outcome of effort]; and there is no special reason to show whether sound comes into existence after effort, or there is only manifestation of it (after effort); and the opposition set up on the basis of this fact of both these (production and manifestation) being equally the "products of effort," is ["balancing the effect"].

38. Effort did not give rise to the second kind of effect [e.g., manifestation], because there was no cause of non-perception.

[or]

Effort cannot be regarded as the cause (of the manifestation of

[1] This is a free reading of the commentary.

sound), as there is not present (in the case of sound) any cause of its non-apprehension.

39. The same defect, we say, attaches to the opposition too.

. . . if an argument is to be set aside owing to an ambiguous meaning of the word "effect," why is not the opposition too set aside on the same ground? . . . [S.B.H.]

40. The same may be said by the first party in answer to all (futile rejoinders). [Jha]

In connection with all that may be taken as the basis of the futile rejoinders—e.g., "similarity" and the rest—whenever no special corroborative reason may be found—the contention may be put forward (by the first party) that both views stand on the same footing.

41. Defect attaches to the opposition of the opposition just as it attaches to the opposition.

42. If one admits the defect of his opposition in consequence of his statement that an equal defect attaches to the opposition of the opposition, it will be called "admission of an opinion" [or: "confession of the contrary opinion"].

43. "Admission of an opinion" also occurs when the disputant, instead of employing reasons to rescue his side from the defect with which it has been charged, proceeds to admit the defect in consequence of his statement that the same defect belongs to his opponent's side as well.

Book V—Chapter II

Examination of clinchers and causes for rebuke

1. The occasions for rebuke are the following:—(1) hurting the proposition, (2) shifting the proposition, (3) opposing the proposition, (4) renouncing the proposition, (5) shifting the reason, (6) shifting the topic, (7) the meaningless, (8) the unintelligible, (9) the incoherent, (10) the inopportune, (11) saying too little, (12) saying too much, (13) repetition, (14) silence, (15) ignorance, (16) non-ingenuity, (17) evasion, (18) admission of an opinion, (19) overlooking the censurable, (20) censuring the non-censurable, (21) deviating from a tenet, and (22) the semblance of a reason.

2. "Hurting the proposition" occurs when one admits in one's own example the character of a counter-example.

3. "Shifting the proposition" arises [when] upon the instance of

one's proposition being opposed one defends it by importing a new character to one's example and counter-example.

4. "Opposing the proposition" occurs when the proposition and its reason are opposed to each other.

5. A proposition being opposed, if one disclaims its import, it will be called "renouncing the proposition."

6. "Shifting the reason" occurs when, the reason of a general character being opposed, one attaches a special character to it.

7. "Shifting the topic" is an argument which, setting aside the real topic, introduces one which is irrelevant.

8. "The meaningless" is an argument which is based on a non-sensical combination of letters into a series.[1]

9. "The unintelligible" is an argument, which, although repeated three times, is understood neither by the audience nor by the opponent.

10. "The incoherent" is an argument which conveys no connected meaning on account of the words being strung together without any syntactical order.

11. "The inopportune" is an argument the parts of which are mentioned without any order of precedence.

12. If an argument lacks even one of its parts [or: is wanting in any one of the factors of reasoning], it is called "saying too little" [or: "the incomplete"].

13. "Saying too much" ["the redundant"] is an argument which consists of more than one reason or [and/or] example.

14. "Repetition" is an argument in which (except in the case of reinculcation] the word or the meaning is said over again.

15. "Repetition" consists also in mentioning a thing by name although the thing has been indicated through presumption.

16. "Silence" is an occasion for rebuke which arises when the opponent makes no reply to a proposition although it has been repeated three times by the disputant within the knowledge of the audience.

17. "Ignorance" is the non-understanding of a proposition.

18. "Non-ingenuity" consists in one's inability to hit upon a reply.

19. "Evasion" arises if one stops an argument on the pretext of going away to attend another business.

[1] An example is the effort to convince in a foreign language a person ignorant of that language.

20. If the party admits the flaw in his own thesis, and then urges the same in that of the opponent,—this is a case of ["the admission of an opinion"]. [Jha]

21. "Overlooking the censurable" consists in not rebuking a person who deserves rebuke.

22. "Censuring the non-censurable" consists in rebuking a person who does not deserve rebuke.

23. A person who, after accepting a tenet, departs from it in the course of his disputation, is guilty of "deviating from a tenet."

24. "The fallacies of reason" already explained[1] do also furnish occasions for rebuke.

B. *NYĀYA KUSUMĀÑJALI*

Now although with regard to that Being whom all men alike worship, whichever of the (four well-known) ends of man[2] they may desire,—(thus the followers of the Upaniṣads [worship it] as the very knower,—the disciples of Kapila as the perfect first Wise,—those of Patañjali as Him who, untouched by pain, action, fruit or desert, having assumed a body in order to create, revealed the tradition of the Veda and is gracious to all living beings,—the Mahāpāśupatas[3] as the Independent one, undefiled by vaidic [Vedic] or secular violations,—the Śaivas as Śiva,—the Vaiṣṇavas[4] as Puruṣottama,—the followers of the Purāṇas[5] as the great Father (Brahmā),—the Ceremonialists as the Soul of the sacrifice,—the Saugatas[6] as the Omniscient,—the Jainas as the Unobstructed,—the Mīmāṁsakas as Him who is pointed out as to be worshipped,—the Cārvākas as Him who is established by the conventions of the world,—the followers of the Nyāya as Him who is all that is said worthy of Him,—why farther detail? whom even the artizans themselves worship as the great artizan, Viśvakarman)—although, I say, with regard to that Being, the adorable Śiva, whom all recognise throughout the world as universally acknowledged like castes, families, family invocations of Agni, schools, social customs, &c., how can there arise any doubt? and what then is there to be ascertained? (Introductory commentary, I.3.)

I.3. Still this logical investigation may be well called the contemplation of God, and this is really worship when it follows the hearing of the *śruti* ([revealed scriptures]).[7]

[1] See above, *sūtras* I.ii.4–9.

[2] That is, righteousness (*dharma*), wealth (*artha*), pleasure (*kāma*), and liberation (*mokṣa*).

[3] Members of an ancient religious sect.

[4] Followers of Viṣṇu.

[5] Ancient legendary texts.

[6] Members of an ancient religious sect.

[7] Brackets within parentheses indicate additions made by the editors. Brackets alone are those of the translator.

Therefore that adorable one who hath been often heard mentioned in the *śruti*, *smṛti* ([traditional texts]), narrative poems, Purāṇas, &c., must now be contemplated, according to such a *śruti* as "He is to be heard and to be contemplated," and such a *smṛti* as "by the Veda, inference and the delight of continued meditation,—in this threefold manner producing knowledge, a man obtains the highest concentration." Now there is, in short, a fivefold opposition to our theory,—based, first, on the non-existence of any supernatural cause of another world (as *adṛṣṭa*, the merit and demerit of our actions);[1]—or secondly, on the possibility of our putting in action certain causes of another world (as sacrifices),[2] even if God be allowed to be non-existent;—or thirdly, on the existence of proofs which show the non-existence of God;—or fourthly, on the opinion that, even if God does exist, he cannot be a cause of true knowledge to us;—or fifthly, on the absence of any argument to prove his existence.[3]

I.4 From dependence,—from eternity,—from diversity,—from universal practice,—and from the apportionment to each individual self, —mundane enjoyment implies a supernatural cause [i.e., "desert"].

Our proposition is that there exists a supernatural cause of another world, i.e., a cause beyond the reach of the senses. (*a*) First of all, then, to establish the class of causes in general, he says, "from dependence." Dependence means here that the effect is occasional. All effects must have a cause since they are occasional, like the gratification produced by food; [otherwise, if they did not depend on a cause, they could be found anywhere and always], (*b*) ([Objection:]) "But if the cause of a jar, &c. were eternal, would it not follow that the jar, &c. would also be eternal, and therefore we must assume the jar's cause to be itself only occasional, and therefore the perpetual series of causes must be all occasional, each dependent on its previous cause?" To meet this objection of a *regressus ad infinitum*, he says, "from the eternity [of the succession of cause and effect]," like the continued series of seed and shoot,—the meaning being that a *regressus ad infinitum* ceases to be a fault, if, like this one alleged in our illustration, it can be proved by the evidence of our senses. (*c*) ([Objection:]) "But [if you require a cause], why not say [with the Vedāntin] that *Brahma* ([*Brahman*]) alone is the cause, or [with the Sāṁkhya] Nature in the form of various individual intellects"? To meet this, he says, "from the diversity [of effects, as heaven, hell, &c.]"—as the effects imply a diversity of causes, from their being diverse as effects. (*d*) ([Objection:]) "But why not accept a visible cause as sacrifices, &c.—why have recourse to an invisible desert (*adṛṣṭa*)?" To meet this, he adds, "from the universal

[1] That is, there is no supernatural cause of rewards and punishments, corresponding to the merits and demerits of our actions, a cause that is called "*adṛṣṭa*" (an unseen force) in some systems.

[2] That is, sacrificial offerings may bring about rewards and punishments.

[3] The five objections serve as the topics of the five chapters of the *Kusumāñjali*. All of the objections are considered in the text in full detail. In the selections given here, only the main statements in reply to the objections are given.

practice," i.e., from the fact that all men, desiring fruit in another world, do engage in sacrifices, &c. It is only the conviction that they do produce heaven, &c. as their fruit, which makes men engage in sacrifices, &c.; and these [passing away when the action is over] cannot produce this fruit unless by means of some influence which continues to act after the rite is over,—and hence is this invisible influence, called merit or demerit, established. (*e*) ([Objection:]) "But why not say that this desert does not reside in the same subject as the enjoyment [i.e., the individual self], but produces the enjoyment by abiding in the thing enjoyed?" He replies, "from the apportionment to each self." Since the enjoyment resides in each word severally, we should be unwarranted to attribute its production to a desert residing elsewhere.

The second objection was that there is no proof of God, since the means of attaining paradise can be practised independently of any such being. That is to say "sacrifices, which are the instruments of obtaining paradise, can be performed even without a God, since it is proved in the Veda that sacrifices are a means of obtaining heaven, and the Veda possesses authority from its eternity and freedom from defects, and we can also gather its authority from its having been accepted by great saints [as Manu and others] and therefore you cannot establish the existence of God on the ground that he is the author of the Veda; or we may suppose that the Veda was made by sages like Kapila and others, who gained omniscience by their preeminence in concentrated devotion."—He replies, (Introductory commentary, II.1.)

II.1. Since right knowledge requires an external source, since creation and destruction take place, and since none other than He can be relied on,—there is no other way open.

The right knowledge caused by testimony is one which is produced by a quality in the speaker, viz., his knowledge of the exact meaning of the words used; hence the existence of God is proved, as he must be the subject of such a quality in the case of the Veda. ([Objection:]) "But may we not allow that such a quality as the knowledge of the exact meaning of the words used is required in the case of an effect which implies an agent; but in the case of the uncreated Veda it is its freedom from defects which produces its authoritativeness, and we can know its authoritativeness from its having been accepted by great saints?" He replies, "because creation and destruction take place." After a mundane destruction, when the former Veda is destroyed, how can the subsequent Veda possess authority, since there will then be no possibility of its having been accepted by great saints?... ([Objection:]) "Well, then, let us say that at the beginning of a creation Kapila and others were its authors, who had acquired omniscience by the power of merit gained by the practice of concentrated devotion in the former aeon." He replies, "none other than He can be relied on." If you mean by omniscient beings, those endowed with the various superhuman faculties of assuming infinitesimal size, &c. and capable of creating everything, then we reply that the law of parsimony bids us assume only one such, namely Him, the adorable Lord. There can be no confidence in a non-eternal and non-omniscient being, and hence it follows that according to the system which rejects God, the tradition of the Veda is simultaneously overthrown,—"there is no other way open."

The third objection was that there were positive arguments to prove God's non-existence. "Just as we infer a jar's absence in a given space of ground [i.e., its non-existence there,] so we infer God's non-existence from His not being perceived. If you reply that 'the Supreme Being is not a legitimate object of perception, and, therefore, since we cannot here have a valid non-perception, we cannot assume His non-existence,'—we retort that in the same way we might prove that a hare's horns may exist since we have only to maintain that it is not a legitimate object of our perception." He answers, (Introductory commentary, III.1.)

III.1. In an illegitimate object [of perception] how can there be a valid non-perception? and still more, how can you establish your contradiction? How can the hare's horn be precluded as absurd if it is an illegitimate object? and how can you have an inference without a subject to base it on?

In the case of the Supreme Being who is not a legitimate object, how can there be a valid non-perception?. It is only *this* which precludes a thing's existence; but the absence of perception which obtains in the case of God cannot exert this precluding influence, as otherwise we should equally be forced to deny the existence of ether, merit, demerit, &c. But a horn must be a legitimate object of perception,—how then can your retort contradict our argument? If you say that a hare's horn is an illegitimate object of perception, then of course its existence is not necessarily precluded,—there is only an absence of proof to establish it; but this cannot be retorted against *us* as the fifth Cluster ([chapter]) will fully show that there are positive arguments to establish God's existence. ([Objection:]) "But may we not infer God's non-existence from the absence, in His case, of a body, and also of any assignable motive for action?" He replies,—how can you have an inference where the minor term is itself controverted? while on the other hand the very proof which will establish the existence of the subject (God) is itself sufficient to debar your subsequent inference [that there is no God].

The fourth objection was that even if God did exist, he could not be a cause of right knowledge to us. "God cannot be an authority to us, because he has no right knowledge, as his knowledge lacks the indispensable characteristic of cognizing an object uncognized before; hence he neither possesses right knowledge himself nor can produce it in us, and who would trust the words of a being who cannot be a cause of right knowledge?" He replies, (Introductory commentary, IV.1.)

IV.1. Cognizing for the first time is no true mark, as it is both too narrow and too wide; we hold right knowledge to be an independent impression which corresponds to the reality.

Your "cognizing an object uncognized before" is not an indispensable characteristic mark of right knowledge, as it fails to apply in such an affirmative instance as repeated knowledge [i.e., seeing a thing a second or third time], and wrongly applies to such a negative instance as the erroneous judgment that "this [nacre before me] is silver."...

([Objection:]) "May we not, however, still maintain that God's knowledge is not properly 'right knowledge' since it is not produced by proof; and therefore God can neither be a right knower Himself nor be a cause of right knowledge to us, since the essential conditions for both are absent in Him?" He replies, (Introductory commentary, IV.5.)

IV.5. Right knowledge is accurate comprehension and right knowing is the possession thereof; authoritativeness is, according to Gautama's school ([Nyāya]), the being separated from all absence thereof.

Right knowledge is a notion corresponding to the object; and this is not inconsistent with God's knowledge, even though His knowing be not produced [but eternal]. "Right knowing"...means the being connected with right knowledge by intimate relation...and this can be established of God, even though He be not a cause of right knowledge to us. In the same way God is an authority as being Himself ever connected with right knowledge, i.e., as being ever "separated from all absence thereof." There is no need to include as absolutely necessary in your definition that He must be an instrument of right knowledge to others, since God's authoritativeness is thus declared in the *Nyāya Sūtra* (II.i.68). "The fact of the Veda being an authority [i.e., an instrument of right knowledge], like the spells [against poison, &c.,] and the medical science, follows from the authoritativeness of the fit person (who gave it)."...

The fifth objection was "from the absence of positive proof." "May we not say that there are no proofs to establish God's existence?" He replies, (Introductory commentary, V.1.)

V.1. From effects, combination, support, &c., traditional arts, authoritativeness, *śruti* (revealed scriptures), the sentences thereof, and particular numbers,—an everlasting omniscient Being is to be established.

(*a*) The earth, &c., must have had a maker because they have the nature of "effects," like a jar; by a thing's having a maker we mean that it is produced by some agent who possesses the wish to make, and has also a perceptive knowledge of the material cause out of which it is to be made. (*b*) "Combination" is an action, and therefore the action which produced the conjunction of two atoms, initiating the binary compound, at the beginning of a creation, must have been accompanied by the volition of an intelligent being, because it has the nature of an action, like the actions of bodies such as ours. (*c*) "Support, &c." The world depends upon some being who possesses a volition which hinders it from falling, because it has the nature of being supported, like a stick supported by a bird in the air; by being supported we mean the absence of falling in the case of bodies possessing weight. By the "&c." we include destruction. Thus the world can be destroyed by a being possessed of volition, because it is destructible, like cloth which is rent. (*d*) "From traditional arts."...The traditional arts now current, as that of making cloth, &c., must have been originated by an independent being, from the very fact that they are traditional usages like the tradition of modern modes of writing [invented by men independently, as systems of short-hand, &c.]. (*e*) "From authoritativeness." The knowledge produced by the Veda is produced by a virtue residing in its cause, because it is right knowledge, just as is the case in the right knowledge produced by perception, &c. (*f*) "From *śruti*," i.e., the Veda. The Veda must have been produced by a person from its having the nature of a Veda like the *Āyur Veda* [...treating of medical science]. (*g*) Again, the Veda must have been produced by a person because it has the nature of "sentences," like the *Mahābhārata*; or, in other words, the sentences of the Veda were produced by a person because they have the nature of sentences, just as the sentences of beings like ourselves. (*h*) "From particular numbers." The measure of a binary compound is produced by number since it is a derived [not eternal] measure and at the same time is not produced by measure or aggregation,...the measure of an atom does not produce measure because its measure is eternal [and therefore incapable of change] or because it is the measure of an atom. Hence at the beginning of a creation there must be the number of duality abiding in the atoms, which is the cause of the measure of the binary compound, but this number cannot be produced at that time by the distinguishing perception of beings like ourselves. Therefore we can only assume this distinguishing faculty as then existing in God.—By the last words of the text it is meant that it is the Being, possessed of this attribute [of omniscience], who is everlasting, and hence is established his eternal omniscience.

([Objection:]) "But how does the fact of a thing's being an effect necessitate that it should have been produced by volition?" He replies, (Introductory commentary, v.4.)

v.4. If it [the atom] acts independently, it ceases to be brute matter; if there be no cause there is no effect; a particular effect has a particular cause.

There cannot be an effect without a causer. If the atom were endued with volition it would follow that the atom was intelligent, since an unintelligent thing can produce an effect only when impelled by an intelligent being;...

v.6. Activity is really volition, and this springs from the desire to act, and this from knowledge, and the object of this knowledge is a command, or [as he would hold] it is rather that which causes a command to be inferred.

v.14. The primary meaning of the potential used imperatively, &c., ([i.e., the true meaning of a command]) is the will of the speaker in the form of a command enjoining activity or cessation therefrom, while we conclude by inference that it is the means to a desired end for the doer.

The will of a fit person, i.e., God, having for its object engagement in the performance of an act [i.e., as in command] or refraining therefrom [i.e., as in prohibition], is the primary meaning of the affix of the potential, &c.; and from these is to be inferred that it is the means to obtain a desired end, [and hence the existence of "command" proves the existence of a commander, God...].

CHAPTER XI

VAIŚEṢIKA

THIS system takes its name from "*viśeṣa*" (particularity); it emphasizes the significance of particulars or individuals, and is decidedly pluralistic. The Vaiśeṣika is mainly a system of physics and metaphysics. It adopts a sixfold classification of the objects of experience (*padārthas*): substance, quality, activity, generality, particularity, and inherence, to which later Vaiśeṣikas added a seventh, non-existence. We find that three of these (substance, quality, and activity) possess real objective existence and we can intuit them; the others (generality, particularity, and inherence) are the products of intellectual discrimination. They are logically inferred, not directly perceived.

Reality consists of substances possessed of qualities. Substances are substrates of qualities, but are distinct from the qualities which they possess. Earth, water, light, air, ether (*ākāśa*), time, space, soul (or self), and mind are the nine substances which comprise all corporeal and incorporeal things.

The existence of soul is inferred from the fact that consciousness cannot be a property of the body, the sense-organs, or the mind. Though the soul is all-pervading, its life of knowing, feeling, and willing resides only where the body is. The plurality of souls is inferred from their differences in status and their variety of conditions. Each soul experiences the consequences of its own deeds, and the Vaiśeṣika system uses this fact as proof of the plurality of souls. Each soul has its characteristic individuality (*viśeṣa*). Even the freed souls exist with specific features.

The Vaiśeṣika adopts the atomic view. Things are composed of invisible eternal atoms which are incapable of division. There are four kinds of atoms: earth, water, light, and air.

The Vaiśeṣika has been regarded as non-theistic. Kaṇāda (or Kāśyapa), the author of the *Vaiśeṣika Sūtra* (much older than Nyāya but later than 300 B.C.), does not mention God, but later commentators felt that the immutable atoms could not by themselves produce an ordered universe unless a presiding God regulated their activities. The authorship of the Vedas and the conventions of the meanings of words also require us to postulate a prime mover. The world cannot be explained by the activities of the atoms alone or by the operation of *karma*. The system therefore adopts the view of God which is found in the Nyāya.

The selections are taken from (A) *The Vaiśeṣika Sūtras of Kaṇāda*, with the *Commentary* of Śaṁkara Miśra, extracts from the *Gloss* of Jayanārāyaṇa, and the *Bhaṣya* of Candrakānta, translated by Nandalal Sinha, The Sacred Books of the Hindus, vi (Allahabad: The Panini Office, 2nd ed., 1923); (B) *The Padārthadharmasaṁgraha of Praśastapāda* (4th century A.D.), with the *Nyāyakandalī* (A.D. 991) of Śrīdhara, translated by Ganganatha Jha (Allahabad: E. J. Lazarus & Co., 1916).

Topics, such as logic and related subjects, which are treated extensively in the selections from the Nyāya system are not included in any detail here.

A. THE *VAIŚEṢIKA SŪTRA*

Book I—Chapter 1

1. Now, therefore, we shall explain *dharma* (righteousness).

2. *Dharma* (is) that from which (results) the accomplishment of exaltation and of the supreme good.

3. The authoritativeness of the Veda (arises from its) being the Word of God [or being an exposition of *dharma*].[1]

4. The Supreme Good [of the Predicables] (results) from the knowledge, produced by a particular *dharma*, of the essence of the predicables, substance, attribute, action, genus, species, and combination [inherence], by means of their resemblances and differences.

5. Earth, water, fire, air, ether, time, space, self (or soul), and mind (are) the only substances.

6. Attributes are color, taste, smell, and touch, numbers, measures, separateness, conjunction and disjunction, priority and posteriority, understandings, pleasure and pain, desire and aversion, and volitions.

7. Throwing upwards, throwing downwards, contraction, expansion, and motion are actions.

8. The resemblance of substance, attribute, and action lies in this that they are existent and non-eternal, have substance as their combinative cause, are effect as well as cause, and are both genus and species.

9. The resemblance of substance and attribute is the characteristic of being the originators of their congeners.[2]

10. Substances originate another substance, and attributes another attribute.

[1] The text does not use the word "God." It uses "*tat*" which means "that."

[2] A preferable translation would be: The resemblance between substances [and substance] and between attribute [and attributes] lies in their giving rise to [members of] their own class.

11. Action, producible by action, is not known.

12. Substance is not annihilated either by effect or by cause.

13. Attributes (are destroyed) in both ways.

14. Action is opposed by its effect.

15. It possesses action and attribute, it is a combinative cause—such (is) the mark of substance.

16. Inhering in substance, not possessing attribute, not an independent cause in conjunctions and disjunctions,—such is the mark of attribute.

17. Residing in one substance only, not possessing attribute, an independent cause of conjunctions and disjunctions—such is the mark of action.

18. Substance is the one and the same cause of substance, attribute, and action.

19. Similarly attribute (is the common cause of substance, attribute, and action).

20. Action is the common cause of conjunction, disjunction, and impetus.

21. Action is not the cause of substances.

22. (Action is not the cause of substance) because of its cessation.

23. A single substance may be the common effect of more than one substance.

25. Duality and other numbers, separateness, conjunction, and disjunction (are originated by more than one substance).

27. Substance is the joint effect of many conjunctions.

29. Throwing upwards (is the joint product) of gravity, volition, and conjunction.

30. Conjunctions and disjunctions also (are individually the products) of actions.

31. Under the topic of causes in general, action has been stated to be not a cause of substances and actions.

Book I—Chapter 2

1. Non-existence of effect (follows) from the non-existence of cause.

2. But non-existence of cause (does) not (follow) from the non-existence of the effect.

3. The notions, genus and species, are relative to the understanding.

4. Existence, being the cause of assimilation only, is only a genus.

5. Substantiality, and attribute-ness and action-ness are both genera and species.

6. (The statement of genus and species has been made) with the exception of the final species.

7. Existence is that to which are due the belief and usage, namely "(it is) existent," in respect of substance, attribute, and action.

8. Existence is a different object from substance, attribute, and action.

9. And as it exists in attributes and actions, therefore it is neither attribute nor action.

10. (Existence is different from substance, attribute, and action) also by reason of the absence of genus-species in it.

12. (Substantiality is distinct from substance, attribute, and action) also by reason of the absence of genera-species in it.

13. (That attribute-ness is distinct from substance, attribute, and action is) explained from its existence in attributes.

14. (Attribute-ness is distinct from substance, attribute, and action) also by reason of the absence of genera-species in it.

16. (Action-ness is distinct from substance, attribute, and action) also by reason of the absence of genera-species in it.

17. Existence is one, because of the uniformity of the mark, viz., that it is existent and because of the absence of any distinguishing mark.

Book II—Chapter 1

1. Earth possesses color, taste, smell, and touch.

2. Waters possess color, taste, and touch, and are fluid and viscid.

3. Fire possesses color and touch.

4. Air possesses touch.

5. These (characteristics) are not in ether.

9. And touch (is a mark) of air.

11. Air is a substance, because it does not contain or reside in substance.

13. The eternality (of air) is evident from its not combining with other substances.

18. But name and effect are the mark (of the existence) of beings distinguished from ourselves.

19. Because name and effect follow from perception.

20. Egress and ingress—such is the mark (of the existence) of ether.

23. Action is not produced on account of conjunction.

24. The attribute of the effect is seen to be preceded by the attribute of the cause.

25. Sound is not an attribute of things possessing touch, because of the non-appearance of (similar) other effects.

26. Because it combines with other objects, and because it is an object of sense-perception, therefore sound is neither an attribute of self nor an attribute of mind.

27. By the method of exhaustion (sound) is the mark of ether.

29. The unity (of ether is explained) by (the explanation of the unity of) existence.

30. (Ether is one), because there is no difference in sound which is its mark, and because there exists no other distinguishing mark.

31. And individuality also belongs to ether, since individuality follows unity.

Book II—Chapter 2

2. Smell is established in earth.

4. Hotness (is the characteristic) of fire.

5. Coldness (is the characteristic) of water.

6. "Posterior" in respect of that which is posterior, "simultaneous," "slow," "quick,"—such (cognitions) are the marks of time.

7. The substantiality and eternality (of time) are explained by (the explanation of the substantiality and eternality of) air.

8. The unity (of time is explained), by (the explanation of the unity of) existence.

9. The name time is applicable to a cause, inasmuch as it does not exist in eternal substances and exists in non-eternal substances.

10. That which gives rise to such (cognition and usage) as "This (is remote, etc.) from this,"—(the same is) the mark of space.

11. The substantiality and eternality (of space are) explained by (the explanation of the substantiality and eternality of) air.

12. The unity (of space is explained) by (the explanation of the unity of) existence.

21. Sound is that object of which the organ of apprehension is the ear.

23. (Sound) is not a substance, since it resides in one substance only.

25. The resemblance (of sound), although it is an attribute, with actions, consists in its speedy destruction.

26. (Sound does not exist before utterance), because there is no mark of (sound as) existent (before utterance),

27. (Sound is not something which only requires to be brought to light), because it differs in property from what is eternal.

28. And sound is non-eternal (because it is observed to be produced) by a cause.

29. Nor is (the dependence of sound upon a cause) disproved by its modifications.

30. (Sound is not eternal), because the theory that it requires to be revealed only will entail a defect.

31. Sound is produced from conjunction, from disjunction, and from sound also.

32. Sound is non-eternal also because of its mark.

37. The existence of number (in sound) is with reference to the genus.

Book III—Chapter 1

1. The objects of the senses are universally known.

2. The universal experience of the objects of the senses is the mark of (the existence of an) object different from the senses and their objects.

3. Perception (as a mark inferring the body or the senses as its substratum) (is) a false mark.

4. (The body or the senses cannot be the seat of perception), because there is no consciousness in the causes [i.e., the component parts, of the body].

5. Because (there would be) consciousness in the effects.

6. And because it is not known (that any minute degree of consciousness exists in the water-pot, etc.).

8. (Although a mark is quite different from that of which it is a mark, still they are not wholly unconnected), for any one thing cannot be a mark of any other thing.

19. And activity and inactivity, observed in one's own self, are the marks of (the existence of) other selves.

Book III—Chapter 2

1. The appearance and non-appearance of knowledge, on contact of the self with the senses and the objects are the marks (of the existence) of the mind.

2. The substantiality and eternality of mind are explained by (the explanation of the substantiality and eternality of) air.

3. From the non-simultaneity of volitions, and from the non-simultaneity of cognitions, (it follows that there is only) one (mind) (in each organism).

4. The ascending life-breath, the descending life-breath, the closing of the eye-lids, the opening of the eye-lids, life, the movement of the mind, and the affections of the other senses, and also pleasure, pain, desire, aversion, and volition are marks (of the existence) of the self.

5. Its substantiality and eternality are explained by (the explanation of the substantiality and eternality of) air.

6. There is no visible mark (of the existence of the self), because there being contact (of the senses with the body of Yajñadatta) perception does not arise (that this self is Yajñadatta).

7. And from a commonly-observed mark (there is) no (inference of anything in) particular.

8. Therefore (the self is) proved by revelation.

9. (The proof of the existence of the self is not solely) from revelation, because of the non-application of the word "I" (to other designates or objects).

10. If (there are) such sensuous observations (or perceptions) as "I am Devadatta," "I am Yajñadatta," (then there is no need of inference).

11. As in the case of other percepts, so, if the self, which is grasped by perception, is also accompanied with, or comes at the top of, marks (from which it can be inferred), then, by means of confirmation, the intuition becomes fastened to one and only one object.

12. "Devadatta goes," "Yajñadatta goes,"—in these cases, the belief (that their respective bodies go) is due to transference.

13. The transference, however, is doubtful.

14. Because the intuition "I" exists in one's own self, and because it does not exist otherwise, therefore the intuition has the individual self as the object of perception.

18. (The self is) not proved (only) by revelation, since, (as ether is proved by sound, so) (the self is) proved in particular by the innate as well as the sensible cognition in the form of "I," accompanied by the invariable divergence (of such cognition from all other things), as is the case with sound.

20. Plurality of selves is proved by status.

21. (Plurality of selves follows) also from the authority or significance of the Śāstras [authoritative texts].

Book IV—Chapter 1

1. The eternal is that which is existent and uncaused.

2. The effect is the mark (of the existence) of the ultimate atom.

5. (It is) an error (to suppose that the ultimate atom is not eternal).

Book V—Chapter 1

17. The first action of the arrow is from impulse; the next is from resultant energy produced by that [i.e., the first] action; and similarly the next, and the next.

Book V—Chapter 2

1. Action in earth (results) from impulse, impact, and conjunction with the conjunct.

2. (If action in earth happens) with a particular consequence, it is caused by *adṛṣṭa* [destiny].[1]

3. The falling of waters, in the absence of conjunction, is due to gravity.

4. Flowing (results) from fluidity.

5. The sun's rays (cause) the ascent (of water), through conjunction with air.

6. (Particles of water fly upwards), by means of concussion with impulse, and of conjunction with the conjunct.

7. The circulation (of water) in trees is caused by *adṛṣṭa*.

12. The action of fire and the action of air are explained by the action of earth.

14. The action of the mind is explained by the action of the hand.

15. Pleasure and pain (results) from contact of self, sense, mind, and object.

16. Non-origination of that (follows) on the mind becoming steady in the self; (after it, there is) non-existence of pain in the embodied self. (This is) that *yoga*.

17. Egress and ingress (of life and mind, from and into, body), conjunctions [i.e., assimilation] of food and drink, and conjunctions of other products,—these are caused by *adṛṣṭa*.

[1] *Adṛṣṭam*: literally, the invisible. Often translated as "destiny."

18. *Mokṣa* [emancipation] consists in the non-existence of conjunction with the body, when there is at the same time no potential body existing, and consequently, re-birth cannot take place.

21. Space, time, and also ether are inactive, because of their difference from that which possesses activity.

23. (The relation) of the inactive [i.e., attribute and action] (to substance), is combination [inherence], (which is) independent of actions.

Book VI—Chapter 1

5. ["Result (of action) indicated by the *Śāstra* (accrues) to the performer"] because there is no causality of the attributes of one self in (the attributes of) another self.

6. That [the reward of action] does not exist [i.e., accrue] where the impure are entertained.

7. Impurity (lies) in killing.

8. Demerit results from association with him [i.e., an impure *brāhmin*].

Book VI—Chapter 2

1. (Of actions) of which the motives are visible and invisible, the motive, where no visible (motive) exists, (tends) to exaltation.

2. Ablution, fast, *brahmacarya* [abstinence], residence in the family of the preceptor, life of retirement in the forest, sacrifice, gift, oblation, directions, constellations, seasons, and religious observances conduce to invisible fruit.

3. The observance of the four *āśramas* [stages of life] (has been already mentioned). Faith and lack of faith are also (sources of *adṛṣṭa* [destiny] or *dharma* [merit] and *adharma* [demerit].[1]

4. *Upadhā* or impurity (denotes) impurity of emotion, or of the self; *anupadhā* [purity] (denotes) purity.

5. The pure is that which possesses prescribed color, taste, smell, and touch, and is sprinkled with water along with the recitation of sacred hymns, and also without it, or is sprinkled with water both with pronation and with supination.

6. Impure,—such is the form of the negation of the pure.

7. (It is) also something else.

8. To the unrestrained, exaltation does not accrue from eating what is pure, inasmuch as there is an absence of self-restraint; and

[1] Revised translation.

it accrues (where there is self-restraint), inasmuch as self-restraint is a different thing (from eating).

9. (Self-restraint alone is not the cause of exaltation), for there is non-existence (of exaltation), where (the eating of pure food) does not exist.

12. (Desire and aversion arise) from *adṛṣṭa* also.

14. Application to *dharma* [merit] and *adharma* [demerit] has for its antecedents desire and aversion.

15. Conjunction (of self with body, sense, and life), produced by them (i.e., *dharma* and *adharma*), (is called birth); disjunction (of body and mind, produced by them, is called death).

16. (It has been) declared that the actions of the self having taken place, salvation (results).

Book VII—Chapter 1

2. The color, taste, smell, and touch of earth, water, fire, and air, are also non-eternal, on account of the non-eternality of their substrata.

22. Ether, in consequence of its vast expansion, is infinitely large. So also is the self.

23. In consequence of non-existence of universal expansion, mind is atomic or infinitely small.

24. By attributes, space is explained (to be all-pervading).

25. Time (is the name given) to (a specific, or a universal) cause. (Hence, in either case it is all-pervading.)

Book VII—Chapter 2

1. Because of its difference from color, taste, smell, and touch, unity is a different object.

2. Similarly, separateness (is a different object).

4. Actions and attributes being void of number, universal unity does not exist.

5. That [i.e., the cognition of unity in action and attribute] is erroneous.

6. In consequence of the non-existence of unity, however, secondariness would not exist.

9. Conjunction is produced by action of any one of two things, is produced by action of both, and is produced by conjunction, also.

10. By this disjunction is explained.

21. The prior and the posterior (are produced by two objects) lying in the same direction, existing at the same time, and being near and remote.

22. (Temporal priority and temporal posteriority are said, by suggestion, to arise respectively) from priority of the cause and from posteriority of the cause.

26. That is combination by virtue of which (arises the intuition) in the form of "This is here," with regard to effect and cause.

27. The negation of substantiality and attribute-ness (in combination) is explained by existence.

28. The unity (of combination is explained) by existence.

Book VIII—Chapter 1

2. Among substances, the self, the mind and others are not objects of perception.

4. Substance is the cause of the production of cognition, where attributes and actions are in contact (with the senses).

6. (Cognition which is produced) in respect of substance, attributes and action, (is) dependent upon genus and species.

Book VIII—Chapter 2

5. By reason of (its) predominance, and of possession of smell, earth is the material cause of the olfactory sense.

6. In like manner, water, fire and air (are the material causes of the sense-organs of taste, color and touch), inasmuch as there is no difference in the taste, color and touch (which they respectively possess, from what they respectively apprehend).

Book IX—Chapter 1

1. In consequence of the non-application of action and attribute (to it), (an effect is) non-existent prior (to its production).

3. (The existent is) a different object (from the non-existent), inasmuch as action and attribute cannot be predicated of the non-existent.

5. And that which is a different non-existent from these, is (absolutely) non-existent.

9. That which has not been produced, does not exist;—this is an identical proposition.

11. Perceptual cognition of the self (results) from a particular conjunction of the self and the mind in the self.

12. Perceptual (cognition is) similarly (produced) in the case of the other substances.

Book IX—Chapter 2

6. Reminiscence (results) from a particular conjunction between the soul and the mind and also from impression or latency.

10. False knowledge (arises) from imperfection of the senses and from imperfection of impression.

11. That (i.e., *avidyā*) is imperfect knowledge.

12. (Cognition) free from imperfection, is (called) *vidyā* or scientific knowledge.

13. Cognition of advanced sages, as also vision of the Perfected Ones, (results) from *dharma* or merits.

Book X—Chapter 2

1. "(It is the combinative) cause"—such (intuition and usage), with regard to substance, (arise) from the combination [inherence] of effect (in it).

2. And, through conjunction, (substance becomes the efficient or conditional cause also).

3. Through combination in the (combinative) cause, actions (are non-combinative causes).

8. The performance of acts of observed utility and of acts the purpose whereof has been taught (in the sacred writings) is for the production of *adṛṣṭa* [destiny], (as these teachings are authoritative being the word of God in whom) the defects found in ordinary speakers do not exist.

B. *THE PADĀRTHADHARMASAṀGRAHA*

Chapter I: Introductory

Having bowed to Īśvara, the Cause, and then to the sage Kaṇāda, I am going to describe the nature of things leading to the best of results. [Introductory text.]

Question: Well, what is this highest result?
[Reply]: . . . the "highest result" is the absolute cessation of pain.

1. A knowledge of the true nature of the six categories—substance, quality, action, generality, individuality and inherence—through

their similarities and dissimilarities,—is the means of accomplishing the highest bliss. (I.i.4)[1]

Abhāva, negation, is not mentioned separately, simply because it is dependent (for its conception) upon *bhāva* (the six categories enumerated), and not because there is no such category.

2. This knowledge proceeds from *dharma* [moral law] manifested by the injunctions of the Lord.

Chapter II: Enumeration and Classification of Categories

3. Question:—"Which are the categories, 'substance and the rest'?"

4. Answer:—Among these the substances are—earth, water, light, air, ether, time, space, self (or soul) and mind. These, mentioned in the *sūtra* [aphorism of Kaṇāda] by their general as well as specific names, are nine only; as besides these none other is mentioned by name. (I.i.5)

5. The qualities are:—colour, taste, odour, touch, number, dimension, separateness, conjunction, disjunction, distance, proximity, intellect, pleasure, pain, desire, aversion and effort; these are the seventeen that are directly mentioned in the *sūtra*. The word "*ca*" (and) (in the *sūtra*), however, indicates the other seven: viz., gravity, fluidity, viscidity, faculty [speed] [*saṁskāra*], the two-fold invisible force [*dharma* and *adharma*, virtue and vice], and sound. These make up the twenty-four qualities. (I.i.6)

6. Throwing upwards, throwing downwards, contracting, expanding, and going—these are the only five actions. . . : all such actions as gyrating, evacuating, quivering, flowing upwards, transverse falling, falling downwards, rising and the like, being only particular forms of going, and not forming distinct classes by themselves. (I.i.7)

7. Of generality, or community [universality], there are two kinds, the higher and the lower; and it serves as the basis of inclusive or comprehensive cognition. The higher (or highest) generality is that of "being"; as it is this that extends over the largest number of

[1] These parenthetical citations refer to *Vaiśeṣika Sūtra* of Kaṇāda, upon which the present text is technically a commentary. This work is not so much a commentary on the *Sūtra* as an important independent work on the subject. It is difficult to defend the position that Praśastapāda's mature views are simply the development of the suggestions contained in Kaṇāda's work.

things; and also because it is this alone that is a generality pure and simple, always serving, as it does, as the basis of comprehensive cognitions. The lower generalities are "substance" and the rest [quality, action, generality, individuality, and inherence], which extend over a limited number of things. These latter, being the basis of inclusive as well as exclusive cognitions, are sometimes regarded as individualities also. (I.ii.1–5)

8. Unique particularities reside in the ultimate substances. They are the factors that make for ultimate distinctions among these substances. [Revised tr.]

9. Inherence [*samavāya*: intimate union, coming together inseparably] is the relationship subsisting among things that are inseparable, standing to one another in the character of the container and the contained,—such relationship being the basis of the idea that "this is in that."

Chapter III: Similarities and Dissimilarities among Categories

11. To all the six categories belong the properties of being-ness, predicability, and cognisability.

12. The character of being dependent (upon something else) belongs to all things except the eternal [ultimate] substances.

13. To the five, substance and the rest [quality, action, generality, and individuality], belong the characters of inherability and plurality.

14. To the five, quality and the rest [action, generality, individuality, and inherence], also belong the character of being devoid of qualities, and that of being without action [chiefly motion].

15. To the three, substance and the rest [quality and action], belong the relationship with being, the character of having communities [universals] and individualities. . . .

16. The character of being an effect and that of being non-eternal belong only to those (substances, qualities and actions) that have causes.

17. The quality of being the cause belongs to all (substances, qualities and actions) except the "atomic measure," &c.

18. The character of subsisting in substances (belongs to substances, qualities and actions) with the exception of the eternal substances.

19. The three beginning with generality [individuality and inherence] have the character—of having their sole being within

themselves, having *buddhi* or the cognitive faculty as their sole indicator, of not being an effect, of not being the cause, of having no particular generalities, of being eternal, and of not being expressible by the word "*artha*" (thing). (I.ii.10, 12, 14, 16; VII.ii.26)

"Having *buddhi* as their sole indicator": i.e., their only proof lies in the intellect. . . whereas for the existence of substance and the rest [quality, action, generality, individuality, and inherence], we would have other grounds for our belief—in the shape of the effects brought about by these, for instance.

20. All the nine, earth and the rest,[1] have the character of—(1) belonging to the class "substance," (2) self-productiveness or bringing about effects in themselves, (3) having qualities, (4) not being destructible by their causes and effects, and (5) being connected with ultimate individualities.

(I.i.9, 10, 12, 15, 18; X.ii.1–2)

21. The character of not being dependent and that of being eternal belong to all (substances) except those that are made up of certain constituent parts.

22. To earth, water, fire, air, soul[2] and mind, belongs the character of being many, and also that of having lower or less extensive generalities [sub-species].

23. To earth, water, fire, air and mind, belong the character of having actions, being corporeal, having distance and proximity, and having speed. (V.ii.1–7, 14; V.i.17; VII.ii.21)

24. To *ākāśa* (ether), time and space belong the characters of—being all-pervasive, having the largest dimensions, and being the common receptacle of all corporeal things. (VII.i.22, 24, 25)

25. To the five beginning with earth [water, fire—or light—, air, and ether] belong the characters of—being material, being the main material principle of the sense-organs, and being endowed with such specific qualities as are each perceptible by each of the external organs of perception. (VIII.ii.5–6)

[1] See above, I.i.5.

[2] Henceforth we shall translate the word "*ātmā*" [or *ātman*] by the word "soul"; as in the sense of the *jīvātmā* [living soul or self] at any rate, "soul" is more easily intelligible to English readers than "self."—Tr. In spite of this statement the translator does not use "soul" consistently. In this case "self" will be used consistently.

Chapter V: Of the ultimate substances

40. We are now going to describe the process of the creation and destruction of the four ultimate material substances [earth, water, fire, air]. . . . The four gross elements having thus been brought into existence, there is produced, from the mere thought (mental picturing) of the Supreme Lord, the Great egg, from out of the fire-atoms mixed up with the atoms of earth; and in this egg having produced all the worlds and the Four-faced Brahmā, the Grandfather of all creatures; the Supreme Lord assigns to him the duty of producing the various creatures. . . .

Question: "What are the proofs for the existence of God?"

This proof is in the form of scriptural authority and inferential reasoning.

This inferential reasoning is—The four great elementary substances are preceded by someone having a knowledge of them, because they are effects,—anything that is an effect is preceded by one having a cognition of it, as, for instance, the jar (which is always preceded by the potter),—and the four great elementary substances are effects,—hence they must be preceded by one having a knowledge of them.

Objection: "The premiss of this inference (that the elementary substances are effects) is not duly cognised by any means of right knowledge,—for instance, the fact of the earth being an effect cannot be regarded as duly established."

Reply: This is not right; as the earth, &c., are made up of parts; and everything that has parts is an effect, as for instance the jar; the earth, &c., have parts,—hence they must be effects.

Objection:—"An inferential reasoning is operative only when the invariable concomitance (upon which it is based) has been duly recognised; as for the invariable concomitance of the *character of an effect* and *that of being preceded by one having knowledge* of it, this can never be known from the case of the jar and such other substances; as in the case of the sprouting of the seed we find that the sprouting appears *at the same time* as the cognition of the sprout by the person who had sown the seed; and hence in this case we do not find any *precedence* of the doer with the knowledge of the effect over the appearance of the effect. Nor could the sprout, &c., be included in the subject of the inference in question; as it is only after the invariable concomitance has been duly cognised, and the inference has begun to operate, that we proceed to distinguish the subject and predicate, &c., of the inference, for the benefit of the opponent; while in the case in question (of the sprout) it is found to be always included in a cognition contrary to the concomitance; and as such, there could be no cognition of the necessary concomitance."

Reply: If there be no recognition of the invariable concomitance simply on account of there being no perception of duality or difference (between the time of the appearance of the sprout and the knowledge thereof by the sower),—then, in that case, we could never rightly arrive at the... inference of the moving of the Sun,...it is merely the fact of the stars, &c., having assumed different positions, and not that of their having *moved*, that is perceived at the same time as the cognition of their other positions preceded by the movement of *Devadatta* (the observer) from one place to another....

Objection: "Then again, does the inferential reasoning establish the creator, or a creator capable of creating the Earth, &c.? If it prove a mere creator, then what is desired is not accomplished. As what you seek to prove is not a mere agent, like ourselves; any such person having a limited vision could not create the Earth, &c...."

Reply: This objection does not apply to the case, as what the inference is sought to prove is not any particular kind of creator. All that the premiss put forward proves is the fact of the substances under consideration being preceded by an intelligent being in general; and this necessarily establishes his particular character in the shape of the capability of creating the Earth, &c.—as the existence of no general entity can be proved without the accompaniment of a particular characteristic...[for example] no universal essence of fire could have an existence apart from a particular fire.

The objector's standpoint may be summed up: "...For instance, the inference cannot prove the fact of the effects (earth, &c.) being preceded by a body (of the God); because, if there be a body, it would necessarily contain the sense-organs; and having these organs, the God could not have any knowledge of the material causes (atoms), the accessories (in the shape of the karmic tendencies of selves) and the potencies of various instrumentalities—all of which are supersensuous,—in the matter of the creation of Earth &c.; and as such He could not be the creator of these. Then as for the creation not being preceded by a body (of God), it is absolutely impossible to prove this; because, as a matter of fact, we find that what a *doer* (of any act) does is—(1) to ascertain the power or capability of the instruments, (2) to desire to fulfil the particular act by means of those instruments, (3) to put forth an effort, (4) to put the body into action, (5) to supervise over the various causes (material and others), & (6) to do the act; and if he does not *ascertain*, or desire, or put forth his effort, or put his body into action, he does not do the act. And from these affirmative and negative universal instances (of the *acting* with the *ascertaining*, &c.) we conclude that like the intelligence (of God), the body also would be a necessary means to the production of effects,...

To the above we make the following reply: Does the nature of the *actor* necessarily consist in being bodied? or does it consist in the character of being the operator of instruments recognised as capable of bringing about the necessary effects? The former alternative could not be accepted; as in that case a person in deep sleep, or one who is not doing anything towards an action, would also have to be regarded as the "actor" (as even in these conditions he would have his body all the same). We must then accept the second alternative; as it is only when this character is present that we find the effect coming about. This character can belong to a bodiless being also; as we find in the case of the self (which is an immaterial thing) operating towards the moving of the body. It might be argued that the body belongs to the self, who has obtained it through its previous deeds (and as such the operating self cannot be regarded as strictly bodiless). True, the body belongs to the self; but it is not the body that supplies the force impelling itself, as any such impulsion by itself would involve a contradiction. It may be urged that the body may be regarded as the means of impulsion, in as much as it is the object of the impelling. But in the case of God also we have the atom as the object to be impelled or operated upon.

Objection: "The impelling of the self's body is found to be brought about by desire and effort; and not when the body does not exist; and from this we infer that the body is the means or author of its own impelling, through the said desire and effort."

Reply: Not so; as the body can be only accepted as impelling or giving rise to desire and effort (and not to its own operations). After the desire and effort have been brought about, and when these begin to operate towards impelling (the body to a certain course of action), the body ceases to be the impelling agent; as the body being the *object* of this impelling could not, at the same time, be its *doer*. And thus we find that there is no similarity between the action of the self and that of the body. Then again, we often meet with cases where certain inanimate things are moved to action by an intelligent being, merely through his own desire and effort, independently of all actions of the body. On the other hand, we never find any action apart from an intelligent being. All these facts go to establish the existence of God.

41. *Ākāśa* (ether), time and space, having no lower species, these are three technical names given to the individuals themselves. (II.i.27, 29–31)

Of *ākāśa* the qualities are—sound, number, dimension, separateness, conjunction and disjunction. (VII.i.22)

Sound cannot be the property of those substances that can be touched. . . . It cannot be regarded as belonging to the self. . . . It cannot be the quality of space, time and mind, . . . (II.i.24–7)

As the distinguishing feature of sound is common to all *ākāśa*, this is regarded as one only. (II.i.30)

From this unity follows its individual separateness or isolation. (II.i.31)

Ākāśa being spoken of as "*vibhu*" (omnipresent or all-pervading), it points to its dimension being the largest or highest. (VII.i.22)

In as much as *ākāśa* is spoken of as the cause of sound, it follows that it has conjunction and disjunction. (II.i.31)

Thus, then, being endowed with qualities, and not being located in anything else, it is regarded as a substance. And in as much as it has no cause, either homogeneous or heterogeneous, it is eternal. (II.i.18)

42. Time is the cause of the [relative] notions of "priority," "posteriority," or "simultaneity" and "succession," and of "late" and "soon." In as much as there is no other cause or basis for these notions, as appearing with regard to these objects,—notions which differ in character from all notions described before,—we conclude "time" to be the basis of these. (II.ii.6)

Time is the cause or basis of the production, persistence and destruction (or cessation) of all produced things; as all these are spoken of in terms of time.... (II.ii.9)

The fact of time being a substance and that of its being eternal are proved as in the case of *ākāśa*. (II.ii.7)

Though from the uniformity of the distinguishing character of time, time is directly by itself, one only, yet, it is indirectly, or figuratively, spoken of as manifold, on account of the diversity among the conditions afforded by the production, persistence and cessation of all produced things;...

43. Space is the cause of the notions of East, West, &c. That is to say, it is that from which arise the ten notions—of East, South-East, South, South-West, West, North-West, North, North-East, Below and Above—with regard to one corporeal (material) object considered with reference to another material object as the starting point or limit. Specially so, as there is no other cause available (for these notions). (II.ii,12; II.i.31; VII.i.24; VII.ii.22)

44. *Ātmā* [or *ātman*], self, is that which belongs to the class "*ātmā*" [or *ātman*]. (VIII.i.2; III.i.2)

In as much as it is extremely subtile in its character, and as such imperceptible, its cognition is brought about by means of the organs of hearing, &c.,—as inferred from the perception of sound, &c.;—aided by the fact of such instruments as the axe and the like being always operated by a doer or agent.

In the cognitions of sound, &c., also we infer a "cogniser." This character cannot belong to the body, or to the sense-organs, or to the mind; because all these are unintelligent or unconscious. Consciousness cannot belong to the body, as it is a material product, like the jar; and also as no consciousness is found in dead bodies.

Nor can consciousness belong to the sense-organs; because these are mere instruments, and also because we have remembrances of objects even after the sense-organ has been destroyed, and even when the object is not in contact with the organ.

Nor can it belong to the mind; because if the mind be regarded as functioning independently of the other organs, then we would have perception and remembrance simultaneously presenting themselves (and if the mind be regarded as functioning through the other organs, then it would be the same as *ātmā* [*ātman* [self]); and also because the mind itself is a mere instrument.

And thus the only thing to which consciousness could belong is the self, which thus is cognised by this consciousness.

As from the motion of the chariot we infer the existence of an intelligent guiding agent in the shape of the charioteer, so also we infer an intelligent guiding agent for the body, from the activity and cessation from activity appearing in the body, which have the capacity of acquiring the desirable and avoiding the undesirable object. (III.i.19)

The intelligent agent is also inferred from the actions of breathing, &c. "How?" (1) When we perceive a variegated functioning of the air contained in the body, (we infer the existence of a guiding agent), who would act like the blower of the wind-pipe. (2) From the regular action of winking up and down, we infer the existence of the agent, who would be like the puller of a pulley. (3) From the fact of the wounds of the body being healed up, we infer the existence of the agent who would be like the master of a house repairing it. (4) From the action of the mind towards the contact of the sense-organs apprehending desirable objects, we infer the existence of the agent, who would be like the boy in a corner of the house throwing a ball (to another ball stuck in the ground). (5) When we see an object by the eye, and then, recalling the taste of that object, we find a certain modification appearing in the organ of taste; from this we infer the existence of a single guiding agent for the two operations, like a person looking through two windows. (6) Then again, from the qualities of pleasure, pain, desire, aversion and effort, we infer the existence of one to whom these qualities belong. These qualities cannot belong either to the body, or to the sense-organs: (*a*) because these are found to be coexistent with the notion of "I"; (*b*) because these qualities exist only in certain parts of the object to which they belong; (*c*) because they are not coeval with their substratum;

(*d*) because they are not perceptible by the external organs of perception. (7) The existence of the self (as a distinct substance) is also proved by the fact of its being spoken of by means of the word "I" which is wholly distinct from the words "earth," "water," &c.

(III.ii.4–13)

The qualities of the self are, these: intelligence, pleasure, pain, desire, aversion, effort, virtue, vice, tendency, number, dimension, separateness, conjunction and disjunction.... The presence of virtue and vice is indicated by the mention [in the *sūtra*] of the fact of the qualities of one self not being the cause of the appearance of a quality in another self. The existence of tendency is indicated by the mention of this as being the cause in the bringing about of remembrance.... The fact of pleasure, &c. being due to contact proves the existence of conjunction in the self; and disjunction is the destroyer of that conjunction. (III.ii.4, 20–21; VI.i.5; IX.ii.6; VII.i.22)

Objection: "As a matter of fact we find that the existence of a perceptible object is always accompanied by a cognition of its shape or form; in the case of the self we find there is no cognition of the shape of the self; and hence not finding its invariable concomitant, we cannot but reject the existence of the self;...

Reply: There is no reason for setting aside the notion of the existence of self; because the absence of the sense-perception of it is implied in its very nature. On the other hand, for its existence we have a proof in the shape of inference....

Objection: "Consciousness may be a quality of the mind; as it applies to all objects, and is eternal; and as such the unification of cognitions... would be quite possible in this case."

Reply: ...If the mind be believed to cognise, by the help of some organ of perception other than the eye, &c., then your theory differs from me only in name (you applying the name "mind" to what we call "self"). As what this other organ would be is the mind; and the mind which you hold to be the substratum of consciousness would be what we call "self."...

For the following reason also consciousness cannot belong to the mind; *because the mind is itself of the nature of an instrument*. That is to say, mind is not conscious, because it is an instrument of consciousness, like the jar.

Objection: "The fact of the mind being an instrument has not been accepted (by both parties) as it is held to be the *doer* or *agent*."

Reply: If the mind were the *doer*, then for the perception of pleasure, &c., we should find some other instrument, like the eye for the perception of colour; as no action can ever be produced without an instrument. And if you agree to accept the existence of some such organ, then there would be a difference in name only; as you would also admit the existence of a *doer* (calling it "mind" while we call it "self"), and a distinct instrument (calling it something else while we call it "mind").

Not for the above reasons alone, but also because of the properties of the pleasure, pain, desire, aversion and effort, which lead to the inference of something to which these properties belong,—all these qualities are cognised as co-extensive with the notion of "I"—being always cognised as "I am pleased," "I am pained" and the like, where we find that it is the object "I" which is characterised by pleasure. The notion of "I" could not refer to the body; because it is not found to apply to the body of another person. Nor could it be said to apply to *one's own* body alone. . . . If the notion of "I" referred to the body, then just as another man's body being as perceptible as our own body,—the notion of fatness appearing equally with reference to both,—the other man's body would also be capable of being spoken of as "I"; specially as in both, the shape is the same. . . . Then again, if the notion of "I" referred to the body, it could not appear in our consciousness as something internal.

. . . just as the self is inferred from pleasure, &c., so also it is inferred from the notion of "I." We find the word "I" used in the Veda as well as in ordinary parlance, by learned persons; and this word could not be without something that it would denote. Its own form could not form its denotation, as that would involve the incongruity of its operation bearing upon itself; as has been well declared—"no word ever denotes itself." And hence that something which is denoted by the word "I" would be the self.

. . . its use with regard to the body must be regarded as secondary or figurative, based upon the fact of the body being a useful instrument for the self; . . .

. . . We have the *sūtra* "there is a multiplicity of selves because of variety of conditions": this *sūtra* points out the multiplicity of selves; and that shows that *multiplicity* of number is one of its properties.

Now what is meant by this "variety"? It means the non-recognition of the cognitions and pleasure, &c. belonging to several persons. That is to say, in the case of our own pleasure, &c. we have the recognition, in old age, of our experiences of the past, as our own; as we often have the idea—"I enjoyed such and such a pleasure" and the like; and if the experience were one and the same in all bodies, then we could have a similar idea with reference to the experiences of other persons: as a matter of fact however we have no such recognition; and from this we infer that there is a distinct self in each body.

Objection: "Just as in the case of *ākāśa* we find that though it is one only, yet on account of the diversity of the limitations in the shape of the ear-cavities, we have a diversity in the sound-experiences—so, in the case of the one self also we may explain the diversity of experiences as being due to the diversity in the limitations of the body, &c."

Reply: The instance is not quite analogous; the diversity of sound-experience might well be explained as due to the diversity of sound-comprehending agencies of the ear-cavity and the rest which have been brought about by the *dharma* and *adharma* [merit and demerit], which again are restricted to each individual person. In the case of the One Self on the other hand, there would be no diversity in the *adharma* and *dharma* (since all these would belong to one and the same self); and as such there being no diversity in the bodies (which are brought about by the *dharma* and *adharma* of the self ensouling the body),—what would be the cause of the diversity of the pleasure and pain experienced by different persons? specially as the self being one, the contact of the mind also would be common to all persons. For one, however, who admits of many selves, even though all selves, being omnipresent, would be present in all bodies, yet his experiences would not be common to all of them; as each of them would experience only such pleasures, &c., as would appear in connection with the particular body that will have been brought about by the previous *karma* of that self,—and not those belonging to the other bodies. And the *karma* also belongs to that self by whose body it has been done. Hence the restriction of body is due to the restriction of *karma* and *vice versa*,—the mutual interdependence going on endlessly (and hence not objectionable).

It might be argued that, "the difference between the Supreme and the human selves may be explained as being due to ignorance; and the differentiations of ignorance with regard to the human selves are beginningless."

But whose "ignorance" is this? Is it of *Brahma* [*Brahman*], or of the human selves? It could not belong to *Brahma* [*Brahman*]; as That is by Its very nature *pure* and *intelligent*. And if it belonged to the human selves, then there would be an interdependence,—differentiation of human selves being due to ignorance, and this latter belonging to the differentiated human selves.

Objection: "The human self also, like *Brahma* [*Brahman*], is beginningless and endless, being a mere reflection of *Brahma* [*Brahman*]; and hence on the strength of the text—'all things shine after that shines, and all this shines by Its light' &c., we hold that it is the endless and beginningless essence of *Brahma* [*Brahman*] that appears in all bodies."

Reply: That is not right; as if such were the case, then the diversity in question would be absolutely inexplicable. Hence it was quite right for the author of the *sūtra* to declare—"*Nānātmāno vyavasthātaḥ*" [the manyness of the *ātman* will result]; and as for the texts laying down the non-difference of selves, they must be taken as figurative.

45. The mind [inner sense, *manas*] is so called, because of its belonging to the class "mind." (III.ii.1)

Even when there is a proximity of the object to the self and the sense-organ, we find that cognition, pleasure, &c., do not appear, and from this we infer the necessity of an instrumentality other than the aforesaid proximity. Then again, we find that due remembrance appears even when there is no functioning of the organs of hearing &c.; and that the objects of this means or instrument are pleasure &c. which are not cognisable by the external sense-organs: and from these two facts we infer the fact of that instrument being internal.

(III.ii.3; VII.i.23; V.ii.17)

The qualities of the mind are—number, dimension, separateness, conjunction, disjunction, priority, posteriority and faculty [tendency or speed].

The *sūtra* asserts the non-simultaneity of effort and knowledge; and this proves that there is one mind to each body. From this follows separateness. The *sūtra* speaking of the "absence" in the mind, of that (largeness) indicates its atomic dimension. The mention of moving to and moving away indicates the presence in it of conjunction and disjunction. Its corporeal or material character indicates priority and posteriority, as also faculty [*saṁskāra*, tendency].

(VII.ii.21)

The mention of the absence of tangibility indicates its being unproductive of substances.

Having action it must be corporeal or material. It must be regarded as unconscious; as otherwise the whole body would be the common ground (of all experiences or sensations). Being an instrument it must be subservient to the purpose of something else. (III.ii.22)

Having qualities it must be regarded as a substance. And it must move quickly, in as much as it includes within itself all effort and the unseen forces (of the self's) actions.

...The self is at one and the same time in contact with all the sense-organs; the sense-organs too have contacts with objects in proximity to themselves; and yet we find that while we cognise one of the various objects in contact with the various sense-organs, we have no cognition or pleasure, &c., with regard to others; hence it follows that for such cognition &c., there is some means or instrumental cause other than the contact of the object, the sense-organs, and the self;—the proximity of which other cause brings about the cognition &c., which do not appear otherwise. The argument may be put forward thus: The contacts of the objects, the sense-organ and the self depend upon some other cause, in the bringing about of the due effect,—because even when the former contacts exist, the necessary effect does not appear,—as in the case of the threads &c. And this instrumentality upon which they depend is that of the *mind*.

...there is one mind with each body....If there were many minds, there would be a multiplicity of the contacts of the self and the mind; and as such we would find the same man having many cognitions and putting forth many efforts at one and the same time. As a matter of fact however we find these appearing only gradually, one after the other;...

In certain cases we have a notion of more than one cognition appearing at one and the same time; but that is due to the fact of the cognitions following each other very quickly....

...the *sūtra* declares the *ākāśa* [ether] and the self to be all-pervading and very large, and then adds "on account of the absence of these characters in the mind, it is atomic in its nature." And hence it is proved that the mind is atomic in its dimensions; specially as an eternal substance, which is not all-pervading, could not but be atomic, (all intervening dimensions belonging to transient things). The absence of the all-pervading character in the mind is inferred from the nonsimultaneity of cognitions; as if the mind were all-pervading, then it would be in contact with all the sense-organs, at one and the same time; and hence there would be simultaneous cognitions of colour, and taste, &c....

...the absence of all-pervading character in the mind proves its corporeality [or materiality];...

Though the materiality of the mind has already been proved by showing that it is atomic, yet the author has added this in order to make it still clearer.

If the mind were the *cogniser*, then, the body would become a common ground of experiences (of all kinds of sensation; or of the mind and the self the two being two distinct cognisers). As a matter of fact, however, we do not find this to be the case, in as much as the activity or inactivity of the body is found to follow the purposes of a single agent (or the motive of a single sensation). Hence the mind cannot be regarded as conscious....

Chapter VI: On Qualities: Similarities and Dissimilarities

46. To the qualities, colour and the rest, belong the (common) character of belonging to the class "quality," of inhering in substances, of being devoid of qualities, and of being devoid of action.

47. Colour, taste, smell, touch, priority, posteriority, gravity, fluidity and viscidity, and speed are qualities that belong to corporeal objects.

48. Intellect, pleasure, pain, desire, aversion, effort, virtue, vice, faculty [tendency, *saṁskāra*], and sound belong to immaterial things.

49. Number, dimension, separateness, conjunction and disjunction belong to both.

52. Colour, taste, smell, touch, viscidity, natural fluidity, intellect,[1] pleasure, pain, desire, aversion, effort, virtue, vice, faculty [tendency] and sound are the "*vaiśeṣika*" [specific] qualities.

[1] A better translation of the original *jñāna* would be knowledge or cognition.

53. Number, dimension, separateness, conjunction, disjunction, priority, posteriority, gravity, caused fluidity and speed are the "*sāmānya*" [generic] qualities.

54. Sound, touch, colour, taste and smell are each perceptible by each one of the external sense-organs (respectively).

55. Number, dimension, separateness, conjunction, disjunction, priority, posteriority, fluidity, viscidity and speed are each perceptible by two sense-organs.

56. Intellect, pleasure, pain, desire, aversion, effort are perceptible by the internal organ [mind].

. . . Some people hold that intellect [knowledge] is an object of inferential knowledge and is not perceived by the mind. But this is not right; as there would be no distinguishing mark—middle term—by which intellect [knowledge] could be inferred. . . .

85. Number forms the basis of such usages as "one" and the rest. It inheres in one and in many substances. The number inhering in one substance has its eternal and transient manifestations in the same manner as those of the colour &c. of the atom of water and the rest. The number inhering in many substances begins with "two" and ends with "*parārdha*" (100,000,000,000,000,000). . . . The same process would also apply to the case of the notions of "three" and the rest. As these also proceed out of unities as accompanied by the idea of many substances; . . .

86. Dimension is that which forms the basis of all measurement. It is of four kinds: (1) minute, (2) large, (3) long, and (4) short. (VII.i.8, 17.) The large again is of two kinds: eternal and non-eternal. To the eternal kind belongs the highest extensiveness of the *ākāśa*, space, time and self; while the non-eternal exists in the triad and the rest.[1] (VII.i.22, 24, 25.) The minute again is of two kinds—eternal and non-eternal. The eternal is that in the atom and in the mind; and this is what is known as the atomic measure. The non-eternal is the diad.[1] (VII.i.11, 13, 17.) . . .

Of the non-eternal dimensions, all the four (the long, the short, the large and the small) are caused by (1) number, (2) dimension and (3) aggregation.

[1] The phrase "the triad and the rest" means any combination of three or more atoms; "the diad" is any combination of two atoms. Since any combination is non-eternal, the diad is the smallest non-eternal, and the triad or any other combination is non-eternal and in the class of "large."

(1) The plurality of number appears in the atoms and the diads, according to the will of God; and when these atoms and diads bring about the effects in the shape of the triad and the like, the said plurality creates in these a certain length and largeness, simultaneously with colour and the other qualities. (2) In a case where the created object is caused by two large components, as also when it is caused by many large components, the largeness of the object is due to largeness of the component parts, and not to their plurality; as even in a case where the number of the components in two objects is the same, we find a difference in their magnitudes (if there happens to be a difference in the volumes of the components of those objects). (3) As for aggregation, we have it in the case where two balls of cotton are rolled into a single ball,—where what the conglomeration produces in this single double ball, is, not plurality and largeness, but largeness only, by means either of conjunctions of the loose particles composing the balls of cotton, or of the mutual conjunction of the particles of one ball with those of the other. We infer this from the fact that even in a case where the number, the largeness (or magnitude) and the dimension of the components of two objects are the same, there is yet a difference in the magnitudes of the objects themselves [i.e., in two objects where the conglomeration of particles is loose and closely compact].

It is the duality of two atoms which produces the minuteness in the diad. In the triad, its length is produced, just like its largeness, by means of the plurality, the largeness and homogeneous conglomeration, of its material cause (the component molecules). In the diad, shortness is produced, just like its minuteness, through the duality of number. . . .

88. Conjunction forms the basis of the idea of two things being "joined together." It is the cause of substances, qualities and actions. . . .

[A discussion is here started as to whether it is only a previously existing entity that is produced by causes, or something that did not exist before, which is produced.—Eds.]

The Sāṁkhyas hold the following view (*Sāṁkhya-kārikā*, 9):—Effect subsists (antecedently to the operation of cause): for what exists not can by no operation of cause be brought into existence. Materials, too, are selected which are fit for the purpose; everything is not by every means possible; what is capable does that for which it is competent; and like is produced from like.[1]

[1] The translation of this paragraph has been revised.

To the above we make the following reply: If even before the operation of the cause, the cloth already exists in the threads, then how is it that we do not see it, even when we seek for it, and our organs of vision are all right? It might be said that we do not see it because of its not having become manifested. But, what is this "non-manifestation"? If by this you mean merely "want of perception," then it is this very want of perception that we have put forward as inexplicable in accordance with your theory; and hence that same fact cannot be accepted as a right explanation of itself. If however by "non-manifestation" be meant "the absence of such form as would be perceptible and capable of effective action," then this would amount to an acceptance of the non-existence of the effect (prior to causal operation), as what this means is that something, in the shape of that form, which did not exist before, is brought into existence by the operation of the cause.

Objection: "For the perception of the cloth, we need the aid of such accessories as the action of the weaver, and the like, just as much as that of the organs of perception; and hence as long as these have not functioned, the cloth, even though extant, is not perceived."

Reply: "This can not be: because the action of its causes would always be possible (and hence the cloth should be always perceptible).

Objection: "Yes; but even this action of the causes which remains unmanifested at first, comes to be manifested by means of causes and then alone does it serve to render the cloth perceptible."

Reply: If this "manifestation" of the cause were non-existent before, then (according to you) how could it be brought about by any causes? And if it were existent, then the thing would also be always perceptible. Hence the perception of something not perceptible before could not be possible, until some peculiarity, that did not exist there before, were produced in it. . . .

Question: "If the thing were non-existent before, then how does it come to have existence?"

Answer: By the force of the operations of the causes. There is a peculiar power in the shuttle &c. on account of which, whenever they come together and function in unison, there appears some thing that did not exist before—viz., the cloth.

Objection: "If something not existing before, and hence not in any way connected with the causes, were to be produced by these, then there would be a great disorder and confusion (any causes giving rise to any effects)."

Reply: This could not be; as the cause in the form of the (thread) has its efficiency restricted to the effect in the form of "cloth" alone.

. . . there is a limitation or restriction as to the natural causes of definite things;—the potency of one class of things towards a certain definite class of things being ascertained by means of invariable concomitance, both positive and negative.

Then again, it has been argued above that, the effect being nondifferent from the cause, the existence of the cause would mean the existence of the effect also. But this is far from proved;...it is a patent fact that the effect differs from the cause, in point of form, potency and position. Then too, if the effect were in every way non-different from the cause, then the whole world, which is held by the Sāṁkhya to be a product of primordial matter, would be imperceptible, as primordial matter is held to be so.

Then, as for the fact of the effect occupying the same extension in space as the cause, this idea is merely due to the fact of the effect resting in, having its receptacle in, the cause. This will be enough, and we need not press the "old people" (the Sāṁkhyas) any further.

89. Disjunction is the basis of the idea of two things being "disjoined."

It consists in the separation of two things that have hitherto been in contact. It is of three kinds: (1) produced by the action of any one of the two things, (2) by the action of both, and (3) by another disjunction....

90. Distance and proximity form the basis of the notions of "prior" and "posterior." They are of two kinds: (1) due to space, and (2) due to time. Those which are due to space afford ideas of particular directions; and those which are due to time afford ideas of age.

92. *Buddhi* has various forms, as objects are endless, and it appertains to each individual object.

93. Though there are many kinds of *buddhi*, yet briefly it is of two kinds, in the form of knowledge [*vidyā*] and non-knowledge or ignorance [*avidyā*]. Of these ignorance is of four kinds, in the shape of (1) doubt, (2) misconception, (3) indefinite or indistinct cognition, and (4) dream.

98. Right knowledge also is of four kinds: (1) directly sensuous,[1] (2) inferential, (3) recollective, and (4) superhuman.

(III.i.8; IX.ii.1, 6, 23)

99. Of these, that which proceeds from the sense-organs is "directly sensuous." The sense-organs are six—the nose, the tongue, the eye, the skin, the ear and the mind.

This knowledge appears with regard to substance and the other categories....

As for persons unlike ourselves—e.g., *yogis* in the ecstatic condition—there appear precisely true cognitions of the real forms of such things as their own self as well as the selves of others, *ākāśa* (ether), space, time, atoms, wind, mind,—the qualities, actions, generalities and individualities inhering in these,—and inherence; and the cogni-

[1] A better translation here and in all succeeding passages would be "sensory.

tion of these is brought about by the mind as aided by properties or faculties born of *yoga*.... [See selections from *Yoga Sūtra*—Eds.]

With regard to generalities and individualities, the only means of direct sensuous knowledge is the perception or cognition of the mere form; the cognisables are substance and other categories; the cogniser is the self; and the cognition is the knowledge of substance, etc.

In the appearance of the cognition of generalities and individualities, the means of direct sensuous cognition consists in mere contact of the sense-organ and the object; for this there is no other means of knowledge; as it is not in the form of resultant cognition. Or, the means of direct sensuous cognition may be defined as any and every true and undefinable cognition of all objects, following from fourfold contact; substance and other categories are the cognisables; the self is the cogniser; and the recognition of the good (pleasant), bad (unpleasant) and indifferent character (of the things perceived) is the cognition.

110. Negation...is mere inference; just as the appearance of the effect becomes "indicative" of the existence of the cause, so also does the non-appearance of the effect become "indicative" of the non-existence of the cause. (IX.ii.5)

Some people hold that for the cognition of the *absence* of a thing there is a distinct means in the shape of negation, which consists in the non-appearance of sense-perception and the four means of knowing the *presence* of things....He also who regards negation as a distinct means of knowledge, does not maintain that the cognition of the absence or non-existence of a thing follows from mere non-appearance of its cognition; as if it were so then, a thing that is at a great distance from the observer (and is *not cognised*) would come to be cognised as *non-existent* (there being an absence of its cognition). What he would hold is that, when all causes and conditions of cognising it are present, if there is non-appearance of the due cognition of an object which is cognisable, then its non-cognition would lead to the cognition of its non-existence. There is however no difference in nature between the non-cognition of the cognisable and that of the non-cognisable object; as there are no varying grades of negation; and hence a negation cannot, by itself, like the sense-organs, bring about the cognition of anything; what constitutes a difference between the two however is that *the non-cognition of the cognisable object* is never found to fail in its concomitance with the *absence or non-existence* of that object; whereas the non-cognition of the *non-cognisable* object is found to fail in such concomitance; as even when the non-cognisable object *exists*, there is *non-cognition* of it; and it is on account of this difference that it is the non-cognition of the cognisable object, and not that of the non-cognisable object, that brings about the cognition (of the non-existence of the object).

And thus negation becomes merely an "inferential indicative," as it would stand in need of the due recognition of invariable concomitance; if it did not require this invariable concomitance, then there would be nothing to prevent the undesirable contingency that all negation is equally liable to bring about the cognition (of the absence of things; which the opponent cannot admit).

..."non-existence" is of four kinds: (1) previous non-existence, (2) destruction, (3) mutual negation, and (4) absolute non-existence.

(3) The negation of the cow in the horse, and *vice versa*, constitutes "mutual negation."...

(4) "Absolute non-existence" consists in the negation of what has no existence at all.

133. *Dharma* [merit or virtue] is the property of man; it brings about to the agent happiness, means of happiness and final deliverance; it is supersensuous; it is destructible by the experiencing of the last item of happiness; it is produced by the contact of the man with the internal organ, by means of pure thoughts and determinations; and with regard to the different castes and conditions of men there are distinct means of accomplishing it.

(I.i.2; VI.ii.1; VI.i.5; X.ii.8)

The means of *dharma* consist in various substances, qualities and actions, laid down in the Veda and the Law-Books,—some as belonging in common to all men, and some as pertaining specially to distinct castes and conditions. Among the common ones we have the following: faith in *dharma*, harmlessness, benevolence, truthfulness, freedom from desire for undue possession, freedom from lust, purity of intentions, absence of anger, bathing, use of purifying substances, devotion to deity, fasting, and non-neglect (of duties).

(VI.ii.2, 5, 8, 9)

What is known as "*dharma*" or "merit" is a property belonging to man; and it is not a potency residing in the action performed.

Dharma is the direct cause of happiness, of the means of happiness and also of final deliverance,—this last consisting in the absolute destruction of all fresh specific qualities of the self....

Dharma is destructible by the experiencing of the last item of happiness. In as much as *dharma* is an effect, it must come to an end;...The results of *dharma* are such as can be experienced, in some cases, during thousands of years; and, under the circumstances, if such a *dharma* were to be destroyed by its very first result, there would be nothing left to produce the remaining factors of its result; nor is it possible for *dharma* to be destroyed in parts; as it is an absolutely impartite entity....

Dharma is also destroyed by true knowledge. Some people hold *dharma* to be absolutely indestructible; but for these people there could be no final deliverance; as there would be no end of *dharmas* and *adharmas* (and hence of the results of these in the shape of worldly experiences).

In reality the self is neither the doer nor the enjoyer; it is wholly indifferent. And it is only when it becomes connected with such limitations as those of the body and the sense-organs, that it comes to have such notions, as "I" and "mine," of its being the doer and the enjoyer; and such notions cannot but be regarded as false; as they represent things as what in reality they are not. From these notions of "I" and "mine" follow an affection for the pleasant, and aversion to the unpleasant thing; these affections and aversions give rise to activity and cessation from activity; thence follow *dharma* and *adharma*; and this lands the self into the cycle of birth and rebirth....

That every self in earthly life is under the influence of beginningless tendencies and impressions, and as such is by its very nature as it were "bound"—is a directly perceptible cognition that has a very firm hold on the minds of the people. The knowledge of self, however, that is acquired by mere verbal teaching, has but a momentary existence, and is not tested and found compatible with actual experience, and is indirect....

Hence with a view to acquire the direct knowledge of self, it becomes necessary to have recourse to meditation; and when meditation has reached the perfect stage, the true nature of the self, preclusive of all notions of its being the doer or the enjoyer, becomes distinctly cognisable;...

134. *Adharma* (lack of merit, demerit) also is a quality of the self; it is conducive to sin and undesirable results; it is imperceptible; destructible by the cognition of the last item of pain (resulting from it). Its causes are—(1) the doing of actions which are prohibited in the scriptures and which are contrary to the causes of *dharma*; e.g., harmfulness, untruthfulness, undue possession; (2) the non-performance of actions enjoined in the scriptures; and (3) neglect [of duties]. These, along with impurity of motives,—tend to the mind-contact[1] bringing about *adharma*. (VI.ii.3, 4, 6, 7; VI.i.5, 7, 8)

135. When the man does not attain true knowledge, and is still under the influence of affections and aversions, the doing of excellent virtuous deeds endowed with great motive power, accompanied by a slight taint of sin, leads him to contact with desirable bodies and sense-organs and consequent experience of pleasures &c., in accordance with the impressions (left by his previous actions)—in such regions as those of Brahmā, of Indra, of Prajāpati, of *pitṛs* [ancestors], or of men. Similarly the performance of bad sinful acts, accompanied

[1] That is, these impurities contaminate the mind.

by a slight touch of virtue, brings about his contact with bodies and sense-organs and consequent experience of pains &c., in such regions as those of ghosts and of the lower animals. And thus by the performance of such virtuous deeds as are in the form of outgoing activity (of the self), accompanied by sin, the man passes through the various divine, human and animal regions, again and again; and this is what constitutes his "wheel of bondage." (vi.ii.15)

136. When a man with due knowledge (intelligently) performs acts of *dharma* without any thought of the result to follow therefrom, he comes to be born in a pure family; and being thus born he has a longing for finding out the means for the absolute removal of pain; and with this end in view, he betakes himself to a properly qualified teacher, and obtains from him the true knowledge of the six categories, which removes his ignorance; then having acquired thorough dispassion, he becomes free from all affections, aversions and other such like feelings; and the absence of these puts a stop to the production of any *dharma* or *adharma*; the *dharma* and *adharma* of his previous lives being exhausted, by his experiences of pleasures and pains, and all affections &c. having ceased, all his actions henceforth are only such as are of the nature of pure "*dharma*" tending towards "cessation" or "peace"; and these actions produce in him the happiness of contentment and a disregard for the body; and having brought about happiness due to the vision of highest truth, this *dharma* also disappears. And thus there being a complete cessation, the self becomes "seedless" and the present body falling off, it takes no other bodies, and this cessation of equipment with bodies and organs, being like the extinguishing of fire on all its fuel being burnt up, constitutes what is called "*mokṣa*" ("final deliverance"). (vi.ii.16; v.ii.16.18)

Question: "What is the true nature of the self, the resolution whereunto would constitute deliverance?"

Some people hold that the nature of the self consists in bliss. But this theory is not correct; as it will not bear an examination of the possible alternatives.

For instance, is this bliss actually experienced in the state of deliverance, or not? If it is not experienced, then, even though extant it is as good as non-existent; for the simple reason that it is not enjoyable. If it is experienced in the state of deliverance, then it becomes necessary for you to point out the cause of this experience. You cannot find any such cause, in the absence of the absolute disappearance of bodies and organs. It might be argued that the contact of the internal organ would be the cause of this experience; but this would not be possible; as the internal organ or mind aids in this manner only when it is influenced by *dharma* and *adharma*; and when the mind is such as has all seeds of good and evil rooted out of it, it can never function towards any purpose of the self. It might be urged that the mind favours the self by the force of *dharma* born of Yogic practices. But even such *dharma* being a product, should be transient; and when this would be destroyed, what would be there to help the mind?

137. Sound[1] is the property of *ākāśa* (II.i.27). It is perceptible by the ear (II.ii.21). It is momentary; and counteracted by its effect, by its cause and by both; it is produced by conjunction, disjunction and another sound; it has a limited existence; and is brought about by homogeneous and heterogeneous causes. (II.ii.25–32)

It is of two kinds (1) in the form of letters and (2) in the form of noise in general;...

Chapter VI (Section 2): On Actions

138. Throwing upwards and the other four[2] are all related (belong) to the genus "action" (or motion).[3] (I.i.7)

They belong to a single substance (at a time) (I.i.17); they are momentary (II.ii.25); they reside only in corporeal substances (II.i.21); are without qualities (I.i.17); are produced by gravity, fluidity, effort and conjunction (I.i.29); are counteracted by conjunction produced by themselves (I.i.14); are the independent causes of conjunctions and disjunctions (I.i.17, 20, 30); they serve only as non-material causes (X.ii.3); are productive of effects inhering in their own substrates as well as in the substrates of others; they never produce effects of the same kind as themselves (I.i.11, 25, 31); they are not productive of substances (I.i.21, 22, 31); they belong to distinct well-defined classes. The distinctive feature of each of the five kinds of actions, consists in the direction in which its effect is produced.

Chapter VII: On Community, the Universal

154. Community [universality][4] is of two kinds—"higher" and "lower."

It pervades over all its objectives; has identically the same form

[1] This apparently disconnected text constitutes the treatment, in order, of the last of the twenty-four qualities listed in text no. 5.

[2] See above, text no. 6.

[3] In text no. 1, the six categories were given as substance, quality, action, generality, individuality, and inherence. The present text begins the treatment of "action."

[4] Hereafter in this chapter "universal" will be used for the translator's "community."

(in all cases) inhering in many individuals; it brings about the idea of its own form in one, two or many things; and it is the cause or basis of the notion of inclusion, inhering as it does in all its substrates simultaneously.

Question: "How so?"

Answer: It is so because as a matter of fact we find that when we cognise [all] individual objects as belong simultaneously to a particular class, and we have such cognitions repeatedly, then there is produced in our minds an impression; and when in view of this impression we review those past cognitions, we come to recognise a certain factor that inheres in every one of the objects cognised; and it is this factor that constitutes the universal. (I.ii.3)

The universal of "being" is the highest; in as much as it is the cause of inclusive cognitions only. In the case of a number of totally different things, such, for instance, as pieces of leather, of cloth, of blanket and so forth,—if all of them are possessed of the same quality of "blueness," with regard to each one of these we have the notion that "it is blue"; and in the same manner, in the case of the totally different categories, substance, quality and action, we find that with regard to each one of them we have the notion that "it exists"; and this all-inclusive notion could not but be due to something apart from the three categories themselves; and this something is what we called "being." And it is by reason of the presence of "being" that we have the inclusive notion of a number of things as "existing"; hence this "Being" cannot but be regarded as a universal.

(I.ii.4, 7–10, 17)

The lower universals are the classes of "substance," "quality," "action," and so forth. As these give rise to inclusive as well as exclusive notions, they are regarded as universals as well as individualities. For instance "substance" is a universal, in as much as it serves as the basis of an inclusive notion with regard to such mutually different things as earth, water and the like; and it is an individuality in as much as it serves as the basis of a notion exclusive of qualities and actions. Similarly "quality" is a universal by reason of its giving rise to a notion including all qualities such as colour and the rest; and it is an individuality, on account of its serving as the basis of a notion exclusive of substances and actions. In the same manner, "action" is a universal by reason of its serving as the basis of a notion inclusive of all the several actions of "throwing upwards" and the rest, and it is an individuality, in as much as it is exclusive of qualities and actions.

155. That these universals belong to a category distinct from substance, quality and action, is proved by the fact of their having a character totally different from these latter. For this same reason too they are eternal. These again are different from one another, by reason of each of them residing in a different set of things,—substances, qualities and actions,—and also by reason of people having a distinct notion with regard to each of them.

CHAPTER VIII: ON INDIVIDUALITIES [PARTICULARITIES]—*VIŚEṢA*

156. Individualities are the ultimate [i.e., final] specificatives or differentiatives of their substrates. They reside in such beginningless and indestructible eternal substrates, as the atoms, *ākāśa*, time, space, self, and mind,—inhering in their entirety in each of these, and serving as the basis of absolute differentiation or specification. Just as we have with regard to the bull as distinguished from the horse, certain distinct cognitions—such, for instance, as (1) that it is a "bull," which is a cognition based upon its having the shape of other bulls, (2) that it is "white," which is based upon a quality, (3) that it is "running swiftly," which is based upon action, (4) that it has a "fat hump," which is based upon "constituent parts," and (5) that it carries a "large bell," which is based upon conjunction; so have the *yogis*, who are possessed of powers that we do not possess, distinct cognitions based upon similar shapes, similar qualities and similar actions—with regard to the eternal atoms, the liberated selves and minds; and as in this case no other cause is possible, those causes by reason whereof they have such distinct cognitions,—as that "this is a peculiar substance," "that a peculiar self," and so forth—and which also lead to the recognition of one atom as being the same that was perceived at a different time and place,—are what we call the "ultimate individualities."

Objection: "Why cannot you assume a self-differentiation in the atoms themselves, as you do in the 'individualities'?"

Reply: The atoms themselves could not be the cause of these distinct cognitions; because of all atoms having the same nature; that is to say, as a matter of fact we find that the cognitions that a certain thing brings about are with regard to things other than itself;

e.g., the lamp brings about the cognition of the jar; and certainly one lamp is never rendered cognisable by another lamp. And just as the flesh of the cow and the horse are unclean by themselves, and other things become unclean by coming in contact with them,—so in the case in question, the "ultimate individualities," though of the same nature, are differentiated by themselves, and the atom &c., become differentiated by reason of their contact with these "individualities." (I.ii.6)

Chapter IX: On Inherence

157. Inherence is the relationship between things that are inseparably connected, and which stand to each other in the relation of the container and the contained,—the relationship, namely, that serves as the ground of the notion that "such and such a thing subsists in this." That is to say, the relationship named "inherence" is that from which proceeds the notion that "this subsists in this,"—with regard to substances, qualities, actions, universals and individualities, that appear in the form of causes and effects, as well as those that do not appear as causes and effects, which are inseparably connected; and also that relationship from which proceeds the interdependence of things of limited extension upon something else, from which they are known to be different. As for instance, the notion that "there is curd in this pot" is found to be present only when there is a distinct relationship between the two things; so also the notions—"the cloth is in these threads," "the mat is in these reeds," "this quality and that action are in this substance," "being is in these substances, qualities and actions," "there is the general character of substance in this substance," "the general character of quality in this quality," "the general character of action in this action," "the ultimate individualities in this eternal substance"; and from all such notions we infer the existence of the relationship in question.

(VII.ii.26, 27, 28; V.ii.23)

158. Inherence is not mere conjunction; (1) because the members of this relationship are inseparably connected; (2) because this relationship is not caused by the action of any of the members related; (3) because it is not found to end with the disjunction of the members; and (4) because it is found subsisting only between the container and the contained.

159. Inherence is a category distinct from substance and the rest; as, like "being," it has a character different from these. That is to

say, as in the case of "being" we find that bringing about notions of itself in regard to the substrates of the classes of "substance" and the rest, it differs from its substrates, as also from other classes,—so also inherence, being the cause of the notion that "this subsists in that," with regard to the other five categories, must be regarded as something different from these. Nor is there a multiplicity of inherences, as there is of conjunctions; because like "being," inherence has the same distinguishing feature, and also because there are no reasons for making distinctions in regard to it; for these reasons inherence, like "being," must be regarded as one only.

161. Even though the members related are transient, the inherence is not transient, like conjunction; because like being, it is not brought about by any cause. That is to say, in the case of being we have found that it is eternal, because we cannot cognise any cause for it, by any of the valid means of knowledge; and the same may be said to be the case with inherence also; as by none of the valid means of knowledge can we find any cause for it.

Objection: "By what relation does inherence subsist in substance &c.? This relation can not be that of conjunction; as conjunction being a quality can reside in substance only (and inherence is not a substance); nor can the relation be that of inherence; as the latter is one only; and there is no third relation by which it can subsist."

Reply: Not so; as it is itself of the nature of relation or subsistence. In the case of "being" with regard to substances, qualities and actions, we have seen that it has no connection with any other "being"; and in the same manner, inherence, being inseparable (from its substrate) and of the very nature of a subsisting relation, could have no other relation; and hence it is regarded as self-sufficient. For this reason it has been regarded as imperceptible by the sense-organs; specially as it is not found to have an existence in the perceptible substances in the same manner that "being" &c. have; and as it is not perceptible by itself, we conclude that it is only inferable from the notion that "this is in that."

All reverence to that Kaṇāda who, having pleased Maheśvara by the superb character of his meditation and austerities, propounded the philosophy of the Vaiśeṣika system!

Thus ends the *Padārthadharmasaṁgraha* of Praśastapāda.

CHAPTER XII

SĀṀKHYA

THIS system is notable for its theory of evolution, which is accepted by many other Indian systems, and for the reduction of the numerous categories of the Nyāya and Vaiśeṣika systems to the two fundamental categories of *puruṣa* and *prakṛti*, subject and object. All experience is based on the duality of the knowing subject, *puruṣa*, and the known object, *prakṛti*. *Prakṛti* (usually translated "Nature") is the basis of all objective existence, physical and psychical. As the changing object, *prakṛti* is the source of the world of becoming. In it all determinate existence is implicitly contained. It is pure potentiality. It is not being but force, a state of tension of the three constituents (*guṇas*), *sattva*, *rajas*, and *tamas*. *Prakṛti* is, as it were, a string of three strands. *Sattva* is potential consciousness; *rajas* is the source of activity, and *tamas* is the source of that which resists activity. They produce pleasure, pain, and indifference, respectively. All things, as products of *prakṛti*, consist of the three *guṇas* in different proportions. The varied interaction of the *guṇas* accounts for the variety of the world. When the three elements are held in equipoise there is no action. When there is a disturbance of the equilibrium, the process of evolution begins.

The evolution of unconscious *prakṛti* can take place only through the presence of conscious *puruṣa*. The presence of *puruṣa* excites the activity of *prakṛti*, and, thus upsetting the equilibrium of the *guṇas* in *prakṛti*, passively starts the evolutionary process. The union of *puruṣa* and *prakṛti* is compared to a lame man of good vision mounted on the shoulders of a blind man of sure foot.

The development of this process of evolution follows a law of succession. *Mahat* (literally "the great" or "the great one") is the first product of the evolution of *prakṛti*. It is the basis of the intelligence (*buddhi*) of the individual. *Mahat* brings out the cosmic aspect, and *buddhi* the psychological counterpart of *mahat* in the individual. *Buddhi* is not *puruṣa*, the self. It is the subtle substance of all mental processes. *Ahaṁkāra* or self-sense, which develops out of *buddhi*, is the principle of individuation.

Three different lines of development arise from *ahaṁkāra*. From its *sattva* aspect arise *manas* (the mind), the five organs of perception, and the five organs or instruments of action; from its *tamas* aspect arise the five fine or subtle elements. From these the gross elements develop by a preponderance of the quality of *tamas*. Its *rajas* aspect supplies the energy for both of these developments.

Creation is the unfolding of the different effects from the original *prakṛti*, and destruction is the dissolution of them into the original *prakṛti*.

Prakṛti and its products are unconscious. They cannot discriminate between themselves and *puruṣa*, the self. The individual is not body, life, or mind, but the informing self, silent, peaceful, eternal. The self is pure spirit. If it were liable to change, knowledge would be impossible. By the light of *puruṣa's* consciousness, we become conscious of *prakṛti*. *Buddhi*, *manas*, etc., are the instruments of consciousness and are not themselves conscious. As there are many conscious beings in the world, the Sāṁkhya adopts the view of the plurality of selves, both in the condition of bondage and in that of release.

The empirical individual, the *jīva*, is the self limited by the body and the senses. It is a member of the natural world. Each ego possesses, within the gross material body which suffers dissolution at death, a subtle body formed of the psychical apparatus, including the senses. These subtle bodies are products of *prakṛti* and possess the three *guṇas*. The empirical self is thus the composite of free spirit and *prakṛti*, where the *puruṣa* forgets its true nature and is deluded into the belief that it thinks, feels, and acts. *Buddhi*, by means of the reflection of *puruṣa* which is adjacent to it, becomes verily of its form and experiences objects.

Salvation in the Sāṁkhya system is only phenomenal, for the true self is always free. Bondage is the activity of *prakṛti* toward one not possessing discrimination, that is, the knowledge of the distinction of *puruṣa* and *prakṛti*. Release is the inactivity of *prakṛti* toward one possessing discriminate knowledge. Freedom consists in the removal of the obstacle which hinders the full manifestation of the light of *puruṣa*. Freedom is obtained by discriminative knowledge, but it is not theoretical. It is the result of the practice of virtue and *yoga*. The Yoga system (to be presented in the next chapter) constitutes, as it were, the practical side of the Sāṁkhya-Yoga philosophy; it enunciates and elaborates the practical methods which lead to discriminative knowledge and thus to release.

Tradition ascribes the authorship of the Sāṁkhya system to Kapila, an almost legendary figure, said by some to be the son of Brahmā, by others to be an incarnation of Viṣṇu, and by still others to be an incarnation of Agni. He probably lived during the seventh century B.C. There is no evidence to show that the *Sāṁkhya-pravacana Sūtra*, which is attributed to him, was written by him. The *Sāṁkhya-kārikā* of Īśvarakṛṣṇa is the earliest available text on the Sāṁkhya philosophy. It is a work of the third century A.D.

The selections in section A of this chapter are taken from *The Sāṅkhya-kārikā of Īśvara Kṛṣṇa* (3rd century A.D.), edited and translated by S. S. Suryanarayana Sastri (Madras: University of Madras, 1935); and *The Tattva-kaumudī* (Vācaspati Miśra's Commentary [850 A.D.] on the *Sāṁkhya-kārikā*), translated by Ganganatha Jha (Poona: The Oriental Book

Agency, 2nd ed. rev., 1934). Some *kārikās* are taken from Jha's translation as noted in the text.

The selections in section B are taken from *The Sāṁkhya Philosophy*, containing (1) *Sāṁkhya-pravacana Sūtra* (14th century A.D.), with the *Vṛtti* of Aniruddha (15th century A.D.), and the *Bhāṣya* of Vijñāna Bhikṣu (16th century A.D.), and extracts from the *Vṛtti-sāra* of Mahādeva Vedāntin (18th century A.D.); (2) *Tattva-samāsa*; (3) *Sāṁkhya-kārikā*; and (4) *Pañca-śikha Sūtra*, translated by Nandalal Sinha, Sacred Books of the Hindus, XI (Allahabad: The Panini Office, 1915).

A. THE *SĀṀKHYA-KĀRIKĀ*

I. From torment by three-fold misery arises the inquiry into the means of terminating it; if it be said that it is fruitless, the means being known by perception,[1] no [we reply], since in them there is not certainty or finality.[2]

The three kinds of pain constitute [what is ordinarily called] the "triad of pain." These are: (1) the intrinsic (*ādhyātmika*), (2) the extrinsic (*ādhibhautika*) and (3) the divine or superhuman (*ādhidaivika*). Of these, the intrinsic is two-fold, bodily and mental. Bodily pain is caused by the disorder of the several humours, wind, bile and phlegm; and mental pain is due to desire, wrath, avarice, affection, fear, envy, grief, and the non-perception of particular objects. All these are called intrinsic on account of their being amenable to internal remedies. Pains amenable to external remedies are two-fold: extrinsic and superhuman. The extrinsic are caused by men, beasts, birds, reptiles, and inanimate things; and the superhuman ones are due to the evil influence of planets and the various elementals.[3]

An objection is raised: "...Hundreds of remedies for bodily pains are laid down by eminent physicians; for mental pains also we have easy remedies in the shape of the attainment of the objects of enjoyment—such as women, desirable food and drink, unguents, dress, ornaments, and the like. Similarly, of extrinsic pains we have easy remedies—such as expert knowledge of moral and political science, residence in safe places, etc. In the same manner, of superhuman troubles we have remedies in the shape of charms, incantations, and the rest."

[Reply] ...though easily available, the obvious means do not effect absolute and final removal of pain. Consequently, the present enquiry is not superfluous.

[1] Perhaps a better translation of *dṛṣṭi* would be "being obvious," instead of "being known by perception."

[2] The translations of the *kārikās* (verses) and the commentary are free rather than literal. The translators have placed in parentheses many words and phrases necessarily implied in the Sanskrit. For the sake of facility of reading, the editors have omitted the parentheses, but have put into brackets words and phrases which are purely explanatory additions.

[3] For "elementals," read "spirits."

II. The scriptural means of terminating misery is also like the perceptible;[1] it is verily linked with impurity, destruction,[2] and surpassability;[3] different therefrom and superior thereto is that means derived from the discriminative knowledge of the evolved,[4] the unevolved,[5] and the knower.

...The host of religious rites laid down in the Veda is equal to the obvious remedies [mentioned before];—both being equally inefficient in the absolute and final removal of the three kinds of pain....

...The *impurity* lies in the fact of the *Soma* and other sacrifices being accompanied by the killing of animals and the destruction of grains and seeds....

The properties—"*decay*" and "*inequality*"—belong really to the effect, but are here attributed to the means. This *liability to decay* is inferred from the fact of heaven being a positive entity and a product. Further, the *Jyotiṣṭoma* and other sacrifices are the means to the attainment of heaven only, whereas the *Vājapeya* and others lead to the attainment of the kingdom of heaven [or "self-sovereignty"]. This is what constitutes the *inequality* spoken of. The greatness of the magnificence of one man is a source of pain to another of lesser magnificence.

The literal meaning of the words of the *kārikā* is as follows: The means of removing pain, consisting in the direct discriminative knowledge of the spirit (*puruṣa*) as apart from matter, is contrary to the Vedic means, and hence is better. The Vedic remedy is good inasmuch as it is authorised by the Veda and as such capable of removing pain to a certain extent; the discriminative knowledge of the spirit as distinct from matter is also good; and, of these two, the latter is better, superior.

III. Primal Nature (*prakṛti*)[6] is not an evolute; the seven,[7] beginning with the Great One [i.e., *mahat*, the intellect] are both evolvents and evolutes; the sixteen [i.e., the five organs of sense, the five of action, the mind, and the five gross elements] are only evolutes; the spirit is neither evolvent nor evolute.

...of this matter itself there can be no root; or else we would be landed in an unwarranted *regressus ad infinitum*.

IV. Three varieties are recognised of the means of correct knowledge—perception, inference, and valid testimony, all means of correct knowledge being comprehended in these; the knowledge of what is to be known depends, verily, on the means of correct knowledge.

[1] See p. 426, footnote 1.
[2] Or "decay."
[3] Or "inequality."
[4] Or "manifested."
[5] Or "unmanifested."
[6] *Prakṛti* may also be translated "root-matter" or "primordial matter" or "matter," as in Jha.
[7] The "seven" are intellect, individuation, and the five subtle elements—to be described later.

v. Perception is the ascertainment of objects [which are in contact with sense-organs]; inference, which follows on the knowledge of the characteristic mark (*liṅga*) [i.e., the middle term] and that which bears the mark [i.e., the major and minor terms] is said to be of three kinds;[1] as for valid testimony, it is incontrovertible knowledge derived from verbal statement.

...Inference that has been just defined in its general form has three special forms, called (1) *a priori* ("*pūrvavat*"), (2) *a posteriori* ("*śeṣavat*"), and (3) based on general observation ("*sāmānyatodṛṣṭa*").

...all the other means of cognition,—such as "analogy" and the rest,— which have been posited in the other philosophical systems, are all included among those that have been described above.

vi. Knowledge of objects beyond the senses comes from inference based on analogy; what knowledge is obscure and not attainable even thereby is gained by valid testimony.

vii. Non-perception may be because of extreme distance, extreme proximity, injury to the organs, non-steadiness of the mind, subtlety, veiling, suppression, and blending with what is similar.

viii. The non-perception of that [i.e., Primal Nature] is due to its subtlety, not to its non-existence, since it is perceived in its effects; the great one (*mahat*) [i.e., the intellect] and the rest are its effects, which are both like and unlike their cause—Nature.[2]

ix. The effect is existent; (1) because what is "non-existent" cannot be produced; (2) because there is a definite relation of the cause with the effect; (3) because all is not possible; (4) because the efficient can do only that for which it is efficient; (5) because the effect is of the same essence as the cause. [Jha]

x. The evolved is caused, non-eternal, non-pervasive, mobile, manifold, dependent,[3] mergent, conjunct [i.e., with parts] and heteronomous;[4] the unevolved is the reverse of all these.

xi. The manifest is "with the three attributes" (*guṇas*),[5] "undistinguishable" (or "non-separative"), "objective," "common," "insentient" and "productive." So also is Nature. The spirit is the reverse, and yet also [in some respects] similar. [Jha]

"*With the three attributes*"—That is to say, the manifest has the three attributes of pleasure, pain, and delusion. By this assertion are set aside all those theories that attribute pleasure and pain to the spirit.

[1] See *Nyāya Sūtra*.

[2] See *kārikā* xxiii.

[3] Or "supported."

[4] Or "dependent."

[5] The term "*guṇas*" may be translated "attribute" or "quality," but technically they are not qualities distinguishable from substance; they are constituents rather than qualities.

"*Undistinguishable*"; just as Nature cannot be distinguished from itself, so also the Great Principle (*buddhi*),[1] being connate with Nature, cannot be distinguished from Nature....

Some people have held that it is idea (*vijñāna*) alone that constitutes pleasure, pain, and delusion, and that there exists nothing besides this idea that could possess these [pleasure, etc.,] as its attributes. In opposition to this view it is asserted that the manifest is "*objective*"; "*objective*" here stands for "what can be apprehended." That is, it is exterior to the idea.—And because it is "objective," therefore, "*common*"—i.e., apprehended simultaneously by several persons. If it were nothing more or less than the idea, then in that case,—in as much as ideas, being in the form of "functions," belong specially to particular individuals,—all that is "manifest" would have to belong specially to particular individuals. That is to say, as a matter of fact, the idea of one person is not apprehended by another, the cognition of another person being always uncognisable. In the case of [manifest substance such as] the glance of a dancing girl, it is found that many persons continue to stare at it at the same time. This could not be the cause if it were otherwise [i.e., if the glance were a mere idea].

"*Yet also similar*"; that is to say, though there are points of similarity, such as being "without cause" and the rest, yet there are points of dissimilarity also, in the form of being devoid of the three attributes and the rest.

XII. The attributes are of the nature of pleasure, pain, and delusion; they serve the purpose of illumination, action, and restraint; and they are mutually subjugative, and supporting, and productive, and co-operative.[2] [Jha]

Now to explain: (1) "*mutually subjugative*"—The attributes are so constituted that when one is brought into play for some purpose, it subjugates the other;... (2) "*mutually supporting*"...what is meant by "support" here is that the operation of one is dependent upon the other. (3) "*mutually productive*." That is to say, one can produce its effects only when resting on the other two. By *production* here is meant modification, and this is always of the same character as the parent attribute. This is the reason why this "modification" is not regarded as "caused" [produced], what brings it about not being essentially different from itself; nor is it non-eternal, transient,—there being no merging of it into anything essentially different from itself. (4) "*mutually co-operative*." That is to say, they are mutual concomitants not existing apart from one another.

XIII. The *sattva* attribute is held to be buoyant and illuminating; the *rajas* attribute exciting and mobile; and the *tamas* attribute

[1] That is, the intellect. *Mahat* (the Great Principle) and *buddhi* represent the cosmic and the individual aspects of intellect.

[2] Read *kārikā* XIII with XII.

sluggish and enveloping. Their functioning is for a single purpose, like that of the lamp. [Jha]

We have all observed how the wick and the oil—each, by itself, opposed to the action of fire—co-operate, when in contact with fire, for the single purpose of giving light;...the three attributes, though possessed of mutually contradictory properties, co-operate towards a single end;—"for the single purpose" of the emancipation of the spirit.

XIV. The properties of being "undistinguishable" and the rest are proved by the existence of the three attributes[1] and by the non-existence of these [i.e., the three attributes] in their absence.[2] And the existence of the unmanifest [i.e., Nature] too is established on the ground of the properties of the effect being of the same nature as those of the cause. [Jha]

..."*by the non-existence of these in their absence*"; that is, where the said properties of "being undistinguishable" and the rest are absent,—as in the *spirit*,—the three attributes of *sattva* etc., are non-existent.

XV. Because of the finite nature of specific objects, because of homogeneity, because of evolution being due to the efficiency of the cause, because of separation between cause and its product, and because of the merging of the whole world (of effects),—there is the Unmanifest as the cause. [Jha]

This "distinguishing" or separation from the final cause, the highest Unmanifest, of the whole world of effects—related to it either mediately [as with earth, etc.] or immediately [as with the Great Principle]—is what is meant by the "distinction between the cause and its product." Similarly, at counter-evolution or dissolution, the product,...merges into its cause,...and thereby disappears,...and finally when the Great Principle merges into its cause, Nature, it renders this latter unmanifest. In as much as there is no merging of Nature itself into anything else, it is unmanifest pure and simple....

"*Because of the finite nature of specific objects*";..."because of being measured, i.e., finite." [The reasoning is stated in the syllogistic form]—The specific objects in question, the Great Principle and the rest, have an unmanifested entity for their cause [i.e., they have a cause in which they exist in their unmanifested state],—because they are finite,—like the jar and other things:—the jar and other things are found to have, for their cause, clay and other things, in which inhere the unmanifested state of the effects; we have already shown that the cause is that wherein the effect already exists in the unmanifested state. Under these circumstances, the cause of the Great Principle must be that highest unmanifest which must be the final cause, for there is no ground for postulating a further unmanifested reality.

[1] That is, in Nature (*prakṛti*). [2] That is, in the spirit (*puruṣa*).

..."*because of homogeneity*."—"homogeneity" consists in the similarity of the different objects. The Great Principle and the rest—manifesting themselves as "volition" and the rest—are found to be "homogeneous" in the sense that they consist in pleasure, pain, and delusion. And whatever is invariably connected with a certain form must have, for its cause wherein it inheres, something which has that form for its constituent element. Thus it becomes established that of the specific objects, the unmanifested [i.e., Nature] is the cause.

XVI. There is the unmanifest as the cause gone before; it operates through the three attributes, by blending and modification, like water, on account of the difference arising from the predominance of one or the other of the attributes. [Jha]

"*By modification like water*";—we all know how the water falling from the clouds, though naturally of itself having one taste, becomes sweet, sour, saline, bitter, pungent, and hot, according as it comes into contact with different modifications of earth and becomes transformed into the juice of fruits such as cocoanut, palm, wood-apples, and so forth; in the same manner [owing to the blending and the mutual suppression of the attributes], the attributes of Nature come to be predominant one by one and thereby bring about various modifications in the state of various products.

XVII. (*a*) Because all composite objects are for another's use, (*b*) because there must be absence of the three attributes and other properties, (*c*) because there must be control, (*d*) because there must be someone to experience and (*e*) because there is a tendency towards "isolation" or final beatitude, therefore, the spirit must be there.

The spirit must be there, apart from the unmanifest (Nature) and other things. (a) "*Because all composite objects are for another's use*"—This reason, when reduced to the syllogistic form, would stand thus—Nature, the Great Principle, the "I-principle," and other things must exist for another's use, because they are composite like the bedstead, the chair, the unguent, and other things. Nature and the rest are all "composite," being composed as they are, of pleasure, pain, and delusion.

"*Because there must be absence of the three attributes and other properties*."—That is to say, if from the fact of Nature, &c., "being for another's use," we were to infer only another composite object, then in that case, we would have to assume such composite objects *ad infinitum*;...Thus then, in order to escape the *regressus ad infinitum*, if we accept the non-composite nature of spirit, we find ourselves constrained to attribute to it the properties of being "without the three attributes," "distinguishable," "non-objective" [i.e., subjective], "uncommon" [i.e., specific], "sentient," and "not productive." Because "being with three attributes" and other properties are always accompanied by that of "being composite," which latter being absent in the spirit, must lead to the inference of the absence of the three attributes,...

"*Because there must be control*"; that is to say, because the objects constituted by the three attributes are such as "are always controlled";—as a matter of fact it is found that everything consisting in pleasure, pain, and delusion [i.e., in the three attributes] is controlled by something else—e.g., the chariot by the charioteer; and the Great Principle and the rest have been proved to "consist in pleasure, pain, and delusion"; therefore, they must have a "controller"—and this "controller" must be beyond the three attributes and independent;—and this is the spirit.

Again there must be the spirit "*because there must be someone to experience.*" The term "someone to experience" indicates the *objects* of experience in the shape of pleasure and pain. The objects of experience are pleasure and pain, which are felt by everyone as agreeable and disagreeable respectively. That is to say, there must be something other than the feelings themselves to which they can be agreeable or otherwise. Feelings cannot be agreeable or disagreeable to the Great Principle and other products, as that would involve the anomaly of things operating upon themselves, as the Great Principle and the rest are all themselves integrally composed of pleasure, pain, and delusion. Thus, then, something else, which does not consist of pleasure, etc., must be the one to whom things are agreeable or disagreeable; and this something else must be the spirit.

...in as much as there is a tendency in all scriptures and among all intelligent persons towards "*isolation*," there must be something beyond (pleasure, etc., and hence) the Great Principle and the rest,—and this is the spirit.

XVIII. The plurality of spirits certainly follows from the distributive nature of the incidence of birth and death and of the endowment of the instruments of cognition and action, from bodies engaging in action, not all at the same time, and also from differences in the proportion of the three constituents.

...Some persons abounding in the *sattva* attribute represent aggregates of that attribute—e.g., the deities and saints; others abound in the *rajas* attribute,—such as men; others again in the *tamas* attribute,—such as beasts. This "diversity" or "differentiation" due to the distribution of the attributes in the various entities, could not be explained if the spirit were one and the same in all. On the hypothesis of plurality, however, there is no difficulty.

XIX. And from that contrast,[1] it follows that the spirit is "witness," and has "isolation," "neutrality," and is the "seer," and "inactive." [Jha]

Thus, the "*contrast*" of the character of "having the three attributes, etc.," and the rest...connotes the spirit's property of being without the

[1] This contrast is that which has been explained in *kārikā* XI.

three attributes and being "distinguishable," "non-objective," "not common," "sentient," and "non-objective." Now the characters being "sentient" and "non-objective" also indicate the characters of being "witness," and "seer." Since it is only a "sentient" being that can be a "seer," and one can be a "seer," and one can be a "witness" only when the things have been shown to him, as in daily life we find the two parties of a dispute showing the object of their dispute to the *witness*, similarly does the Nature exhibit its creations before the spirit, which latter, therefore, becomes the *witness*. And again, no object can be shown to one who is himself an object and insentient; and since the spirit is both sentient and non-objective, it becomes the *witness*. For the same reasons, the spirit is also the "seer."

Further, from *the absence of the three attributes* in the spirit follows its *isolation*—by which is meant the final and absolute removal of the three kinds of pain; and this property, as belonging to the spirit, is a necessary deduction from the fact of the spirit being by its very nature without the three attributes, and hence without pleasure, pain, or delusion.

From the absence of the attributes, again, follows *neutrality*; since this latter property is such as cannot belong either to the happy and satisfied, or to the sad and grumbling. It is only one who is devoid of both pleasure and pain who can be called *neutral*—also called *udāsīna* (indifferent). Lastly, the *inactivity* of the spirit follows from its being "distinguishable" and "non-productive."

xx. Thus from this union, the insentient "evolute" appears as if "sentient"; and similarly, from the activity really belonging to the attributes, the spirit, which is neutral, appears as if it were active. [Jha]

The word "evolute" ("*liṅga*"), here stands for everything from the Great Principle down to the primary elements to be described later on. The cause of the mistake is said to be the "union," i.e., proximity of the spirit with the "evolute."

xxi. For the perception of Nature by the spirit and for the isolation of the spirit, there is union of both,—like that of the halt and the blind; and from this union proceeds evolution. [Jha]

"*For the isolation of the spirit*"—The spirit, while in union with the "enjoyable" Nature, believes the three kinds of pain—the constituents of Nature—to be his own; and from this [self-imposed bond] he seeks liberation, isolation; this isolation is dependent upon due discrimination between the spirit and the three attributes; this discrimination is not possible without the Nature... thus it is that for his own isolation the spirit needs Nature.

"*From this union proceeds evolution.*" The said "union" [of spirit with Nature] cannot by itself suffice either for "enjoyment" or "isolation" if the Great Principle and the rest be not there; hence the *union* itself brings about the evolution for the sake of "enjoyment" and "isolation."

xxii. From *prakṛti* (primordial matter, Nature) issues *mahat* (*buddhi*, the Great Principle); from this issues *ahaṁkāra* (I-principle); from which proceed the "set of sixteen"; from five of this "set of sixteen" proceed the five elementary substances. [Jha][1]

...The "set of sixteen" is made up of the eleven sense-organs, to be described later on, and the five primary elements. Out of these sixteen, from the five primary elements proceed respectively the five elementary substances (*ākāśa* [ether], earth, water, air, and fire).

xxiii. Intellect is determinative. Virtue, wisdom, non-attachment, and the possession of lordly powers constitute its *sāttvika* form [i.e., its form when the constituent *sattva*, goodness, predominates]; the reverse of these are of its *tāmasa* form [i.e., of its nature, when *tamas*, darkness, preponderates].

...Now "determination" consists in the notion that "this should be done," and it belongs to, and forms the characteristic function of, *buddhi* (the "Great Principle," will),[2] which acquires sentience from its proximity to the sentient faculty of the spirit; and "*buddhi*" is regarded as not different from the said "determination"...this also constitutes the "definition"...of *buddhi*, in as much as it distinguishes it from all like and unlike things.

Having thus defined *buddhi*, the author, in order to help the attainment of discriminative wisdom, states the properties of *buddhi*, as abounding in the *sattva* and *tamas* attributes: "*Virtue*, etc. etc.," Virtue "leads to prosperity and the highest Good,—that brought about by the performance of sacrifices, charity, and the like lead to the former, and that due to the practice of eight-fold *yoga* lead to the latter. Wisdom consists in the knowledge of the difference between the attributes (as constituting Nature) and the spirit. Dispassion is absence of attachment [or love].

Power also is a property of *buddhi*, and it is to this that the perfections, attenuation and the rest (*aṇimā*, etc.) are due.

These four are the properties of *buddhi*, abounding in the *sattva* attribute. Those abounding in the *tamas* attribute are the reverse of these—viz., vice, ignorance, passion, and weakness.

xxiv. Individuation is conceit in the ego. Therefrom, creation[3] proceeds in two ways, as the eleven-fold aggregate and as the five-fold subtle elements.

xxv. The "set of eleven" abounding in the *sattva* attribute, evolves out of the "*vaikṛta*" form of the "I-principle"; the set of rudimentary

[1] See *kārikā* iii.

[2] The word "will" used in Jha's translation stands for "*buddhi*," which is usually translated as "intellect."

[3] "Evolution" should be substituted for "creation" throughout the text.

substances from the "*bhūtādi*" form of the "I-principle"; and both of them from the "*taijasa*" form of the "I-principle."[1]

"The set of eleven," the sense-organs, being illuminative and buoyant, is said to abound in the *sattva* attribute; and it proceeds from the "*vaikṛta*" "I-principle." From the "I-principle" as dominated by the *tamas* attribute proceeds the set of rudimentary substances. How so? Because these substances abound in the *sattva* attribute. That is to say—though the I-principle is one and uniform, yet by reason of the domination or suppression of one or other of these attributes it evolves products of diverse kinds.

. . . from the "*taijasa* form," that is, from the form abounding in the *rajas* attribute, proceed both, the "set of eleven" as also the "set of rudimentary substances." Even though there is no separate product from the *rajas* attribute exclusively by itself, yet [it is a necessary factor as] the *sattva* and *tamas* attributes are, by themselves, absolutely inert and as such do not perform their functions at all; it is only when they are energised and moved by the *rajas* attribute that they perform their functions; thus the *rajas* attribute is instrumental in the evolving of both the sets of products mentioned above, through the exciting of activity of the other two attributes, *sattva* and *tamas*. Thus it is not true that the *rajas* attribute serves no useful purpose.

XXVI. Eye, ear, nose, tongue, and skin are called organs of cognition; voice, hands, feet, and the organs of excretion and generation are said to be the organs of action.

XXVII. Of these [sense-organs] mind partakes of the nature of both [sensory and motor]: it is the "observing" principle, and is called a "sense-organ" since it has properties common to sense-organs. Its multifariousness, as also its diverse external forms, are due to the particular modifications of the attributes. [Jha]

"*Partakes, etc.*"—Among the eleven sense-organs the mind partakes of the nature of both—i.e., it is an organ of sensation, as well as one of action, since the eye and the other sensory organs, as well as speech and other motor organs, are able to operate on their respective objects only when influenced by the mind.

. . . "*It is the observing principle*"—That is to say, mind is defined by observation; when a certain object has been just vaguely apprehended by a sense-organ as "a thing," there follows the definite cognition in the form "it is such and such a thing, not that"; and it is this observing, i.e., the perception of definite properties as belonging to the thing apprehended,—that is done through the mind.

[1] (a) "*vaikṛta*," (b) *bhūtādi* and (c) *taijasa* are purely technical term-names applied to the three forms or states of the "I-principle." When the "I-principle" is dominated by the *sattva* attribute, it is called "*vaikṛta*"; when it is dominated by the *tamas* attribute, it is called "*bhūtādi*"; and when it is dominated by the *rajas* attribute, it is called "*taijasa*." These are mere technical names, and do not connote anything—Gauḍapāda.

"*It is a sense-organ.*" Why? "Because it has properties common to sense-organs." The property meant is that consisting in its having for its constituent cause the "I-principle" abounding in the *sattva* attribute,...

XXVIII. Bare awareness, in respect of sound, etc., is acknowledged to be the function of the five organs of cognition, while of the five organs of action, the functions are speech, grasping, motion, excretion, and sexual enjoyment.

XXIX. Of the three [the internal organs—intellect, individuation, and mind], the functions consist of their respective characteristics; this is peculiar to each. The function common to the organs consists in the five breaths (*prāṇa*) and the rest.

...the sense...is that the property which serves as the distinguishing feature of each of the three internal organs also denotes its respective function; thus "determination" of the will, "egoism" of the I-principle, and "observation" of the mind.

..."*The five breaths constitute the common function.*" The five "vital airs" i.e., the *life* itself—form the common function of the three internal organs, since the latter exists while the former do and ceases to exist when these are absent....

XXX. With regard to perceptible things, the functions of the whole set of the four organs[1] are said to be simultaneous, as well as gradual; with regard to imperceptible [as well as perceptible] things, the functions of the three internal organs are preceded by that [i.e., the cognition of some perceptible object]. [Jha]

With regard to imperceptible things, on the other hand, the [three] internal organs operate without the aid of the external organs. "*The functions of the three are preceded by that,*" i.e., *the instantaneous* as well as the *gradual* functions of the three internal organs are preceded by some perception of a visible object; since inference, testimony, and remembrance—which are the means of cognising imperceptible things,—operate only when they have for their background some sort of perception [of perceptible things]. The sense is that in regard to "perceptible" as well as "imperceptible" things the functioning of the internal organs is always preceded by the perception of some external object.

XXXI. The organs, external and internal, discharge their respective functions, prompted by mutual impulsion; the goal of the spirit is alone the cause; by nothing else is any instrument actuated.

XXXII. Instruments [or organs] are of thirteen varieties; they function by grasping, sustaining, and disclosing; their objects, which are of the nature of what is grasped, sustained, or disclosed, are ten-fold.

[1] That is, the three internal organs and the organ of one outer sense.

The "thirteen organs" consist of the eleven sense-organs, the I-principle, and the will...."Having the functions of seizing, sustaining, and illuminating,"—respectively; that is to say, the motor organs have the function of seizing, that is, they take up their respective objects; i.e., extend their activities over them;—the will, the I-principle, and the mind "sustain" things through their function in the shape of the vital airs and the rest [mentioned before]; and lastly, the sensory organs "illumine" [or render perceptible] their respective objects.

XXXIII. The internal organs are three; and the external, ten, exhibiting objects to the former three. The "external" organs act at the present time, and the "internal" at all the three points of time. [Jha]

XXXIV. Of these, the five sensory organs are concerned with objects specific as well as non-specific. Speech is concerned with sound; the rest are concerned with five objects. [Jha]

...The term "specific" here stands for the gross sound [touch, colour, taste, and odour] in their "calm," "turbulent," and "deluding" forms, as manifested in the form of earth [water, air, fire and *ākāśa*];—and "*non-specific*" stands for the subtile forms of sound, etc., manifested as the rudimentary elements.

"*The rest*," i.e., the four other motor-organs—the arms, the generative organ, the hands, and the feet—are "*concerned with five objects*"; because the jar and such other objects, which are what are dealt with by those organs, are all made up of the five primary elements of sound, colour, touch, taste, and odour.

XXXV. For the reason that the intellect with the other internal organs ascertains the nature of objects of sense, the internal organs are the principal ones, while the rest of the organs are the entrances thereto.

XXXVI. [The external organs together with the mind and the I-principle], characteristically different from one another and being different modifications of the attributes, resemble a lamp in action; [and as such] having first illumined [or rendered manifest] the whole of the spirit's purpose, present it to the will. [Jha]

XXXVII. In as much as it is the will that accomplishes the spirit's experiences, and again it is will that discriminates the subtle difference between Nature and spirit [it is will that is regarded as superior to the other two]. [Jha]

XXXVIII. The rudimentary elements are "non-specific"; from these five proceed the five gross elements; these latter are said to be "specific," because they are calm, turbulent, and deluding. [Jha]

...what the particle "*mātra*" [in the term "*tanmātra*," which is the name of the rudimentary elements] connotes is that these subtle elements are devoid of that "specific character" consisting of the "calmness, turbulence, and delusiveness" which would make them objects of direct experience.

..."*From these, etc.*," from the five rudimentary elements of sound, touch, colour, taste, and odour proceed respectively the five gross elements —*ākāśa*, air, fire, water, and earth—these "five" proceeding from the aforesaid "five" rudimentary elements.

...The sense is that, in as much as among the gross elements, *ākāśa* and the rest, some abounding in the *sattva* attribute are calm, pleasing, illuminating, and buoyant; others abounding in the *rajas* attribute are turbulent, painful, and unstable; the rest abounding in the *tamas* attribute are deluded, confounded, and sluggish. These gross elements, thus perceived to be distinguished from one another, are said to be *specific* and *gross*. The rudimentary elements on the contrary cannot be similarly distinguished by ordinary people; and as such they are said to be *non-specific* and *subtle*.

XXXIX. (1) The "subtle" bodies, (2) "those born of parents," and (3) the "gross" elements,—these are the three kinds of the "specific." Of these, the "subtle" bodies are everlasting, and "those born of parents" are perishable. [Jha]

...(1) subtle bodies which [are not visible, but] are postulated [in order to explain certain phenomena];...Thus subtle bodies form the first kind of "specific" objects, "bodies born of parents" the second kind, and the "gross elements" the third kind. Ordinary things like the jar are included in this last.

XL. The "mergent" [subtle] body formed primevally, unconfined, lasting, composed of will and the rest down to rudimentary elements, migrates, is devoid of experiences, and is invested with dispositions.

"*Formed primevally*";—when the emanations from Nature began, the first object to evolve therefrom, was the subtle body, one for each spirit. This body is "*unconfined*," untrammeled; as such, it can enter even a solid piece of stone. It is "lasting," since it continues to exist all the time from the first evolution to the final dissolution....

"*It migrates*," i.e., the subtle body goes on deserting and occupying one six-sheathed physical body after the other.—"But why?"—Because it is "*devoid of experience*," that is to say, because the subtle body by itself without a corresponding physical body of six sheaths to afford the vehicle of experience would be devoid of experience; that is why it migrates.

...The "*dispositions*" are virtue and vice, wisdom and ignorance, passion and dispassion, power and weakness; and it is the will which is endowed, that is, directly connected with them; and the subtle body is connected with the will; hence the subtle body becomes invested with those dispositions:...

"Why should not the subtle body—like Nature—last even after the final dissolution?"

Because it is "*mergent*," that is to say, because it dissolves into Nature. This mergent character of the subtle body is inferred from the fact of its being a product; i.e., having a cause, it must merge into it.

XLI. Just as a picture does not exist without a substrate, or a shadow without a post or the like, so too the cognitive apparatus [*liṅga*: intellect, etc.], does not subsist supportless, without what is specific [i.e., a subtle body].

The term "*liṅga*" here stands for the will, the I-principle, and the rudimentary elements, because they are the means of knowing and these cannot subsist without a substrate....

XLII. Formed for the sake of the spirit's purpose the subtle body acts like a dramatic actor, on account of the connection of "causes and effects" and by union with the all-embracing power of Nature. [Jha]

"*Formed for the spirit's purpose*," the subtle body acts like a *dramatic actor*, on account of its connection with the "*causes*" in the shape of virtue, vice, etc.,—and "*effects*" in the shape of the taking up of different kinds of physical bodies, the latter being the effects of virtue, etc. That is to say, just as a dramatic actor, playing different parts, acts like Paraśurāma or Yudhiṣṭhira or Vatsarāja, so does the subtle body, occupying various physical bodies, act like a man or a brute or a tree.

XLIII. Virtue and other dispositions are—(*a*) natural, which are innate, and (*b*) incidental; and these are related to the "cause"; and the ovum, etc., related to the "effect." [Jha]

...The "*incidental*" dispositions, on the other hand, are not innate; that is to say, they are brought about by the personal effort of the man;...

The aggregate formed of the ovum, foetus, flesh, blood, etc., of the child in the mother's womb is related to the gross physical body; that is to say, they are particular states of the latter; so also are the childhood, youth and old age of the person after birth.[1]

XLIV. By virtue is obtained ascent to higher planes, by vice, descent to the lower; from wisdom results the highest good, and bondage from the reverse. [Jha]

XLV. From dispassion results "mergence into Nature"; from attachment which abounds in the *rajas* attribute, transmigration;

[1] Gauḍapāda has taken the *kārikā* as setting forth *three* kinds of dispositions—(1) "*sāṁsiddhika*," innate, (2) "*prākṛtika*," natural due to the operation of Nature, primordial matter, and (3) "*vaikṛtika*," incidental.

from power, non-impediment; and from the reverse, the contrary. [Jha]

"*From dispassion results mergence into Nature.*" Those who are free from passion, but are ignorant of the true nature of the spirit, become merged into Nature. "Nature" here stands for the whole set consisting of Nature, will, I-principle, the elements, and the sense-organs. Those who worship these as "spirit," become absorbed into these [i.e., those mistaking the senses for the spirit become absorbed in the senses, and so on]; that is to say, they rest there till, in the course of time, they are born again.

XLVI. This aggregate of sixteen—[eight causes and eight effects, mentioned in the last two verses]—is a creation of the intellect, and is distinguished as ignorance, infirmity, complacency, and attainment [or success]. Their varieties due to the suppression of one or more of the constituents, because of their relative inequalities in strength, are fifty in number.

XLVII. Five are the varieties of ignorance; the varieties of infirmity due to organic defect are twenty-eight; complacency [or contentment] is nine-fold, and attainment eight-fold.

XLVIII. Of error there are eight forms; as also of delusion; extreme delusion is ten-fold; gloom is eighteen-fold, and so is also "blind gloom."[1]

XLIX. Injuries to the eleven organs along with the injuries to the intellect are declared to constitute infirmity; the injuries to the intellect are seventeen resulting from the failure of the nine-fold complacency[2] and the eight-fold attainment.

. . . Contentment being nine-fold, the disabilities caused by its reversion are also nine-fold; and similarly, success being eight-fold, the disability caused by its reversion is eight-fold, thus making the seventeen disabilities proper of the will.

L. The nine forms of contentment have been held to be the following: Four internal, named Nature (*prakṛti*), (2) means (*upādāna*), (3) time (*kāla*), and (4) luck (*bhāgyā*); and five external due to the abstinence from objects. [Jha]

The *contentment* called "Nature" consists in that feeling of satisfaction which the disciple has on being told that "discriminative wisdom is only a modification of Nature and, as such, would come to every one in the natural course of events, and there is no need of having recourse to the practice of meditation, etc. So, my child, remain as you are! . . ."

[1] Or "utter darkness."

[2] Or "contentment."

The second form of *contentment* arises from the following instruction: "Wisdom cannot be attained in the ordinary course of nature, because, if it were so, then everybody would attain to wisdom at all times as the course of Nature functions equally for all individuals; such wisdom can only be attained through renunciation, and so, O long-living one, thou must have recourse to renunciation and give up all practice of meditation. The satisfaction arising from this instruction is named means. . . .

The *contentment* that follows upon the feeling of satisfaction arising from the instruction that renunciation also cannot bring about emancipation at once; renunciation also will bring you success only when the time is ripe for it; there is no need for undergoing the troubles of renunciation. . . . [This is the third form of contentment.]

The fourth form of *contentment* is the feeling of satisfaction arising from the following: "Discriminative wisdom proceeds neither from Nature nor from any other *means* [such as renunciation], nor does it depend solely upon *time*, but it comes only by *luck*; . . ."

The external forms of *contentment* are next described: The *external* forms are five, arising from abstinence from sound, odour, etc.,—the five objects of sense.

LI. The eight attainments are the proper use of reasoning, oral instruction from a teacher, study, the three-fold suppression of the three kinds of misery, the intercourse of friends, and purity; those mentioned before [viz., ignorance, infirmity, and complacency] are the three-fold curb on attainment.

LII. Without the "subjective," there would be no "objective," and without the "objective" there would be no "subjective." Therefore, there proceeds two-fold evolution, the "objective" and the "subjective." [Jha]

The term "objective" (*liṅga*) stands for the evolution out of the rudimentary elements, and "subjective" (*bhāva*) for the evolution out of the will.

That is to say, experience, which is the purpose of the spirit, is not possible unless there are the objects of experience and also the vehicle of experience in the form of the two bodies [subtle and physical]. Hence the necessity of the *objective* evolution;—conversely, that same experience is not possible without the organs of experience, in the shape of the sense-organs and the internal organs; and these are not possible without virtue and the other dispositions. Lastly, the discriminative wisdom, which leads to the final end [emancipation], is not possible without both these forms of evolution. Thus is the need for both forms of evolution established.

LIII. The "celestial" evolution has eight forms, the "animal" has five; the "human" has only one form; thus in brief is the "material" evolution. [Jha]

LIV. In the worlds above, there is predominance of *sattva* (goodness); in the sphere of the lower order of creation, *tamas* (darkness) predominates; in the middle, *rajas* (passion) predominates; this is so from Brahmā down to a blade of grass.

LV. Therein does the sentient spirit experience pain arising from decay and death, due to the non-discrimination of the spirit from the body [or, until the dissolution of the subtle body]; thus pain is in the very nature of things. [Jha]

"*Therein*"—in the body. Among corporeal beings the body is the vehicle of various forms of pleasure; and yet the pain of "decay and death" is the common lot of all. The fear of death,—"may I not cease to be; may I continue to be," etc.,—being common to man as well as to the smallest insect; and the cause of fear constituting pain, death is a source of pain.

LVI. This evolution from the will down to the specific elements, is brought about by the modifications of Nature (*prakṛti*). This work is done for the emancipation of each spirit, and thus is for another's sake, though appearing as if it were for the sake of Nature herself. [Jha]

. . . "*this*" *evolution*—from the will onwards down to the elements—is brought about by Nature itself; it is neither produced by a God [as held by the Naiyāyika] nor is it an evolution from *Brahman* [as held by the Vedāntin]; nor is it without cause [as held by the atheist]. If it were the latter, there would never be any evolution at all or it would be eternally going on;—nor can it be said to be evolved from *Brahman* [the Vedānta view], for there can be no modification of what is pure intelligence [which is *Brahman*, as postulated by Vedānta]. Nor, again, can evolution be brought about by Nature, as controlled by God, as no controlling can be done by one who is not active, e.g., an inactive carpenter does not manipulate his tools.

Objection: "Granted that the evolution is due to Nature alone. But Nature is eternally active, and, as such, her operations should never cease; so that there would be no emancipation for the spirit."

Answer:—"*The evolution is for the emancipation of each spirit, and appearing as if it were for Nature's own sake is really for the sake of another.*" A cook having finished the cooking in which he was engaged retires from the work; similarly Nature, being urged to action for the emancipation of the spirit, brings about this emancipation and thereafter stops her operations with regard to that spirit whom she has already liberated [and, thus emancipation is not impossible]. This action for another's sake is just like the action for one's own benefit.

Objection: "Granted all this. But it is only a sentient being that acts either for its own or for another's purpose; and Nature, being insentient, cannot act in the manner described; and, as such, she requires a sentient controller [over her blind force]; the spirits residing in the bodies cannot be such controllers, because such conditioned spirits are ignorant of the true character of Nature; consequently there must be some other omniscient sentient being who controls *ab extra* the operations of Nature,—and to this Being we give the name of God."

LVII. As the insentient milk flows out for the growth of the calf, so does Nature act towards the emancipation of the spirit.

It is a fact of observation that insentient objects also act towards definite ends; e.g., the milk, which is insentient, flows for the nourishment of the calf. Similarly, Nature though insentient, could act towards the emancipation of the spirit.

It would not be right to urge that "the flow of the milk being due to the superintending care of God, its action does not afford an instance vitiating the general proposition that the actions of insentient things are due to the control of sentient beings";—the activity of every sentient being is always found to be due either to selfishness, or to benevolence; neither of these is applicable to the case of the "creation of the Universe," and, therefore, it follows that the said creation cannot be due to the action of a sentient agent. Further, God, being the Lord of the Universe, has all that He requires and, as such, in the creating of the world, He can have no selfish motive; nor can His action be said to be due solely to benevolence or pity; for pity consists in a desire for the removal of others' pains; but before creation, the spirits would be without bodies, organs, and objects as such, without pain; for the removal of what then would God's compassion be roused? And if the pain subsequent to creation be held to be the cause of creation, then we should be in the inextricable noose of "interdependence": creation due to pity, and pity due to creation! and, again, if God were moved to creation by pity, then He would create only happy mortals, not mortals with variegated experiences. And if the diversity of men's experiences be attributed to their past deeds, then what is the necessity of postulating an intelligent controller of such deeds? The mere absence of the control of an intelligent agent would mean [according to the opponent] that the *deeds* of men could not have any activity, which would mean that their effects, in the shape of men's bodies, organs, and objects, could not be produced,—and the result of this would be that there would be no pain; so that the removal of pains would be very easy! [and there would be no ground for God's compassion].

As regards the action of the insentient Nature, on the other hand, it is due neither to selfishness nor to pity; and thus, in this case, none of the above incongruities arise; the only motive of Nature is the fulfilment of another's purpose. Thus, therefore, the instance cited in the *kārikā* is quite appropriate.

LVIII. Just as in the world one undertakes action in order to be rid of desire by satisfying it, even so does the Unevolved[1] function for the release of the spirit.

[1] Or Unmanifest.

LIX. As a dancer desists from dancing, having exhibited herself to the audience, so does Primal Nature desist, having exhibited herself to the spirit.

LX. Generous Nature, endowed with attributes, brings about by manifold means, without benefit to herself, the good of the spirit, who is devoid of attributes, and confers no benefit in return. [Jha]

LXI. It is my belief that there is not any other being more bashful than Primal Nature, who because of the realisation "I have been seen" never again comes into the view of the spirit.

LXII. Of a certainty, therefore, not any spirit is bound or liberated, not does any migrate; it is Primal Nature, abiding in manifold forms, that is bound, is liberated, and migrates.

Verily no spirit is bound; nor does any migrate; nor is any emancipated. Nature alone, having many vehicles, is bound, migrates, and is released. Bondage, migration and release are ascribed to the spirit, in the same manner as defeat and victory are attributed to the king, though actually occurring to his soldiers, because it is the servants that take part in the undertaking, the effects of which—grief or profit—accrue to the king. In the same manner, experience and emancipation, though really belonging to Nature, are attributed to the spirit, on account of the non-discrimination of spirit from Nature, as has been already explained....

LXIII. Nature by herself binds herself by means of seven forms; and by means of one form she causes deliverance for the benefit of the spirit. [Jha]

"*Nature binds herself by means of seven forms*"; i.e., by virtue and other dispositions[1] [all properties of the will] except wisdom. For the benefit of the spirit in the shape of experience and final release, she releases herself by herself, "*by means of one form*," i.e., by wisdom—by discrimination. That is to say, she does not again bring about the experience or emancipation of that same spirit

LXIV. Thus, from the repeated study of the truth, there results that wisdom, "I do not exist, naught is mine, I am not," which leaves no residue to be known, is pure, being free from ignorance, and is absolute.

..."*I am not*" merely precludes all action from the spirit;...And since there is no action of the spirit, there arises the idea of "not-I"; "I" here stands for active agency in general,...

Or we may interpret the three forms in another way. The sentence, "I am not," means that "I am the spirit, *not productive*" and because non-productive, "I have no action"—"Not I"; and since without action, "I can have no possessions," hence "naught is mine."

[1] See *kārikās* XXIII and XLV and the commentary on *kārikā* LXV.

LXV. Thereby does the pure spirit, resting like a spectator, perceive Primal Nature, which has ceased to be productive, and, because of the power of discriminative knowledge, has turned back from the seven forms [i.e., dispositions].

...The seven forms of evolution,—virtue, vice, error, dispassion, passion, power and weakness—are all due to erroneous knowledge....

LXVI. "She has been seen by me," thinks the one and hence loses all interest; "I have been seen," thinks the other, and ceases to act. Hence, though their connection is still there, there is no motive for further evolution. [Jha]

..."*There is no motive for evolution.*" A "motive" is that which moves Nature to act towards evolution; and no such motive is possible, when there is no "purpose of the spirit."

LXVII. Virtue and the rest having ceased to function as causes, because of the attainment of perfect wisdom, the spirit remains invested with the body, because of the force of past impressions, like the whirl of the potter's wheel, which persists for a while by virtue of the momentum imparted by a prior impulse.

LXVIII. When the separation from the body has at length been attained, and by reason of the purpose having been fulfilled, Nature ceases to act,—then he attains eternal and absolute isolation. [Jha]

LXIX. This abstruse doctrine which is accessory to the attainment of the goal of the spirit, and wherein are considered the existence, origin, and dissolution of beings, has been fully expounded by the Great Sage [Kapila].

LXX. This supreme purifying knowledge, the sage first handed on, in compassion, to Āsuri; Āsuri passed it on to Pañcaśikha; by him the doctrine was elaborated.

LXXI. This which was handed down through a succession of pupils has been compendiously set down in Āryā metre, after fully comprehending the final doctrine, by Īśvara Kṛṣṇa, whose intellect had approximated to the truth.

LXXII. The subjects of the seventy verses are, verily, those of the entire science of sixty topics, exclusive of illustrative tales, and omitting also the discussion of rival views.

B. *SĀṀKHYA-PRAVACANA SŪTRA*

I.19. Without the conjunction of *prakṛti*, there can be no conjunction of bondage in the self (*puruṣa*) who is, by nature, eternal, and eternally pure, enlightened, and unconfined [unbound].

I.20. Nor does bondage result from ignorance also, because of the impossibility of bondage by means of a non-entity.

Vṛtti:...For ignorance denotes either...that knowledge has not yet been acquired but that it may be acquired afterwards, or that knowledge which was acquired has been afterwards lost. And, either way, it is a non-entity.

I.27. His bondage, moreover, is not caused by means of the tint (*vāsanā*) reflected from objects from all eternity.

Vṛtti: The author refutes the Bauddha [Buddhist] view.

It cannot be maintained that "his," i.e., of the self, bondage will be caused by the instrumentality of the tendency to or longing for objects from all eternity or of which no beginning can be traced. With us there can be, by no means, connection of the self with such tendency or longing, and consequently bondage cannot result from it. While in the Bauddha system, since a permanent self does not exist, and tendency or longing does not endure forever, who will be bound?

I.34. [Objection of the Buddhist]: Since there is no proof of[1] a permanent effect, the momentariness of bondage is to be admitted.

I.35. Nay. [Things are not momentary in their duration], as [in that case] there would be obstruction to knowing them over again.[2]

I.36. And things are not momentary also because this is contradicted by the Veda and by logic.

Vṛtti: The Veda says: There exists the self, the experiencer of the objects of experience in a different birth.

Logic also: Whoso will exert himself in an act which is incapable of enjoyment or in the employment of means for its accomplishment?

I.38. There can be no relation of effect and cause between two things simultaneously produced.

Vṛtti: ...on the theory of momentariness...no production is possible.

I.39. [The relation of effect and cause cannot subsist between temporary things even though they be successive] because, on the passing away of the precedent, there can be no causal connection with the subsequent.

[1] Or "no such thing as."

[2] Or "impossibility of recognition."

1.42. The world is not a mere idea, on account of the intuition[1] of objective reality.

Bhāṣya: Other unbelievers, again, say: There is no existence of an entity which is not an idea. Therefore, bondage also is a mere idea, like an object seen in a dream. Hence, it being absolutely unreal, there is no cause of it.

1.43. If the one [i.e., external reality] does not exist, the other [i.e., the world of ideas] also does not exist; therefore, reality is a void.[2]

1.44. Reality is void; existence passes away, it being the nature of things to pass away.[3]

Vṛtti: [The Śūnyavādin, Buddhist negativist, goes on]...

1.45. ["Existence passes away"—] this is a meaningless statement on the part of the unenlightened.[4]

1.46. This theory also should be rejected, because it possesses no more worth than the other two theories [viz., transciency and idealism].

Vṛtti: This also, the theory of the void, should be set aside, because it possesses as much strength as the theory of momentariness and the theory of idealism. As momentary existence is contravened by the recognition of things previously perceived, as ideal existence is contravened by the perception of external entities, in like manner this also, the theory of the void, should be contravened by the observation of the entire universe in perception itself.

1.61. *Prakṛti* is the state of quiescence [equilibrium] of *sattva*, *rajas*, and *tamas*. From *prakṛti* evolves *mahat* (intellect); from *mahat*, *ahaṁkāra* (I-consciousness); from *ahaṁkāra*, the five *tanmātras* (subtle elements) and the two sets of *indriyas* (senses or instruments); from the five *tanmātras*, the gross elements. Then there is the self. Such is the group of the twenty-five principles.

1.67. Since the root (*mūla*) has no root, the root is root-less.

1.68. Even in the case of a succession, there must be a stop at some one point, and so it [*prakṛti*, the root cause] is merely a name [that is given to such a point].

1.77. [*Prakṛti* is the cause of all things, and not the atoms], also because there are Vedic declarations about the production of this [i.e., the world] from that [i.e., the root cause].[5]

[1] Preferably, "perception."
[2] Revised translation.
[3] Revised translation.
[4] Revised translation.
[5] Revised translation.

I.79. The world is not unreal, because there is no fact contradictory to its reality, and also because it is not the product of [depraved] causes.[1]

Bhāṣya: Nor can it be said that the cognition of the reality of the world is the result of depraved senses, etc., as it is in the case of the yellowness of a conch-shell, because there is no reason for the supposition of such depravation; hence, the effect, i.e., world, is not unreal.

I.93. Proof of His existence is not possible, because He can be neither free nor bound, nor anything else.[2]

Vṛtti: Is He [Īśvara, personal God] bound or is He free? If bound, He cannot be Īśvara, owing to conjunction of merit and demerit. If free, He cannot be the agent or doer, on account of the absence of particular cognitions and desire to act and effort. Hence Īśvara is above proof.

I.94. Either way also He would be inefficient.

Bhāṣya: If He were free, He would be unequal to the task of creation, etc., as He would not possess the will-to-be and the will-to-do, desires, etc., which instigate to creation, etc. And, again, if He were bound, He would be under delusion, and so, unequal to the task of creation. Such is the meaning.

I.95. [The sacred texts which speak of Īśvara, are] either glorification of the free self or homages paid to the perfect ones.

Bhāṣya: But, then, one may ask, what becomes of the Vedic texts which establish Īśvara? To this the author replies.

I.96. The superintendence is through proximity to *prakṛti*, as in the case of the loadstone.[3]

Vṛtti: Nor is proof of Īśvara, declares the author, from the argument that the non-intelligent cannot act without the superintendence of the intelligent.

Bhāṣya: . . . superintendence in the form of creativeness, etc., is through proximity, as is the case with the loadstone. As the loadstone acts as the attracter of iron by mere proximity, and not by volition, etc., similarly, by the mere conjunction of the original self, takes place the modification or *prakṛti* into the form of *mahat*. And it is this alone in which consists His being the creator of His own adjunct.

I.149. Multiplicity of selves is proved from the several allotments of births, etc.

[1] Preferably, "faulty senses."

[2] Revised translation. The last sentence quoted from the commentary ("Hence Īśvara is above proof") should be translated "Hence Īśvara is not amenable to proof." In the *Vṛtti* to this *sūtra*, "above proof" probably means "incapable of proof."

[3] Revised translation.

Bhāṣya: Since there is no other reason for the distribution or differentiation of selves made in the Veda and the *smṛti* (traditional texts), namely, that a virtuous self is born in heaven, that a vicious one in hell, that an ignorant self is bound, that a knowing one is released, etc., it follows that selves are manifold.

I.150. [The Vedāntins maintain that] from difference of investments[1] also arises the appearance of multiplicity of the one Self; as of ether (*ākāśa*), by reason of water pots, etc., [which divide it into many parts].

Bhāṣya: Even in the case of differences of investments, connection with manifold investments would be really of the one Self only; as, for example, connection with manifold investments such as the water pot, walls, etc., is of the one ether only. Hence, by means of the difference of determining conditions, it is of the one Self only that diverse births, deaths, etc., would take place, as in the case of the physical organisms, etc. So that distribution of births, etc., such as one self is born and not another, would not be possible. Such is the meaning.

Moreover, since a portion of the Self which has been freed from one investment would still be liable to be confined by other investments, the irregularity of bondage and release is also in the same state [of defectiveness];...

I.151. The investment is different, but not the holder thereof [i.e., the self].[2]

I.152. Thus, [i.e., on the theory of the multiplicity of selves, as held by the Sāṁkhyas], there is no imputation of contradictory properties, [as is entailed in the case] of one universal Self [of the Vedāntins].

Bhāṣya: . . . it is . . . not reasonable to introduce the simultaneous presence of contradictory properties in the form of birth, death, etc., in the case of the Self present everywhere by reason of its unity.

I.154. There is no contradiction [by the Sāṁkhya theory of the multiplicity of selves] of the Vedic declarations of non-duality of the self, because the reference in these declarations is to the genus of the self.

Bhāṣya: . . . the Vedic declarations on non-duality being only to the genus of self which consists of oneness of form in general [in other words, of the general characteristic of being the self], and not to its entireness, since there is no reason or necessity for reading such a reference in them.

[1] A better translation of *upādhi* would be "conditions" or "determining conditions."

[2] The *sūtra* is probably incomplete. It is likely that the full meaning of the *sūtra* would be contained in the unexpressed additional statement, "but this is absurd."

In the Vedic texts... the reference to non-difference in the form of non-difference in property [i.e., absolute identity] is, in our opinion, to be observed of such sayings as "I am Viṣṇu," "I am Śiva," etc., but not also of sayings like "Thou art that," "I am *Brahman*," etc.; for, among such passages, the phrase, for instance, "Thou art that," as heard, expressed, in the theory of the Sāṁkhyas, the sense of a passage like this, that thou art eternal and eternally pure and eternally released, since, in the theory of the Sāṁkhyas, it is the perfect self existing at the time of dissolution that alone is the object denoted by the words "That" and the like.

III.56. For He [Īśvara] becomes the all-knower and the all-doer.

Vṛtti: Of what form, one may ask, is the Supreme Self? To this the author replies.

Bhāṣya: The author gives the proof also of the rising again of the self after his absorption into *prakṛti.*

For, he who was, in a previous creation, absorbed into the cause [i.e., *prakṛti*] becomes, in another creation, the original self, [bearing the character of Īśvara or the Lord, all-knowing and all-doing; because, by reason of his absorption into *prakṛti*, it is but fitting that he alone should reach the status of *prakṛti* [the primal evolvent], as declared in the *śruti* (scriptures).

III.57. Knowledge of such an Īśvara is proved. [Or:] Such proof of an Īśvara is admitted.

Bhāṣya: But, then, one may object, if that be so, the denial of Īśvara is not established. To this the author replies:

It is verily agreed on all hands that, of the existence of an *emergent* Īśvara previously absorbed into *prakṛti*, there is proof from the *śruti* such as, "He who is all-knower, all-wise, whose penance consists in knowledge" [*Muṇḍaka Up.*, I.i.9], for the subject of dispute [between the Sāṁkhyas and the others] is the existence of an *eternal* Īśvara. Such is the meaning.

V.2. The accomplishment of results [*phala*] is not under the superintendence of a Lord [Īśvara] because that is effected by *karma.*[1]

Vṛtti: Were Īśvara an independent creator, he would create even without the aid of *karma*, [but this is not so]. If you say that he creates, having *karma* as an auxiliary, then let *karma* itself be the cause: what need of Īśvara? Nor can an auxiliary obstruct the power of the principal agent, since, in that case, there would be a contradiction of its independence.

Moreover, activity is seen to proceed from egoistic and altruistic motives. Neither can any egoistic motive belong to Īśvara. And were his motives altruistic, then, he being compassionate, there would be no justification for a creation which is full of pain. Nor is there any activity which is purely altruistic, because such activity proceeds from a desire for selfish gain even by means of doing good to others, etc.

[1] New translation.

v.3. Because of his own benefit, Īśvara's superintendence will be like that of man.

Vṛtti: The author shows this: [that all activity is ultimately selfish]. Nor does personal benefit exist consistently with him who is eternal.

v.4. Otherwise, Īśvara will be like a human lord.

v.5. [Otherwise, Īśvara will be like a human lord], or nominal [technical].

Bhāṣya: In spite of the existence of worldly life, were he still to be Īśvara, then "Īśvara" will, as with us, so with you also, be a mere technical name to denote the self who is produced at the beginning of creation; because, owing to the contradiction of being worldly and of having unobstructed will, eternal Īśvara-hood will not be proved. Such is the meaning.

v.6. Without passion,[1] superintendence is not established, because passion is the invariable and unconditioned cause of all activity.

v.7. On the admission, again, of connection with passion, he will not be eternally free.

v.8. If [you say that the condition of being Īśvara arises] through connection with the powers of *prakṛti*, then there will be the implication of his attachment.

v.9. If [it be said that the condition of being Īśvara may arise] through the mere existence of *prakṛti* by the side of the self, then the condition of being Īśvara will belong to all selves.

v.10. On account of the non-existence of evidence, there is no proof of an eternal Īśvara.

v.11. Owing to the non-existence of pervasion,[2] there is no inference of Īśvara.

Vṛtti: Since the general proposition as to the pervasion of one thing by another or their universal going together must have sense-perception to precede it, in the absence thereof [as stated in the preceding aphorism], how can there be the apprehension of the universal relation in the case of an uncommon thing?

v.12. The *śruti* (scriptures) also speak of this [i.e., the world] as the product of *prakṛti*.[3]

Bhāṣya: Nor is there verbal testimony, also, says the author.
In respect of the web of creation, there exists *śruti* or Vedic declaration of its being the product of *prakṛti*, but not of its having an intelligent being as its cause.

[1] Or "intense desire."
[2] *Saṁbandha*—invariable concomitance.
[3] Revised translation.

v.61. There is no non-duality of the Self because there is cognition of differences through different marks.[1]

v.62. There is no non-distinction of Self and non-Self because that is disproved by perception.[2]

vi.45. Multiplicity of selves is established from allotment [of bondage and liberation].[3]

vi.46. If external investment (*upādhi*) is acknowledged, then, on the establishment thereof, there is again duality.

Vṛtti: But diversity of multeity will be, it may be contended, according to differences of external investment. In regard to this, the author says: "On the establishment thereof," that is, on the establishment of difference. In the case of external investment being an unreality, where is the establishment of difference? While in the case of its reality, by means of that itself, there will again result duality.

vi.47. Even by the two,[4] there is contradiction of the evidence of non-duality.

Bhāṣya: But then, the external investments also will be, may contend our opponent, constituted by ignorance, and, therefore, there will be no breach of non-duality by them. There being room for such an apprehension, the author says:

The self and ignorance,—by those two also, being acknowledged, the contradiction of the *śruti* which is the evidence for non-duality is in the very same state. Such is the meaning.

vi.52. The reality of the world follows from its being the product of not-imperfect causes,[5] and from the absence of any impediment to its reality.[6]

Bhāṣya: The author tells us that the teachers of non-duality are to be rejected not only by means of the argument set forth above, but also by means of the non-existence of any proof to lead to the cognition of the unreality of the universe.

[1] New translation.

[2] New translation.

[3] Revised translation.

[4] The two, i.e., the self (*ātman*) and ignorance (*ajñāna*)

[5] That is, non-defective senses.

[6] That is, there is no denial of its reality in scripture.

CHAPTER XIII

YOGA

THE word *yoga* has become well known in the West, though its different meanings and its deeper significance and purpose are not well understood. For Patañjali (2nd century B.C.), the founder of the Yoga system and the author of the basic text, the *Yoga Sūtra*, *yoga* is discrimination between subject and object, *puruṣa* (self or spirit) and *prakṛti* (Nature), which means the establishment of the self in its purity. *Yoga*, according to Patañjali, is a methodical effort to attain perfection, through the control of the different elements of human nature, physical and psychical.

The main interest of Patañjali is not metaphysical theorizing, but the practical motive of indicating how salvation can be attained by disciplined activity. The Yoga system accepts the Sāṁkhya psychology and metaphysics. However, it is definitely more theistic than the Sāṁkhya, as evidenced by the addition of God to the Sāṁkhya's twenty-five elements of reality.

What the Sāṁkhya calls *mahat* (the great one, or *buddhi* as described in the previous chapter) is called *citta* (mind-stuff) in the Yoga system. It undergoes modifications when it is affected by objects through the senses. The consciousness of *puruṣa* reflected in it (*citta*) gives rise to the impression that it is the experiencer. *Citta* is really the spectacle of which the self is by reflection the spectator. We have as many *cittas* as there are selves. The ego is different from the self and is dependent on the experience of the world. The life of the ego is restless and unsatisfied, being subject as it is to the five afflictions of (1) ignorance or the mistaking of the non-eternal for the eternal, (2) the erroneous identification of oneself with the instruments of body and mind, (3) attachment to pleasant things, (4) hatred of unpleasant things, and (5) the instinctive love of life and the dread of death. When the self is freed from *citta* it withdraws itself into its own pure nature.

The special feature of the Yoga system is its practical discipline, by which the suppression of mental states is brought about through the practice of spiritual exercises and the conquest of desire. The Yoga gives us the eightfold method of abstention, observance, posture, breath-control, withdrawal of the senses, fixed attention, contemplation, and concentration. The first two of these refer to the ethical prerequisites for the practice of *yoga*. We should practice non-violence, truthfulness, honesty, continence, and non-acceptance of gifts. We should observe purification (internal and external), contentment, austerity, and devotion to God. Posture is a physical aid to concentration. Breath-control aids serenity of mind. Abstraction of the senses from their natural functions helps to keep the mind still. These five steps are indirect or external means to *yoga*. In fixed attention we get the mind focussed on a particular object. Contemplation or meditation leads to concentration. *Yoga* is identified with concentration (*samādhi*), where the self regains its eternal and pure free status. This is the meaning of freedom or release or salvation in the Yoga system.

Through yogic practices, one can attain supernormal powers. The classical authors do not encourage the acquisition of these powers, as they consider spiritual calm and moral virtue to be superior to magical powers, which are only incidental to the attainment of the true goal of spiritual freedom

For the source from which selections are taken, see footnote 1.

THE *YOGA SŪTRA*[1]

CHAPTER 1: CONCENTRATION (*SAMĀDHI*)

1. Now a revised text of *yoga*.[2]

Yoga is contemplation (*samādhi*),[3] and it is a characteristic of the mind pervading all its planes. The planes of the mind are:—

Wandering (*kṣipta*); forgetful (*mūḍha*); occasionally steady or distracted (*vikṣipta*); one-pointed (*ekāgra*); and restrained (*niruddha*).

Of these the contemplation in the occasionally steady mind does not fall under the heading of *yoga*, because of unsteadiness appearing in close sequence.... *Y.B.*[4]

The commentator now removes the doubt as to the meaning of the word "*yoga*," which arises from its ordinary connotation. Thus says he, "*Yoga* is contemplation." The word "*yoga*" is derived from the root *yuj*, to contemplate, and not from the root *yujir*, to join, in which latter case it would mean conjunction.[4] *T.V.*

2. *Yoga* is the restraint of mental modifications.

The mind is possessed of the "three qualities,"[5] showing as it does the nature of illumination, activity, and inertia.... *Y.B.*

[1] Selections are taken from *The Yoga Sūtras of Patañjali*, with the *Yoga-bhāṣya* of Vyāsa (4th century A.D.) and the *Tattva-vaiśāradī* of Vācaspati Miśra (*ca.* 850 A.D.), translated by Rama Prasada, Sacred Books of the Hindus, IV (Allahabad: The Panini Office, 3rd ed., 1924). All the *sūtras* are quoted, with commentary where necessary for explanation or clarity.

[2] Or "Now an explanation of *yoga*."

[3] *Samādhi* may be translated variously: as contemplation, concentration, trance, superconscious state, etc.

[4] For convenience, the *Yoga-bhāṣya* is indicated by "*Y.B.*" and the *Tattva-vaiśāradī* by "*T.V.*"

[5] These are the three *guṇas* or constituent elements of things. They are described fully in the selections from the Sāṁkhya system in Chapter XII.

That particular state of the mind in which the manifestations of real cognition, &c., have been restrained, is the state of *yoga*. *T.V.*

3. Then the seer stands in his own nature.

...The objects of the *puruṣa* (self)[1] are discriminative knowledge and the experience of the objective world. These two no longer exist in the state of inhibition (*nirodha*).... *T.V.*

4. Identification with modifications elsewhere.

...The conscious principle (*puruṣa*) is not unaffected by whatever may be the modifications of the mind in the state of outgoing activity. And so in the aphorism: "Knowledge is but one; discrimination alone is knowledge."

The mind is like a magnet energized by nearness alone. Being seen it becomes the possession of its lord, the *puruṣa*. Therefore the reason for knowing the modifications of the mind is the eternal relation of the *puruṣa*. *Y.B.*

...The notions, "I am calm," "I am ruffled," "I am forgetful," appear by fastening the modifications of the will-to-be upon the conscious principle, by taking the will-to-know and the conscious principle to be one on account of proximity, as in the case of the white crystal and the Japa [Chinese rose] flower. This happens in the same way as one looking at his face reflected in a dirty mirror becomes anxious, and thinks, "I am dim...." And similarly does this *ātmā* [or *ātman*] (self) appear to possess false knowledge, although in reality he has no false knowledge. He appears as the enjoyer, although he is not the enjoyer. He appears as possessed of discriminative knowledge, and illuminated thereby, although devoid of it in reality. *T.V.*

5. The modifications are five-fold, painful and not-painful.

...The painful are those that cause the afflictions and become the field for the growth of the vehicle of actions (*karmāśaya*). The not-painful are those that have discrimination for their object and which oppose the functioning of the "qualities...." *Y.B.*

6. Real cognition, unreal cognition, imagination, deep sleep, and memory.[2]

7. Perception, verbal cognition, and inference are real cognitions.

8. Unreal cognition is the knowing of the unreal, possessing a form not its own.

9. Imagination is followed in sequence by verbal expression and knowledge, and is devoid of objective substratum.

[1] "*Puruṣa*" (self or spirit) will not be translated in this chapter. For a complete explanation of the concept, see selections from the Sāṁkhya system in Chapter XII.

[2] These are the five modifications referred to in *sūtra* 5, above.

There being no objective substratum for either the distinction or the absence thereof, imagination shows an unreal image of the substratum; and it is not, therefore, an act of real cognition. Nor is it unreal cognition, because it differs from it in being recognised as such in practice. *T.V.*

10. Sleep is the mental modification which has for its objective substratum the cause of non-existence.

The non-existence spoken of is of the modifications of the waking and dreaming states. *T.V.*

11. Memory is the not stealing away along with objective mental impression [retained] [i.e., the reproducing of not more than what has been impressed upon the mind].

. . . Right cognition and others all cause the knowledge of an object unknown, either in the ordinary or in some particular way. Memory, however, does not pass over the limitation of the former knowledge. It is that former knowledge or something less than that which is its object, never something more. . . . *T.V.*

12. They are restrained by practice and desirelessness.

The stream of mind flows both ways: it flows towards good and it flows towards evil. That which flows on to perfect independence (*kaivalya*) down the plane of discriminative knowledge is named the stream of happiness. That which leads to rebirth and flows down the plane of undiscriminative ignorance is the stream of sin.

Among those[1] the flow of the desirables is thinned by desirelessness; the flow of discrimination is rendered visible by habituating the mind to the experience of knowledge.

Hence suppression of the mental modification is dependent upon both. *Y.B.*

13. Of these, practice is the effort to secure steadiness.

14. And this is firmly rooted, being well attended to for a long time without interruption and with devotion.

15. Desirelessness is the consciousness of supremacy in him who is free from thirst for perceptible and scriptural enjoyments.

A mind free from attachment to perceptible enjoyments, such as women, foods, drinks, and power, and having no thirst for scriptural enjoyables, such as heaven and the attainment of the states of the *videha* (disembodied) and the *prakṛtilaya* (absorbed in Nature), has, when it comes into contact with such divine and worldly objects, a consciousness of its supremacy, due to an understanding of the defects of the objects, brought about by virtue of intellectual illumination. This consciousness of power is the same

[1] "Those," i.e., the modifications.

as the consciousness of indifference to their enjoyment, and is devoid of all desirable and undesirable objects as such. This mental state is desirelessness (*vairāgya*). *Y.B.*

16. The same is higher, when there is indifference to the "qualities," due to the knowledge of the *puruṣa*.

There are two forms of desirelessness. Of these the latter is but the light of spiritual knowledge. . . .Desirelessness is but the highest perfection of spiritual knowledge; and absolute independence (*kaivalya*) is nothing else. *Y.B.*

17. The cognitive trance (*samādhi*) is accompanied by the appearances of philosophical curiosity,[1] meditation,[2] elation, and egosim.

Philosophical curiosity (*vitarka*) is a superficial attempt of the mind to grasp any object.

Meditation is a subtle attempt. Elation is bliss. Egoism is the consciousness of being one with the self.

. . .All these trances have something to grasp (*ālambana*). *Y.B.*

18. Preceded by the constant repetition of the notion of cessation is the other; in which the residual potencies only remain.

The ultra-cognitive trance is that state of mental restraint in which all its modifications cease from action and remain only *in posse*. Its means is the higher desirelessness.

. . .The trance, being thus seedless, is the ultra-cognitive. *Y.B.*

19. [This] is caused by objective existence for the *videhas* and *prakṛtilayas*.

This is of two descriptions:—brought about by objective existence and brought about by the practice of the means. In the case of *yogis* it is brought about by the practice of the means. In the case of the *videhas* and the *prakṛtilayas* it is caused by objective existence. *Y.B.*

. . .They are called the *videhas* (disembodied) because they are free from the physical bodies. It is they who, with a mind capable of moving only along the line marked by habit, enjoy a state of something like absolute freedom, but are without the physical body. . . .

. . .The *prakṛtilayas*, having their minds merged in *prakṛti* [Nature], with its work still undone, enjoy a state of something like absolute freedom as long as they do not come back by virtue of the work yet to be done. Although the mind has become similar to *prakṛti*, yet they come back when the limit has been reached. . . . *T.V.*

[1] A better translation of *vitarka* would be "wrong reasoning."

[2] A better translation of *vicāra* would be "thinking" or "reasoning."

20. For others it is preceded by faith, energy, memory, trance, and discernment.

It is brought about by the means of achievement for the *yogis*. Faith is the pleasing wishful contact of mind with the object of pursuit. It sustains the *yogi*, like a mother. Energy is born in him who pursues knowledge with faith. Memory comes to help when he is possessed of energy. On the appearance of memory, the mind ceases to be disturbed and passes into trance. When the mind is entranced, discrimination appears, by which it knows an object as it is.... *Y.B.*

21. Proximate for those whose consciousness of supremacy is keen.

...Of these, the attainment of trance and the fruit of trance are near to those who are intensely energetic in their application to the means of achievement and possess a keen consciousness of supremacy. *Y.B.*

22. There is a further differentiation also—mild, middling, and intense.[1]

23. Or, by feeling the omnipresence of God (Īśvara).[2]

24. Īśvara is a distinct *puruṣa*, untouched by the vehicles of affliction, action, and fruition.

Are all those, then, who have reached the state of absolute freedom Īśvaras, and there are many such for they have reached the state of absolute freedom after cutting the three bonds? No, Īśvara never had, or will have, any relation to these bonds. As former bondage is known in the case of the emancipated, not so in the case of Īśvara. Or, as future bondage is possible in the case of the *prakṛtilayas*, not so in the case of Īśvara. He is ever free, ever the Lord.

...Hence he alone is Īśvara whose divinity is free from equality or excess, and He is a distinct *puruṣa*. *Y.B.*

The world is made of the conscious and the unconscious principles only. There is none else that goes to make it. If Īśvara is unconscious, He must be the *mūlaprakṛti* (root Nature), comprehending as it does all the non-intelligent modifications. If this be so, then it is impossible, by reason of his being non-intelligent, that he should be brought face to face with the devotee.[3] If, on the other hand, he is intelligent, then too it is impossible that he should be brought face to face with the devotee, because the power of consciousness is by nature indifferent, and because Īśvara is not like other *puruṣas* in evolution, on account of the absence of any connection with the principles of egoism, &c. Furthermore, how is it possible that he should possess a wish for the attainment [of trance by the devotee]? *T.V.*

25. In Him the seed of the omniscient is not exceeded.

...Wherever knowledge reaches the highest limit, that is the omniscient and that is a distinct *puruṣa*. Inference is of service only in establishing the general idea.... *Y.B.*

[1] The translation has been revised slightly.

[2] Or "by devotion to God."

[3] The translation has been revised slightly.

26. He is the teacher of the ancients too, not being limited by time.

27. The sacred word[1] connotes Him.

28. Its repetition and the understanding of its meaning.

. . . The mind of the *yogi* who constantly repeats the sacred syllable and habituates the mind to the constant manifestation of the idea it carries becomes one-pointed. . . . *Y.B.*

29. Thence the understanding of the individual self and the absence of obstacles too.

. . . Whatever obstacles there may be—diseases, &c.—cease to be by feeling the omnipresence of the Lord; and the true nature of himself is also seen. It is known that just as Īśvara is a *puruṣa*, pure, calm, free and without appendants, such is this *puruṣa* also, the self underlying the individual manifestation of the will-to-be. *Y.B.*

30. Disease, languor, indecision, carelessness, sloth, sensuality, mistaken notion, missing the point, instability,—these, causing distractions, are the obstacles.

31. Pain, despair, shakiness, inspiration, and expiration are the companions of these distractions.

32. For their prevention, habituation to one truth.

33. By cultivating habits of friendliness, compassion, complacency, and indifference towards happiness, misery, virtue, and vice, respectively, the mind becomes pure.

34. Optionally, by the expulsion and retention of breath.

Expulsion is the throwing out of the air in the lungs through the nostrils by special effort. Retention is the control of breath (*prāṇāyāma*), the lengthening of the duration of the stay of the air outside the lungs. Let mental steadiness be optionally cultivated by these. *Y.B.*

. . . By thus exhaling and inhaling air the body becomes light, and the mind thence attains the state of steadiness. . . .[2] *T.V.*

35. Or, higher sense-activity appearing, mental steadiness results.[3]

The power to cognize superphysical (*divya*) smell, which one gets by concentrating upon the forepart of the nose, is the higher olfactory sense-activity. By concentration upon the forepart of the tongue, the power to cognize taste; over the palate, cognition of colour; in the middle of the tongue, cognition of touch; in the root of the tongue, cognition of sound. *Y.B.*

[1] The sacred word is "*Om*"—or "*Aum*."

[2] The translation has been revised slightly.

[3] The translation has been revised slightly.

36. Or, the state of painless lucidity.

"Or, the state of painless lucidity" appearing as a higher activity, causes the steadiness of the mind.

This two-fold higher activity, the painless sensuous and the purely egoistic, is called lucidity. By this the *yogi's* mind reaches the state of steadiness. *Y.B.*

37. Or, the mind having desirelessness for its object.

38. Or, having the knowledge of dream and sleep as its object of study.

39. Or, by meditating according to one's predilection.

40. His power reaches down to the minutest, and up to the largest.

41. Becoming like a transparent crystal on the modifications disappearing, the mind acquires the power of thought-transformation (*samāpatti*), the power of appearing in the shape of whatever object is presented to it, be it the knower, the knowable, or the act of knowing.

"Like a transparent crystal":—This is the statement of an analogy. As the crystal becomes coloured by the colour of the object placed beside it, and then shines according to the form of the object, so the mind is coloured by the colour of the object presented to it and then appears in the form of the object.

This, then, is *samāpatti* [thought-transformation]—the mind showing itself like a transparent crystal, in the form of the object it comes in contact with, be it the knower, the knowable, or the acts of knowledge. *Y.B.*

42. There the thought-transformation in which the options of word, meaning, and idea are mixed up, is called indistinct (verbal).

And that as follows:—The cow as a word, the cow as an object, and the cow as an idea, although different from one another, are cognized as indistinct . . . if an object, such as a cow, is present in the trans-consciousness[1] of the *yogi* who has reached this state of thought-transformation, being pierced through by the indeterminate notions of word, meaning, and idea, then the thought-transformation is mixed up and is called indistinct.

When, however, the mind becomes free from the memories of verbal convention, and trans-consciousness is devoid of the options of inferential and verbal cognitions, the object makes its appearance in the mind in its own distinct nature [unmixed with word and meaning], the thought-transformation is called distinct (*nirvitarka*). . . . *Y.B.*

43. Distinct [i.e., wordless] thought-transformation is that in which the mind shines out as the object alone on the cessation of memory, and, [as] it were, devoid of its own nature.

[1] Or "super-consciousness."

...The thought-transformation becomes distinct at the time when the memory of the fictions of verbal convention and verbal and inferential knowledge ceases; when the mind is coloured by the nature of the object; when it, as it were, gives up its own nature of conscious cognition; and when, therefore, it only shows out the nature of the object, and has, as it were, transformed into the shape of the object itself.... *Y.B.*

44. By this the meditative and the ultra-meditative, having the subtle for their objects, are also described.

Of these, the indistinct and distinct thought-transformations have to operate upon things extended in time and space; the meditative and the ultra-meditative operate upon the subtle elements.... *Y.B.*

45. And the province of the subtle reaches up to the noumenal.

Does the range of thought-transformation with reference to objective appearances extend up to the subtle elements only? No. "And the province of subtle reaches up to the noumenal." *T.V.*

46. They are the seeded trance only.

These four descriptions of thought-transformations have their origin [seed] in external objects. Therefore, is the trance, too, "seeded." In the case of the gross objects it is the indistinctive and the distinctive. In the subtle objects it is the meditative and the ultra-meditative. Thus is trance described to be four-fold. *Y.B.*

47. The undisturbed flow of the ultra-meditative causes subjective luminosity.

48. Therein the faculty of essential cognition.

The cognitive faculty which shows itself in that state in the mind of the wise bears the name of essential cognition. The term itself expresses the definition. It always cognizes the essence, the truth. There is not even a trace of false knowledge. *Y.B.*

49. It has different objects from those of verbal and inferential cognition, as it refers to particulars.

Verbal cognition refers to knowledge received from another. It has the generals for its objects. It is not possible to describe the particulars by words. Why? Because there is no conventional denotation of the particular in words.

...Nor can it be said that this particular does not exist for want of authority....Hence this cognition has different objects from those of inferential and verbal cognitions, because it has the particulars for its objects. *Y.B.*

50. Residual potencies born therefrom impede other residual potencies.

When the trance cognition has been reached, the *yogi* acquires by the exercise of that cognition, newer and newer residual potencies. . . . The potency born of trance impedes the outgoing vehicle of potencies. By overpowering the outgoing tendencies, notions due to them cease to exist. On the suppression of these notions the trance faculty gains in power. Then again the activity of trance cognition. Then again residual potencies caused by the act of cognition. In this way the vehicle of potencies is being constantly renewed. *Y.B.*

. . . When, however, the power which springs from the manifestation of trance cognition entirely roots out the vehicles of action and affliction and the mind for that reason exists in the state of having mostly fulfilled its objects, the only object that then remains for it to achieve is the attainment of discriminative knowledge. Therefore, the potencies of the mind due to the practice of the trance cognition cannot generate the habits of returning to the duties of enjoyment. . . . The action of the mind lasts only up to the attainment of discriminative knowledge. The mind only works for enjoyment as long as it does not experience discriminative knowledge. When, however, discriminative knowledge is born, the afflictions are removed, and the duty of causing enjoyment is over. *T.V.*

51. By the suppression of that, too, all beings suppressed, comes the seedless trance.[1]

Chapter 2: Methods (*Sādhanā*)

1. Purificatory action,[2] study, and making God the motive of action, constitute the *yoga* of action.[3]

2. For the purpose of bringing about trance and for the purpose of attenuating afflictions.

3. The afflictions are nescience, egoism, attachment, aversion, and love of life.

Nescience [ignorance] is unreal cognition itself. Egoism and the others also carry nescience with them and cannot exist without it. They too are therefore unreal cognitions. The meaning is that for this reason they are destroyed with the destruction of nescience. He says now that the reason for their destruction[4] exists in their being the cause of repeated births: . . . *T.V.*

4. Nescience is the field for the others, whether dormant, tenuous, alternated, or fully operative.

[1] The translation has been revised.

[2] The word *tapas* has been translated as "purificatory action," because *tapas* means that which burns up impurities.

[3] The translation has been revised slightly.

[4] "Destruction" is to be preferred to the translator's "destructibility."

Of these, nescience is the field, the breeding ground for the others that follow, the egoism, &c., having a four-fold possible mode of their existence, as the dormant, the tenuous, the alternated, and the fully operative.

What is dormancy? It is the existence in the mind as power alone in the germinal state. It is awake when it turns its face towards its objects. In the case of him who possesses discriminative knowledge, the germs of the afflictions are singed, and, therefore, even on the object coming in front, they do not come into operation. How can the burned-up seed sprout? Hence, the wise man, whose afflictions are gone, is said to have had his birth....

Tenuity is now described. The afflictions become tenuous on being cut down by habituation to contraries.

And they are alternated, inasmuch as they disappear and appear over and over again in the same condition....

The fully operative is that which has found manifestation in the object.

All these do not pass beyond the sphere of affliction....

...The afflictions appear only in the form which is put upon an object by nescience. They are found existing simultaneously with the cognition of the unreal; and they disappear when nescience disappears. *Y.B.*

5. Nescience is the taking of the non-eternal, the impure, the painful, and the not-self to be the eternal, the pure, the pleasurable, and the self.

6. Egoism is the appearance of identity in the natures of the subjective power of consciousness and the instrumental power of seeing.

7. Attachment is the sequential attraction to pleasure.

8. Aversion is the sequential repulsion from pain.

9. Flowing on by its own potency, established all the same even in the wise, is love of life.

10. These, when but potential, are destroyed along with the passing out of activity.

These five afflictions, when their seed-power has, as it were, been burnt up, disappear of themselves along with that *yogi's* mind, when, having fulfilled the purpose of its existence, it becomes latent. *Y.B.*

...The destruction of the potential state is not within the sphere of man's effort. It is, on the contrary, to be destroyed by the passing out of activity; that is, by the mind passing back into its cause, the principle of egoism. *T.V.*

11. Their modifications are destroyed by meditation.

...As the gross dirt of clothes is at first shaken off, and then the fine dirt is washed off, by effort and appliance, so the gross essential modifications need but small antagonistic efforts, whereas the potential ones need very powerful antagonists. *Y.B.*

12. The vehicle of actions has its origin in afflictions, and is experienced in visible and invisible births.

Here the vehicle of good and bad actions is born of lust, avarice, forgetfulness, and anger. Its operation is left in the visible as well as in the invisible birth.... *Y.B.*

13. It ripens into life-state, life-time, and life-experience, if the root exists.

14. They have pleasure or pain as the fruit, by reason of virtue or vice.

They, i.e., life-state, life-period and life-experience, have pleasure for their fruit when caused by virtue, and have pain for their fruit when caused by vice. *Y.B.*

15. By reason of the pains of change, anxiety, and habituation, and by reason of the contrariety of the functionings of the "qualities," all indeed is pain to the discriminating.

...It is not possible to make the powers of action, &c., free from desire by the frequent repetition of enjoyments, because attachment increases in consequence of the repetition of enjoyments and so also does the dexterity of the powers. The repetition of enjoyment is, therefore, no cause of pleasure....

This is the pain of change. In the state of pleasure even, it produces a contrary effect and thus afflicts a *yogi* alone.

What, again, is the painfulness of habituation? By the enjoyment of pleasure comes into being the vehicle of the potency of pleasure. By the feeling of pain comes the vehicle of the potency of pain. By thus experiencing the fruition of actions in the shape of pleasures and pains, the vehicle of actions grows.

Further, by reason of the contrariety of the functionings of the qualities, "all is indeed pain to the discriminating." The qualities of the will-to-know, being of the nature of essentiality, activity and inactivity, become dependent upon mutual help, and set the formation of either a quiescent, a disturbed, or a delusive notion possessed of the three qualities themselves. And the functioning of the qualities being changeful, the mind is said to possess the nature of changing quickly. The intensities of their natures and the intensities of their functionings are contradictory to one another. The ordinary, however, function together with the intense. Thus do these qualities bring about the notions of pleasure, pain, and delusion by each subserving the others, and all thus enter into the formations of the others. It is by the quality which is the leading factor, that the difference is introduced. It is for this reason that all is pain to the discriminating. *Y.B.*

16. Pain not-yet-come is the avoidable.

17. The conjunction of the knower and the knowable is the cause of the avoidable pain.

...The eternal conjunction of the power of knowing and the capacity of being known, brought about by the purpose of existence, is the cause of the avoidable pain...for example, the soles of the feet possess the capacity of being pierced, and the thorn possesses the power of piercing. The remedy consists in not putting the foot on the thorn, or putting it with a shoe on.... *Y.B.*

18. The knowable is of the nature of illumination, activity, and inertia; it consists of the elements and the powers of sensation, action, and thought; its objects are emancipation and experience.

...The object of the "knowable" is, of course, the fulfilment of the objects of the *puruṣa*, experience and emancipation. Of these, experience consists in obtaining the knowledge of the nature of the desirable and undesirable phenomena of the qualities, which knowledge, however, does not recognize them as only the modifications of the qualities. Emancipation is the ascertainment of the nature of the enjoyer, the *puruṣa*. Beyond the knowledge of these two there is no wisdom....

Well, but how can either experience or emancipation, which being both of them the works of the will-to-be (*buddhi*), live in the will-to-be alone, be predicated of the *puruṣa*? As victory and defeat, existing in the soldiers, are predicated of their master, because it is he who enjoys the fruit thereof, so are bondage and freedom existing in the will-to-be alone predicated of the *puruṣa*, because he is the enjoyer of their fruit. It is of the will-to-be alone that the bondage exists until the object of the *puruṣa* is fulfilled, and it is fulfilment of the object that is emancipation (*mokṣa*). Similarly have perception, retention, judgment, rejection, knowledge of realities, and the distinction of unrealities their existence fastened onto the *puruṣa* although they have their existence in the will-to-be, because he is the enjoyer of their fruit. *Y.B.*

19. The specialized, the unspecialized, the undifferentiated phenomenal, and the noumenal are the stages of "the qualities."

20. The seer is consciousness only; even though pure, he cognizes ideas by imitation.

"Consciousness only": This means that he is nothing other than the power of becoming conscious; that is to say, he is not touched by the qualities. This *puruṣa* cognizes the will-to-be by reflex action. He is neither quite similar nor quite dissimilar to the will-to-be (*buddhi*). "He is not quite similar." Why? The will-to-be, having for its sphere of action objects known and not yet known, is of course changeful. The changefulness is shown by its objects, such as the cow and the jar, &c., being both known and unknown....

..."He is not quite dissimilar." Why? "Even though pure, he sees the ideas after they have come into the mind." Inasmuch as the *puruṣa* cognizes the ideas as the will-to-be, seized of consciousness, is transformed into them, he appears by the act of cognition to be as it were the very self of the will-to-be, although in reality he is not so.... *Y.B.*

21. For his purpose only is the being of the "knowable."

...For this reason the existence of the knowable is for his purpose only, i.e., for the purpose of the knower alone, and not for the purpose of the knowable.

It is because the being of the knowable is for the purpose of the *puruṣa* and not for the purpose of the knowable itself that its nature acts to that purpose until that purpose of the *puruṣa* is achieved; and ceases to act when that purpose has been achieved.... *T.V.*

22. Although destroyed in relation to him whose objects have been achieved, it is not destroyed, being common to others.

...Although it is destroyed to the *puruṣa* who has attained wisdom, it is not destroyed in relation to *puruṣas* who have not attained wisdom, as it has not done its duty by them yet.... *Y.B.*

23. Conjunction is that which brings about the recognition of the natures of the power of owning and the capacity of being owned.

...The *puruṣa* is the owner. "The knowable" is whatever is owned. The former is conjoined to the latter for the purpose of knowing. The cognition of the knowable which follows from the conjunction is enjoyment. The knowledge, however, of the nature of the knower is emancipation. Conjunction, therefore, ends when it has caused knowledge. Knowledge is, therefore, called the cause of separation. Knowledge is the contradictory of ignorance. Therefore, ignorance is said to be the reason for conjunction. Here knowledge is not the cause of freedom (*mokṣa*), because the absence of ignorance itself, meaning as it does the absence of bondage, is freedom (*mokṣa*).... *Y.B.*

24. Nescience is its effective cause.

25. Removal [of bondage] is the disappearance of conjunction on account of the disappearance of nescience, and that is the absolute freedom of the knower.[1]

...The meaning is that on the disappearance of the conjunction of the *puruṣa* and the will-to-be being brought about by the disappearance of ignorance, bondage is forever removed. This is removal. This is the freedom of the seer (*puruṣa*).... *Y.B.*

26. The means of the removal is discriminative knowledge undisturbed.

Discriminative knowledge is the recognition of the distinct natures of the *puruṣa* and the essence of matter (*sattva*)....It is this discriminative knowledge undisturbed that is the means of the removal. By this it is clear that the means of removal, the path of *mokṣa* (absolute freedom), is the burning of the seed of false knowledge, so that it may not sprout again. *Y.B.*

[1] The translation has been revised.

27. His discrimination becoming final at each stage is seven-fold.

. . . This is as follows:—(1) The pain to be removed is known. Nothing further remains to be known of it. (2) The causes of pain to be removed have been done away with. (3) Removal has become a fact of direct cognition by means of inhibitive trance. (4) The means of knowledge in the shape of discriminative knowledge has been understood.

This is the four-fold freedom of conscious discrimination from external phenomena. The freedom from the mind itself is three-fold. The will-to-be has done its duty. The "qualities," tending to become latent into their cause, disappear along with it, finding no support . . . like stones rolled down from the edge of a hilltop. Nor once passed into latency, do they come back to life again, there being no object for it. In this state, the *puruṣa*, having passed beyond the limits of the relation with the "qualities," remains only the light of his own pure nature and is free.

The *puruṣa* who has seen successively these seven stages of discrimination is called "adept" (*kuśala*). He remains free and wise even when the mind is resolved into its cause, because he has passed beyond the sphere of the "qualities." *Y.B.*

28. On the destruction of impurity by the sustained practice of the accessories[1] of *yoga*, the light of wisdom reaches up to discriminative knowledge.

The accessories of *yoga* are eight, to be further named. By their sustained practice is destroyed the five-fold unreal cognition, which is of the nature of impurity. . . . *Y.B.*

29. Restraint, observance, posture, regulation of breath, abstraction [of the senses], concentration, meditation, and trance are the eight accessories of *yoga*.[2]

30. Of these, the restraints (*yama*) are: abstinence from injury (*ahiṁsā*), veracity, abstinence from theft, continence, and abstinence from avariciousness.

31. They are the great vow, universal, and not-limited by life-state, space, time, and circumstance.

Of these, abstinence from injury is limited to life-state, as, for example, the injury inflicted by a fisherman is limited to fish alone, and to none else. The same is limited to space, as, for example, in the case of a man who says to himself, "I shall not injure at a sacred place." The same is limited to time, as for example, in the case of a man who says to himself, "I shall not cause injury on the sacred day of the *caturdaśī* (the fourteenth) of the lunar fortnight."

[1] "Parts" or "limbs" would be a better translation of "*aṅga*."

[2] See p. 454, n. 3. The three basic terms, *dhāraṇā*, *dhyāna*, and *samādhi*, are variously translated and interpreted by different translators and writers on *yoga*.

The same in the case of a man who has given up the three injuries is limited by circumstance, as, for example, when a man says to himself, "I shall cause injury only for the sake of gods and *brāhmins* and not in any other way." Or, as for example, injury is caused by soldiers in battle alone and nowhere else. . . . Universal is that which pervades all conditions of life, everywhere, always, and is nowhere out of place. They are called the great vow. *Y.B.*

32. The observances (*niyama*) are cleanliness, contentment, purificatory action, study, and the making of the Lord the motive of all action.

Of these, cleanliness is external when brought about by earths and water, &c., and consists in the eating of pure things, &c. It is internal when it consists in the washing away of impurities of the mind.

Contentment is the absence of desire to secure more of the necessaries of life than one already possesses.

Study is the reading of the sciences of liberation (*mokṣa*), or the repetition of the sacred syllable, *Aum*.

The making of Īśvara the motive of all actions means the doing of all actions to fulfil the purpose of that great teacher. . . . *Y.B.*

33. Upon thoughts of sin troubling, habituation to the contrary.

When during the practice of the restraints and observances sinful thoughts give trouble, the mind is to be habituated to the contrary ideas. *Y.B.*

34. The sins are the causing of injury to others and the rest. They are done, caused to be done, and permitted to be done; they are preceded by desire, anger, and ignorance; they are slight, middling, and intense; their result is an infinity of pain and unwisdom; thus comes the habit of thinking to the contrary.

. . . Thus making himself familiar with undesirable consequences of these sins, he no longer allows his mind to rest over evil acts. The habituation to the contrary tendencies becomes the cause of removing the sins. . . . *Y.B.*

35. [The habit of] not causing injury being confirmed, hostilities are given up in his presence.

36. Veracity being confirmed, action and fruition become dependents.

37. [The habit of] not stealing being confirmed, all jewels approach him.

38. Continence being confirmed, vigour is obtained.

39. Non-covetousness being confirmed, knowledge of the succession of births is obtained.[1]

[1] The translation has been revised.

. . . It means the perfect knowledge of the past, the present, and of all that is beyond ken, together with their modes. *T.V.*

40. By cleanliness is meant disgust with one's body, and cessation of contact with others.[1]

41. And upon the essence [of mind] becoming pure, come high-mindedness, one-pointedness, control of the senses, and fitness for the knowledge of the self.

42. By contentment, the acquisition of extreme happiness.

43. By purificatory actions, the removal of impurity and the attainments of the physical body and the senses.

44. By study comes communion with the desired deity.

45. The attainment of trance, by making Īśvara the motive of all actions.

46. Posture is steadily easy.

47. By slackening of effort and by thought-transformation as infinite.

. . . Posture becomes perfect when effort to that end ceases, so that there may be no more movement of the body. Or, when the mind is transformed into the infinite, that is, makes the idea of infinity its own, it brings about the perfection of posture. *Y.B.*

48. Thence cessation of disturbance from the pairs of opposites.

When posture has been mastered he is not disturbed by the pairs of opposites such as heat and cold. *Y.B.*

49. Regulation of breath (*prāṇāyāma*) is the stoppage of the inhaling and exhaling movements [of breath] which follows when that[2] has been secured.[3]

50. Manifestation as external, internal, and total restraint [of breath] is regulated by place, time, and number; and thus it becomes long in duration and subtle.

. . . The cessation of the motion of breath which precedes exhalation is external. The cessation of the motion of breath which precedes inhalation is internal. The third manifests total restraint where cessation of both these motions takes place by a single effort. . . . *Y.B.*

51. The fourth is that which follows when the spheres of the external and internal have been passed.

52. Thence the cover of light is destroyed.

[1] The translation has been revised.

[2] "That" refers to posture.

[3] "Inspiring" and "expiring" have been replaced by "inhaling" and "exhaling" respectively.

...This *karma* of the *yogi* which covers up the light and binds him to repeated births, becomes weak by the practice of control of breath every moment, and is then destroyed.... *Y.B.*

53. And the fitness of the mind for concentration (*dhāraṇā*).

54. Abstraction [of the senses] (*pratyāhāra*) is that by which the senses do not come into contact with their objects and follow as it were the nature of the mind.

...The senses are restrained, like the mind, when the mind is restrained. *Y.B.*

55. Thence the senses are under the highest control.

Chapter 3: Attainments (*Vibhūtis*)

1. Concentration (*dhāraṇā*) is the steadfastness of the mind.

...Concentration means the mind becoming fast in such places as the sphere of the navel, the lotus of the heart, the light in the brain, the fore-part of the nose, the fore-part of the tongue, and such like parts of the body; or by means of the modifications only in any other external object only. *Y.B.*

Trance (*samādhi*) and the means of its attainment have been described in the first and second chapters. In the third chapter are to be described the attainments which follow in their wake and which are the means of generating faith. The attainments are achieved by *saṁyama*. *Saṁyama* consists of concentration, meditation, and trance together. As means for the achievement of attainment, these three accessories are more intimate than the five external ones, and, thus being internal, they are described here, in order that they may be specifically mastered. Among these, too, concentration, meditation, and trance are related to one another as cause and effect consecutively, and their order of causation is fixed.... *T.V.*

2. The continuation there of the mental effort [to understand] is meditation (*dhyāna*).

...Continuance of the mental effort means one-pointedness. *T.V.*

3. The same, when shining with the light of the object alone, and devoid, as it were, of itself, is trance [or contemplation] (*samādhi*).

When on account of the object of contemplation taking entire possession of the mind, contemplation shows forth only the light of the form of the contemplated object, and is devoid, as it were, of its nature of self-cognition, then it is called trance [or contemplation]. *Y.B.*

4. The three together are *saṁyama*.[1]

[1] *Saṁyama* literally means "inner discipline."

5. By the achievement thereof comes the visibility of the cognition.

. . . As *saṁyama* becomes firmer and firmer so does the trance-cognition become more and more lucid. *Y.B.*

6. Its application is to the planes.[1]

When one plane has been conquered by *saṁyama*, it is applied to the next immediately following. No one who has not conquered the lower plane can jump over the plane immediately following, and then achieve *saṁyama* with reference to the plane further off. . . . *Y.B.*

When the indistinct trance-cognition, having the gross world for its sphere, has been achieved by *saṁyama*, the application of *saṁyama* is to be the yet unconquered distinct trance. When that has been conquered, the application is to be to the meditative transformation. Similar is the application to the ultra-meditative. *T.V.*

7. The three are more intimate than the preceding.[2]

8. Even that is non-intimate to the seedless.

This intimate triad of means too becomes an external accessory of the seedless trance. . . . *Y.B.*

9. The suppressive modification is the conjunction of the mind with the moment of suppression (*nirodha*), when the outgoing and suppressive potencies disappear and appear, respectively.

The outgoing potencies are the characteristics of the mind. It is not that they are suppressed by the restraints of the acts of cognition, being of the nature of the acts of cognition, [as they are not of the nature of the acts of cognition]. The potencies of suppression too are characteristics of the mind. The respective suppression and appearance of these two, when the characteristics of the outgoing potencies are destroyed and the potencies of suppression acquired, is the moment of suppression which the mind appears in conjunction with.[3] This acquiring of different potencies by the one mind every moment is the suppressive change. In that state the potencies alone are left in the mind. This has been described as the suppressive trance. *Y.B.*

10. By potency comes its undisturbed flow.

11. The trance-modification of the mind is the destruction and rise of all-pointedness and one-pointedness, respectively.

All-pointedness is a characteristic of the mind. One-pointedness is also a characteristic of the mind. . . . This mind, then, following alone both these

[1] Or "stages."

[2] "The preceding," that is, the preceding five steps, *yama*, *niyama*, etc.

[3] A different translation may serve to clarify this passage somewhat: "When these two [states of the mind-stuff] become visible or become invisible, [that is when] the subliminal impressions of emergence are withdrawing and the subliminal impressions of restriction are being brought into place." J. H. Woods, *The Yoga System of Patañjali*, Harvard Oriental Series, Vol. 17 (Cambridge, Mass.: Harvard University Press, 1927), p. 209.

characteristics of destruction and manifestation which make its very nature, inclines towards contemplation. This is the trance modification of the mind. *Y.B.*

12. Thence, again, comes the mental modification of one-pointedness, when the subsiding and rising cognitive acts are similar.

Again, when, trance having been achieved, the later state of trance becomes the former, the former subsides and the later cognitive trance modification arises. That is to say, one becomes the past and the other the present. When both these cognitive acts of him who has become inclined towards trance become similar to each other, it [the mind] becomes one-pointed. This shows the achievement of trance, and also of one-pointedness itself.... *T.V.*

13. By this are described the changes of characteristic (*dharma*), secondary quality (*lakṣaṇa*), and condition (*avasthā*) in the objective and instrumental phenomena.

By this must be understood the three-fold change in the objective and instrumental phenomena, due to the conception of a distinction between the characteristic and the characterized. In reality, however, there is but one change, because the characteristic is the very being itself of the characterized; and it is the change of the characterized alone that is detailed by means of the characteristic. It is only the characteristic present in the characterized object that changes states in the past, the present, and the future; the substance is not changed. Thus when a vessel of gold is broken to be made into something else, it is only the condition that changes, not the gold. *Y.B.*

14. "The object characterized" is that which is common to the latent, the rising, and the unpredicable characteristic.

Now of the characteristics of an object that are either latent, rising, or unpredicable, the latent are those that have been in operation and ceased. The rising characteristics are those that are in operation. They are immediate consequents of the yet unmanifested secondary quality. Those that have passed are the consequents of the present ones....

"The characterized object" is that constant nature thereof which remains common to all these manifested and unmanifested characteristics and which is the substratum of both the generic and the specific. In the case of him, however, to whom this is a characteristic only without a substratum, there must be absence of experience.... *Y.B.*

The word "characteristics" is used here to denote characteristic, secondary quality, and condition, because that is the basic quality....

Having thus divided the characteristics, he now describes the substratum as being common to all these states:—"The characterized object is that common, &c." The generic is the nature of the characterized, the substratum; and the specific is the characteristic. The substratum is of the nature of both these. This is the meaning. *T.V.*

15. The distinctness of succession is the reason for the distinctness of modifications.

The succession of a characteristic is that characteristic which comes before it immediately. The kneaded lump of clay disappears and the jar appears in close sequence. This is the order of the sequence of the changes of the characteristic. The order of the change of secondary qualities is the sequential appearance of the present state of a jar out of its yet-unmanifested state of existence. Similarly is there a succession for the passing into its past state, of the present state of the kneaded lump of clay. There is no succession for the past. . . .

Such is also the succession in the case of the change of condition. . . .

When, however, the characterized object is spoken of as being what it really is, as not distinct from the characteristic, then, by virtue of that conception, the object itself is described as a characteristic; and then the succession appears to be one only. *Y.B.*

16. By *saṁyama* over[1] the three-fold change, comes the knowledge of the past and the future.

By *saṁyama* on the changes of characteristic, secondary quality, and condition, comes to the *yogis* the knowledge of the past and the future. . . . When direct knowledge of the three-fold change is obtained by means of *saṁyama*, knowledge of their past and present is obtained. *Y.B.*

17. The word, the object, and the idea appear as one, because each coincides with the other; by *saṁyama* on their distinction comes the knowledge of the sounds of all living beings.

18. By bringing residual potencies into consciousness, the knowledge of previous life-state (*jāti*).

19. Of the notions, the knowledge of other minds.

By *saṁyama* on the notions [or ideas] and thus by obtaining the direct knowledge of the notions comes the knowledge of other minds. But not of its object, that not being the direct object of the *yogi's* mind. . . . *Y.B.*

20. By *saṁyama* on the form of the body, on perceptibility being checked, and thus there being no contact with the light of the eye, comes disappearance.

By *saṁyama* on the form of the body, he checks the perceptibility of the form. On perceptibility being checked, and thus there being no longer contact with the light which carries it to the eye, disappearance of the *yogi* is brought about. . . . *Y.B.*

21. *Karma* is either fast in fruition or slow; by *saṁyama* on these comes knowledge of death; or, by portents.

[1] Or "By performing *saṁyama* on. . . ." Hereafter, "over" is changed to "on."

...By *saṁyama* on that *karma*, that is, on virtue and vice, accrues the knowledge of death. By this the *yogi* knows his fast-fructifying *karma*, and then makes many bodies for himself and thereby enjoys the fruit thereof as fast as he likes and dies whenever he pleases. *T.V.*

22. On friendliness, &c., the powers.

...By the performance of *saṁyama* on friendliness, &c., the powers of friendliness, &c., come to him. Of these, the power which comes by the practice of the feeling of friendliness is that by which he can make the whole living world happy, and hence becomes the well-wisher of all. *T.V.*

23. On the powers, the powers of elephant, &c.

By *saṁyama* with reference to the strength of an elephant he comes to possess the strength of an elephant. *Y.B.*

24. The knowledge of the subtle, the veiled, the remote, by directing the light of higher sense-activity towards them.

25. By *saṁyama* on the sun, knowledge of the regions.

26. On the moon, the knowledge of the starry systems.

27. On the pole-star, the knowledge of their movements.

...let him know the movement of the stars by performing *saṁyama* with reference to the pole-star. *Y.B.*

28. On the plexus of the navel, the knowledge of the system of the body.

Let him know the system of the body by performing *saṁyama* on the plexus of the navel. *Y.B.*

29. On the pit of the throat, subdual of hunger and thirst.

30. On the tortoise tube (*kūrmanāḍi*), steadiness.

31. On the coronal light, vision of the Perfected-Ones.

32. Or, all knowledge by prescience (*pratibhā*).

...When *saṁyama* is performed with the object of attaining the highest intellection, then, at the time of the height of practice, there takes its rise a power which, as it were, draws in all knowledge. The *yogi* knows everything by that. *T.V.*

33. On the heart, the knowledge of the mind.

34. Experience consists in the absence of the notion of distinction between the *puruṣa* and objective essence [*sattva*],[1] which are really quite distinct from each other, because it [*sattva*] exists for another. By *saṁyama* on his own object, comes the knowledge of the *puruṣa*.

[1] *Sattva*, translated here as "objective essence," is another name for *buddhi* (intellect or will) or *mahat* (the Great Principle) both of which were discussed at length in the Sāṁkhya system in Chapter XII.

...Widely different from that changing objective existence also in characteristic is the *puruṣa* who appears as pure consciousness. They are quite distinct from each other. Experience consists in the notion of the two not being taken as distinct, because the objects are shown to him. The notion of enjoyment is the knowable, because the essence of matter exists for another. There is another notion, however, the notion of the *puruṣa*, which is quite distinct from this, and which appears as pure consciousness.

By *saṁyama* with reference to this notion is born the knowledge of the *puruṣa*. The *puruṣa* is not known by that notion of itself, which is the selfsame as the objective *buddhi*. The *puruṣa* only sees that notion of self by himself.... *Y.B.*

35. Thence proceed prescience, higher hearing, touch, vision, taste, and smell.

By prescience comes the knowledge of the subtle, the intercepted, the remote, and the past and future. By higher hearing comes the hearing of divine sounds, by touch, the knowledge of divine touch;... *Y.B.*

36. They are obstacles to trance, but perfections to the outgoing mind.

They, the powers of prescience, &c., prove to be obstacles when they appear in a mind which has reached the state of trance, because they oppose the knowledge obtained in that state. When, however, they appear in a mind which is active in going out, they are attainments. *Y.B.*

It is only he whose mind is active in going out that becomes proud of the possession of these as attainments. A beggar in life may think that the possession of a little wealth is the fulness of riches. The *yogi*, however, who is inclined to the attainment of trance must reject them whenever they come. He has vowed the removal of all the three descriptions of pain to their utmost limit. That being the object of the *puruṣa*, how can he take pleasure in the attainments which are the opponents of that state of being? *T.V.*

37. The mind may enter another body, on relaxation of the cause of bondage, and by knowledge of the passages of the mind.

...By the destruction of the bonds imposed by *karma*, and by knowing the method of the mind acting upon the body, the *yogi* withdraws his mind from his own body and throws it into the body of another. As the mind is thus thrown into another body, the powers of sensation, &c., follow it. *Y.B.*

38. By mastery over *udāna*, ascension and non-contact with water, mud, thorns, &c.

Life which shows itself as the operations of *prāṇa* (vital breath) and others, is the manifestation of all the powers of sensation and action. Its action is five-fold. The *prāṇa* moves through the mouth and the nose, and manifests itself within the chest. The *samāna* manifests up to the navel.

It is so called because it carries equally (*sama*) [to all parts of the body, the juice of food, &c.]. Manifesting down to the soles of feet [all over] is the *apāna*, so called because it carries away (*apa*). Manifesting up to the head is the *udāna*, so called because it carries upward (*ut*). The *vyāna* is so called because it pervades the whole body in every direction. Of these, the *prāṇa* is the chief. *Y.B.*

39. By mastery over *samāna* comes effulgence.

He who has obtained mastery over *samāna* blows the fire into flame and thus shines. *Y.B.*

40. By *saṁyama* on the relation between *ākāśa* (space) and the power of hearing comes the higher power of hearing.

41. By *saṁyama* on the relation between the body and the *ākāśa*, or by attaining to [the state of thought transforming as] the lightness of cotton, &c., passage through space (*ākāśa*).

Wherever there is the body, there is the *ākāśa*. The body becomes related to the *ākāśa*, because the latter gives room to the former. Having mastered the relation by the attainment of the state of thought transforming into light things such as cotton, &c., down to the atom, the *yogi* becomes light. Thence does he get the power of roaming through space and walking over water with his feet. He walks over a spider's web, and then walks over the rays of light. Then does he get the power of roaming through space at will. *Y.B.*

42. Actual passing out and acting outside the body is the great excorporeal; by that is destroyed the veil of light.

That form of concentration in which the mind acts upon something outside the body, is named excorporeal concentration.

This excorporeal concentration, if taking place by merely the mind functioning, while yet staying in the body, is called fancied (*kalpita*) excorporeal.

That, however, in which the mind has no need of the body left and passes out of the body and then functions outside the body, is called the actual excorporeal concentration.

Of these, the actual excorporeal, which is also called the great excorporeal, is attained by means of the fancied excorporeal. It is by this that the *yogis* effect their entrance into other bodies. By this concentration the veil of the luminous essence of the will-to-be, in the shape of the three vehicles of affliction, action, and fruition, which has its origin in the *rajas* (activity) and *tamas* (inertia), is destroyed. *Y.B.*

43. By *saṁyama* on the gross, the substantive, the astral, conjunction, and purposefulness, is obtained mastery over the elements (*bhūtas*).

44. Thence the manifestation of attenuation (*aṇimā*) and the other

[powers]; as also the perfection of the body and non-resistance by their characteristics.

Although he possesses the power, he does not interfere to set the objects of the world topsy-turvy. Why not? Because his desire with reference to them is the same always which another *siddha*[1] of the same power has formerly willed. These are the eight attainments. The perfection of the body will be described. "Non-resistance by their characteristics":—The *pṛthivī* (earth) does not by cohesion interfere with the action of a *yogī's* body. He might even enter a stone in virtue of the use of his powers. The waters with their viscidity do not wet him. The fire does not burn him by its heat. The air moves him not by its motion. Even in *ākāśa*, which naturally offers no obstruction, his body might become obstructed to sight. Even the *siddhas* may fail to see him. *Y.B.*

45. The perfection of the body consists in beauty, grace, strength, and adamantine hardness.

46. By *saṁyama* on the act, the substantive appearance, egoism, the conjunction, and purposefulness [of sensation] comes mastery over them.[2]

47. Thence come quickness as of mind, non-instrumental perception, and mastery over the *pradhāna* (first cause).[3]

Non-instrumental perception means the action of the senses at any time or place without the necessity of the presence of the body.

Mastery over the *pradhāna* means the power of control over all the modifications of the *prakṛti*. . . . *Y.B.*

48. To him who recognizes the distinction between consciousness and pure objective existence comes supremacy over all states of being and omniscience.

Omniscience means the simultaneously discriminative knowledge of the "qualities" being as they are of the nature of all phenomena, and showing forth as they do separately the quiescent, the disturbed, and the unpredicable characteristics. This attainment is known as the "sorrowless" (*viśoka*).

Reaching this, the *yogi* moves omniscient and powerful, with all his afflictions ended. *Y.B.*

49. The seed of bondage having been destroyed by desirelessness even for that, comes absolute independence (*kaivalya*).

Then all the seeds of afflictions pass, together with the mind, into latency. When they have become latent, the *puruṣa* does not then suffer

[1] One who has attained powers.

[2] A better translation would be: By *saṁyama* on the act of knowing, on the nature of knowledge, on egoity, on contact with the object of knowledge, and on the purpose of knowledge, comes mastery over them.

[3] Or, root matter; another name for *prakṛti*.

from the triad of pain. This, then, the state, that is to say, in which the qualities manifest in the mind as afflictions, actions, and fruitions do not, having fulfilled their object, come back to action, is the final separation of consciousness from the qualities. This is the state of absolute independence, when the *puruṣa* remains consciousness alone, as in its own nature. *Y.B.*

50. When the presiding deities invite, there should be no attachment and no smile of satisfaction; contact with the undesirable being again possible.

51. By *saṁyama* on the moments and their succession, comes knowledge born of discrimination.

...The succession of moments is the non-cessation of the flow thereof. ...This time, which is not a substantive reality in itself, but is only a mental concept, and which comes into the mind as a piece of verbal knowledge only, appears to people whose minds are given to out-going activities, as if it were an objective reality....

...the moments that have passed and those that have yet to come should be described as existing in consequence of universal change in evolution. For this reason the whole world undergoes change every moment; all these characteristics are relatively established in that one moment of time. By *saṁyama* on the moments and their succession, direct knowledge is obtained of them both, and thence is manifested discriminative knowledge. *Y.B.*

52. Two similars are thereby distinguished when not separately distinguishable by genus, differentia, and position in space.

...For ordinary men the difference of genus is the cause of the knowledge of distinction. When genus, such as the characteristic of a cow, is the same; when also space, such as presence in the east, &c., is the same; then the distinction of the black-eyed and the auspicious is the other means of distinction....[1]

Inasmuch as it has been said that the differences of genus, position and time, &c., are known by the intellect of the ordinary man, it is said that the difference of moment of time (*kṣaṇa*) is known by the intellect of the *yogi* alone. The word "alone" signifies the difference of the moment of time, not that of the intellect of the *yogi*.... *T.V.*

53. And it, the intuitional, has everything for its sphere of operation; has all conditions for its sphere of operation; has no succession. This is the entire discriminative knowledge.

54. When the purity of the objective essence and that of the *puruṣa* become equal, it is absolute independence.

[1] That is, the *yogi* has subtle perception of distinctions not possessed by ordinary men.

CHAPTER 4: ABSOLUTE INDEPENDENCE (*KAIVALYA*)[1]

1. The attainments are by birth, drugs, incantations, purificatory action (*tapas*), or trance.

Attainments by birth exist in the body.

By drugs, in the houses of the Asuras [demons], by elixir, and such like....

By incantations, motion in space and the powers of attenuation (*aṇimā*), &c.

By purificatory action, the achievement of wishes. He takes such forms and goes to such places as he may like, and other similar things.

The attainments born of trance have been described. *Y.B.*

2. Change to another life-state by the filling up of the creative causes (*prakṛtyāpūra*).

The attainments due to trance have been described in the previous chapter. It is now desirable to say that the change into another life-state brought about by the four classes of attainments due to the use of herbs, &c., is also of the same body and the powers thereof. This, however, does not come about by mere material causes. The material itself, so far as it goes, does not prove to be competent to intensify or weaken the state of the divine and the not-divine in him. It is plain that a cause having no elements of difference in itself cannot operate to produce different effects....

The creative causes of the body are the elements of *pṛthivī* (earth), &c. The creative cause of the "powers" is the principle of egoism.

"Filling up" means the sequential showing forth, entrance therein, of these causes. By this comes about the change. *T.V.*

3. The creative causes are not moved into action by any incidental cause; but that pierces the obstacle from it like the husbandman.

As the husbandman, desirous of carrying water from an already well-filled bed to another, does not draw the water with his own hands to places which are on the same or a lower level; but simply removes the obstacles, and thereupon the water flows down of itself to the other bed, so it pierces through vice, which is the obstacle to virtue, and, that being pierced through, the creative causes pass through their respective changes. *Y.B.*

4. Created minds proceed from egoism alone.

5. There being difference of activity, one mind the director of the many.

It should not be said that there is no use in more minds than one, that is, one for each body, when one such mind is posited; nor should it be

[1] *Kaivalya* may be variously translated: as "absolute independence," "absolute freedom," or "isolation."

said that there is no use in making a directing mind, because one's mind can serve that purpose. The reason is that that which has been proved to exist by right reasoning, need no more be subjected to the test of being placed in consonant and dissonant positions. *T.V.*

6. Of these the meditation-born is free from the vehicles.

The created mind is five-fold, as said:—"The attainments are by birth, drugs, incantations, purificatory action, or trance." Of these, the one that is born of meditation is alone free from the vehicles. It does not possess the vehicles, which cause the manifestation of desire, &c. Thence is there no coming into relationship with virtue and vice, inasmuch as the afflictions of a *yogi* have ceased to exist. *Y.B.*

7. A *yogi's karma* is neither white nor black; of the others it is three-fold.

This class of actions has four locations:[1] the black, the black-white, the white, neither white nor black. Of these, the black is of the wicked. The black-white is brought about by external means, as in this the vehicle of actions grows by means of causing pain to, or acting kindly towards, others.

The white is of those who resort to the means of improvement of study and meditation. This is dependent upon the mind alone. It does not depend upon external means and is not, therefore, brought about by injuring others.

The one which is neither white nor black exists in the case of those who have renounced everything, whose afflictions have been destroyed, and whose present body is the last one they will have. It is not white in the case of a *yogi*, because he gives up the fruit of action; and it is not black, because he does not perform actions. Of the other creatures, it is of the three former descriptions only. *Y.B.*

8. Thence proceed the residual potencies competent to bring about their fruition alone.

"Thence" means from the three-fold *karma*. *Y.B.*

9. Memory and potential-residua being the same in appearance, there is sequential non-interruption, even when there is distinction of life-state, locality, and time.

...Why? Because even if there be an interval between them, the residua are manifested by the similar manifesting *karma* becoming the operative cause thereof....Thus, even though separated in time, &c., there is sequential non-interruption, inasmuch as the relation of cause and effect does not break. *Y.B.*

10. And there is no beginning for them, the desire to live being eternal.

[1] Or "is of four types."

11. Being held together by cause, motive, substratum, and object, they disappear on the disappearance of these.

The cause:—By virtue comes pleasure, by vice, pain. From pleasure comes attachment; from pain, aversion. Thence comes effort. Thereby, acting by mind, body, and speech, one either favours or injures others. Thence come again virtue and vice, pleasure and pain, attachment and aversion. Thus it is that revolves the six-spoked wheel of the world. And the driver of this wheel is nescience, the root of the afflictions. This is the cause.

Motive or fruit is that with a view to which appropriate virtue, &c., are brought about. There is no non-sequential manifestation.

The substratum is the mind which has yet a duty to perform. It is there that the residua live. They no longer care to live in a mind which has already performed its duty; their substratum is gone.

The object of the residua is the substance which when placed in contact calls them forth.

Thus are all the residua held together by cause, fruit, substratum, and object.

When these exist not, the residua which depend upon them for existence disappear too. *Y.B.*

12. The past and the future exist in reality, there being difference of the paths of being of the characteristics.

The future is the manifestation which is to be. The past is the appearance which has been experienced. The present is that which is in active operation. It is this three-fold substance which is the object of knowledge. If they did not exist in reality, there would not exist the knowledge thereof....

...Hence the existence of the three paths of being does not come out of non-existence. *Y.B.*

13. They are manifested and subtle, and of the nature of the qualities.

They, i.e., these characteristics which are possessed of the three paths of being, are of the nature of the manifested when they exist in the present, and are of the nature of the subtle when they pass into the past or are yet unmanifested.... *Y.B.*

14. The reality of the object[1] on account of the unity of modification.

There are people who try to do away with the reality of objects by this reasoning, saying that objects are but the fabrications of the mind, like the fancies of a dream, and that they are nothing real. The objective world is present by its own power. How is it that they give up the objective world on the strength of imaginative cognition, and even then go on talking nonsense about it?... *Y.B.*

[1] Or "the object is real."

...The cow, the horse, the buffalo, the elephant, all of them modify into a single substance, the salt, when they are thrown into a mine of salt. Wick, oil, and fire change into a lamp. In this way, although the qualities are more than one, a single modification does take place. For this reason, the subtle elements (*tanmātra*), the elements, and the objects made of the elements have each a real unity. *T.V.*

15. There being difference of mentality[1] in the case of the external object being the same, their ways of being are different.

16. And if an object dependent upon one mind were not cognized by that, would it then exist?

...For this reason, the object is self-dependent, and common to all the *puruṣas*. Minds also are self-dependent. They come into relationship with the *puruṣas*. By their relationship is secured perception which is enjoyment. *Y.B.*

17. The mind needing to be coloured thereby an object may be known or unknown.

...Objects are in nature similar to that of loadstone; the mind is similar in characteristic to iron. Objects coming into contact with the mind colour it. Whatever objects colour the mind, that object becomes known. That which becomes known is an object. That which is not thus known is the *puruṣa* and is unknown. The mind is changeful, because it assumes the natures of known and unknown objects. *Y.B.*

18. To its lord, the *puruṣa*, the modifications of the mind are always known on account of unchangeability.

19. It is not self-illuminating, being the knowable.

A doubt may arise that the mind itself may be self-illuminating as well as the illuminator of the objects, as in fact it is believed by the Vaināśikas to be like fire, which illuminates itself as well as other objects. Therefore [the author] says:—"It is not self-illuminating, being the knowable...." *Y.B.*

20. Nor can both be cognized at the same time.

And it is not proper that in one moment both one's own nature and the nature of other objects may be ascertained.... *Y.B.*

21. In the case of being knowable by another mind, there will be too many wills-to-know the wills-to-know; and there will be confusion of memories.

...If the mind be cognized by another mind, by what may the wills-to-know the wills-to-know be cognized. Even that by another; and that again by another. There will thus be too many of such wills-to-know. And there will be confusion of memories.... *Y.B.*

[1] Or "differences of impressions (or ideas)."

22. Consciousness knows its own will-to-be by transforming its appearance, though not itself moving from place to place.

...The knowing by the *puruṣa* of his will-to-be is achieved when the will-to-be takes the form of the *puruṣa*, i.e., when it takes on the appearance thereof by receiving into itself the reflection of the *puruṣa*. Similar is the case with the moon, reflected in pure water. Although the moon is not in motion, yet she appears to be in motion on account of the movements of the water, without any action of her own. In the same way, without any sort of action on the part of consciousness, the mind in which the reflection of consciousness has taken its place, shows the power of consciousness to be active by its own movements, and makes it appear to be following itself, although in reality it does not follow it. It is by acting in this way that the mind brings about the experience of the *puruṣa* and gives him the nature of the enjoyer.... *T.V.*

23. The mind being coloured by the knower and the knowable is omni-objective (*sarvārtha*).

...The mind is of course coloured by the objects of thought. The mind being itself an object comes into relationship with the subjective *puruṣa* through its modification as self. Thus it is that the mind is coloured by both subjectivity and objectivity, the knower and the knowable; it assumes the nature of both the conscious and the unconscious. Although it is of the very nature of the objective, it appears as if it were consciousness. Being of the nature of the crystal, it is termed omni-objective.

It is by this similarity of mental appearance that some people are deceived into saying that the mind itself is the conscious agent. There are others again who say that all this is but the mind only and that there is nothing in the existence of the objective world, such as the cow or jar, all of which are governed by the law of causation. They are to be pitied.... *Y.B.*

24. And the mind exists for another, also because it is variegated by innumerable residua, inasmuch as it acts by combination.

...As a house which has assumed its shape as such by various materials being brought together cannot come into existence for itself, so also the mind which assumes a particular shape by more things than one coming together. The mental phenomenon of pleasure does not exist for its own sake; nor does knowledge exist for itself. On the contrary, both these exist for the sake of another. That other is the *puruṣa* who has objects to achieve in the shape of enjoyment and emancipation. It cannot be another of the same class.... *Y.B.*

25. For the seer of the distinction ceases the curiosity as to the nature and relations of the self.

The curiosity as to the nature of the self ceases in the case of him who possesses that curiosity, when he sees the distinction between the subjective *puruṣa* and the objective existence, by the practice and effective achievement of the means of the *yoga*.... *T.V.*

26. Then the mind inclines towards discrimination and gravitates towards absolute independence (*kaivalya*).

Now [the author] describes the nature of the mind of him who sees the distinction:—"The mind" is then inclined towards discrimination and gravitates towards absolute independence.... *T.V.*

27. In the breaks[1] arise other thoughts from residua.

In the mind inclining towards discriminative knowledge of the notions, and which has just entered the stream of the discriminative knowledge of the *puruṣa* and objective existence, other thoughts appear in the intervals, such as "I am," "This is mine," "I know," &c. Whence? From previous residua, whose seeds are being destroyed. *Y.B.*

28. Their removal has been described like that of the afflictions.

29. Having no interest left even in the highest intellection, there comes from constant discrimination the trance known as the cloud of virtue.

...By that highest intellection, he does not desire the possession of anything, even of the power of becoming the master of all existence. Nay he begins to feel pain even there. Having become desireless even there by seeing the defect of change, he comes to the possession of constant discriminative knowledge [undisturbed].... *T.V.*

30. Thence the removal of actions and afflictions.

By the attainment thereof, the afflictions of nescience, etc., are removed, even to the very root. And the good and bad vehicles of action are utterly uprooted. On the afflictions and the actions being removed, the wise man becomes free even while alive (*jīvan-mukta*).... *Y.B.*

31. The knowable is but little then, because of knowledge having become infinite, on account of the removal of all obscuring impurities.

Knowledge, when rid of all the impurities of affliction and action, becomes infinite....When knowledge becomes infinite, but little remains to know, like the shining insect in space.... *Y.B.*

32. By that, the qualities having fulfilled their object, the succession of their changes ends.

By that, i.e., by the rise of the cloud of virtue, the succession of the changes of the qualities is over, inasmuch as they have fulfilled their object by having achieved experience and emancipation, and their succession having ended, they no longer care to stay even for a moment. *Y.B.*

[1] Or "intervals."

33. Succession is the uninterrupted sequence of moments, cognised as distinct on the cessation of evolutionary change.

Well, but what is this succession? "Succession is the uninterrupted flow of moments"; it is taken in by the last end, the cessation of changes. A cloth which has not undergone the succession of moments does not give up its newness and become old all at once in the end.

Further, succession is found in the permanent also. This permanence is two-fold, the eternal in perfection and the eternal in evolution. Of these, the perfect eternity belongs to the *puruṣa.* The evolutionary eternity belongs to the qualities. The permanent or eternal is that in which the substance is not destroyed by changing appearances. Both are permanent because their substance is never destroyed. *Y.B.*

...The meaning is that succession is that which is the support of a group of moments. There can of course be no succession ascertained without the existence of that of which it is the succession. Nor can there be a succession of moment only.... *T.V.*

34. Absolute freedom comes when the qualities, becoming devoid of the object of the *puruṣa*, become latent; or the power of consciousness becomes established in its own nature.

...Absolute freedom is the becoming latent, by inverse process, of the qualities, when they are devoid of the object of the *puruṣa*, after having achieved the experience and emancipation of the self. *Y.B.*

CHAPTER XIV

PŪRVA MĪMĀṀSĀ

THE central problem of this system is the investigation of *dharma*, duty, especially as it is stated in the Vedas. It sets forth some important philosophical speculations, though they are subservient to its main practical interest.

As the Vedas are the main source of *dharma* they are said to be eternally valid. The Vedas are not the work of God. They are uncreated, and the seers apprehend and transmit them. Elaborate discussions about sounds, words, and meanings are to be found in Mīmāṁsā works—in the course of studies or demonstrations of the validity and eternality of the Vedas.

As the Vedic injunctions hold out promises of rewards to be enjoyed in another world, they assume the reality of selves. The self is distinct from the body, the senses, and the understanding.

Acts are enjoined with a view to their fruits. Between an act and its result there is a necessary connection. An act performed today may achieve its result at some later date, and in the meantime the result is in the form of an unseen force or *apūrva*, which may be regarded either as the imperceptible antecedent of the fruit or the after-state of the act itself. The deferred fruition of acts is possible only through the force of *apūrva*.

Liberation for the Mīmāṁsā is life in heaven, and not the state of ultimate release found in most other systems of Indian thought. Later Mīmāṁsā thinkers, however, were not untouched by the prevalent tendency in other systems of thought. Prabhākara (7th century A.D.) defines liberation as "the absolute cessation of the body caused by the disappearance of all *dharma* and *adharma* (merit and demerit)." For Kumārila Bhaṭṭa (7th century A.D.) it is the state of the self free from pain. Jaimini, the author of the *Mīmāṁsā Sūtra* (*ca.* 400 B.C.), admits the reality of the Vedic deities, to whom sacrifices are offered, but does not argue for the existence of a supreme God. He does not so much deny God as ignore Him. Some later Mīmāṁsakas admit the reality of God. Others, however, argue extensively against the existence and the necessity of God, as, for example, does Kumārila in the *Ślokavārtika* (see section B of selections).

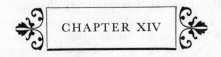

In the field of logic and epistemology, later Mīmāṁsā made some notable contributions. Unlike the Nyāya and other systems of Hindu philosophy, it believes in six—instead of the usual four—means of valid knowledge. The two that are added are knowledge by *arthāpatti* (presumption or postulation) and knowledge by *abhāva* (absence, negation, or non-existence). It is argued that these two valid means of knowledge are not accounted for by the usual valid means of knowledge. A more interesting factor, however, of the Mīmāṁsā philosophy is its unique epistemological theory of the validity of all cognition as such. It is held that all knowledge is *ipso facto* true. Thus, what is to be proved is not the truth of a cognition but its falsity. Not only did the Mīmāṁsakas make very great use of this theory to establish the unchallengeable validity of the Vedas, but later Vedāntists also drew freely upon this great Mīmāṁsā contribution.

The selections are from Jaimini, *Mīmāṁsā Sūtra*, with the commentary of Śabara (1st century B.C.), English translation, *Śabara-Bhāṣya*, by Ganganatha Jha, Gaekwad's Oriental Series, Vols. LXVI, LXX, LXXIII (Baroda: Oriental Institute, 1933, 1934, 1936); and Kumārila Bhaṭṭa, *Ślokavārtika*, translated by Ganganatha Jha (Calcutta: Asiatic Society of Bengal, 1909), pp. 355–63, 553–55.

A. THE *MĪMĀṀSĀ SŪTRA*

Topic: Propounding of the enquiry.

I.i.1. Next, therefore, comes the enquiry into *dharma* (duty).

I.i.2. *Dharma* is that which is indicated by means of the Veda as conducive to the highest good.

Topic: *Dharma* not amenable to such means of cognition as sense-perception and the like.

I.i.4. That cognition by a person which appears when there is contact of the sense-organs is "sense-perception," and it is not a means of knowing *dharma*, as it apprehends only things existing at the present time.

. . . *Dharma*, however, is something that is yet to come, and it does not exist at the time that it is to be known. . . hence sense-perception cannot be the means (of knowing) *dharma*.

Topic: *Dharma* cognisable by means of verbal injunctions.

I.i.5. The relation of the word with its denotation is inborn—instruction is the means of knowing it (*dharma*)—infallible regarding all that is imperceptible; it is a valid means of knowledge, as it is independent, according to Bādarāyaṇa.[1]

"*Autpattika*" ("inborn"),—what we mean by this is "constant." It is *existence* (presence) that is figuratively spoken of as "*origin*." What is

[1] Author of the *Brahma Sūtra*.

meant is that the relation between word and its meaning is *inseparable.*—It becomes the *means of knowing* ["*jñāyatē anena iti jñānam*" says the *Śloka-vārtika* 5.9] *Dharma* in the shape of *Agnihotra* and such acts, which are not known by means of sense-perception and such other means of knowledge. —"How so?"—Because there is "*instruction*"; "instruction stands for the speaking of a particular set of words. [Thus it is the *Word*, in the form of instruction or injunction, which is the means of knowing *Dharma.*]—Of this "means of knowledge" there is "*infallibility*"; i.e., the cognition brought about by that means never fails (is never wrong); when a cognition is not found to be wrong, it cannot be said with regard to it that "this is not so," or "the real thing is not as it is represented by this cognition," or "the real thing is otherwise than what is represented in this cognition," or "it may be that the idea in the mind of the speaker is different from what is expressed by his words," or "the words used give rise to contradictory ideas, representing the same thing as *existing* and as *non-existing*."—For these reasons (since cognition brought about by words is not fallible), it is "*a valid means of knowledge, as it is independent.*" That is, when a cognition has been brought about by means of words, there is no need for any other cognition (to corroborate it), or of any other person as having the same cognition.

[Ed. Note: In this connection, the commentator discusses extensively the relation of Word as a means of knowledge and the other recognized means of right knowledge. Included in this discussion is a description of "postulation" and "negation" as well as the four widely accepted methods of perception, inference, analogy, and testimony. The text says:]

"*Arthāpatti*," "presumption," also consists in the presuming of something not seen, on the ground that a fact already perceived or heard would not be possible without that presumption; for instance, it is found that Devadatta who is alive is not in the house, and this *non-existence in the house* leads to the presumption that he is somewhere outside the house [as without this, the aforesaid fact of his being alive and not in the house could not be explained.]

Abhāva, "Negation," "Non-apprehension," stands for the non-existence (non-operation) of the (five) means of cognition (described above); and it is what brings about the cognition that "it does not exist," in regard to things not in contact with the senses. [That is, in a case where sense-perception and the other means of cognition are not found to be operative towards bringing about the notion of the *existence* of a certain thing, we have the notion of the *non-existence* of that thing; and the means by which this notion is brought about is called "*abhāva*"—*Ślokavārtika*, *Abhāva* 1.]

From all this it follows that (all) means of cognition being well-known, they need not be examined.

Topic: Eternality of words.

I.i.6. [*Pūrvapakṣa* or objection to Mīmāṁsā]—"Word is a product (non-eternal), because it is seen to follow (after effort),"—so say some people.

...finding that there is an invariable concomitance (between the appearance of the word and human effort, the word appearing only when there is human effort) we infer that the word "is produced" by the effort....

I.i.7. [Objection *continued*]—"Because it does not persist."

I.i.8. [Objection *continued*]—"Also, because of the term 'to make' [being used in connection with words]."

I.i.9. [Objection *continued*]—"Also because there is simultaneity (of the perception of the word) in diverse places."

...this could not be possible if the word were only one and *eternal*. Unless there is something special there can be no plurality of what is eternal;...

I.i.10. [Objection *continued*]—"Also because there are original forms and modifications."

...whatever is liable to modification must be non-eternal.

I.i.11. [Objection *concluded*]—"Further, there is an augmentation for the word (sound), due to the multiplicity of its producers (speakers)."

If the word were only *manifested* (and not *produced*, by the utterance), then the sound heard would always be the same, whether it were uttered by many or fewer persons. From this we conclude that some portion of the word is *produced* by each of the speakers,...

I.i.12. [*Siddhānta* or true *Mīmāṁsā* teaching]—[*Answer to sū. 6*]—But the fact of being "seen" is equal in both cases.

...the word is *manifested* (not *produced*) by human effort; that is to say, if, before being pronounced, the word was not manifest, it becomes manifested by the effort (of pronouncing). Thus it is found that the fact of word being "seen after effort" is equally compatible with both views.

I.i.13. [*Answer to sū. 7*]—What happens (when the word ceases to be heard) is that there is no perception of the extant word on account of the non-reaching of the object (by the manifesting agency).

I.i.14. [*Answer to sū. 8*]—The term refers to the using.

...if it is beyond doubt that word is eternal, then the meaning of these expressions would be "make *use* of the word."...

I.i.15. [*Answer to sū. 9*]—The simultaneity is as in the case of the sun.

Look at the sun....Being only one he is seen as if occupying several places.

I.i.16. [*Answer to sū. 10*]—It is a different letter, not a modification.

I.i.17. [*Answer to sū. 11*]—The "augmentation" spoken of is the augmentation of the noise (not of the word).

I.i.18. [*Final siddhānta*]—In fact (the word) must be eternal; as (its) utterance is for the purpose of another.

...i.e., for the purpose of making known the meaning to "another." If the word ceased to exist as soon as uttered, then no one could speak of (make known) anything to others; and in that case the word could not be uttered for the purpose of another.

I.i.19. There is simultaneity throughout.

Whenever the word "*go*" ("cow") is uttered, there is a notion of all cows simultaneously. From this it follows that the word denotes the class. And it is not possible to *create* the relation of the word to a class; because, in creating the relation, the creator would have to lay down the relation by pointing to the class;...

If, however, the word "*go*" is eternal, it is the same word that is uttered many times and has been previously heard also many times, as applied to other individual cows; and thus by a process of positive and negative concomitance the word comes to be recognised as denoting the particular class. For this reason also, the word must be eternal.

I.i.20. Because there is no number (in connection with a word).

People speak of the word "*go*" being *pronounced eight times*; they never speak of the word "*go*" itself being *eight in number*....

I.i.21. Because it is not dependent.

...In the case of the word,...we do not perceive any material cause, on the destruction whereof the word itself would be regarded as ceasing to exist.

I.i.22. Also because there is no idea of the connection (of the word, with any material cause).

[Objection]—The word may be the product of air; in fact it is air which, through certain conjunctions and disjunctions, becomes the word.

[It is in answer to this that we have the *sūtra*]—It cannot be so; if the word were the product of air, then it could only be air in a particular shape. As a matter of fact, however, we do not recognise any particle of air in the constitution of the word....If the word were a product of air, then we could perceive it with our tactile organ (as we perceive air); and yet we do not feel by touch any air-particles in the word. Hence word cannot be a product of air. Therefore it must be eternal.

I.i.23. Also because we find indicative texts.

We also actually find a Vedic text indicating the eternality of word—e.g., "By means of word which is eternal, etc."...

From all this we conclude that word is eternal.

I.i.24. [Objection]—"Even though they (word, its meaning, and the relation between the two) be eternal, they could not be expressive of the Vedic subject-matter (of the Vedic injunction, *dharma*); because they are not efficient for that purpose."

...as the Vedic injunction, which is the sole means of knowing *dharma*, is always in the form of *sentence*,—until the same fact is established regarding *sentences*, the validity of the injunction as a means of knowing *dharma* remains doubtful.

I.i.25. [*Answer to the objector's arguments*]—[In the sentence] there is only a predication (or mention) of words with definite denotations along with a word denoting an action; as the meaning (of the sentence) is based upon that (i.e., the meaning of the words).

Topic: The Veda is not the work of any person.

I.i.27. [Objection]—"Some people regard the Vedas to be modern, because they are named after persons."

I.i.28. [Objection *concluded*]—"Also because we find ephemeral things (mentioned in the Veda)."

I.i.29. [True view]—It has already been explained that there is an unbroken continuity of the text.

We have already explained (under *sū.* 5) that there is an unbroken tradition of the text among the students of the Veda [which proves that the Veda is eternal]; all that we have to do here is to answer the objections....

I.i.30. The name is due to expounding.

It has been urged by the *pūrvapakṣin* (objector) that such names of Vedic texts as "*Kāṭhaka*" and the like must be indicative of the *author*.[1]—Our answer to this is as follows:—No such presumption (of the author) is justifiable; as people might call a text by the name of one who is not the author at all; it is possible that all that Kaṭha and other persons (whose names are applied to certain Vedic texts) have done is such superior *expounding* of the text as has not been done by any one else; and there are people who call texts by the names of such exceptional expounders.

I.i.32. On account of passages being correlated to actions, the passages in question would be of use in regard to an act.

Asks the opponent—"How do you know that all this (Veda) is not like the utterance of lunatics and children? As a matter of fact, we find in it such sentences as 'Trees sat at the sacrificial session,' 'Serpents sat at the sacrificial session,' 'The old bull sings maddening songs.' Now, how

[1] See also section B of this chapter.

could the 'old bull' sing? How too could 'trees' or 'serpents' sit at sacrifices?"

The answer to this is as follows:—As a rule we find the sentences occurring in the Veda laid down as mutually connected.—"How so?"—Having stated the word "*Jyotiṣṭoma*" [name of ritual], the term "should be performed" is added;—then the question arising as to the means of the performance—"by what is it to be performed?"—the term "by means of the *Soma*" is added;—then arises the question, "for what purpose?"—and in answer there is the term "for the purpose of attaining heaven";—then comes the question, "in what manner?"—and the answer is "thus, by this process." Thus seeing that the entire passage affords an idea which is the sum total of what is expressed by each of the terms described above, how could we say that it is like the utterance of a lunatic or a child?

"But the statement that we find to the effect that 'Trees sat at the sacrificial session' is clearly absurd."

It is not absurd. In the first place, even if this particular statement were absurd, that would not make all other statements—such as "Desiring heaven, one should perform the *Agnihotra*"—absurd, but in reality, even such statements as "Trees sat at the sacrificial session" are not absurd. They serve to eulogise the sacrificial session; the sense being, "even such inanimate things as trees performed this sacrifice, what to say of learned *brāhmins*?" Just as in common parlance we say "At eveningtime even animals do not graze, what to say of learned *brāhmins*?"—Further, the teaching in the Veda being found irreproachable, wholesome and definite, how could it ever be suspected to be like the utterance of lunatics and children?

For these reasons, it becomes established that "*Dharma is what is indicated by Vedic injunctions as conducive to the highest good.*"

I.ii.1. [Objection]—"The purpose of the Veda lying in the enjoining of actions, those parts of the Veda which do not serve that purpose are useless; in these therefore the Veda is declared to be non-eternal (unreliable)."

I.ii.2. [Objection *continued*]—"Also because there is contradiction of the scriptures and of directly perceived facts."

"There are such passages in the Veda as—(*a*) 'The mind is a thief,' 'Speech is a liar' and so forth. These passages, containing mere descriptions of accomplished things, cannot serve as the means of knowing *dharma*. Even if some indirect meaning could be assumed by the indirect methods of interpretation, the only injunction of actions that could be derived from these would be—(*a*) that 'one should commit theft,' and that (*b*) 'one should tell lies'; and the acts thus enjoined cannot be performed without transgressing the prohibitions of stealing and of telling lies. Nor could the two (stealing and not-stealing, or lying and not-lying) be taken as optional alternatives, as the two do not stand on the same footing: in the case of one (i.e., stealing) the injunction is assumed (on the basis of the *arthavāda*[2] 'the mind is a thief'), while in that of the other (not-stealing), we have the direct injunction ('thou shalt not steal').

"Then again, there is contradiction of directly perceived facts also: For example—'During the day, it is only the smoke of the fire that is seen, not its flame, and during the night only the flame of the fire is seen, not the smoke' (*Taitt. Brā.* II.i.2) and in support of this statement we have the further assertion—'The fire going forth from this world enters the sun, and during the night the sun enters the fire'—Both these statements (of the fire entering the sun and the sun entering the fire) are contrary to perceptible facts; and hence cannot prove the aforesaid restrictive assertion that 'it is *the smoke alone*' or '*the flame alone*' that is seen.

"Another example of the contradiction of perceptible facts we have in the passage—'we know not whether we are *brāhmins* or non-*brāhmins*' (*Gopatha Brāhmaṇa* v.21). In the first place, this sentence, not laying down anything in regard to any action, is useless. Secondly, if it actually means that 'we do not know whether we are *brāhmins* or non-*brāhmins*,' then it is contrary to a perceptible fact, and as such cannot be true.

"An example of the contradiction of what is stated in the scriptures we have in the passage—'who knows whether one lives in the other world or not' (*Taitt. Saṁ.* 7.ii.2; 6.i.1). If it is a mere question, then, serving no purpose regarding any act, it is useless. If it expresses a real uncertainty, then it is contrary to what is declared in the scriptures regarding men going, after death, to regions other than the earth. And thus being contrary to well-ascertained facts, the statement cannot be true."

I.ii.3. [Objection *continued*]—"Also because of the absence of results."

I.ii.4. [Objection *continued*]—"Because of the uselessness of other (acts)."

"There are the following three texts—(1) 'By pouring the final oblation one fulfills all desires' (*Taitt. Brā.* III.viii.10); (2) 'One who performs the *Paśubandha* sacrifice wins all regions'; (3) 'He passes beyond death, he passes beyond the sin of *brāhmin*-slaughter, who performs the *Aśvamedha* sacrifices, as also one who knows this.'—Now if these are mere descriptions of established facts, then they are useless. If they lay down the actual results following from the acts mentioned, then there is no use for any other acts."

I.ii.5. [Objection *continued*]—"Also because of the prohibiting of what cannot be prohibited."

"Such passages as 'The fire shall not be kindled on the earth, nor in the sky, nor in heaven'. . . prohibits things which are incapable of being prohibited. . . ."

I.ii.6. [Objection *concluded*]—"Because of the mention of non-eternal things."

[1] That is, the theory of meaning.

In connection with the authoritative character of the Veda, the objection that there is mention of non-eternal things in the Veda has been answered by the declaration that "it is merely a similarity of sounds" (*sū.* I.i.21).—The same objection is raised here again in support of the attack upon some parts of the Veda—on the basis of the mention in the Veda, of such apparently ephemeral things as "Babara, the son of Pravāhaṇa, desired" (*Taitt. Saṁ.* VII.i.10).

I.ii.7. [True view]—Being construed along with injunction, they would serve the purpose of commending those injunctions.

...such passages are glorifications, to be taken along with injunctive passages, and as such help in the knowledge of *dharma*;...

The following text is found in the Veda—"One desiring prosperity should sacrifice the animal *Śveta* dedicated to Vāyu (wind);—Vāyu is the eftest deity;...he leads the man to prosperity" (*Taitt. Saṁ.* II.i.1). Though the sentence "Vāyu is the eftest deity" does not indicate any action (to be done), or anything connected with an action, yet it becomes a valid means of knowledge by being construed with an injunctive sentence;...

It may be asked—"Why should there be commendation (of the enjoined act)?"—There is commendation for the purpose of making the act attractive and hence performed.

I.ii.9. The incongruity (urged by the opponent) [in *sū.* I.ii.2] is not applicable (to the *siddhānta* [true view]); because the incongruity could be there only if an action were indicated (by the commendatory words); as a matter of fact, however, what these words indicate is not an action. Hence it is all right.

Hence all these texts—"The mind is a thief." "The speech is a liar"—are all right (not incongruous).

I.ii.10. Then there is indirect application (figurative expression).

I.ii.11. (*a*) On the similarity in form, and (*b*) on the character of the greater part [is the indirect signification based].

[This answers the first two objections urged under *sū.* I.ii.2.]

There is an injunction to the effect that "one should hold the gold-piece in one's hand and then he (the priest) takes it"...; this injunction stands in need of aid, which is supplied by its auxiliary in the shape of the statement that "the mind is a thief, and speech is a liar." This deprecatory assertion serves the purpose of commending the gold;...—"But even for decrying it, why should the mind, which is *not* a thief, be spoken of as *thief*? Why too the speech, which is not a liar, be spoken of as liar?"—The answer is that this also is "figurative expression," based (*a*) "*upon the similarity of form*,"—as thieves remain hidden, so mind also remains unseen, the term "thief" being taken in the figurative sense of "one who remains hidden,"—and "*upon the character of the greater part*,"—for the most part what people speak is *untrue*.

I.ii.12. Because of the greatness of distance.

[This answers the third objection urged under *sū.* I.ii.2.]

As an example of a statement (in the Veda) contrary to directly perceived facts, the opponent has cited the passage—"During the day only the smoke of fire was perceived, not the flame, and during the night only the flame of fire was perceived, not the smoke."...

It is the fact of their being at a "great distance" that is figuratively spoken of as the "not seeing" of the *smoke* and the *flame.*

I.ii.15. It is praise of knowledge.

[This answers the objection urged under *sū.* I.ii.3.]

I.ii.16. The mention of "all" refers to the fact of the man being entitled (to perform all acts and obtain all their rewards).

[This answers the objections urged under *sū.* I.ii.4.]

The mention of the results (in the injunctive text itself) is purely commendatory.

When the text speaks of the man "attaining all desires," it is only a figurative way of stating that he performs the acts bringing about the reward in the shape of the attaining of all desires. And though "*all*" is not meant, yet the word "all" is used, in the sense of all that the man may be *entitled to.*

I.ii.17. The result being accomplished by means of actions, the difference in the results could be due to the magnitude of the actions.

This is a bold assertion (in answer to the same objection that has been answered in the preceding *sū.*).—Even if one takes the statement in question (to the effect that "All desires are obtained by the final oblation") as laying down the results actually following from the oblation,—the statement would be quite reasonable even in its direct literal sense; and even though all results might really follow from the oblation, yet there would be a difference in the quantity and quality (of the results as obtained by the simple act of the final oblation, and as obtained by means of the more elaborate sacrifices; and hence the actual performance of the latter would not be superfluous).

Topic: The authority of *smṛtis* [remembrances or traditional texts] in general.

I.iii.1. [Objection]—"Inasmuch as *dharma* is based upon the Veda, what is not Veda should be disregarded."

I.iii.2. [True view]—But (*smṛti*) is trustworthy, as there would be inference (assumption, of the basis in the Veda) from the fact of the agent being the same.

...what we could infer (as the ground for reliability) is the text (Vedic) itself [which would have provided the *smṛti*-writers with the previous cognition necessary for the remembrance, *smṛti*, which would thus have its basis in that inferred Vedic text];—this inference being drawn from the fact (premiss) that "the agent is the same";—i.e., the "agent," author, of the *smṛti* is the same as the "agent," performer, of the acts prescribed in the Veda.

Topic: *Śruti* (Veda) more authoritative than *smṛti*.

I.iii.3. When there is conflict (between Veda and *smṛti*), the *smṛti* should be disregarded; because it is only when there is no such conflict that there is an assumption (of Vedic text in support of *smṛti*).

Topic: No authority attaches to *smṛtis* prompted by worldly motives.

I.iii.4. If worldly motives are discernible the *smṛti*-rules cannot be regarded as trustworthy.

Topic: There is such a thing as *apūrva*,[1] transcendental potency.

II.i.5. There is *apūrva*, because action (is enjoined).

. . . there is such a thing as *apūrva*,—because action is enjoined—in such injunctions as "Desirous of Heaven, one should sacrifice." Otherwise,—if there were no such thing as *apūrva*—such an injunction would be meaningless, as the act of the *sacrifice* itself is perishable, so that if the sacrifice were to perish without bringing into existence something else, then the cause having ceased to exist, the result (in the shape of heaven) could never come about.—From this it follows that the sacrifice does bring into existence something (some force or potency which continues to exist and operate till such time as the result is actually brought about).

Thus then, the only possible alternative is that the act (of sacrifice) subsists in the material substance (offered), and this substance has perished (ceased to exist); and when the substratum (in the shape of the substance) has perished, it is understood that the act (sacrifice) itself has perished.—If it be urged that "the substratum (substance) has not perished,"—that cannot be true, as all that is found to be left of the substance (offered at the sacrifice) is mere ash.—It might be argued that "even while the ash is there the substance is there (in the form of that ash),"—that cannot be right; because what exists must be perceived, and yet the substance is *not* perceived (in the ashes).—"The very fact of the bringing about of the result would be indicative of the presence of the substance (at the time of the appearance of the result)."—In that case, it is necessary for the other party to answer the objection that there is no perception of the substance. It might be argued that "the non-perception might be due to one or the other of the various reasons of non-perception, such as the subtle character of the substance [or "being too remote," or "too near," or "the inefficiency of the perceptive organ," or "absent-mindedness"—

[1] Literally, not having existed before, and therefore something new.

enumerated in *Sāṁkhya-kārikā*].—If such is the view, then it comes to this, that something has to be assumed; and the question to be considered is—Is it the *apūrva* that should be assumed—or some reason for the non-perception of the existing substance? There is always some justification for making a general assumption, and none for a particular one [so that while there may be some justification for the assuming of a general potency in the shape of the *apūrva*, there can be none for assuming a reason for the non-perception of every particular object, as there will have to be a separate reason for every particular case of non-perception].

IV.iii.15. That one result would be "heaven," as that is equally desirable for all.

"But why so?"—Because "heaven" is happiness, and everyone seeks for happiness.

IV.iii.16. Also because *such is the common* notion (of people).

VI.i.3. Further, inasmuch as the act (of sacrifice) must be related (to something), it should be taken as related to the desired thing (heaven); hence the text should be taken as enjoining the act (of sacrifice, as a means to the attainment of heaven).

If the sacrifice is not taken as enjoined in reference to heaven, then,—and the sacrifice thereby being something fruitless,—the "desire for heaven," even though laid down in the text, would be entirely useless; and in that case the whole injunction would be pointless.

Topic: Only human beings are entitled to perform such acts as the "sacrifice."

VI.i.4. [Objection]—"Inasmuch as an act is performed for the purpose of obtaining results, all beings should be entitled to perform the acts prescribed in the scriptures."

VI.i.5. [True view]—In reality, the injunction of an act should be taken to apply to only such an agent as may be able to carry out the entire details of the act; because such is the sense of the Vedic texts.

VI.i.8. In reality, it is the whole genus [that is entitled],—says Bādarāyaṇa,—because there is no ground for distinction; hence the woman also should be regarded (as entitled to perform sacrifices), as the genus is equally present in all (human beings).

Topic: The *śūdra* [lowest caste] is not entitled to the performance of sacrifices.

VI.i.25. [Objection]—"All the four castes [are entitled to the performance of sacrifices],—there being no distinction."

VI.i.26. [True view]—In reality, the acts in question can be performed by the three (higher) castes only; as in connection with the "Installation of Fire" these three only have been mentioned; [the *śūdra*] therefore can have no connection with sacrifices; the Veda being applicable to the *brāhmin* (and the other two castes) only;—such is the opinion of Ātrēya.

B. *ŚLOKAVĀRTIKA*[1]

1. On God's not being the creator of the world

41. To all persons ignorant (of the relation of a word with a certain meaning), the relation comes in a well-established form, through previous traditions (i.e., from people who have known it before them, and so on *ad infinitum*); and therefore there can be no beginning of the (application of the) relation (to the word); and (as such it must be held to be eternal).

42. The theory, of the accomplishment (of the relation) based upon (conventional rules made with) each utterance (of the word), has been rejected in the *Bhāṣya* [Commentary]. And as for the fixing (of the relation) at the beginning of creation,—(this cannot be; since) we do not admit of any such time (the world being eternal and as such having no beginning in time).

43–4. *Objection:* "But, if there be such a Person as would create the world, and then set going the processes of *dharma* and *adharma*, and the uses and relations of words, for the sake of the world,—then, such a fact would not in any way vitiate the Veda."

Reply: Yet this theory is as difficult to prove as an omniscient person; hence we have not admitted it (in the Mīmāṁsā system).

45. At a time when all this (earth, water, etc.,) did not exist, what could have been the condition of the universe? As for Prajāpati himself, what could be his position? And what his form?

46. And at that time (when no men existed) who would know Him and explain His character to the later created persons? (If it be held that He cannot be perceived by any man, then) without perception (or cognition of some sort, by some person), how can we determine this (fact of His existence)?

47. Then again, in what manner do you believe the world to have had a beginning in time? (If it be held that it is brought about by

[1] Section 16: *Saṁbandhākṣepa-parihāra.*

a desire on the part of Prajāpati, then) since Prajāpati is (held to be) without a material body, etc., how could He have any desire towards creation?

48–9. And if He has a body, assuredly this body could not have been created by Himself; thus then we would have to postulate another creator (for his body) (and so on, *ad infinitum*). If Prajāpati's body be held to be eternal, then (we ask)—so long as earth (water, etc.,) have not been produced, of what material would that body be composed?

49–50. Then again, in the first place, how is it that He should have a desire to create a world which is to be fraught with all sorts of troubles to living beings? For at that time (of the beginning of creation) he has not got any guiding agencies, in the shape of the virtue (or sin), etc., of the living beings themselves. Nor can any creator create any thing, in the absence of means and instruments.

51. Even the production of the spider's net is not held to be without some sort of a (material) basis; as (the net is spun out of) the saliva, which is produced out of the body of the animals (flies, etc.,) eaten (by the spider).

52. (If it be held that Prajāpati creates the world, out of pity, then, we say) in the absence of objects of compassion (in the shape of living persons), no pity (or compassion) could be possible for Him. And if He were urged to creation by pure compassion, then He would create only happy beings.

53. If it be urged that "without some pain, neither the creation nor the continuation of the world would be possible,"—then (we reply that) when everything depends upon the mere will of the Creator Himself, what could be impossible for Him?

54. And if He were to depend upon laws and agencies, then this fact would deprive Him of His (boasted) independence. (You say He desires to create the world,—will you let me know) what is that end which He desires, and which could not be gained without creating the world?

55. For without some end in view, even a fool does not act. Then if He were to act so (without any end in view), then what would be the good of his intelligence?

56. If the activity of the Creator were due to a desire for mere amusement, then that would go against his ever-contentedness. And (instead of affording any amusement), the great amount of work (required for creation) would be a source of infinite trouble to Him.

57. And His desire to destroy the world (at *pralaya*) [time of destruction] too would be hardly explicable. And (above all) such a Creator could never be known by anybody.

58. Even if He were known in form, the fact of His being the Creator could never be known. Because at that time (i.e., in the infancy of creation) what could the living beings, appearing at the beginning of creation, understand?

59. They could not understand wherefrom they have been born; nor could they know the state of the world prior to creation, or the fact of Prajāpati being the Creator.

60. Nor could the idea that they would derive from His own assertion (with regard to His being the Creator) be altogether trustworthy, because even though He may not have created the world, He might speak of having done so, in order to show off His great power.

61. In the same manner the Veda that would proceed from Him would only be doubtful, and hence could not be admitted as a sure proof of His existence (and creative power). And as for that (Veda) which is eternal, how could it make a mention (of facts and processes with reference to the creation of living beings, etc.)?

62. For, if the Veda existed before the objects (created), then there can be no connection between this (Veda) and the objects created. Therefore the passages (occurring in the Veda) (which appear to describe the process of creation) must be interpreted as praising up something else (i.e., some injunctions of sacrifices, etc.).

63. The idea common among ordinary people (that the Veda mention of the creation as proceeding from Prajāpati) is a mistaken one, caused by certain valedictory passages (praising up certain injunctions). Because whenever a passage is not duly considered and interpreted together with the passages that precede and follow it, it is bound to give rise to a misconception.

64. The use of the *Mahābhārata*, etc., too, to the matter of *dharma*, etc., is in the form of telling stories (exemplifying and praising up certain duties and sacrifices), just like that of the Vedic passages (which seem to mention certain processes, while they only praise up certain sacrifices). Therefore the notion (of the creation proceeding from Prajāpati) got from these (i.e., passages occurring in the Purāṇas, etc.,) would also be only a mistaken one.

65. Because mere story-telling cannot have any use, therefore in all these (stories making up the Purāṇas) we must admit of something

that could be the object of praise or dispraise (embodied in the stories);—and this *something* may be that which is enjoined either in the Veda, or in the Purāṇas themselves.

66. If there were any such thing as the *first activity* of the Veda (towards injunction, etc.,) (this would mean that the Veda has had a beginning, and) then we could never have an idea of the fact of its not being composed by anybody (but being eternal in itself). The theory, too, that during universal dissolution the Veda resides in (the person of) Prajāpati, could, at best, only be considered doubtful.

67. If, however, you assume the eternality of the Creator and the processes of creation and dissolution,—then too, we could only admit of a gradual process of creation, such as we see in the case of present living beings (creating the jar, etc.).

68. And as for a "*pralaya*" in the form of universal destruction, we find no proofs for admitting it. Nor could such an action (of destruction) on the part of Prajāpati serve any useful purpose.

69–70. And for such souls as have (the load of) actions (*dharma* and *adharma*) upon them, there can be no existence during which there is no enjoyment of their results. Nor can the results of one action be restrained by any other action (in the shape of the Creator's desire, as held by the Vaiśeṣika); and it is not possible for all actions to continue to remain devoid of their results. Nor is there any single action, the result of which could be the non-fruition of all other actions (and which single action would thereby keep the other actions in check).

71. Then again, if all the actions (of persons) were to be destroyed (at the dissolution), then no future creation would be possible; for, under the circumstances (i.e., if actions were destroyed), what could be the means of bringing out these actions (out of their latent state)?

72. If the desire of God be held to be such a means, then that (desire) in itself could be an efficient cause of the creation of souls. And if creation were dependent upon God's wish, it would be useless to assume the (agency of) actions (*dharma* and *adharma*).

73. And it is not possible for God's desire too to be produced without any cause. If there be any such cause (of the production of God's desire), then that could also be the cause of the (production of the worldly) elements also.

74. If one were to argue that "the production of the bodies of living beings is controlled by an intelligent agency (in the form of

God's desire),—because they are made up of certain constituent parts,—like a house, etc.,"—then, he should be answered thus:

75–6. If by "control" is meant only the fact of some intelligent agency being the cause of creation,—then, inasmuch as all creation could be accomplished by the actions of all living beings (which are intelligent agents), your argument would become redundant (proving a fact already proved; for no one denies the fact that the diversity of the world is regulated by the actions of living persons). (And you have the same redundancy) even if by "control" you mean that the creation of bodies is preceded by the desire of an intelligent agent, because the actions (of living beings) too are preceded by it (i.e., a desire to act, on the part of the acting persons).

If, however, you mean that the creation follows immediately after the desire, then (we say that) there is no such immediate sequence even in the case of your own instance (the making of a *house* not following immediately after the desire of the builder).

77. Your premisses too are inconclusive (i.e., deficient and doubtful), with regard to the body of God Himself. For His body too must have had a beginning, inasmuch as it is also a body, like ours (made up of constituent parts).

78. If it be argued that "the production of God's body too is controlled by His own intelligence, and as such this (case of God's body) does not go against the conclusion (of the argument mentioned in K. [*kārikā*] 74),"—then (we reply that) the bodiless God, being like an emancipated soul, could not exercise any control.

79. And if in the case of the jar, etc. (that you cite as an instance) you refer to the superintendence of the potter, etc., then the control of God would not apply to these (and as such the instance could not prove the fact of the creation of the body being controlled by God); if, on the other hand, you mean that the making of the jar *is* controlled by God, then you would have the deficiency of the major term (that is to say, the fact of the jar, etc., being controlled by God is not recognised by us, and hence these could not serve as instances to prove the same with regard to the body, etc.).

80. And if you take the instance (of jar, etc.), as it is commonly recognised, then the premiss would contradict (the conclusion); inasmuch as in that case (the instance would lead to the conclusion that) the body, etc., are produced by one who is not a God, and who is himself perishable.

81–2. If it be held that God does not Himself carry on any operations, as the potter does (towards making the jar),—then, how could an insentient entity (in the shape of the atoms) follow His desire? Therefore the creation of the atoms, etc., could never be brought about by a mere desire of His.

82–3. Of a Person who is Himself extremely pure, the modifications (in the shape of this universe) could not be impure (as the world is found to be). *Dharma*, etc., too being absolutely under His power, it is not right (and reasonable) that there should be pain (in this world). And if the activity (of the world) were to be dependent upon (i.e., regulated by) these (*dharma*, etc.), then that would be accepting something else (i.e., an agency other than God's desire).

84. God himself being absolutely pure, and there being no other object (at the time of creation), what could bring about the activity of nescience, which (in falsity) resembles a dream?

85. If the mobility (to activity) were held to be due to something other (than *Brahman*), then you would have duality (since you would be admitting the existence of *Brahman* and something else to stimulate the activity of nescience). And if nescience itself were only natural (and as such not requiring any stimulation from without), then none could strike it off (and we could not have any deliverance).

86. A natural existence (like that of nescience) could be destroyed only by the influence of something unique (i.e., some such agencies as those of meditation, etc.). But for those who have their only means (of deliverance from nescience) in the Self, there cannot be any unique agency.

87. Even for those (the *Sāṁkhyas*) who hold the person (soul) to be inactive, how could there be any functioning of the attributes, at the beginning (of creation)? Because till then there would be no *karma* (of the souls).

On the Veda being without an author[1]

1. *Objection:*—"Finding the Vedic assertions to be similar to ordinary assertions, we have a general idea of the Veda having an author; and this becomes specified by the names 'Kaṭha,' etc., given to the different sections of the Veda.

2. "In the 21st *sūtra* it has been shown (in the *Bhāṣya*) that the fact of words being caused entities is based upon their having forms; and this is equally applicable to the Veda also, inasmuch as it makes

[1] Aphorisms XXVII–XXXII.

mention of caused entities (such as the names of certain persons, etc., which can never be eternal)."

3. *Reply:* Inasmuch as we have neither any remembrance of an author nor any need of any such,—no author is wanted for the Veda...; and since the ideas of particular authorship (as of Kaṭha, etc.) depend upon the general notion (of such authorship), no names (such as "Kaṭha" and the like) can point to any authors of the Veda.

4. Inasmuch as the names "Kaṭha," etc., may be explained as signifying the fact of certain portions of the Veda being explained by such people,—these names cannot necessarily point to an author; specially as the affix (in the word "Kaṭha") is also laid down (by Pāṇini)[1] as denoting the fact of being expounded (by Kaṭha).

5. And thus *name*, being weaker than direct assertion and the rest, cannot set aside the facts based upon these latter. And further, inasmuch as this (name) is a part of the Veda, it can never possibly set aside the whole of the Veda (by pointing to the fact of its having an author).

6. Or these ("Kaṭha," etc.) may be taken as conventional names, given, without any reason, to particular sections of the Veda. And the fact of these names (appearing with regard to certain sections of the Veda) being only similar in *sound*, the same words (as signifying the fact of being composed by Kaṭha, etc.) is not to be denied on pain of any punishment (i.e., there is no law which lays down that the two do not resemble [each other] in sound only).

7. Even though the explanation of the Veda is common to all persons (and not restricted particularly to Kaṭha alone), yet the name may be given to certain sections of the Veda, simply on the ground of the possibility (of their being explained by Kaṭha); just as the *Jyotiṣṭoma* is called "*Vairūpāsāmā*" (though many other *sāmas* are chanted in the *Jyotiṣṭoma*), simply because the particular *sāma* "Vairūpa" also appears in it.

8. The names "Kaṭha," etc., indicating the fact of Kaṭha, etc., being the explainers, are not such as to restrict the explicability of those sections of the Veda to those teachers alone, inasmuch as all that the name does is to show that the section of the Veda has been explained by that particular teacher *also* among others,—just as the mother of Ḍittha is not the mother of Kapittha, but that she is also the mother of Ḍittha, among others).

9. The fact that, even though the relation of the section with all

[1] An outstanding grammarian.

teachers is the same, yet it is named after one of them only, is due to the fact that such naming is not a qualification of the agent (i.e., the teacher) and as such it is not necessary to repeat it with regard to all the teachers); hence the naming (in accordance with teachers) being (a qualification) for the sake of another (i.e., the sections of the Veda), the mention of only one of them is necessary.

10. (Even if the name "Kaṭha" were taken as implying the authorship of Kaṭha with regard to the Veda, then too) it is only an already existing cause (in the shape of Kaṭha) that is signified (by the name "Kaṭha"); and it does not signify the production of something previously non-existent.

And (as for the meaning of Vedic sections according to the name of only one teacher, it is similar to the case where) a certain sacred place, though visited by many people, is named in accordance with only one of its visitors (such as "Somatīrtha," etc.).

11. And if the name "Kaṭha" be not due to human agency, then it cannot indicate non-eternality; and if it be due to human agency, then how can its truthfulness be ascertained?

12. Or "Kaṭha" as a *class* (of *brāhmins*) is held by us to be eternal; and it is this *class* (as denoted by "Kaṭha") which appears in the name "Kāṭhaka" which (means that the particular section of the Veda belongs to the particular class of *brāhmins*, called "Kaṭha" and) serves to distinguish that particular section from other sections of the Veda.

13–14. The Veda naturally abandons the denotation of non-eternal meanings,—inasmuch as such denotation is found to be impossible with regard to the Veda, by considering alternatives of eternality and non-eternality with regard to it. Because if the Veda be eternal its denotation cannot but be eternal; and if it be non-eternal (caused), then it can have no validity (which is not possible, as we have already proved the validity of the Veda); and as for the theory that the Veda consists of assertions of intoxicated (and senseless) people, this theory has been already rejected above—(and as such the validity and hence the eternality of the Veda cannot be doubted.)

15. Thus up to this place, we have established by arguments, the fact of the Veda being the means of arriving at the right notion of "*dharma*."

CHAPTER XV

VEDĀNTA

THE Vedānta philosophy, in one or another of its forms, is closely bound up with the religion of India. While Jaimini's Pūrva Mīmāṁsā deals with the *karmakāṇḍa* or the duties enjoined by the Veda Bādarāyaṇa's Uttara Mīmāṁsā or the Vedānta (between 500 and 200 B.C.) deals with the religious and philosophical speculations of the Upaniṣads. The two together form a systematic account of the contents of the Veda. The *Vedānta Sūtra* deals with Vedānta or the final aim of the Veda. It is also called the *Brahma Sūtra*, since it deals with the doctrine of *Brahman*, and the *Śārīraka Sūtra*, since it deals with the embodiment of the unconditioned Self.

In the 555 *sūtras* an attempt is made to systematize the teachings of the Upaniṣads. These *sūtras*, which consist of two or three words each, cannot be understood without a commentary. The different commentators develop different interpretations in the light of their own preconceived opinions. The chief commentators, who are dealt with in this book, are Śaṁkara, Rāmānuja, and Madhva.

Śaṁkara's Non-dualism

Śaṁkara is generally assigned to the eighth century (788–820?) A.D., and his system is traceable to Gauḍapāda's *Kārikās* (verses) (8th century A.D.) on the *Māṇḍūkya Upaniṣad*. A creative thinker of the first rank, Śaṁkara says that he is merely expounding what is contained in the Vedas.

In the introduction to his commentary on the *Vedānta Sūtra* he asks whether there is anything in experience which may be regarded as foundational. Our senses may deceive us; our memory may be an illusion. The forms of the world may be pure fancy. The objects of knowledge may be open to doubt, but the doubter himself cannot be doubted. "All means of knowledge exist only as dependent on self-experience and since such experience is its own proof there is no necessity for proving the existence of self."[1] It cannot be proved, because it is the basis of all proof. The self is self-established and is different from all else, physical and mental. As the subject it is not the object. It has being in itself and for itself. It is undifferentiated consciousness, which remains unaffected even when the

[1] See S. Radhakrishnan, *Indian Philosophy,* II, p. 476. (London: George Allen & Unwin, Ltd., 2nd rev. ed., 1931.)

body is reduced to ashes and the mind perishes. The Self (*Ātman*) is existence, knowledge, and bliss. It is universal and infinite.

The object-world is dependent. It is changing but is not a mental fiction. We perceive objects; we do not invent the corresponding ideas. The world perceived is as real as the individual perceiver. Śaṁkara repudiates the subjectivism of the Yogācāras (Buddhist idealists). He also holds that the world is not non-existent. It is not *abhāva* (non-existent) or *śūnya* (void). Nevertheless, the world is not ultimate reality.

Our ignorance is born of a confusion of the transcendental subject (*Ātman*) with empirical existence (*anātman*).

When we start from the cosmic end, as it were, we find that the world is bound up by the categories of space, time, and cause. These are not self-contained or self-consistent. They point to something unalterable and absolute, which remains identical with itself in all its manifestations. *Brahman* is the basis and ground of all experience. *Brahman* is different from the space-time-cause world. *Brahman* has nothing similar to it, nothing different from it, and no internal differentiation, for all these are empirical distinctions. *Brahman* is the non-empirical, the non-objective, the wholly other, but it is not non-being. It is the highest being. With Śaṁkara, *Ātman* is the same as *Brahman*; the essence of the subject, the deepest part of our being, is one with the essence of the world.

The empirical world cannot exist by itself. It is wholly dependent on *Brahman*, but the changes of the empirical order do not affect the integrity of *Brahman*. The world depends on *Brahman*, but *Brahman* depends on nothing. Ignorance affects our whole empirical being. It is another name for finitude.

To remove ignorance is to realize the truth. We reach wisdom when error is dissipated. While absolute truth is *Brahman*, empirical truth is not false. The highest representation of absolute being through logical categories is Īśvara, the creator and governor of the universe; *Brahman*, cast through the molds of logic, is Īśvara or *saguṇa Brahman* (*Brahman* with qualities), determinate *Brahman*. *Brahman*, as the Absolute *nirguṇa Brahman* (qualityless *Brahman*) is the basis of the phenomenal world, presided over by Īśvara. In this empirical universe, we have God (Īśvara), selves, and the world.

The individual self is the agent of activity. It is the universal Self or *Ātman* limited or individuated by the object. It is connected with *buddhi* or understanding, and this connection lasts until release is attained.

By the practice of ethical virtues and by the pursuit of devotion and knowledge we reach the goal of self-realization (*mokṣa*). *Mokṣa* (self-realization or freedom) is the direct realization of the truth which has been there from eternity. On the attainment of freedom nothing happens to the world; only our view of it changes. *Mokṣa* is not the dissolution of the world but is the displacement of a false outlook (*avidyā*) by the right outlook, wisdom (*vidyā*).

Rāmānuja's Qualified Non-dualism

Rāmānuja (11th century) fixes his attention on the world, self, and God. For him all these are real, but the world and the selves depend on God. Rāmānuja believes in the continued individual existence of the released selves. While *Brahman* is eternally free from all imperfections, matter is unconscious, and the individual selves are subject to ignorance and suffering prior to release. They (God, selves, and the world) form a unity, as matter and selves have existence only as the body of *Brahman*. *Brahman* is the self and the controlling power of the body, which includes the world and the selves. Apart from *Brahman* they are nothing. The individual self and inanimate nature are essentially different from God, though they have no existence or purpose to serve apart from him or his service. Rāmānuja's theory, therefore, is a non-dualism with a difference, namely, that the one *Brahman* has two forms: selves and matter.

Rāmānuja rejects the doctrine of the phenomenality of the world, admits the inalienable individuality of selves, and holds that the Supreme *Brahman* is personal. For him, there can be no such thing as undifferentiated *Brahman*. Knowledge is always of the determinate.

Though Śaṁkara did not mean by knowledge theoretical learning, there was a tendency among his followers to emphasize it. Rāmānuja stresses devotion (*bhakti*).

Salvation, according to Rāmānuja, is not the disappearance of the self but its release from limiting barriers. The self cannot be dissolved into God. One substance cannot be dissolved into another. However high a man may rise, there will always be God superior to him, whom he should reverence, worship, and adore. The released self has a permanent intuition of God. Its essential nature, which is obscured by ignorance and passion in the state of bondage, is manifested in the state of release.

Madhva's Dualism

Madhva (1197–1276) holds that God, selves, and the world exist permanently, but the latter two are subordinate to God and dependent on Him. *Brahman* or God possesses all perfection and is identified with Viṣṇu. The Supreme directs the world. He is endowed with a supernatural body and is regarded as transcendent to the world as well as immanent in it, since he is the inner ruler of all selves.

Madhva's system, as contrasted with other schools of Vedānta, is noted for its doctrine of five fundamental differences: (1) between God and the individual self; (2) between God and matter; (3) between individual selves; (4) between selves and matter; and (5) between individual material substances.

For Madhva, everything on earth is a living organism. The self is not an absolute agent, since it is of limited power and is dependent on God. It is by nature blissful, though it is subject to pain and suffering on account of its connection with a material body due to its past *karma*. So long as it is not freed from impurities it wanders about in changing forms of existence. No two selves are alike.

God cannot be approached directly, Vāyu, whose ancestry can be traced to the Vedic air, being in Madhva's system the mediator. The divine will is supreme. It sets men free or casts them into bondage.

Salvation, for Madhva, consists in the perpetuation of the individual self in the condition of release, where the self takes delight in adoration and worship of God.

Selections for this chapter have been taken from *The Vedānta Sūtras with the Commentary by Śaṅkarākārya*, translated by George Thibaut, Sacred Books of the East, XXXIV and XXXVIII (Oxford: Clarendon Press, 1890, 1896); *The Vedānta Sūtras with the Commentary of Rāmānuga*, translated by George Thibaut, Sacred Books of the East, XLVIII (Oxford: Clarendon Press, 1904); and *Vedānta-sūtraș with the Commentary of Sri Madhwacharya*, translated by S. Subba Rao (Tirupati: Sri Vyasa Press, 2nd ed. rev., 1936).

A. THE NON-DUALISM OF ŚAṀKARA

It is a matter not requiring any proof that the object and the subject whose respective spheres are the notion of the "Thou" (the non-ego) and the "ego," and which are opposed to each other as much as darkness and light are, cannot be identified.... In spite of this it is on the part of man a natural procedure—which has its cause in wrong knowledge—not to distinguish the two entities (object and subject) and their respective attributes, although they are absolutely distinct, but to superimpose upon each the characteristic nature and the attributes of the other, and thus, coupling the real and the unreal, to make use of expressions such as "That am I," "That is mine."—But what have we to understand by the term "superimposition"? —the apparent presentation, in the form of remembrance, to consciousness of something previously observed, in some other thing.

...definitions [of superimposition] agree in so far as they represent superimposition as the apparent presentation of the attributes of one thing in another thing. And therewith agrees also the popular view which is exemplified by expressions such as the following: "Mother-of-pearl appears like silver," "The moon although one only appears as if she were double." But how is it possible that on the interior Self which itself is not an object there should be superimposed objects and their attributes? For every one superimposes an object only on such other objects as are placed before him (i.e., in contact with his sense-organs), and you have said before that the interior Self which is entirely disconnected from the idea of the Thou (the non-ego) is never an object. It is not, we reply, non-object in the absolute sense. For it is the object of the notion of the ego, and the interior Self is well known to exist on account of its immediate (intuitive) presentation.[1]

This superimposition thus defined, learned men consider to be ignorance,[2] and the ascertainment of the true nature of that which is (the Self) by means of the discrimination of that (which is superimposed on the Self), they call knowledge. . . . But how can the means of right knowledge such as perception, inference, &c., and scriptural texts have for their object that which is dependent on ignorance?—Because, we reply, the means of right knowledge cannot operate unless there be a knowing personality, and because the existence of the latter depends on the erroneous notion that the body, the senses, and so on, are identical with, or belong to, the Self of the knowing person. For without the employment of the senses, perception and the other means of right knowledge cannot operate. And without a basis (i.e., the body) the senses cannot act. Nor does anybody act by means of a body on which the nature of the Self is not superimposed. Nor can, in the absence of all that, the Self which, in its own nature is free from all contact, become a knowing agent. . . .

With a view to freeing one's self from that wrong notion which is the cause of evil and attaining thereby the knowledge of the absolute unity of the Self the study of the Vedānta-texts is begun. . . .

I.i.1. Then there is the enquiry into *Brahman.*

. . . It therefore is requisite that something should be stated subsequent to which the enquiry into *Brahman* is proposed.—Well, then, we maintain that the antecedent conditions are the discrimination of what is eternal and what is non-eternal, the renunciation of all desire to enjoy the fruit (of one's actions) both here and hereafter, the acquirement of tranquillity, self-restraint, and the other means, and the desire of final release. If these conditions exist, a man may, either before entering on an enquiry into active religious duty or after that, engage in the enquiry into *Brahman* and come to know it; but not otherwise. . . .

. . . the complete comprehension of *Brahman* is the highest end of man,

[1] Translated according to the *Bhāmatī*. We deny, the objector says, the possibility of superimposition in the case of the Self, not on the ground that it is not an object because self-luminous (for that it may be an object although it is self-luminous you have shown), but on the ground that it is not an object because it is not manifested either by itself or by anything else.—It is known or manifest, the Vedāntin replies, on account of its immediate presentation i.e., on account of the intuitional knowledge we have of it.

[2] "Ignorance" is substituted throughout these selections for the translator's "Nescience" (for *avidyā*).

since it destroys the root of all evil such as ignorance, the seed of the entire *saṁsāra*. Hence the desire of knowing *Brahman* is to be entertained.

But, it may be asked, is *Brahman* known or not known (previously to the enquiry into its nature)? If it is known we need not enter on an enquiry concerning it; if it is not known we can not enter on such an enquiry.

We reply that *Brahman* is known. *Brahman*, which is all-knowing and endowed with all powers, whose essential nature is eternal purity, intelligence, and freedom, exists. . . . Moreover, the existence of *Brahman* is known on the ground of its being the Self of every one. For every one is conscious of the existence of (his) Self, and never thinks "I am not." If the existence of the Self were not known, every one would think "I am not." And this Self (of whose existence all are conscious) is *Brahman*. But if *Brahman* is generally known as the Self, there is no room for an enquiry into it! Not so, we reply, for there is a conflict of opinions as to its special nature.

I.i.2. (*Brahman* is that) from which the origin, &c., (i.e., the origin, subsistence, and dissolution) of this (world proceed).

. . . That omniscient omnipotent cause from which proceed the origin, subsistence, and dissolution of this world—which world is differentiated by names and forms, contains many agents and enjoyers, is the abode of the fruits of actions, these fruits having their definite places, times, and causes, and the nature of whose arrangement cannot even be conceived by the mind,—that cause, we say, is *Brahman*. . . .

The origin, &c., of a world possessing the attributes stated above cannot possibly proceed from anything else but a Lord possessing the stated qualities; not either from a non-intelligent *pradhāna* [eternal fundamental substance], or from atoms, or from non-being, or from a being subject to transmigration; nor, again, can it proceed from its own nature (i.e., spontaneously, without a cause), since we observe that (for the production of effects) special places, times, and causes have invariably to be employed. . . .

. . . the comprehension of *Brahman* is effected by the ascertainment, consequent on discussion, of the sense of the Vedānta-texts, not either by inference or by the other means of right knowledge. While, however, the Vedānta-passages primarily declare the cause of the origin, &c., of the world, inference also, being an instrument of right knowledge in so far as it does not contradict the Vedānta-texts, is not to be excluded as a means of confirming the meaning ascertained. Scripture itself, moreover, allows argumentation; for [certain] passages, . . . declare that human understanding assists scripture.

. . . as *Brahman* is not an object of the senses, it has no connection with those other means of knowledge. For the senses have, according to their nature, only external things for their objects, not *Brahman*. If *Brahman* were an object of the senses, we might perceive that the world is connected with *Brahman* as its effect; but as the effect only (i.e., the world) is perceived, it is impossible to decide (through perception) whether it is connected with *Brahman* or something else.

I.i.3. (The omniscience of *Brahman* follows) from its being the source of scripture.

I.i.4. But that (*Brahman* is to be known from scripture), because it is connected (with the Vedānta-texts) as their purport.

. . . *Brahman* is eternal, all-knowing, absolutely self-sufficient, ever pure, intelligent and free, pure knowledge, absolute bliss. From the devout meditation on this *Brahman* there results as its fruit, final release, which, although not to be discerned in the ordinary way, is discerned by means of the *Śāstra* [treatise]. . . .

. . . this (*mokṣa* [release]) is eternal in the true sense, i.e., eternal without undergoing any changes. . . omnipresent as ether, free from all modifications, absolutely self-sufficient, not composed of parts, of self-luminous nature. That bodiless entity in fact to which merit and demerit with their consequences and threefold time do not apply is called release; . . . It . . . is, therefore, the same as *Brahman* in the enquiry into which we are at present engaged. . . .

. . . even if *Brahman* were altogether different from a person's Self still it would not be something to be obtained; for as it is omnipresent it is part of its nature that it is ever present to every one, just as the (all-pervading) ether is. Nor, again, can it be maintained that release is something to be ceremonially purified, and as such depends on an activity. For ceremonial purification (*saṁskāra*) results either from the accretion of some excellence or from the removal of some blemish. The former alternative does not apply to release as it is of the nature of *Brahman*, to which no excellence can be added; nor, again, does the latter alternative apply, since release is of the nature of *Brahman*, which is eternally pure. . . . What is purified by. . . actions is that self merely which is joined to the body, i.e., the Self in so far as it is under the power of ignorance. . . . And as nobody is able to show any other way in which release could be connected with action, it is impossible that it should stand in any, even the slightest, relation to any action, excepting knowledge.

. . . neither from that part of the Veda which enjoins works nor from reasoning, anybody apprehends that self which, different from the agent that is the object of self-consciousness, merely witnesses it; which is permanent in all (transitory) beings; uniform; one; eternally unchanging; the Self of everything. Hence it can neither be denied nor be represented as the mere complement of injunctions; for of that very person who might deny it it is the Self. And as it is the Self of all, it can neither be striven after nor avoided. All perishable things indeed perish, because they are mere modifications, up to (i.e., exclusive of) the self. But the self is imperishable, as there is no cause why it should perish; and eternally unchanging, as there is no cause for its undergoing any modification; hence it is in its essence eternally pure and free. . . .

As. . . the application of the conception of the ego to the body on the part of those who affirm the existence of a Self different from the body is simply false, not figurative, it follows that the embodiedness of the Self is (not real but) caused by wrong conception, and hence that the person who has reached true knowledge is free from his body even while still alive.... the man who has once comprehended *Brahman* to be the Self, does not belong to this transmigratory world as he did before. He, on the other hand, who still belongs to this transmigratory world as before, has not comprehended *Brahman* to be the Self.

I.i.5. On account of seeing (i.e., thinking being attributed in the Upaniṣads to the cause of the world; the *pradhāna*) is not (to be identified with the cause indicated by the Upaniṣads; for) it is not founded on scripture.

...just as in consequence of connexion of the latter kind such conceptions and terms as "the hollow (space) of a jar," &c., are generally current, although the space inside a jar is not really different from universal space, and just as in consequence thereof there generally prevails the false notion that there are different spaces such as the space of a jar and so on; so there prevails likewise the false notion that the Lord and the transmigrating self are different; a notion due to the non-discrimination of the (unreal) connexion of the self with the limiting conditions, consisting of the body and so on....

I.i.10. On account of the uniformity of view (of the Vedānta-texts, *Brahman* is to be considered the cause).

I.i.11. And because it is directly stated in scripture (therefore the all-knowing *Brahman* is the cause of the world).

...*Brahman* is apprehended under two forms; in the first place as qualified by limiting conditions owing to the multiformity of the evolutions of name and form (i.e., the multiformity of the created world); in the second place as being the opposite of this, i.e., free from all limiting conditions whatever.... [Many passages] declare *Brahman* to possess a double nature, according as it is the object either of knowledge or of ignorance. As long as it is the object of ignorance, there are applied to it the categories of devotee, object of devotion, and the like. The different modes of devotion lead to different results, some to exaltation, some to gradual emancipation, some to success in works; those modes are distinct on account of the distinction of the different qualities and limiting conditions. And although the one highest Self only, i.e., the Lord distinguished by those different qualities, constitutes the object of devotion, still the fruits (of devotion) are distinct, according as the devotion refers to different qualities....

Although one and the same Self is hidden in all beings movable as well as immovable, yet owing to the gradual rise of excellence of the minds which form the limiting conditions (of the Self), scripture declares that the Self, although eternally unchanging and uniform, reveals itself in a graduated series of beings, and so appears in forms of various dignity and power;...

I.i.17. And on account of the declaration of the difference (of the two, the *ānandamaya* [Self of bliss] cannot be the transmigrating self).

...(Nor can it be said that the Lord is unreal because he is identical with the unreal individual soul; for) the Lord differs from the soul (*vijñānātman*) which is embodied, acts and enjoys, and is the product of ignorance, in the same way as the real juggler, who stands on the ground, differs from the illusive juggler, who, holding in his hand a shield and a sword, climbs up to the sky by means of a rope; or as the free unlimited ether differs from the ether of a jar, which is determined by its limiting adjunct (viz., the jar). With reference to this fictitious difference of the highest Self and the individual self, the two last *sūtras* have been propounded.

I.i.19. And, moreover, it (i.e., scripture) teaches the joining of this (i.e., the individual self) with that (i.e., the Self consisting of bliss), on that (being fully known).

...if he sees in that Self consisting of bliss even one small difference in the form of non-identity, then he finds no release from the fear of transmigratory existence. But when he, by means of the cognition of absolute identity, finds absolute rest in the Self consisting of bliss, then he is freed from the fear of transmigratory existence. But this (finding absolute rest) is possible only when we understand by the Self consisting of bliss, the highest Self, and not either the *pradhāna* or the individual self....

I.ii.8. If it is said that (from the circumstance of *Brahman* and the individual self being one) there follows fruition (on the part of *Brahman*); we say, no; on account of the difference of nature (of the two).

...From the circumstance that *Brahman* is connected with the hearts of all living beings it does not follow that it is, like the embodied Self, subject to fruition. For, between the embodied Self and the highest Self, there is the difference that the former acts and enjoys, acquires merit and demerit, and is affected by pleasure, pain, and so on; while the latter is of the opposite nature, i.e., characterised by being free from all evil and the like. On account of this difference of the two, the fruition of the one does not extend to the other.

I.iii.19. If it be said that from the subsequent (chapter it appears that the individual self is meant), (we point out that what is there referred to is) rather (the individual self in so far) as its true nature has become manifest (i.e., as it is non-different from *Brahman*).

...That same highest *Brahman* constitutes—as we know from passages such as "that art thou"—the real nature of the individual self, while its second nature, i.e., that aspect of it which depends on fictitious limiting conditions, is not its real nature. For as long as the individual self does not free itself from ignorance in the form of duality—which ignorance may be compared to the mistake of him who in the twilight mistakes a post for a man—and does not rise to the knowledge of the Self, whose nature is unchangeable, eternal cognition—which expresses itself in the form "I am *Brahman*"—so long it remains the individual self. But when, discarding the aggregate of body, sense-organs and mind, it arrives, by means of scripture, at the knowledge that it is not itself that aggregate, that it does not form part of transmigratory existence, but is the True, the Real, the Self, whose nature is pure intelligence; then knowing itself to be of the nature of unchangeable, eternal cognition, it lifts itself above the vain conceit of being one with this body, and itself becomes the Self, whose nature is unchanging, eternal cognition. As is declared in such scriptural passages as "He who knows the highest *Brahman* becomes even *Brahman*" (*Mu. Up.* III.ii.9). And this is the real nature of the individual self by means of which it arises from the body and appears in its own form....

...Before the rise of discriminative knowledge the nature of the individual self, which is (in reality) pure light, is non-discriminated as it were from its limiting adjuncts consisting of body, senses, mind, sense-objects and feelings, and appears as consisting of the energies of seeing and so on....Manifestation and non-manifestation of its nature of a different kind are not possible, since its nature is nothing but its nature (i.e., in reality is always the same). Thus the difference between the individual self and the highest Lord is owing to wrong knowledge only, not to any reality, since, like ether, the highest Self is not in real contact with anything....

I.iv.3. (...a previous seminal condition of the world may be admitted) on account of its dependency on him (the Lord); (for such an admission is) according to reason.

...If we admitted some antecedent state of the world as the independent cause of the actual world, we should indeed implicitly admit the *pradhāna* doctrine.[1] What we admit is, however, only a previous state dependent on the highest Lord, not an independent state. A previous stage of the world such as the one assumed by us must necessarily be admitted, since it is according to sense and reason. For without it the highest Lord could not be conceived as creator, as he could not become active if he were destitute of the potentiality of action. The existence of such a causal potentiality renders it moreover possible that the released selves should not enter on new courses of existence, as it is destroyed by perfect knowledge. For that causal potentiality is of the nature of ignorance; it is rightly denoted by the term "undeveloped"; it has the highest Lord for its substratum; it is of the nature of an appearance;[2] it is a universal sleep in which are lying the transmigrating selves destitute for the time of the consciousness of their individual character. This undeveloped principle is sometimes denoted by the term *ākāśa*, ether;...Sometimes, again, it is

[1] That is, the doctrine that all is derived from an eternal fundamental substance.
[2] "Appearance" is substituted for the translator's "illusion."

denoted by the term *akṣara*, the imperishable;...Sometimes it is spoken of as *māyā*, appearance;...For *māyā* is properly called undeveloped or non-manifested since it cannot be defined either as that which is or that which is not.

I.iv.14. (Although there is a conflict of the Vedānta-passages with regard to the things created, such as) ether and so on, (there is no such conflict with regard to the Lord) on account of his being represented (in one passage) as described (in other passages), viz., as the cause (of the world).

...a conflict of statements [in Vedānta-passages] regarding the world would not even matter greatly, since the creation of the world and similar topics are not at all what scripture wishes to teach....the passages about the creation and the like form only subordinate members of passages treating of *Brahman*.

I.iv.15. On account of the connexion (with passages treating of *Brahman*, the passages speaking of the non-being do not intimate absolute non-existence).

The passage "Non-being indeed was this in the beginning" (*Taitt. Up.* II.7) does not declare that the cause of the world is the absolutely non-existent which is devoid of all Selfhood. For in the preceding sections of the *Upaniṣad Brahman* is distinctly denied to be the non-existing, and is defined to be that which is ("He who knows the *Brahman* as non-existing becomes himself non-existing. He who knows the *Brahman* as existing him we know himself as existing"); it is further, by means of the series of sheaths, viz., the sheath of food, &c., represented as the inner Self of everything. This same *Brahman* is again referred to in the clause, "He wished, may I be many"; is declared to have originated the entire creation; and is finally referred to in the clause, "Therefore the wise call it the true." Thereupon the text goes on to say, with reference to what has all along been the topic of discussion, "On this there is also this *śloka* [verse], non-being indeed was this in the beginning," &c. If here the term "non-being" denoted the absolutely non-existent, the whole context would be broken; for while ostensibly referring to one matter the passage would in reality treat of a second altogether different matter. We have therefore to conclude that, while the term "being" ordinarily denotes that which is differentiated by names and forms, the term "non-being" denotes the same substance previous to its differentiation, i.e., that *Brahman* is, in a secondary sense of the word, called non-being, previously to the origination of the world....We, moreover, must assume that the world was evolved at the beginning of the creation in the same way as it is at present seen to develop itself by names and forms, viz., under the rulership of an intelligent creator; for we have no right to make assumptions contrary to what is at present actually observed.

I.iv.20. (The circumstance of the self being represented as the object of sight) indicates the fulfillment of the promissory statement; so Āśmarathya thinks.

The fact that the text proclaims as the object of sight that Self which is denoted as something dear indicates the fulfilment of the promise made in the passages, "When the Self is known all this is known," "All this is that Self." For if the individual self were different from the highest Self, the knowledge of the latter would not imply the knowledge of the former, and thus the promise that through the knowledge of one thing everything is to be known would not be fulfilled. Hence the initial statement aims at representing the individual Self and the highest Self as non-different for the purpose of fulfilling the promise made.—This is the opinion of the teacher Āśmarathya.[1]

I.iv.21. (The initial statement identifies the individual self and the highest Self); thus Auḍulomi thinks.

The individual self which is inquinated by the contact with its different limiting adjuncts, viz., body, senses, and mind, attains through the instrumentality of knowledge, meditation, and so on, a state of complete serenity, and thus enables itself, when passing at some future time out of the body, to become one with the highest Self; hence the initial statement in which it is represented as non-different from the highest Self. This is the opinion of the teacher Auḍulomi.—Thus scripture says, "That serene being arising from this body appears in its own form as soon as it has approached the highest light" (*Ch. Up.* VIII.xii.3).—In another place scripture intimates, by means of the simile of the rivers, that name and form abide in the individual self, "As the flowing rivers disappear in the sea, having lost their name and their form, thus a wise man freed from name and form goes to the divine Person who is greater than the great" (*Mu. Up.* III.ii.8). I.e., as the rivers losing the names and forms abiding in them disappear in the sea, so the individual self also losing the name and form abiding in it becomes united with the highest person. That the latter half of the passage has the meaning here assigned to it follows from the parallelism which we must assume to exist between the two members of the comparison.[2]

[1] The comment of the *Bhāmatī* on the *sūtra* runs as follows: As the sparks issuing from a fire are not absolutely different from the fire, because they participate in the nature of the fire; and, on the other hand, are not absolutely non-different from the fire, because in that case they could be distinguished neither from the fire nor from each other; so the individual selves also—which are effects of *Brahman*—are neither absolutely different from *Brahman*, for that would mean that they are not of the nature of intelligence; nor absolutely non-different from *Brahman*, because in that case they could not be distinguished from each other, and because, if they were identical with *Brahman* and therefore omniscient, it would be useless to give them any instruction. Hence the individual selves are somehow different from *Brahman* and somehow non-different.—The technical name of the doctrine here represented by Āśmarathya is *bhedābhedavāda* [the theory of difference—non-difference].

[2] *Bhāmatī:* The individual self is absolutely different from the highest Self; it is inquinated by the contact with its different limiting adjuncts. But it is spoken of, in the

I.iv.22. (The initial statement is made) because (the highest Self) exists in the condition (of the individual self); so Kāśakṛtsna thinks.

Because the highest Self exists also in the condition of the individual self, therefore, the teacher Kāśakṛtsna thinks, the initial statement which aims at intimating the non-difference of the two is possible. That the highest Self only is that which appears as the individual self, is evident from the Brāhmaṇa-passage, "Let me enter into them with this living Self and evolve names and forms," and similar passages. We have also *mantras* to the same effect, for instance, "The wise one who, having produced all forms and made all names, sits calling the things by their names" (*Taitt. Ār.* III.xii.7). And where scripture relates the creation of fire and the other elements, it does not at the same time relate a separate creation of the individual self; we have therefore no right to look on the self as a product of the highest Self, different from the latter.—In the opinion of the teacher Kāśakṛtsna the non-modified highest Lord himself is the individual self, not anything else. Āśmarathya, although meaning to say that the self is not (absolutely) different from the highest Self, yet intimates by the expression, "On account of the fulfilment of the promise"—which declares a certain mutual dependence—that there does exist a certain relation of cause and effect between the highest Self and the individual soul.[1] The opinion of Auḍulomi again clearly implies that the difference and non-difference of the two depend on difference of condition.[2] Of these three opinions we conclude that the one held by Kāśakṛtsna accords with scripture, because it agrees with what all the Vedānta-texts (so, for instance, the passage, "That art thou") aim at inculcating. Only on the opinion of Kāśakṛtsna immortality can be viewed as the result of the knowledge of the self; while it would be impossible to hold the same view if the self were a modification (product) of the Self and as such liable to lose its existence by being merged in its causal substance. For the same reason, name and form cannot abide in the self (as was above attempted to prove by means of the simile of the rivers), but abide in the limiting adjunct and are ascribed to the self itself in a figurative sense only. For the same reason the origin of the selves from the highest Self, of which scripture speaks in some places as analogous to the issuing of sparks from the fire, must be viewed as based only on the limiting adjuncts of the self.

The last three *sūtras* have further to be interpreted so as to furnish replies to the second of the *pūrvapakṣin's* arguments, viz., that the *Bṛhadāraṇyaka* passage represents as the object of sight the individual self, because it

Upaniṣad, as non-different from the highest Self because after having purified itself by means of knowledge and meditation it may pass out of the body and become one with the highest Self. The text of the Upaniṣad thus transfers a future state of non-difference to that time when difference actually exists. Compare the saying of the Pāñcarātrikas: "Up to the moment of emancipation being reached the self and the highest Self are different. But the emancipated self is no longer different from the highest Self, since there is no further cause of difference."—The technical name of the doctrine advocated by Auḍulomi is *satyabhedavāda*.

[1] And not the relation of absolute identity.

[2] I.e., upon the state of emancipation and its absence.

declares that the great Being which is to be seen arises from out of these elements. "There is an indication of the fulfilment of the promise; so Āśmarathya thinks." The promise is made in the two passages, "When the Self is known, all this is known," and "All this is that Self." That the Self is everything, is proved by the declaration that the whole world of names, forms, and works springs from one being, and is merged in one being; and by its being demonstrated, with the help of the similes of the drum, and so on, that effect and cause are non-different. The fulfilment of the promise is then, finally indicated by the text declaring that that great Being rises, in the form of the individual self, from out of these elements; thus the teacher Āśmarathya thinks. For if the self and the highest Self are non-different, the promise that through the knowledge of one everything becomes known is capable of fulfilment.—"Because the self when it will depart is such; thus Auḍulomi thinks." The statement as to the non-difference of the self and the Self (implied in the declaration that the great Being rises, &c.) is possible, because the self when—after having purified itself by knowledge, and so on—it will depart from the body, is capable of becoming one with the highest Self. This is Auḍulomi's opinion.—"Because it exists in the condition of the self; thus Kāśakṛtsna opines." Because the highest Self itself is that which appears as the individual self, the statement as to the non-difference of the two is well-founded. This is the view of the teacher Kāśakṛtsna.

But, an objection may be raised, the passage, "Rising from out of these elements he vanishes again after them. When he has departed there is no more knowledge," intimates the final destruction of the self, not its identity with the highest Self!—By no means, we reply. The passage means to say only that on the self departing from the body all specific cognition vanishes, not that the Self is destroyed. For an objection being raised—in the passage, "Here thou hast bewildered me, Sir, when thou sayest that having departed there is no more knowledge"—scripture itself explains that what is meant is not the annihilation of the Self, "I say nothing that is bewildering. Verily, beloved, that Self is imperishable, and of an indestructible nature. But there takes place non-connexion with the *mātrās*." That means: The eternally unchanging Self, which is one mass of knowledge, cannot possibly perish; but by means of true knowledge there is effected its dissociation from the *mātrās*, i.e., the elements and the sense organs, which are the product of ignorance. When the connexion has been solved, specific cognition, which depended on it, no longer takes place, and thus it can be said, that "When he has departed there is no more knowledge."

The third argument also of the *pūrvapakṣin*, viz., that the word "knower" —which occurs in the concluding passage, "How should he know the knower?"—denotes an agent, and therefore refers to the individual self as the object of sight, is to be refuted according to the view of Kāśakṛtsna. —Moreover, the text after having enumerated—in the passage, "For where there is duality as it were, there one sees the other," &c.—all the kinds of specific cognition which belong to the sphere of ignorance declares

—in the subsequent passage, "But when the Self only is all this, how should he see another?"—that in the sphere of true knowledge all specific cognition such as seeing, and so on, is absent. And, again in order to obviate the doubt whether in the absence of objects the knower might not know himself, Yājñavalkya goes on, "How, O beloved, should he know himself, the knower?" As thus the latter passage evidently aims at proving the absence of specific cognition, we have to conclude that the word "knower" is here used to denote that being which is knowledge, i.e., the Self.—That the view of Kāśakṛtsna is scriptural, we have already shown above. And as it is so, all the adherents of the Vedānta must admit that the difference of the self and the highest Self is not real, but due to the limiting adjuncts, viz., the body, and so on, which are the product of name and form as presented by ignorance. That view receives ample confirmation from scripture; compare, for instance, "Being only, my dear, this was in the beginning, one, without a second" (*Ch. Up.* vi.ii.1); "The Self is all this" (*Ch. Up.* vii.xxv.2); "*Brahman* alone is all this" (*Mu. Up.* ii.ii.11); "This everything is that Self" (*Bṛ. Up.* ii.iv.6); "There is no other seer but he" (*Bṛ. Up.* iii.vii.23); "There is nothing that sees but it" (*Bṛ. Up.* iii.viii.11).—It is likewise confirmed by *smṛti*; compare, for instance, "Vāsudeva is all this" (*B.G.* vii.19); "Know me, O Bhārata, to be the self in all bodies" (*B.G.* xiii.2); "He who sees the highest Lord abiding alike within all creatures" (*B.G.* xiii.27).—The same conclusion is supported by those passages which deny all difference; compare, for instance, "If he thinks, that is one and I another; he does not know" (*Br. Up.* i.iv.10); "From death to death he goes who sees here any diversity" (*Br. Up.* iv.iv.19). And, again, by those passages which deny all change on the part of the Self; compare, for instance, "This great unborn Self, undecaying, undying, immortal, fearless is indeed *Brahman*" (*Bṛ. Up.* iv.ii.4).—Moreover, if the doctrine of general identity were not true, those who are desirous of release could not be in the possession of irrefutable knowledge, and there would be no possibility of any matter being well settled; while yet the knowledge of which the Self is the object is declared to be irrefutable and to satisfy all desire, and scripture speaks of those, "Who have well ascertained the object of the knowledge of the Vedānta" (*Mu. Up.* iii.ii.6). Compare also the passage, "What trouble, what sorrow can there be to him who has once beheld that unity?" (*Īś. Up.* vii).—And *smṛti* also represents the mind of him who contemplates the Self as steady (*B.G.* ii.54).

As therefore the individual self and the highest Self differ in name only, it being a settled matter that perfect knowledge has for its object the absolute oneness of the two; it is senseless to insist (as some do) on a plurality of Selves, and to maintain that the individual self is different from the highest Self, and the highest Self from the individual self. For the Self is indeed called by many different names, but it is one only. Nor does the passage, "He who knows *Brahman* which is real, knowledge, infinite, as hidden in the cave" (*Taitt. Up.* ii.1), refer to some one cave (different from the abode of the individual self). And that nobody else but *Brahman* is hidden in the cave we know from a subsequent passage, viz., "Having sent forth he entered into it" (*Taitt. Up.* II.6), according to which the creator only entered into the created beings.—Those who insist on the distinction of the individual and the highest Self oppose themselves to the true sense of the Vedānta-texts, stand thereby in the way of perfect knowledge, which is the door to perfect beatitude, and groundlessly assume release to be something effected, and therefore non-eternal.[1] (And if they attempt to show that *mokṣa*, although effected, is eternal) they involve themselves in a conflict with sound logic.

I.iv.23. (*Brahman* is) the material cause also, on account of (this view) not being in conflict with the promissory statements and the illustrative instances.

...The promissory statement chiefly meant is the following one, "Have you ever asked for that instruction by which that which is not heard becomes heard; that which is not perceived, perceived; that which is not known, known?" (*Ch. Up.* VI.i.3). This passage intimates that through the cognition of one thing everything else, even if (previously) unknown, becomes known. Now the knowledge of everything is possible through the cognition of the material cause, since the effect is non-different from the material cause. On the other hand, effects are not non-different from their operative causes; for we know from ordinary experience that the carpenter, for instance, is different from the house he has built.... Ordinarily material causes, indeed, such as lumps of clay and pieces of gold, are dependent, in order to shape themselves into vessels and ornaments, on extraneous operative causes such as potters and goldsmiths; but outside *Brahman* as material cause there is no other operative cause to which the material cause could look; for scripture says that previously to creation *Brahman* was one without a second.—The absence of a guiding principle other than the material cause can moreover be established by means of the argument made use of in the *sūtra*, viz., accordance with the promissory statements and the illustrative examples. If there were admitted a guiding principle different from the material cause, it would follow that everything cannot be known through one thing, and thereby the promissory statements as well as the illustrative instances would be stultified.—The Self is thus the operative cause, because there is no other ruling principle, and the material cause because there is no other substance from which the world could originate.

II.i.5. But (there takes place) denotation of the superintending (deities), on account of the difference and the connexion.

From all this[2] it follows that this world is different in nature from *Brahman*, and hence cannot have it for its material cause.

To this objection...the next *sūtra* replies.

[1] While release, as often remarked, is eternal, it being in fact not different from the eternally unchanging *Brahman*.

[2] That is, from the elaborate commentary explaining the *sūtra*, but of little philosophical significance.

II.i.6. But it is seen.

Your assertion that this world cannot have originated from *Brahman* on account of the difference of its character is not founded on an absolutely true tenet. For we see that from man, who is acknowledged to be intelligent, non-intelligent things such as hair and nails originate, and that, on the other hand, from avowedly non-intelligent matter, such as cow-dung, scorpions and similar animals are produced. . . . If absolute equality were insisted on (in the case of one thing being the effect of another), the relation of material cause and effect (which after all requires a distinction of the two) would be annihilated. If, again, it be remarked that in the case of men and hair as well as in that of scorpions and cow-dung there is one characteristic feature, at least, which is found in the effect as well as in the cause, viz., the quality of being of an earthy nature, we reply that in the case of *Brahman* and the world also one characteristic feature, viz., that of existence, . . . is found in ether, &c., (which are the effects) as well as in *Brahman* (which is the cause). . . .

. . . *Brahman*, as being devoid of form and so on, cannot become an object of perception; and as there are in its case no characteristic marks (on which conclusions, &c., might be based), inference also and the other means of proof do not apply to it; but, like religious duty, it is to be known solely on the ground of holy tradition. . . .

. . . if it has been maintained above that the scriptural passage enjoining thought (on *Brahman*) in addition to mere hearing (of the sacred texts treating of *Brahman*) shows that reasoning also is to be allowed its place, we reply that the passage must not deceitfully be taken as enjoining bare independent ratiocination, but must be understood to represent reasoning as a subordinate auxiliary of intuitional knowledge.

II.i.7. If (it is said that the effect is) non-existent (before its origination); we do not allow that because it is a mere negation (without an object).

. . . If you deny[1] the existence of the effect previous to its actual origination, your denial is a mere denial without an object to be denied. The denial (implied in "non-existent") can certainly not have for its object the existence of the effect previous to its origination, since the effect must be viewed as "existent," through and in the Self of the cause, before its origination as well as after it; for at the present moment also this effect does not exist independently, apart from the cause; according to such scriptural passages as, "Whosoever looks for anything elsewhere than in the Self is abandoned by everything" (*Bṛ. Up.*, II.iv.6). In so far, on the other hand, as the effect exists through the Self of the cause, its existence is the same before the actual beginning of the effect (as after it).—But *Brahman*, which is devoid of qualities such as sound, &c., is the cause of this world (possessing all those qualities)!—True, but the effect with all

[1] "Deny" and "denial" are substituted for the translator's "negative" and "negations," respectively.

its qualities does not exist without the Self of the cause either now or before the actual beginning (of the effect); hence it cannot be said that (according to our doctrine) the effect is non-existing before its actual beginning.

II.i.8. On account of such consequences at the time of reabsorption (the doctrine maintained hitherto) is objectionable.

The *pūrvapakṣin* [objector] raises further objections.—If an effect which is distinguished by the qualities of grossness, consisting of parts, absence of intelligence, limitation, impurity, &c., is admitted to have *Brahman* for its cause, it follows that at the time of reabsorption (of the world into *Brahman*) the effect, by entering into the state of non-division from its cause, inquinates the latter with its properties. As therefore—on your doctrine—the cause (i.e., *Brahman*) as well as the effect is, at the time of reabsorption, characterised by impurity and similar qualities, the doctrine of the Upaniṣads, according to which an omniscient *Brahman* is the cause of the world, cannot be upheld.... If you finally say, "Well, let this world remain distinct from the highest *Brahman* even at the time of reabsorption," we reply that in that case a reabsorption will not take place at all, and that, moreover, the effect's existing separate from the cause is not possible. —For all these reasons the Vedānta doctrine is objectionable.

II.i.9. Not so; as there are parallel instances.

...As the magician is not at any time affected by the magical effect[1] produced by himself, because it is unreal, so the highest Self is not affected by the world-[effects (or appearances)]. And as one dreaming person is not affected by the illusory visions of his dream because they do not accompany the waking state and the state of dreamless sleep; so the one permanent witness of the three states (viz., the highest Self which is the one unchanging witness of the creation, subsistence, and reabsorption of the world) is not touched by the mutually exclusive three states. For that the highest Self appears in those three states is a mere illusion, not more substantial than the snake for which the rope is mistaken in the twilight....

...With regard to the...objection, viz., that if we assume all distinctions to pass (at the time of reabsorption) into the state of non-distinction there would be no special reason for the origin of a new world affected with distinctions, we likewise refer to the "existence of parallel instances." For the case is parallel to that of deep sleep and trance. In those states also the self enters into an essential condition of non-distinction; nevertheless, wrong knowledge being not yet finally overcome, the old state of distinction re-establishes itself as soon as the self awakes from its sleep or trance....

II.i.11. If it be said that, in consequence of the ill-foundations of reasoning, we must frame our conclusions otherwise; (we reply that) thus also there would result non-release.

[1] "Effect" is substituted for the translator's "illusion."

In matters to be known from scripture mere reasoning is not to be relied on for the following reason also. As the thoughts of man are altogether unfettered, reasoning which disregards the holy texts and rests on individual opinion only has no proper foundation. We see how arguments, which some clever men had excogitated with great pains, are shown, by people still more ingenious, to be fallacious, and how the arguments of the latter again are refuted in their turn by other men; so that, on account of the diversity of men's opinions, it is impossible to accept mere reasoning as having a sure foundation. Nor can we get over this difficulty by accepting as well-founded the reasoning of some person of recognised mental eminence, may he now be Kapila or anybody else; since we observe that even men of the most undoubted mental eminence, such as Kapila, Kaṇāda, and other founders of philosophical schools, have contradicted one another.

...The true nature of the cause of the world on which final emancipation depends cannot, on account of its excessive abstruseness, even be thought of without the help of the holy texts; as already remarked, it cannot become the object of perception, because it does not possess qualities such as form and the like, and as it is devoid of characteristic signs, it does not lend itself to inference and the other means of right knowledge.

II.i.13. If it be said that from the circumstance of (the objects of enjoyment) passing over into the enjoyer (and *vice versa*) there would result non-distinction (of the two); we reply that (such distinction) may exist (nevertheless) as ordinary experience shows.

Another objection, based on reasoning, is raised against the doctrine of *Brahman* being the cause of the world.—Although scripture is authoritative with regard to its own special subject-matter (as, for instance, the causality of *Brahman*), still it may have to be taken in a secondary sense in those cases where the subject-matter is taken out of its grasp by other means of right knowledge;...Analogously reasoning is to be considered invalid outside its legitimate sphere; so, for instance, in the case of religious duty and its opposite.—Hence scripture cannot be acknowledged to refute what is settled by other means of right knowledge. And if you ask, "Where does scripture oppose itself to what is thus established?" we give you the following instance. The distinction of enjoyers and objects of enjoyment is well known from ordinary experience, the enjoyers being intelligent, embodied selves, while sound and the like are the objects of enjoyment.... The distinction of the two would be reduced to non-existence if the enjoyer passed over into the object of enjoyment, and *vice versa*. Now this passing over of one thing into another would actually result from the doctrine of the world being non-different from *Brahman*. But the sublation of a well-established distinction is objectionable, not only with regard to the present time when that distinction is observed to exist, but also with regard to the past and the future, for which it is inferred. The doctrine of *Brahman's* causality must therefore be abandoned, as it would lead to the sublation of the well-established distinction of enjoyers and objects of enjoyment.

To the preceding objection we reply, "It may exist as in ordinary experience." Even on our philosophic view the distinction may exist, as ordinary experience furnishes us with analogous instances. We see, for instance, that waves, foam, bubbles, and other modifications of the sea, although they really are not different from the sea-water, exist, sometimes in the state of mutual separation, sometimes in the state of conjunction, etc. From the fact of their being non-different from the sea-water, it does not follow that they pass over into each other; and again, although they do not pass over into each other, still they are not different from the sea. So it is in the case under discussion also. . . . The conclusion is that the distinction of enjoyers and objects of enjoyment is possible, although both are non-different from *Brahman*, their highest cause, as the analogous instance of the sea and its waves demonstrates.

II.i.14. The non-difference of them (i.e., of cause and effect) results from such terms as "origin" and the like.

The refutation contained in the preceding *sūtra* was set forth on the condition of the practical distinction of enjoyers and objects of enjoyment being acknowledged. In reality, however, that distinction does not exist because there is understood to be non-difference (identity) of cause and effect. The effect is this manifold world consisting of ether and so on; the cause is the highest *Brahman*. Of the effect, it is understood that in reality it is non-different from the cause, i.e., has no existence apart from the cause.—How so?—"On account of the scriptural word 'origin' and others." The word "origin" is used in connexion with a simile, in a passage undertaking to show how through the knowledge of one thing everything is known; viz., *Ch. Up.* VI.i.4, "As, my dear, by one clod of clay all that is made of clay is known, the modification (i.e., the effect; the thing made of clay) being a name merely which has its origin in speech, while the truth is that it is clay merely; thus," &c.—The meaning of this passage is that, if there is known a lump of clay which really and truly is nothing but clay, there are known thereby likewise all things made of clay, such as jars, dishes, pails, and so on, all of which agree in having clay for their true nature. For these modifications or effects are names only, exist through or originate from speech only, while in reality there exists no such thing as a modification. In so far as they are names (individual effects distinguished by names) they are untrue; in so far as they are clay they are true.—This parallel instance is given with reference to *Brahman*; applying the phrase "having its origin in speech" to the case illustrated by the instance quoted we understand that the entire body of effects has no existence apart from *Brahman*.—Later on again the text, after having declared that fire, water, and earth are the effects of *Brahman*, maintains that the effects of these three elements have no existence apart from them, "Thus has vanished the specific nature of burning fire, the modification being a mere name which has its origin in speech, while only the three colours are what is true" (*Ch. Up.* VI.iv.1).—Other sacred texts also whose purport it is to intimate the unity of the Self are to be quoted here, in accordance with the "and others" of the *sūtra.* Such texts are, "In that all this has its Self; it is the True, it is the Self, thou art that" (*Ch. Up.* VI.viii.7); "This everything, all is that Self" (*Bṛ. Up.* II.iv.6); "Brahman alone is all this" (*Mu. Up.* II.ii.11); "The Self is all this" (*Ch. Up.* VII.xxv.2); "There is in it no diversity" (*Bṛ. Up.* IV.iv.25).—On any other assumption it would not be possible to maintain that by the knowledge of one thing everything becomes known (as the text quoted above declares). We therefore must adopt the following view. In the same way as those parts of ethereal space which are limited by jars and water-pots are not really different from the universal ethereal space, and as the water of a mirage is not really different from the surface of the salty steppe —for the nature of that water is that it is seen in one moment and has vanished in the next, and moreover, it is not to be perceived by its own nature (i.e., apart from the surface of the desert)—; so this manifold world with its objects of enjoyment, enjoyers, and so on, has no existence apart from *Brahman.*—But—it might be objected—*Brahman* has in itself elements of manifoldness. As the tree has many branches, so *Brahman* possesses many powers and energies dependent on those powers. Unity and manifoldness are therefore both true. Thus, a tree considered in itself is one, but it is manifold if viewed as having branches; so the sea in itself is one, but manifold as having waves and foam; so the clay in itself is one, but manifold if viewed with regard to the jars and dishes made of it. On this assumption, the process of final release resulting from right knowledge may be established in connexion with the element of unity (in *Brahman*), while the two processes of common worldly activity and of activity according to the Veda—which depend on the *karmakāṇḍa* (texts of injunction)—may be established in connexion with the element of manifoldness. And with this view the parallel instances of clay &c., agree very well.

This theory, we reply, is untenable because in the instance (quoted in the *Upaniṣad*) the phrase "as clay they are true" asserts the cause only to be true while the phrase "having its origin in speech" declares the unreality of all effects. And with reference to the matter illustrated by the instance given (viz., the highest cause, *Brahman*) we read, "In that all this has its Self"; and, again, "That is true"; whereby it is asserted that only the one highest cause is true. The following passage again, "That is the Self; thou art that, O Śvetaketu"! teaches that the embodied self (the individual self) also is *Brahman.* (And we must note that) the passage distinctly teaches that the fact of the embodied self having its Self in *Brahman* is self-established, not to be accomplished by endeavour. This doctrine of the individual self having its Self in *Brahman*, if once accepted as the doctrine of the Veda, does away with the independent existence of the individual self, just as the idea of the rope does away with the idea of the snake (for which the rope has been mistaken). And if the doctrine of the independent existence of the individual self has to be set aside, then the opinion of the entire phenomenal world—which is based on the individual self—having an independent existence is likewise to be set aside. But only for the establishment of the latter an element of manifoldness would have to be assumed in *Brahman*, in addition to the element of unity.—Scriptural passages also (such as, "When the Self only is all this, how should he see another?" *Bṛ. Up.* II.iv.13) declare that for him who sees that everything has its Self in *Brahman* the whole phenomenal world with its actions, agents, and results of actions is non-existent. Nor can it be said that this non-existence of the phenomenal world is declared (by scripture) to be limited to certain states; for the passage "Thou art that" shows that the general fact of *Brahman* being the Self of all is not limited by any particular state. Moreover, scripture, showing by the instance of the thief (*Ch. Up.* VI.16) that the false-minded is bound while the true-minded is released, declares thereby that unity is the one true existence while manifoldness is evolved out of wrong knowledge. For if both were true how could the man who acquiesces in the reality of this phenomenal world be called false-minded?[1] Another scriptural passage ("from death to death goes he who perceives therein any diversity," *Bṛ. Up.* IV.iv.19) declares the same, by blaming those who perceive any distinction.—Moreover, on the doctrine which we are at present impugning, release cannot result from knowledge, because the doctrine does not acknowledge that some kind of wrong knowledge, to be removed by perfect knowledge, is the cause of the phenomenal world. For how can the cognition of unity remove the cognition of manifoldness if both are true?

Other objections are stated.—If we acquiesce in the doctrine of absolute unity, the ordinary means of right knowledge, perception, &c., become invalid because the absence of manifoldness deprives them of their objects; just as the idea of a man becomes invalid after the right idea of the post (which at first had been mistaken for a man) has presented itself. Moreover, all the texts embodying injunctions and prohibitions will lose their purport if the distinction on which their validity depends does not really exist. And further, the entire body of doctrine which refers to final release will collapse, if the distinction of teacher and pupil on which it depends is not real. And if the doctrine of release is untrue, how can we maintain the truth of the absolute unity of the Self, which forms an item of that doctrine?

These objections, we reply, do not damage our position because the entire complex of phenomenal existence is considered as true as long as the knowledge of the *Brahman* being the Self of all has not arisen; just as the phantoms of a dream are considered to be true until the sleeper wakes. For as long as a person has not reached the true knowledge of the unity of the Self, so long it does not enter his mind that the world of effects with its names and objects of right knowledge and its results of actions is untrue; he rather, in consequence of his ignorance, looks on mere effects (such as body, offspring, wealth, &c.) as forming part of and belonging to his Self, forgetful of *Brahman* being in reality the Self of all. Hence, as long as true

[1] In the passage alluded to he is called so by implication, being compared to the "false-minded" thief who, knowing himself to be guilty, undergoes the ordeal of the heated hatchet.

knowledge does not present itself, there is no reason why the ordinary course of secular and religious activity should not hold on undisturbed. The case is analogous to that of a dreaming man who in his dream sees manifold things, and, up to the moment of waking, is convinced that his ideas are produced by real perception without suspecting the perception to be a merely apparent one.—But how (to restate an objection raised above) can the Vedānta-texts if untrue convey information about the true being of *Brahman*? We certainly do not observe that a man bitten by a rope-snake (i.e., a snake falsely imagined in a rope) dies, nor is the water appearing in a mirage used for drinking or bathing.—This objection, we reply, is without force (because as a matter of fact we do see real effects to result from unreal causes), for we observe that death sometimes takes place from imaginary venom, (when a man imagines himself to have been bitten by a venomous snake), and effects (of what is perceived in a dream) such as the bite of a snake or bathing in a river take place with regard to a dreaming person.—But, it will be said, these effects themselves are unreal!—These effects themselves, we reply, are unreal indeed; but not so the consciousness which the dreaming person has of them. This consciousness is a real result; for it is not sublated by the waking consciousness. The man who has risen from sleep does indeed consider the effects perceived by him in his dream such as being bitten by a snake, bathing in a river, &c., to be unreal, but he does not on that account consider the consciousness he had of them to be unreal likewise.—(We remark in passing that) by this fact of the consciousness of the dreaming person not being sublated (by the waking consciousness) the doctrine of the body being our true Self is to be considered as refuted.—Scripture also (in the passage, "If a man who is engaged in some sacrifice undertaken for some special wish sees in his dream a woman, he is to infer therefrom success in his work") declares that by the unreal phantom of a dream a real result such as prosperity may be obtained. And, again, another scriptural passage, after having declared that from the observation of certain unfavourable omens a man is to conclude that he will not live long, continues "if somebody sees in his dream a black man with black teeth and that man kills him" intimating thereby that by the unreal dream-phantom a real fact, viz., death, is notified.—It is, moreover, known from the experience of persons who carefully observe positive and negative instances that such and such dreams are auspicious omens, others the reverse. And (to quote another example that something true can result from or be known through something untrue) we see that the knowledge of the real sounds A., &c., is reached by means of the unreal written letters. Moreover, the reasons which establish the unity of the Self are altogether final, so that subsequently to them nothing more is required for full satisfaction.[1] An injunction as, for instance, "He is to sacrifice"

[1] As long as the "*vyavahāra*"—phenomenon—presents itself to our mind, we might feel inclined to assume in *Brahman* an element of manifoldness whereby to account for the *vyavahāra*; but as soon as we arrive at true knowledge, the *vyavahāra* vanishes, and there remains no longer any reason for qualifying in any way the absolute unity of *Brahman*.

at once renders us desirous of knowing what is to be effected, and by what means and in what manner it is to be effected; but passages such as, "Thou art that," "I am *Brahman*," leave nothing to be desired because the state of consciousness produced by them has for its object the unity of the universal Self. For, as long as something else remains, a desire is possible; but there is nothing else which could be desired in addition to the absolute unity of *Brahman*. Nor can it be maintained that such states of consciousness do not actually arise; for scriptural passages such as, "He understood what he said" (*Ch. Up.* VII.xviii.2), declare them to occur, and certain means are enjoined to bring them about, such as the hearing (of the Veda from a teacher) and the recital of the sacred texts. Nor, again, can such consciousness be objected to on the ground either of uselessness or of erroneousness, because, firstly, it is seen to have for its result the cessation of ignorance, and because, secondly, there is no other kind of knowledge by which it could be sublated. And that before the knowledge of the unity of the Self has been reached the whole real-unreal course of ordinary life, worldly as well as religious, goes on unimpeded, we have already explained. When, however, final authority having intimated the unity of the Self, the entire course of the world which was founded on the previous distinction is sublated, then there is no longer any opportunity for assuming a *Brahman* comprising in itself various elements.

But—it may be said—(that would not be a mere assumption, but) scripture itself, by quoting the parallel instances of clay and so on, declares itself in favour of a *Brahman* capable of modification; for we know from experience that clay and similar things do undergo modifications.—This objection—we reply,—is without force, because a number of scriptural passages, by denying all modifications of *Brahman*, teach it to be absolutely changeless (*kūṭastha*). Such passages are, "This great unborn Self, undecaying, undying, immortal, fearless, is indeed *Brahman*" (*Bṛ. Up.* IV.iv.25); "That Self is to be described by No, no" (*Bṛ. Up.* III.ix.26); "It is neither coarse nor fine" (*Bṛ. Up.* III.viii.8). For to the one *Brahman* the two qualities of being subject to modification and of being free from it cannot both be ascribed. And if you say, "Why should they not be both predicated of *Brahman* (the former during the time of the subsistence of the world, the latter during the period of reabsorption) just as rest and motion may be predicated (of one body at different times)?" we remark that the qualification, "absolutely changeless" (*kūṭastha*), precludes this. For the changeless *Brahman* cannot be the substratum of varying attributes. And that, on account of the negation of all attributes, *Brahman* really is eternal and changeless has already been demonstrated.—Moreover, while the cognition of the unity of *Brahman* is the instrument of final release, there is nothing to show that any independent result is connected with the view of *Brahman*, by undergoing a modification, passing over into the form of this world. Scripture expressly declares that the knowledge of the changeless *Brahman* being the universal Self leads to a result; for in the passage which begins, "That Self is to be described by No, no," we read later on, "O Janaka, you have indeed reached fearlessness" (*Bṛ. Up.*

IV.ii.4). We have then to accept the following conclusion that, in the sections treating of *Brahman*, an independent result belongs only to the knowledge of *Brahman* as devoid of all attributes and distinctions, and that hence whatever is stated as having no special fruit of its own—as, for instance, the passages about *Brahman* modifying itself into the form of this world—is merely to be applied as a means for the cognition of the absolute *Brahman*, but does not bring about an independent result; according to the principle that whatever has no result of its own, but is mentioned in connexion with something else which has such a result is subordinate to the latter. For to maintain that the result of the knowledge of *Brahman* undergoing modification would be that the Self (of him who knows that) would undergo corresponding modifications would be inappropriate, as the state of final release (which the self obtains through the knowledge of *Brahman*) is eternally unchanging.

But, it is objected, he who maintains the nature of *Brahman* to be changeless thereby contradicts the fundamental tenet according to which the Lord is the cause of the world, since the doctrine of absolute unity leaves no room for the distinction of a ruler and something ruled.—This objection we ward off by remarking that omniscience, &c., (i.e., those qualities which belong to *Brahman* only in so far as it is related to a world) depend on the evolution of the germinal principles called name and form, whose essence is ignorance. The fundamental tenet which we maintain (in accordance with such scriptural passages as, "From that Self sprang ether," &c.; *Taitt. Up.* II.1) is that the creation, sustentation, and reabsorption of the world proceed from an omniscient, omnipotent Lord, not from a non-intelligent *pradhāna* or any other principle. That tenet we have stated in I.i.4 and here we do not teach anything contrary to it.—But how, the question may be asked, can you make this last assertion while all the while you maintain the absolute unity and non-duality of the Self?—Listen how. Belonging to the Self, as it were, of the omniscient Lord, there are name and form, the figments of ignorance, not to be defined either as being (i.e., *Brahman*), nor as different from it, the germs of the entire expanse of the phenomenal world, called in *śruti* (scripture) and *smṛti* (secondary texts) the appearance (*māyā*), power (*śakti*), or Nature (*prakṛti*) of the omniscient Lord himself, as we learn from scriptural passages such as the following, "He who is called ether is the revealer of all forms and names; that within which these forms and names are contained is *Brahman*" (*Ch. Up.* VIII.xiv.1); "Let me evolve names and forms" (*Ch. Up.* VI.iii.2); "He, the wise one, who having divided all forms and given all names, sits speaking (with those names)" (*Taitt. Ār.* III.xii.7); "He who makes the one seed manifold" (*Śve. Up.* VI.12).—Thus the Lord depends (as Lord) upon the limiting adjuncts of name and form, the products of ignorance; just as the universal ether depends (as limited ether, such as the ether of a jar, &c.) upon the limiting adjuncts in the shape of jars, pots, &c. He (the Lord) stands in the realm of the phenomenal in the relation of a ruler to the so-called *jīvas* (individual souls [or selves]) or cognitional selves (*vijñānātman*), which indeed are one with his own Self—

just as the portions of ether enclosed in jars and the like are one with the universal ether—but are limited by aggregates of instruments of action (i.e., bodies) produced from name and form, the presentations of ignorance. Hence the Lord's being a Lord, his omniscience, his omnipotence, &c., all depend on the limitation due to the adjuncts whose self is ignorance; while in reality none of these qualities belong to the Self whose true nature is cleared, by right knowledge, from all adjuncts whatever. Thus scripture also says, "Where one sees nothing else, hears nothing else, understands nothing else, that is the Infinite" (*Ch. Up.* VII.xxiv.1); "But when the Self only has become all this, how should he see another?" (*Bṛ. Up.* II.iv.13). In this manner the Vedānta-texts declare that for him who has reached the state of truth and reality the whole apparent world does not exist. The *Bhagavad-gītā* also ("The Lord is not the cause of actions, or of the capacity of performing actions, or of the connexion of action and fruit; all that proceeds according to its own nature. The Lord receives no one's sin or merit. Knowledge is enveloped by ignorance; hence all creatures are deluded"; (*B.G.* v.14–15) declares that in reality the relation of ruler and ruled does not exist. That, on the other hand, all those distinctions are valid, as far as the phenomenal world is concerned, scripture as well as the *Bhagavad-gītā* states; compare *Bṛ. Up.* IV.iv.22, "He is the Lord of all, the king of all things, the protector of all things; he is a bank and boundary, so that these worlds may not be confounded"; and *B.G.* XVIII.61, "The Lord, O Arjuna, is seated in the region of the heart of all beings, turning round all beings, (as though) mounted on a machine, by his delusion." The Sūtrakāra also asserts the non-difference of cause and effect only with regard to the state of reality; while he had, in the preceding *sūtra*, where he looked to the phenomenal world, compared *Brahman* to the ocean, &c., that comparison resting on the assumption of the world of effects not yet having been refuted (i.e., seen to be unreal).—The view of *Brahman* as undergoing modifications will, moreover, be of use in the devout meditations on the qualified (*saguṇa*) *Brahman.*

II.i.15. And because only on the existence (of the cause) (the effect) is observed.

...only when the cause exists the effect is observed to exist, not when it does not exist. For instance, only when the clay exists the jar is observed to exist, and the cloth only when the threads exist. That it is not a general rule that when one thing exists another is also observed to exist, appears, for instance, from the fact, that a horse which is other (different) from a cow is not observed to exist only when a cow exists. Nor is the jar observed to exist only when the potter exists; for in that case non-difference does not exist, although the relation between the two is that of an operative cause and its effect....

II.i.26. Either the consequence of the entire (*Brahman* undergoing change) has to be accepted, or else a violation of the texts declaring *Brahman* to be without parts.

II.i.27. But (this is not so), on account of scriptural passages, and on account of (*Brahman*) resting on scripture (only).

. . .—our opponent will say—even the holy texts cannot make us understand what is contradictory. *Brahman*, you say, which is without parts undergoes a change, but not the entire *Brahman*. If *Brahman* is without parts, it does either not change at all or it changes in its entirety. If, on the other hand, it be said that it changes partly and persists partly, a break is effected in its nature, and from that it follows that it consists of parts. . . we reply, . . . that the (alleged) break in *Brahman's* nature is a mere figment of ignorance. By a break of that nature a thing is not really broken up into parts, not any more than the moon is really multiplied by appearing double to a person of defective vision. By that [appearance] of plurality which is the [product] of ignorance, which is characterised by name and form, which is evolved as well as non-evolved, which is not to be defined either as the existing or the non-existing, *Brahman* becomes the basis of this entire apparent world with its changes, and so on, while in its true and real nature it at the same time remains unchanged, lifted above the phenomenal universe. And as the distinction of names and forms, the [product] of ignorance, originates entirely from speech only, it does not militate against the fact of *Brahman* being without parts.—Nor have the scriptural passages which speak of *Brahman* as undergoing change the purpose of teaching the fact of change; for such instruction would have no fruit. They rather aim at imparting instruction about *Brahman's* Self as raised above this apparent world; that being an instruction which we know to have a result of its own. . . .

II.i.32. (*Brahman* is) not (the creator of the world), on account of (beings engaging in any action) having a motive.

Another objection is raised against the doctrine of an intelligent cause of the world.—The intelligent highest Self cannot be the creator of the sphere of this world, "on account of actions having a purpose."—We know from ordinary experience that man, who is an intelligent being, begins to act after due consideration only, and does not engage even in an unimportant undertaking unless it serves some purpose of his own; much less so in important business. There is also a scriptural passage confirming this result of common experience, "Verily everything is not dear that you may love everything; but that you may love the Self therefore everything is dear" (*Bṛ. Up.* II.iv.5). Now the undertaking of creating the sphere of this world, with all its various contents, is certainly a weighty one. If, then, on the one hand, you assume it to serve some purpose of the intelligent highest Self, you thereby sublate its self-sufficiency vouched for by scripture; if, on the other hand, you affirm absence of motive on its part, you must affirm absence of activity also.—Let us then assume that just as sometimes an intelligent person when in a state of frenzy proceeds, owing to his mental aberration, to action without a motive, so the highest Self also created this world without any motive.—That, we reply, would contradict the omniscience of the highest Self, which is vouched for by scripture.—Hence the doctrine of the creation proceeding from an intelligent Being is untenable.

II.i.33. But (*Brahman's* creative activity) is mere sport, such as we see in ordinary life.

The word "but" discards the objection raised.—We see in every-day life that certain doings of princes or other men of high position who have no unfulfilled desires left have no reference to any extraneous purpose, but proceed from mere sportfulness, as, for instance, their recreations in places of amusement. We further see that the process of inhalation and exhalation is going on without reference to any extraneous purpose, merely following the law of its own nature. Analogously, the activity of the Lord also may be supposed to be mere sport, proceeding from his own nature, without reference to any purpose. For on the ground neither of reason nor of scripture can we construe any other purpose of the Lord. Nor can his nature be questioned.—Although the creation of this world appears to us a weighty and difficult undertaking, it is mere play to the Lord, whose power is unlimited. And if in ordinary life we might possibly, by close scrutiny, detect some subtle motive, even for sportful action, we cannot do so with regard to the actions of the Lord, all whose wishes are fulfilled, as scripture says.—Nor can it be said that he either does not act or acts like a senseless person; for scripture affirms the fact of the creation on the one hand, and the Lord's omniscience on the other hand. And, finally, we must remember that the scriptural doctrine of creation does not refer to the highest reality; it refers to the apparent world only, which is characterised by name and form, the figments of ignorance, and it, moreover, aims at intimating that *Brahman* is the Self of everything.

II.i.34. Inequality (of dispensation) and cruelty (the Lord can) not (be reproached with), on account of his regarding (merit and demerit); for so (scripture) declares.

...The Lord...cannot be reproached with inequality of dispensation and cruelty, "because he is bound by regards." If the Lord on his own account, without any extraneous regards, produced this unequal creation, he would expose himself to blame; but the fact is, that in creating he is bound by certain regards, i.e., he has to look to merit and demerit. Hence the circumstance of the creation being unequal is due to the merit and demerit of the living creatures created, and is not a fault for which the Lord is to blame....

II.i.36. (The beginninglessness of the world) recommends itself to reason and is seen (from scripture).

The beginninglessness of the world recommends itself to reason. For if it had a beginning it would follow that, the world springing into existence without a cause, the released selves also would again enter into the circle of transmigratory existence; and further, as then there would exist no determining cause of the unequal dispensation of pleasure and pain, we should have to acquiesce in the doctrine of rewards and punishments being allotted, without reference to previous good or bad actions. That the Lord is not the cause of the inequality, has already been remarked. Nor can ignorance by itself be the cause, as it is of a uniform nature. On the other hand, ignorance may be the cause of inequality, if it be considered as having regard to merit accruing from action produced by the mental impressions of wrath, hatred, and other afflicting passions. Without merit and demerit nobody can enter into existence, and again, without a body merit and demerit cannot be formed; so that—on the doctrine of the world having a beginning—we are led into a logical see-saw. The opposite doctrine, on the other hand, explains all matters in a manner analogous to the case of the seed and sprout, so that no difficulty remains.

II.i.37. And because all qualities (required in the cause of the world) are present (in *Brahman*).

The teacher has now . . . established as the real sense of the Veda . . . that the intelligent *Brahman* is the cause and matter of this world . . . his view should be accepted . . . because, if that *Brahman* is acknowledged as the cause of the world, all attributes required in the cause (of the world) are seen to be present—*Brahman* being all-knowing, all-powerful, and possessing the great power of *māyā* [phenomenality or appearance].

II.ii.28. The non-existence (of the external things) cannot be maintained, on account of (our) consciousness of them.

. . . In every act of perception we are conscious of some external thing corresponding to the idea, whether it be a post or a wall or a piece of cloth or a jar, and that of which we are conscious cannot but exist.

II.ii.29. And on account of their difference of nature (the ideas of the waking state) are not like those of a dream.

. . . The things of which we are conscious in a dream are negated by our waking consciousness. . . . Those things, on the other hand, of which we are conscious in our waking state, such as posts and the like, are never negated in any state. . . .

II.ii.30. The existence (of mental impressions) is not possible (on the Bauddha view) on account of the absence of perception (of external things).

II.ii.31. And on account of the momentariness (of the *ālayavijñāna* [ideation store], it cannot be the abode of mental impressions).

II.ii.32. And on account of its general deficiency in probability.

No further special discussion is in fact required. From whatever new points of view the Bauddha system is tested with reference to its probability, it gives way on all sides, like the walls of a well dug in sandy soil. It has, in fact, no foundation whatever to rest upon, and hence the attempts to use it as a guide in the practical concerns of life are mere folly.—Moreover, Buddha by propounding the three mutually contradictory systems, teaching respectively the reality of the external world, the reality of ideas only, and general nothingness, has himself made it clear either that he was a man given to make incoherent assertions, or else that hatred of all beings induced him to propound absurd doctrines by accepting which they would become thoroughly confused.—So that—and this the *sūtra* means to indicate—Buddha's doctrine has to be entirely disregarded by all those who have a regard for their own happiness.

II.iii.16. But the designation (as being born and dying) abides in the (bodies of beings) moving and non-moving; it is secondary (metaphorical) if applied to the self, as the existence (of those terms) depends on the existence of that (i.e., the body).

II.iii.17. The (living) self [the individual self] is not (produced) as there is no scriptural statement, and as it is eternal according to them (i.e., scriptural passages).

II.iii.43. (The self is) a part of the Lord, on account of the declarations of difference....

We have shown that the individual self and the Lord stand to each other in the relation of what is being acted upon and what is acting upon....

...the self must be considered a part of the Lord, just as a spark is a part of the fire. By "part" we mean "a part as it were," since a being not composed of parts cannot have parts in the literal sense....

II.iii.46. (As the self is affected by pleasure and pain) not so the highest (Lord);...

...The pain of the individual self also is not real, but imaginary only, caused by the error consisting in the non-discrimination of (the Self from) the body, senses, and other limiting adjuncts which are due to name and form, the effects of ignorance.

II.iii.48. (The possibility of) injunctions and prohibitions (results) from the connexion (of the Self) with bodies;...

...Of what kind then is that connexion?—It consists in the origination in the Self of the erroneous notion that the Self is the aggregate consisting of the body and so on. This erroneous notion is seen to prevail in all living beings, and finds its expression in thoughts such as the following: "I go," "I come," "I am blind," "I am not blind," "I am confused," "I am not confused." That erroneous notion cannot be removed by anything but perfect knowledge, and before the latter supervenes, it remains spread among all living beings. And thus, although the Self must be admitted to be one only, injunctions and prohibitions are possible owing to the difference effected by its connexion with bodies and other limiting adjuncts, the products of ignorance.—It then follows that for him who has obtained perfect knowledge, injunctions and prohibitions are purportless.—No, we reply, (they are not purportless for him, but they do not refer to him), since to him who has obtained the highest aim no obligation can apply.

III.i.25. Should it be said that (sacrificial work is) unholy; we deny this on the ground of scripture.

...our knowledge of what is duty and the contrary of duty depends entirely on scripture. The knowledge of one action being right and another wrong is based on scripture only; for it lies out of the cognizance of the senses, and there moreover is, in the case of right and wrong, an entire want of binding rules as to place, time, and occasion. What in one place, at one time, on one occasion is performed as a right action, is a wrong action in another place, at another time, on another occasion; none therefore can know, without scripture, what is either right or wrong....

III.ii.14. ...(*Brahman*) is merely devoid of form, on account of this being the main purport of scripture.

III.ii.15. And as light (assumes forms as it were by its contact with things possessing form, so does *Brahman*); since (the texts ascribing form to *Brahman*) are not devoid of meaning.

Just as the light of the sun or the moon after having passed through space enters into contact with a finger or some other limiting adjunct, and, according as the latter is straight or bent, itself becomes straight or bent as it were; so *Brahman* also assumes, as it were, the form of the earth and the other limiting adjuncts with which it enters into connexion. Hence there is no reason why certain texts should not teach, with a view to meditative worship, that *Brahman* has [any particular] form. We thus escape the conclusion that those Vedic passages which ascribe form to *Brahman* are devoid of sense, a conclusion altogether unacceptable since all parts of the Veda are equally authoritative, and hence must all be assumed to have a meaning.

III.ii.18. For this very reason (there are applied to *Brahman*) comparisons such as that of the images of the sun and the like.

Because that Self is of the nature of intelligence, devoid of all difference, transcending speech and mind, to be described only by denying of it all other characteristics, therefore the Mokṣa-śāstras [treatises on liberation] compare it to the images of the sun reflected in the water and the like, meaning thereby that all difference in *Brahman* is unreal, only due to its limiting conditions. Compare, e.g., out of many, the two following passages: "As the one luminous sun when entering into relation to many different waters is himself rendered multiform by his limiting adjuncts; so also the one divine unborn Self"; and "The one Self of all beings separately abides in all the individual beings; hence it appears one and many at the same time, just as the one moon is multiplied by its reflections in the water."

III.ii.20. Since (the highest *Brahman*) is inside (of the limiting adjuncts), it participates in their increase and decrease; owing to the appropriateness (thus resulting) of the two (things compared) it is thus (i.e., the comparison holds good).

The parallel instance (of the sun's reflection in the water) is unobjectionable, since a common feature—with reference to which alone the comparison is instituted—does exist.[1] Whenever two things are compared, they are so only with reference to some particular point they have in common. Entire equality of the two can never be demonstrated; indeed if it could be demonstrated there would be an end of that particular relation which gives rise to the comparison. . . .

III.ii.21. And on account of the declaration (of scripture).

What then, it may be asked, is the meaning of those Vedic passages which speak of the highest *Brahman* as something to be seen, to be heard, and so on?—They aim, we reply, not at enjoining the knowledge of truth, but merely at directing our attention to it. . . . Even when a person is face to face with some object of knowledge, knowledge may either arise or not; all that another person wishing to inform him about the object can do is to point it out to him; . . . . True knowledge . . . which is produced by the means of true knowledge and is comformable to its object, can neither be brought about by hundreds of injunctions nor be checked by hundreds of prohibitions. For it does not depend on the will of man, but merely on what really and unalterably exists.—For this reason also injunctions of the knowledge of *Brahman* cannot be admitted.

III.ii.22. For (the clause "Not so, not so") denies (of *Brahman*) the suchness which forms the topic of discussion; . . .

We suppose, the *pūrvapakṣin* [objector] says, that the negative statement denies *Brahman* as well as its two forms [material and immaterial]; . . .

To this we make the following reply. It is impossible that the phrase, "Not so, not so!" should deny both, since that would imply the doctrine of a general Void. Whenever we deny something unreal, we do so with reference to something real; the unreal snake, e.g., is denied with reference to the real rope. But this (denial of something unreal with reference to something real) is possible only if some entity is left. If everything is denied, no entity is left, and, if no entity is left, the denial of some other entity which we may wish to undertake becomes impossible, i.e., that latter entity becomes real and as such cannot be denied. . . . The phrase that *Brahman* transcends all speed and thought does certainly not mean to say that *Brahman* does not exist; . . .

[1] That is, the dependence of the reflection on the sun.

. . . *Brahman* is that whose nature is permanent purity, intelligence, and freedom; it transcends speech and mind, does not fall within the category of "object," and constitutes the inward Self of all. Of this *Brahman* our text denies all plurality of forms; but *Brahman* itself it leaves untouched.

. . . the clause, "Not so, not so!" denies not absolutely everything, but only everything but *Brahman.*

III.ii.26. Hence (the self enters into unity) with the infinite (i.e., the highest Self); for this scripture indicates.

Hence i.e., because the non-difference of all selves is essential and their difference due to ignorance only, the individual self after having dispelled ignorance by true knowledge passes over into unity with the highest Self.

III.ii.38. From him (i.e., the Lord, there comes) the fruit (of works); for (that only) is possible.

. . . actions, on the other hand, which pass away as soon as done, have no power of bringing about results at some future time, since nothing can spring from nothing. . . . Nor, in the second place, have we the right to assume that the fruit will, at some future time, spring from the so-called supersensuous principle (*apūrva*),[1] which itself is supposed to be a direct result of the deed; for that so-called supersensuous principle is something of non-intelligent nature, comparable to a piece of wood or metal, and as such cannot act unless moved by some intelligent being.

III.iii.54. There is separation (of the Self from the body) because its existence does not depend on the existence of that (viz., the body), but there is not (non-separation); as in the case of perceptive consciousness.

. . . For if from the circumstance that they are where the body is you conclude that the qualities of the Self are qualities of the body, you also must conclude from the fact that they are not where the body is that they are not qualities of the body, because thereby they show themselves to be different in character from the qualities of the body. . . . The qualities of the body, again, such as form and so on, are perceived by others; not so the qualities of the Self, such as consciousness, remembrance, and so on . . . it is possible that even after this body has died the qualities of the Self should continue to exist by passing over into another body. The opposite opinion is thus precluded also for the reason of its being a mere hypothesis. . . . Should he [opponent] say that consciousness is the perception of the elements and what springs from the elements, we remark that in that case the elements and their products are objects of consciousness and that hence the latter cannot be a quality of them, as it is contradictory that anything should act on itself. Fire is hot indeed but does not burn itself . . . as we admit the existence of that perceptive consciousness which has the material elements and their products for its objects, we also must admit the separate-

[1] The force which in the Mīmāṁsā system brings about the future effects of actions.

ness of that consciousness from the elements. And as consciousness constitutes the character of our Self, the Self must be distinct from the body. That consciousness is permanent follows from the uniformity of its character (and we therefore may conclude that the conscious Self is permanent also, as also follows) from the fact that the Self, although connected with a different state, recognises itself as the conscious agent—a recognition expressed in judgments such as "I saw this,"—and from the fact of remembrance and so on being possible.

...Moreover, perceptive consciousness takes place where there are certain auxiliaries such as lamps and the like, and does not take place where those are absent, without its following therefrom that perception is an attribute of the lamp and the like. Analogously the fact that perception takes place where there is a body, and does not take place where there is none, does not imply that it is an attribute of the body....Nor is it even true that the body is absolutely required as an auxiliary of perception; for in the state of dream we have manifold perceptions while the body lies motionless....

III.iv.1. The purpose of man (is effected) thence (i.e., through the mere knowledge of *Brahman*),...

III.iv.26. And there is need of all (works), on account of the scriptural statement of sacrifices and the like;...

...knowledge has regard for all works enjoined on the *āśramas* [stages of life] and...there is not absolute non-regard.—But do not the two *sūtras* thus contradict each other?—By no means, we reply. Knowledge having once sprung up requires no help towards the accomplishment of its fruit, but it does stand in need of something else with a view to its own origination.

III.iv.27. But all the same he (who is desirous of knowledge) must be possessed of calmness, subjection of the senses, etc., since those (states) are enjoined as auxiliaries to that (viz., knowledge), and must (on that account) necessarily be accomplished.

III.iv.51. In this life also (the origination of knowledge takes place) if there is no obstruction of what is ready at hand, on account of this being seen (in scripture).

Beginning from *sūtra* 26 of the present *pāda* [chapter or section] we have discussed the various means of knowledge. We are now to consider whether knowledge—the fruit of those means—when accomplishing itself accomplishes itself only here in this life, or sometimes in the next life only.—The *pūrvapakṣin* maintains that it accomplishes itself here in this life only. For, he argues, knowledge has for its antecedent the learning of scripture and so on, and nobody applies himself to learning, &c., with the intention that knowledge should result therefrom in the next life only; we rather observe that men begin to learn with a view to knowledge already springing up in this life. And also sacrifices and the like produce knowledge only mediately through learning and so on; for knowledge can be produced (directly) through the means of right knowledge only. Hence the origination of knowledge takes place in this life only.—To this we reply, "The origination of knowledge takes place in this life if there is no obstruction of that which is ready at hand." That means: When the means of knowledge which is operative is not obstructed by some other work the results of which are just then reaching maturity, knowledge already reaches maturity in this life. But when such an obstruction takes place, then in the next life. And a work's reaching maturity depends on place, time, and operative cause presenting themselves. Nor is there any binding rule according to which the same time, place and operative cause which ripen one work should ripen another work also; for there are works the fruits of which are opposed to each other. And scripture also goes only so far as to teach what the fruit of each work is, without teaching the special conditions of place, time, and operative cause. And owing to the specific strength of the means employed the supersensuous power of one work manifests itself (i.e., the fruit of that work realizes itself), while that of another is obstructed thereby and comes to a standstill.

Nor is there any reason why a man should not form, with regard to knowledge, an unspecified intention; for we may freely form the intention that knowledge should spring up from us either in this life or in some subsequent life. And knowledge although springing up through the mediation of learning and so on, springs up only in so far as learning destroys the obstacles in the way of knowledge. Thus scripture also declares the difficulty of knowing the Self, "He of whom many are not even able to hear, whom many even when they hear of him do not comprehend; wonderful is a man when found who is able to teach him; wonderful is he who comprehends him when taught by an able teacher" (*Ka. Up.* I.ii.7).—Moreover scripture relates that Vāmadeva already became *Brahman* in his mother's womb, and thus shows that knowledge may spring up in a later form of existence through means procured in a former one; for a child in the womb cannot possibly procure such means in its present state.

The same is shown by *smṛti*. Vāsudeva being asked by Arjuna, "What will be the fate of him, O Kṛṣṇa, who has not reached perfection?" replies, "None who performs good works undergoes an evil fate"; declares thereupon that such a man reaches the world of the blessed and is, later on, born again in a good family; and finally states just what we at present maintain in the passage beginning, "There he obtains that knowledge which corresponds to his former bodily existence," and closing, "Perfected by many states of existence he then goes the highest way."—It therefore is an established conclusion that knowledge originates, either in the present or in a future life, in dependence on the evanescence of obstacles.

III.iv.52. No such definite rule (exists) as to the fruit which is release, on account of the assertions as to that condition, on account of the assertions as to that condition.

We have seen that in the case of persons desirous of release who rely upon the means of knowledge there exists a definite difference of result, in so far as the knowledge resulting springs up either in this life or a future life according to the degree of strength of the means employed. It might now be supposed that there exists a similar definite difference with regard to the fruit characterised as final release, owing to the superior or inferior qualification of the persons knowing.

With reference to this possible doubt the *sūtra* now says, "No such definite rule as to that fruit which is release." That means: We must not suppose that in the case of that fruit which is release there exists an analogous definite rule of difference.—Why?—"On account of the assertions (by scripture) about that condition." For all Vedānta-texts assert the state of final release to be of one kind only. The state of final release is nothing but *Brahman*, and *Brahman* cannot be connected with different forms since many scriptural passages assert it to have one nature only. Compare e.g., "It is neither coarse nor fine" (*Bṛ. Up.* III.viii.8); "That Self is to be described by No, no" (*Bṛ. Up.* III.ix.26); "Where one sees nothing else" (*Ch. Up.* VII.xxiv.1); "That immortal *Brahman* is before" (*Mu. Up.* II.ii.11); "This everything is that Self" (*Bṛ. Up.* II.iv.6); "This great unborn Self, undecaying, undying, immortal, fearless, is indeed *Brahman*" (*Bṛ. Up.* IV.iv.25); "When the Self only is all this how should he see another?" (*Bṛ. Up.* IV.v.15).—Moreover the means of knowledge might perhaps, according to their individual strength, impart a higher (or lower) degree to their result, viz., knowledge, but not to the result of knowledge, viz., release; for, as we have explained more than once, release is not something which is to be brought about, but something whose nature is permanently established, and is reached through knowledge. Nor does, in reality, knowledge admit of lower or higher degree; for it is, in its own nature, high only, and would not be knowledge at all if it were low. Although therefore knowledge may differ in so far as it originates after a long or short time, it is impossible that release should be distinguished by a higher or lower degree. And from the absence of difference of knowledge also there follows absence of definite distinction on the part of the result of knowledge (viz., release). The whole case is analogous to that of the results of works. In that knowledge which is the means of release there is no difference as there is between works. In those cognitions, on the other hand, which have the qualified *Brahman* for its object—such as "he who consists of mind, whose body is *prāṇa* [breath]"—a difference is possible according to the addition or omission of qualities, and hence there may be a definite distinction of results, just as there is between the results of actions. This is also indicated by the passage, "according as they meditate on him they become." But in meditations on *Brahman* devoid of qualities it is otherwise. Thus *smṛti* also says, "No higher road is possible for any one; for they speak of inequality only where there are qualities." —The repetition of the clause "on account of the assertions as to that condition" indicates the termination of the *Adhyāya* [Book].

IV.i.14. Of the other (i.e., good works) also there is, in the same way, non-clinging; but at death.

. . . Scripture . . . declares that good works are extinguished no less than evil ones, and the extinction of works which depends on the cognition of the Self not being an agent is the same in the case of good and of evil works, . . . As it is established that good as well as evil works—which are both causes of bondage—do, owing to the strength of knowledge, on the one hand not cling and on the other hand undergo destruction, there necessarily results final release of him who knows, as soon as death takes place.

IV.i.15. But only those former (works) whose effects have not yet begun (are destroyed by knowledge); because (scripture states) that (i.e., the death of the body) to be the term.

Those works, on the other hand, whose effects have begun and whose results have been half enjoyed—i.e., those very works to which there is due the present state of existence in which the knowledge of *Brahman* arises—are not destroyed by that knowledge.

IV.i.19. But having destroyed by fruition the two other (sets of work) he becomes one with *Brahman.*

It has been shown that all good and evil deeds whose effects have not yet begun are extinguished by the power of knowledge. "The two others," on the other hand, i.e., those good and evil works whose effects have begun, a man has at first to exhaust by the fruition of their consequences, and then he becomes one with *Brahman.* This appears from scriptural passages such as "For him there is delay so long as he is not delivered (from the body), then he will become one with *Brahman*" (*Ch. Up.* VI.xiv.2); and "Being *Brahman* he goes to *Brahman*" (*Bṛ. Up.* IV.iv.6).—But, an objection is raised, even when perfect intuition has risen the practical intuition of multiplicity may continue after the death of the body, just as it continued before death; analogously to the visual appearance of a double moon (which may continue even after it has been cognized as false).—Not so, we reply. After the death of the body there no longer exists any cause for such continuance; while up to death there is such a cause, viz., the extinction of the remainder of works to be enjoyed.—But a new aggregate of works will originate a new fruition!—Not so, we reply; since the seed of all such fruition is destroyed. What, on the death of the body, could originate a new period of fruition is only a new set of works, and works depend on false knowledge; but such false knowledge is completely destroyed by perfect intuition. When therefore the works whose effects have begun are destroyed, the man who knows necessarily enters into the state of perfect isolation.

IV.iv.22. (Of them) there is non-return, according to scripture; non-return, according to scripture.

It is a settled matter that those who through perfect knowledge have dispelled all mental darkness and are devoted to the eternally perfect *nirvāṇa* do not return. And as those also who rely on the knowledge of the qualified *Brahman* in the end have recourse to that (*nirvāṇa*), it follows that they also do not return.

B. THE QUALIFIED NON-DUALISM (VIŚIṢṬĀDVAITA) OF RĀMĀNUJA

I.i.1. Then therefore the enquiry into Brahman.

. . . we [*pūrvapakṣins* (objectors)] [1] sum up our view as follows.—Eternal, absolutely non-changing consciousness, whose nature is pure non-differenced intelligence, free from all distinction whatever, owing to error illusorily manifests itself . . . as broken up into manifold distinctions—knowing subjects, objects of knowledge, acts of knowledge. And the purpose for which we enter on the consideration of the Vedānta-texts is utterly to destroy what is the root of that error, i.e., ignorance, and thus to obtain a firm knowledge of the oneness of *Brahman*, whose nature is mere intelligence—free, pure, eternal.

The Great Siddhānta [True view]

This entire theory rests on a fictitious foundation of altogether hollow and vicious arguments, incapable of being stated in definite logical alternatives, . . . The theory therefore must needs be rejected by all those who, through texts, perception and the other means of knowledge—assisted by sound reasoning—have an insight into the true nature of things.

There is no proof of non-differenced substance

To enter into details.—Those who maintain the doctrine of a substance devoid of all difference have no right to assert that this or that is a proof of such a substance, for all means of right knowledge have for their object things affected with difference.—Should any one, taking his stand on the received views of his sect, assert that the theory of a substance free from all difference (does not require any further means of proof but) [2] is immediately established by one's own consciousness, we reply that he also is refuted by the fact, warranted by the witness of the Self, that all consciousness implies difference: all states of consciousness have for their object something that is marked by some difference, as appears in the case of judgments like "I saw this." And should a state of consciousness—although directly apprehended as implying difference—be determined by some fallacious reasoning to be devoid of difference, this determination could be effected only by means of some special attributes additional to the quality of mere Being; and, owing to these special qualities on which

[1] The *pūrvapakṣins* in this case are those who hold the Advaita Vedānta view of Śaṁkara.
[2] Parenthetical statements are those of the translator.

the determination depends, that state of consciousness would clearly again be characterised by difference. . . . To thought there at any rate belongs the quality of being thought and self-illuminatedness, for the knowing principle is observed to have for its essential nature the illumining (making to shine forth) of objects. . . . Moreover, you yourself admit that to consciousness there actually belong different attributes such as permanency (oneness, self-luminousness, &c.), and of these it cannot be shown that they are only Being in general. And even if the latter point were admitted, we observe that there takes place a discussion of different views, and you yourself attempt to prove your theory by means of the differences between those views and your own. It therefore must be admitted that reality is affected with difference well established by valid means of proof.

Speech (śabda) proves difference

As to sound (speech; *śabda*), it is specially apparent that it possesses the power of denoting only such things as are affected with difference. Speech operates with words and sentences. Now, a word originates from the combination of a radical element and a suffix, and as these two elements have different meanings it necessarily follows that the word itself can convey only a sense affected with difference. And further, the plurality of words is based on plurality of meanings; the sentence, therefore, which is an aggregate of words expresses some special combination of things (meanings of words), and hence has no power to denote a thing devoid of all difference.—The conclusion is that sound cannot be a means of knowledge for a thing devoid of all difference.

Perception (pratyakṣa) proves difference

Perception in the next place—with its two subdivisions of non-determinate and determinate perception—also cannot be a means of knowledge for things devoid of difference. Determinate perception clearly has for its object things affected with difference, for it relates to that which is distinguished by generic difference and so on. But also non-determinate perception has for its object only what is marked with difference, for it is on the basis of non-determinate perception that the object distinguished by generic character and so on is recognised in the act of determinate perception. . . .

View of simultaneous difference and non-difference (bhedābheda) is untenable

The same arguments tend to refute the view that there is difference and absence of difference at the same time (the so-called *bhedābheda* [difference-non-difference] view). Take the judgment "This is such and such"; how can we realise here the non-difference of "being this" and "being such and such"? The "such and such" denotes a peculiar make [structure] characterised, e.g., by a dewlap; the "this" denotes the thing distinguished by that peculiar make; the non-difference of these two is thus contradicted by immediate consciousness. . . .

Inference teaches difference

Perception thus having for its object only what is marked by difference, inference also is in the same case, for its object is only what is distinguished by connexion with things known through perception and other means of knowledge....

Perception does not reveal mere being

Moreover, if perception made us apprehend only pure Being, judgments clearly referring to different objects—such as "Here is a jar," "There is a piece of cloth"—would be devoid of all meaning. And if through perception we did not apprehend difference—as marked by generic character, &c., constituting the structure or make of a thing—why should a man searching for a horse not be satisfied with finding a buffalo?...

If all acts of cognition had one and the same object only, everything would be apprehended by one act of cognition; and from this it would follow that there are no persons either deaf or blind!

...Hence there is not any source of knowledge causing us to apprehend mere Being. If, moreover, the senses had for their object mere Being free from all difference, it would follow that scripture which has the same object would (not be originative of knowledge but) perform the function of a mere *anuvāda* [statement], i.e., it would merely make statements about something, the knowledge of which is already established by some other means. And further, according to your own doctrine, mere Being, i.e., *Brahman*, would hold the position of an object with regard to the instruments of knowledge; and thus there would cling to it all the imperfections indicated by yourself—non-intelligent nature, perishableness and so on.... we adhere to the conclusion that generic character is nothing but structure. By "structure" we understand special or distinctive form; and we acknowledge different forms of that kind according to the different classes of things....

Plurality is not unreal

Next as to the assertion that all difference presented in our cognition—as of jars, pieces of cloth and the like—is unreal because such difference does not persist. This view, we maintain, is altogether erroneous, springs, in fact, from the neglect of distinguishing between persistence and non-persistence, on the one hand, and the relation between what sublates and what is sublated, on the other hand. Where two cognitions are mutually contradictory, there the latter relation holds good, and there is non-persistence of what is sublated. But jars, pieces of cloth and the like, do not contradict one another, since they are separate in place and time. If on the other hand the non-existence of a thing is cognised at the same time and the same place where and when its existence is cognised, we have a mutual contradiction of two cognitions, and then the stronger one sublates the other cognition which thus comes to an end. But when, of a thing that is perceived in connexion with some place and time, the non-existence is perceived in connexion with some other place and time, there arises no contradiction; how, then, should the one cognition sublate the other? or how can it be said that of a thing absent at one time and place there is absence at other times and places also? In the case of the snake-rope,[1] there arises a cognition of non-existence in connexion with the given place and time; hence there is contradiction, one judgment sublates the other and the sublated cognition comes to an end. But the circumstance of something which is seen at one time and in one place not persisting at another time and in another place is not observed to be invariably accompanied by falsehood, and hence mere non-persistence of this kind does not constitute a reason for unreality. To say, on the one hand, that what is is real because it persists, is to prove what is proved already, and requires no further proof.

Being and consciousness are not one

Hence mere Being does not alone constitute reality. And as the distinction between consciousness and its objects—which rests just on this relation of object and that for which the object is—is proved by perception, the assertion that only consciousness has real existence is also disposed of....

Consciousness is the attribute of a permanent conscious self

...the essential character of consciousness or knowledge is that by its very existence it renders things capable of becoming objects, to its own substrate, of thought and speech. This consciousness...is a particular attribute belonging to a conscious self and related to an object; as such it is known to every one on the testimony of his own self—as appears from ordinary judgments such as "I know the jar," "I understand this matter," "I am conscious of (the presence of) this piece of cloth." That such is the essential character of consciousness you yourself admit; for you have proved thereby its self-luminousness. Of this consciousness which thus clearly presents itself as the attribute of an agent and as related to an object, it would be difficult indeed to prove that at the same time it is itself the agent; as difficult as it would be to prove that the object of action is the agent.

...we clearly see that this agent (the subject of consciousness) is permanent (constant), while its attribute, i.e., consciousness, not differing herein from joy, grief, and the like, rises, persists for some time, and then comes to an end. The permanency of the conscious subject is proved by the fact of recognition, "This very same thing was formerly apprehended by me." The non-permanency of consciousness, on the other hand, is proved by thought expressing itself in the following forms, "I know at

[1] This refers to the mistaking of the rope for a snake. This illustration is used to illustrate the one-sided dependence of the world on *Brahman* and not *vice versa*. The existence of the rope does not depend on the appearance of the snake but the appearance of the snake is dependent upon the rope. So, also, is the world dependent upon *Brahman*, but *Brahman* is not dependent upon the world. The changes in the world do not affect the integrity of *Brahman*.

present," "I knew at a time," "I, the knowing subject, no longer have knowledge of this thing." How, then, should consciousness and the conscious subject be one?...

View that the conscious subject is unreal is untenable

...if things were as you describe them, the conscious "I" would be cognised as co-ordinate with the state of consciousness "I am consciousness"; just as the shining thing presenting itself to our eyes is judged to be silver. But the fact is that the state of consciousness presents itself as something apart, constituting a distinguishing attribute of the I, just as the stick is an attribute of Devadatta who carries it. The judgment "I am conscious" reveals an "I" distinguished by consciousness; and to declare that it refers only to a state of consciousness—which is a mere attribute—is no better than to say that the judgment "Devadatta carries a stick" is about the stick only....

The conscious subject persists in the state of release

To maintain that the consciousness of the "I" does not persist in the state of final release is again altogether inappropriate. It, in fact, amounts to the doctrine—only expressed in somewhat different words—that final release is the annihilation of the self.[1] The "I" is not a mere attribute of the self so that even after its destruction the essential nature of the self might persist—as it persists on the cessation of ignorance; but it constitutes the very nature of the self. Such judgments as "I know," "Knowledge has arisen in me," show, on the other hand, that we are conscious of knowledge as a mere attribute of the self.—Moreover, a man who, suffering pain, mental or of other kind—whether such pain be real or due to error only—puts himself in relation to pain—"I am suffering pain"—naturally begins to reflect how he may once for all free himself from all these manifold afflictions and enjoy a state of untroubled ease; the desire of final release thus having arisen in him he at once sets to work to accomplish it. If, on the other hand, he were to realise that the effect of such activity would be the loss of personal existence, he surely would turn away as soon as somebody began to tell him about "release."...Nor must you maintain against this that even in the state of release there persists pure consciousness;...No sensible person exerts himself under the influence of the idea that after he himself has perished there will remain some entity termed "pure light"!—What constitutes the "inward" self thus is the "I," the knowing subject.

This "inward" self shines forth in the state of final release also as an "I," for it appears to itself. The general principle is that whatever being appears to itself appears as an "I"; both parties in the present dispute establish the existence of the transmigrating self on such appearance. On the contrary, whatever does not appear as an "I," does not appear to

[1] The word "self" has been substituted for "soul" denoting the individual embodied self throughout the remainder of the selection from Rāmānuja.

itself, as jars and the like. Now, the emancipated self does thus appear to itself, and therefore it appears as an "I." Nor does this appearance as an "I" imply in any way that the released self is subject to ignorance and implicated in the *saṁsāra* [cycle of existence]; for this would contradict the nature of final release, and, moreover, the consciousness of the "I" cannot be the cause of ignorance and so on. Ignorance is either ignorance as to essential nature, or the cognition of something under an aspect different from the real one (as when a person suffering from jaundice sees all things yellow), or cognition of what is altogether opposite in nature (as when mother of pearl is mistaken for silver). Now the "I" constitutes the essential nature of the self; how, then, can the consciousness of the "I," i.e., the consciousness of its own true nature, implicate the released self in ignorance, or, in the *saṁsāra*? The fact, rather, is that such consciousness destroys ignorance, and so on, because it is essentially opposed to them....

No scriptural texts teach a Brahman devoid of all difference

We now turn to the assertion that certain scriptural texts, as e.g., "Being only was this in the beginning," are meant to teach that there truly exists only one homogeneous substance, viz., intelligence free from all difference. —This we cannot allow....the passage "the higher knowledge is that by which the Indestructible is apprehended, etc." (*Mu. Up.* I.i.5) first denies of *Brahman* all the evil qualities connected with *prakṛti*, and then teaches that to it there belong eternity, all-pervadingness, subtilty, omnipresence, omniscience, imperishableness, creativeness with regard to all beings, and other auspicious qualities. Now, we maintain that also the text "True, knowledge, infinite is *Brahman*," does not prove a substance devoid of all difference,...Now whether we take the several terms, "true," "knowledge," "infinite," in their primary sense, i.e., as denoting qualities, or as denoting modes of being opposed to whatever is contrary to those qualities, in either case we must needs admit a plurality of causes for the application of those several terms to one thing....

You have further maintained the following view:—In the text, "one only without a second," the phrase "without a second" denies all duality on *Brahman's* part even in so far as qualities are concerned....What the phrase "without a second" really aims at intimating is that *Brahman* possesses manifold powers, and this it does by denying the existence of another ruling principle different from *Brahman*....If it were meant absolutely to deny all duality, it would deny also the eternity and other attributes of *Brahman*....the...passage "He who knows the bliss of that *Brahman* from whence all speech, together with the mind, turns away unable to reach it," hence must be taken as proclaiming with emphasis the infinite nature of *Brahman's* auspicious qualities....We thus conclude that all scriptural texts enjoin just the knowledge of *Brahman* for the sake of final release. This knowledge is, as we already know, of the nature of meditation, and what is to be meditated on is *Brahman* as possessing qualities....

We now turn to the numerous texts which, according to the view of our opponent, deny the existence of plurality.—"Where there is duality as it were" (*Bṛ. Up.* IV.v.15); "There is not any plurality here; from death to death goes he who sees here any plurality" (*Bṛ. Up.* IV.iv.19); "But when for him the Self alone has become all, by what means, and whom, should he see?" (*Bṛ. Up.* IV.v.15) &c.,—But what all these texts deny is only plurality in so far as contradicting that unity of the world which depends on its being in its entirety an effect of *Brahman*, and having *Brahman* for its inward ruling principle and its true Self. They do not, on the other hand, deny that plurality on *Brahman's* part which depends on its intention to become manifold—a plurality proved by the text "May I be many, may I grow forth" (*Ch. Up.* VI.ii.3). Nor can our opponent urge against this, that, owing to the denial of plurality contained in other passages, this last text refers to something not real; for it is an altogether laughable assertion that scripture should at first teach the doctrine, difficult to comprehend, that plurality as suggested by perception and other means of knowledge belongs to *Brahman* also, and should afterwards deny this very doctrine!

Nor do smṛti and Purāṇa teach such a doctrine

...texts teach that the highest *Brahman* is essentially free from all imperfection whatsoever, comprises within itself all auspicious qualities, and finds its pastime in originating, preserving, reabsorbing, pervading, and ruling the universe; that the entire complex of intelligent and non-intelligent beings (selves and matter) in all their different estates is real, and constitutes the form, i.e., the body of the highest *Brahman*, as appears from those passages which co-ordinate it with *Brahman* by means of terms such as body (*śarīra*), form (*rūpa*), body (*tanu*), part (*aṁśa*), power (*śakti*), manifestation of power (*vibhūti*), and so on;—that the selves which are a manifestation of *Brahman's* power exist in their own essential nature, and also, through their connexion with matter, in the form of embodied selves; —and that the embodied selves, being engrossed by ignorance in the form of good and evil works, do not recognise their essential nature, which is knowledge, but view themselves as having the character of material things.—The outcome of all this is that we have to cognise *Brahman* as carrying plurality within itself, and the world, which is the manifestation of his power, as something real.

The theory of ignorance cannot be proved

We now proceed to the consideration of ignorance.—According to the view of our opponent, this entire world, with all its endless distinctions of ruler, creatures ruled, and so on, is, owing to a certain defect, fictitiously super-imposed upon the non-differenced, self-luminous Reality; and what constitutes that defect is beginningless ignorance, which invests the Reality, gives rise to manifold illusions, and cannot be defined either as being or non-being. . . .

Now, this theory of ignorance is altogether untenable. In the first place we ask, "What is the substrate of this ignorance which gives rise to the great error of plurality of existence?" You cannot reply "the individual self," for the individual self itself exists in so far only as it is fictitiously imagined through ignorance. Nor can you say "*Brahman*," for *Brahman* is nothing but self-luminous intelligence, and hence contradictory in nature to ignorance, which is avowedly sublated by knowledge....

...If our opponent should argue that the knowledge of the falsity of whatever is other than *Brahman* is contradictory to non-knowledge, we ask whether this knowledge of the falsity of what is other than *Brahman* is contradictory to the non-knowledge of the true nature of *Brahman*, or to that non-knowledge which consists in the view of the reality of the apparent world. The former alternative is inadmissible; because the cognition of the falsity of what is other than *Brahman* has a different object (from the non-knowledge of *Brahman's* true nature) and therefore cannot be contradictory to it; for knowledge and non-knowledge are contradictory in so far only as they refer to one and the same object. And with regard to the latter alternative we point out that the knowledge of the falsity of the world is contradictory to the non-knowledge which consists in the view of the reality of the world; the former knowledge therefore sublates the latter non-knowledge only, while the non-knowledge of the true nature of *Brahman* is not touched by it....From all this it follows that *Brahman*, whose essential nature is knowledge, cannot be the substrate of ignorance: the theory, in fact, involves a flat contradiction....

Whether we view non-knowledge as a positive entity or as the antecedent non-existence of knowledge, in either case it comes out as what the word indicates, viz., non-knowledge. Non-knowledge means either absence of knowledge, or that which is other than knowledge, or that which is contradictory to knowledge; and in any of these cases we have to admit that non-knowledge presupposes the cognition of the nature of knowledge. Even though the cognition of the nature of darkness should not require the knowledge of the nature of light, yet when darkness is considered under the aspect of being contrary to light, this presupposes the cognition of light. And the non-knowledge held by you is never known in its own nature but merely as "non-knowledge," and it therefore presupposes the cognition of knowledge no less than our view does, according to which non-knowledge is simply the negation of knowledge....

The assertion, again, that non-knowledge as a positive entity is proved by inference, also is groundless. But the inference was actually set forth!—True; but it was set forth badly. For the reason you employed for proving *ajñāna* [non-knowledge] is a so-called contradictory one (i.e., it proves the contrary of what it is meant to prove), in so far as it proves what is not desired and what is different from *ajñāna* (for what it proves is that there is a certain knowledge, viz., that all knowledge resting on valid means of proof has non-knowledge for its antecedent). (And with regard to this knowledge, again, we must ask whether it also has non-knowledge for its antecedent.) If the reason (relied on in all this argumentation) does not prove, in this case also, the antecedent existence of positive non-knowledge, it is too general (and hence not to be trusted in any case). If, on the other hand, it does prove antecedent non-knowledge, then this latter non-knowledge stands in the way of the non-knowledge (which you try to prove by inference) being an object of consciousness, and thus the whole supposition of *ajñāna* as an entity becomes useless.

Scripture does not teach that release is due to knowledge of a non-qualified Brahman

Nor can we admit the assertion that scripture teaches the cessation of ignorance to spring only from the cognition of a *Brahman* devoid of all difference.... For the reason that *Brahman* is characterised by difference all Vedic texts declare that final release results from the cognition of a qualified *Brahman.* And that even those texts which describe *Brahman* by means of negations really aim at setting forth a *Brahman* possessing attributes, we have already shown above.

The meaning of "Tat tvam asi."

In texts, again, such as "Thou art that," the co-ordination of the constituent parts is not meant to convey the idea of the absolute unity of a non-differenced substance; on the contrary, the words "that" and "thou" denote a *Brahman* distinguished by difference. The word "that" refers to *Brahman* omniscient, etc., which had been introduced as the general topic of consideration in previous passages of the same section, such as "It thought, may I be many"; the word "thou," which stands in co-ordination to "that," conveys the idea of *Brahman* in so far as having for its body the individual selves connected with non-intelligent matter. This is in accordance with the general principle that co-ordination is meant to express one thing subsisting in a twofold form. If such doubleness of form (or character) were abandoned, there could be no difference of aspects giving rise to the application of different terms, and the entire principle of co-ordination would thus be given up.... If the text "Thou art that" were meant to express absolute oneness, it would, moreover, conflict with a previous statement in the same section, viz. "It thought, may I be many"; and, further, the promise (also made in the same section) that by the knowledge of one thing all things are to be known could not be considered as fulfilled. It, moreover, is not possible (while, however, it would result from the absolute oneness of "*tat*" and "*tvam*") that to *Brahman*, whose essential nature is knowledge, which is free from all imperfections, omniscient, comprising within itself all auspicious qualities, there should belong ignorance; and that it should be the substrate of all those defects and afflictions which spring from ignorance.... If... the text is understood to refer to *Brahman* as having the individual selves for its body, both words ("that" and "thou") keep their primary denotation; and, the text thus making a declaration about one substance distinguished by two aspects, the fundamental principle of "co-ordination" is preserved. On this interpretation the text further intimates that *Brahman*—free from all imperfection and comprising within itself all auspicious qualities—is the internal ruler of the individual selves and possesses lordly power. It moreover satisfies the demand of agreement with the teaching of the previous part of the section, and it also fulfils the promise as to all things being known through one thing, viz. in so far as *Brahman* having for its body all intelligent and non-intelligent beings in their gross state is the effect of *Brahman* having for its body the same things in their subtle state....

...the individual self also has *Brahman* for its Self, owing to the fact of *Brahman* having entered into it.—From all this it follows that the entire aggregate of things, intelligent and non-intelligent, has its Self in *Brahman* in so far as it constitutes *Brahman's* body. And as, thus, the whole world different from *Brahman* derives its substantial being only from constituting *Brahman's* body, any term denoting the world or something in it conveys a meaning which has its proper consummation in *Brahman* only: in other words all terms whatsoever denote *Brahman* in so far as distinguished by the different things which we associate with those terms on the basis of ordinary use of speech and etymology.—The text "that art thou" we therefore understand merely as a special expression of the truth already propounded in the clause "in that all this has its Self".

Ignorance cannot be terminated by the simple act of cognising Brahman as the Universal Self

The doctrine, again, that ignorance is put an end to by the cognition of *Brahman* being the Self of all can in no way be upheld, for as bondage is something real it cannot be put an end to by knowledge. How, we ask, can any one assert that bondage—which consists in the experience of pleasure and pain caused by the connexion of selves with bodies of various kind, a connexion springing from good or evil actions—is something false, unreal?...the cessation of such bondage is to be obtained only through the grace of the highest Self pleased by the devout meditation of the worshipper,...

I.ii.12. And on account of distinctive qualities.

...Those, however, who understand the Vedānta, teach as follows: There is a highest *Brahman* which is the sole cause of the entire universe, which is antagonistic to all evil, whose essential nature is infinite knowledge and blessedness, which comprises within itself numberless auspicious qualities of supreme excellence, which is different in nature from all other beings, and which constitutes the inner Self of all. Of this *Brahman*, the individual selves—whose true nature is unlimited knowledge, and whose only essential attribute is the intuition of the supreme Self—are modes, in so far, namely, as they constitute its body. The true nature of these selves is, however, obscured by ignorance, i.e., the influence of the beginningless chain of works; and by release then we have to understand that intuition of the highest Self, which is the natural state of the individual selves, and which follows on the destruction of ignorance....

II.ii.3. And because from the independence (of the *pradhāna*) there would follow the non-existence of what is different (from creation, i.e., of the *pralaya* [dissolution or destruction] condition).

. . . The divine Supreme Person, all whose wishes are eternally fulfilled, who is all-knowing and the ruler of all, whose every purpose is immediately realised, having engaged in sport befitting his might and greatness and having settled that work is of a two-fold nature, such and such works being good and such and such being evil, and having bestowed on all individual selves bodies and sense-organs capacitating them for entering on such work and the power of ruling those bodies and organs, and having himself entered into those selves as their inner self, abides within them, controlling them as an animating and cheering principle. The selves, on their side, endowed with all the powers imparted to them by the Lord and with bodies and organs bestowed by him, and forming abodes in which he dwells, apply themselves on their own part, and in accordance with their own wishes, to works either good or evil. The Lord, then, recognising him who performs good actions as one who obeys his commands, blesses him with piety, riches, worldly pleasures, and final release; while him who transgresses his commands he causes to experience the opposites of all these. There is thus no room whatever for objections founded on deficiency, on the Lord's part, of independence in his dealings with men, and the like. Nor can he be arraigned with being pitiless or merciless. For by pity we understand the inability, on somebody's part, to bear the pain of others, coupled with a disregard of his own advantage. When pity has the effect of bringing about the transgression of law on the part of the pitying person, it is in no way to his credit; it rather implies the charge of unmanliness (weakness), and it is creditable to control and subdue it. For otherwise it would follow that to subdue and chastise one's enemies is something to be blamed. What the Lord himself aims at is ever to increase happiness to the highest degree, and to this end it is instrumental that he should reprove and reject the infinite and intolerable mass of sins which accumulates in the course of beginning and endless aeons, and thus check the tendency on the part of individual beings to transgress his laws. . . .

II.iii.18. Not the Self, on account of scriptural statement, and on account of the eternity (which results) from them.

The *sūtras* so far have stated that this entire world, from ether downwards, originates from the highest *Brahman*. It now becomes a matter for discussion whether the individual self also originates in the same way or not.—It does so originate, the *pūrvapakṣin* maintains. For on this assumption only the scriptural statement as to the cognition of all things through the cognition of one thing holds good, and moreover scripture declares that before creation everything was one. . . .

. . . To this the *sūtra* replies, "Not the Self, on account of scriptural statement." The Self is not produced, since certain texts directly deny its origination; cp. "the intelligent one is not born nor does he die" (*Ka. Up.*

I.ii.18); "There are two unborn ones, one intelligent and strong, the other non-intelligent and weak" (*Śvet. Up.* I.9). And the eternity of the self is learned from the same texts, cp. "There is one eternal thinker," &c. (*Ka. Up.* II.v.13); "Unborn, eternal, everlasting is that ancient one; he is not killed though the body is killed" (*Ka. Up.* I.ii.18).—For these reasons the self is not produced.

But how then about the declaration that through the cognition of one thing everything is known?—There is no difficulty here, since the self also is an effect, and since effect and cause are non-different.—But this implies that the self is an originated thing just like ether and so on!—Not so, we reply. By a thing being an effect we mean its being due to a substance passing over into some other state; and from this point of view the self also is an effect. There is, however, the difference, that the "other condition" which is represented by the self is of a different kind from that which constitutes non-sentient things, such as ether and so on. The "otherness" on which the self depends consists in the contraction and expansion of intelligence; while the change on which the origination of ether and so on depends is a change of essential nature. And change of the latter kind is what we deny of the self. We have shown that there are three entities of distinct nature, viz., objects of fruition, enjoying subjects, and a ruler; that origination and so on which are characteristic of the objects do not belong to the subjects, and that the latter are eternal; that the characteristic qualities of the objects and likewise those of the subjects —viz., liability to pain and suffering—do not belong to the ruler; that the latter is eternal, free from all imperfections, omniscient, immediately realising all his purposes, the Lord of the lords of the organs, the highest Lord of all; and that sentient and non-sentient beings in all their states constitute the body of the Lord while he constitutes their Self. While *Brahman* thus has for its modes. . . the sentient and non-sentient beings in which it ever is embodied, during certain periods those beings abide in so subtle a condition as to be incapable of receiving designations different from that of *Brahman* itself; *Brahman* then is said to be in its causal state. When, on the other hand, its body is constituted by all those beings in their gross state, when they have separate, distinct names and forms, *Brahman* is said to be in its effected condition. When, now, *Brahman* passes over from the causal state into the effected state, the aggregate of non-sentient things which in the causal state were destitute of name and form undergoes an essential change of nature—implying the possession of distinct names and so on—so as to become fit to constitute objects of fruition for sentient beings; the change, on the other hand, which the sentient beings (the selves) undergo on that occasion is nothing more than a certain expansion of intelligence (or consciousness), capacitating them to experience the different rewards or punishments for their previous deeds. The ruling element of the world, i.e., the Lord, finally, who has the sentient and non-sentient beings for his modes, undergoes a change in so far as he is, at alternating periods, embodied in all those beings in their alternating states. The two modes, and he to whom the modes belong, thus undergo a common change in so far as in the case of all of them the causal condition passes over into a different condition.

II.iii.45. But as in the case of light and so on. Not so is the highest.

. . . The individual self is a part of the highest Self; as the light issuing from a luminous thing such as fire or the sun is a part of that body; or as the generic characteristics of a cow or horse, and the white or black colour of things so coloured, are attributes and hence parts of the things in which those attributes inhere; or as the body is a part of an embodied being. For by a part we understand that which constitutes one place (*deśa*) of some thing, and hence a distinguishing attribute (*viśeṣaṇa*) is a part of the thing distinguished by that attribute. Hence those analysing a thing of that kind discriminate between the distinguishing element or part of it, and the distinguished element or part. Now, although the distinguishing attribute and the thing distinguished thereby stand to each other in the relation of part and whole, yet we observe them to differ in essential character. Hence there is no contradiction between the individual and the highest Self—the former of which is a distinguishing attribute of the latter—standing to each other in the relation of part and whole, and their being at the same time of essentially different nature. This the *sūtra* declares "not so is the highest," i.e., the highest Self is not of the same nature as the individual self. For as the luminous body is of a nature different from that of its light, thus the highest Self differs from the individual self which is a part of it. It is this difference of character—due to the individual self being the distinguishing element and the highest Self being the substance distinguished thereby—to which all those texts refer which declare difference. Those texts, on the other hand, which declare non-difference are based on the circumstance that attributes which are incapable of separate existence are ultimately bound to the substance which they distinguish, and hence are fundamentally valid. . . .

C. MADHVA'S DUALISM

I.i.1. Then therefore enquiry into *Brahman*.

And in the *Bhāgavata Tantra* eligibility is thus described—"The eligible persons are in fact of three classes, the lowest, . . . the middling, . . . and the highest. . . . He is said to belong to the lowest class who with devotion to the highest Lord has studied the Vedas; he is of the middling class who markedly unites unto these the qualifications of tranquillity, &c.; and he is accounted to be of the highest class who, in addition, realises the futility and the perishable character of all things from the four-faced Brahmā[1] down to the clump of grass, and who, thus rising above desires, resigns himself to the feet of the Lord Viṣṇu, and in Him sees all his works secure. . . .

[1] The figure of Brahmā is usually represented as having four faces corresponding to the four directions.

. . . the term *Brahman* primarily denotes Viṣṇu only: for there are Vedic passages which run thus: "He who abiding in the sea is but just known by the wise, who transcends comprehension, who is eternal, who holds sway over all beings, from whom the Great Mother of the world issued forth, and by whom the selves[1] are brought into the world of life bound up with their actions, and imprisoned in the five elements."—And after this, "He is the embodiment of pure wisdom; He is consciously active, and is, according to the wise, the one Lord of the world." [*Mahānārāyaṇa Upaniṣad* 1.] From the subsequent statement (We know Nārāyaṇa, we contemplate Vāsudeva), and therefore, may Viṣṇu impel us (towards good).[2] [*Mn. Up.*] It is evident that Viṣṇu is referred to in the previous passage. . . .

. . . all the Vedas declare Him alone. "In the Vedas, in the *Rāmāyaṇa*, in the Purāṇas and in the *Mahābhārata*, in the beginning, in the middle and at the end, yea everywhere, Viṣṇu is sung." . . .

I.i.4. Only that (*Brahman* only) is the subject of all scripture because it is primarily connected with [i.e., conveyed by] (all the texts in their comprehensive sense if properly construed).

"Scripture enjoins duties as My worship, uses Indra and all other names as My appellations, the texts that prescribe, as well as those that prohibit acts, point to Me; so, of such statements, none other than Myself can understand the true meaning." . . .

I.i.5. Since it is the object of seeing, i.e., knowing, it is not what cannot be spoken of.

. . . The statement that *Brahman* is indescribable, etc., however, proceeds from the absence of thorough comprehension of *Brahman*. "The wise see the form of (Mount) Meru and still do not see it (for they cannot see all over, in and out). (Similarly) it (*Brahman*) cannot be described, reasoned out, and known (entirely as such and such). So the *Garuḍa Purāṇa* says, 'For want of thorough comprehension, *Brahman* though declared by the whole body of scripture and capable of being known and inferred by reasoning, is said to be beyond the reach of words, reasoning and knowledge.'" . . .

I.i.6. If it (that which is spoken of) is said to be the *saguṇa* (qualified) *Brahman*, we deny that, on account of the word *Ātman* (used in the text to denote the cause of the world).

It is not proper to hold that it is the qualified *Brahman* that is spoken of as capable of being seen and described, and not the *nirguṇa* (unqualified); for the word *Ātman* [Self] used to denote the Lord (precludes this view). The *Vāmana Purāṇa* says, "He is called *Ātman* who is unassailed by the three qualities[3] of matter and unapproached by faults, with regard to

[1] Throughout this section "self" meaning the embodied self is substituted for *jīva*.

[2] Parenthetical statements are those of the translator.

[3] Throughout this section "qualities" is substituted for "*guṇas*."

whom the complex notion of abandoning and seeking together is incompatible; and, on the other hand, in the opinion of the wise, he is *anātman* who is of the opposite character. . . .

I.i.7. Because it is taught that he obtains final release who is devoted to it, (*Brahman* is referred to by the word *Ātman*).

Indeed release cannot be obtained by him who is devoted to the *saguṇa* (qualified) (*Brahman*). For in the *Bṛhadāraṇyaka Upaniṣad*, "release is obtained by him who is devoted to *Ātman*." . . .

Brahman and others are called selves, and *Ātman* is but one who is Janārdana (the saviour). In the case of others, the word *Ātman* is used only in a secondary sense. By means of the direct realisation of that *Ātman*, it is said, release is obtained. The others (selves) are bound up with qualities, it is said, and their knowledge does not lead to release. For the highest and perfect Lord is Viṣṇu. Hence the sages say that release comes through His grace.

I.i.8. And because of the absence of any statement to the effect that it is a thing to be set aside or abandoned.

The *Atharvaṇa Upaniṣad* says, "Know that Him only, the one *Ātman* only, as the (supreme) one; abandon other words; He is the bridge of immortality." [II.ii.5] and from this injunction not to discard Him, *Ātman* is not the *saguṇa* (qualified) (*Brahman*).

I.i.9. On account of His merging into Himself.

. . . The glorious Lord, who is superior to and different from the persons of the world, and not limited by the three qualities, shows himself as many, and again the Lord untouchable by any defect, the first cause, becomes one again and goes to rest. Thus there is the scriptural declaration of His (*Ātman's*) withdrawing Himself into Himself. For it cannot be that the pure Lord merges into the *Ātman* bound down with qualities. . . .

I.i.11. And because (it is so) declared in scripture.

"He is the one supreme and illustrious Lord, who is imperceptibly present in every being, who is all-pervading who actuates all beings from within, who is the master of all action, who is essentially intelligence and who is unmixed with matter, and untouched by qualities." [*Śvet. Up.* VI.11.] For what cannot be conveyed by words cannot be declared by the *śruti* [authoritative texts]; and it is not fit to assume what is not established by authority; for it is not possible that words indicate anything which is not named (denoted directly) by any word. . . .

I.i.15. And (because) that only (i.e., *Brahman* only) which is (distinctly) described by the *Mantrovarṇa* (the Vedic text) is sung as *annamaya* [food], etc.).

. . . in the term *annarasamaya* (He who is the perfect essence of good), the word "*rasa*" used to distinguish food, etc., (from ordinary food, etc.,) shows that only the pure spiritual essence of *Brahman* is meant, which is present in all the various things....

I.i.16. (*Ānandamaya* is) not any other, on account of impossibility.

For through the knowledge of any other, release is impossible; and in support of it, *śruti* has been quoted, that is, "Whoever thus knows Him becomes immortal. There is no other path that leads unto Him" [*Taitt. Ār.* III.xii.7].

I.i.17. And on account of the declaration of difference.

(Of the two, *ānandamaya* cannot be the self.)

For, "a hundred times the bliss of Prajāpati (is the unit of *Brahman's* bliss)." "He who fearlessly takes his stand on Him who is beyond comprehension, independent, not fully explained, unsupported by other things, —he (the votary) attains to the fearless (state). And He who is in the self" [*Taitt. Up.* II.7–8]. These and other texts draw distinction (between the Lord, [i.e.,] *ānandamaya*, and the limited self); nor is there any conflict here with the texts, "That thou art," [*Ch. Up.* VI.8], "I am *Brahman*," [*Bṛ. Up.* I.iv.10]....Again, the *Bhāgavata* has [that] knowledge is the understanding of the separateness (from the self) of the Lord, and by the perception of separateness, by intense devotion and by duties performed irrespective of fruits, (the votary rejoices in heaven). "When the self sees the Lord worshipped by the gods as different from the selves and perceives His unlimited glory, he becomes liberated from miseries." [*Ath. Up.* III.i.2.] "He who is not all, is as if He were all, He who is indeed the inner guide appears as if he were no guide (guided), He who is the inward ruler appears as if He were the outward one (the ruled), He who is known as one and many,—He is the *Puruṣa* dwelling in all bodies; He is the Lord of all powers; He is *Brahman*. Viṣṇu who rules all from within is named all, and said to be all; He is denoted by all names (words) as 'that,' 'I,' 'thou,' 'He,' etc., but not as being essentially identical with all."...

[*Bṛ. Up.* IV. iv. 6]

I.ii.3. ...the (all-pervading) one is not the embodied self, as it is quite impossible (to predicate omnipresence of him).

(That is,) it is impossible and against fact and reason that one and the same self could be in all the bodies (at the same time).

I.ii.5. On account of the emphatic use of the word (*Brahman*) and of the particle of emphasis being used to restrict the word (*Brahman*).

I.ii.8. (Then) if it be said that (the two) should equally partake (of the experiences), it is denied on account of the difference.

(That is,) if the two, the self and the Supreme Lord, being in the same body should be supposed to undergo equally the experiences (of that body), the view is refuted on the ground that their power differs. This is also said in the *Garuḍa Purāṇa*, "There is no equality in experience between the Lord and the self; for the Lord is all-knowing, all-powerful, and absolute; while the self is of little understanding, of little power and absolutely dependent," and so on....

I.ii.11. The two who have entered into the cave, are indeed both *Ātman* (the Lord), from this very well-known characteristic, and from scripture to that effect.

The two in the cave (heart) that are drinking (the essence of bliss) are only the two forms of Viṣṇu....This dwelling in the cavity of the heart is a well-known attribute of Viṣṇu (*Brahman*) in such texts as "He who knows that *Brahman* as present in the cave of the heart," [*Taitt. Up.* II.1]....

I.ii.12. And on account of the distinguishing attributes.

...The excellent qualities of the Lord cannot be one by one described; for they are (verily) innumerable. Hence He is called *Brahman*, which means absolutely perfect, so that all His qualities may be (at least) collectively denoted. And for this reason, this word *Brahman* (is invariably used to denote Viṣṇu as distinguished from other deities). For except the supreme Lord, none are of infinite qualities (*Brāhma Purāṇa*)....

...From these references and arguments (it would appear), the distinction (between the Lord and the self) is not unreal....

I.ii.22. And from the distinctive attributes and the statement of difference, the other two (are not described by the attributes of being invisible, etc.).

Prakṛti [Nature] of lifeless character is called the lower *akṣara* [imperishable]. The spiritual *prakṛti* dependent upon Viṣṇu is called the higher *prakṛti* or *Śrī* whom they call higher *akṣara*; and consequently they call Hari perfect in excellences, the (Imperishable) *akṣara* higher than the higher; thus three *akṣaras* (imperishable entities) are spoken of. From this explanation found in the *Skānda Purana*, of the three *akṣaras*, "The one higher than the higher *akṣara*" is indeed a distinguishing attribute (of *Brahman*). And from the text, "He is rid of misery who sees Īśa [the Lord] to be the other (than the self), worshipped by the gods, and contemplates His glory" [*Ath. Up.* III.i.2], the express mention of separateness by the word *anya* ("other"), precludes taking the internal ruler to be Rudra, though suggested by (the use of) the word "Īśa."

I.ii.26. If it be objected that (Vaiśvānara) is not *Brahman* on account of the word (scriptural passages) dedicated to Agni, etc. and other (characteristics of Agni), and from reference to the function of the one abiding within; (we reply the objection) is not valid on account of the teaching that *Brahman* is to be contemplated as such, and on account of the impossibility (of finding in Agni the attributes declared in the beginning of the scriptural passages); and also for the reason that some *śākhins* [followers] read of Him (Vaiśvānara) as (the Person of the description given in the Puruṣa Sūkta) [*Ṛg Veda* x.90].

Not being accepted as perfect and falling short of perfection in attributes of excellence, all others (gods) are considered non-*Brahman*, and Viṣṇu only is *Brahman*, the Lord. . . . these attributes and acts cannot be predicated of others, and so Viṣṇu alone is Vaiśvānara.

I.iii.1. The abode (support) of heaven, etc., (is *Brahman* only), from (the use of) the word *Ātman* which is restricted to Viṣṇu alone.

I.iii.4. Nor [is the abode of heaven] the self; (nor *prāṇa* the chief [of breaths]).

I.iii.5. From the declaration of difference.

The view of absolute identity cannot be taken; for the text, "He who sees the Lord worshipped by the gods as different from himself and understands His glory," declares the difference (between the self worshipping and the Lord worshipped).

I.iii.6. From the context (i.e., the subject matter of the passages being *Brahman*).

For the passage has for its subject *Paramātman* [Supreme Self], whose knowledge is to be acquired by the higher study spoken of in the passage beginning with "There are two kinds of study to be known, etc." [*Ath. Up.* I.i.4].

I.iii.7. And (also) on account of the two conditions of standing, [namely,] being present and eating (described).

In the text, "(The two like unto two birds, which are inseparably connected and live together, embrace the same tree; of these one eats the insipid fruit as sweet; the other without eating shines all round)." Thus the Lord is said to stand (to be merely present) shining; while the self is subject to the experience of the consequences of his works: (thereby the difference between the Lord and the self is declared). . . .

I.iii.13. (The *Sat* [Being]) is only He (Viṣṇu), the act of seeing being predicated of it, (for the purpose of creation).

In the text, "He saw that," etc., the act of seeing (as well as the authorship of creation being predicated of *Sat*, by *Sat* Viṣṇu only is meant (but not the lifeless matter). And this characteristic belongs to Him alone as supported by the following text; "There is none seeing absolutely other than He" [*Bṛ. Up.* III.vii.23]; there is none other than that that can see [*Bṛ. Up.* III.viii.11].

I.iii.18. If it be said that from the reference to the other, it is the self (that is in the lotus of the heart), we say "no," on account of the impossibility (absence of the attributes in him).

I.iii.19. But if it be again said that it is the self which is in the subtle ether, from the subsequent passage showing the attribute of being "free from sin" possible in the self, we say "no," for (the subject of the subsequent passage) is the released (self), (the self whose essential nature has been delivered from mundane bondage).

From the subsequent text, "There he goes about, eating, sporting, rejoicing," [*Ch. Up.* VIII.xii.3] the self only is, it appears, fit to be taken (as referred to); but it cannot be done, for even there, the released (self) who has attained to his essential state as pure spirit, through the grace of the supreme Lord, is declared....

I.iv.25. And (*prakṛti* is *Brahman* only) on account of His (divine) will being called (*prakṛti* or of His being spoken of as Will, i.e., *prakṛti*).

"Let him know the Lord's will to be *prakṛti* and the supreme Lord to be the master of the Will." [*Ṛg Veda* V.iv.10] O Eternal One, Thy will is variously designated as *mahāmāyā* [great power], *avidyā* [ignorance], the decree, or *mohinī*, that which stupifies, *prakṛti* and *vāsanā* [great desire]." According to this statement, it is only the will of the Lord that is spoken of as *prakṛti*....

I.iv.26. And because He (Viṣṇu) is directly spoken of as both (*prakṛti* and *puruṣa* [self]).

"He is woman; He is man; He is *prakṛti*; He is the Lord (*puruṣa*); He is *Brahman*; He is the support; He is the light, who is the Lord Hari, the cause of all; Himself without beginning or end, but the end of all; the highest of the high; the original present in all."...

I.iv.27. (*Prakṛti* is *Brahman* only) also for the reason that He moulds forms out of (*prakṛti*, the material cause), in which He (also) exhibits Himself in various forms (ways), and makes (everything).

I.iv.28. And because *Brahman* is called the Source.

The state of being *prakṛti* consists in being the immediate means of bringing forth; and this is indeed declared only of Him, as in the text, "Whom the wise clearly find to be the immediate source of beings."...

II.i.12. If it be said that as there is no limit to controversial reasoning, something to the contrary may always be inferred, we say "no," for even if that be (adopted), absence of final release would have to be admitted.

"So far only reasoning goes and no farther." No such limit can be assigned to reasoning by any authority; consequently when one position is advanced, it is possible to make inferences to the contrary also.

But this view cannot be held. For, if that should be true, the release which is a fact made known by settled authorities, the contrary being possible to be inferred, would come to be given up as impossible. Wherefore things are facts as authorities prove, and nothing else (should be surmised). So it is said in the *Vāmana Purāṇa* "Whatever is settled to be true by authorities is to be accepted as such and not to be abandoned. For in the absence of authority (settled means of proof) it would be impossible to prove or disprove anything...."

II.i.14. If it be said that on account of the statement that (on release) the self, the subject of the experiences of mundane life, becomes one with the Supreme Being, there is absolute identity, we deny it; for (the statement bears an explanation) according to the usage of the world.

In the text, "The works and the intelligent self all become one in the immutable Supreme Lord" [*Ath. Up.* III.ii.7], the emancipated self is said to become the Supreme Being. Hence the absolute identity of the two (is established). Wherefore it may be understood to be even before emancipation, (i.e., in the embodied state) the self is the same Lord, for it would not do to accept that one essentially different might become identical with another. This view we refute; for the non-distinction spoken of in the text may arise as in other cases under observation. For instance, there is actually distinction in details though the world may speak of a certain quantity of water becoming one with another quantity; so is it here too. Accordingly the *śruti* says, "Just as pure water poured on to (another quality of) pure water, becomes only such (water)" [*Ka. Up.* IV.15].... "Even so the self too, though said to be in a state of non-distinction from *Brahman*, does not, however, become absolutely the Lord Himself; for there exist the attributes of absolute independence, wisdom, etc., which differentiate *Brahman* from the self." And, "O Hari, thou art of that pure essence and character to which it is not possible for Brahmā, and Rudra and other gods to attain." "Lord, they do not make approaches to Thy glory." [*Ṛg Veda* VII.99.1] "O Viṣṇu, no one that was, is or will be, etc." [*Ṛg Veda* VII.99.2]...

II.i.18. If it be said that (before creation) there was nothing (none of the means) on account of the statement of absolute non-existence of all things other than *Brahman*, we say "no"; for other things are so spoken of with reference to certain attributes (in certain aspects), (as may be seen) from the complementary sentences.

In the text, "Nor was there *asat* (the non-existent)" [*Ṛg Veda* x.129.1], the non-existence of everything being declared, other things, it may be stated, absolutely had no existence (before creation). But this view cannot be held: for the whole body of other things is spoken of as *asat* or non-existent on account of some particular attributes (in certain aspects), viz., the state of being not manifest, of being absolutely dependent, etc.,"... "Without beginning or end (through eternity) this world has continued to exist as such. There is nothing here to be questioned. In no place or time was this world ever observed otherwise by anybody in the past, nor will it be, in the future." "They say that the world is unreal, baseless, without a Lord." [*Gītā* XVI.8.] The ignorant say that the world is unreal, for they are really ignorant of the supreme power of Hari the Lord, who, boundless in wisdom, having created such a world of real existence, has become the author of real work. Therefore they call Him the author of real work, because He indeed creates this world a perfect reality. And also they call Him the Maker of things eternal, for He always makes things eternal. "The world which thou hast made is real indeed, for it is not empty." [*Ṛg Veda* x.55.6] From such *śrutis* and *smṛtis* [traditional texts], it is clear that besides *Brahman* there were other things in the beginning.

"If there appears a conflict between (different) statements (of *śruti*), the understanding of the subject should be guided in the light of the judgment conveyed by that statement which is consistent with reason. But no reasoning independent of Testimony of the Word is admissible" (*Bṛhat-Saṁhitā*). Further on it says, "Where Vedic passages mutually appear conflicting, there the meaning should be sought out on the strength of the collated evidence and accurate direct perception."

. . . When contradictory statements occur in the Vedas and in the works that follow in the footsteps of the Vedas, one of them must be interpreted differently from what it may seem to convey, so as to reconcile it with the statement (or statements) of which the meaning is otherwise determined. . . .

II.i.29. And in the Lord only find place such (inconceivably) vast and various wonderful (powers).

Only the Supreme Lord and no other (not the self) has such extraordinary and inconceivable powers (which make what is impossible elsewhere possible in Him). This is clearly declared in the following texts. "The eternal Lord is possessed of wonderful powers; and like powers cannot be found in others." . . .

II.ii.28. The non-existence (of external things, i.e., of the world) cannot be maintained, on account of our being conscious of them.

Further it cannot be said that the world itself is non-being, or non-being itself the world, for it is actually perceived (as entity), being the object of accurate knowledge (as existing).

II.ii.29. And on account of the difference of characteristics (the world is not non-existent), as those of dreams, etc., are.

And it cannot be said that as the creatures of a dream, etc., (are), the world too, though an object of perception, is non-entity; for, unlike the world, the creations of a dream, etc., are objects of a widely different perception thus: "This is a mere dream, this is not the serpent," and so on. And there is no such authority here (as would prove non-existence of the world).

II.ii.30. The world is not *vijñāna* (consciousness or thought), for it is not so perceived.

The world is not a mere mode of the mind; for nobody has perceived it to be such in his experience.

II.ii.31. And because of its (of consciousness) momentary duration.

Vijñāna or consciousness is only of a moment's duration, whereas the objects have been shown to be (and are) permanent. Hence, too, the mind and the world outside cannot be said to be identical.

II.ii.32. And because of the absence of, and of the conflict with, reason and all authorities, in every position (the systems opposed to *śruti* are to be rejected).

II.iii.18. The Intelligent Being (the self too) is indeed born from the Supreme Lord only, (as seen from . . . the same scriptural passage).

II.iii.19. And also on account of the possibility (of considering the self as having a birth).

Though the self is eternal, still it is possible to speak of him as being born, with reference to the (embodied) condition (to which he is subjected). . . .

II.iii.23. And (the text declaring pervasion refers to *Brahman*, not to the self) on account of the term belonging to Himself (directly expressing Viṣṇu) and (of His characteristic) of being immeasurable.

. . . From the term *Ātman* and the characteristic of being immeasurable found in the subsequent sentence of the Vedic passage, the pervasion spoken of in the previous text is only predicated of the Lord with reference to one and all of his forms. . . .

II.iii.27. The extending beyond of parts is as in the case of odour; and thus scripture also declares.

Just as fragrance goes forth separated from the flower, so from the individual self parts go forth separated by the inconceivable power of the Lord. . . .

"That thou art." [*Ch. Up.* VI.viii.7); "I am *Brahman*." [*Bṛ. Up.* III.iv.10]. In these and like texts, identity of the self with the Supreme Being seems to be (declared). On the other hand, separateness appears to be stated in such texts as, "The eternal of the eternal, the intelligent of the intelligent" [*Śvet. Up.* VI.13], "Two birds which are inseparable friends, etc." [*Śvet. Up.* IV.6]. To remove this contradiction, the following *sūtra* proceeds.

II.iii.28. The self is separate from (not one with, *Brahman*), from the statements in *śruti*.

"The Supreme Lord is absolutely separate from the whole class of selves; for He is inconceivable, exalted far above the selves, most high, perfect in excellences and He is eternally blessed, while from that Lord this self has to seek release from bondage." From this *Kauśika śruti*,[1] embodying a reasoning, it is plain that the self is separate from the Lord, not one with him.

II.iii.29. Only on account of having for his essence qualities similar to those of *Brahman*, the self is spoken of as *Brahman*, as in the case of the all-wise *Brahman*.

Since the essence (i.e., the very nature) of the self consists only of wisdom, bliss and other qualities similar (in some degree) to those of *Brahman*, there proceeds the statement that the self is one with (like) *Brahman*;...

Origination has been predicated also of the self; hence he cannot be said to have the eternal association of *karma* (actions) or to attain to eternal existence....

II.iii.30. The contradiction affecting the authoritativeness of *śruti* does not arise, since the self has existed all along with the Supreme Being, it being thus observed also in *śruti*.

...The power to do (everything)...has been predicated only of the Lord. But in the text, "According as he does work, he attains to the result" [*Bṛ. Up.* IV.iv.5] it is predicated of the self. To reconcile this contradiction, the Sūtrakāra says. [Introductory commentary to II.iii.33]:

II.iii.33. (The self too) is an agent, for (then only) *śruti* (consisting of permission and prohibition) has a (real) purport; (otherwise it would be purportless).

II.iii.34. (The self is an agent in reality) on account of *śruti* declaring the blissful activities (of the released self).

For instance in the text, "With women, or in vehicles, or with those who obtain release along with him, or those that had obtained release before him, (he diverts himself)" [*Ch. Up.* VIII.xii.3], &c., (his real activity is spoken of) even in heaven.

II.iii.35. (Here too, the self is a real agent) on account of his adapting (means to ends).

Further, since the self is seen (in this world) to adapt means, etc., to ends (for obtaining salvation as well as accomplishing the desired results), he is a real agent.

II.iii.36. The self is an agent, also on the ground of his being directed to do the work of meditation,...

[1] *Kauṣītaki Upaniṣad.*

. . . Then how does this agree with the statement that the Lord is the sole agent? In reply to this question, the Sūtrakāra says:

II.iii.37. He has not the freedom (absolute power) of action, as of perception.

II.iii.39. And on account of the absence of the feeling in him of being perfect (accomplished).

And because the dependent state appears from the absence of the sense of being accomplished (i.e., the feeling of satisfaction and confidence in himself), therefore (the absolute agentship of the Lord and the dependent agentship of the self) must be distinctly understood.

II.iii.40. And even as the carpenter (the self is an agent) in double fashion.

As the carpenter is an agent under the master who asks him to work and is also an agent by himself, so in the case of the self there is the guidance of the Lord, as well as his own capacity for action.

II.iii.42. . . . The Lord impels the self to action, only according to (the tendency of) his previous actions and his effort (or aptitude), so that the injunctions and prohibitions are not purportless, etc.

II.iii.43. . . . The self is a part of the Lord, on account of his being declared to be variously related to him; also declared otherwise (as unrelated); . . .

II.iii.46. (The Supreme Being, with regard to His manifestations) does not thus (consist of separate parts); just as (the superior deities presiding over) superior light, etc., are not.

. . . selves and the manifestations of the Lord are both spoken of as parts, . . . (not-different from Himself); just as the idea of part cannot be the same with regard to both the great fire at the end of the world (which is but a part of fire) and the fire-fly which is also considered a part of fire; . . .

II.iii.50. Also for the reason that the self is but a reflection (of the Lord), . . .

III.ii.18. And (if it be said that), for the self-same reasons, the similarity (between the Lord and selves) is the similarity, i.e., absolute identity (which exists between the Lord and His manifestations), it is denied; for it (absolute identity) cannot be, just as (it does not exist) between Sūrya (the sun), etc., and their images.

It may appear that since there is thus no difference whatever between the manifestations of the Lord mutually and since there is similarity in the self also, the same non-difference (absolute identity of the self with *Brahman*) might be supposed. To refute such as upposition the Sūtrakāra, having stated that the self is an image of the Lord,...shows that he is quite distinct from Him. *Śruti* and *smṛti* declare the same thus: "The selves stand as so many reflections with regard to the different forms of the Lord." [*Bṛ. Up.* IV.v.19] "Just as the many images reflected on the surface of water are like the sun, so are the little selves of the world said to be like the Lord," and so on.

For the same reasons, that is, on account of separateness, of dependence upon, and of likeness to, the Lord, the comparison of the images of the sun, etc., is instituted in the case of the self, not as being conditioned by anything (like a mirror, etc.)....

III.ii.32. (The qualities of *Brahman* are of a different nature), on account of His being declared as the bridge, as that which is beyond measure (absolutely perfect), as related (the original of the reflected qualities in the self), and as being quite distinct from those of the world.

III.ii.39. The fruit (is obtained) from Him only, for this is possible (reasonable).

Only hence, (that is, from the Lord alone) the fruit is obtained; for it cannot be from the inanimate *karma* [principle of cause and effect], which is incapable of independent activity.

III.ii.41. *Dharma* [righteousness] is the rewarder and it springs only from Him; Jaimini holds this view from such (*śruti*).

Only that *karma* springs from the Lord which is the cause of fruit. Thus Jaimini thinks, from the Vedic statement, "Indeed He only causes the self to do the righteous deed, etc." [*Kauṣītaki Up.* v.iii.8].

III.ii.42. Bādarāyaṇa says the aforesaid (*Brahman*) (as well as *dharma* are the cause of fruit) as they are declared to be such (in general terms); but with a difference (viz., *Brahman* is the agent and *karma* is the means).

Though the Supreme Being and *karma* (action)[1] are both the cause of fruit, *karma* does not guide the Supreme Being; on the other hand it is the Supreme Being that guides and rules (our) action....And the glorious Lord confers knowledge (on the devoted self) for his righteousness, and absolves him from sin and leads him to eternal bliss; (such is the boundless mercy of the Lord). The mere instrumentality of *karma* has been already spoken of in the text, "Matter, action, time, etc., exist or cease to exist at the pleasure of the Lord."

[1] *Karma* means both action and the law of cause and effect as bringing about the fruits of action. See above, III.ii.39.

III.iii.1. (*Brahman*) is the object of that knowledge which results from the conclusion of an enquiry into ALL *śruti*; for the injunctions, etc., are not special.

...For, "Meditate on Him as the *Ātman* only" [*Bṛ. Up.* III.iv.7]—this and similar injunctions and the reasoning comprehended by them are not of a special character (i.e., they apply equally to all grades of devotees)....

III.iii.43. Discernment (accurate perception) of truth and conclusive understanding of the Vedas are different from the direct perception of that (*Brahman*); and their direct (immediate) result is indeed the removal of obstacles (to direct perception).

Decisive ideas of all that is true and the conclusive understanding of all *śruti* that such and such is the meaning and no other, are both quite different from the direct perception of *Brahman*. By the term "indeed," the Sūtrakāra points to the *śruti*, "Verily the *Ātman* is to be seen, heard, thought and meditated on" [*Bṛ. Up.* IV.iv.5]—the consequence of hearing, etc., (study, etc.,) is the removal of obstacles to seeing *Brahman*, such as ignorance, wrong knowledge, doubt, etc. And the *Brahmatarka* has the following: "By hearing (studying *śruti*), by reasoning and by contemplation, having expelled the gloom of ignorance, wrong knowledge, and doubt, he obtains sight of *Brahman*."

III.iii.48. Knowledge only is the means of release (as seen from the emphatic statement).

"Having known Him thus, he overcomes death, and there is no way leading unto Him (to release) other than knowledge" [*Śvet. Up.* III.8]. From this emphatic statement, only by means of knowledge, it is clear, release is to be obtained.

III.iii.49. And from the (actual) seeing (of the Lord), as *śruti* says.

III.iii.51. (The perception of *Brahman*) arises also from devotion, etc.

III.iii.53. Though all the forms of *Brahman* are identical, from the ordinary sight (of any form) final release cannot result, as from death (at any time); nor does attaining to other regions (constitute final release) indeed.

III.iii.54. (That perception is, however, caused) only by the Supreme; (still) such a declaration of *śruti* (is admissible), for devotion is (indeed) the pre-eminent (means).

As the Supreme Being of His own accord shows Himself in consideration of the self's devotion and bestows upon him final beatitude, devotion becomes the foremost of all the means, and consequently it is spoken of as the only means....

III.iv.26. The requisiteness of all the duties is only towards the production of knowledge, as that of the horse in journeying, since it is seen from the text, "By sacrifice, etc."

There is the need for the performance of all the duties towards the production of knowledge as it is seen from the *śruti*: "They seek to know Him by means of sacrifices, distribution of gifts, penance (or the imparting of knowledge), by abstinence" (*Bṛ. Up.* VI.iv.22); just as only for the purpose of journeying the horse and other (conveyances) are required, not for the act of getting into the village, etc., when he has journeyed the distance.

III.iv.27. Notwithstanding, the wise man shall be possessed of devotional tranquility, control of senses, etc., on account of these being specially enjoined upon him (the wise), and on account of their being the cause of enhancing the effect of knowledge and, as such, being fit to be necessarily observed.

IV.i.5. *Ātman* is to be contemplated as *Brahman* (the perfect); for (this) is the best, (i.e., to contemplate Him as perfect is the best means of gaining His perfect grace).

IV.i.13. On the attainment of the sight of that (*Brahman*), the non-clinging of all subsequent sin and the destruction of all previous sin result, (as seen) from Vedic declaration to that effect.

IV.ii.7. The intelligent *prakṛti* is not withdrawn into the Lord; for she is co-existent with the Person (the Lord) (in time and space), never subject to mundane bondage; and she is eternally blessed, but not in consequence of meditation.

IV.ii.9. . . . the Lord is greater than she in point of subtlety and in the extent of qualities; (they are not equals); as seen from the *śruti* announcing it.

IV.ii.10. Hence without prejudice (to the supremacy, i.e., the special attributes of the Lord, there is the aforesaid equality between *prakṛti* and the Lord).

IV.ii.12. If it be said that the equality with the Lord being denied of all, (*prakṛti*, too, cannot be on an equality with Him), it is to be denied, for the equality with the Lord is denied of the individual self.

IV.ii.16. (For, of the released) there is no division (i.e., there is oneness of will, purpose, etc.,) on account of the statement (to that effect).

The *Gaupavana śruti* says: "These Gods having entered into the Lord become eternal; are of real desires and of real thoughts; and at their pleasure go everywhere, within and without." Thus from the above statement, it is plain that the desires of the released are real, because those desires are not different from (i.e., they are at one with) the desires, etc., of that Supreme Lord of all.... It is also said in the *Brāhma*[1] "The attribute of having real desires as well as real power possessed by the released is true only because they are at one (agree) with those of the perfect Lord; but nothing else (more) is predicated of them."

IV.iv.6. Auḍulomi[2] thinks that the released enjoy blessings by their absolutely intelligent (and essential) personality, for they are of such essence.

IV.iv.10. Bādari[3] considers that the released have no physical frame (and their enjoyment proceeds with the essentially intelligent body), for *śruti* speaks to that effect.

Bādari says that, except one of pure intelligence, the released have no other body, for it is said in the *Kauntharavya śruti* thus: "Indeed he then becomes destitute of body; and him that is without a body, pleasure and pain do not touch, with which indeed this embodied being is afflicted."

IV.iv.11. Jaimini[4] asserts the existence of a physical body (too), on account of alternatives declared (in the *śruti*).

Jaimini thinks that there is also the other body (i.e., other than the body consisting of pure intelligence) in the case of the released as optional assumption of such a body is spoken of in the *Uddālaka śruti* thus: "He who thus knows the Supreme Lord, when released, sees Him, hears Him distinctly, with a lustrous body consisting only of intelligence or non-intelligent matter (*śuddhasattva*), everlasting or temporary; and thereby he becomes simply blessed and blessed only, and nothing that is not blissful touches him."

IV.iv.12. Hence (i.e., on account of both being facts as stated in scripture) Bādarāyaṇa accepts both the views....

...the enjoyment of blessings by the released may take place by means of an external body as well as by the body of pure intelligence identical with (each) self. Thus Bādarāyaṇa judges.

IV.iv.13. In the absence of an external body, it (the experience of enjoyment) may arise as in the *sandhyā* (the state of dreaming).

IV.iv.14. When the external body is present (i.e., is assumed by the *mukta* [the freed self] at his will) (the enjoyment may take place) as in the state of wakefulness.

[1] *Brāhma* is an abbreviation for the *Brāhma Purāṇa*.

[2] An Upaniṣadic philosopher.

[3] A Sāṁkhya philosopher.

[4] Author of the *Pūrva Mīmāṁsā Sūtra*.

IV.iv.15. Their entering into a body is like the presence of the flame (in the wick), (is only for the enjoyment of blessings), for *śruti* shows that.

Though they enter a body, they light it up (with their own lustre) and enjoy only blessings that are the results of virtues (practised after the sight of *Brahman*), and are never liable to the experience of miseries, etc., just as the lustrous flame in a lamp, etc., consumes only the oil, etc., in it but not the soot, etc. For the *śruti* declares thus: "For then, indeed, the self has got over all miseries and become directly related to the Lord who is seated in the heart of all." [*Bṛ. Up.* VI.iii.22.]

And it should not be supposed that the above statement refers to him that has attained to *svarga* [heaven] and other regions, on the strength of such texts as "In the world of *svarga* there is no fear whatever." [*Ka. Up.* I.12.]

IV.iv.17. The released self obtains all wishes except the power of (creating) the world, etc.

IV.iv.20. And (they have) no control over the effected world, for thus (*śruti*) declares.

Addendum

IV.i.3. But as the Self (scriptural texts) acknowledge and make us comprehend (the Lord). [Śaṁkara]

The Sūtrakāra now considers the question whether the highest Self whose characteristics scripture declares is to be understood as the "I" or as different from me.—But how can a doubt arise, considering that scripture exhibits the term "Self" whose sphere is the inward Self?

The highest Lord must be understood as the Self. In [this] light . . . texts have to be viewed which . . . acknowledge the Lord as the Self, such as "I am *Brahman*" (*Bṛ. Up.* I.iv.10) . . . , "Thy Self is this which is within all" (*Bṛ. Up.* II.iv.1), "He is thy Self, the ruler within, the immortal" (*Bṛ. Up.* III.vii.3), "That is the True, that is the Self, thou art that" (*Ch. Up.* VI.viii.7) . . . , "From death to death goes he who here perceives any diversity" (*Bṛ. Up.* IV.iv.19), "Whosoever looks for anything elsewhere than in the Self is abandoned by everything" (*Bṛ. Up.* II.iv.6). . . . Nor is there any force in the objection that things with contrary qualities cannot be identical; for this opposition of qualities can be shown to be false. Nor is it true that from our doctrine it would follow that the Lord is not a Lord. For in these matters scripture alone is authoritative, and we, moreover, do not at all admit that scripture teaches the Lord to be the Self of the transmigrating self, but maintain that by denying the transmigrating character of the self it aims at teaching that the self is the Self of the Lord. From this it follows that the non-dual Lord is free from all evil qualities, and that to ascribe to him contrary qualities is an error. . . .

IV.i.3. But as the Self; this (the ancient Devotees) acknowledge (since the texts) make (them) apprehend (in that way). [Rāmānuja]

Is *Brahman* to be meditated upon as something different from the meditating Devotee, or as the Self of the latter? *Brahman* is rather . . . to be meditated upon as being the Self of the meditating Devotee. As the meditating individual self is the Self of its own body, so the highest *Brahman* is the Self of the individual self—this is the proper form of meditation. Why? Because the great Devotees of olden times acknowledged this to be the true nature of meditation; compare the text "Then I am indeed thou, holy divinity, and thou art me." But how can the Devotees claim that *Brahman* which is a different being is their "Ego"?—Because the texts enable them to apprehend this relation as one free from contradiction. "He who dwelling within the Self is different from the Self, whom the Self does not know, of whom the Self is the body, who rules the Self from within; he is thy Self, the inner ruler, the immortal one" (*Bṛ. Up.* III.vii.3)—all [such] texts teach that all sentient and non-sentient beings spring from *Brahman*, are merged in him, breath through him, are ruled by him, constitute his body so that he is the Self of all of them. In the same way therefore as, on the basis of the fact that the individual self occupies with regard to the body the position of a Self, we form such judgments of co-ordination as "I am a god—I am a man," the fact of the individual Self being of the nature of Self justifies us in viewing our own Ego as belonging to the highest Self . . . our view implies a denial of difference in so far as the individual "I" is of the nature of the Self; and it implies an acknowledgment of differences in so far as it allows the highest Self to differ from the individual self in the same way as the latter differs from its body.

IV.i.3. *Ātman* (Viṣṇu) is to be meditated on as the Lord; for the wise know Him and contemplate Him as such and instruct (their pupils accordingly). [Madhva]

It is indispensable that those who seek release should by all means instruct their pupils that *Ātman* is the Lord and they (themselves) meditate on Him as such; for the wise understand Him thus: "I shall not think of another, I would know only *Ātman*, I contemplate *Ātman*; for *Ātman* is my Lord." They instruct their pupils thus: "Meditate on only *Ātman* as the Lord; know Him only as the Lord; do not think of any other thing; for He is (thy) Lord." This is said in the Bhaviṣyat Parvan: "By those that seek after release the contemplation of *Ātman* as the Lord should by all means be practised. A person should not forget at least this to do, though he may be beset with various difficulties." "The meditation that Viṣṇu is the Lord, taking the word *Ātman* to be an attribute of the Lord, should be practised by all seeking after release, and the instruction also should be similar. Abandoning this, no one can obtain release" (Brāhma).

CONTEMPORARY THOUGHT

CHAPTER XVI

SRI AUROBINDO

Sri Aurobindo (Arabinda Ghose, 1872–1950) was widely accepted as the great mystic-philosopher of present-day India. Attained by mystical insight and expressed in brilliant literary and rational form, the philosophy of Sri Aurobindo constitutes a point of view which he considers to be original Vedānta but which stands in strong opposition to the Advaita Vedānta of Śaṁkara on several basic issues.

His synthetic doctrine is one which calls for the universal expression of the Absolute in, and the development of the Absolute through, a series of grades of reality from matter up to the absolute spirit. Sri Aurobindo rejects categorically what he considers to be the illusionism of Śaṁkara as untrue to Vedānta and as untrue to his own vision of reality. The descent of the Absolute into the finite, which would be inexplicable on the basis of Śaṁkara's negativistic interpretation, is necessitated in Sri Aurobindo's view as the inevitable expression of the essential power of *Brahman*.

There is no part of reality which is not in some degree infused with the absolute spirit. For this reason, evolution of lower forms into higher forms, as well as the reverse process of involution, is almost inevitable, although great effort is demanded on the part of man to rend the veil which seems to separate the Absolute from the finite. Man's task on earth is to achieve identity with the Absolute by passing beyond the realm of the mental through a supra-mental change; the mental level does not constitute the limit of man's progress because it does not constitute the limit of his fundamental nature. To achieve this identity, however, it is necessary for man to prepare himself for the leap by an elaborate discipline of *yoga*—called "integral *yoga*" by Sri Aurobindo because of its comprehensive and all-inclusive transformation of the state of mind and the life of the individual. As Sri Aurobindo says, "This illumination and change must take up and re-create the whole being, mind, life and body; it must be not only an inner experience of the Divinity, but a remoulding of both the inner and outer existence by its power." Such preparation is however, not sufficient. Man must prepare himself, but the Supreme Being alone is capable of enabling man to achieve his ultimate destiny.

These are the basic principles of Sri Aurobindo's general point of view of reconciliation between matter and spirit, God and man, the finite world and absolute reality, and the one and the many.

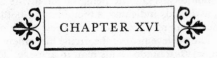

Man must progress from mind to supermind and is to achieve the life of what Sri Aurobindo calls Gnostic Being or the divine life. This divine life, constituting, as already indicated, a remolding of both the inner and the outer existence of man, is to produce "a new order of beings and a new earth-life." The achievement of the divine life, among men on earth, is the goal which Sri Aurobindo wants man to achieve. From the larger point of view, not the individualistic, this means essentially that the mind-life of men must be prepared to receive the divine inner life on earth by a complete transition from the point of view of worldliness and materiality to a realization of their spiritual nature and by establishing the complete dominance of the spirit in the physical, vital, and mental life on earth. For Sri Aurobindo, as for most Indian thinkers, it is not enough to realize that this is the ultimate truth; for him, the truth must be lived—the truth of the spiritual essence of all reality must be made the motivating force of all life.

As said above, Sri Aurobindo is a mystic-philosopher. Part of the meaning of this characterization is that Sri Aurobindo has gained his enlightenment concerning the ultimate truth from his own intuitive mystic vision. He insists that all ultimate truth must be achieved in this way. Reason and science are limited in their perspectives and in their possibilities and cannot achieve the ultimate vision which transcends the physical, the vital, and the mental. Reason is significant in its own sphere, but truth of spirit transcends truth of life and can be achieved only by the direct experience of mystic insight. On the basis of his mystic vision, Sri Aurobindo formulates a philosophy which—like the rationally grounded philosophy of Radhakrishnan to be described in the next chapter—eliminates the alleged negativism and illusionism of traditional Indian philosophy and thus prepares the way for a more positive way of life for the Indian people and which makes possible a much greater mutual philosophical understanding of India and the West, and eventually—possibly—a significant synthesis of Eastern and Western thought. (C. A. M.)

Selections in this chapter are taken from *Arya* and from *The Life Divine*, American edition (New York: The Greystone Press, 1949). Now published by E. P. Dutton & Co., Inc.

1. *The Value of Philosophical Thought*

There is no greater error than to suppose, as the "practical" man is wont to do, that thought is only a fine flower and ornament of life and that political, economic and personal interests are the important and effective motors of human action. We recognise that this is a world of life and action and developing organism; but the life that seeks to guide itself only by vital and material forces is a slow, dark and blundering growth. It is an attempt to approximate man to the method of vegetable and animal existence. The earth is a world of life and matter but man is not a vegetable nor an animal; he is a spiritual and a thinking being who is set here to shape and use the animal mould for higher purposes, by higher motives, with a more divine instrumentation.

Therefore by his very nature, he serves the working of a Thought within him even when he is ignorant of it in his surface self. The practical man who ignores or despises the deeper life of the Idea, is yet serving that which he ignores or despises.

The problem of thought therefore is to find out the right idea and the right way of harmony; to restate the ancient and eternal spiritual truth of the Self, so that it shall re-embrace, permeate and dominate the mental and physical life; to develop the most profound and vital methods of psychological self-discipline and self-development so that the mental and psychical life of man may express the spiritual life through the utmost possible expansion of its own richness, power and complexity; and to seek for the means and motives by which his external life, his society and his institutions may remould themselves progressively in the truth of the spirit and develop towards the utmost possible harmony of individual freedom and social unity.

Throughout the world there are plenty of movements inspired by the same drift, but there is room for an effort of thought which shall frankly acknowledge the problem in its integral complexity and not be restrained in the flexibility of its search by attachment to any cult, creed or extant system of philosophy.

The effort involves a quest for the truth that underlies existence and the fundamental law of its self-expression in the universe—the work of metaphysical philosophy and religious thought; the sounding and harmonising of the psychological methods of discipline by which man purifies and perfects himself—the work of psychology, not as it is understood in Europe, but the deeper practical psychology called in India *yoga*; and the application of our ideas to the problems of man's social and collective life.

Philosophy and religious thought must be the beginning and foundation of any such attempt; for they alone go behind appearances and processes to the truth of things. The attempt to get rid of their supremacy must always be vain. Man will always think and generalise and try to penetrate behind the apparent fact, for that is the imperative law of his awakened consciousness; man will always turn his generalisations into a religion, even though it be only a religion of positivism or of material law. Philosophy is the intellectual search for the fundamental truth of things, religion is the attempt to make the truth dynamic in the soul of man. They are essential to each other; a religion that is not the expression of philosophic truth degenerates into superstition and obscurantism, and a philosophy which does not dynamise itself with the religious spirit is a barren light, for it cannot get itself practised.

Unity for the human race by an inner oneness and not only by an external association of interests; the resurgence of man out of the merely animal and economic life or the merely intellectual and aesthetic into the glories of the spiritual existence; the pouring of the power of the spirit into the physical mould and mental instrument, so that man may develop his manhood into that true supermanhood which shall exceed our present state as much as this exceeds the animal state from which science tells us that we have issued. These three are one; for man's unity and man's self-transcendence can come only by living in the spirit. (*Arya*, Aug. 15, 1915, pp. 2–9.)

All philosophy is concerned with the relations between two things, the fundamental truth of existence and the forms in which existence presents itself to our experience. The deepest experience shows that the fundamental truth is truth of the spirit; the other is the truth of life, truth of form and shaping force and living idea and action. Here the West and the East have followed divergent lines. The West has laid most emphasis on truth of life and for a time came to stake its whole existence on truth of life alone, to deny the existence of Spirit or to relegate it to the domain of the unknown and unknowable; from that exaggeration it is now beginning to return. The East has laid most emphasis on truth of the spirit and for a time came, at least in India, to stake its whole existence upon that truth alone, to neglect the possibilities of life or to limit it to a narrow development of a fixed status; the East too is beginning to return from this exaggeration. The West is reawaking to the truth of the spirit and the spiritual possibilities of life, the East is reawaking to the truth of life and tends towards a new application to it of its spiritual knowledge. Our view is that the antinomy created between them is an unreal one. Spirit being the fundamental truth of existence, life can be only its manifestation; Spirit must be not only the origin of life but its basis, its pervading reality and its highest and total result. But the forms of life as they appear to us are at once its disguises and its instruments of self-manifestation. Man has to grow in knowledge till they cease to be disguises and grow in spiritual power and quality till they become in him its perfect instruments. To grow into the fulness of the divine is the true law of human life and to shape his earthly existence into its image is the meaning of his evolution. (*Arya*, July 15, 1918, pp. 764–5.)

2. *The Search for Reality through Aspiration, Senses, Reason, and Intuition*[1]

The earliest preoccupation of man in his awakened thoughts and, as it seems, his inevitable and ultimate preoccupation,—for it survives the longest periods of scepticism and returns after every banishment,—is also the highest which his thought can envisage. It manifests itself in the divination of Godhead, the impulse towards perfection, the search after pure truth and unmixed bliss, the sense of a secret immortality. The ancient dawns of human knowledge have left us their witness to this constant aspiration; today we see a humanity satiated but not satisfied by victorious analysis of the externalities of Nature preparing to return to its primeval longings. The earliest formula of wisdom promises to be its last,—God, light, freedom, immortality. (*The Life Divine*, p. 3.)

. . . To know, possess and be the divine being in an animal and egoistic consciousness, to convert our twilit or obscure physical mentality into the plenary supramental illumination, to build peace and a self-existent bliss where there is only a stress of transitory satisfactions besieged by physical pain and emotional suffering, to establish an infinite freedom in a world which presents itself as a group of mechanical necessities, to discover and realise the immortal life in a body subjected to death and constant mutation,—this is offered to us as the manifestation of God in matter and the goal of Nature in her terrestrial evolution. To the ordinary material intellect which takes its present organisation of consciousness for the limit of its possibilities, the direct contradiction of the unrealised ideals with the realised fact is a final argument against their validity. But if we take a more deliberate view of the world's workings, that direct opposition appears rather as a part of Nature's profoundest method and the seal of her completest sanction. (*ibid.*, p. 4.)

We arrive at the conception and at the knowledge of a divine existence by exceeding the evidence of the senses and piercing beyond the walls of the physical mind. . . . (*ibid.*, p. 58.)

[1] This and following sectional headings are editorial additions.

...To correct the errors of the sense-mind by the use of reason is one of the most valuable powers developed by man and the chief cause of his superiority among terrestrial beings.

The complete use of pure reason brings us finally from physical to metaphysical knowledge. But the concepts of metaphysical knowledge do not in themselves fully satisfy the demand of our integral being. They are indeed entirely satisfactory to the pure reason itself, because they are the very stuff of its own existence. But our nature sees things through two eyes always, for it views them doubly as idea and as fact and therefore every concept is incomplete for us and to a part of our nature almost unreal until it becomes an experience....

...In reality, all experience is in its secret nature knowledge by identity; but its true character is hidden from us because we have separated ourselves from the rest of the world by exclusion, by the distinction of ourself as subject and everything else as object, and we are compelled to develop processes and organs by which we may again enter into communion with all that we have excluded. We have to replace direct knowledge through conscious identity by an indirect knowledge which appears to be caused by physical contact and mental sympathy. This limitation is a fundamental creation of the ego and an instance of the manner in which it has proceeded throughout, starting from an original falsehood and covering over the truth of things by contingent falsehoods which become for us practical truths of relation.

From this nature of mental and sense knowledge as it is at present organised in us, it follows that there is no inevitable necessity in our existing limitations. They are the result of an evolution in which mind has accustomed itself to depend upon certain physiological functionings and their reactions as its normal means of entering into relation with the material universe....It is possible for the mind—and it would be natural for it, if it could be persuaded to liberate itself from its consent to the domination of matter,—to take direct cognisance of the objects of sense without the aid of the sense-organs. This is what happens in experiments of hypnosis and cognate psychological phenomena. Because our waking consciousness is determined and limited by the balance between mind and matter worked out by life in its evolution, this direct cognisance is usually impossible in our ordinary waking state and has therefore to be brought about by throwing the waking mind into a state of sleep which liberates the true or subliminal mind. Mind is then able to assert its true character as the one and all-sufficient sense and free to apply to the objects of sense its pure and sovereign instead of its mixed and dependent action. Nor is this extension of faculty really impossible but only more difficult in our waking state,—as is known to all who have been able to go far enough in certain paths of psychological experiment.

...It is possible, once we have entered by any of the senses into relation with an external object, so to apply the *manas* [mind] as to become aware of the contents of the object, for example, to receive or to perceive the thoughts or feelings of others without aid from their utterance, gesture, action or facial expressions and even in contradiction of these always partial and often misleading data. Finally, by an utilisation of the inner senses,—that is to say, of the sense-powers, in themselves, in their purely mental or subtle activity as distinguished from the physical which is only a selection for the purposes of outward life from their total and general action,—we are able to take cognition of sense-experiences, of appearances and images of things other than those which belong to the organisation of our material environment....

None of them [these extensions of faculty], however, leads to the aim we have in view, the psychological experience of those truths that are "beyond perception by the sense but seizable by the perceptions of the reason," *buddhigrāhyam atīndriyam.*[1] They give us only a larger field of phenomena and more effective means for the observation of phenomena. The truth of things always escapes beyond the sense. Yet is it a sound rule inherent in the very constitution of universal existence that where there are truths attainable by the reason, there must be somewhere in the organism possessed of that reason a means of arriving at or verifying them by experience. The one means we have left in our mentality is an extension of that form of knowledge by identity which gives us the awareness of our own existence....

...We have to go beyond the mind and the reason. The reason active in our waking consciousness is only a mediator between the subconscient All that we come from in our evolution upwards and the superconscient All towards which we are impelled by that evolution. The subconscient and the superconscient are two different formulations of the same All. The master-word of the subconscient is Life, the master-word of the superconscient is Light. In the subconscient knowledge or consciousness is involved in action, for action

[1] *Bhagavad-gītā* VI.21.

is the essence of Life. In the superconscient action re-enters into Light and no longer contains involved knowledge but is itself contained in a supreme consciousness. Intuitional knowledge is that which is common between them and the foundation of intuitional knowledge is conscious or effective identity between that which knows and that which is known; it is that state of common self-existence in which the knower and the known are one through knowledge. But in the subconscient the intuition manifests itself in the action, in effectivity, and the knowledge or conscious identity is either entirely or more or less concealed in the action. In the superconscient, on the contrary, Light being the law and the principle, the intuition manifests itself in its true nature as knowledge emerging out of conscious identity, and effectivity of action is rather the accompaniment or necessary consequent and no longer masks as the primary fact. Between these two states reason and mind act as intermediaries which enable the being to liberate knowledge out of its imprisonment in the act and prepare it to resume its essential primacy. When the self-awareness in the mind applied, both to continent and content, to own-self and other-self, exalts itself into the luminous self-manifest identity, the reason also converts itself into the form of the self-luminous intuitional knowledge. This is the highest possible state of our knowledge when mind fulfils itself in the supramental. (*ibid.*, pp. 59–63.)

...Ancient Vedānta seized this message of the intuition and formulated it in the three great declarations of the Upaniṣads, "I am He," "Thou art That, O Śvetaketu," "All this is the *Brahman*; this Self is the *Brahman*." (*ibid.*, p. 65.)

An unknowable which appears to us in many states and attributes of being, in many forms of consciousness, in many activities of energy, this is what Mind can ultimately say about the existence which we ourselves are and which we see in all that is presented to our thought and senses. It is in and through those states, those forms, those activities that we have to approach and know the Unknowable. But if in our haste to arrive at a unity that our mind can seize and hold, if in our insistence to confine the Infinite in our embrace we identify the reality with any one definable state of being however pure and eternal, with any particular attribute however general and comprehensive, with any fixed formulation of consciousness however vast in its scope, with any energy or activity however boundless its application, and if we exclude all the rest, then our thoughts sin against

Its unknowableness and arrive not at a true unity but at a division of the Indivisible. (*ibid.*, pp. 34–5.)

...Only, the positive and synthetic teaching of the Upaniṣads beheld *sat* [existence] and *asat* [non-existence] not as opposites destructive of each other, but as the last antinomy through which we look up to the Unknowable. And in the transactions of our positive consciousness, even unity has to make its account with multiplicity; for the many also are *Brahman.* It is by *vidyā*, the knowledge of the oneness, that we know God; without it *avidyā*, the relative and multiple consciousness, is a night of darkness and a disorder of ignorance. Yet if we exclude the field of that ignorance, if we get rid of *avidyā* as if it were a thing non-existent and unreal, then knowledge itself becomes a sort of obscurity and a source of imperfection. We become as men blinded by light so that we can no longer see the field which that light illumines. (*ibid.*, p. 35.)

3. *What is Reality? The One or the Many?*

...They [the ancient sages of the Upaniṣads] had the patience and strength to find and to know; they had also the clarity and humility to admit the limitation of our knowledge. They perceived the borders where it has to pass into something beyond itself. It was a later impatience of heart and mind, vehement attraction to an ultimate bliss or high masterfulness of pure experience and trenchant intelligence which sought the one to deny the many and because it had received the breath of the heights scorned or recoiled from the secret of the depths. But the steady eye of the ancient wisdom perceived that to know God really, it must know Him everywhere equally and without distinction, considering and valuing but not mastered by the oppositions through which He shines.

We will put aside then the trenchant distinctions of a partial logic which declares that because the One is the reality, the Many are an illusion, and because the Absolute is *sat*, the one existence, the relative is *asat* and non-existent. If in the many we pursue insistently the one, it is to return with the benediction and the revelation of the one confirming itself in the many.

We will guard ourselves also against the excessive importance that the mind attaches to particular points of view at which it arrives in its more powerful expansions and transitions. The perception of the spiritualised mind that the universe is an unreal dream can have no more absolute a value to us than the perception of the materialised mind that God and the beyond are an illusory idea. In the one case the mind, habituated only to the evidence of the senses and associating reality with corporeal fact, is either unaccustomed to use other means of knowledge or unable to extend the notion of reality to a supraphysical experience. In the other case the same mind, passing beyond to the overwhelming experience of an incorporeal reality, simply transfers the same inability and the same consequent sense of dream or hallucination to the experience of the senses. But we perceive also the truth that these two conceptions disfigure. It is true that for this world of form in which we are set for our self-realisation, nothing is entirely valid until it has possessed itself of our physical consciousness and manifested on the lowest levels in harmony with its manifestation on the highest summits. It is equally true that form and matter asserting themselves as a self-existent reality are an illusion of ignorance. Form and matter can be valid only as shape and substance of manifestation for the incorporeal and immaterial. They are in their nature an act of divine consciousness, in their aim the representation of a status of the spirit.

In other words, if *Brahman* has entered into form and represented Its being in material substance, it can only be to enjoy self-manifestation in the figures of relative and phenomenal consciousness. *Brahman* is in this world to represent Itself in the values of Life. Life exists in *Brahman* in order to discover *Brahman* in itself. Therefore man's importance in the world is that he gives to it that development of consciousness in which its transfiguration by a perfect self-discovery becomes possible. To fulfil God in life is man's manhood. He starts from the animal vitality and its activities, but a divine existence is his objective.

But as in thought, so in life, the true rule of self-realisation is a progressive comprehension. *Brahman* expresses Itself in many successive forms of consciousness, successive in their relation even if coexistent in being or coeval in Time, and Life in its self-unfolding must also rise to ever-new provinces of its own being. But if in passing from one domain to another we renounce what has already been given us from eagerness for our new attainment, if in reaching the mental life we cast away or belittle the physical life which is our basis, or if we reject the mental and physical in our attraction to the spiritual, we do not fulfil God integrally, nor satisfy the conditions of His self-manifestation. We do not become perfect, but only shift the field of our imperfection or at most attain a limited altitude.

However high we may climb, even though it be to the non-being itself, we climb ill if we forget our base. Not to abandon the lower to itself, but to transfigure it in the light of the higher to which we have attained, is true divinity of nature. *Brahman* is intergral and unifies many states of consciousness at a time; we also, manifesting the nature of *Brahman*, should become integral and all-embracing.

Besides the recoil from the physical life, there is another exaggeration of the ascetic impulse which this ideal of an integral manifestation corrects. The nodus of Life is the relation between three general forms of consciousness, the individual, the universal and the transcendent or supracosmic. In the ordinary distribution of life's activities the individual regards himself as a separate being included in the universe and both as dependent upon that which transcends alike the universe and the individual. It is to this transcendence that we give currently the name of God, who thus becomes to our conceptions not so much supracosmic as extra-cosmic. The belittling and degradation of both the individual and the universe is a natural consequence of this division: the cessation of both cosmos and individual by the attainment of the transcendence would be logically its supreme conclusion.

The integral view of the unity of *Brahman* avoids these consequences. Just as we need not give up the bodily life to attain to the mental and spiritual, so we can arrive at a point of view where the preservation of the individual activities is no longer inconsistent with our comprehension of the cosmic consciousness or our attainment to the transcendent and supracosmic. For the World-Transcendent embraces the universe, is one with it and does not exclude it, even as the universe is one with it and does not exclude it, even as the universe embraces the individual, is one with him and does not exclude him. The individual is a centre of the whole universal consciousness; the universe is a form and definition which is occupied by the entire immanence of the formless and indefinable.

This is always the true relation, veiled from us by our ignorance or our wrong consciousness of things. When we attain to knowledge or right consciousness, nothing essential in the eternal relation is changed, but only the inview and the outview from the individual centre is [*sic*] profoundly modified and consequently also the spirit and effect of its activity. The individual is still necessary to the action of the transcendent in the universe and that action in him does not cease to be possible by his illumination. On the contrary, since the conscious manifestation of the transcendent in the individual is the means by which the collective, the universal is also to become conscious of itself, the continuation of the illumined individual in the action of the world is an imperative need of the world-play. If his inexorable removal through the very act of illumination is the law, then the world is condemned to remain eternally the scene of unredeemed darkness, death and suffering. And such a world can only be a ruthless ordeal or a mechanical illusion.

It is so that ascetic philosophy tends to conceive it. But individual salvation can have no real sense if existence in the cosmos is itself an illusion. In the monistic view the individual soul is one with the Supreme, its sense of separateness an ignorance, escape from the sense of separateness and identity with the Supreme its salvation. But who then profits by this escape? Not the supreme Self, for it is supposed to be always and inalienably free, still, silent, pure. Not the world, for that remains constantly in the bondage and is not freed by the escape of any individual soul from the universal illusion. It is the individual soul itself which effects its supreme good by escaping from the sorrow and the division into the peace and the bliss. There would seem then to be some kind of reality of the individual soul as distinct from the world and from the Supreme even in the event of freedom and illumination. But for the illusionist the individual soul is an illusion and non-existent except in the inexplicable mystery of *māyā*. Therefore we arrive at the escape of an illusory non-existent soul from an illusory non-existent bondage in an illusory non-existent world as the supreme good which that non-existent soul has to pursue! For this is the last word of the knowledge, "There is none bound, none freed, none seeking to be free." *Vidyā* turns out to be as much a part of the Phenomenal as *avidyā*; *māyā* meets us even in our escape and laughs at the triumphant logic which seemed to cut the knot of her mystery.

These things, it is said, cannot be explained; they are the initial and insoluble miracle. They are for us a practical fact and have to be accepted. We have to escape by a confusion out of a confusion. The individual soul can only cut the knot of ego by a supreme act of egoism, an exclusive attachment to its own individual salvation which amounts to an absolute assertion of its separate existence in *māyā*. We are led to regard other souls as if they were figments of our mind and their salvation unimportant, our soul alone as if it were entirely real and its salvation the one thing that matters. I come to regard my personal escape from bondage as real while other souls who are equally myself remain behind in the bondage!

It is only when we put aside all irreconcilable antinomy between Self and the world that things fall into their place by a less paradoxical logic. We must accept the many-sidedness of the manifestation even while we assert the unity of the Manifested. And is not this after all the truth that pursues us wherever we cast our eyes, unless seeing we choose not to see? Is not this after all the perfectly natural and simple mystery of Conscious Being that It is bound neither by its unity nor by its multiplicity? It is "absolute" in the sense of being entirely free to include and arrange in its own way all possible terms of its self-expression. There is none bound, none freed, none seeking to be free,—for always That is a perfect freedom. It is so free that it is not even bound by its liberty. It can play at being bound without incurring a real bondage. Its chain is a self-imposed convention, its limitation in the ego a transitional device that it uses in order to repeat its transcendence and universality in the scheme of the individual *Brahman.*

The Transcendent, the Supracosmic is absolute and free in Itself beyond time and space and beyond the conceptual opposites of finite and infinite. But in cosmos It uses Its liberty of self-formation, Its *māyā*, to make a scheme of Itself in the complementary terms of unity and multiplicity, and this multiple unity It establishes in the three conditions of the subconscient, the conscient and the superconscient. For actually we see that the many objectivised in form in our material universe start with a subconscious unity which expresses itself openly enough in cosmic action and cosmic substance, but of which they are not themselves superficially aware. In the conscient the ego becomes the superficial point at which the awareness of unity can emerge; but it applies its perception of unity to the form and surface action and, a failing to take account of all that operates behind, fails also to realise that it is not only one in itself but one with others. This limitation of the universal "I" in the divided ego-sense constitutes our imperfect individualised personality. But when the ego transcends the personal consciousness, it begins to include and be overpowered by that which is to us superconscious; it becomes aware of the cosmic unity and enters into the Transcendent Self which here cosmos expresses by a multiple oneness.

The liberation of the individual soul is therefore the keynote of the definite divine action; it is the primary divine necessity and the pivot on which all else turns. It is the point of light at which the intended complete self-manifestation in the many begins to emerge. But the liberated soul extends its perception of unity horizontally as well as vertically. Its unity with the transcendent one is incomplete without its unity with the cosmic many. And that lateral unity translates itself by multiplication, a reproduction of its own liberated state at other points in the multiplicity. The divine soul reproduces itself in similar liberated souls as the animal reproduces itself in similar bodies. Therefore, whenever even a single soul is liberated, there is a tendency to an extension and even to an outburst of the same divine self-consciousness in other individual souls of our terrestrial humanity and,—who knows?—perhaps even beyond the terrestrial consciousness. Where shall we fix the limit of that extension? Is it altogether a legend which says of the Buddha that as he stood on the threshold of *nirvāṇa*, of the non-being, his soul turned back and took the vow never to make the irrevocable crossing so long as there was a single being upon earth undelivered from the knot of the suffering, from the bondage of the ego?

But we can attain to the highest without blotting ourselves out from the cosmic extension. *Brahman* preserves always Its two terms of liberty within and of formation without, of expression and of freedom from the expression. We also, being That, can attain to the same divine self-possession. The harmony of the two tendencies is the condition of all life that aims at being really divine. Liberty pursued by exclusion of the thing exceeded leads along the path of negation to the refusal of that which God has accepted. Activity pursued by absorption in the act and the energy leads to an inferior affirmation and the denial of the Highest. But what God combines and synthetises, wherefore should man insist on divorcing? To be perfect as He is perfect is the condition of His integral attainment.

Through *avidyā*, the multiplicity, lies our path out of the transitional egoistic self-expression in which death and suffering predominate; through *vidyā* consenting with *avidyā* by the perfect sense of oneness even in that multiplicity, we enjoy integrally the immortality and the beatitude. By attaining to the Unborn beyond all becoming we are liberated from this lower birth and death; by accepting the becoming freely as the divine, we invade mortality with the immortal beatitude and become luminous centres of its conscious self-expression in humanity. (*ibid.*, pp. 35–41.)

4. *The Power of Illusion, Māyā*

...The mind of humanity, ever seeking, ever active, never arrives at a firmly settled reality of life's aims and objects or at a settled reality of its own certitudes and convictions, an established foundation or firm formation of its idea of existence.

At a certain point of this constant unrest and travail even the physical mind loses its conviction of objective certitude and enters into an agnosticism which questions all its own standards of life and knowledge, doubts whether all this is real or else whether all, even if real, is not futile; the vital mind, baffled by life and frustrated or else dissatisfied with all its satisfactions, overtaken by a deep disgust and disappointment, finds that all is vanity and vexation of spirit and is ready to reject life and existence as an unreality, all that it hunted after as an illusion, *māyā*; the thinking mind, unbuilding all its affirmations, discovers that all are mere mental constructions and there is no reality in them or else that the only reality is something beyond this existence, something that has not been made or constructed, something absolute and eternal,—all that is relative, all that is of time is a dream, a hallucination of the mind or a vast delirium, an immense cosmic illusion, a delusive figure of apparent existence. The principle of negation prevails over the principle of affirmation and becomes universal and absolute. Thence arise the great world-negating religions and philosophies; thence too a recoil of the life-motive from itself and a seeking after a life elsewhere flawless and eternal or a will to annul life itself in an immobile reality or an original non-existence. In India the philosophy of world-negation has been given formulations of supreme power and value by two of the greatest of her thinkers, Buddha and Śaṁkara. There have been, intermediate or later in time, other philosophies of considerable importance, some of them widely accepted, formulated with much acumen of thought by men of genius and spiritual insight, which disputed with more or less force and success the conclusions of these two great metaphysical systems, but none has been put forward with an equal force of presentation or drive of personality or had a similar massive effect. The spirit of these two remarkable spiritual philosophies—for Śaṁkara in the historical process of India's philosophical mind takes up, completes and replaces Buddha,—has weighed with a tremendous power on her thought, religion and general mentality: everywhere broods its mighty shadow, everywhere is the impress of the three great formulas, the chain of *karma*, escape from the wheel of rebirth, *māyā*. It is necessary therefore to look afresh at the Idea or Truth behind the negation of cosmic existence and to consider, however briefly, what is the value of its main formulations or suggestions, on what reality they stand, how far they are imperative to the reason or to experience. For the present it will be enough to cast a glance on the principal ideas which are grouped around the conception of the great cosmic illusion, *māyā*, and to set against them those that are proper to our own line of thought and vision; for both proceed from the conception of the One Reality, but one line leads to a universal illusionism, the other to a universal realism,—an unreal or real-unreal universe reposing on a transcendent reality or a real universe reposing on a reality at once universal and transcendent or absolute.

In itself and by itself the vital being's aversion, the life-mind's recoil from life cannot be taken as valid or conclusive. Its strongest motive is a sense of disappointment and an acceptance of frustration which has no greater claim to conclusiveness than the idealist's opposite motive of invariable hope and his faith and will to realise. Nevertheless there is a certain validity in the mental support of this sense of frustration, in the perception at which the thinking mind arrives that there is an illusion behind all human effort and terrestrial endeavour, the illusion of his political and social gospels, the illusion of his ethical effort at perfection, the illusion of philanthropy and service, the illusion of works, the illusion of fame, power, success, the illusion of all achievement. Human, social and political endeavour turns always in a circle and leads nowhere; man's life and nature remain always the same, always imperfect, and neither laws nor institutions nor education nor philosophy nor morality nor religious teachings have succeeded in producing the perfect man, still less a perfect humanity,—straighten the tail of the dog as you will, it has been said, it always resumes its natural curve of crookedness. Altruism, philanthropy and service, Christian love or Buddhist compassion have not made the world a whit happier, they only give infinitesimal bits of momentary relief here and there, throw drops on the fire of the world's suffering. All aims are in the end transitory and futile, all achievements unsatisfying or evanascent; all works are so much labour of effort and success and failure which consummate nothing definitive: whatever changes are made in human life are of the form only and these forms pursue each other in a futile circle;

for the essence of life, its general character remains the same for ever. This view of things may be exaggerated, but it has an undeniable force; it is supported by the experience of man's centuries and it carries in itself a significance which at one time or another comes upon the mind with an overwhelming air of self-evidence. Not only so, but if it is true that the fundamental laws and values of terrestrial existence are fixed or that it must always turn in repeated cycles,—and this has been for long a very prevalent notion,—then this view of things in the end is hardly escapable. For imperfection, ignorance, frustration and suffering are a dominant factor of the existing world-order, the elements contrary to them, knowledge, happiness, success, perfection are constantly found to be deceptive or inconclusive: the two opposites are so inextricably mixed that, if this state of things is not a motion towards a greater fulfilment, if this is the permanent character of the world-order, then it is hard to avoid the conclusion that all here is either the creation of an inconscient energy, which would account for the incapacity of an apparent consciousness to arrive at anything, or intentionally a world of ordeal and failure, the issue being not here but elsewhere, or even a vast and aimless cosmic illusion.

Among these alternative conclusions the second, as it is usually put before us, offers no ground for the philosophic reason, since we have no satisfying indication of the connection between the here and the elsewhere which are posited against each other but not explained in the inevitability of their relations, and there is no light cast on the necessity or fundamental significance of the ordeal and failure. It could only be intelligible,—except as the mysterious will of an arbitrary Creator,—if there was a choice by immortal spirits to try the adventure of the ignorance and a necessity for them to learn the nature of a world of ignorance in order that they might reject it. But such a creative motive, necessarily incidental and quite temporary in its incidence, with the earth as its casual field of experience, could hardly by itself account for the immense and enduring phenomenon of this complex universe. It can become an operative part of a satisfactory explanation if this world is the field for the working out of a greater creative motive, if it is a manifestation of a divine truth or a divine possibility in which under certain conditions, an initiating ignorance must intervene as a necessary factor, and if the arrangement of this universe contains in it a compulsion of the ignorance to move towards knowledge, of the imperfect manifestation to grow into perfection, of the frustration to serve as steps towards a final victory, of the suffering to prepare an emergence of the divine delight of being. In that case the sense of disappointment, frustration, illusion and the vanity of all things would not be valid; for the aspects that seem to justify it would be only the natural circumstances of a difficult evolution: all the stress of struggle and effort, success and failure, joy and suffering, the mixture of ignorance and knowledge would be the experience needed for the soul, mind, life and physical part to grow into the full light of a spiritual perfected being. It would reveal itself as the process of an evolutionary manifestation; there would be no need to bring in the fiat of an arbitrary omnipotence or a cosmic illusion, a phantasy of meaningless *māyā*.

But there is too a higher mental and spiritual basis for the philosophy of world-negation and here we are on more solid ground: for it can be contended that the world is in its very nature an illusion and no reasoning from the features and circumstances of an illusion could justify it or raise it into a reality,—there is only one reality, the transcendent, the supracosmic: no divine fulfilment, even if our life were to grow into the life of gods, could nullify or cancel the original unreality which is its fundamental character; for that fulfilment would be only the bright side of an illusion. Or even if not absolutely an illusion, it would be a reality of an inferior order and must come to an end by the soul's recognition that the *Brahman* alone is true, that there is nothing but the transcendent and immutable Absolute. If this is the one truth, then all ground is cut away from under our feet; the divine manifestation, the victory of the soul in matter, its mastery over existence, the divine life in Nature would itself be a falsehood or at least something not altogether real imposed for a time on the sole true reality. But here all turns on the mind's conception or the mental being's experience of reality and how far that conception is valid or how far that experience is imperative,—even if it is a spiritual experience, how far it is absolutely conclusive, solely imperative.

The cosmic illusion is sometimes envisaged—though that is not the accepted position—as something that has the character of an unreal subjective experience; it is then—or may be—a figure of forms and movements that arises in some eternal sleep of things or in a dream-consciousness and is temporarily imposed on a pure and featureless self-aware existence; it is a dream that takes place in the Infinite. In the philosophies of the Māyāvādins [illusionists]—for there are several systems alike in their basis but not altogether and at every point coincident with each other,—the analogy of dream is given, but as an analogy only, not as the intrinsic character of the world-illusion. . . .

Dream is felt to be unreal, first, because it ceases and has no further validity when we pass from one status of consciousness to another which is our normal status. But this is not by itself a sufficient reason: for it may well be that there are different states of consciousness each with its own realities; if the consciousness of one state of things fades back and its contents are lost or, even when caught in memory, seem to be illusory as soon as we pass into another state, that would be perfectly normal, but it would not prove the reality of the state in which we now are and the unreality of the other which we have left behind us. If earth circumstances begin to seem unreal to a soul passing into a different world or another plane of consciousness, that would not prove their unreality; similarly, the fact that world-existence seems unreal to us when we pass into the spiritual silence or into some *nirvāṇa*, does not of itself prove that the cosmos was all the time an illusion. The world is real to the consciousness dwelling in it, an unconditioned existence is real to the consciousness absorbed in *nirvāṇa*; that is all that is established. But the second reason for refusing credit to our sleep experience is that a dream is something evanescent without antecedents and without a sequel; ordinarily, too, it is without any sufficient coherence or any significance intelligible to our waking being. If our dreams wore like our waking life an aspect of coherence, each night taking up and carrying farther a past continuous and connected sleep experience as each day takes up again our waking world-experience, then dreams would assume to our mind quite another character. There is therefore no analogy between a dream and waking life; these are experiences quite different in their character, validity, order. . . . (*ibid.*, pp. 373–8.)

. . . It may be said, however, that our dreams are not themselves realities but only a transcript of reality, a system of symbol-images, and our waking experience of the universe is similarly not a reality but only a transcript of reality, a series or collection of symbol-images. It is quite true that primarily we see the physical universe only through a system of images impressed or imposed on our senses and so far the contention is justified; it may also be admitted that in a certain sense and from one view-point our experiences and activities can be considered as symbols of a truth which our lives are trying to express but at present only with a partial success and an imperfect coherence. If that were all, life might be described as a dream experience of self and things in the consciousness of the Infinite. But although our primary evidence of the objects of the universe consists of a structure of sense images, these are completed, validated, set in order by an automatic intuition in the consciousness which immediately relates the image with the thing imaged and gets the tangible experience of the object, so that we are not merely regarding or reading a translation or sense-transcript of the reality but looking through the sense-image to the reality. This adequacy is amplified too by the action of a reason which fathoms and understands the law of things sensed and can observe scrupulously the sense-transcript and correct its errors. Therefore we may conclude that we experience a real universe through our imaged sense-transcript by the aid of the intuition and the reason,—an intuition which gives us the touch of things and a reason which investigates their truth by its conceptive knowledge. But we must note also that even if our image view of the universe, our sense-transcript, is a system of symbol images and not an exact reproduction or transcription, a literal translation, still a symbol is a notation of something that is, a transcript of realities. Even if our images are incorrect, what they endeavour to image are realities, not illusions; when we see a tree or a stone or an animal, it is not a non-existent figure, a hallucination that we are seeing; we may not be sure that the image is exact, we may concede that other-sense might very well see it otherwise, but still there is something there that justifies the image, something with which it has more or less correspondence. But in the theory of illusion the only reality is an indeterminable featureless pure Existence, *Brahman*, and there is no possibility of its being translated or mistranslated into a system of symbol-figures, for that could only be if this Existence had some determinate contents or some unmanifested truths of its being which could be transcribed into the forms or names given to them by our consciousness: a pure indeterminable cannot be rendered by a transcript, a multitude of representative differentiae, a crowd of symbols or images; for there is in it only a pure identity, there is nothing to transcribe, nothing to symbolize, nothing to image. Therefore the dream analogy fails us altogether and is better put out of the way; it can always be used as a vivid metaphor of a certain attitude our mind can take towards its experiences, but it has no value for a metaphysical enquiry into the reality and fundamental significances or the origin of existence. (*ibid.*, pp. 384–5.)

If we scrutinise other illustrations or analogies that are offered to us for a better understanding of the operation of *māyā*, we detect in all of them an inapplicability that deprives them of their force and value. The familiar instance of mother-of-pearl and silver turns also, like the rope and snake analogy, upon an error due to a resemblance between a present real and another and absent real; it can have no application to the imposition of a multiple and mutable unreality upon a sole and unique immutable Real. In the example of an optical illusion duplicating or multiplying a single object, as when we see two moons instead of one, there are two or more identical forms of the one object, one real, one—or the rest—an illusion: this does not illustrate the juxtaposition of world and *Brahman*; for in the operation of *māyā* there is a much more complex phenomenon,—there is indeed an illusory multiplication of the identical imposed upon its one and ever-unalterable identity, the one appearing as many but upon that is imposed an immense organised diversity in nature, a diversity of forms and movements which have nothing to do with the original Real. Dreams, visions, the imagination of the artist or poet can present such an organised diversity which is not real; but it is an imitation, a mimesis of a real and already existent organised diversity, or it starts from such a mimesis and even in the richest variation or wildest imagination some mimetic element is observable. There is here no such thing as the operation attributed to *māyā* in which there is no mimesis but a pure and radically original creation of unreal forms and movements that are non-existent anywhere and neither imitate nor reflect nor alter and develop anything discoverable in the reality. There is nothing in the operations of mind illusion that throws light upon this mystery; it is, as a stupendous cosmic illusion of this kind must be, *sui generis* without parallel. What we see in the universe is that a diversity of the identical is everywhere the fundamental operation of cosmic Nature; but here it presents itself, not as an illusion, but as a various real formation out of a one original substance. A reality of oneness manifesting itself in a reality of numberless forms and powers of its being is what we confront everywhere. There is no doubt in its process a mystery, even a magic, but there is nothing to show that it is a magic of the unreal and not a working of a consciousness and force of being of the omnipotent real, a self-creation operated by an eternal self-knowledge. (*ibid.*, pp. 387–8.)

Existence that acts and creates by the power and from the pure delight of its conscious being is the reality that we are, the self of all our modes and moods, the cause, object and goal of all our doing, becoming and creating. As the poet, artist or musician when he creates does really nothing but develop some potentiality in his unmanifested self into a form of manifestation and as the thinker, statesman, mechanist only bring out into a shape of things that which lay hidden in themselves, was themselves, is still themselves when it is cast into form, so is it with the world and the Eternal. All creation or becoming is nothing but this self-manifestation. . . .

. . . Therefore whatever comes into the world, seeks nothing but this, to be, to arrive at the intended form, to enlarge its self-existence in that form, to develop, manifest, increase, realise infinitely the consciousness and the power that is in it, to have the delight of coming into manifestation, the delight of the form of being, the delight of the rhythm of consciousness, the delight of the play of force and to aggrandise and perfect that delight by whatever means is possible, in whatever direction, through whatever idea of itself may be suggested to it by the existence, the conscious-force, the delight active within its deepest being. (*ibid.*, pp. 105–6.)

. . . Infinite consciousness in its infinite action can produce only infinite results; to settle upon a fixed truth or order of truths and build a world in conformity with that which is fixed, demands a selective faculty of knowledge commissioned to shape finite appearance out of the infinite reality.

This power was known to the Vedic seers by the name of *māyā*. *Māyā* meant for them the power of infinite consciousness to comprehend, contain in itself and measure out, that is to say, to form—for form is delimitation—name and shape out of the vast illimitable truth of infinite existence. It is by *māyā* that static truth of essential being becomes ordered truth of active being,—or, to put it in more metaphysical language, out of the supreme being in which all is all without barrier of separative consciousness emerges the phenomenal being in which all is in each and each is in all for the play of existence with existence, consciousness with consciousness, force with force, delight with delight. This play of all in each and each in all is concealed at first from us by the mental play or the illusion of *māyā* which persuades each that he is in all but not all in him and that he is in all as a separated being not as a being always inseparably one with the rest of existence. Afterwards we have to emerge from this error into the supramental play or the truth of *māyā* where the "each" and the "all" coexist in the inseparable unity of the one truth and the multiple symbol. The lower, present and deluding mental *māyā* has first to be embraced, then to be overcome; for it is God's play with division and darkness and limitation, desire and strife and suffering in which He subjects Himself to the force that has come out of Himself and by her obscure suffers Himself to be obscured. That other *māyā* concealed by this mental has to be overpassed, then embraced; for it is God's play of the infinities of existence, the splendours of knowledge, the glories of force mastered and the ecstasies of love illimitable where He emerges out of the hold of force, holds her instead and fulfils in her illumined that for which she went out from Him at the first.

This distinction between the lower and the higher *māyā* is the link in thought and in cosmic fact which the pessimistic and illusionist philosophies miss or neglect.... (*ibid.*, 108–9.)

5. *The Supermind or Truth-Consciousness*

Still, when we have found that all things are *Saccidānanda* [existence-consciousness-force-bliss], all has not yet been explained. We know the reality of the universe, we do not yet know the process by which that reality has turned itself into this phenomenon....For this existence, conscious-force, delight does not work directly or with a sovereign irresponsibility like a magician building up worlds and universes by the mere fiat of its word. We perceive a process, we are aware of a law.

...When we perceive that force is a self-expression of existence, we are bound to perceive also that this line which force has taken, corresponds to some self-truth of that existence which governs and determines its constant curve and destination. And since consciousness is the nature of the original existence and the essence of its force, this truth must be a self-perception in conscious-being and this determination of the line taken by force must result from a power of self-directive knowledge inherent in consciousness which enables it to guide its own force inevitably along the logical line of the original self-perception. It is then a self-determining power in universal consciousness, a capacity in self-awareness of infinite existence to perceive a certain truth in itself and direct its force of creation along the line of that truth, which has presided over the cosmic manifestation. (*ibid.*, p. 107.)

...A truth of conscious being supports these forms and expresses itself in them, and the knowledge corresponding to the truth thus expressed reigns as a supramental truth-consciousness organising real ideas in a perfect harmony before they are cast into the mental-vital-material mould. Mind, life and body are an inferior consciousness and a partial expression which strives to arrive in the mould of a various evolution at that superior expression of itself already existent to the beyond-mind. That which is in the beyond-mind is the ideal which in its own conditions it is labouring to realise. . . .

Mind is not sufficient to explain existence in the universe. Infinite consciousness must first translate itself into infinite faculty of knowledge or, as we call it from our point of view, omniscience; but mind is not a faculty of knowledge nor an instrument of omniscience; it is a faculty for the seeking of knowledge, for expressing as much as it can gain of it in certain forms of a relative thought and for using it towards certain capacities of action. Even when it finds, it does not possess; it only keeps a certain fund of current coin of truth—not truth itself—in the bank of memory to draw upon according to its needs. For mind is that which does not know, which tries to know and which never knows except as in a glass darkly. It is the power which interprets truth of universal existence for the practical uses of a certain order of things; it is not the power which knows and guides that existence and therefore it cannot be the power which created or manifested it. (*ibid.*, pp. 109–10.)

A principle of active will and knowledge superior to mind and creatrix of the worlds is then the intermediary power and state of being between that self-possession of the one and this flux of the many. . . .

. . . But since this consciousness is creatrix of the world, it must be not only state of knowledge, but power of knowledge, and not only a will to light and vision, but a will to power and works. And since mind too is created out of it, mind must be a development by limitation out of this primal faculty and this mediatory act of the supreme consciousness and must therefore be capable of resolving itself back into it through a reverse development by expansion. For always mind must be identical with supermind, . . . however different or even contrary it may have become in its actual forms and settled modes of operation. . . . (*ibid.*, pp. 114–15.)

. . . This intermediary term is therefore the beginning and end of all creation and arrangement, . . . the starting-point of all differentiation, the instrument of all unification, originative, executive and consummative of all realised or realisable harmonies. It has the knowledge of the One, but is able to draw out of the one its hidden multitudes; it manifests the many, but does not lose itself in their differentiations. And shall we not say that its very existence points back to something beyond our supreme perception of the ineffable unity,—something ineffable and mentally inconceivable not because of its unity and indivisibility, but because of its freedom from even these formulations of our mind,—something beyond both unity and multiplicity? That would be the utter Absolute and real which yet justifies to us both our knowledge of God and our knowledge of the world. (*ibid.*, pp. 117–18.)

In supermind being, consciousness of knowledge and consciousness of will are not divided as they seem to be in our mental operations; they are a trinity, one movement with three effective aspects. Each has its own effect. Being gives the effect of substance, consciousness the effect of knowledge, of the self-guiding and shaping idea, of comprehension and apprehension; will gives the effect of self-fulfilling force. But the idea is only the light of the reality illumining itself; it is not mental thought nor imagination, but effective self-awareness. It is real-idea.

In supermind knowledge in the idea is not divorced from will in the idea, but one with it—just as it is not different from being or substance, but is one with the being, luminous power of the substance. As the power of burning light is not different from the substance of the fire, so the power of the idea is not different from the substance of the being which works itself out in the idea and its development. (*ibid.*, p. 121.)

6. *The Ascending Series of Substance*

. . . if there is, as there must be in the nature of things, an ascending series in the scale of substance from matter to spirit, it must be marked by a progressive diminution of these capacities most characteristic of the physical principle and a progressive increase of the opposite characteristics which will lead us to the formula of pure spiritual self-extension. . . . Drawing away from durability of form, we draw towards eternity of essence; drawing away from our poise in the persistent separation and resistance of physical matter, we draw near to the highest divine poise in the infinity, unity and indivisibility of spirit. Between gross substance and pure spirit substance this must be the fundamental antinomy. In matter *cit* or conscious-force masses itself more and more to resist and stand out against other masses of the same conscious-force; in substance of spirit pure consciousness images itself freely in its sense of itself with an essential indivisibility and a constant unifying interchange as the basic formula even of the most diversifying play of its own force. Between these two poles there is the possibility of an infinite gradation. (*ibid.*, p. 233.)

Even within the formula of the physical cosmos there is an ascending series in the scale of matter which leads us from the more to the less dense, from the less to the more subtle. Where we reach the highest term of that series, the most supra-ethereal subtlety of material substance or formulation of force, what lies beyond? Not a *nihil*, not a void; for there is no such thing as absolute void or real nullity and what we call by that name is simply something beyond the grasp of our sense, our mind or our most subtle consciousness. Nor is it true that there is nothing beyond, or that some ethereal substance of matter is the eternal beginning; for we know that matter and material force are only a last result of a pure substance and pure force in which consciousness is luminously self-aware and self-possessing and not as in matter lost to itself in an inconscient sleep and an inert motion. What then is there between this material substance and that pure substance? For we do not leap from the one to the other, we do not pass at once from the inconscient to absolute consciousness. There must be and there are grades between inconscient substance and utterly self-conscious self-extension, as between the principle of matter and the principle of spirit. (*ibid.*, pp. 234–5.)

In the next grade of substance the initial, dominating, determining fact is no longer substantial form and force, but life and conscious desire. Therefore the world beyond this material plane must be a world based upon a conscious cosmic vital energy, a force of vital seeking and a force of desire and their self-expression and not upon an inconscient or subconscient will taking the form of a material force and energy. All the forms, bodies, forces, life-movements, sense-movements, thought-movements, developments, culminations, self-fulfilments of that world must be dominated and determined by this initial fact of conscious-life to which matter and mind must subject themselves, must start from that, base themselves upon that, be limited or enlarged by its laws, powers, capacities, limitations; and if mind there seeks to develop yet higher possibilities, still it must then too take account of the original vital formula of desire-force, its purpose and its demand upon the divine manifestation.

So too with the higher gradations. The next in the series must be governed by the dominating and determining factor of mind. Substance there must be subtle and flexible enough to assume the shapes directly imposed upon it by mind, to obey its operations, to subordinate itself to its demand for self-expression and self-fulfilment. The relations of sense and substance too must have a corresponding subtlety and flexibility and must be determined, not by the relations of physical organ with physical object, but of mind with the subtler substance upon which it works. The life of such a world would be the servant of mind in a sense of which our weak mental operations and our limited, coarse and rebellious vital faculties can have no adequate conception. There mind dominates as the original formula, its purpose prevails, its demand overrides all others in the law of the divine manifestation. At a yet higher reach supermind—or, intermediately, principles touched by it—or, still higher, a pure bliss, a pure conscious Power or pure Being replace mind as the dominant principle, and we enter into those ranges of cosmic existence which to the old Vedic seers were the worlds of illuminated divine existence and the foundation of what they termed immortality. . . .

The principle which underlies this continually ascending experience and vision uplifted beyond the material formulation of things is that all cosmic existence is a complex harmony and does not finish with the limited range of consciousness in which the ordinary human mind and life is content to be imprisoned. Being, consciousness, force, substance descend and ascend a many-runged ladder on each step of which being has a vaster self-extension, consciousness a wider sense of its own range and largeness and joy, force a greater intensity and a more rapid and blissful capacity, substance gives a more subtle, plastic, buoyant and flexible rendering of its primal reality. For the more subtle is also the more powerful,—one might say, the more truly concrete; it is less bound than the gross, it has a greater permanence in its being along with a greater potentiality, plasticity and range in its becoming. Each plateau of the hill of being gives to our widening experience a higher plane of our consciousness and a richer world for our existence.

But how does this ascending series affect the possibilities of our material existence? It would not affect them at all if each plane of consciousness, each world of existence, each grade of substance, each degree of cosmic force were cut off entirely from that which precedes and that which follows it. But the opposite is the truth; the manifestation of the spirit is a complex weft and in the design and pattern of one principle all the others enter as elements of the spiritual whole. Our material world is the result of all the others, for the other principles have all descended into matter to create the physical universe, and every particle of what we call matter contains all of them implicit in itself; their secret action, as we have seen, is involved in every moment of its existence and every movement of its activity. And as matter is the last word of the descent, so it is also the first word of the ascent; as the powers of all these planes, worlds, grades, degrees are involved in the material existence, so are they all capable of evolution out of it. It is for this reason that material being does not begin and end with gases and chemical compounds and physical forces and movements, with nebulae and suns and earths, but evolves life, evolves mind, must evolve eventually supermind and the higher degrees of the spiritual existence. Evolution comes by the unceasing pressure of the supra-material planes on the material compelling it to deliver out of itself their principles and powers which might conceivably otherwise have slept imprisoned in the rigidity of the material formula. This would even so have been improbable, since their presence there implies a purpose of deliverance; but still this necessity from below is actually very much aided by a kindred superior pressure.

Nor can this evolution end with the first meagre formulation of life, mind, supermind, spirit conceded to these higher powers by the reluctant power of matter. For as they evolve, as they awake, as they become more active and avid of their own potentialities, the pressure on them of the superior planes, a pressure involved in the existence and close connection and interdependence of the worlds, must also increase in insistence, power and effectiveness. Not only must these principles manifest from below in a qualified and restricted emergence, but also from above they must descend in their characteristic power and full possible efflorescence into the material being; the material creature must open to a wider and wider play of their activities in matter, and all that is needed is a fit receptacle, medium, instrument. That is provided for in the body, life and consciousness of man.

Certainly, if that body, life and consciousness were limited to the possibilities of the gross body which are all that our physical senses and physical mentality accept, there would be a very narrow term for this evolution, and the human being could not hope to accomplish anything essentially greater than his present achievement. But this body, as ancient occult science discovered, is not the whole even of our physical being; this gross density is not all of our substance. The oldest Vedāntic knowledge tells us of five degrees of our being, the material, the vital, the mental, the ideal, the spiritual or beatific and to each of these grades of our soul there corresponds a grade of our substance, a sheath as it was called in the ancient figurative language. A later psychology found that these five sheaths of our substance were the material of three bodies, gross physical, subtle and causal, in all of which the soul actually and simultaneously dwells, although here and now we are superficially conscious only of the material vehicle. But it is possible to become conscious in our other bodies as well and it is in fact the opening up of the veil between them and consequently between our physical, psychical and ideal personalities which is the cause of those "psychic" and "occult" phenomena that are now beginning to be increasingly though yet too little and too clumsily examined, even while they are far too much exploited....

Behind all these terms of ancient psycho-physical science lies the one great fact and law of our being that whatever be its temporary poise of form, consciousness, power in this material evolution, there must be behind it and there is a greater, a truer existence of which this is only the external result and physically sensible aspect. Our substance does not end with the physical body; that is only the earthly pedestal, the terrestrial base, the material starting-point. As there are behind our waking mentality vaster ranges of consciousness subconscient and superconscient to it of which we become sometimes abnormally aware, so there are behind our gross physical being other and subtler grades of substance with a finer law and a greater power which support the denser body and which can by our entering into the ranges of consciousness belonging to them be made to impose that law and power on our dense matter and substitute their purer, higher, intenser conditions of being for the grossness and limitation of our present physical life and impulses and habits. If that be so, then the evolution of a nobler physical existence not limited by the ordinary conditions of animal birth and life and death, of difficult alimentation and facility of disorder and disease and subjection to poor and unsatisfied vital cravings ceases to have the appearance of a dream and chimera and becomes a possibility founded upon a rational and philosophic truth which is in accordance with all the rest that we have hitherto known, experienced or been able to think out about the overt and secret truth of our existence.

So it should rationally be; for the uninterrupted series of the principles of our being and their close mutual connection is too evident for it to be possible that one of them should be condemned and cut off while the others are capable of a divine liberation. The ascent of man from the physical to the supramental must open out the possibility of a corresponding ascent in the grades of substance to that ideal of causal body which is proper to our supramental being, and the conquest of the lower principles by supermind and its liberation of them into a divine life and a divine mentality must also render possible a conquest of our physical limitations by the power and principle of supramental substance. And this means the evolution not only of an untrammelled consciousness, a mind and sense not shut up in the walls of the physical ego or limited to the poor basis of knowledge given by the physical organs of sense, but a life-power liberated more and more from its mortal limitations, a physical life fit for a divine inhabitant and,—in the sense not of attachment or of restriction to our present corporeal frame but an exceeding of the law of the physical body,—the conquest of death, an earthly immortality. For from the divine bliss, the original delight of existence, the Lord of immortality comes pouring the wine of that bliss, the mystic *Soma*, into these jars of mentalised living matter; eternal and beautiful, he enters into these sheaths of substance for the integral transformation of the being and nature. (*ibid.*, pp. 236–40.)

7. *The Gnostic Being and The Divine Life*

As there has been established on earth a mental consciousness and power which shapes a race of mental beings and takes up into itself all of earthly nature that is ready for the change, so now there will be established on earth a gnostic consciousness and power which will shape a race of gnostic spiritual beings and take up into itself all of earth-nature that is ready for this new transformation. It will also receive into itself from above, progressively, from its own domain of perfect light and power and beauty all that is ready to descend from that domain into terrestrial being. For the evolution proceeded in the past by the upsurging, at each critical stage, of a concealed power from its involution in the inconscience, but also by a descent from above, from its own plane, of that power already self-realised in its own higher natural province.... (*ibid.*, p. 859.)

A supramental or gnostic race of beings would not be a race made according to a single type, moulded in a single fixed pattern; for the law of the supermind is unity fulfilled in diversity, and therefore there would be an infinite diversity in the manifestation of the gnostic consciousness although that consciousness would still be one in its basis, in its constitution, in its all-revealing and all-uniting order.... (*ibid.*, p. 862.)

The gnosis is the effective principle of the spirit, a highest dynamis of the spiritual existence. The gnostic individual would be the consummation of the spiritual man; his whole way of being, thinking, living, acting would be governed by the power of a vast universal spirituality....All his existence would be fused into oneness with the transcendent and universal Self and Spirit; all his action would originate from and obey the supreme Self and Spirit's divine governance of Nature.... (*ibid.*, p. 863.)

The supramental being...would act in a universal awareness and a harmony of his individual self with the total self, of his individual will with the total will, of his individual action with the total action. For what we most suffer from in our outer life and its reactions upon our inner life is the imperfection of our relations with the world, our ignorance of others, our disharmony with the whole of things, our inability to equate our demand on the world with the world's demand on us.... (*ibid.*, p. 865.)

...Delight of the manifestation of the spirit in its truth of being would be the sense of the gnostic life. All its movements would be a formulation of the truth of the spirit, but also of the joy of the spirit,—an affirmation of spiritual existence, an affirmation of spiritual consciousness, an affirmation of spiritual delight of being.... (*ibid.*, p. 866.)

An evolution of gnostic consciousness brings with it a transformation of our world-consciousness and world-action: for it takes up into the new power of awareness not only the inner existence but our outer being and our world-being; there is a remaking of both, an integration of them in the sense and power of the spiritual existence. There must come upon us in the change at once a reversal and rejection of our present way of existence and a fulfilment of its inner trend and tendency.... (*ibid.*, pp. 867–8.)

...The peace of God within will be extended in the gnostic experience of the universe into a universal calm of equality not merely passive but dynamic, a calm of freedom in oneness dominating all that meets it, tranquillising all that enters into it, imposing its law of peace on the supramental being's relations with the world in which he is living. Into all his acts the inner oneness, the inner communion will attend him and enter into his relations with others, who will not be to him others but selves of himself in the one existence, his own universal existence. It is this poise and freedom in the spirit that will enable him to take all life into himself while still remaining the spiritual self and to embrace even the world of the ignorance without himself entering into the ignorance. (*ibid.*, p. 869.)

. . . A gnostic being will possess not only a truth-conscious control of the realised spirit's power over its physical world, but also the full power of the mental and vital planes and the use of their greater forces for the perfection of the physical existence. This greater knowledge and wider hold of all existence will enormously increase the power of instrumentation of the gnostic being on his surroundings and on the world of physical Nature. (*ibid.*, p. 870.)

As a consequence of the total change and a reversal of consciousness establishing a new relation of spirit with mind and life and matter, and a new significance and perfection in the relation, there will be a reversal, a perfecting new significance also of the relations between the spirit and the body it inhabits. . . .

This new relation of the spirit and the body assumes—and makes possible—a free acceptance of the whole of material Nature in place of a rejection; the drawing back from her, the refusal of all identification or acceptance, which is the first normal necessity of the spiritual consciousness for its liberation, is no longer imperative. To cease to be identified with the body, to separate oneself from the body consciousness, is a recognised and necessary step whether towards spiritual liberation or towards spiritual perfection and mastery over Nature. But, this redemption once effected, the descent of the spiritual light and force can invade and take up the body also and there can be a new liberated and sovereign acceptance of material Nature. . . . (*ibid.*, pp. 874–6.)

There can undoubtedly be a spiritual life within, a kingdom of heaven within us which is not dependent on any outer manifestation or instrumentation or formula of external being. The inner life has a supreme spiritual importance and the outer has a value only in so far as it is expressive of the inner status . . . but still, from the point of view of a spiritual evolution, this would be only an individual liberation and perfection in an unchanged environmental existence: for a greater dynamic change in earth-nature itself, a spiritual change of the whole principle and instrumentation of life and action, the appearance of a new order of beings and a new earth-life must be envisaged in our idea of the total consummation, the divine issue. Here the gnostic change assumes a primary importance; all that precedes can be considered as an upbuilding and a preparation for this transmuting reversal of the whole nature. For it is a gnostic way of dynamic living that must be the fulfilled divine life on earth, a way of living that develops higher instruments of world-knowledge and world action for the dynamisation of consciousness in the physical existence and takes up and transforms the values of a world of material Nature. (*ibid.*, pp. 903–4.)

To be and to be fully is Nature's aim in us; but to be fully is to be wholly conscious of one's being: unconsciousness, half consciousness or deficient consciousness is a state of being not in possession of itself; it is existence, but not fullness of being. . . .

But also, since consciousness carries in itself the force of existence, to be fully is to have the intrinsic and integral force of one's being; it is to come into possession of all one's force of self and of all its use. . . .

Lastly, to be fully is to have the full delight of being. Being without delight of being, without an entire delight of itself and all things is something neutral or diminished; it is existence, but it is not fullness of being. This delight too must be intrinsic, self-existent, automatic; it cannot be dependent on things outside itself: whatever it delights in, it makes part of itself, has the joy of it as part of its universality. All undelight, all pain and suffering are a sign of imperfection, of incompleteness; they arise from a division of being, an incompleteness of consciousness of being, an incompleteness of the force of being. To become complete in being, in consciousness of being, in force of being, in delight of being and to live in this integrated completeness is the divine living. (*ibid.*, pp. 907–9.)

These things are impossible without an inward living; they cannot be reached by remaining in an external consciousness turned always outwards, active only or mainly on and from the surface. . . . If there is a being of the transcendence in us, it must be there in our secret self; on the surface there is only an ephemeral being of nature, made by limit and circumstance. If there is a self in us capable of largeness and universality, able to enter into a cosmic consciousness, that too must be within our inner being; the outer consciousness is a physical consciousness bound to its individual limits by the triple cord of mind, life and body: any external attempt at universality can only result either in an aggrandisement of the ego or an effacement of the personality by its extinction in the mass or subjugation to the mass. It is only by an inner growth, movement, action that the individual can freely and effectively universalise and transcendentalise his being.... In men, says the Upaniṣad, the Self-Existent has cut the doors of consciousness outward, but a few turn the eye inward and it is these who see and know the Spirit and develop the spiritual being. Thus to look into ourselves and see and enter into ourselves and life within is the first necessity for transformation of nature and for the divine life. (*ibid.*, pp. 910–11.)

...The spiritual individual acts out of that sense of oneness which gives him immediate and direct perception of the demand of self on other self, the need of the life, the good, the work of love and sympathy that can truly be done. A realisation of spiritual unity, a dynamisation of the intimate consciousness of one-being, of one self in all beings, can alone found and govern by its truth the action of the divine life. (*ibid.*, p. 913.)

There is a reality, a truth of all existence which is greater and more abiding than all its formations and manifestations; to find that truth and reality and live in it, achieve the most perfect manifestation and formation possible of it, must be the secret of perfection whether of individual or communal being. This reality is there within each thing and gives to each of its formations its power of being and value of being.... (*ibid.*, p. 929.)

...A perfected community also can exist only by the perfection of its individuals, and perfection can come only by the discovery and affirmation in life by each of his own spiritual being and the discovery by all of their spiritual unity and a resultant life unity. There can be no real perfection for us except by our inner self and truth of spiritual existence taking up all truth of the instrumental existence into itself and giving to it oneness, integration, harmony. As our only real freedom is the discovery and disengagement of the spiritual reality within us, so our only means of true perfection is the sovereignty and self-effectuation of the spiritual reality in all the elements of our nature. (*ibid.*, p. 931.)

It is almost universally supposed that spiritual life must necessarily be a life of ascetic spareness, a pushing away of all that is not absolutely needed for the bare maintenance of the body; and this is valid for a spiritual life which is in its nature and intention a life of withdrawal from life. Even apart from that ideal, it might be thought that the spiritual turn must always make for an extreme simplicity, because all else would be a life of vital desire and physical self-indulgence. But from a wider standpoint this is a mental standard based on the law of the ignorance of which desire is the motive; to overcome the ignorance, to delete the ego, a total rejection not only of desire but of all the things that can satisfy desire may intervene as a valid principle. But this standard or any mental standard cannot be absolute nor can it be binding as a law on the consciousness that has arisen above desire; a complete purity and self-mastery would be in the very grain of its nature and that would remain the same in poverty or in riches: for if it could be shaken or sullied by either, it would not be real or would not be complete. The one rule of the gnostic life would be the self-expression of the Spirit, the will of the Divine Being; that will, that self-expression could manifest through extreme simplicity or through extreme complexity and opulence or in their natural balance,—for beauty and plenitude, a hidden sweetness and laughter in things, a sunshine and gladness of life are also powers and expressions of the Spirit. In all directions the spirit within determining the law of the nature would determine the frame of the life and its detail and circumstance. In all there would be the same plastic principle; a rigid standardisation, however necessary for the mind's arrangement of things, could not be the law of the spiritual life. A great diversity and liberty of self-expression based on an underlying unity might well become manifest; but everywhere there would be harmony and truth of order. (*ibid.*, pp. 944–5.)

If there is an evolution in material Nature and if it is an evolution of being with consciousness and life as its two key-terms and powers, this fullness of being, fullness of consciousness, fullness of life must be the goal of development towards which we are tending and which will manifest at an early or later stage of our destiny. . . . (*ibid.*, p. 947.)[1]

[1] Except for capitalization and Sanskrit transliteration, which have been modified to conform with the style used throughout this volume, the selections in this chapter follow the original texts literally—in spelling, hyphenation, and construction.

CHAPTER XVII

SARVEPALLI RADHAKRISHNAN

SARVEPALLI RADHAKRISHNAN (1888–) is a versatile genius, universally recognized and acclaimed for his remarkable ability as teacher, lecturer, scholar, and administrator, as philosopher, statesman, and India's cultural ambassador throughout the East and the West. His deep learning, his brilliant style, and his absolute tolerance have brought him recognition not only as the greatest living interpreter of Indian philosophy, religion, and culture, but also as an original and creative thinker of the first order. In essence, his philosophy is absolute idealism, but in a form and with a dynamic character which, instead of nullifying the great richness of the many facets of life and experience in terms of a wholly transcendent Absolute, recognizes the reality and the meaning of the many aspects and grades of experience. In all phases of his philosophy, he reveals a synthesizing ability which enables him, in conformity with the essence of the great Indian tradition, to avoid all extremes. In this spirit, Radhakrishnan resolves the traditional oppositions between the Absolute and the non-absolute, God and the world, appearance and reality, intuition and reason, philosophy and religion, and philosophy and life, as well as contradictions and oppositions among the various religious and philosophical systems. Radhakrishnan stands as a profound critic of all forms of exclusiveness, one-sided perspective, dogmatism, and intolerance. He supports this with a philosophical perspective which avoids mere eclecticism through a truly enlightened integration.

Radhakrishnan's greatest contributions are, first, his re-interpretation of the doctrine of *māyā* in the Advaita Vedānta of Śaṁkara, and, second, the exposition of a profound philosophy of the religion of the spirit. According to Radhakrishnan, *māyā* has not meant to Indian philosophers, even to Śaṁkara, that the world is illusion. The world of everyday events and things is not ultimate reality, to be sure, but neither is it unreality.[1] He has defended the reality of the empirical world; it finds its basis in the Absolute. The Absolute is the source of its many transformations but these transformations in the world of the here-and-now do not, in turn, affect the integrity or absoluteness of *Brahman*. In this way he overcomes the greatest obstacle to Western cordiality to the most highly-developed

[1] See his *Indian Philosophy* (London: George Allen & Unwin Ltd., 2nd revised edition, 1931), Vol. II, chap. VIII.

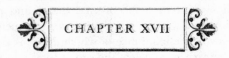

philosophy in India, Śaṁkara's Advaita Vedānta, and in this way paves the way for much greater understanding of India's greatest heights of thought and for a possible meeting of the minds of East and West.

His religion of the spirit, accompanied by a deep religious fervor and conviction, provides him with the belief that the essence of all religions is the same, since, as he says, "...religion is not a creed or code but an insight into reality." In this attitude, Radhakrishnan has taken religion out of the realm of conflicts and bickerings, out of the realm of dogmas and authoritarianism, and has made it into a living philosophy of the spirit, in which he has imbued religion with depth and meaning and practicality both for India and for all mankind.

Interpreting, purifying, and extending the wisdom of the ancient Indian tradition, and looking at truth and reality from the total perspective of the wisdom of East and West, Radhakrishnan has given man a comprehensive philosophy of the spirit which may well be the basis of the future peace of the world and the unity of mankind. (C. A. M.)

Extensive selections from the writings of Radhakrishnan are not required in a book of this type, since all his major works are still in print and are readily available. The brief selection given here is his most concentrated presentation of his religion of the spirit and is to be found in Chapter III of *An Idealist View of Life* (London: George Allen & Unwin Ltd., 1929). (C. A. M.)

RELIGIOUS EXPERIENCE AND ITS AFFIRMATIONS

What is Philosophy of Religion? The Essence of Religion—Personal Experience of God—Its Character and Content—Experience and the Variety of Expressions—God and Self—The World a Harmony—Self-Recognition and the Way to It—The Life of the Reborn—Rebirth—Salvation—Summary.

Philosophy of Religion

Philosophy of religion is religion come to an understanding of itself. It attempts a reasoned solution of a problem which exists directly only for the religious man who has the spiritual intuition or experience and indirectly for all those who, while they have no personal share in the experience, yet have sufficient belief that the experience does occur and is not illusory. The direct apprehension of God seems to be as real to some men as the consciousness of personality or the perception of the external world is to others. The sense of communion with the divine, the awe and worship which it evokes, which to us are only moments of vision or insight, seem to be normal and all-pervading with the saints. If philosophy of religion is to become scientific, it must become empirical and found itself on religious experience.

Before thinking can start there must be something thought about. Thinking does not produce its object but has it offered to it as a datum. If thought cuts itself away from the compulsion of fact, to that extent it ceases to be thought and becomes imagination. Just as there can be no geometry without the perception of space, even so there cannot be philosophy of religion without the facts of religion.

As we have seen, sometimes psychology of religion professes to serve as a substitute for philosophy and repudiates the validity of religious intuitions by tracing them to psychological factors as subconscious desires. To trace the psychological conditions of a belief is not to determine its validity. To say that our sense perceptions answer to reality, while spiritual intuitions do not, is for psychology a gratuitous assumption. Psychologically the experience we have of the world before us or of the British constitution or of the categorical nature of duty is on the same level as St Paul's vision on the road to Damascus or Augustine's in the Italian garden. In the experience itself no question is raised whether the object experienced is real or not. Professor Alexander says: "It is for the worshipper as much a fact as a green leaf or the sun is for a dispassionate observer. The religious feeling and its object are given in one and the same experience."[1] It is for philosophy of religion to find out whether the convictions of the religious seers fit in with the tested laws and principles of the universe.

It is sometimes urged that while the psychological experiences rationalised by science are more or less uniform for all observers, the data for philosophy of religion are diverse and discordant. Stones are hard and the sky is blue for all. But God is Buddha to some and Christ to some others. This difference means that the facts are more complex and require closer study. Just as we attempt to formulate in precise terms our sense experience in the natural sciences, even so philosophy of religion attempts to define the world to which our religious experiences refer. There is no reason why the intuitions of the human soul with regard to the ultimate reality should be studied in any other spirit or by any other method than those which are adopted with such great success in the region of positive science. When we speak of matter, life or mind, we refer to a certain type of

[1] *Hibbert Journal*, January 1928, p. 251.

experiences. Matter means a set of experiences with a certain definite character and we account for it by the hypothesis of electric energy or other kinds of resistance. The same is true of life and mind. Religious experiences possess their own distinctive character and we seem to be in touch with reality other than that of matter, life or mind. We cannot say that we know matter, life and mind and not God or ultimate spirit. As a matter of fact, we do not know precisely what matter or life is. We know that they are objects of experience though their real nature is hidden from us. So also we may not know the ultimate meaning of God, though we may know something about God or what answers to God in reality through religious experience. The creeds of religion correspond to theories of science. The physicist attempts to account for physical phenomena by the hypothesis of the electron and feels that his mental picture of it is like the real thing. However, we are realising that it is simply impossible to form any picture at all of the ultimate nature of the physical world. The theories are symbolic and are accepted because they work. Similarly, we have certain experiences which we try to account for by the assumption of God. The God of our imagination may be as real as the electron but is not necessarily the reality which we immediately apprehend. The idea of God is an interpretation of experience.

Purely speculative theology which cuts itself off from religious tradition and experience and works from premises which are held to be universally valid cannot serve as an adequate philosophy of religion. The proofs of God's existence from premises of a general character yield not the God of religion but a supreme first cause or being who can be construed into the object of religious experience only if we start with the latter.[1] A category of thought with no basis in fact is not an experienced certainty. No stable conviction can be built on mere dialectic. Speculative theology can conceive of God as a possibility; it is religion that affirms God as a fact.

In dogmatic theology, on the other hand, the theologian regards himself as an expositor of traditional doctrine accepted as revealed and his task is limited to the elimination of contradictions in it. He takes his stand on one set of facts and ignores elements of reality that his scheme does not recognise. Within limits the theologian is allowed

[1] "What in the end does the most complete teleology prove?" asks Kant. "Does it prove that there is such an intelligent Being? No. It only proves that according to the constitution of our cognitive fa ulties we can form absolutely no concept of the possibility of such a world as this save by thinking a designedly-working supreme cause thereof." (*Critique of Judgment*, Bernard's E.T., p. 311.)

freedom to interpret doctrines and elucidate their implications, but his investigations should always confirm the dogmas. While the methods are optional, the conclusions are obligatory.

Philosophy of religion as distinct from dogmatic theology refuses to accept any restricted basis but takes its stand on experience as wide as human nature itself. It rejects the high *a priori* road of speculative theology and adopts a scientific view of religious experience and examines with detachment and impartiality the spiritual inheritance of men of all creeds and of none. Such an examination of the claims and contents of religious consciousness, which has for its background the whole spiritual history of man, has in it the promise of a spiritual idealism which is opposed to the disintegrating forces of scientific naturalism on the one hand and religious dogmatism on the other.

The Essence of Religion

Religion has been identified with feeling, emotion and sentiment, instinct, cult and ritual, perception, belief and faith, and these views are right in what they affirm, though wrong in what they deny. Schleiermacher is not wrong in saying that there is a predominant feeling element in the religious consciousness. Religious feeling, however, is quite distinct from any other kind of feeling. Nor is it to be identified with a sense of creaturely dependence; for then Hegel might retort that Schleiermacher's dog may be more pious than his master. If we assimilate religious experience to the moral consciousness, as Kant is inclined to do, we overlook the distinctive characters of the two activities. Religion is not mere consciousness of value. There is in it a mystical element, an apprehension of the real and an enjoyment of it for its own sake which is absent in the moral consciousness. Religion is not a form of knowledge as Hegel sometimes urged. While religion implies a metaphysical view of the universe, it is not to be confused with philosophy.

When Professor Whitehead defines religion as "what the individual does with his own solitariness,[1] he is urging that it is not a mere social phenomenon. It is not an apologetic for the existing social order; nor is it a mere instrument for social salvation. It is an attempt to discover the ideal possibilities of human life, a quest for emancipation from the immediate compulsions of vain and petty moods. It is not true religion unless it ceases to be a traditional view and becomes

[1] *Religion in the Making* (1926), p. 6.

personal experience. It is an independent functioning of the human mind, something unique, possessing an autonomous character. It is something inward and personal which unifies all values and organises all experiences.[1] It is the reaction of the whole man to the whole reality. We seek the religious object by the totality of our faculties and energies. Such functioning of the whole man may be called spiritual life, as distinct from a merely intellectual or moral or aesthetic activity or a combination of them. The spiritual sense, the instinct for the real, is not satisfied with anything less than the absolute and the eternal. It shows an incurable dissatisfaction with the finiteness of the finite, the transiency of the transient. Such integral intuitions are our authority for religion. They reveal a Being who makes himself known to us through them and produces revolt and discontent with anything short of the eternal.

Personal Experience of God

All the religions owe their inspiration to the personal insights of their prophet founders. The Hindu Religion, for example, is characterised by its adherence to fact. In its pure form, at any rate, it never leaned as heavily as other religions do on authority. It is not a "founded" religion; nor does it centre round any historical events. Its distinctive characteristic has been its insistence on the inward life of spirit. To know, possess and be the spirit in this physical frame, to convert an obscure plodding mentality into clear spiritual illumination, to build peace and self-existent freedom in the stress of emotional satisfactions and sufferings, to discover and realise the life divine in a body subject to sickness and death has been the constant aim of the Hindu religious endeavour. The Hindus look back to the Vedic period as the epoch of their founders. The Veda, the wisdom, is the accepted name for the highest spiritual truth of which the human mind is capable. It is the work of the *ṛṣis* or the seers. The truths of the *ṛṣis* are not evolved as the result of logical reasoning or systematic philosophy but they are the products of spiritual intuition, *dṛṣṭi* or vision. The *ṛṣis* are not so much the authors of the truths recorded in the Vedas as the seers who were able to discern the eternal truths

[1] When Croce declines to regard religion as an autonomous form of experience, and veiws it as an immature misunderstood form of philosophy, when Gentile treats it as a stage, though essential in our spiritual development, they are voicing their protest against the transcendental conceptions of God. The God before whose majesty we abase ourselves, or to whose love we surrender ourselves, is completely immanent, is the spirit in man objectified.

by raising their life-spirit to the plane of the universal spirit. They are the pioneer researchers in the realm of spirit who saw more in the world than their fellows. Their utterances are based not on transitory vision but on a continuous experience of resident life and power.[1] When the Vedas are regarded as the highest authority, all that is meant is that the most exacting of all authorities is the authority of facts.

If experience is the soul of religion, expression is the body through which it fulfils its destiny. We have the spiritual facts and their interpretations by which they are communicated to others, *śruti* or what is heard, and *smṛti* or what is remembered. Śaṁkara equates them with *pratyakṣa* or intuition and *anumāna* or inference. It is the distinction between immediacy and thought. Intuitions abide, while interpretations change. *Śruti* and *smṛti* differ as the authority of fact and the authority of interpretation. Theory, speculation, dogma, change from time to time as the facts become better understood. Their value is acquired from their adequacy to experience. When forms dissolve and the interpretations are doubted, it is a call to get back to the experience itself and reformulate its content in more suitable terms. While the experiential character of religion is emphasised in the Hindu faith, every religion at its best falls back on it.

The whole scheme of Buddhism centres on Buddha's enlightenment. Moses saw God in the burning bush, and Elijah heard the still small voice. In Jeremiah we read: "This is the covenant which I will make with the house of Israel after those days, saith the Lord. I will put my hand in their inward parts, and in their heart will I write it."[2] Jesus' experience of God is the basic fact for Christianity: "As he came up out of the river he saw the heavens parted above him and the spirit descending like a dove towards him: and he heard a voice sounding out of the heavens and saying 'Thou art my beloved son. I have chosen thee.'" According to St. Mark, the baptism in the Jordan by John was to Jesus the occasion of a vivid and intense religious experience, so much so that he felt that he had to go for a time into absolute solitude to think it over.[3] He obviously spoke of the ineffable happening, the sudden revelation, the new peace and joy in words that have come down to us. He emphasises the newness of the reborn soul as something which marks him off from all those who are religious only at second hand. "Verily I say unto you, among men born of women there hath not arisen a greater than John

[1] *Sadā paśyanti sūrayaḥ.* [2] xxxi. 37. [3] Mark i.10.

the Baptist; but the least in the Kingdom of God is greater than he."[1] The vision that came to Saul on the Damascus road and turned the persecutor into an apostle[2] is another illustration. Faith means in St. James acceptance of dogma; in St. Paul it is the surrender of heart and mind to Christ; but in the Epistle to the Hebrews, faith is defined as that outreaching of the mind by which we become aware of the invisible world.[3] The life of Mohammad is full of mystic experiences. Witnesses to the personal sense of the divine are not confined to the East. Socrates and Plato, Plotinus and Porphyry, Augustine and Dante, Bunyan and Wesley, and numberless others, testify to the felt reality of God. It is as old as humanity and is not confined to any one people. The evidence is too massive to run away from.

Character of Religious Experience

To study the nature of this experience is rather a difficult matter. All that one can hope to do is to set down a few general impressions. It is a type of experience which is not clearly differentiated into a subject-object state, an integral, undivided consciousness in which not merely this or that side of man's nature but his whole being seems to find itself. It is a condition of consciousness in which feelings are fused, ideas melt into one another, boundaries broken and ordinary distinctions transcended.[4] Past and present fade away in a sense of timeless being. Consciousness and being are not there different from each other. All being is consciousness and all consciousness being. Thought and reality coalesce and a creative merging of subject and object results. Life grows conscious of its incredible depths. In this fulness of felt life and freedom, the distinction of the knower and the known disappears.[5] The privacy of the individual self is broken

[1] See also Matt. xi.11.

[2] Acts ix.1–9.

[3] See also I Cor. xiii.12; Romans viii.18–25; Rev. xiii.22.

[4] "In this intelligible world, everything is transparent. No shadow limits vision. All the essences see each other and interpenetrate each other in the most intimate depth of their nature. Light everywhere meets light. Every being contains within itself the entire Intelligible world, and also beholds it entire in any particular being. . . . There abides pure movement; for He who produces movement, not being foreign to it, does not disturb it in its production. Rest is perfect, because it is not mingled with any principle of disturbance. The Beautiful is completely beautiful there, because it does not dwell in that which is not beautiful" (*Enneads*, v.8.4).

[5] "To have seen that vision is reason no longer. It is more than reason, before reason, and after reason, as also is the vision which is seen. And perhaps we should not here speak of sight; for that which is seen—if we must needs speak of seer and seen as two and not one—is not discerned by the seer, nor perceived by him as a second thing. Therefore this vision is hard to tell of; for how can a man describe as other than himself that which, when he discerned it, seemed not other, but one with himself indeed?" (*Enneads*, vi.9 and 10).

into and invaded by a universal self which the individual feels as his own.

The experience itself is felt to be sufficient and complete. It does not come in a fragmentary or truncated form demanding completion by something else. It does not look beyond itself for meaning or validity. It does not appeal to external standards of logic or metaphysics. It is its own cause and explanation. It is sovereign in its own rights and carries its own credentials. It is self-established (*svataḥsiddha*), self-evidencing (*svasaṁvedya*), self-luminous (*svayamprakāśa*). It does not argue or explain but it knows and is. It is beyond the bounds of proof and so touches completeness. It comes with a constraint that brooks no denial. It is pure comprehension, entire significance, complete validity. Patañjali, the author of the *Yoga Sūtra*, tells us that the insight is truth-filled, or truth-bearing.[1]

The tension of normal life disappears, giving rise to inward peace, power and joy. The Greeks called it ataraxy, but the word sounds more negative than the Hindu term "*śānti*" or peace, which is a positive feeling of calm and confidence, joy and strength in the midst of outward pain and defeat, loss and frustration. The experience is felt as profoundly satisfying, where darkness is turned into light, sadness into joy, despair into assurance. The continuance of such an experience constitutes dwelling in heaven which is not a place where God lives, but a mode of being which is fully and completely real.

However much we may quarrel about the implications of this kind of experience, we cannot question the actuality of the experience itself. While the profound intuitions do not normally occur, milder forms are in the experience of all who feel an answering presence in deep devotion or share the spell which great works of art cast on us. When we experience the illumination of new knowledge, the ecstasy of poetry or the subordination of self to something greater, family or nation, the self-abandonment of falling in love, we have faint glimpses of mystic moods. Human love perhaps takes us nearest to them. It can become an experience deep and profound, a portal through which we enter the realm of the sublime. "My life, My all, My more," said Sappho to Philaenis. To have one's heart and mind absorbed in love seems to unveil the mystery of the universe. We forget the sense of the outward world in our communion with the grandeur beyond. Religious mysticism often falls into the language of passionate love. It has been so from the Upaniṣads and the Song of Songs.

[1] *Ṛtambharā tatra prajñā* (*Yoga Sūtra* 1.48).

Since the intuitive experiences are not always given but occur only at rare intervals, they possess the character of revelation. We cannot command or continue them at our will. We do not know how or why they occur. They sometimes occur even against our will. Their mode of comprehension is beyond the understanding of the normal, and the supernormal is traced to the supernatural. Those who are gifted with the insight tend to regard themselves as the chosen ones, the privileged few. Conscious of a light which other men had not, they feel inclined to believe that the light has been directed on them and that they are not only the seekers but the sought. "Only he who is chosen by the Supreme is able to realise it."[1]

If all our experience were possessed of intrinsic validity (*svataḥ-prāmāṇya*) there would be no question of truth and falsehood. There would be nothing with which our experience will have to cohere or to correspond. There would not arise any need or desire to test its value. All our experience will be self-valid, i.e. all reality will be present in its own immediate validity. But even the noblest human minds have had only glimpses of self-valid experiences. The moments of vision are transitory and intermittent. We therefore do not attain an insight, permanent and uninterrupted, where reality is present in its own immediate witness. But we are convinced that such an ideal is not an impossible one.

So long as the experience lasts, the individual remains rapt in contemplation, but no man can rest in that state for all time. Life is restless surge. Scarcely is the seer assured of the unique character of the experience than he is caught in the whirl of desire and temptation, discord and struggle. During the vision, its influence was so potent and overwhelming that he had neither the power nor the desire to analyse it. Now that the vision is no more, he strives to recapture it and retain in memory what cannot be realised in fact. The process of reflection starts. He cannot forget the blessed moments which have a weight for the rest of his life and give to his beliefs a power and a vividness that nothing can shake. The individual adopts an attitude of faith which is urged by its own needs to posit the transcendental reality. He affirms that the soul has dealings, direct, intimate and luminous, with a plane of being different from that with which the senses deal, a world more resplendent but not less real than the conventional one. The experience is felt as of the nature of a discovery or a revelation, not a mere conjecture or a creation.

[1] *Yamaivesa vṛṇute tena labhyaḥ.*

The real was there actually confronting us, it was not conjured out of the resources of our mind.[1] He claims for his knowledge of reality an immediate and intuitive certainty, transcending any which mere reason can reach. No further experience or rational criticism can disturb his sense of certainty. Doubt and disbelief are no more possible. He speaks without hesitation and with the calm accents of finality. Such strange simplicity and authoritativeness do we find in the utterances of the seers of the Upaniṣads, of Buddha, of Plato, of Christ, of Dante, of Eckhart, of Spinoza, of Blake. They speak of the real, not as the scribes, but as those who were in the immediate presence of "that which was, is and ever shall be." St. Theresa says: "If you ask how it is possible that the soul can see and understand that she has been in God, since during the union she has neither sight nor understanding, I reply that she does not see it then, but that she sees it clearly later, after she has returned to herself, not by any vision, but by a certitude which abides with her and which God alone can give her."[2]

In addition to the feeling of certitude is found the sense of the ineffability of the experience. It transcends expression even while it provokes it. It is just what it is and not like anything else. There is no experience by which we can limit it, no conception by which we can define it. The *Kena Upaniṣad* says that "it is other than the known and above the unknown."[3] As Lao Tze expresses it at the beginning of his *Tao Têh King*: "The Tao which can be expressed is not the unchanging Tao; the Name which can be named is not the unchanging Name."

The unquestionable content of the experience is that about which nothing more can be said.[4] Indian scriptures give cases of teachers who dispelled the doubts of their pupils by assuming an attitude of silence on this question.[5] When we hear enthusiastic descriptions about the ultimate reality, let us remember the dictum of Lao Tze

[1] *Bhūtam brahma na puruṣavyāpāratantram* (Śaṁkara on *Brahma Sūtra* I.i.1).

[2] James: *Varieties of Religious Experience* (1906), p. 409.

[3] I.3.

[4] "There is an endless world, O my brother, and there is the Being, of whom nought can be said.
Only he knows it who has reached that region: it is other than all that is heard and said.
No form, no body, no length, no breadth is seen there: how can I tell you that which it is?"
(*Kabir*: Rabindranath Tagore's E.T., 76)

[5] *Maunavyākhyāprakatitāparabrahmatattvam.*
Guros tu maunam vyākhyānam śiṣyās tu chinnasaṁsayāḥ.
Cp. also Lao Tze: "To teach without words and to be useful without action, few among men are capable of this."

that he who knows the *Tao* may be recognised by the fact that he is reluctant to speak of it.

Conceptual substitutes for ineffable experiences are not adequate. They are products of rational thinking. All forms, according to Śaṁkara, contain an element of untruth and the real is beyond all forms. Any attempt to describe the experience falsifies it to an extent. In the experience itself the self is wholly integrated and is therefore both the knower and the known, but it is not so in any intellectual description of the experience. The profoundest being of man cannot be brought out by mental pictures or logical counters.[1] God is too great for words to explain. He is like light, making things luminous but himself invisible.

And yet we cannot afford to be absolutely silent. Though the tools of sense and understanding cannot describe adequately, creative imagination with its symbols and suggestions may be of assistance. The profoundest wisdom of the past is transmitted to us in the form of myths and metaphors which do not have any fixed meaning and therefore can be interpreted as life requires. The seers who were at least as wise and as subtle as ourselves, by letting their imagination work on the experience, devised symbolic conceptions such as crossing the ocean of *saṁsāra*, ascending into heaven, meeting God face to face. Plato expressed his deepest convictions, which were incapable of proof, in the language of poetry, saying, "Not this perhaps, but something like this must be true." If we insist on interpreting these symbols literally, difficulties arise. But if we go behind the words to the moods they symbolise, agreement is possible.

The symbols and suggestions employed are derived from the local and historical traditions. An Orphic describes to us Charon and the spring on either side of the road and the tall cypress tree. The Vaiṣṇava speaks to us of the cowherd, the Brindāvan and the river Yamunā. The myths require to be changed as they lose their meaning with the lapse of time, but they are in no case to be accepted as

[1] Cp. St. Paul's words of his own experience in II Cor. xii.2–4; also the following from Middleton Murry's *God* (1929), p. 36: "What happened then? If I could tell that, I should tell a secret indeed. But a moment came when the darkness of that Ocean changed to light, the cold to warmth; when it swept in one great wave over the shores and frontiers of myself; when it bathed me and I was renewed; when the room was filled with a presence and I knew I was not alone—that I never could be alone any more, that the universe beyond held no menace, for I was part of it, that, in some way for which I had sought in vain so many years, I belonged and because I belonged I was no longer I, but something different, which could never be afraid in the old ways or cowardly with the old cowardice."

literal truths. They require to be interpreted "according to their meaning and not their lisping expression," as Aristotle suggests in speaking of Empedocles. Much of the rationalistic criticism of the sacred scriptures is due to a confusion between symbolic statements and literal truths. It is easy to prove that the world was not made in seven days or that Eve was not made out of Adam's rib. What they say is not scientifically true; but what they mean is a different matter. The recent excitement about the *Green Pastures* is rather undeserved. If God works in an office, employing charwomen and smoking cigars, it is only a metaphor, rather crude perhaps, as much as glassy seas or many mansions.

Experience and the Variety of Expressions

If all our experiences were adequately intuited at once, such immediate intuitions could not be doubted under any circumstances; but, as it is, we are compelled to relate our intuitive experiences with others and here we are obliged to employ formulas. The pedestrian function of consolidation and revaluation seems to be indispensable. The only way to impart our experiences to others and eludicate their implications for the rest of our life and defend their validity against hostile criticism is by means of logic. When we test the claim of the experience to truth, we are really discussing the claims of the forms or propositions in which the nature of the experience is unfolded. In the utterances of the seers, we have to distinguish the given and the interpreted elements. What is regarded as immediately given may be the product of inference. Immediacy does not mean absence of psychological mediation but only non-mediation by conscious thought. Ideas which seem to come to us with compelling force, without any mediate intellectual process of which we are aware, are generally the results of previous training in traditions imparted to us in our early years. Our past experience supplies the materials to which the new insight adds fresh meanings. When we are told that the souls have felt in their lives the redeeming power of Kṛṣṇa or Buddha, Jesus or Mohammad, we must distinguish the immediate experience or intuition which might conceivably be infallible and the interpretation which is mixed up with it. St. Theresa tells us that after her experience she learned to understand the Trinity. Surely she would not have recognised the revelation as that of the Trinity if she had not already known something of the Trinity.[1] Similarly,

[1] Evelyn Underhill: *Mysticism*, 5th ed., p. 132.

if Paul had not learned something about Jesus, he would not have identified the voice that came to him on the Damascus road as Jesus'. We must distinguish the simple facts of religion from the accounts which reach us through the depth of theological preconceptions. That the soul is in contact with a mighty spiritual power other than its normal self and yet within and that its contact means the beginning of the creation of a new self is the fact, while the identification of this power with the historic figures of Buddha or Christ, the confusion of the simple realisation of the universal self in us with a catastrophic revelation from without, is an interpretation, a personal confession and not necessarily an objective truth. Something is directly experienced, but it is unconsciously interpreted in the terms of the tradition in which the individual is trained. The frame of reference which each individual adopts is determined by heredity and culture.

Again, there is no such thing as pure experience, raw and undigested. It is always mixed up with layers of interpretation. The alleged immediate datum is psychologically mediated. The scriptural statements give us knowledge, or interpreted experience, a that-which. The "that" is merely the affirmation of fact, of a self-existent spiritual experience in which all distinctions are blurred and the individual seems to overflow into the whole and belong to it. The experience is real though inarticulate.

Among the religious teachers of the world, Buddha is marked out as the one who admitted the reality of the spiritual experience and yet refused to interpret it as a revelation of anything beyond itself. For him the view that the experience gives us direct contact with God is an interpretation and not an immediate datum. Buddha gives us a report of the experience rather than an interpretation of it, though strictly speaking there are no experiences which we do not interpret. It is only a question of degree. But Buddha keeps closest to the given and is content with affirming that a deeper world of spirit penetrates the visible and the tangible world. Such a world certified as valid by the witness of perfect intuition exists beyond or rather within the world of multiplicity and change which the senses and understanding present to us. The primary reality is an unconditional existence beyond all potentiality of adequate expression by thought or description by symbol, in which the word "existence" itself loses its meaning and the symbol of *nirvāṇa* alone seems to be justified. The only liberty in which Buddha indulges when obliged to give a positive content to it is to identify it with Eternal righteousness (*dharma*), which is the principle of the universe[1] and the foundation of all conduct. It is on account of it that we have the implicit belief in the worth of life.

The Hindu thinkers admit the ineffability of the experience but permit themselves a graduated scale of interpretations from the most "impersonal" to the most "personal." The freedom of interpretation is responsible for what may be called the hospitality of the Hindu mind. The Hindu tradition by its very breadth seems to be capable of accommodating varied religious conceptions.

Hinduism admits that the unquestionable content of the experience is a *that* about which nothing more can be said. The deeper and more intimate a spiritual experience, the more readily does it dispense with signs and symbols. Deep intuition is utterly silent. Through silence we "confess without confession" that the glory of spiritual life is inexplicable and beyond the reach of speech and mind. It is the great unfathomable mystery and words are treacherous.[2]

The empirical understanding is quite competent within its own region, but it cannot be allowed to criticise its foundation, that which it, along with other powers of man, takes for granted. The Supreme is not an object presented to knowledge but is the condition of knowledge. While for Buddha, who was ethically disposed, the eternal spirit is righteousness or *dharma*, in the strength of which we live and struggle, for many Hindu thinkers it is the very condition of knowledge. It is the eternal light which is not one of the things seen but the condition of seeing. The ultimate condition of being where all dualities disappear, where life and death do not matter since they spring from it, where spirit seems to enjoy spirit and reason does not stir, can be expressed only in negative terms. The Upaniṣads and Śaṁkara try to express the nature of the ultimate being in negative terms. "The eye goes not thither nor speech nor mind."[3]

[1] See Appendix to the writer's work on *Indian Philosophy*, I, 2nd ed., 1929.

[2] Plutarch has preserved for us the inscription on a statue of Isis in the Egyptian city of Sais, which runs: "I am all that hath been, and that is, and that shall be, and no mortal hath ever raised my veil." Hooker in his *Ecclesiastical Polity* (i.2) observes: "Dangerous it were for the feeble brain of man to wade far into the doings of the Most High; whom although to know be life, and joy to make mention of his name; yet our soundest knowledge is, to know that we know him not as indeed he is, neither can know him; and our safest eloquence concerning him is our silence, when we confess without confession, that his glory is inexplicable, his greatness above our capacity and reach. He is above, and we upon earth. Therefore it behoveth our words to be wary and few."

[3] *Bṛhadāraṇyaka Upaniṣad* III.viii.8. For Śaṁkara it is *nirguṇa* (without qualities), *nirākāra* (without form), *nirviśeṣa* (without particularity), *nirupādhika* (without limitations). It is what it is. Isaiah's words are true, "Verily, thou art a God that hidest thyself." For Dionysius the Areopagite, God is the nameless supra-essential one elevated above goodness itself. St. Augustine speaks of the Absolute, selfsame One, that which is.

There is a danger in these negative descriptions. By denying all attributes and relations we expose ourselves to the charge of reducing the ultimate being to bare existence which is absolute vacuity. The negative account is intended to express the soul's sense of the transcendence of God, the "wholly other," of whom naught may be predicated save in negations, and not to deprive God of his positive being. It is the inexhaustible positivity of God that bursts through all conceptual forms. When we call it nothing we mean that it is nothing which created beings can conceive or name and not that it is nothing absolutely. The scriptures do not demonstrate or describe him but only bear witness to him. The three noteworthy features of spiritual experience are reality, awareness and freedom. If some parts of our experience come to us with these characteristics, it implies the possibility that all experience is capable of being received in the same manner. The consciousness to which all experience is present in its own immediacy, revealedness and freedom from anything which is not itself is the divine consciousness, that which is our ideal. We picture it as a glowing fire, a lucid flame of consciousness ever shining and revealing itself. In the divine status reality is its own immediate witness, its own self-awareness, its own freedom of complete being. There is nothing which is not gathered up in its being, nothing which is not revealed in it, and there is utter absence of all discord. It is perfect being, perfect consciousness and perfect freedom, *sat*, *cit* and *ānanda*.. Being, truth and freedom are distinguished in the divine but not divided. The true and ultimate condition of the human being is the divine status. The essence of life is the movement of the universal being; the essence of emotion is the play of the self-existent delight in being; the essence of thought is the inspiration of the all-pervading truth; the essence of activity is the progressive realisation of a universal and self-effecting good. Thought and its formations, will and its achievements, love and its harmonies are all based on the Divine Spirit. Only the human counterparts involve duality, tension, strain, and so are inadequate to the fulness of the divine. The supreme is real, not true, perfect, not good. Its freedom is its life, its essential spontaneity.

God and Self

While the fulness of spiritual being transcends our categories, we are certain that its nature is akin to the highest kind of being we are aware of in ourselves. If the real were utterly transcendent to the self of man, it would be impossible for us to apprehend even dimly its presence. We would not be able to say even that it is "wholly other." There is in the self of man, at the very centre of his being, something deeper than the intellect, which is akin to the Supreme. God's revelation and man's contemplation seem to be two sides of one fact. The spiritual glimpses are prophetic indications of an undeveloped power of apprehension in the human mind as well as of an underlying reality with which it is unable to establish permanent contact without an adequate development of that power. There is a real ground in man's deepest being for the experience of reality. Man as a microcosm has relations with every form of existence. While the spiritual apprehension appears in the course of our ordinary life, it is not due to it. It has its source elsewhere though it exhibits its force on the plane of the ordinary consciousness. It is due to that part of the soul which is timeless being. The consubstantiality of the spirit in man and God is the conviction fundamental to all spiritual wisdom. It is not a matter of inference only. In the spiritual experience itself, the barriers between the self and the ultimate reality drop away. In the moment of its highest insight, the self becomes aware not only of its own existence but of the existence of an omnipresent spirit of which it is, as it were, a focussing. We belong to the real and the real is mirrored in us. The great text of the Upaniṣad affirms it—*Tat tvam asi* (That art Thou). It is a simple statement of an experienced fact. The Biblical text, "So God created man in his own image; in the image of God created he him,"[1] asserts that in the soul of man is contained the true revelation of God. "The spirit of man is the candle of the Lord."[2] According to Plato man is potentially a participator in the eternal mode of being which he can make his own by living in detachment from the fleeting shadows of the earth. In the *Theaetetus* Socrates declares that we should strive to become "like unto the divine." "I and my Father are one," "All that the Father hath are mine," is the way in which Jesus expressed the same profound truth. It is not a peculiar relation between any one chosen individual and God but an ultimate one binding every self to God. It was Jesus' ambition to make all men see what he saw and know what he knew. In the Gospel according to St. Matthew, Jesus sums up the various ethical demands in the general requirement: "Be ye therefore perfect as your heavenly Father also is perfect." As Paul says, he was the first-born among many brethren.

[1] Genesis i.27. [2] Proverbs xx.27.

Recognising us all as children of God and made in his image, Jesus shows us by his own example that the difference between God and man is only one of degree. St. John spoke of the spirit as "the light that lighteth every man that cometh into the world," the "spirit that guides unto all the truth." The phrase in I Peter of a birth "of the incorruptible seed by the word of God" refers to the divine in man. Plotinus' last words to his physician Eristochius are: "I was waiting for you before that which is divine in me departs to unite with itself the Divine in the Universe."[1] The Quakers believe in the divine spark or the apex in the soul. Descartes asks: "How could I doubt or desire, how could I be conscious, that is to say, that anything is wanting in me, and that I am not altogether perfect, if I had not within me the idea of a being more perfect than myself, by comparison with whom I recognise the defects of my own nature."[2] According to Eckhart: "There is something in the soul which is above the soul, divine, simple, an absolute nothing.... This light is satisfied only with the supraessential essence. It is bent on entering into the simple ground, the still waste wherein is no distinction, neither Father nor Son nor Holy Ghost, into the unity where no man dwelleth." Augustine says: "And being admonished to return into myself, I entered even into my inmost self. Thou being my guide, I entered and beheld with the eye of my soul, above the same eye of my soul, above my mind, the light unchangeable."[3] St. Catherine of Genoa says: "God is my being, my life, my strength, my Beatitude, my Goal, my Delight." "All minds partake of one original mind," says Cudworth.[4] The individuals are the reproductions of an eternal consciousness according to Green. William James, in his *Varieties of Religious Experience*, writes: "The overcoming of all the usual barriers between the individual and the Absolute is the great mystic achievement. In mystic states we become one with the Absolute and we become aware of our oneness. This is the everlasting and triumphant mystic tradition, hardly altered by differences of clime and creed. In Hinduism, in Neoplatonism, in Sufism, in Christian mysticism, in Whitmanism, we have the same recurring note, so that there is about mystical utterances an eternal unanimity which ought to make a

[1] Witness also the last testament of Labadie: "I surrender my soul heartily to my God, giving it back like a drop of water to its source, and rest confident in him, praying God, my origin and ocean, that he will take me into himself and engulf me eternally in the divine abyss of his being" (Inge, *Philosophy of Plotinus* (1918), I, 121 n).

[2] *Third Meditation.*

[3] *Confessions,* vii.10. See also vii.32.

[4] *Intellectual System,* iii.62.

critic stop and think, and which brings it about that the mystic classics have, as has been said, neither birthday nor native land. Perpetually telling of the unity of man and God, their speech antedates language, nor do they grow old." The immanence of God, the revelation of the meaning and mystery of life in the soul of man, is the substance of the mystic testimony.

We generally identify ourselves with our narrow limited selves and refer to spiritual experience as something given or revealed to us, as though it did not belong to us. We separate the power of spiritual apprehension from the rest of our nature and refer to it as something divine. Such a separation is unfair to humanity. The insight of the best moments reveals the deepest in us. It is wrong to regard human nature as its very self when it is least inspired and not its true self when it is most. If our self finds in these moments of vision its supreme satisfaction, and is intensely alive while they last, then that self is our true self. We cannot limit our being to the physical or the vital, the customary or the conventional. The divine in us is the source and perfection of our nature.

The Divine is both in us and out of us. God is neither completely transcendent nor completely immanent. To bring about this double aspect, contradictory accounts are given. He is divine darkness as well as "unencompassed light." The philosophers with their passion for unity emphasise the immanent aspect, that there is no barrier dividing man from the real. The unity of man and God is the fundamental thesis of the great philosophic tradition which has come down to us from the Upaniṣads and Plato. Aristotle, Plotinus, Śaṁkara, Spinoza, Bradley and a host of others are witnesses to it.

Those who emphasise the transcendence of the Supreme to the human insist on the specifically religious consciousness, of communion with a higher than ourselves with whom it is impossible for the individual to get assimilated. Devotional religion is born of this haunting sense of otherness. We may know God but there is always a something still more that seems unknown and remains unspoken. A profound impression of the majesty of God always remains with the devotee who is certain that we can never reach the divine level of glory. Some of the seers of the Upaniṣads, the author of the *Bhagavad-gītā*, St. Theresa, John of the Cross, represent this type. For them the experiences themselves are due to the grace of God. God speaks to us, commands us, comforts us, and we speak to him in praise and prayer, reverence and worship. There are many degrees in this personal relationship, from the feeling of utter humiliation in the presence of the numinous, the other than ourselves, to the communion with a supreme Love on whose grace the worst sinner can count.

There cannot be a fundamental contradiction between the philosophical idea of God as an all-embracing spirit and the devotional idea of a personal God who arouses in us the specifically religious emotion. The personal conception develops the aspect of spiritual experience in which it may be regarded as fulfilling the human needs. Man finds his rest and strength in the spiritual experience and so he knows the spirit as that which fulfils his needs. God is represented as possessing the qualities which we lack. In a sense the Freudians are not wrong when they assert that our religion is the projection of the desires of grown-up children. Justice, love and holiness are the highest qualities we know and we imagine God as possessing them, though these qualities exist in God in a different sense from their existence in us.

To compare the Supreme with the highest kind of being we know is nearer the truth than comparing him with anything lower. Though the supreme spirit in its essential aspect is the changeless noumenal reality, its representation in the form of a personal God who is the source, guide and destiny of the world seems to be the highest open to the logical mind. The difference between the Supreme as spirit and the Supreme as person is one of standpoint and not of essence, between God as he is and God as he seems to us. When we consider the abstract and impersonal aspect of the Supreme, we call it the Absolute; when we consider the Supreme as self-aware and self-blissful being, we get God. The real is beyond all conceptions of personality and impersonality. We call it the "absolute" to show our sense of the inadequacy of all terms and definitions. We call it "God" to show that it is the basis of all that exists and the goal of all. Personality is a symbol and if we ignore its symbolic character it is likely to shut us from the truth. Even those who regard personality as the ultimate category of the universe recognise that God is vast and mysterious, mighty and ultimate.[1]

[1] Calvin says: "God treats sparingly of his essence. His essence is indeed incomprehensible by us. Therefore let us willingly leave to God the knowledge of his own essence" (*Institute of the Christian Religion*).

A Bengali poet sings:

"I have searched the Vedas and the Vedāntas, the Tantras and the Mantras, yet nowhere have I found thy fulness.

"As Rāma thou dost take the bow, as Śyāma the Black (Kṛṣṇa) thou dost seize the sword. (*continued overleaf*)

Our myths and metaphors "do him wrong, being so majestical," and the spiritual seers know it; it is their intellectual followers who ignore it.

In the history of thought we have had different interpretations of the spiritual experience, such as Buddha's conception that it is the reality we are to accept with reverence; Aristotle's view of the Unmoved First Mover whose supreme perfection draws the universe towards himself as the beauty of the beloved draws the lover;[1] Spinoza's God who is that than which nothing is more real, which we are called upon to love without expecting anything in return, a personal God who is a creature of moods and passions, an ethical God who is the highest good at which men aim, and a knightly God who begs of us the favour of helping him in his great designs. The monotheists are quite certain that the gods of the polytheists are symbolic if not mythological presentations of the true God, but they are loath to admit that their own God is at bottom a symbol. All religion is symbolic, and symbolism is excluded from religion only when religion itself perishes. God is a symbol in which religion cognises the Absolute. Philosophers may quarrel about the Absolute and God, and contend that God, the holy one who is worshipped, is different from the Absolute which is the reality demonstrated by reason. But the religious consciousness has felt that the two are one.[2]

The World a Harmony

Besides the affirmation of a spiritual reality which is variously interpreted and its consubstantiality with the deepest self of man, we have also the conviction of the unity of the universe. We see the one spirit overarching us. The earth and the sky, the world and the animals—all become suddenly strange and wonderful. For our eyes are opened and they all declare the presence of the one Supreme.

"O mother, mother of the universe, art thou male or female? Who can say? Who knows thy form?

"Nīlakantha's mind ever thinks of thee as chief of the Creators" (E. J. Thomson and A. M. Spencer: *Bengali Religious Lyrics*, 9.78).

A modern poet writes:

"Some seek a Father in the heavens above;
Some ask a human image to adore;
Some crave a spirit vast as life and love;
Within thy mansions we have all and more."

(G. Matheson, quoted in Bulcock: *Religion and its New Testament Explanation* (1928), p. 278).

[1] *Metaphysics*, A. 7.

[2] Cp. Thomas à Kempis: "He to whom the eternal word speaks is set at liberty from a multitude of opinions."

The universe seems to be alive with spirit, aglow with fire, burning with light. All that there is comes out of life and vibrates in it.[1] The Upaniṣad says: "When all this is turned into the self, who is to be known by whom?"[2] The supreme spirit is inescapable. It is "above, below, behind, before, to the right and to the left."[3] "The reborn soul is as the eye which, having gazed into the sun, thenceforward sees the sun in everything," says Eckhart. George Fox asks us to "learn to see all things in the universal spirit." God is everywhere, even in the troubled sea of human history, in the tragedy and injustice of the world, in its suffering and sorrow. When we experience the harmony, the discord with which we are familiar seems unreal.

If the universe is essentially spirit, how do we account for its appearance as non-spirit? If the experience gives us the joyful awareness of the universe as a harmony, why do we have the tension, the discord and the cleavage in the universe? The world of science and common sense seems so different from the freedom of the self. Is it an illusion or is it a reality? Those who are pragmatically inclined take the practical life as the reality and treat spiritual experience as a mere dream, so deep seems to be the division between them. Some of the more careful trace the appearance of the multiple universe to the limitations of human intelligence, *avidyā,* nescience. The human mind, being what it is, tries to reconstruct the universe from the intellectual point of view into an organic whole. For the intellect, the unity is only a postulate, an act of faith. For the spirit, the harmony is the experienced reality. It belongs to the nature of things and we have had partial and momentary premonitions of it, and we can work up the harmony if we remember that the world of ordinary experience is a feeble representation of the perfect world, a combination of light and darkness, a reflection of the pure idea in an incomplete material form. The hasty logic which declares because the one is the real, the many are an illusion, is corrected in the view that the one reveals itself in the many.

Self-Recognition and the Way to It

If in spite of this identity of kinship between the soul and God the latter appears so far away, it is because the soul is immersed in what is alien to it, and finds it difficult to get at self-knowledge. Having drunk of the waters of Lethe (forgetfulness), man has forgotten his

[1] *Yat kiñca yad idam sarvam prāṇa ejati niḥsṛtam.*

[2] "*Yatra sarvam idam ātmaivābhūt tat kena kaṁ paśyet?*"

[3] *Chāndogya Upaniṣad* VIII.24.

heavenly origin. He is an exile from heaven, clothed in what seems an alien garment of flesh. We have to discover the spirit in us by stripping off all that is extraneous to it. The assertion of the self as something other than the true reality of God is the fall or the original sin (*avidyā*). The obstacles to self-discovery are the stresses of the personal will and they can be overcome only by the replacement of the selfish will by an impersonal universalised will. The endeavour of religion is to get rid of the gulf between man and God and restore the lost sense of unity. It is a progressive attempt at self-realisation, the lifting of the empirical ego into the transcendental plane, mind in its immediacy into mind in its ideal perfection. A strict ethical discipline is insisted on. The apprehension of spiritual truth depends on the quality of the soul of him who sees,[1] and this quality can be raised only by the cultivation of the intellect, the emotions and the will through prayer and contemplation. No one can know the truth without being the truth. An absolute inward purity demanding self-mastery and self-renunciation is demanded. "He who has not first turned away from frivolity, who is restless and uncollected, who has not a peaceful mind, cannot through searching reach Him."[2] The soul forgets its true origin if it fancies itself as part of the drift of events and is swept in its currents and eddies. The Hindu thinkers ask us to abstract from all definite manifestations of life, outward and inward, from our sense-impressions and feelings, thoughts and aspirations, let ourselves sink into the pure silent spirit from which the turbid stream of our present being wells forth.[3] Such is the way to get inwardly into touch with the source of universal life. Buddha prescribes the eightfold path of morality and tells us that men with unpurified minds and unchastened sensibilities cannot rise into the domain of spiritual experience. The cultivation of the interior life is not a fad of the oriental mind. Every great religion asks us to retire from the world and be alone and prescribes a discipline for assisting the individual to come into vital contact with the spiritual environment. The Orphics and the Pythagoreans tried to secure the recovery of the soul to its

[1] "The sun's light when he unfolds it depends on the organ that beholds it" (Blake).

[2] *Kaṭha Up.* II.24.

[3] Cp. *Kaṭha Up.*: "The self-existent pierced the openings of the senses so that they turn outwards. Therefore man looks outward, not inward, into himself; some wise man, however, with his eyes closed and wishing for immortality, saw the self behind" (IV.1). "The mind which sees the divine essence must be totally and thoroughly absolved from all commerce with the corporeal senses, either by *Death*, or some *ecstatical* and *Rapturous Abstraction*" (Norris: *Reason and Religion* [1689], quoted in Stewart, *The Myths of Plato* [1905], p. 481).

original condition by means of purifications. By exalting contemplative life above practical activity, the Greeks suggest that the most perfect of all objects could be apprehended only by those whose powers of spiritual apprehension are perfected.[1] "Religion is the art and theory of the internal life of man" according to Whitehead, "so far as it depends on the man himself and on what is permanent in the nature of things."[2] By doctrine, devotion and worship our life is awakened to the unseen reality. Salvation is attained not so much by placating God as by transforming our being, by achieving a certain quality and harmony of the passions through severe self-discipline. The effort is costly. No tricks of absolution or payment by proxy, no greased paths of smooth organs and stained-glass windows can help us much. The spirit has to be stripped bare if it is to attain its goal.

Meditation is the way to self-discovery. By it we turn our mind homeward and establish contact with the creative centre. To know the truth we have to deepen ourselves and not merely widen the surface. Silence and quiet are necessary for the profound alteration of our being and they are not easy in our age. Discipline and restraint will help us to put our consciousness into relation with the Supreme. What is called *tapas* is a persistent endeavour to dwell in the divine and develop a transfigured life. It is the gathering up of all dispersed energies, the intellectual powers, the heart's emotions, the vital desires, nay the very physical being itself, and concentrating them all on the supreme goal.[3] The rapidity of the process depends on the intensity of the aspiration, the zeal of the mind for God.

[1] Commenting on the text "About the going down of the sun, a deep sleep fell upon Abraham," Philo says: "This describes what happens to the man who goes into the state of enthusiasm, the state of being carried away by God. The sacred scripture bears witness that it is to every virtuous man that prophecy belongs, for a prophet utters nothing of his own; in all his word there is to be discovered the voice of another. It would not be lawful for any not virtuous man to become the interpreter of God so that by the fitness of things no vicious man is capable of the state of enthusiasm. Such things belong to the wise alone, because the wise man alone is the sounding instrument of God, struck and played by God after an invisible sort" (quoted in Edwin Bevan's *Sybils and Seers* [1928], p. 188). There is a well-known passage in Plotinus: "Oftentimes when I awake out of the slumber of the body, and come to a realising sense of myself, and, retiring from the world outside, give myself up to inward contemplation, I behold a wonderful beauty. I believe, then, that I belong to a higher and better world, and I strive to develop within me a glorious life and to become one with the Godhead. And by this means I receive such an energy of life that I rise above the world of things" (quoted in Rufus Jones's *New Studies in Mystical Religion*, pp. 43–4).

[2] *Religion in the Making* (1926), p. 6.

[3] A true religious culture will train the body also so as to develop rhythm and balance, grace and strength.

No man on earth has ever maintained spiritual poise all through his life. The Jesus who declared that men must not resist evil if they are to become the sons of the Father who makes his sun shine upon good men and bad, and his rain to fall upon the just and the unjust, was the same Jesus who cursed the fig-tree and drove the tradesmen from the temple. There are moments in the life of the best of us as the one in Gethsemane when we shrink from the ordeal before us and pray if possible to escape from it, and it requires some effort before we can bring ourselves to say, "Thy will be done." To keep one's balance in the face of an uncomprehending and hostile world is not a light affair. It is possible only if we get back to the depths constantly, and develop a disinterestedness of mind which no pleasure can entice nor pain overpower.

The mystics emphasise being more than doing. While their lives escape triviality, pettiness and intolerance, it is possible that they may exaggerate a negative self-feeling and non-aggressiveness. They are more inclined to surrender their rights than fight for them, but their gentleness is born of courage and strength and not fear and cowardice. But in the heart of asceticism there is a flame of spiritual joy which is of the very essence of religion. Withdrawal is not the whole of the religious tradition; there is also participation, enjoyment. The *Īśā Upaniṣad* asks us to enjoy by renouncing. It is a deep and disinterested acceptance of the world and a joyful recognition that no part of it may be refused. We renounce the world in order to return to it with the knowledge of its oneness to sustain us....

Rebirth

The way to realisation is a slow one. Hindu and Buddhist thought, the Orphic mysteries, Plato and some forms of early Christianity maintain that it takes a long time for realising the holy longing after the lost heaven. The souls that have fallen from the higher estate and that now dwell on earth as in a prison pass up and down in their wanderings so that the deeds of an earlier life condition the existence of the following one. The Hindu holds that the goal of spiritual perfection is the crown of a long patient effort. Man grows by countless lives into his divine self-existence. Every life, every act, is a step which we may take either backward or forward. By one's thought, will and action one determines what one is yet to be. According to Plato, the wise man turns away from the world of the senses, and keeps his inward and spiritual eye ever directed to the world of the eternal idea, and if only the pursuit is maintained, the individual becomes freed from the bonds of sensualism, and after death his released spirit slowly mounts up higher and higher until at last it finds its way back to the home of the eternal light.[1] Our feet are set on the path of the higher life, though they wander uncertainly and the path is not seen clearly. There may be the attraction of the ideal but no assent of the whole nature to it. The utter self-giving which alone can achieve the end is not easy. But no effort is wasted. We are still far from realising the implications of the spiritual dignity of man in matters of conduct, individual and social. It requires an agelong effort carried on from life to life and from plane to plane.

Salvation

It is the aim of religion to lift us from our momentary meaningless provincialism to the significance and status of the eternal, to transform the chaos and confusion of life to that pure and immortal essence which is its ideal possibility. If the human mind so changes itself as to be perpetually in the glory of the divine light, if the human emotions transform themselves into the measure and movement of the divine bliss, if human action partakes of the creativity of the divine life, if the human life shares the purity of the divine essence, if only we can support this higher life, the long labour of the cosmic process will receive its crowning justification and the evolution of centuries unfold its profound significance. The divinising of the life of man in the individual and the race is the dream of the great religions. It is the *mokṣa* of the Hindus, the *nirvāṇa* of the Buddhists,[2] the kingdom of heaven of the Christians. It is for Plato the life of

[1] Dean Inge writes: "The disbelief in the pre-existence of the soul, a doctrine which for Greek thought stands or falls with the belief in survival after death, is more important and may be partly attributable to Jewish influence. But pre-existence does not seem to have been believed by the majority of Greeks, and in fact almost disappears from Greek thought between Plato and the Neo-Platonists. It is possible that the Pythagorean and Platonic doctrine may still have a future." (*The Legacy of Greece* [1922], ed. by Livingstone, p. 44.)

[2] The *Udāna* states clearly the Buddhist view: "There is a stage (*āyatana*) where there is neither earth nor water, nor fire nor wind, nor the stage of the infinity of space, nor the stage of the infinity of consciousness, nor the stage of nothingness, nor the stage of neither consciousness nor nonconsciousness. There is not this world nor the other world, not sun nor moon. That I call neither coming nor going nor staying nor passing away nor arising; without support or going on or basis is it. This is the end of pain. There is an unborn, an unbecome, an unmade, an uncompounded; if there were not, there would be no escape from the born, the become, the made and the compounded" (VIII.1–4). For a detailed discussion of the Buddhist view of *nirvāṇa*, see the author's *Indian Philosophy*, I, 2nd ed. (1929).

the untroubled perception of the pure idea. It is the realisation of one's native form, the restoration of one's integrity of being. *Tadā draṣṭuḥ svarūpe 'vasthānam*, as the *Yoga Sūtra* has it. Heaven is not a place where God lives but an order of being, a world of spirit where the ideas of wisdom, love and beauty exist eternally, a kingdom into which we all may enter at once in spirit, which we can realise fully in ourselves and in society though only by long and patient effort. The expectation of the second advent is the expression of the soul's conviction of the reality of the spiritual. The world process reaches its consummation when every man knows himself to be the immortal spirit, the son of God and is it. Till this goal is reached, each saved individual is the centre of the universal consciousness. He continues to act without the sense of the ego. To be saved is not to be moved from the world. Salvation is not escape from life. The individual works in the cosmic process no longer as an obscure and limited ego, but as a centre of the divine or universal consciousness embracing and transforming into harmony all individual manifestations. It is to live in the world with one's inward being profoundly modified. The soul takes possession of itself and cannot be shaken from its tranquillity by the attractions and attacks of the world. The spiritual illumination does not make the individual life impossible. If the saved individuals escape literally from the cosmic process, the world would be forever unredeemed. It would be condemned to remain for all time the scene of unending strife and darkness. The Hindus assert different degrees of liberation, but the complete and final release of all is the ultimate one. Mahāyāna Buddhism declares that Buddha standing on the threshold of *nirvāṇa* took the vow never to make the irrevocable crossing so long as there was a single undelivered being on earth. The *Bhāgavata Purāṇa* records the following prayer: "I desire not the supreme state with all its eight perfections nor the release from rebirth; may I assume the sorrow of all creatures who suffer and enter into them so that they may be made free from grief." The self-fulfilment which they aspire to is inconsistent with the failure to achieve similar results in others. This respect for the individual as individual is not the discovery of modern democracy, so far as the religious sphere is concerned. When the cosmic process results in the revelation of all as the sons of God, when all the Lord's people become prophets, when this universal incarnation takes place, the great cosmic rebirth of which nature strives to be delivered will be consummated.

We may now bring together the several affirmations of religious experience.

There is a mode of consciousness which is distinct from the perceptual, imaginative or intellectual, and this carries with it self-evidence and completeness. Religious men of all ages have won their certainty of God through this direct way of approach to the apprehension of reality.

The larger environment is of the nature of one's own self, with which the individual occasionally comes into contact. There are differences regarding the interpretation of the nature of this spiritual environment, while this at any rate is true, that it offers the only justification for a life of truth seeking and good realising.

The intuition of the all-pervading unity of the self and the universe is emphasised sometimes to the extent of rejecting a God who can reciprocate our love or a self which has real independence.

Those who have this consciousness are the saintly souls whose lives are characterised by an unshakable faith in the supremacy of spirit, invincible optimism, ethical universalism and religious toleration.

The attainment of steady spiritual insight is the aim of religious endeavour and the means to it are an ethical life and the art of meditation. . . .

APPENDICES

A. PRONUNCIATION AND ACCENT

WITH a few exceptions, the foreigner may approximate the correct pronunciation of Sanskrit words by giving to the consonants their English value and to the vowels and diphthongs their Italian or German value.

Exceptions:

a — like u in but.
ṛ — properly like ur in the Scottish pronunciation of "hurt"; but now often pronounced in India as "ri".
c — like ch in check, but not so strongly aspirated.
th and ph — somewhat as in boa*th*ouse and u*ph*ill, never as in thin and phase.
ś (or ç) — like sh in shut.
ḥ — occurs only at the end of syllables and is a light h-sound.
ṁ or ṃ — serves to nasalize the preceding vowel.

The reader may accent Sanskrit words correctly by observing the following rules. The accent falls normally on the last heavy syllable of the word. A heavy syllable is one containing a long vowel or diphthong (a, i, u, e, o, ai, au) or a short vowel followed by two or more consonants (kh, gh, th, ph, bh count as only one consonant). If a word contains no heavy syllable, it is accented on the third syllable from the end. Examples: *Mahābhā́rata*, Rāmā́nuja, Abhinavagúpta, *viśiṣṭhādvaíta*, *párama*, *abhigámana*.

a — like u in but	g — like g in go
ā — like a in father	gh — like gh in loghut
i — like i in pin	ṅ or ñ — like n in sing
ī — like i in police	c — like ch in check
u — like u in pull	ch — like chh in churchhill
ū — like u in rude	j — like j in jump
ṛ — like Ri in Rita	jh — like dgeh in hedgehog
e — like e in prey	ñ — like n in singe
ai — like ai in aisle	ṭ* — like t in time
o — like o in go	ṭh — like th in boathouse
au — like ou in house	ṁ, ṃ, or ṅ — semi-nasal sound
k — like k in kind	ḍ — like d in drum
kh — like kh in inkhorn	ḍh — like dh in madhouse

* For all practical purposes Western Sanskritists do not insist on a sharp distinction between the dental (t, th, d, dh) and the linguals or cerebrals (ṭ, ṭh, ḍ, ḍh).

ṇ — like n in nice
t* — like t in water
th — like th in nuthook
d — like d in dice
dh — like dh in adhere
n — like n in not
p — like p in put
ph — like ph in uphill
b — like b in bear
bh — like bh in abhor
m — like m in mad
y — like y in yes
r — like r in red
l — like l in lull
v — like v in very (like w after consonant)
ś or ç (palatal) — like sh in shut
ṣ (sibilant) — like sh in shut but with the tip of the tongue turned backward
s — like s in since
h — like h in him
ḥ — final h aspirate sound

B. ORIGINAL SOURCES OF ENGLISH TRANSLATIONS USED

(In the order in which selections appear in this text.)

Ṛg Veda Saṁhitā *page* 3
Īśā Upaniṣad 39
Kena Upaniṣad 41
Kaṭha Upaniṣad 42
Praśna Upaniṣad 50
Muṇḍaka Upaniṣad 51
Māṇḍūkya Upaniṣad 55
Taittirīya Upaniṣad 57
Aitareya Upaniṣad 63
Chāndogya Upaniṣad 64
Bṛhadāraṇyaka Upaniṣad 77
Śvetāśvatara Upaniṣad 89
Kauṣītaki Upaniṣad 92
Maitri Upaniṣad 93
Bhagavad-gītā (by Veda-vyāsa) 101
Mahābhārata (by Veda-vyāsa) 164
Manu Smṛti (or *Manu Saṁhitā*) (by Manu) 172
Arthaśāstra (by Kauṭilya) 193
Sarvadarśanasaṁgraha (by Madhavācārya) 228
Sarvasiddhāntasaṁgraha (ascribed to Śaṁkara) 234
Tattvopaplavasiṁha (by Jayarāśi Bhaṭṭa) 236
Prabodha-candrodaya (by Kṛṣṇa Miśra) 247
Tattvārthādhigama Sūtra (by Umāsvāti) 252
Syādvādamañjarī (by Malliṣeṇa) *page* 260
Sanmati Tarka (by Siddhasena Divākara) 269
Saṁyutta-nikāya 274, 278, 280, 286
Majjhima-nikāya 275, 289
Visuddhi-magga 279, 284, 289
Milindapañha 281
Dhammapada 292
Iti Vuttaka 325
Udāna (by Vasubandhu) 327
Vijñaptimātratāsiddhi-viṁśatikā (by Vasubandhu) (Chinese version: Hsüan Tsang's *Wei-shih-er-shih lun*) 328
Vijñaptimātratāsiddhi-triṁśikā (by Vasubandhu) (*Wei-shih-san-shih lun*) 333
Mahāyāna-viṁśaka (by Nāgārjuna) 338
Mādhyamika-śāstra (by Nāgārjuna) 340
Nyāya Sūtra (by Gautama) 358
Nyāya-kusumāñjali (by Udayana) 379
Vaiśeṣika Sūtra (by Kaṇāda) 387
Padārthadharmasaṁgraha (by Praśastapāda) 397

C. ENGLISH TRANSLATIONS OF SELECTIONS USED

Lord Chalmers, trans., *Further Dialogue of the Buddha*, Part II, The Sacred Books of the Buddhists, Vol. VI (London: Oxford University Press, Humphrey Milford, 1927).

Siddhasena Divākara, *Sanmati Tarka*; Pandita Sukhlalji Sanghavi and Pandita Bechardasji Doshi, trans., *Siddhasena Divākara's Sanmati Tarka* (Bombay: Shri Jain Shivetambar Education Board, 1939).

Gautama, *Nyāya Sūtra*; S. C. Vidyābhuṣaṇa, trans. *The Nyāya Sūtras of Gotama*, The Sacred Books of the Hindus, Vol. VIII (Allahabad: The Panini Office, 1930).

——— *Nyāya Sūtra*; Ganganatha Jha, trans., *Gautama's Nyāyasūtras* (Poona: Oriental Book Agency, 1939).

R. T. H. Griffith, trans., *The Hymns of the Rigveda*, 2 vols. (Benares: E. J. Lazarus & Co., 3rd ed., 1920–1926).

R. E. Hume, trans., *The Thirteen Principal Upanishads* (London: Oxford University Press, Humphrey Milford, 1921).

Īśvara Kṛṣṇa, *Sāṁkhya Kārikā*; S. S. Suryanarayana Sastri, trans., *The Sāṅkhyakārikā of Īśvara Kṛṣṇa* (Madras: University of Madras, 1935).

Jaimini, *Mīmāṁsā Sūtra*; Śabara, *Śabara-bhāṣya*; Ganganatha Jha, trans., *Śabara-Bhāṣya*, The Gaekwad's Oriental Series, Vols. LXVI, LXX, LXXIII (Baroda: Oriental Institute, 1933, 1934, 1936).

Kaṇāda, *Vaiśeṣika Sūtra*; Nandalal Sinha, trans., *The Vaiśeṣika Sūtras of Kaṇāda*, The Sacred Books of the Hindus, Vol. VI (Allahabad: The Panini Office, 2nd ed., 1923).

Kapila, *Sāṁkhya-pravacana-sūtra*; Nandalal Sinha, trans., *The Sāṁkhya Philosophy*, The Sacred Books of the Hindus, Vol. XI (Allahabad: The Panini Office, 1915).

Kauṭilya, *Arthā-śāstra*; R. Shamasastry, trans., *Kauṭilya's Arthaśāstra* (Mysore: Wesleyan Mission Press, 2nd ed., 1923).

Kumārila Bhaṭṭa, *Ślokavārtika*; Ganganatha Jha, trans., Çlokavārtika (Calcutta: Royal Asiatic Society of Bengal, 1909).

A. A. Macdonell, trans., *Hymns from the Rigveda* (London: Oxford University Press; Calcutta: Association Press, 1922).

Mādhava Ācārya, *Sarvadarśanasaṁgraha*; E. B. Cowell and A. E. Gough, trans. (London: Kegan Paul, Trench, Trübner & Co., Ltd., 1904).

Madhva, *Brahma-sūtra-bhāṣya*; S. Subba Rao, trans., *Vedanta-sutras with the Commentary of Sri Madhwacharya* (Tirupati: Sri Vyasa Press, 2nd ed., rev., 1936).

Manu, *Manu Smṛti*: G. Bühler, trans., *The Laws of Manu*, The Sacred Books of the East, Vol. xxv (Oxford: The Clarendon Press, 1886).

Kṛṣṇa Miśra, *Prabodha-candrodaya*; J. Taylor, trans. (Bombay: no publisher, 1811).

Vācaspati Miśra, *Tattva-kaumudī*; Ganganatha Jha, trans., *The Tattva-kaumudī* (Poona: Oriental Book Agency, 2nd ed., rev., 1934).

Nāgārjuna, *Mādhyamika-śāstra* (Chapters I and XXV) with commentary by Candrakīrti; Th. Stcherbatsky, trans., *The Conception of Buddhist Nirvāṇa* (Leningrad: Academy of Sciences of the USSR, 1927).

———, *Mahāyāna Viṁśaka*; Susumu Yamaguchi, trans., *Nāgārjuna's Mahāyāna Viṁśaka*, in *The Eastern Buddhist*, Vol. IV, No. 2, 1927.

Hermann Oldenberg, trans., *Vedic Hymns*, Part II, Sacred Books of the East, Vol. XXVI (Oxford: The Clarendon Press, 1897).

Patañjali, *Yoga Sūtra*; Vyāsa, *Yoga-bhāṣya*; Vācaspati Miśra, *Tattva-vaiśāradī*; Rama Prasada, trans., *The Yoga Sūtras of Patañjali*, The Sacred Books of the Hindus, Vol. IV (Allahabad: The Panini Office, 3rd ed., 1924).

Praśastapāda, *Padārthadharmasaṁgraha*, with the *Nyāyakandalī* of Śrīdhara; Ganganatha Jha, trans., *The Padārthadharmasaṁgraha of Praçastapāda* (Allahabad: E. J. Lazarus & Co., 1916).

S. Radhakrishnan, trans., *The Bhagavadgītā* (New York: Harper & Bros., 1948).

———, *The Dhammapada* (London, New York, Toronto: Oxford University Press, 2d imp., 1954).

Rāmānuja, *Śrī-bhāṣya*; George Thibaut, trans., *The Vedānta Sūtras with the Commentary of Rāmānuga*, The Sacred Books of the East, Vol. XLVIII (Oxford: The Clarendon Press, 1904).

Pratap Chandra Ray, trans., *The Mahābhārata* (Calcutta: Bharata Press, 1890).

Śaṁkara, *Śārīraka-bhāṣya*; George Thibaut, trans., *The Vedānta Sūtras with the Commentary by Śaṅkarācārya*, The Sacred Books of the East, Vols. XXXIV, XXXVIII (Oxford: The Clarendon Press, 1890, 1896).

Śaṁkara, *Sarvasiddhāntasaṁgraha*; Prem Sundar Bose, trans. (Calcutta: Navavidhan Press, 1929).

Edward J. Thomas, *The Life of Buddha as Legend and History* (New York: Alfred A. Knopf, 1927).

———, *Vedic Hymns*, Wisdom of the East Series (London: John Murray, 1923).

Udayana Ācārya, *Kusumāñjali*, with the commentary of Hari Dāsa Bhattacārya; E. B. Cowell, trans., *The Kusumāñjali or Hindu Proof of the Existence of a Supreme Being* (Calcutta: Baptist Mission Press, 1864).

Śrī Umāśvātī Ācārya, *Tattvārthādhigama Sūtra*; J. L. Jaini, trans., The Sacred Books of the Jainas, Vol. II (Arrah, India: The Central Jaina Publishing House, 1920).

Vasubandhu, *Viṁśatikā*; Clarence H. Hamilton, trans., *Wei Shih Er Shih Lun*, or *The Treatise in Twenty Stanzas on Representation-Only*, American Oriental Series, Vol. XIII (New Haven: American Oriental Society, 1938).

H. C. Warren, trans., *Buddhism in Translations*, Harvard Oriental Series, Vol. III (Cambridge, Mass.: Harvard University Press, 6th issue, 1915).

F. L. Woodward, trans., *The Minor Anthologies of the Pali Canon*, Part II, The Sacred Books of the Buddhists, Vol. VIII (London: Oxford University Press, Humphrey Milford, 1935).

BIBLIOGRAPHY

GENERAL

Emil Abbeg, *Indische Psychologie.* Zurich: Rascher, 1945.

Ananda Acharya, *Brahmadarsanam, an Introduction to the Study of Hindu Philosophy.* New York: The Macmillan Co., 1917.

Paramanheri Sundaram Sivasvami Aiyar, *Evolution of Hindu Moral Ideals.* Calcutta: University of Calcutta, 1935.

Swami Akhilananda, *Mental Health and Hindu Psychology.* New York: Harper & Bros., 1951.

Lionel David Barnett, *The Heart of India; Sketches in the History of Hindu Religion and Morals.* W of E Series, 1908, 1913, 1924.

Benimadhab Barua, *A History of Pre-Buddhistic Indian Philosophy.* Calcutta: University of Calcutta, 1921.

Allan Bennet, *The Wisdom of the Aryans.* London: Kegan Paul, Trench, Trübner & Co., Ltd., 1923.

Theos Bernard, *Hindu Philosophy.* New York: Philosophical Library, 1947.

Ramkrishna Gopal Bhandarkar, *Vaisnavism, Saivism, and Minor Religious Systems.* Strasbourg: K. J. Trübner, 1913.

Asutosh Sastri Bhattacharya, *Studies in Post-Sankara Dialectics.* Calcutta: University of Calcutta, 1936.

Nalini Kanta Brahma, *The Philosophy of Hindu Sadhana.* London: Kegan Paul, Trench, Trübner & Co., Ltd., 1932.

Note. Although apparently rather comprehensive, this bibliography must be selective because of the great amount of material in the field. Works included in this source book complete or in part are not cited in the bibliography. English translations used in this volume are listed in Appendix C. All authors and titles are listed exactly as they appear in the volumes cited, and spelling and diacritical marks are often inconsistent. In a few cases, the date of publication and the publisher are not available.

The following abbreviations are used: (1) HOS for Harvard Oriental Series, edited with the cooperation of various scholars by Charles Rockwell Lanman (present editor, Daniel Henry Holmes Ingalls). Cambridge, Mass.: Harvard University Press, various dates, as noted. (2) SBE for The Sacred Books of the East, translated by various Oriental scholars and edited by F. Max Müller. Oxford: Oxford University Press, various dates, as noted. (3) SBH for The Sacred Books of the Hindus, translated by various Sanskrit scholars and edited by Major B. D. Basu. Allahabad: The Panini Office, various dates, as noted. (4) W of E Series for Wisdom of the East Series, edited by J. L. Cranmer-Byng and S. A. Kapadia. London: John Murray, various dates, as noted.

Great appreciation is hereby expressed to Professor Daniel H. H. Ingalls, Chairman of the Department of Sanskrit and Indian Studies of Harvard University, for his extensive and cordial assistance in the compilation of this bibliography. My thanks also to Mr Masatoshi Nagatomi for his assistance in double checking all items, and to Miss Jean Akimoto for much clerical assistance. (C.A.M.)

D. Mackenzie Brown, *The White Umbrella—Indian Political Thought from Manu to Gandhi.* Berkeley: University of California Press, 1953.

Paul Brunton, *Indian Philosophy and Modern Culture.* New York: E. P. Dutton & Co., Inc., 1939.

Joseph Estlin Carpenter, *Theism in Medieval India.* London: Williams & Norgate, 1921.

Satischandra Chatterjee, *The Fundamentals of Hinduism: a Philosophical Study.* Calcutta: Das Gupta & Co., Ltd., 1950.

Jagadish Chandra Chatterji, *The Hindu Realism; being an Introduction to the Metaphysics of the Nyaya-Vaiseshika System of Philosophy.* Allahabad: The Indian Press, 1912.

Surendra Nath Dasgupta, *Hindu Mysticism: Six Lectures.* Chicago, London: The Open Court Publishing Co., 1927.

———, *A History of Indian Philosophy.* Cambridge: Cambridge University Press, Vol. I, 1922; Vol. II, 1932; Vol. III, 1940; Vol. IV, 1949; Vol. V, 1955.

———, and S. K. De, *History of Sanskrit Literature (Classical Period).* Calcutta: University of Calcutta, 1947.

———, *Indian Idealism.* Cambridge: The University Press, 1933.

Dhirendra Mohan Datta, *Six Ways of Knowing; a Critical Study of the Vedanta Theory of Knowledge.* London: George Allen & Unwin, Ltd., 1932.

Paul Deussen, *Outlines of Indian Philosophy: with an Appendix on the Philosophy of the Vedanta in its Relations to Occidental Metaphysics.* Berlin: Karl Curtins, 1907.

———, *Allgemeine Geschichte der Philosophie, mit besonderer Berücksichtigung der Religionen.* Leipzig: F. A. Brockhaus, 1920.

Gai Eaton, *The Richest Vein, Eastern Tradition and Modern Thought.* London: Faber & Faber, Ltd., 1949.

Sir Charles Norton Edgecumbe Eliot, *Hinduism and Buddhism; an Historical Sketch.* London: E. Arnold & Co., 1921. 3 vols.

Murray Barnson Emeneau, *A Union List of Printed Indic Texts and Translations in American Libraries.* New Haven: American Oriental Society, 1935.

John Nicol Farquhar, *An Outline of the Religious Literature of India.* London: Oxford University Press, 1920.

E. Frauwallner, *Geschichte der indischen Philosophie.* Salzburg: Otto Müller Verlag, 1953–56. 2 vols.

Geoffrey Theodore Garratt, ed., *The Legacy of India.* Oxford: The Clarendon Press, 1933.

Helmuth von Glasenapp, *Brahma und Buddha.* Berlin: Deutsche Buchgemeinschaft, 1926.

———, *Der Stufenweg zum Göttlichen.* Baden-Baden: Bühlar Verlag, 1948.

———, *Die Philosophie der Inder.* Stuttgart: Alfred Kröner Verlag, 1949.

———, *Entwicklungsstufen des indischen Denkens: Untersuchungen über die Philosophie der Brahmanen und Buddhisten.* Halle: M. Niemeyer, 1940.

Helmuth von Glasenapp, *Der Hinduismus; Religion und Gesellschaft in heutigem Indien.* Munich: K. Wolff, 1922.

Upendra Nath Goshal, *A History of Hindu Political Theories.* London: Oxford University Press, Humphrey Milford, 1927.

Hervey De Witt Griswold, *Brahman: A Study in the History of Indian Philosophy.* Cornell University Studies in Philosophy, Vol. II. New York: The Macmillan Co., 1900.

René Grousset, *Les philosophies indiennes, les systèmes.* Paris: Desclée De Brower et Cie, 1931.

René Guénon, *Introduction générale à l'étude des doctrines hindoues.* Paris: M. Rivière, 1921.

———, *ibid.*, trans. by Marco Pallis, *Introduction to the Study of Hindu Doctrines.* London: Luzac & Co., 1945.

———, *Orient et Occident.* Paris: Payot, 1924.

———, *ibid.*, trans. by William Massey, *East and West.* London: Luzac & Co., 1941.

Max Hunter Harrison, *Indian Monism and Pluralism.* London, Bombay, Calcutta, Madras: Oxford University Press, Humphrey Milford, 1932.

Betty Heimann, *Indian and Western Philosophy, a Study in Contrasts.* London: George Allen & Unwin, Ltd., 1937.

———, *Studien zur Eigenart des indischen Denkens.* Tübingen: J. C. B. Mohr, 1930.

Mysore Hiriyanna, *Outlines of Indian Philosophy.* London: George Allen & Unwin, Ltd., 1932.

———, *The Essentials of Indian Philosophy.* London: George Allen & Unwin, Ltd., 1932; New York: The Macmillan Co., 1949.

Edward Washburn Hopkins, *Ethics of India.* New Haven: Yale University Press, 1924.

Hermann Jacobi, *Entwicklung der Gottesidee bei den Indern.* Bonn: K. Schroeder, 1923.

Maximilian Kern, *Licht des Ostens.* Stuttgart: Union deutsche Verlagsgesellschaft, 1922.

Louis de La Vallée-Poussin, *Le Brahmanisme: Notions sur les religions de l'Inde.* Paris: Bloud, 1910.

Ernst Leumann, *Buddha und Mahāvīra, die beiden indischen Religionsstifter.* Munich-Neubiberg: O. Schloss, 1922.

Arthur Anthony Macdonnell, *A History of Sanskrit Literature.* Appleton Dollar Library. New York, London: D. Appleton & Co., 1929.

Nicol Macnicol, *Indian Theism from the Vedic to the Mohammedan Period.* London: Oxford University Press, Humphrey Milford, 1915.

T. M. P. Mahadevan, *Time and the Timeless.* Madras: Upanishad Vihar, 1953.

Sushil Kumar Maitra, *The Ethics of the Hindus.* Calcutta: University of Calcutta, 1925.

S. K. Maitra, *The Spirit of Indian Philosophy.* Benares: the author, 1947.

Paul Masson-Oursel, *Comparative Philosophy.* International Library of Psychology, Philosophy and Scientific Method. New York: Harcourt, Brace & Co., Inc.; London: Kegan Paul, Trench, Trübner & Co., Ltd., 1926.

John McKenzie, *Hindu Ethics: a Historical and Critical Essay.* The Religious Quest of India Series. London, New York: Oxford University Press, Humphrey Milford, 1922.

Rohit Mehta, *The Intuitive Philosophy.* Adyar: The Theosophical Publishing House, 1950.

Charles A. Moore, ed., *Essays in East-West Philosophy: an Attempt at World Philosophical Synthesis.* Honolulu: University of Hawaii Press, 1951.

A. C. Mukerji, *The Nature of Self.* Allahabad: The Indian Press, Ltd., 1938.

Friedrich Max Müller, *The Six Systems of Indian Philosophy.* London, New York: Longmans, Green & Co., latest ed., 1928.

Filmer S. C. Northrop, *The Meeting of East and West, an Inquiry Concerning World Understanding.* New York: The Macmillan Co., 1946.

Hermann Oldenberg, *Die indische Philosophie.* Allgemeine Geschichte der Philosophie. Kultur der Gegenwart, de Hinneberg. Leipzig: B. G. Teubner, 1913.

Rudolf Otto, *West-östliche Mystik.* Gotha: L. Klotz, 1926.

———, *ibid.*, trans. by Bertha L. Bracey and Richenda C. Payne, *Mysticism East and West.* New York: The Macmillan Co., 1932.

Kanti Chandra Pandey, *Comparative Aesthetics*; Vol. I, *Indian Aesthetics.* The Chowkhamba Sanskrit Studies, Vol. II. Banaras: Chowkhamba Sanskrit Series Office, 1950.

Jwala Prasad, *Indian Epistemology.* The Punjab Oriental Series, No. XXV. Lahore: The Punjab Sanskrit Book Depot, 1939.

James Bissett Pratt, *India and its Faiths.* Boston, New York: Houghton Mifflin, Co., 1915.

Sarvepalli Radhakrishnan *et al.*, eds., *A. R. Wadia: Essays in Philosophy Presented in his Honour.* Madras: G. S. Press, 1954.

——— and John Henry Muirhead, eds., *Contemporary Indian Philosophy.* The Muirhead Library of Philosophy. 2nd ed. New York: The Macmillan Co., 1952.

——— *et al.*, eds., *History of Philosophy Eastern and Western.* The Ministry of Education, Government of India. London: George Allen & Unwin, Ltd., 1952, 1953. 2 vols.

Poola Tirupati Raju, *Idealistic Thought of India.* Cambridge: Harvard University Press, 1953.

Ramchandra Dattatraya Ranade, *Indian Mysticism: Mysticism in Maharashtra.* Poona: Bilvakunja Publishing House, 1933.

Malur Rao Bahadur Rangacarya, trans., *The Sarva-siddhānta-saṅgraha of Śaṅkarācārya.* Madras: Government Press, 1909.

Shri Krishna Saksena, *Nature of Consciousness in Hindu Philosophy.* Benares: Nand Kishore & Bros., 1944.

Benoy Kumar Sarkar, *Hindu Achievement in Exact Science.* New York: Longmans, Green & Co., 1918.

———, *The Positive Background of Hindu Sociology*, Book I: *Non-Political.* SBH, XVI, 1914.

———, *The Positive Background of Hindu Sociology*, Book II: *Political.* SBH, XXV, 1921.

———, *The Positive Background of Hindu Sociology*, Book I: *Introduction to Hindu Positivism.* SBH, XXXII, 1937.

Dittakavi Subrahmanya Sarma, *Studies in the Renaissance of Hinduism in the Nineteenth and Twentieth Centuries.* Benares: The Benares Hindu University, 1944.

———, *What is Hinduism?* Madras: The Madras Law Journal Office, 1945.

N. Sivarama Sastry and G. Hanumantha Rao, eds., *Prof. Mysore Hiriyanna Commemoration Volume.* Mysore: Prof. Mysore Hiriyanna Commemoration Volume Committee, 1952.

Friedrich Otto Schrader, *Über den Stand der indischen Philosophie zur Zeit Mahāvīras und Buddhas.* Doctordissertation. Strasbourg: K. J. Trübner, 1902.

Albert Schweitzer, *Die Weltanschauung der indischen Denker.* Munich: C. H. Beck'sche Verlagsbuchhandlung, 1935.

———, *ibid.*, trans. by Mrs Charles E. B. Russell, *Indian Thought and Its Development.* New York: Henry Holt & Co., 1936.

Sir Brajendranath Seal, *The Positive Sciences of the Ancient Hindus.* London, New York: Longmans, Green & Co., 1915.

Chandradhar Sharma, *Indian Philosophy.* Banaras: Nand Kishore & Bros., 1952.

D. S. Sharma, *Dialectic in Buddhism and Vedānta.* Banaras: Nand Kishore & Bros., 1952.

Prabhu Dutt Shastra, *The Essentials of Eastern Philosophy.* New York: The Macmillan Co., 1928.

Jadunath Sinha, *History of Indian Philosophy*, Vol. II. Calcutta: Central Book Agency, 1952.

———, *Introduction to Indian Philosophy.* Agra: Lakshmi Narain Agarwal, 1949.

———, *Indian Realism.* London: Kegan Paul, Trench, Trübner & Co., Ltd., 1938.

Nandalal Sinha, trans., *Bhakti Sastra. The Bhakti Sūtras of Nārada with Explanatory Notes*; Manmathanath Paul, trans., *The One Hundred Aphorisms of Sāṇḍilya with the Commentary of Svapneśvara*; "a Professor of Sanskrit", trans., *The Bhakti-ratnāvali with the Commentary of Viṣṇu Purī.* SBH, VII, 1911–1912.

Otto Strauss, *Indische Philosophie.* Munich: E. Reinhardt, 1925.

———, *Kausalitätsproblem in der indischen Philosophie.* Acta Orientalia, I. Leiden: Lagduni Batavorum, apud E. J. Brill, 1922.

Luigi Suali, *Introduzione allo studio della filosofia indiana.* Pavia: Mattei & Co. 1912.

Srisa Chandra Vidyarnava, *A Catechism of Hindu Dharma*. SBH, Extra III, 1919.

——— (Rai Bahadur Srisa Chandra Vidyārnava), trans., *The Śiva Saṃhitā*. 2nd ed. SBH, XV, 1923.

Swami Vijnanananda, alias Hari Prasanna Chatterji, trans., *Srī Narada Pancharatam — the Jnanamrita Sara Samhita*. SBH, XXIII, 1921.

Moriz Winternitz, *Geschichte der indischen Literatur*. Leipzig: C. F. Amelangs Verlag, 1908–1922.

———, *ibid.*, trans. by S. Ketkar, Vol. I (1927) and S. Ketkar and H. Kohn, Vol. II (1933), *A History of Indian Literature*. Calcutta: University of Calcutta.

Heinrich Zimmer. Joseph Campbell, ed., *Philosophies of India*. Bollingen Series, XXVI. New York: Pantheon Books, 1951.

VEDAS

Abel Bergaigne, *La religion védique d'après les hymnes du Rig-Véda*. Paris: F. Vieweg, 1878–83. 3 vols.

Maurice Bloomfield, trans., *Hymns of the Atharva-veda, together with Extracts from the Ritual Books and the Commentaries*. SBE, XLII, 1897.

———, *The Religion of the Veda, the Ancient Religion of India (from Rig-Veda to Upanishads)*. New York, London: G. P. Putnam's Sons, 1908.

Karl Friederich Geldner, *Der Rigveda aus dem Sanskrit ins Deutsche übersetzt*. HOS, XXXIII–XXXV, 1951.

Hervey De Witt Griswold, *The Religion of the Ṛigveda*. London, New York: Oxford University Press, Humphrey Milford, 1923.

Martin Haug, trans., *The Aitareya Brahmanam of the Rigveda*. SBH, Extra IV, 1922.

A. Kaegi, *The Rig Veda: the Oldest Literature of the Indians*. Boston: Ginn & Co., 1886.

Arthur Berriedale Keith, *The Religion and Philosophy of the Veda and Upanishads*, First Half, Chapters 1–19. HOS, XXXI, 1925.

———, *The Religion and Philosophy of the Veda and Upanishads*, Second Half, Chapters 20–29. HOS, XXXII, 1925.

Louis de La Vallée-Poussin, *Notions sur les religions de l'Inde: Le Védisme*. Paris: Bloud, 1909.

Arthur Anthony Macdonnell, *Vedic Mythology*. Strasbourg: K. J. Trübner, 1897.

Friedrich Max Müller, trans., *Vedic Hymns*; Part I, *Hymn to the Maruts, Rudra, Vāyu, and Vāta*. SBE, XXXII, 1889.

Hermann Oldenberg, *Die Religion des Veda*. Berlin: W. Hertz, 1894.

Radhabinode Pal, *The Hindu Philosophy of Law in the Vedic and Post-Vedic Times Prior to the Institutes of Manu*. Calcutta: Bishwabhander Press, n.d.

Peter Peterson, trans., *Hymns from the Rigveda*, ed. with Sayana's commentary and notes. Bombay: Government Central Book Agency, 1888; Poona: Bhandarkar Oriental Research Institute, new imp., 1924.

Louis Renou, *Bibliographie védique*. Paris: Adrien-Maisonneuve, 1931.

Vishnu Sistam Sukthankar, *Ghate's Lectures on the Rig-Veda*. Poona: Oriental Book Agency, 1926.

William Dwight Whitney, trans., revised and edited by Charles Rockwell Lanman, *Atharva-veda Saṃhitā*, First Half, Introduction, Books I to VII. HOS, VII, 1905.

———, trans., *Atharva-veda Saṃhitā*, Second Half, Books VIII to XIX. HOS, VIII, 1905.

UPANIṢADS

T. R. Srinivasa Aiyangar, trans., *Śaiva Upaniṣads*. Madras: The Adyar Library, 1953.

———, trans., *Vaiṣṇava Upaniṣads*. Madras: The Adyar Library, 1945.

———, trans., *Yoga Upaniṣads*. Madras: The Adyar Library, 1952.

———, trans., *Sāmānya Vedānta Upaniṣads*. Madras: The Adyar Library, 1941.

K. Narayanasvami Aiyar, trans., *Thirty Minor Upanishads*. Madras: The Vasanta Press, 1914.

S. C. Chakravarti, *The Philosophy of the Upanishads*. Calcutta: University of Calcutta, 1935.

Paul Deussen, *Allgemeine Einleitung und Philosophie des Veda bis auf die Upanishads*. Leipzig: F. A. Brockhaus, 1894.

———, *Die Philosophie der Upanishads*. Leipzig: F. A. Brockhaus, 1899.

———, *ibid*., trans. by A. S. Geden, *The Philosophy of the Upanishads*. The Religion and Philosophy of India Series. Edinburgh, New York: T. & T. Clark, 1906, 1908.

———, *Sechzig Upanishads des Veda*. Leipzig: F. A. Brockhaus, 1899.

Friedrich Heiler, *Die Mystik in den Upanishaden*. Munich-Neubiberg: O. Schloss, 1925.

Mysore Hiriyanna, trans., *Kenopanishad with the Commentary of Srī Sankarāchārya*. Srirangam: Sri Vain Vials Press, 1912.

Charles Johnston, *The Great Upanishads*, Vol. I. New York: Quarterly Book Department, 1927.

T. M. P. Mahadevan, *The Upanishads, Selections from the 108 Upanishads with English Translation*. Madras: G. A. Natesan & Co., n.d.

R. Gordon Milburn, *The Religious Mysticism of the Upanishads*. London: Theosophical Publishing House, Ltd., 1924.

Friedrich Max Müller, trans., *The Khandogya-upanishad, the Talavakāra-upanishad, the Aitareya-āranyaka, the Kaushītaki-brāhmaṇa-upanishad, and the Vāgasaneyi-samhitā-upanishad*. SBE, I, 1900; 2nd imp., 1926.

———, trans., The Upanishads; Part II, *The Katha-upanishad, the Mundaka-upanishad, the Taittirīyaka-upanishad, the Brihadāranyaka-upanishad, the the Śvetāsvatara-upanishad, the Praśna-upanishad, and the Maitrāyana-brahmana-upanishad*, 2nd imp. SBE, XV, 1926.

Swami Nikhilananda, trans., *The Upanishads*. New York: Harper & Bros., 1949, 1951. 2 vols.

Hermann Oldenberg, *Die Lehre der Upanishaden und die Anfänge des Buddhismus*. Göttingen: Vandenhoeck & Ruprecht, 1915.

Ramchandra Dattatraya Ranade, *A Constructive Survey of Upanishadic Philosophy*. Poona: Oriental Book Agency, 1926.

Joseph Nadin Rawson, *The Katha Upaniṣad*. Oxford: Oxford University Press, 1934.

Pandit Mohan Lal Sandal, *Philosophical Teachings in the Upanisats*. SBH, Extra v, 1926.

S. Sitaram Sastri (Vols. I, II, V) and Ganganatha Jha (Vols. III, IV), trans., *The Upanishads and Sri Sankara's Commentary*. Madras: V. C. Seshacherri, 1898–1901.

Rai Bahadur Srisa Chandra Vidyarnava and Pandit Mohan Lal Sandal, trans., *Aitareya Upaniṣat and the Taitirīya Upaniṣat*, Parts I–III. SBH, XXX, 1925.

———, (Srisa Chandra Basu), trans., *Chāndogya Upaniṣad*. (Also translation of Madhva's Commentary.) SBH, III, 1910.

———, trans., *Isa, Kena, Katha, Prasna, Mundaka and Manduka*. 3rd ed. SBH, I, 1924.

——— and Pandit Mohan Lal Sandal, trans., *The Kauṣitaki Upaniṣat and the Maitri Upaniṣat*. SBH, XXXI, 1925–1926.

EPICS AND LAW

Sir Edwin Arnold, trans., *The Song Celestial; or, Bhagavad-Gītā*. Philadelphia: David McKay Co., 1934.

Lionel David Barnett, trans., *Bhagavad-gītā; or, The Lord's Song*. London: J. M. Dent & Sons, 1920, 1926.

Annie Besant and Bhagavan Das, trans., *The Bhagavad-Gītā*. 3rd ed. Adyar: Theosophical Publishing House, 1940.

Mahadev Desai, trans., *The Gospel of Selfless Action, or the Gītā according to Gandhi*. Ahmedabad: Navajivan Publishing House, 1946.

Manmatha Nath Dutt, trans., *The Dharma Sūtras*. Calcutta: Society for the Resuscitation of Indian Literature, 1908.

———, trans., *The Garuda Puranam*. Calcutta: Society for the Resuscitation of Indian Literature, 1908.

———, trans., *A Prose English Translation of the Mahabharata*. Calcutta: H. C. Dass, 1895–1905.

———, trans., *The Ramayana*. Calcutta: Wealth of India, 1892–1894.

Franklin Edgerton, *The Bhagavad Gītā Translated and Interpreted*. HOS, XXXVIII–XXXIX, 1944.

Ralph Thomas Hotchkin Griffith, trans., *The Rāmāyana of Vālmiki*. London: Trübner & Co., 1870–1874. 5 vols.

William Douglas Penneck Hill, trans., *The Bhagavadgītā*. London: Oxford University Press, Humphrey Milford, 1928.

Edward Washburn Hopkins, *The Great Epic of India*. New Haven: Yale University Press, 1928.

Charles Johnston, trans., *Bhagavad Gītā, "The Songs of the Master."* New York: Quarterly Book Department for the author, 1908.

Julius Jolly, trans., *The Institutes of Vishnu*. SBE, VII, 1880.

Julius Jolly, trans., *Nāradīya Dharmaśāstra, or the Institutes of Nārada.* London: Trübner & Co., 1876.

Pandurang Vaman Kane, *History of Dharmaśāstra (Ancient and Medieval Religious and Civil Law in India).* Bombay: Bhandarkar Oriental Research Institute, 1930–1953. 4 vols.

Étienne Lamotte, *Notes sur la Bhagavad Gītā.* Paris: Paul Geuthner, 1929.

Swami Nikhilananda, trans., *The Bhagavad Gītā.* New York: Ramakrishna-Vivekananda Centre, 1944.

Rudolf Otto, J. E. Turner, trans. and ed., *The Original Gītā.* London: George Allen & Unwin Ltd., 1939.

S. Subba Rau, trans., *The Bhagavad-gītā (Translation and Commentaries in English according to Sri Madwacharya's Bhashya).* Madras: Minerva Press, 1906.

Arthur William Ryder, trans., *The Bhagavad-gītā.* Chicago: University of Chicago Press, 1929.

Benoy Kumar Sarkar, trans., *The Sukranīti (Nitiśāstra* by Sukra). SBH, XIII, 1914.

Dittakavi Subrahmanya Sarma, *Lectures on the Bhagavad-gita, with an English Translation of the Gita.* London: Luzac & Co., 1938.

Alladi Mahadeva Sastri, trans., *The Bhagavad-gītā with the Commentary of Shri Shankarāchārya.* Madras: Minerva Press, 1897.

Otto Strauss, *Ethische Probleme aus dem Mahābhārata.* Giornale della Societa Asiatica Italiana. Florence: Tipografia Galileiana, 1912.

Swami Swarupananda, trans., *Śrīmad-Bhagavad-gītā.* 2nd ed., Mayavati: Swami Pragnananda, 1891; 5th ed., Mayavati: Advaita Ashrama, 1933.

Kashinath Trimbak Telang, trans., *The Bhagavadgītā, with the Sanatsugātīya, and the Anugītā.* SBE, VIII, 1908.

Edward Joseph Thomas, trans., *The Song of the Lord: Bhagavadgita.* W of E Series, 1931.

Ernest Wood and S. V. Subrahmanyam, trans., *The Garuḍa Purāṇa.* SBH, IX, 1911.

Horace Hayman Wilson, trans., *The Vishnu Purāṇa, a System of Hindu Mythology and Tradition.* London: John Murray, 1840.

Alkondavilli Govindacarya, trans., *Śrī Bhagavad-gītā with Śrī Rāmānujāchārya's Visishtādvaita Commentary.* Madras: Vaijayanti Press, 1898.

Johannes Adrianus Bernardus Van Buitenen, *Rāmānuja on the Bhagavadgītā, a Condensed Rendering of his Gitabhashya with Copious Notes and an Introduction.* Leiden: 's-Gravenhage, 1954.

Srisa Chandra Vasu, trans., *Yajnavalkya's Smriti with the Commentary of Vijnanesvara called the Mitaksara and the Gloss of Bālambhaṭṭa.* SBH, II, 1909.

——— (Śriśa Chandra Vidyārṇava), trans., *Yajnavalkya Smriti with the Commentary of Vijnaneśvara called the Mitaksara and Notes from the Gloss of Bālambhaṭṭa*; Book I, *The Āchāra Adhyāya.* SBH, XXI, 1918.

Bhalchandra Sitaram Sukthankar, trans., *The Gītā-rahasya (of Bal Ganga Tilak).* Bombay: Bombay Vaibhav Press, 1935.

CĀRVĀKA

Edward Byles Cowell, "Charvaka System", *Journal of Asiatic Society of Bengal*, XXXI (1862), pp. 371–390.

Alfred Hillebrandt, "Zur Kenntnis der indischen Materialisten", *Festschrift für Ernst Kuhn*. Munich: M. & H. Marcus, 1916.

Dakshinaranjan Shastri, *A Short History of Indian Materialism, Sensationalism and Hedonism*. Calcutta: Calcutta Book Co., 1930.

———, trans., *Chārvāka-Shasti* (*Indian Materialism*). Calcutta: The Calcutta Book Co., n.d.

Luigi Suali, trans., "The Section on the Carvakas of the Saddarsanasamuccaya of Haribhadra", *Bibliothèque du Muséon*, IX (1939), pp. 277–298.

Giuseppe Tucci, *Linee di una storia del materialismo indiano*. R. A. N. dei Lincei. Rome: 1924.

JAINISM

Barodia, *History and Literature of Jainism*. Bombay: 1909.

———, *Outline of Jainism*. London: 1916.

Mohanlal Dalichand Desai, trans., *The Naya-karnika* (by Sri Vinaya Vijaya Maharaj). Arrah: Central Jaina Publishing House, 1915.

Helmuth von Glasenapp, *Der Jainismus*. Berlin: Alf Häger, 1925.

Armand Guerinot, *Essai de Bibliographie Jaina*. Paris: E. Leroux, 1906.

Hermann Jacobi, "Eine Jaina Dogmatik" (Umasvati's *Tattvārthādhigama-Sūtra*). *Zeitschrift der Deutschen Morgenländischen Gesellschaft*, 60. Leipzig: F. A. Brockhaus, 1906.

———, trans., *Gaina-Sūtras*; Part I, *The Ākārānga-Sūtra and the Kalpa-Sūtra*. SBE, XXII, 1884.

———, trans., *The Gaina Sūtras*; Part II, *The Uttarādhyayana Sūtra, the Sūtrakṛitānga Sūtra*. SBE, XLV, 1895.

J. Jaini, *Outlines of Jainism*. Cambridge: Cambridge University Press, 1916.

Helen Moore Johnson, trans., *Trisaṣṭiśalākāpuruṣacarita*; Vol. I, *Ādīśvaracarita*. Gaekwad's Oriental Series, Vol. LI. Baroda: Oriental Institute, 1931.

Mohan Lal Mehta, *Outlines of Jaina Philosophy*. Bangalore: Jain Mission Society, 1954.

Satkari Mookerji, *The Jaina Philosophy of Non-Absolutism: a Critical Study of Anekāntavāda*. Calcutta: Bharati Mahavidyalaya, 1944.

Walther Schubring, *Die Lehre der Jainas*. Berlin und Leipzig: W. de Gruyter & Co., 1935.

Mrs Sinclair T. Stevenson, *The Heart of Jainism*. London: Oxford University Press, 1915.

Nathmal Tatia, *Studies in Jaina Philosophy*. Sanmati Publication, No. VI. Banaras: Jain Cultural Research Society, 1951.

Satis Chandra Vidyabhusana, trans., *Nyāyāvatāra: the Earliest Jaina Work on Pure Logic (by Siddhasena Divākara)*. Calcutta: Indian Research Society, 1909.

The Sacred Books of the Jainas:[1]

I. Sarat Chandra Ghoshal, ed. and trans., *Davva-saṃgaha (Dravya-saṃgraha) by Nemichandra Siddhāntachakravartī with a Commentary by Brahma-deva*. 1917.

III. A. Chakravartinayanar, ed. and trans., *The Building of the Cosmos, or, Pañchāstikāyasāra (the Five Cosmic Constituents) by Svami Sri Kundakundacharya*. 1920.

IV. Pandit Ajita Prasada, ed. and trans., *Purushārtha-siddhyupāya (Jaina-pravachana-rahasya-kosha) by Shrimat Amrita Chandra Acharya*. 1933.

V. Rai Bahadur J. L. Jaini, assisted by Jaindharmabhushana Brahmachari Sital Prasad Ji, ed. and trans., *Gommaṭasāra Jīva-Kanda (the Soul) by Shri Nemichandra Siddhanta Chakravati*. 1927.

VI. ———, assisted by Jaindharmabhushana Brahmachari Sital Prasada Ji, ed. and trans., *Gommaṭasara Karma-Kanda* (Part I) *by Shri Nemichandra Siddhanta Chakravarti*. 1927.

VII. ———, assisted by Jaindharmabhushana Brahmachari Sital Prasada Ji, ed. and trans., *Ātmānushāsana (Discourse to the Soul) by Shri Gunabhadra Acharya*. 1928.

VIII. ———, assisted by Jaindharmabhushana Sital Prasada Ji, trans., *Samayasāra (the Soul-essence) by Shri Kunda Kunda Acharya*. 1930.

IX. Uggar Sain, assisted by Jaindharmabhushana Brahmachari Sital Prasada Ji, trans., *Niyamsāra (the Perfect Law) by Shri Kunda Kunda Acharya*. 1931.

X. Brahmachari Sital Prasada Ji, assisted by Pandit Ajit Prasada, trans., *Gommatasāra Karma-kaṇḍa* (Part II) *by Shri Nemichandra Siddhanta Chakravarti*. 1937.

XI. Sarat Chandra Ghoshal, trans., *Parīkṣāmukha by Mānikyanandī*. 1940.

BUDDHISM

Shwe Zan Aung und Max Walleser, *Dogmatik des modernen südlichen Buddhismus*. Materialien zur Kunde des Buddhismus. Heft 5. Heidelberg: in Kommission bei O. Harrassowitz, 1924.

Irving Babbitt, trans., *Dhammapada*. New York, London: Oxford University Press, 1936.

Benimadhab Barua, *Prolegomena to a History of Buddhist Philosophy*. Calcutta: University of Calcutta, 1918.

Samuel Beal, trans., *A Catena of Buddhist Scriptures from the Chinese*. London: Trübner & Co., 1871.

[1] Edited with the cooperation of various scholars by Sarat Chandra Ghoshal. Arrah and Lucknow: The Central Jaina Publishing House, various dates, as noted.

Cecil Bendall and William Henry Denham Rouse, trans., *Siksha-samuccaya by Santideva.* London: John Murray, 1922.

Vidhuskekhara Bhattacharya, *The Basic Conception of Buddhism.* Calcutta: University of Calcutta, 1934.

E. A. Burtt, ed., *The Teachings of the Compassionate Buddha.* New York: The New American Library, 1955.

Paul Carus, *The Gospel of Buddha.* Religion of Science Library, No. 14. Chicago, London: The Open Court Publishing Co., 1921.

Lord Chalmers, ed., *Buddha's Teaching: being the Suttanipata or Discourse-Collection.* HOS, XXXVII, 1933.

Edward Conze, trans., *Abhisamayālaṅkāra.* Serie Orientale Rome, 6. Rome: Istituto italiano per il Medio ed Estremo Oriente, 1954.

———, *Buddhism, Its Essence and Development.* New York: Philosophical Library, 1954.

———, *Buddhist Texts Through the Ages.* New York: Philosophical Library, 1954.

Ananda Kentish Coomaraswamy, *Buddha and the Gospel of Buddhism.* London: Harrap, 1928.

Paul Dahlke, *Buddhism and its Place in the Mental Life of Mankind.* London: Macmillan & Co., Ltd., 1927.

Caroline Augusta Foley Rhys Davids, *Buddhism, a Study of the Buddhist Norm.* New York: Henry Holt & Co., 1912; revised: *Buddhism: Its Birth and Dispersal.* London: Thornton Butterworth, 1934.

———, trans., *A Buddhist Manual of Psychological Ethics, being a Translation of Dhamma-sangaṇi (Compendium of States or Phenomena).* London: Royal Asiatic Society, 1900.

———, *Buddhist Psychology.* 2nd ed. The Religious Quest of India Series. London: G. Bell & Sons, Ltd., 1914; London: Luzac & Co. 1924.

———, *A Manual of Buddhism.* London: Sheldon Press, 1932.

———, *Outlines of Buddhism, a Historical Sketch.* London: Methuen, 1934.

Thomas William Rhys Davids, *Buddhism: Its History and Literature.* Rev. ed. New York: G. P. Putnam's Sons, 1926.

———, *Buddhist India.* New York: G. P. Putnam's Sons, 1903.

———, trans., *Buddhist Suttas*; Part I, *The Mahaparinibbāna Suttanta*; Part II, *The Dhamma-kakka-ppavattana Sutta*; Part III, *The Tevigga Suttanta*; Part IV, *The Ākankheyya Sutta*; Part V, *The Ketokhila Sutta*; Part VI, *The Mahasudassana Suttanta*; Part VII, *The Sabbāsava Sutta.* SBE, XI, 1881.

———, trans., *The Questions of King Milinda*, Part I. SBE, XXXV, 1890.

———, trans., *The Questions of King Milinda*, Part II. SBE, XXXVI, 1894.

Manmatha Nath Dutt, *Aspects of Mahāyāna Buddhism and Its Relation to Hīnayāna.* London: Luzac & Co., 1930.

William Gemmell, trans., *The Diamond Sutra (Chin-kang-ching), or Prajna Paramita.* London: Kegan Paul, Trench, Trübner & Co., 1912; New York: E. P. Dutton & Co., 1913.

Helmuth von Glasenapp, *Der Buddhismus in Indien und im Fernen Osten.* Berlin, Zürich: Atlantis-verlag, 1936.

Helmuth von Glasenapp, *Die Weisheit des Buddha.* Baden-Baden: H. Bühler, Jr., 1947.

Dwight Goddard, ed., *A Buddhist Bible.* Rev. ed. New York: E. P. Dutton & Co., Inc., 1952.

Clarence Herbert Hamilton, ed., *Buddhism, a Religion of Infinite Compassion; Selections from Buddhist Literature.* New York: Liberal Arts Press, 1952.

———, *Buddhism in India, Ceylon, China and Japan, a Reading Guide.* Chicago: University of Chicago Press, 1931.

Friedrich Heiler, *Buddhistische Versenkung.* Munich: E. Reinhardt, 1922.

Edmond Gore Alexander Holmes, *The Creed of Buddha.* New York: John Lane Co., 1908.

Edouard Huber, trans., *Sūtrālaṃkara* (by pseudo-Aśvaghoṣa). Paris: Ernest Leroux, 1908.

Christmas Humphreys, *Buddhism.* A Pelican Book. Harmondsworth: Penguin Books, 1951.

Hermann Jacobi, trans., *Triṃśikāvijnāpti des Vasubandhu mit Bhāṣya des Ācārya Sthiramati.* Stuttgart: W. Kohlhammer, 1932.

Ganganatha Jha, trans., *The Tattvasangraha of Santarkshita.* Gaekwad's Oriental Series, Vol. LXXX (1937), LXXXIII (1939). Baroda: Oriental Institute.

Edward Hamilton Johnston, *The Buddhacarita or Acts of the Buddha,* Part II. Translation. Panjab University Oriental Publications, No. XXXII. Calcutta: 1936.

Arthur Berriedale Keith, *Buddhist Philosophy in India and Ceylon.* Oxford: The Clarendon Press, 1923.

Hendrik Kern. Trans., by Gédéon Huet, *Histoire du Bouddhisme dans l'Inde.* Annales du Musée Guimet. Paris: E. Leroux, 1901–1903. 2 vols.

———, *Manual of Indian Buddhism.* Encyclopedia of Indo-Aryan Research, Vol. III, Part VIII. Strasbourg: K. J. Trübner, 1896.

———, trans., *The Saddharma-pundarīka, or, the Lotus of the True Law.* SBE, XXI, 1884.

Junyu Kitayama, *Metaphysik des Buddhismus* (by Vasubandhu). Stuttgart: W. Kohlhammer, 1934.

Louis de La Vallée-Poussin, *Bouddisme, Études et Matériaux, La Théorie des Douze Causes.* Ghent(?): E. van Goethem; London: Luzac & Co., 1913.

———, *Bouddhisme: Opinions sur l'histoire de la dogmatique.* Paris: G. Beauchesne, 1909.

———, *Le dogme et la Philosophie du bouddhisme.* Paris: G. Beauchesne, 1930.

———, trans., *L'abhidharmakośa de Vasubandhu.* Paris: Paul Geuthner; Louvain: J. B. Istas, 1923–1926. 6 vols.

———, *Morale bouddhique.* Paris: Nouvelle Librairie Nationale, 1927.

———, *Nirvāṇa.* Paris: G. Beauchesne, 1925.

———, trans., *Vimsakakārikā-prakaraṇa* (by Vasubandhu). Louvain: Bureaux du Muséon, 1912.

———, *The Way to Nirvana; Six Lectures on Ancient Buddhism as a Discipline of Salvation.* Cambridge: Cambridge University Press, 1917.

Étienne Lamotte, *La Somme du grand véhicule d'Asanga* (*Mahāyāna-Saṃgraha*). Text translation. Bibliothèque du Muséon, Vol. VII. Louvain: Bureaux du Muséon, 1939.

———, *Le Traité de la Grande Vertu de Sagesse* (*Mahāprajñā-pāramitā-Shāstra*). Bibliothèque du Muséon, Vol. XVIII. Louvain: Bureaux du Muséon, 1944, 1949. 2 vols.

Bimala Charan Law, ed., *Buddhist Studies*. Calcutta, Simla: Thacker, Spink & Co., Ltd., 1931.

Sylvain Lévi, trans., *Mahāyāna sūtrālaṃkāra, exposé de la doctrine du Grand Vehicule selon le système Yogācāra* (by Asaṅga). Bibl. Hautes Études. Paris: H. Champion, 1907–1911.

J. Masuda, *Der individualistische Idealismus der Yogācāra-Schule; Versuch einer genetischen Darstellung*, Materialen zur Kunde des Buddhismus. Heidelberg: Institut für Buddhismus-Kunde, in Kommission bei O. Harrassowitz, 1926.

William Montgomery McGovern, *Introduction to Mahāyāna Buddhism*. London: Kegan Paul, Trench, Trübner & Co., Ltd.; New York: E. P. Dutton & Co., Inc., 1922.

Satkari Mookerjee, *Buddhist Philosophy of Universal Flux*. Calcutta: University of Calcutta, 1935.

Justin Hartley Moore, trans., *Sayings of the Buddha, the Iti-vuttaka*. New York: Columbia University Press, 1908.

Friedrich Max Müller and V. Fausboll, trans., *The Dhammapada, with the Sutta-Nipata* (Friedrich Max Müller, trans., Part I, *The Dhammapada*; V. Fausboll, trans., Part II, *The Sutta-Nipata*). SBE, X, 1881.

T. R. V. Murti, *The Central Philosophy of Buddhism*. London: George Allen & Unwin, Ltd., 1955.

E. Obermiller, *History of Buddhism*. Translated from the Tibetan text entitled *Chos-hbyung by Bu-ston* (A.D. 1290–1364). Materialien zur Kunde des Buddhismus. Hefte 18, 19. Heidelberg: Institut für Buddhismus-Kunde, 1931–1932. 2 vols.

———, trans., *Abhisamayālaṃkāra* (by Maitreya). Acta Orientalia, XI. Leiden: Lugduni Batavorum, apud E. J. Brill, 1932.

———, trans., *Uttaratantra*. *Acta Orientalia*, 9. Leiden: Lugduni Batavorum, apud E. J. Brill, 1931.

Hermann Oldenberg, *Buddha: sein Leben, seine Lehre, seine Gemeinde*. Stuttgart: J. A. Cotta, 1914.

———, *ibid.*, trans. by W. Hoey, *Buddha, His Life, His Doctrine, His Order*. London: Williams & Norgate, 1882.

———, Karl Seidenstücker, und Helmuth von Glasenapp, *Gedanken von Buddha*. Berlin: 1942.

James Bissett Pratt, *The Pilgrimage of Buddhism and a Buddhist Pilgrimage*. New York: The Macmillan Co., 1928.

Otto Rosenberg (Aus dem Russischen übersetzt von Frau E. Rosenberg), *Die Probleme der Buddhistischen Philosophie*. Heidelberg: O. Harrassowitz, 1924.

Magdalene Schott, *Sein als Bewusstsein: ein Beitrag zur Mahāyāna-Philosophie.* Heidelberg: C. Winters, 1935.

Karl Schumacher, *Buddhistische Versenkung und jesuitische Exerzitien.* Stuttgart: K. Kohlhammer, 1928.

Bhikkhu Silacara, trans., *The Majjhima Nikaya.* (The first fifty discourses from the collection of the medium-length discourses of Gautama the Buddha.) Leipzig: Walter Markgraf, 1912; London: Arthur Probsthain, 1913.

Th. Stcherbatsky, *Buddhist Logic.* Leningrad: Academy of Sciences of the USSR, 1932. 2 vols.

———, *The Central Conception of Buddhism and the Meaning of the Word "Dharma".* London: Royal Asiatic Society, 1923.

———, (Aus dem Russischen übersetzt von Otto Strauss). *Erkenntnistheorie und Logik der späteren Buddhisten.* Munich: O. Schloss, 1924.

———, *Rapports entre la théorie bouddhique de la connaissance et l'enseignement des autres écoles philosophiques de l'Inde.* Louvain: Bureau du Muséon, 1904.

Dawsonne Melauchton Strong, trans., *The Udāna.* London: Luzac & Co., 1902.

Beatrice Lane Suzuki, *Mahāyāna Buddhism.* London: The Buddhist Lodge, 1938.

Daisetz Teitaro Suzuki, *Açvagosha's Discourse on the Awakening of Faith in the Mahāyāna.* Chicago: The Open Court Publishing Co., 1900.

———, *The Laṅkāvatāra Sūtra—a Mahāyāna Text.* London: George Routledge & Sons, Ltd., 1932.

———, *Studies in the Laṅkāvatāra Sūtra.* London: George Routledge & Sons, Ltd., 1930.

———, *Outlines of Mahāyāna Buddhism.* London: Luzac & Co., 1907.

———, *Philosophy of the Yogācāra,* Bibliothèque du Muséon. Louvain: Bureau du Muséon, 1904.

Junjiro Takakusu. Wing-tsit Chan and Charles Alexander Moore, eds., *The Essentials of Buddhist Philosophy.* Honolulu: University of Hawaii, 1947.

Narada Thera, trans., *The Dhammapada.* W of E Series, 1954.

Edward Joseph Thomas, trans., *Buddhist Scriptures; a Selection Translated from the Pali with Introduction.* W of E Series, 1931.

———, *History of Buddhist Thought.* London: Kegan Paul, Trench, Trübner & Co., Ltd.; New York: Alfred A. Knopf, 1933.

Giuseppe Tucci, *Il Buddhismo.* Foligno: 1926.

Max Walleser, *Die buddhistische Philosophie in ihrer geschichtlichen Entwicklung.* Heidelberg: C. Winters. I. *Die philosophische Grundlage des alteran Buddhismus,* 1904. II. *Die mittlere Lehre* (*Mādhyamika-śāstra*) *des Nāgārjuna: Nach der Tibetischen Version Übertragen,* 1911. III. *Die mittlere Lehre des Nāgārjuna: Nach der Chinesischen Version übertragen* 1912. IV. *Die Sekten des alten Buddhismus,* 1927.

Friedrich Weller, *Das Leben des Buddha von Açvaghosa.* Leipzig: E. Pfeffer, 1926.

W. D. C. Wagiswara and Kenneth James Saunders, trans., *The Buddha's "Way of Virtue"; a Translation of the Dhammapada from the Pāli Text.* W of E Series, 1912.

C. H. S. Ward, *Buddhism*, Vol. I: *Hīnayāna.* Rev. ed. Great Religions of the East Series. London: The Epworth Press, 1952.

———, *Buddhism*, Vol. II: *Mahāyāna.* Great Religions of the East Series. London: The Epworth Press, 1952.

E. Wolff, *Lehre vom Bewusstsein.* Materialien zur Kunde des Buddhismus, Vol. 17. Heidelberg: Institut für Buddhismus-Kunde, 1930.

Sogen Yamakami, *Systems of Buddhistic Thought.* Calcutta: University of Calcutta, 1912.

Sacred Books of the Buddhists:[1]

- II. Thomas William Rhys Davids, trans., *Dialogues of the Buddha... (Dīgha Nikāya)*, Vol. I, 1899.
- III. ——— and Mrs Caroline Augusta Foley Rhys Davids, trans., *Dialogues of the Buddha...(Dīgha Nikāya)*, Vol. II, 3rd ed., 1952.
- IV. ———, trans., *Dialogues of the Buddha...(Dīgha Nikāya)*, Vol. III, 1921.
- IX. Bimala Charan Law, trans., *Minor Anthologies of the Pali Canon*; Part III, *Buddhavaṃsa: the Lineage of the Buddhas, and Cariyā-piṭaka or Collection of the Ways of Conduct.* 1938.
- X. Isaline Blew Horner, trans., *The Book of Discipline (Vinaya, Suttavibhanga)*, Vol. I, 1938.
- XI. ———, trans., *The Book of Discipline (Vinaya, Suttavibhanga)*, Vol. II, 1940.
- XIII. ———, trans., *The Book of Discipline (Vinaya, Suttavibhanga)*, Vol. III, 1942.
- XIV. ———, trans., *The Book of Discipline (Mahāvagga)*, Vol. IV, 1951.
- XV. E. M. Hare, trans., *Woven Cadences (Suttanipāta).* 2nd ed., 1948.
- XVI. John James Jones, trans., *Mahāvastu Translation*, Vol. I. 1949.
- XVII. Bimala Charan Law, trans., *Sāsanavaṃsa Translation.* 1952.
- XVIII. John James Jones, trans., *Mahāvastu Translation*, Vol. II. 1952.
- XIX. ———, trans., *Mahāvastu Translation*, Vol. III. (In preparation.)
- XX. Isaline Blew Horner, trans., *The Book of Discipline (Cullavagga)*, Vol. V. 1952.

Pali Text Society Translation Series:[2]

- I. Caroline Augusta Foley Rhys Davids, trans., *Psalms of the Early Buddhists*; Part I, *Psalms of the Sisters (Therīgāthā).* 1909, 1949.
- II. Shwe Zan Aung, trans., Caroline Augusta Foley Rhys Davids, rev. and ed., *Compendium of Philosophy, being a Translation of the Abhidhammattha-Saṅgaha.* 1910.

[1] Translated by various Oriental scholars and edited by C. A. F. Rhys Davids. Oxford: Oxford University Press, various dates, as noted. (I. B. Horner is present editor.)

[2] Translated by various Oriental scholars and edited by T. W. Rhys Davids (with C. A. F. Rhys Davids). (Present editor, I. B. Horner.) London: Oxford University Press for Pali Text Society, various dates, as noted.

IV. Caroline Augusta Foley Rhys Davids, trans., *Psalms of the Early Buddhists*; Part II, *Psalms of the Brethren* (*Theragāthā*). 2nd ed., 1937; reprint, 1953.

V. Shwe Zan Aung and Caroline Augusta Foley Rhys Davids, trans., *Points of Controversy or Subjects of Discourse, being a Translation of the Kathā-vatthu from the Abhidhammapiṭaka.* 1915.

VI. Frank Lee Woodward, trans., Caroline Augusta Foley Rhys Davids, ed., *Manual of a Mystic, being a Translation from the Pali and Sinhalese Work entitled Yogāvachara's Manual.* 1916.

VII. Caroline Augusta Foley Rhys Davids, assisted by Sūriyagoda Sumangala Thera, trans., *The Book of Kindred Sayings* (*Sanyutta-nikāya*) *or Grouped Suttas*, Vol. I. 1917.

VIII. Pe Maung Tin, trans., Caroline Augusta Foley Rhys Davids, rev. and ed., *The Expositor* (*Atthasālinī*), *Buddhaghosa's Commentary on the Dhammasangaṇī.* 1920, 1921.

X. Caroline Augusta Foley Rhys Davids, assisted by Frank Lee Woodward, trans., *The Book of Kindred Sayings* (*Sanyuttanikāya*) *or Grouped Suttas*, Vol. II. 1922, 1953.

XI. Pe Maung Tin, trans., *The Path of Purity, being a Translation of Buddhaghosa's Vissudhimagga*, Vol. I. 1922.

XII. Bimala Charan Law, trans., *Designation of Human Types* (*Puggala-paññathi*). 1924.

XIII. Frank Lee Woodward, trans., Caroline A. F. Rhys Davids, ed., *The Book of Kindred Sayings* (*Sanyutta-nikāya*) *or Grouped Suttas*, Vol. III. 1927.

XIV. ———, trans., Caroline A. F. Rhys Davids, ed., *The Book of Kindred Sayings* (*Sanyutta-nikāya*) *or Grouped Suttas*, Vol. IV. 1927.

XV. Lord Chalmers, trans., *Further Dialogues of the Buddha* (*Majjhima-nikāya*). 1926, 1927. Sacred Books of the Buddhists, Vols. V, VI. 2 vols.

XVI. Frank Lee Woodward, trans., *The Book of Kindred Sayings* (*Saṇyutta-nikāya*) *or Grouped Suttas*, Vol. V. 1930.

XVII. Pe Maung Tin, trans., *The Path of Purity, being a Translation of Buddhaghosa's Vissudhimagga*, Vol. II. 1928, 1929.

XXI. ———, trans., *The Path of Purity, being a Translation of Buddhaghosa's Visuddhimagga*, Vol. III. 1931.

XXII. Frank Lee Woodward, trans., *The Book of Gradual Sayings* (*Aṅguttara-nikāya*) *or More-numbered Suttas*, Vol. I. 1932; 1951.

XXIII. Caroline Augusta Foley Rhys Davids, trans., *The Minor Anthologies of the Pali Canon*; Part I, *Dhammapada...and Khuddakapaṭha.* 1931. Sacred Books of the Buddhists, Vol. VII.

XXIV. Frank Lee Woodward, trans., *The Book of Gradual Sayings* (*Anguttara-nikāya*) *or More-numbered Suttas*, Vol. III. 1933, 1953.

XXV. E. M. Hare, trans., *The Book of Gradual Sayings* (*Anguttara-nikāya*) *or More-numbered Suttas*, Vol. III. 1934, 1953.

XXVI. E. M. Hare, trans., *The Book of the Gradual Sayings* (*Anguttara-nikāya*), Vol. IV. 1935, 1955.

xxvii. Frank Lee Woodward, trans., *The Book of the Gradual Sayings* (*Anguttara-nikāya*), Vol. v. 1936, 1955.

xxviii. Bimala Charan Law, trans., *The Debates Commentary* (*on Points of Controversy*). 1941.

xxix. Isaline Blew Horner, trans., *The Middle Length Sayings* (*Majjhima-nikāya*); Vol. i (First Fifty Suttas). 1954.

NYĀYA

Bhikan Lal Atreya, *The Elements of Indian Logic, with the Text and Hindi & English Translations of Tarkasangraha* (*Buddhikhaṇḍa*). 2nd ed. Benares: The Indian Bookshop, 1934.

Sadananda Bhaduri, *Studies in Nyāya-Vaiśeṣika Metaphysics*. Poona: Bhandarkar Oriental Research Institute, 1947.

Satis Chandra Chatterjee, *The Nyāya Theory of Knowledge*. 2nd ed. Calcutta: University of Calcutta, 1950.

Alfred Foucher, *Le Compendium des Topiques* (*Tarkasamgraha d'Annambhatta*). Paris: Maissoneuve, 1949.

Daniel Henry Holmes Ingalls, *Materials for the Study of Navya-Nyāya Logic*. HOS, xl, 1951.

Hermann Jacobi, "Indische Logik", *Nachrichten der Göttinger Gesellschaft der Wissenschaften*. Göttingen: Philologisch-historische Klasse, 1901.

Ganganatha Jha, trans., *The Tarkabhāṣā* (by Keśavamiśra), *or Exposition of Reasoning*. 2nd rev. ed. Poona: Oriental Book Agency, 1924.

———, *The Nyāya Philosophy of Gautama* (Sadholal Lectures). Allahabad: Allahabad University, n.d.

Arthur Berriedale Keith, *Indian Logic and Atomism, an Exposition of the Nyāya and Vaiçeṣika Systems*. Oxford: The Clarendon Press, 1921.

Swami Madhavananda, trans., *Visvanatha Nyayapancanana, Bhasapariccheda with Siddhantamuktavali*. Calcutta: Advaita Ashrama, 1940.

Umesha Mishra, *Conception of Matter according to Nyāya-Vaiśeṣika: with a Foreword by Ganganatha Jha and an Introduction by Gopinath Kaviraj*. Allahabad: M. N. Pandey, 1936.

Herbert Niel Randle, *Indian Logic in the Early Schools*. London: Humphrey Milford, Oxford University Press, 1930.

Walter Ruben, *Zur indischen Erkenntnistheorie: Die Lehre von der Wahrnehmung nach den Nyayasutras*. iii, i. Leipzig: O. Harrassowitz, 1926.

S. Kuppuswami Sastri, *A Primer of Indian Logic according to Annambhatta's Tarkasamgraha*. Madras: P. Varadachary & Co., 1932.

Stanislaus Schayer, "Studien zur indischen Logik i, ii," *Bulletin international de l'Académie polonaise des Sciences et des Lettres*. Classe de philologie, classe d'histoire et de philosophie (1932), pp. 98–102; and (1933), pp. 90–96.

———, "Über die Methode der Nyaya-forschung", *Festschrift Moriz Winternitz*, Otto Stein und Wilhelm Gampert, hrsg. Leipzig: O. Harrassowitz, 1933.

Saileswar Sen, *A Study on Mathuranatha's Tattvacintamanirahasya*. Wageningen: H. Veenman en Zonen, 1924.

Moritz Spitzer, *Begriffsuntersuchungen zum Nyāya-bhāṣya*. Kiel: 1926.

Sadajiro Sugiura and Edgar Arthur Singer, Jr., eds., *Hindu Logic as Preserved in China and Japan*. Philadelphia: University of Pennsylvania, 1900.

Giuseppe Tucci, trans., "Nyāyamukha of Dignāga: the Oldest Buddhist Text on Logic", Materialien zur Kunde des Buddhismus, Heft 15. Heidelberg: Kommission bei O. Harrassowitz, 1930.

———, *Pre-Dinnaga Buddhist Texts on Logic from Chinese Sources*. Baroda: Oriental Institute, 1929.

———, "Buddhist Logic before Dinnaga", *Journal of the Royal Asiatic Society of Great Britain and Ireland* (1929), pp. 451–488.

Satis Chandra Vidyabhusana, *A History of Indian Logic*. Calcutta: University of Calcutta, 1921.

VAIŚEṢIKA

Barend Faddegon, *The Vaiçeṣika System*. Amsterdam: J. Muller, 1918.

Archibald Edward Gough, trans., *The Vaiśeṣika Sūtras of Kaṇāda with Comments from the Upaskāra of Śankara-miśra and the Vivṛitti of Jaya-nārāyaṇa-tarkaparichānana*. Benares: E. J. Lazarus & Co., 1873.

Werner Handt, *Die atomistische Grundlage der Vaiśeṣikaphilosophie*. Rostock: Druck von G. Kreysing in Leipzig, 1900.

Paul Masson-Oursel, "L'atomisme indien", *Revue Philosophique* (1924).

Hakuju Ui, trans., Frederick William Thomas, ed., *The Vaiśeṣika Philosophy according to the Daśopadārtha-śāstra: Chinese Text with Introduction, Translation, and Notes*. Oriental Translation Fund New Series, Vol. XXIV. London: Royal Asiatic Society, 1917.

SĀṀKHYA

Sarat Chandra Banerjee, trans., *The Sānkhya Philosophy: Sānkhyakārikā with Gaudapada's Scolia and Narayana's Gloss*. Calcutta: University of Calcutta, 1909.

Henry Thomas Colebrooke, trans., *The Sānkhya Kārikā*; and Horace Hayman Wilson, trans., *The Bhashya or Commentary of Gaudapada*. Bombay: Tookaram Tatya, 1887.

Joseph Dahlman, *Samkhya-Philosophie*. Berlin: F. L. Dames, 1902.

Richard Garbe, *Die Sāṃkhya Philosophie*. Leipzig: H. Haessel, 1894, 1917.

———, *ibid.*, trans. by R. D. Vadekar, *The Samkhya Philosophy*. Poona.

———, *Aniruddha's Commentary and the Original Parts of Vedāntin Mahādeva's Commentary on the Sāmkhya Sūtras*. Calcutta: Baptist Mission Press, 1892.

———, *Samkhya und Yoga*. Strasbourg: K. J. Trübner, 1896.

Jajineswar Ghosh, *Sāṃkhya and Modern Thought*. Calcutta: The Book Co., Ltd., 1930.

Edward Hamilton Johnston, *Early Samkhya: An Essay on its Historical Development according to the Texts.* London: Royal Asiatic Society, 1937.

Arthur Berriedale Keith, *The Sāṃkhya System.* London: Oxford University Press, 1918. Reprint, Calcutta: Y.M.C.A. Publishing House, 1949.

Jag Mohan Lawl, trans., *The Samkhya Philosophy of Kapila.* Edinburgh: Orpheus Publishing House, 1921.

Abhay Kumar Majundar. Jatindra Kumar Majundar, ed., *The Sāṅkhya Conception of Personality; or, a New Interpretation of the Sāṅkhya Philosophy.* Calcutta: University of Calcutta, 1930.

J. N. Mukerji, *Sāṃkhya or the Theory of Reality: a Critical and Constructive Study of Īśvarakṛṣṇa's Sāṃkhya-Kārikā.* Calcutta: the author, 1931.

Vidyasudhakara Har Dutta Sharma, trans., *The Tattvakaumudi* (*Vacaspati Misra's Commentary on the Samkhya-Karika*). 2nd ed. Poona: Oriental Book Agency, 1934.

YOGA

Kovoor Thomas Behanan, *Yoga, a Scientific Evaluation.* New York: The Macmillan Co., 1937.

Annie Besant, *An Introduction to Yoga.* Madras: Theosophical Publishing House, 1920.

Frances Geraldine Halles Coster, *Yoga and Western Psychology: a Comparison.* London: Oxford University Press, Humphrey Milford, 1935.

Alain Daniélou (Shiva Sharan), *Yoga: The Method of Re-integration.* London: Christopher Johnson, 1949.

Surendra Nath Dasgupta, *The Study of Patanjali.* Calcutta: University of Calcutta, 1920.

———, *Yoga as Philosophy and Religion.* London: Kegan Paul, Trench, Trübner & Co., Ltd.; New York: E. P. Dutton & Co., 1924.

———, *Yoga Philosophy in Relation to Other Systems of Indian Thought.* Calcutta: University of Calcutta, 1930.

Mircel Eliade, *Yoga: essai sur les origines de la mystique indienne.* Paris: P. Geuthner, 1936.

Jacob Wilhelm Hauer, *Yoga als Heilweg.* Stuttgart: W. Kohlhammer, 1932.

Hermann Jacobi, *Ursprüngliches Yogasystem.* Sitzungsberichte der Preussischen Akademie der Wissenschaften. Berlin: in Kommission bei Walter de Gruyter U. Co., 1929, 1930.

Ganganatha Jha, trans., *The Yoga-darśana. The Sūtras of Patañjali with the Bhāshya of Vyāsa.* Bombay: R. T. Tatya for Bombay Theosophical Publication Fund, 1907.

———, trans., *The Yogasārasaṅgraha of Vijñāna Bhikshu.* Bombay: Tattvavivechaka Press for Bombay Theosophical Publication Fund, 1894.

Charles Johnston, trans., *The Yoga Sūtras of Patañjali.* New York: the author, 1912.

Sigurd Lindquist, *Die Methoden des Yoga.* Lund: Ohlssons, 1932.

Shree Purohit Swami, trans., *Aphorisms of Yoga* (by Patañjali). London: Faber & Faber, 1938.

Ernest Wood, *Great Systems of Yoga*. New York: Philosophical Library, 1954.

James Haughton Woods, trans., *The Yoga System of Patañjali, or the Ancient Hindu Doctrine of Concentration of Mind*. 2nd ed. HOS, XVII, 1927.

Paul Tuxen, *Yoga* (in Danish). Copenhagen: H. Hagerups, 1911.

MĪMĀṀSĀ

Franklin Edgerton, trans., *The Mīmāṁsā Nyāya Prakāśa of Āpadevī: a Treatise on the Mīmāṁsā System by Apadeva*. New Haven: Yale University Press, 1929.

Ganganatha Jha, *Prabhākara School of Pūrva Mīmāṁsā*. Indian Thought Series, No. VIII. Benares: Benares Hindu University, 1918.

———, *Pūrva Mīmāṁsā in its Sources: with a Critical Bibliography by Umesha Mishra*. Benares: Benares Hindu University, 1942.

———, trans., *The Pūrva Mīmāṁsā Sūtras of Jaimini*, Chapters I–III. SBH, X, 1916.

Pandurang Vaman Kane, *A Brief Sketch of the Purva-Mimamsa System*. Poona: printed for the author by A. B. Patvardhan at the Arya-bhushan Press, 1924.

Arthur Berriedale Keith, *The Karma Mīmāṁsā*. London: Oxford University Press, 1921.

Pandit Mohan Lal Sandal, trans., *The Mīmāṁsā Sūtras of Jaimini*. SBH, XXVII, 1923–1925.

———, *The Mīmāṁsā Sūtras of Jaimini*. SBH, XXVIII, 1925.

Chitenjoor Kunhan Raja and Sastri Satalur Sundra Suryanarayana, trans., *Manameyodaya*. Madras: The Adyar Library, 1933.

Kisarilala Sarkar, *The Mimamsa Rules of Interpretation: as applied to Hindu Law*. Calcutta: University of Calcutta, 1909.

Pashupatinath Shastri, *Introduction to the Pūrva Mīmāṁsā*. Calcutta: A. N. Bhattacharya, 1923.

Nanikram Vasanmal Thadani, *The Mīmāṁsā: the Sect of the Sacred Doctrines of the Hindus*. Delhi: The Bharati Research Institute, 1952.

VEDĀNTA

Swami Abhedananda, *Vedanta Philosophy*. 4th ed. New York: Vedanta Society, 1899.

Krishnasvami Aiyar, *Shri Madhva and Madhvism*. Madras: G. A. Nateson & Co., n.d.

Bhikan Lal Atreya, *The Philosophy of the Yoga-vāsiṣṭha*. Adyar: The Theosophical Publishing House, 1936.

———, *The Yogavāsiṣṭha and its Philosophy*. 2nd ed. Benares: The Indian Bookshop, 1939.

Rai Bahadur Lala Baijath, trans., *The Adhyatma Ramayana*. SBH, Extra I, 1912.

Lionel David Barnett, *Brahma-Knowledge: an Outline of the Philosophy of the Vedānta as set forth by the Upanishads and by Śankara.* W of E Series. London: John Murray, 1907.

Shripad Krishna Belvalkar, *Shree Gopal Basu Mallik Lectures on Vedānta Philosophy.* Poona: Bilvakunja Publishing House, 1929.

Asutosh Bhattacharya, *Studies in Post-Śaṇkara Dialectics.* Calcutta: University of Calcutta, 1936.

K. C. Bhattacharyya, *Studies in Vedāntism.* Calcutta: University of Calcutta, 1909.

Kokileswar Bhattacharyya, *An Introduction to Adwaita Philosophy.* Calcutta: University of Calcutta, 1924.

Vidhushekhara Bhattacharyya, ed., trans., and annot., *The Āgamaśāstra of Gauḍapāda.* Calcutta: University of Calcutta, 1943.

Roma Bose, trans. and annot., *Vedānta-parijāta and Vedānta-kaustubha of Srīnivāsa. Commentaries on the Brahma-sūtras.* Bibliotheca Indica, Work No. 259. Calcutta: Royal Asiatic Society of Bengal, 1940–1943. 3 vols.

Mohini M. Chatterjee, trans., *Ātmānātma-vivêka... and Ātmabodha by Shrimat Śankarāchārya.* Bombay: Bombay Theosophical Publishing House, 1932.

———, trans., *Viveka-chūdāmaṇi, or Crest-jewel of Wisdom of Sri Śankarāchārya.* Adyar, Madras: Theosophical Publishing House, 1932.

Anil Kumar Ray Chaudhuri, *The Doctrine of Maya.* Calcutta: Das Gupta & Co., 1950.

———, *A Realistic Interpretation of Śaṅkara Vedānta.* Calcutta: University of Calcutta.

———, *Self and Falsity in Advaita Vedanta.* Calcutta: Progressive Publication, 1955.

G. Dandoy, *Essay on the Doctrine of the Unreality of the World in the Advaita.* Calcutta: A. Rome, 1919.

Ras Vihari Das, *The Essentials of Advaitism: Sureśvara's Naiṣkarmyasiddhi, Explained in English.* Lahore: Motilal Banarsi Das, 1933.

———, *The Self and the Ideal.* Calcutta: University of Calcutta, 1935.

Saroj Kumar Das, *A Study of the Vedānta.* Calcutta: University of Calcutta, 1934.

———, *Towards a Systematic Study of the Vedanta.* Calcutta: University of Calcutta, 1931.

Vinayak Hari Date, *Vedānta Explained, Śaṅkara's Commentary on the Brahma-sūtras,* Vol. I. Bombay: Bookseller's Publishing Co., 1954.

Paul Deussen, *Das System des Vedanta.* Leipzig: F. A. Brockhaus, 1921.

———, *ibid.*, trans. by Charles Johnston, *The System of the Vedanta, according to Badarayana's Brahmasutras and Çankara's Commentary.* Chicago: The Open Court Publishing Co., 1912.

———. J. H. Woods, and C. B. Runkel, trans., *Outline of the Vedanta System of Philosophy according to Shankara.* 2nd ed. New York: The Grafton Press, 1906; Cambridge, Mass.: Harvard University Press, 1927.

(A trans. of the chapter "Kurze Übersicht der Vedantalehre" of *Das System des Vedanta*. Leipzig: F. A. Brockhaus, 1883.)

Prahlad Chandrashekha Devanji, trans., *Siddhantabindu by Madhusūdanasarasvati: a Commentary on the Daśaśloki of Śaṁkarācārya*. Gaekwad's Oriental Series, Vol. 64. Baroda: Oriental Institute, 1933.

Nripendra Kumar Dutt, *The Vedanta: Its Place as a System of Metaphysics*. Calcutta: University of Calcutta, 1931.

V. S. Ghate, *Le Védanta: Étude sur les Brahmasutras et leur cinq Commentaires*. Tours: Imp. E. Arrault & Co., 1918.

———, (trans. the above vol. in a slightly different form), *The Vedanta: A Study of the Brahma-Sutras with the Bhasyas of Sankara, Ramanuja, Nimbarka, Madhva and Vallabha*. Poona: Bhandarkar Oriental Research Institute, 1926.

Helmuth von Glasenapp, *Madhvas Philosophie des Vishnu Glaubens, mit einer Einleitung über Madhva und seine Schule*. Geistesströmungen des Ostens, II. Bonn: K. Schroeder, 1923.

Jan Gonda, *Notes on Brahman*. Utrecht: J. L. Beyers, 1950.

René Guénon, *L'homme et son devenir selon le Vēdānta*. Paris: Editions Bossard, 1925.

———, *ibid.*, trans. by Richard C. Nicholson, *Man and His Becoming, according to the Vedanta*. London: Luzac & Co., 1945.

Paul Hacker, "Eigentümlichkeiten der Lehre und Terminologie Śankara's". *Zeitschrift der deutschen Morgendländischen Gesellschaft*, 100 (1950), pp. 246–286.

———, *Untersuchungen über Texte des frühen Advaitavāda*. 1. *Die Schüler Śankaras*. Mainz: Akademie der Wissenschaften und der Literatur, 1950.

Mysore Hiriyanna, ed. and trans., *Vedānta-sāra (by Sadānanda): a Work on Vedanta Philosophy*. Poona: Oriental Book Agency, 1929.

Swami Jagadananda, trans., *A Thousand Teachings of Srī Śaṅkarachārya* (Śaṅkara's Upadeshasāhasrī). Madras: Sri Ramakrishna Math, 1949.

Ganganatha Jha, *Advaitasiddhi of Madhusudana Sarasvati*, translated in *Indian Thought* (Vol. 6, 1914—Vol. 10, 1917).

———, *Khandana-khanda-khadya*, translated in *Indian Thought* (Vol. 1, 1907—Vol. 7, 1915).

———, *Shaṅkara Vedānta*, Allahabad: The Allahabad Law Journal Press, 1939.

J. Johnson, trans., *The Vedāntatattvasāra ascribed to Rāmānujāchārya*. Benares: E. J. Lazarus & Co., 1898.

Charles Johnston, trans., *The Great Jewel of Wisdom (Vivekachūdāmaṇi) attributed to Shaṅkara Āchārya*. New York: Quarterly Book Department, 1925.

Vasudeva Jagannath Kirtikar, *Studies in Vedanta*. Bombay: D. B. Taraporevala Sons, Co., 1924.

Olivier Lacombe, *L'Absolu selon le Védānta*. Paris: P. Geuthner, 1937.

Swami Madhavananda, *Bṛhadāraṇyaka Upaniṣad*. Text with translation of Śaṅkara's Commentary. Calcutta: Advaita Ashrama, 1934.

T. M. P. Mahadevan, *Guaḍapāda: A Study in Early Vedanta.* Madras University Philosophical Series, No. 5. Madras: University of Madras, 1952.

———, *The Philosophy of Advaita, with Special Reference to Bhāratītīrtha-Vidyāraṇya.* London: Luzac & Co., 1938.

Susil Kumar Maitra, *Madhva Logic.* Calcutta: University of Calcutta, 1936.

Ghanshamdas Rattanmal Malkani, *Vedantic Epistemology.* Amalner: The Indian Institute of Philosophy, 1951.

———, Ras Vihari Das and T. R. V. Murti, eds., *Ajñāna.* London: Luzac & Co., 1933.

Nalinimohan Sastri Mukharji, *A Study of Śaṅkara.* Calcutta: University of Calcutta, 1942.

Paramathanath Mukhopadhyaya, *Introduction to Vedānta Philosophy.* Calcutta: The Book Co., Ltd., 1928.

Swami Nikhilananda, *Self Knowledge: an English Translation of Śaṅkarā-chārya's Ātmabodha.* Madras: Sri Ramakrishna Math, 1947.

———, trans., *Vedāntasāra of Sadānanda.* Mayavati, Almora: Advaita Ashrama, 1941.

Padmanabhacharya, *Life and Teachings of Shri Madhvāchārya.*

Kanti Chandra Pandey, *Abhinavagupta, an Historical and Philosophical Study.* Benares: Chowkhamba Sanskrit Series Office, 1935.

V. Ponniah, *The Saiva Siddhanta Theory of Knowledge.* Annamalainagar: The Annamalai University, 1952.

H. N. Raghavendrachar, *Conception of Svatantra.* Mysore: Mysore University, 1943.

———, *Dvaita Philosophy and its Place in the Vedanta.* Mysore: Mysore University, 1941.

Poola Tirupati Raju, *Thought and Reality—Hegelianism and Advaita.* London: George Allen & Unwin Ltd., 1937.

Malur Rao Bahadur Rangacarya, trans., *The Sarva-siddhānta-saṅgraha of Śaṅkarācārya.* Madras: Government Press, 1909.

——— and Varadaraja Aiyangar, trans., *The Vedānta-sūtras with the Srī-Bhāshya of Rāmānujāchārya.* Madras: The Brahmavadin Press, 1919.

B. A. Krishnaswamy Rao, *Outlines of the Philosophy of Sri Madwacharya.* Tumkur: privately published, 1951.

Pandit Mohan Lal Sandal, trans., *The Siddhānta Darśanam of Vyāsa.* SBH, XXIX, 1925.

Sadhu Santinatha, *The Critical Examination of the Non-Dualistic Philosophy* (*Vedānta*). Amalner: the author, 1936.

———, *Māyāvāda; or the Non-Dualistic Philosophy* (*Vedānta*). Poona: the author, 1938.

Nagaraja Sarma, *The Reign of Realism in Indian Philosophy, Exposition of Ten Works by Madhva.* Madras: The National Press, 1937.

Kokileswar Sastri, *An Introduction to Advaita Philosophy.* Calcutta: University of Calcutta, 1926.

———, *A Realistic Interpretation of Śaṅkara-Vedānta.* (The Sreegopal Basu Mallick fellowship lectures for 1930–1931.) Calcutta: University of Calcutta, 1931.

Satalur Sundra Suryanarayana Sastri, trans., *Siddhanta-leśa-saṅgraha.* Madras: University of Madras, 1935.

———, *The Sivādvaita of Śrīkaṇṭha.* Madras: University of Madras, 1930.

Satalur Sundra Suryanarayana Sastri, trans., *Vedanta-Paribhāṣā (of Dharmarajadhvarindra).* Adyar Library Series, 134. Adyar: Adyar Library, 1942.

——— and Saileswar Sen, trans., *Vivaraṇa-prameya-saṅgraha.* Madras: The Sri Vidya Press, 1941.

———, and Chittenjoor Kunhan Raja, trans., *Vācaspati's Bhāmatī.* (Partial translation.) Madras: Theosophical Publishing House, 1933.

——— and T. M. P. Mahadevan, trans., *Bhedadhikkara.* (A free translation under the title *A Critique of Difference.*) Madras: Madras University, 1936.

Prabhu Dutt Shastri, *The Doctrine of Māyā in the Philosophy of the Vedānta.* London: Luzac & Co., 1911.

Siddheswarananda, *Quelques aspects de la philosophie védantique.* Paris: A. Maisonneuve, 1941.

Ram Pratap Singh, *The Vedānta of Śaṅkara—a Metaphysics of Value.* Jaipur: Bharat Publishing House, 1949.

Mahendranath Sircar, *Comparative Studies in Vedantism.* Bombay: Humphrey Milford, Oxford University Press, 1927.

———, *The System of Vedantic Thought and Culture.* Calcutta: University of Calcutta, 1925.

P. N. Srinivasachari, *The Philosophy of Bhedābheda.* 2nd ed., rev. and enl. Adyar Library Series No. 74. Adyar: Adyar Library, 1950.

———, *The Philosophy of Viśiṣṭādvaita.* Adyar Library Series, No. 39. Adyar: Adyar Library, 1943.

A. Govinda Swamin, trans., *Yatīndra-mata-dīpikā* (by Śrinivāsa). Madras: Meykandan Press, 1912.

William Spence Urquhart, *The Vedanta and Modern Thought.* The Religious Quest of India Series. London: Humphrey Milford, Oxford University Press, 1928.

K. C. Varadachari, *Sri Ramanuja's Theory of Knowledge.* Sri Venkatesvara Oriental Institute Studies, No. 1. Tirupati: Tirumalai-Tirupati Devasthanams Press, 1943.

Arthur Venis, trans., *The Vedānta Siddhāntamuktāvalī of Prakāśānanda,* trans. in *The Pandit.* Benares: E. J. Lazarus & Co., 1890.

Rai Bahadur Śriśa Chandra Vasu Vidyārṇava, with the assistance of Pandit Rāmākṣyaya Bhaṭṭāchārya Vidyābhusaṇa, trans., *The Bṛihadāraṇyaka Upaniṣad with the Commentary of Śrī Mādhvāchārya called also Ānandatīrtha.* 2nd ed. SBH, XIV, 1923.

———, *Studies in the Vedānta Sūtras*; Part I, *Studies in the Upaniṣads.* 2nd ed. SBH, XXII, 1933.

———, trans., *The Vedānta-Sūtras of Bādarāyaṇa with the Commentary of Baladeva.* SBH, V, 1912.

Vidyatilaka, trans., *The Brahmopanisat-Sara Sangraha,* Part I (with *Dīpikā*); Siddhesvar Varma Shastri, trans., *The Śvetāśvatara.* SBH, XVIII, 1916.

Swami Vireswarananda, *Brahmasutras.* Text and Translation with Notes. Calcutta: Advaita Ashrama, 1936.

Max Walleser, *Der ältere Vedanta.* Heidelberg: C. Winters Universitätsbuchhandlung, 1910.

SRI AUROBINDO

Essays on the Gītā. Sri Aurobindo Library. Calcutta: Arya Publishing House, 1926–1944, 1950.

The Human Cycle. Pondicherry: Sri Aurobindo Ashram, 1949.

The Ideal of Human Unity. 2nd ed. Pondicherry: Sri Aurobindo Ashram, 1950.

The Life Divine. 3rd ed. Calcutta: Arya Publishing House, 1947. 2 vols.

More Lights on Yoga. Pondicherry: Sri Aurobindo Ashram, 1948.

The Problem of Rebirth. Pondicherry: Sri Aurobindo Ashram, 1952.

The Renaissance in India. 3rd ed. Calcutta: Arya Publishing House, 1946.

The Riddle of the World. 3rd ed. Calcutta: Arya Publishing House, 1946.

Savitri—a Legend and a Symbol. Pondicherry: Sri Aurobindo Ashram, 1951.

The Supramental Manifestation upon Earth. Pondicherry: Sri Aurobindo Ashram, 1952.

The Synthesis of Yoga. Madras: Sri Aurobindo Library, 1948.

Haridas Chaudhuri, *Sri Aurobindo: The Prophet of Life Divine.* Calcutta: Sri Aurobindo Pathamandir, 1951.

———, *The Philosophy of Integralism, or, the Metaphysical Synthesis Inherent in the Teaching of Sri Aurobindo.* Calcutta: Sri Aurobindo Pathamandir, 1954.

S. K. Maitra, *An Introduction to the Philosophy of Sri Aurobindo.* 2nd ed. Benares: Benares Hindu University, 1945.

———, *Studies in Sri Aurobindo's Philosophy.* Benares: Benares Hindu University, 1945.

———, *The Meeting of East and West in Sri Aurobindo's Philosophy.* Pondicherry: Sri Aurobindo Ashram, 1956.

S. RADHAKRISHNAN

East and West in Religion. London: George Allen & Unwin Ltd., 1949.

Eastern Religions and Western Thought. 2nd ed. London: Oxford University Press, Humphrey Milford, 1940.

Education, Politics and War. Poona: International Book Service, 1944.

The Essentials of Psychology. London: Oxford University Press, 1912.

The Ethics of the Vedānta and Its Metaphysical Presuppositions. Madras: The Guardian Press, 1908.

Freedom and Culture. 4th ed. Madras: G. A. Natesan & Co., 1946.

Gautama the Buddha. Bombay: Hind Kitabs, 1945.

Great Indians. Bombay: Hind Kitabs, 1949.

The Heart of Hindusthan. 8th ed. Madras: G. A. Natesan & Co., 1945.

The Hindu View of Life. London: George Allen & Unwin, Ltd., 1927.

Indian Philosophy. London: George Allen & Unwin, Ltd., Vol. I, 1923; rev. 1929; Vol. II, 1927, rev., 1931.

Introduction to Mahatma Gandhi, ed. London: George Allen & Unwin, Ltd. 1939.

Kalki—or the Future of Civilisation. London: Kegan Paul & Co., 1929.

The Philosophy of Rabindranath Tagore. London: Macmillan & Co., Ltd., 1918.

The Philosophy of the Upaniṣads. Rev. ed. London: George Allen & Unwin, Ltd., 1935.

The Principal Upanisads. The Muirhead Library of Philosophy. London: George Allen & Unwin, Ltd., 1953.

The Reign of Religion in Contemporary Philosophy. London: Macmillan & Co., Ltd., 1920.

Religion and Society. 2nd ed. Kamala Lectures. London: George Allen & Unwin, Ltd., 1948.

The Religion We Need. London: Ernest Benn, 1928.

C. E. M. Joad, *Counter Attack from the East, the Philosophy of Radhakrishnan.* London: George Allen & Unwin, Ltd., 1933.

Paul Arthur Schilpp, ed., *The Philosophy of Sarvepalli Radhakrishnan.* The Library of Living Philosophers. New York: Tudor Publishing Co., 1952.

The following index entries should be added:

INDEX

ADDENDUM

The following famous prayer should be added to section 10, page 77—

"From the unreal lead me to the real!
From darkness lead me to light!
From death lead me to immortality."

(*Bṛ. Up.* I.iii.28.)